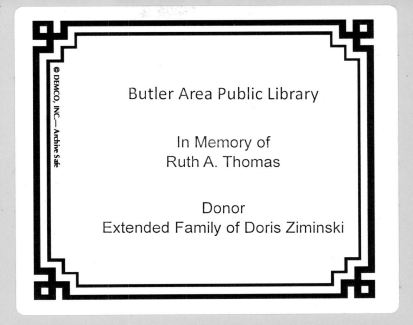

Butler Area Public Library

In Memory of
Ruth A. Thomas

Donor
Extended Family of Doris Ziminski

© DEMCO, INC.— Archive Safe

Butler Area Public Library
218 North McKean Street
Butler PA 16001

P9-AQL-316

THE ADVANCE MAN

A Journey Into the World of the Circus

Butler Area Public Library
218 North McKean Street
Butler PA 16001

2795099

THE ADVANCE MAN

A Journey Into the World of the Circus

Butler Area Public Library
218 North McKean Street
Butler PA 16001

JAMIE MACVICAR

791.3
MAC

BEAR MANOR MEDIA
ALBANY, GEORGIA

· Publishers of Quality Entertainment Biographies ·

The Advance Man: A Journey Into the World of the Circus
Copyright © 2010 by Jamie MacVicar
First Edition
All rights reserved
Printed in the United States of America

Published in conjunction with the documentary, *"A Look Back,"* © 2010 Jamie MacVicar, a production of MacVicar Enterprises, Inc.

No part of this book may be reproduced in any form or by any means, electronic, mechanical, digital, photocopying or recording, except for the inclusion in a review, without the written permission of the copyright holder.

BearManor Media
P.O. Box 71426
Albany, Georgia 31708
www.bearmanormedia.com

Distributed by:
Pathway Book Service
800-345-6665
orders@pathwaybook.com

ISBN 10: 1-59393-203-0
ISBN 13: 978-1-59393-203-9

Library of Congress Cataloging-in-Publication Data

MacVicar, Jamie F., 1951–
    The advance man : a journey into the world of the circus / Jamie MacVicar.
       p.   cm.
    Includes bibliographical references and index.
    ISBN 978-1-59393-203-9
    1. MacVicar, Jamie F., 1951–   2. Circus—United States—Biography.
3. Promoters—United States—Biography.   I. Title.

GV1811.M314A2   2010
791.3—dc22

                                                    2008039213

Photo credits are on page 667

Manufactured by RR Donnelley, Harrisonburg Division
Composition by Coghill Composition Company

Cover photographer: Robert Shafer
Cover illustrator: Bob Lane
Designer: Jonathan Briggs

Typeset in Sabon

Butler Area Public Library
218 North McKean Street
Butler PA 16001

for Errol
who taught me 'to thine own self be true'
and for Harland
who showed me most everything else

Contents

Butler Area Public Library
218 North McKean Street
Butler PA 16001

PART FOUR • SAVANNAH – HEADING SOUTH

PART FIVE • INDIANA

Contents

Introduction

Butler Area Public Library
218 North McKean Street
Butler PA 16001

One week after college graduation, in May of 1974, most of my colleagues, fellow business and marketing majors, were scouting for jobs as junior account executives in established advertising agencies such as J. Walter Thompson or McCann Erickson or hoping to climb the marketing ranks of Proctor and Gamble, Campbell's Soup or IBM. Soap, soup and computers, among other things, were waiting to be sold.

God knows we'd been bred on case study after case study designed to test our problem-solving abilities in marketing such products, but not once do I recall a case study, or even a single sentence uttered by a marketing professor, on how to promote a lion tamer or reassure an irate city mayor that someone was going to clean up the five miles of elephant dumpings leading to city hall or how to negotiate with a recalcitrant star acrobat so he'd do an interview with the media the next day.

I was soon to learn. I was 30,000 feet above the Midwest on my way to Los Angeles on the first day of my job as an advance man for Ringling Brothers and Barnum and Bailey Circus. The excitement, innocence and wide-eyed anticipation I felt made me giddy with expectations. I was out to make my fortune, conquer the marketing world, and for that matter, the world in general, and learn my craft from the masters, people who had forgotten more about promotion, publicity and marketing chutzpa than most people would ever know. For an impressionable twenty-one year old, this was heady stuff. I was also full of piss, vinegar and a fair amount of arrogance, which was how I got hired in the first place.

Management preferred we call ourselves "Regional Marketing Directors," and that was the appellation typeset on our fancy business cards; and these were the fanciest business cards I'd ever seen. On crisp linen stock, two white stallions adorned in ornate headdresses reared up on their hind legs on either side of a red and gold circus wagon. But despite management's more elaborate sobriquet, we called ourselves "advance men" or simply "promoters."

There were only a dozen of us, and our job was to criss-cross the country in front of the circus and somehow, between the time we arrived in town and the show's last performance, figure out how to fill every seat.

We were the modern-day advance men—the same men you read about in children's books—the portly, cigar-smoking, middle-aged men who were illustrated hammering a circus poster to the pole and shouting, "The circus is coming! The circus is coming!" But this was 1974, not 1850, and we were all in our early to mid-twenties, and only one of us was portly, and few of us smoked cigars (except on those rare occasions when we wanted to impress Irvin Feld, our owner, a cigar chain smoker, at which time we looked pretty asinine), and instead of shouting "The circus is coming!," we deployed a grab bag of marketing tools and strategies for mass communication that had been finely tuned over decades of circus hype and promotion.

In 1974 alone, my eleven colleagues and I would sell more than six million circus tickets. It was hucksterism at its finest! When it came to marketing a product, I believed then that these men who had invented the word promotion were the best in the world. And I still believe it today.

This was it! This was the granddaddy of them all, the home of Cecil B. DeMille's "Greatest Show on Earth," P.T. Barnum, the Ringling brothers, the famous Jumbo, Gunther Gebel Williams,

Gargantua, and General Tom Thumb, not to mention the Siamese Twins and the Wild Men of Borneo and now, oddly enough to my friends and family . . . me.

Butler Area Public Library
218 North McKean Street
Butler PA 16001

Butler Area Public Library
218 North McKean Street
PA 16001

Butler Area Public Library
218 North McKean Street
Butler PA 16001

PART ONE

THE BEGINNING

Butler Area Public Library
218 North McKean Street
Butler, PA 16001

Chapter 1
CHARMED OFF A MEAT WAGON

Butler Area Public Library
218 North McKean Street
Butler PA 16001

The ring of the phone interrupted an otherwise lazy campus afternoon. To my surprise, it was Sam Barrett, a fraternity brother who had graduated the previous year. Sam and I were friendly acquaintances, but I didn't expect such an ebullient tone.

"You won't believe what I'm doing," he said.

Intrigued, I waited in silence.

"I'm an advance man for Ringling Brothers and Barnum and Bailey Circus."

"You're kidding!"

"I kid you not. What are you doing next weekend?"

"Nothing I know of."

"Great. We're opening Saturday night at the Hampton Roads Coliseum near Norfolk. Why don't you come up for the weekend? I'll get you front row seats, take you backstage, give you the grand tour."

I hesitated for a moment. It sounded fascinating, but Norfolk was a monotonous four-hour drive on nothing but interstate. I started to decline, but I couldn't help feeling Sam's request was more of a plea than a simple invitation. Besides, I'd fumbled past the time for an appropriate excuse.

"Okay," I declared, "I'll be there."

"Fantastic! By the way, why don't you bring Patti Burke with you?"

Suddenly the mystery was solved. It wasn't as much me as Patti he wanted to see. Patti was a friend of mine whom Sam had dated once or twice. He obviously wanted to see her again and must have figured she'd be easier to entice accompanied by me.

Already committed, I said, "I'll see what I can do."

"Just meet me at the Coliseum. I'll leave two tickets at the 'will call' window. Tell the box office you're looking for the promoter. They'll know where to find me." And then, just as I was wondering how slighted I should feel, he added, "Jamie, I know you. You're going to love this. It's the perfect job for you."

Patti and I arrived just before the start of the show. We picked up our tickets and edged our way through the crowd, breathing in the aroma of buttered popcorn and freshly whipped cotton candy. Barkers were shouting, "Programs for sale!" while others with circus toys raised above their heads wove through the audience. All around us thousands of children chattered in nervous anticipation.

I smiled at Patti as we took our seats next to the center aisle and then waited and watched. Suddenly the lights were dimmed. The audience quieted as a single spotlight illuminated a man standing alone in the center ring dressed in a red-sequined jacket and top hat. In a booming baritone rising slowly to a rousing crescendo, he announced, "Ladies and gentlemen . . . and children of all ages, Irvin Feld and Kenneth Feld proudly present The Greatest Show on Earth!" And as the last of his syllables still echoed in the air, a column of performers suddenly emerged from behind the back curtain. One by one, in dazzling costumes, they paraded around the hippodrome track circling the three rings. The ringmaster sang while the band played music befitting the spectacle as the procession paused for a final salute before filing once again through the backstage curtain.

As the last performer slipped out of view, the music stopped, and the arena again became noticeably quiet. Suddenly, trumpets blared, and I found myself sliding closer to the edge of my seat. The sounds of the reverberating horns transported me back in time, back to the Hollywood version of ancient Rome, where thousands of spectators eagerly awaited the start of events. And then, just as our collective curiosity was reaching its peak, the epitome of a Greek god exploded onto the arena floor. Blonde hair flying in the wind, he rode a white chariot, and with one hand grasping the reins and the other hand cracking a long, twirling whip, circus legend Gunther Gebel Williams careened round and round the hippodrome track.

This was it. He was Ben Hur and this was the reliving of the great Roman Circus Maximus, where it all began. And as the sounds of triumph filled the air, and Gunther raced one final lap around the track, the ringmaster roared, "Let the show begin!"

Sam caught up with us at intermission, and I was further intoxicated by the bedlam of activities backstage. Acrobats stretched while clowns practiced their tumbles, and whole families, some with children in leotards, mingled together in small groups. As I watched a show girl in high heels delicately adjust her plume, a procession of elephants with show girls and clowns high atop were quickly brought into formation. It was obvious everything was a matter of split-second timing, as a man in a tuxedo, wiping sweat from his brow, shouted at the performers to hurry up and take their places in line. The music started again—this time a pulsating African drum roll—and the curtain parted. As the elephants breezed by, the performers broke into smiles and paraded back onto the hippodrome track.

Sam and I exchanged excited glances. He was right. How he got this job, I had no idea, but if he could do it, I could too. I had to become a part of this strange exotic world.

After the show, Sam and Patti and I left the building and began walking across the huge and now vacant parking lot that led to the hotel. It was almost midnight with a gentle mist in the air. As we walked across the pavement with the light rain caught in the glow of the parking lot lights, I pumped Sam for information.

"I knew with your love of advertising you'd react this way," Sam said. "I'll tell you what you do. Work up a resume and mail it to me. The headquarters is located in Washington, D.C. The man who hires the new promoters is named Bradley Rosenberg. I'll see if I can get you an interview." Then Sam turned to me and laughed. "I'd better warn you. Brad can charm a hungry dog off the top of a meat wagon!"

⟐

According to Sam, Brad Rosenberg was the golden-haired boy of Irvin Feld. He could do no wrong. Recently promoted to Director of Sales, Brad was a rapidly rising star. Nothing signified this more than the fact that he alone was entrusted with the annual New York City engagement, a grueling eight-week run, responsible in itself for more than a fourth of the circus' annual revenues.

But as I drove into downtown D.C. for my ten-thirty interview, all of this paled by comparison to another item Sam had casually mentioned. Brad had been a platoon leader in Vietnam.

If this was true, this wasn't a man who'd been behind the front lines calling in logistical support or ordering ordinance or safely typing press releases. This was the real thing. Raw recruits and hardened veterans under his command. Rice paddies . . . jungle . . . fear . . . terror . . . love . . . hate . . . pain and death. After experiencing all that, what could possibly intimidate him?

One thousand fifteen 18th Street, in the heart of downtown D.C., seemed an unlikely place to house the executive offices of Ringling Brothers and Barnum and Bailey Circus. Tucked between L Street and K Street, the area was well known for its row upon row of law offices, accounting firms and associations, all in one way or the other feeding out of the federal government trough.

"Let's meet at 10:30. First thing in the morning," Brad Rosenberg had said, which I gathered for a promoter *was* the first thing in the morning, and I found myself on a wide sidewalk gazing up at a black, glass office building. Duke Ziebert's restaurant, a legendary Washington establishment known for its pricey menus, anchored the building on the left, while a carryout deli secured the building's streetfront on the right. Yet surprisingly, other than the number 1015 in an elongated serif type, nothing on the outside of the building indicated the strange nature of its famous occupant.

Nervously I wandered into the lobby, checking the registry to confirm what I'd been told. The executive offices were located on the eleventh floor, while the marketing office, where my interview would take place, was located on the fifth.

Exiting the elevator, I found at the end of a long hallway a solid white door labeled "Marketing and Sales," next to the globe-shaped Ringling logo. I knocked softly. The door opened, and in front of me stood a pretty, red-haired woman with a pixieish grin.

"Hi, I'm Nancy Pond."

"I'm here for an interview with Brad Rosenberg."

"Yes, he's expecting you," she said, and reaching out a hand, she offered to take my coat.

Inside, another woman, tall and big-boned, worked busily at her desk.

"This is Margot," Nancy said, and the dark-haired woman looked up and smiled.

The room was spacious, more of a working office than a reception area. On one end of the room I could see three executive offices, while behind me I noticed a large, cavernous room with several cubicles.

"Those are for the promoters, whenever they're in town," Nancy said, interrupting my stare. "Follow me."

Brad Rosenberg was on the phone, but he motioned me inside to take a seat. Even though he was occupied with someone else, he fixed me with an interested gaze. Blue-eyed and deeply tanned, he was wearing a light-blue dress shirt embellished by a pair of gleaming gold lion-headed cufflinks. He spoke rapidly, I noticed, punctuated frequently with a short, staccato laugh. He didn't seem to be in any hurry to end the conversation, so I glanced around the room. Except for a photograph on the wall that riveted my attention, the office had little in the way of circus memorabilia. Maybe that was why the photograph was so arresting. It was a black-and-white photo of the marquee announcing Ringling's engagement outside New York City's Madison Square Garden. Lit up in bright lights were the words "Sold Out." Underneath, in equally large letters, were the words "Brad Thanks You!"

Brad hung up the phone, reached over and shook my hand. "Sam Barrett tells me you'd like to become a promoter."

He sat back in a listening pose, my cue, I assumed, to talk about myself.

I was working my way through college, and since I could only afford a small, unknown school, my competitive edge as a marketing major was to have already worked in my field. During my sophomore year, I proceeded to tell him, I approached the owner of a local newspaper and said I'd work for free if he'd let me do something worthwhile. Just as I'd hoped, he took pity on me and offered me minimum wage. By my senior year, between that and other jobs, I'd sold newspaper space, written copy and pasted up ads. And now, as the owner of a one-horse advertising agency, I was making a livable wage placing ads for a few local accounts.

Brad must have admired my spunk, for without any further questions he launched into explaining life as a promoter.

"You'll be living on the road," he said, "your life's belongings in a suitcase. 1015 18th Street will be your home mailing address. Do you think you'd enjoy that?"

"Absolutely," I said.

"There are two things Irvin Feld is adamant about. The first is hirees can't be married," and pointing with a smile to my mustache he said, "and the second is you can't have any facial hair."

My expression must have registered my protest, for he quickly added, "I tried it myself. I'd been away from the office six weeks and had grown a nice mustache. Irvin flew in unexpectedly, and I had until that night to shave it off. I know it sounds quirky. Irvin just associates the clean-cut look with clean-shaven faces."

We talked a few more minutes, and then I said I had three more months to go until graduation.

"Go back, finish up and give me a call. We'll take it from there."

I exited his office, smiling encouragingly at Nancy Pond. As she retrieved my coat, I heard a shrill yell from Brad's office. "Nancy, when are you bringing me the St. Louis files?"

Nancy snapped back, "In a minute. Hold your horses!" And then she glanced up and grinned. "Don't worry. Irvin yells. Bradley yells. We all yell around here."

Graduation was coming up in three short weeks. I was being considered as a trainee by Kaufman Advertising, a leading Washington, D.C. advertising agency, but the lure of the circus was too great.

"Brad, it's me, Jamie MacVicar. I hope you remember me."

"Of course I do."

"Do you have any openings?"

"Probably," he said, sounding delighted to hear from me, "but I don't make the final decision. You'll have to meet with Allen Bloom. He's my boss. The man I report to."

I wondered why he hadn't mentioned him before. "Has he ever not hired someone you recommended?"

Brad hesitated for a second. "Not yet. But I'm sure you'll do fine."

Brad promised he'd arrange the interview, and I hung up the phone. I stared at the receiver, recalling every word of the conversation, trying to measure his every intonation. But the only thing that was certain was when the name Allen Bloom was spoken, it was done so with either reverence or fear.

Chapter 2

IRVIN FELD—A SHREWD BUSINESSMAN

Butler Area Public Library
218 North McKean Street
Butler PA 16001

By the time Brad called to confirm my appointment with Allen Bloom, I had learned the circus was owned by Mattel, the famous toy manufacturer. Irvin Feld, the President and CEO, held an iron-clad, long-term contract with Mattel, placing him in full control of the circus operations. Irvin was a tiny man, no more than five-feet-four and a hundred-and-thirty pounds, with an overweight ego that many said could only be described as a Napoleonic complex.

In appearance, from the pictures I saw, he reminded me of E.T. with a pair of coke-bottle glasses. The glasses magnified his eyes, rendering his face not only somewhat child-like, but also out of all proportion. To me, he certainly didn't fit the physical image of a great showman. In fact, a poster had been illustrated in the program depicting his face diagonally lined up with Barnum and Bailey and the five Ringling brothers, and even he, with his oversized ego, must have realized it looked pretty ridiculous.

But by all accounts, Irvin was a shrewd businessman who loved the mechanics of business as much as he loved the results, amassing a fortune over the years. Yet it appeared he had few interests outside of the circus, and it seemed as though the show consumed his entire life.

But from what Sam had told me, the driving force wasn't just his love of money. Irvin also loved power and recognition. He unabashedly publicized the circus as part and parcel of Irvin Feld. Every item connected with Ringling Brothers was emblazoned in sound or copy with "Produced by Irvin Feld." His publicity department and press releases had no shortage of stories on Irvin, and, just as he gave celebrity status to his performers and others "well known" in show business, he craved the same recognition.

Seldom, I was told, was he seen alone. There was always an entourage of three or four people. And if that didn't clue you in that he wasn't to be viewed as one of the employees—that he was the king and you were the pawn and your behavior had better reflect it—then his chauffeur, who doubled as his bodyguard, confirmed it. Sam Barrett didn't know his chauffeur's name. He just told me, "Don't be surprised if you run into 'Odd Job,'" and then he added as an aside, "friends may come and go, but for men like Irvin, enemies accumulate."

Irvin's personality, according to Sam, could range from extremely quiet and withdrawn to enthusiastically charming to unexplainably furious. And it could change in a matter of seconds. "Thirty minutes with an unhappy Irvin and men would shake for the rest of the day." But it was Irvin's unpredictability coupled with his need for adulation and control that permeated the organization with fear.

According to office legend, Irvin got his first taste of show business as a boy of thirteen, selling snake oil to crowds attending the sideshows of the traveling circuses near his hometown of Hagerstown, Maryland, thirty miles north of Washington, D.C. It was during the Great Depression, and his father, a Russian Jewish immigrant, was struggling to make a living operating a small clothing store. Irvin peddled his cure-all elixir from a colorful stand he'd personally constructed and, according to his press release, in one year made almost eight-thousand dollars. Impressed by his chutzpa, the supply house that provided him with his liquid panacea offered him a job as a full-time salesman. Within a few years, Irvin convinced his employer to advance him the money to open his own retail outlet, and in 1940, along with his brother, Israel, he opened a drugstore in a black neighborhood in Washington, D.C. In order to attract business, he blared gospel music from speakers outside his drug-store, and soon customers wanted to buy more music than tooth-paste. This prompted him to start a record store called Super Music City on H Street, Northeast in 1944.

It wasn't long before he parlayed his business instincts into pro-moting the live acts that visited his store, and by the early 1950s, he was organizing national tours and promoting concerts featuring Fats Domino, Chubby Checker, Frankie Avalon, The Drifters, and The Everly Brothers. As a rock and entertainment promoter, Irvin now spent weeks at a time on the road, and his life became con-sumed by the frenzied world of promotion.

It was during this period Irvin met a relatively unknown Cana-dian singer, Paul Anka, who was only fifteen at the time. But Feld recognized his bankability and placed him on tour, and under Feld's guidance, Paul Anka soared to the top of the record charts.

But the Paul Ankas were few and far between, and rock stars were in and out of popularity faster than he could reconcile his bank account. Irvin wanted a more predictable flow of income. Besides that, the handling and promotion of rock stars had the ear-marks of a sleazy business, and Irvin may have grown tired of lurk-ing around smoke-filled bars and nightclubs trying to find his next meal ticket. So in 1956, when he heard that Ringling Brothers and Barnum and Bailey Circus had declared bankruptcy, his interest peaked considerably.

John Ringling North had been running the show for the past eighteen years, with an understandable mix of triumphs and fail-ures, ever since he'd wrangled control from his uncle John Ring-ling's estate in 1938, but by the early fifties, the business setbacks had begun to take their toll. In 1944 the circus had experienced the devastating Hartford fire in which a flaming canvas tent collapsed on hundreds of people. "It was like you'd opened hell's doors," said one survivor. In a state of chaos and panic, 168 people—many of whom were young children—died as they tried to escape. Lawsuits from the damage totaled almost five-million dollars, and by the time it was paid off six years later, the show's cash reserves were depleted. In fact, the only thing that staved off bankruptcy was Cecil B. DeMille's movie *The Greatest Show on Earth*, released in 1950, netting the circus $1.3 million in royalties.

Nevertheless, by 1955 the show was losing a million dollars a year, largely due to increased costs from labor unions, the railroads, and operating expenses. Business associates desperately tried to convince North to scale back the size of the operation in order to match overhead with revenues, but his personal identity was probably too entwined with the show's grandiosity, and he adamantly refused. One year later, however, with losses continuing unabated, he admitted defeat and announced the show had played its last performance.

Irvin had contacted North six months earlier to negotiate a deal to promote the circus, but North wasn't interested; however, according to Feld, North called him the day he declared the show bankrupt to re-open talks. Irvin said he told him the show had to play indoors if it was to return to the black, eliminating the hundreds of laborers and corresponding exorbitant costs it took to erect the tents. Although Irvin took great personal credit for saving the circus with this insight, the Norths, interestingly, tell a different tale. According to Henry North, his brother John and a close business associate named Art Concello hatched the idea to play indoors, and with $686,000 of John's own money, they re-launched the circus with exactly that intent. In Henry's book *The Circus Kings*, published in 1960, four years after the fact, no mention is made of Irvin Feld.

Nevertheless, North gave Irvin the exclusive contract to book and promote the show with Irvin receiving a percentage of all ticket sales. It wasn't the ownership Irvin desperately wanted, but it was the next best thing, and he threw himself into the challenge. Huge indoor arenas were popping up all over the country, and Irvin began negotiating the contracts, a task far more important than it might appear, because locking in the location—often with caveats that competing circuses couldn't play anywhere near the time of Ringling's run, if at all for that matter—was even more critical than the quality of the show. A hundred competitors with even better acts could be vying for the same audience, but to no avail once Ringling sewed up the arena contract. The smaller circuses were left to play the smaller towns and couldn't produce the revenues to grow, so for all practical purposes, smallness and bigness perpetuated themselves. With this at stake, political contacts were just as important as business contacts, especially since the cities often owned the arenas, and Irvin wisely cultivated both.

But obsessed with his business ambitions, Irvin may not have realized at the time what a shambles his personal life was in. Irvin was married to the former Adele Ruth Schwartz, and together they had two children, Karen and Kenneth. Their home was in the gentile Northwest section of Washington, D.C., but Irvin was seldom around. A younger woman by ten years, Adele was prone to bouts of depression, confiding in friends that she blamed herself for Irvin's inattention. If I were prettier? If I were sexier?

In July of 1958—just two years after Irvin had begun promoting the circus—while he was out of town, she wrote a note saying her marriage was no good, and she was lonely and felt abandoned. She left the note in the house, walked into their garage, turned on the car's engine and lay down among the exhaust fumes.

The maid found her body the next morning near the door. She had apparently changed her mind and struggled to escape, but she was too late. At thirty-one her life was over.

The suicide would haunt Irvin the rest of his life and remain an incident he would never discuss. The children, in accordance with his wife's wishes in the note she'd left behind, were raised first by Adele's parents and then later by Shirley Feld, Irvin's sister-in-law.

Under John Ringling North, Irvin managed the show for ten years and was presumably responsible for its profitability. But although he was paid to assure its financial success, it would have been to Feld's advantage to have it a failure if he could ever convince North to sell him the circus. How Irvin's conscience fared during this obvious conflict of interest, I have no idea, but when Feld finally convinced North to sell him the show in 1967, it was $1.7 million in debt. But because North reportedly couldn't abide Irvin Feld, he demanded a sum of eight million for the show, far more than it was worth. Irvin, nevertheless, was determined and raised part of the money through Wells Fargo Bank of San Francisco and the rest from Judge Roy Hofheinz, the owner of the Houston Astrodome. He hyped the consummation of the purchase, and the signing of the final papers was held in the coliseum in Rome amidst international fanfare and publicity. Now, with ownership finally his, Irvin could focus on turning it into a money maker.

Feld had frequently complained that North wouldn't allow him to touch the production side of the circus. As a result, he needed to revamp the show. His first problem was the age of the performers, the average age of which was forty-six. A few of the show girls were in their fifties. Feld remarked, "A fifty-year-old woman may be fantastic, but a show girl she isn't." And there were now only thirteen clowns, seven of whom were in their seventies and eighties. The youngest was past fifty. Irvin told a reporter, "We know that the clowns can fall down, but can they get up again?"

Irvin fired the show girls, began looking for fresh new acts and created a clown college where the old timers could teach their skills to a new breed. He also needed new headliners. His first dramatic acquisition was Gunther Gebel Williams, at the time an unknown tiger and elephant trainer. But Gunther was unfortunately under contract to Circus Williams. Not to be defeated, Irvin simply bought the whole circus for two-million dollars. It was well worth it, for Gunther became a superstar and a Ringling money-making machine for years.

Irvin realized one circus couldn't possibly play all the cities with arenas in one year, so in an act of mitosis, he created two circuses— the blue show and the red show—each essentially the same size and quality but with different headliners and acts. Since it took a full two years for the shows to play all eighty arenas he had booked, the two circuses could alternately play each year in a city with a completely different show (Irvin again took much publicized credit for this insight despite the fact this had been a customary practice for years, much as the Ringlings did from 1907 to 1919, routing separately The Ringling Brothers Circus and the newly acquired Barnum and Bailey Circus).

In 1971, Irvin, possibly pressured by his partner, Hofheinz, who wanted cash, sold the show to Mattel for fifty million in stock. Not a bad profit considering Irvin's comparatively small original investment. (Although Irvin would later sue Mattel claiming the stock was overvalued.) Irvin, though, in a brilliant move, kept the owner-ship of a separate corporation, Sells-Floto, which sold the programs and concessions, and as part of the agreement, he kept the exclusive rights to sell to Ringling's audiences. Much like movie theaters, where the concessions generate the vast percentage of the profits, Sells-Floto made Irvin millions of dollars in profits. Proving a point, if you ever have to bet money on an entrepreneur versus a corpo-crat, take the entrepreneur every time. In fact, in 1982 Irvin would repurchase the circus from Mattel for $22.6 million in stock, $28 million less than Mattel originally paid him eleven years earlier. And this time, in addition to the circus, the purchase would include two ice shows.

Irvin would go on to apply all of his promotional talents to assur-ing the success of the circus, but despite his acclamations of "fam-ily" and "circus spirit," to many of the old timers, the circus would never again be the same. "They are superior businessmen," said a veteran clown, "but they lack one thing. They have no heart. The heart of the circus is no longer there." Nothing exemplified this more than the 25¢ Feld charged the performers for transportation on the circus bus to and from the arenas. How else, I wondered, were they to get there?

Feld had another shortcoming. There is nothing wrong with self aggrandizement, if at the same time you're delivering the goods, but many in the circus world felt his claim as "The Greatest Showman on Earth" was premature and egotistical, even by circus standards. As a result, he found little acceptance in the world in which he so desperately wanted to belong.

But despite the criticisms, if the golden era of Ringling Brothers and Barnum and Bailey Circus had passed, under Irvin Feld—the ruthless, unpredictable super salesman—I was about to discover another golden age of promotion had just begun.

Chapter 3
DULY-ANOINTED SON

My stomach fluttered as I pushed the elevator button to the eleventh floor executive offices. As the elevator crept past the fifth floor marketing department, it seemed more like weeks than only a few days ago that I was led back to Brad Rosenberg's office by a pretty Nancy Pond. "Eleven o'clock sharp," Brad had said before filling me in on Allen Bloom. I nervously looked at my watch. I was ten minutes early. Then again, I couldn't have been later if I'd chained myself to a cast iron stove.

The elevator rumbled softly to a stop, and the stainless steel doors slid open. Suddenly I had an idea how Dorothy must have felt when she awoke half startled in Munchkin Land. I stepped off the elevator and onto a bright red carpet, finding myself only a few feet away from a white, circular receptionist desk with dozens of round, blinking lights. Floor-to-ceiling mirrors multiplied the effect, and before I could mutter an introduction to the receptionist, I was jolted by the presence of someone else in the room. To my right, outstretched and upright, with a menacing stare, stood a fully grown gorilla. Hundreds of pounds of him, stuffed and encased in glass, glared at me from under the moniker, "Gargantua."

I tried to pry my eyes off the gorilla as I told the receptionist I had an appointment with Allen Bloom, adding apologetically, "I'm a few minutes early."

"Have a seat," she said, pointing to a cushioned bench that ran alongside one wall, and I heard her say into the phone, "Maureen, there is a Jamie MacVicar here to see Allen Bloom."

Ten minutes passed and twenty minutes more, as I slowly became accustomed to the gorilla's glassy-eyed gaze and wondered if I'd be equally rattled meeting Allen Bloom. From what I'd surmised from Brad's history of Allen Bloom, if Brad was Irvin Feld's golden-haired boy, then Allen was his duly-anointed son. Brad informed me that Allen was only eleven years old when he went to work for Irvin Feld; first, simply enough, as an errand boy for Irvin's D.C. drugstore, and then slowly graduating to "program" seller and right-hand man while helping to promote Irvin's concerts. Loyalty and indispensiblity clearly paid off, for now, thirty years later, as Executive Vice President in charge of all marketing, Allen held the second most powerful position in the company.

Just as I was forming a mental picture of what he might look like, a tall, rail-thin woman with tightly curled hair in a style reminiscent of the 1920s appeared.

"How do you do? I'm Maureen," she said, exhibiting a well practiced efficiency. "Mr. Bloom is ready to see you."

I followed her through a door behind the receptionist's desk and past a small outer office that I took to be hers, then turned right into a large adjacent office.

A man greeted me with a warm smile and invited me to sit in one of two swivel chairs in front of his desk. He sat down, leaned back in his chair and, in what I assumed was a familiar pose, propped his feet on the corner of the desk, ankles crossed. Then he reached behind him to a wooden box on top of a credenza, pulled out a cigar and asked if I cared for one.

I politely declined. He snipped off the end, wet it in his mouth and in what appeared to be an enjoyable task began lighting the other end.

"Your desk has no drawers," I commented.

He laughed in between puffs, "I decided a long time ago, drawers collect clutter, so now I just collect it everywhere else."

The surface of his desk was piled high with stacks of paper, but the open look made him seem more accessible. A comfortable feel. It occurred to me, watching him admire his cigar while he slowly turned his attention in my direction, that he had an immediately likeable charm, and it wasn't because of a sophisticated polish. In fact, the few words he'd spoken had a broken, under-educated quality. It was because of an instinctive impression I had that he was genuinely, unmistakably "kind."

Behind him and to his left, shelves rising to the ceiling were lined with more stacks of papers and an assortment of circus products. Stuffed tigers and monkeys, glasses, plates and ashtrays, all emblazoned with the Ringling logo leaned casually against one another at various angles. To the right, a large map of the United States covered half the wall with red and blue pins inserted in a multitude of places, next to what appeared to be several names: Stinson, Collins, Krastner, Barrett and others, some repeating themselves.

"That's how I keep track of my promoters," he said, clearly delighting in the ambience of an operations room the map lent the office. I noticed he even periodically punctuated his comments with wartime metaphors, chortling at one point about an ongoing feud with the accounting department over documentation. "You can't shoot the enemy if you can't find them!"

We talked for several minutes, surprisingly about almost everything *but* the job, and the more we talked, the more fascinated with him I became. Wearing a turtleneck sweater and suede jacket, he told me, "I refuse to wear a tie. They made me wear one for my program photo, and I thought I'd choke to death!" No one could accuse him of looking anything but manly, but when he laughed, the bridge of his nose wrinkled up, rendering him what most women would probably describe as "simply adorable."

But it wasn't just his appearance or his charm that made him so hypnotic. He was a kaleidoscope of mannerisms. At various points in the conversation he would brood like a mafia chieftain, his lips and his gaze turned downward, deep in reflective thought, and yet moments later, with the slightest provocation, he would burst into joyous laughter. Perhaps it was why I was so mesmerized. The forces of light and dark were so readily on display. But beyond his mercurial temperament was an ease and self assuredness that no amount of money or position can buy, an inner peace that comes from having achieved worthy goals.

Finally, without asking if I wanted the job, just assuming correctly that I did, he announced, "I think I'll send you to California to spend some time under Art Ricker. You'll like Art," and then he laughed and said, "Funny thing about Art. I just spoke to him on the phone this morning. When he hangs up, he never says 'goodbye.' He just hangs up." And then, still amused by his observation, he hollered out to Maureen, "Can you arrange a flight to L.A.?"

A moment later, Maureen strode in. "There's a plane leaving Thursday morning at eight A.M."

"Can you be on it?" Allen asked.

"You bet," I said. "Thank you! You won't be disappointed." And as I walked elated out of his office, escorted toward the elevator by Maureen, it dawned on me that Thursday morning was only thirty-six hours away.

PART TWO

California – Learning The Back End

Chapter 4
FOLLOW ME CLOSE BEHIND

What an incredibly lovely sun! I stepped off the plane, strolled across the tarmac and, to my amazement, I wasn't sweating. Ninety-three degrees and I stood on the curb in my black-and-white-checkered sport coat waiting for a cab, and I wasn't sopping wet, as I had been in Washington, D.C.

"Where is the smog I've heard so much about?"

"It's a better day than usual," said the cab driver, acknowledging a thin haze that lingered in the distance. Instead, as we drove along, the sun shimmered in the morning light off the white stucco buildings and red tiled roofs, bathing the palm trees in a healthy glow. It wasn't the kind of sun I was used to, so bright it was almost blinding. I noticed it made everything from the sidewalk bench to the corner cafe look freshly cleaned.

"Here you are," the driver said, "Los Angeles Forum." I gazed across the street at a huge red building surrounded by white columns, shrunken in size by the vastness of the empty parking lot.

"Where would you like to go?"

"I'm not sure . . . the box office, I suppose," I said to the driver, noting a few cars parked near the marquee on the right side of the building.

I stepped out of the cab and approached the arena.

"I'm with the circus," I said to the ticket seller, feeling a little awkward with my large suitcase in hand. "Could you tell me where I might find Art Ricker?"

"Take the elevator to the basement floor. The promoter's office is on your right."

I walked down a long corridor until, as instructed, I noticed a pair of elevator doors and pushed the button marked "Basement." A few yards ahead, I heard the clacking of a typewriter and peeked inside an open door.

"Would this by any chance be Art Ricker's office?"

A freckled woman with an angular face looked up from a black typewriter. "I'm Rachel, Art Ricker's fiancée. Are you the new trainee?"

I smiled, confirming I was, and she indicated I could take a seat. I sat down in front of a paper-strewn desk adjacent to hers, while she busily returned to her typing. The office, I noticed, appeared to be a converted dressing room and a rather depressing one at that. The walls were windowless, painted in a drab yellow, and other than the two wooden desks and chairs, the only things of interest were several overstuffed white binders stacked against the wall.

Rachel, whose attempts at friendliness were short lived, was still typing and largely ignoring me, when a man looking slightly disheveled walked into the room.

"Hi, I'm Art Ricker," he said with a grin, without extending his hand. "You must be Jamie." He slipped into his chair, and despite his large frame, his movements were smooth and unhurried. But unlike Brad Rosenberg or Allen Bloom, he seemed almost shy.

"You must be tired," he said, sounding mildly distracted, and although it was only eleven in the morning, he was right. I'd been up since five, and it seemed more like the end of the day than the beginning.

"Why don't you check into the hotel, get some rest and come back after lunch? I made reservations for you at the Winner's Circle Inn. That's where Rachel and I are staying. You'll find it on the south side of the parking lot."

I thanked him, nodding my appreciation, and strolled back out of his office sooner than I'd anticipated. For a bewildering moment, I stood motionless outside the Forum, wondering which way to go, until a guard pointed to a tall white building in the distance. Like a mirage, it quivered on the horizon. Squinting, I picked up my suitcase and began ambling across the parking lot, shifting the weight from arm to arm.

Halfway across the lot, I sat on my suitcase, wiping my brow. On closer inspection, it was a far fancier hotel than I expected. Perhaps I'll stay one night in the Winner's Circle Inn and then search for the Loser's Group Motel, I mused, wondering anxiously just how I was going to afford it.

"Yes, Mr. Ricker made a reservation for you," the clerk behind the reception desk said, and he handed me a key directing me to the seventh floor.

"Isn't there anything to sign?" I asked.

"No. It's all taken care of," he said nonchalantly, which began to unnerve me, since I was afraid to ask, "What's the rate?"

"Would you like a bellboy, sir?"

"No, I'm fine," I quickly said, asking myself, "How much could it be for one night?"

Turning the key, I opened the door, and although I expected nice quarters, suddenly I felt as though someone had just handed me a plate of peach pie and then asked if I wanted whipped cream. A king-sized bed with thick pillows occupied the center of the room amidst pastel colors of mauve and light green, while tropical rattan furniture served as a dresser and circular table. I threw my suitcase on the bed and quickly drew open the curtains that covered the back wall. Beneath me, seven floors below, a rectangular pool glistened in the morning sun.

I bounced down on the bed, mentally pinching myself. This was unbelievable . . . even if I *could* only afford it for one night.

I showered, changed and hurried downstairs for lunch and a look around. A race track was located just over the hill, and the hotel obviously catered to its clientele. The lobby had a horse racing motif with jockeys' shirts and riding crops hanging on the walls, while in the bar three television sets bolted to the dark paneling gave continuous reruns of the day's events.

I finished my sandwich, the Pimlico Special, and refreshed if not rested, strode across the parking lot back to the Los Angeles Forum.

"How's the room?" Art asked.

"Beautiful! But I'm not sure I can afford it. Is there somewhere less expensive nearby?"

"Don't worry," Art said. "I traded out some tickets for the room. It won't cost you anything . . . at least as long as we're in L.A. Once we head south, you're on your own."

"Traded out tickets?"

"They didn't tell you? Once you've been with the show for a while, you can trade out tickets for your hotel room."

That's a relief, I thought, for more than one reason, since I was being paid the trainee's salary of $200.00 a week, which, even after a cost-of-living adjustment, only netted $186.00. I'd been given a company credit card for airplane tickets and rental cars, but the rest, which included restaurant food and hotels, was up to me. After one year, Brad Rosenberg had promised, my salary would jump to $15,000.00, but first, he intimated, management weeded out the weak from the strong.

"Where's Rachel?" I asked, for some reason feeling relieved Art was alone.

"She went back to the hotel," he said. Then straightening up in his chair, while giving me the impression he'd do his best, but deep down he'd rather not be bothered with a trainee, he gave me a summary of what to expect. "You're going to learn the back end of the business first. I've already been here for four months, so most of the promotional work has been done. Over the next few weeks, we'll be cleaning up loose ends. Then the show arrives in San Diego, moves up to Anaheim, then Long Beach, and finishes here in the Los Angeles Forum. Eight straight weeks of performances in all."

I looked at him blankly, trying to digest what he'd just said.

"Here's the program," he said, handing me a glittery brochure with a montage of clowns and acrobats on the cover. "It's the Blue Show coming to town. I'd suggest you study it," and then he pointed to the stack of white binders on the floor. "One of the binders is filled with the press releases we've been sending to the local newspapers. The other binders contain everything I've done for each of the four cities. You'll find all the media buys, ads, schedules, promotional deals and everything else pertaining to the four dates."

Impressed, I stared at the binders, observing each one was at least four inches thick and overflowing with papers.

Art paused, lighting a cigar, and I interjected out of curiosity, "What about when the show comes to town?"

"That's when we get really busy—performer interviews, promotional agreements, auditing the show—but I'll explain all that later. For now, when I'm not giving you something to do, you're to follow me close behind. When you're not reading the binders, listen to my conversations, watch what I do and absorb what you hear."

It was obvious I wasn't to learn by Art's direct teaching but instead by observing his every move. Even if it was a one-sided phone conversation, I was to soak up his every word. And over the next several days, if Art had suddenly stopped, I'd have broken my nose.

Art spent most of his time on the phone, and if he wasn't on the phone, he was looking for a phone or directing me to find a phone. If nothing else, I soon gained the confidence I could find a phone in the middle of the Mojave Desert. The only problem was, just as Art never said goodbye at the end of a conversation, he didn't get too wordy in the middle either. But between his brief conversations over the phone and the promotional agreements I read in the binders, I learned as a part of his promotional deals that he arranged for local media personalities, politicians, corporate executives and others to participate in the show. A tie-in with a TV station might label the performance "WJLA Night at the Circus" allowing a local anchor person to serve as honorary ringmaster, complete with an honorary whistle for the official start of the show. I noticed in the binders there were several variations on this theme. Children had won contests in local newspapers entitling them to join in a special number, and local media personalities had been promised everything from a ride on an elephant's back to a guest appearance as an honorary clown, with a four-color certificate signed by Irvin Feld himself to cap off their performance. All of these events were negotiated—at the reward of considerable publicity for the circus—and now had to be confirmed and coordinated by the promoter.

In addition, Art had arranged numerous interviews between the performers and the local media, especially at the beginning of each city's run, to maximize our exposure. It soon became apparent that while our unofficial title of "Advance Man" would imply we'd be well on our way to the next town by the time the show appeared, in fact, we were the first to arrive and, by the time we audited the show and settled with the box office, the last to leave.

Art had promoted Southern California along with a few other western cities for the past four years. As a result, even though he had a home in Washington, D.C., he now lived over half of the year on the West Coast. He had trained under a man named Cotton Fenner who had died a year earlier. On the few occasions Art mentioned his name, it appeared as though Cotton had been as much a father figure as a mentor.

Rachel, I came to discover, had quit her job and was now traveling with Art year round. Although he seemed to be relaxed in her company, her hard-edged personality contrasted sharply with his gentle, more laid-back demeanor. Blue-eyed, with his hair prematurely thinning, Art's soft facial features gave him an air of innocence that worked to his advantage, inspiring trust when dealing with others who naturally eyed an advance man with a degree of well deserved suspicion. But Art, at least around me, was quiet—quiet enough to make me uneasy—for I never quite knew if I was pleasing him or not.

To my surprise, Art told me he had been a pilot for the Air Force before joining Ringling, one more item that struck me as unusual for what he now did. But if he didn't *act* the part of a promoter, Art was at least determined to *look* the part. Despite his choir boy image that even a constant cigar couldn't diminish, he had a taste for outlandish clothes. Each day he'd don a different silk suit in shades of purples, greens and blues that seemed flamboyant even by circus measures, accented often by even more outlandish Gatsby-style, two-toned shoes. He clearly lavished a small fortune on his wardrobe, teasing me one day when I wore my black-and-white checkered sports coat for the third day in a row. "Is that the only sports coat you own?"

"Unfortunately," I replied, "it is." The truth of the matter was, until I could afford an all-purpose blue suit, everything I owned plus twenty-three dollars squished easily into a single suitcase.

Art had grown comfortable with his role to the extent that, if people asked what he did for a living, he'd either lie or ignore the question in order to skirt a dialogue on the subject. For me, I was too enamored with the daring, romantic appeal of the job not to broadcast it at the least inquisition. Like barnstormers or stuntmen, it was simply one of those occupations that few others shared. But something else intrigued me: that rich tradition where the past seemed never too far removed from the present.

I suspected that in the circus, with its multiple ethnic groups, there wasn't the self imposed "us versus them" solidarity one might find in groups such as Gypsies or the Amish. But there was nevertheless a culture and language often casually displayed that firmly linked the past to the present. One afternoon, listening to Art on the phone with another Ringling promoter, I heard him ask, "Did you make your nut?" Upon hanging up, I questioned him as to the meaning of the term. Art smiled and said he had asked if the other promoter had met his projections. He proceeded to explain that the term was rooted in the days of old, when circus wagons rolled into town only to have their axle nuts confiscated by the local authorities. Consequently there was no sneaking out in the middle of the night until they had secured enough money to pay all their bills, which was commonly referred to as "making your nut."

When I wasn't studying the binders in the evenings, I'd often find myself thumbing through the Blue Show program, almost as though I'd forget what was coming if I wasn't constantly reminded.

The Red Show that I'd seen in Norfolk largely centered around one main star, Gunther Gebel Williams, while the Blue Show, from what I'd heard, was considered to be the more balanced of the two shows with the attractions spread among four main acts.

If among the four there was one main attraction, it was Michu, the Hungarian lilliputian discovered by Irvin and billed as "the smallest man in the world." Purported to be seven inches shorter than P.T. Barnum's legendary Tom Thumb, Michu was featured gap-toothed and grinning on a life-sized poster folded inside the program.

The second billing was reserved for Elvin Bale, the Blue Show's answer to Gunther Gebel Williams. Elvin didn't have Gunther's name recognition, but with a gymnast's perfect physique and a beach boy's pretty face, he gave Gunther a reason to maintain his competitive edge.

Elvin didn't work with big cats. He wasn't an acrobat, nor was he part of a larger act; he was simply known as a daredevil. Three times, each and every show, Elvin risked his life. Once on a high wire motorcycle that he drove upside down and sideways; once on a swing thirty feet above the arena floor in which he sprang from a sitting position to clutching the bar by only his heels; and once on the "Wheel of Death," a giant hamster cage in which, blindfolded, he ran along the outside mesh while it spun high above the circus rigging.

Featured in one of the press releases sitting at the breakfast table in his trailer along with his stunning German wife, Jeanette Williams, and their two young children, Elvin was described as the perfect family man. But there was one other reason he and Gunther sustained a healthy competition, which in actuality wasn't healthy at all; in fact it was a simmering feud. Jeanette Williams was Gunther's ex-wife.

Charlie Bauman, rising above it all by stature alone, was the show's tiger trainer. He was also the performance director responsible for all the performers and the split-second timing the show required. Art mentioned him frequently, telling me I'd be working with Charlie since the performer interviews and promotional events required his coordination.

Intimidatingly handsome, in Hollywood's version of the testosterone male of the 1950s, Charlie's photos in the program exuded self determination. But the Hollywood stars only acted their parts. They didn't take their powerful hands and use them to pry open the jaws of a man-eating Bengal tiger. Charlie did.

The fourth act that served to balance the show, amidst the clowns and European acrobats and Russian Cossacks, was the crazy antics of the King Charles Troupe.

Originally created by his father but now led by Charlie King, a young man in his early twenties, the King Charles Troupe was the Harlem Globe Trotters of the circus. Straight from the ghettos of

Harlem, a dozen black teenagers had found an escape by playing a madcap version of basketball on unicycles.

Other than one black show girl, the troupe was the only black act in the show. Irvin freely admitted they were his ticket to the black audience, and from what I could determine, Art publicized them to the hilt.

"What would you be doing if you weren't doing this?" I asked.

"I don't know," Art said, "maybe owning a little bed and breakfast somewhere. That's always been a dream of mine." Somehow, coming from Art, it didn't seem out of character.

We talked for a few minutes over lunch, and since he seemed a little more approachable than usual, I found myself teasing him about his upcoming marriage to Rachel.

"Why do you want to get married? You're in the prime of your life!"

My teasing wasn't all innocent, since in Rachel, I feared he was hitching a long-term ride with an ocelot—a hell of a pet till you stepped on its tail.

Art took my ribbing good naturedly, and man-to-man I felt, if nothing else, I had at least done my part.

We finished our lunch, and Art reached for the check. "You'd better get some rest this weekend. Steve Smith, the advance clown, and Vanessa Beal, our publicist, arrive next week. From here on in, the pace will be speeding up."

Chapter 5

SUNLIT BLISS

Jack Sullivan was just the sort of man my father would like. The son of an Irish friend of his, Jack was living on a boat while putting himself through graduate school working odd jobs. That night, sitting by my night stand, I unfolded a piece of paper in which he'd scrawled Jack's name and phone number.

"My father told me you might call," Jack said in a warm, welcoming voice.

"This is the only weekend I'll have free," I said, and Jack immediately responded, suggesting I meet him Sunday morning for a day at the beach.

Jack was living in Port-O-Fino, and as the name would suggest, the yacht club was trendy, with a galaxy of sailboats. Their aluminum masts tinkled in unison, as though they were competing for attention. The sounds accented a gentle breeze in the air, and the sky seemed bluer than usual as I wandered past several piers amidst expensive schooners and turned left at Jack's dock, where he said I'd find his boat. He had described it as an old whaling vessel that the owner had rented to him at a bargain price in return for upkeep. Suddenly I could see why. This had to be the ugliest boat I'd ever seen. It was about fifteen feet at the beam, sixty feet from bow to stern and was missing its mast, which made it look like an old wooden barge. The deck was a mass of tar, epoxy glue, dried-out peeling varnish and marine paint in a patchwork of sun-faded colors. What kept it afloat was frankly beyond me.

I jumped on deck, found a half-opened hatch cover near the mast housing and shouted down for life below. Jack's head popped up along with a lopsided grin, and a rag wiping off a pair of greasy hands.

After an exchange of introductions, he said, "Come on, I'll show you below."

"Why haven't your neighbors sunk you?" I said, as I stepped down a steep ladder.

"That's a good question," Jack laughed, and it was obvious he couldn't care less what others might think. Inside he'd created a cozy, untroubled home with a galley for cooking, a ship's bed made comfortable by the glow of an old lamp and books by the dozen filling the empty spaces.

"Grab these," he said, and he handed me two beach chairs, then lifted an ice chest up the steps and into the back of a beat-up convertible. "The beach is only thirty minutes away."

I liked Jack immediately. He reminded me of the actor Sam Elliott, with his one-sided smile and a mischievous gleam in his eye. Jack spoke in a slow, deep drawl that, combined with a laid-back personality, could tranquilize a rogue elephant. But what made him instantly likeable was a nonjudgemental view of people I'd seldom seen in others.

As we drove down the freeway, I thought about the difference between male friends and female friends. God knows I adored women. In fact, I'm not sure a better friend can be found than a woman who decides she loves you—nor for that matter, a worse enemy when she decides she doesn't. But understanding them is another cup of tea. Sometimes I wondered if men and women were God's idea of a practical joke, making us undeniably, gut-wrenchingly attracted to each other while rendering us so incompatible, with our differing goals and viewpoints, that finding a common ground is virtually impossible.

But with male friends, really good male friends, you can relax. No tension. Just loose kindred spirits. Jack and I sat on the beach watching a shapely figure walk by and then looked at each other with an identical smile, never doubting for a second we knew exactly what the other was thinking.

I slumped back in my chair and stared out past the pier at a group of surfers bobbing serenely on their boards, waiting patiently for the next big wave.

"They're out here all the time. It doesn't matter if it's six a.m. or midnight," Jack said in his slow, scratchy drawl.

"Even weekdays?"

"Even weekdays."

"Oh to be so shallow!" I said. Yet there was something about them in which I was irresistibly drawn. While we worked, they played. I was alone, and they were a group. A virile tribe of muscles and sun-bleached hair. Yet my envy wasn't because while we worked they had fun, or while we glanced all day at our watches, they meandered through the day. It was the fact that *they didn't care*. Surrounded by a world of conventions and expectations, they simply didn't care. Fun, sun, sand and freedom. The embodiment of all that was supposedly California.

Jack and I talked on and off all day, basking at times in a warm silence only two friends can enjoy. Finally, baked and gritty, we called it a day and headed back to the boat. It was almost six o'clock. We cleaned up and strolled over to a bar on the other side of the club. The bar had a long veranda, high up on stilts, that faced westward. We ordered a pitcher of margaritas, salted the rims of our glasses and then propped our feet on the railing and watched the golden California sun set slowly over the horizon. For the first time in months, I felt a sense of inner peace.

In one fell swoop, I could start a new life away from a painful past. The circus offered the perfect escape. New people and new places to go. And unlike the carefree surfers, a chance to prove my worth.

As I watched the sun slip quietly into the sea, I felt content. Here I was, doing what I loved to do, in a beautiful part of the world. Could life get any better?

Chapter 6
THE ADVANCE CLOWN

"If you ever interfere with Art and my's wedding plans again, I'll see to it you'll wish you'd never drawn a breath!"

Rachel's face was crimson with rage, but it didn't stop her from pronouncing each word with measured deliberation. How dare me, a lowly trainee, do anything that could possibly derail her plans. I stared back at her, not saying a word. There was nothing I *could* say. Whatever Art, for some unthinkable reason, had told her about our conversation, my position was indefensible.

"Understood," I muttered and fled the office in search of a safe haven. Well, that's two things I've learned in less than two minutes, I thought. From now on, give Rachel a wide berth and, like a mother bear and her cubs, never stand between a woman and her intended husband-to-be when the hook isn't firmly in place.

I circled back an hour later to find Art alone at his desk. He didn't indicate he knew anything about Rachel's tirade, and I decided I wasn't going to tell him. For all I knew he'd *used* me to express his own doubts to Rachel, and I'll be damned if I'm going to march into that trap again.

"Steve Smith, the advance clown, arrives this afternoon. Here's his schedule," Art said. "I thought you might enjoy taking him around. It will get you out of the office for a few days."

As I reached for the schedule, it occurred to me maybe, on second thought, he did know.

Art and Rachel and I had moved our things the day before into a two-story, ranch-style motel not far from the San Diego Sports Arena. In the center of the motel was a kidney-shaped pool surrounded by a carefully groomed lawn and coconut trees.

I knew my way around San Diego enough by now that with the help of a map, I could chauffeur Steve to the list of activities Art had scheduled over the next two days. Awaiting his arrival, I glanced up periodically from reviewing the list: two hospitals, three elementary schools, one theme park, one recreation center, two senior citizens' homes and two local newspapers.

Art had told me to be on the lookout for a cross-country motor home. Steve and his wife, Robin, would be pulling into the motel parking lot sometime near noon. I'm not sure what I expected, probably a motor home with the Ringling logo and a stream of balloons trailing behind, but just before twelve, a plain-looking camper pulled up in front of the lobby, and a short, wiry man along with an equally short, brown-haired woman jumped out of the cab.

Steve was all business as I introduced myself, asking me where he could park his camper and hook up its generator, while Robin stood to the side radiating an almost childlike curiosity.

"Why don't we have lunch?" I said, after pointing out where to park. "We can meet here in thirty minutes and go over your schedule."

Once Steve had settled his camper, he was in a more talkative mood. But as we slipped into a booth in the restaurant, it seemed Robin was the more animated of the two. Slightly overweight but round-eyed and pretty, she told me they had met while attending Irvin's Clown College. After graduation Steve was offered a job with the circus, but she was not. I looked for a sign of disappointment or competitive resentment, but found none.

"So what should I avoid? Are there things you don't like to do?" I asked, thinking ahead to when it would be my job to schedule his activities.

"Shopping malls and burn wards!"

Steve spoke in a clipped, direct manner, which I instantly appreciated, since I wouldn't have to wonder how he felt. "Don't stick me handing out balloons in a shopping mall. It's degrading. I don't mind hospitals. I'll even visit the terminally ill, but the burn wards . . . that's just too hard to take."

He paused and continued. "And another thing, don't have me perform to a bunch of two and three-year-olds. Their mothers, having seen clowns a thousand times, give their kids no forewarning, plop them in front of me, and the kids promptly burst into tears. They're scared shitless."

"Is there anything else?"

"I guess there's one other thing. Unless it's unavoidable, try not to schedule me for a seven a.m. TV taping. Promoters forget that it takes me two hours to apply all my makeup."

Not trusting his admonitions to memory, I scribbled them down on a napkin and told him I'd pick him up at nine in the morning. We finished lunch, and I returned to the sports arena to see if Art had any last-minute instructions.

"It looks like you've got him scheduled in front of a lot of people," I said.

"That's not what I care about. It's whether or not the local press show up. A hundred kids in an audience is one thing. The evening news is another."

The next morning I knocked gently on the camper's door. Robin answered and said Steve would be out shortly, and a moment later Steve Smith emerged, only now in the form of his alter ego, "Tatters." He stepped gingerly down the aluminum steps, being careful not to trip over his huge, floppy shoes. Dressed in a royal-blue topcoat with bright-yellow buttons and carrying a large, black suitcase, he slipped into the front seat of the car. I stared at him, looking for signs of Steve Smith, but with his newly arched eyebrows, orange wig and huge, red lips and nose, the Steve Smith of yesterday was unrecognizable except for his high pitched voice.

As we drove toward our first stop, an elementary school, Steve said, "I suppose you should know, in case anyone asks, there are two main types of clowns. The 'tramp,' made famous by Emmett

Kelly, is what's called an 'August' clown, as am I. There are numerous variations, but we're the ones in the oversized clothes doing the bumbling, farcical parts of the act. His counterpart, whom he often works with, is the 'white-faced clown.' The white-faced clown is well mannered and wears a more serious expression embellished by red and black paint. If there is such a thing, the white-face is the straight man of the team, with the August spoiling his tricks and appearing at some inopportune time often to trip over one of the props."

"What's Ronald McDonald?" I asked.

"An embarrassment! Professional clowns can't stand him. If there's anything we hate, it's an amateur pretending to be a professional."

The minute Steve entered the school auditorium, his personality changed. In a burst of spontaneous energy, while quipping one-liners and twisting balloons into animal shapes, Steve bounced from one antic to another, never forgetting to announce to the audience the circus was coming, along with the dates and times.

Fortunately, as we drove into the driveway of a senior citizens' home—four stops later and the last appearance of the day—we tallied one TV station and three local newspapers that had recorded the day's events.

A woman greeted us at the door and led us around the building to a side entrance at the back of a small stage. Up until this point, Steve had performed for children all day, and I wondered, as I peered out a slit in the curtains at fifty or sixty elderly men and women, some in wheelchairs, but almost all anxiously alert, what he'd do differently. I took a seat in the audience and watched as the curtains parted, and Steve, alone on the stage except for a small trunk, swept silently, apathetically, while pretending to push an old broom. Wearing a janitor's cap, he occasionally wiped his brow with an invisible handkerchief and while eyeing the trunk curiously, continued to do what appeared to be his daily routine. Finally, the presence of the black trunk proved to be too much for his curiosity, and he timidly opened the lid. Reaching inside, to his amazement, he pulled out a hat—a World War I flying ace helmet, and suddenly, playfully, he is transformed into a World War I fighter pilot. He repeatedly yanks the propeller, starts the engine and climbs while waving to the audience into the shuddering cockpit. Soon he is swerving through the clouds, heroically shooting down the enemy while rattling a machine gun with both thumbs. Next he retrieves an elegant top hat, and bowing to an imaginary well dressed maiden, he waltzes his fair partner round and round the stage, capturing the audience's imagination. A cowboy hat produced a galloping horseback ride so vivid you could almost smell the dust. While feeding a lariat through his hands and skillfully lassoing a steer, he's nearly jerked out of his saddle. A fireman's hat, then a policeman's hat, and with each subsequent hat, the lowly janitor becomes the compelling, dynamic character he only dreams he could be, until unexpectedly, the woman who escorted us into the building lumbers onto the stage. As though she'd misplaced it, she picks up the trunk and casually carts it away. His fantasy lives now gone, he stands frozen in a state of despair, until wistfully he sighs, and resigned to reality, he begins sweeping the stage once again.

Vanessa Beal was a thief. She didn't steal your strength, as did Samson's Delilah, nor your money, since I had none to steal. She stole your reasoning and, as a consequence, your dignity, and for that I resented her.

There should be no earthly reason for a twenty-two-year-old to be attracted to a fifty-two-year-old—yet I was. Partly because she still had a magnetic beauty, dazzling green eyes and a worldly gaze, but mostly because she was a seducer of men - all men—but only until she extracted some words of attraction. Desire. And then she'd accomplished her goal, leaving you feeling a little foolish, as though she'd taken something away you could never win back.

Vanessa had arrived in town a few days earlier, and armed with a stack of "fact sheets"—a one-page flyer with all our raw data, dates, times, location and prices—she schmoozed the local press. Sending out prewritten and customized press releases along with photo slicks and captions, she helped Art strategize our publicity campaign.

Vanessa was a freelance public relations specialist, and though publicity was typically the job of the advertising agencies we hired, in this case, with four cities back-to-back, Art said he needed the additional resource.

Luckily for me, Vanessa served one other purpose. Unbeknownst to her, she served as a buffer. With another woman around, Rachel seemed to ease her hostilities toward me. At least I thought so, until one afternoon, while discussing business over lunch with Art and Rachel and Vanessa, I innocently asked Rachel to pass the salt and pepper. "Get it yourself," she snapped. "Your arm's not broken!" I reached for the salt and pepper while finding myself murmuring involuntarily, "That's not very nice," and to my surprise, Art looked up and said, "Jamie's right. That wasn't very nice."

Rachel didn't say a word. And from that moment on, I took refuge in the fact that whatever admirable traits she had, when it came to the anger that simmered beneath her skin, Art was at least unafraid to confront it.

The next day Vanessa escorted Steve Smith up the coast. and Art and I strolled into the San Diego Sports Arena. Art was holding a map-like piece of paper, which he spread out on the back of one of the empty chairs.

"This is what is called a seating manifest," he said, flicking his cigar ashes onto the concrete floor. "The first thing a promoter does, before reviewing the tickets that headquarters prints, is make sure the seating manifest is accurate."

I looked at the large piece of paper. It was an oval, black-and-white line drawing of every section, row and seat in the arena. Someone had taken magic markers in different colors and divided the chart into three distinct parts, designating each section with its own price—$6.00, $5.00, $4.00.

"Who decides which seats are which price?"

"The home office," Art said. "Unless we spot any obstructions or feel headquarters has weighted the high-priced seats too heavily for the market."

"Who provides the seating manifest?" I asked.

"The box office. That's why we sit here and check every seat." And for the first time I realized, without Art even saying it, the relationship between the promoter and the box office was based on utter distrust.

⟶

"A hungry army is a marauding army," a general once said. Fortunately, Art and I didn't have to feed it.

Due to arrive in just twenty-four hours, the circus train, eighty-six cars in length, was a traveling city with an 18-hour-a-day dining car, "the pie car," a postmaster to receive and distribute the mail and special tutors for the two-dozen children aboard. A blue, ramshackle bus traveled alongside to transport the personnel upon arrival into town for shopping and to and from the arena.

A transportation director in charge of logistical support ordered the food—a bear eats thirty-two loaves of brown bread a day; a single lion devours six 10-ounce steaks; each elephant consumes three 70-pound bales of hay and 40 gallons of water a day. And, of course, electricity is needed to power the generators.

Occasionally the advance man might be required to assist, but as a general rule, Art told me, our two logistical tasks are to provide the transportation director with a list of doctors and dentists willing to serve at a moment's notice, along with the number for an ambulance and the nearest emergency room. And secondly, to make sure adequate security had been provided to help guard the train, especially during the performances, when it was virtually abandoned.

⟶

"Don't forget to set your alarm. We'll need to leave here at four in the morning," Art had said a few hours earlier.

I stood on the motel balcony and looked at Art sitting alone, reflectively, by the courtyard pool. I wondered what it must feel like, after four months of preparations, to finally have the circus train arriving in just a few hours.

I strolled down to the patio and pulled up a chair.

"I hope I'm not intruding."

"No, of course not. Have a seat."

"What do you normally do in the evenings?" I asked, since rarely had I seen him after dark.

"I watch TV."

"You do?" I said, surprised to hear him so casually admit it.

"Yes. I like it. It's entertaining."

There was a moment of silence, and then unable to control my own excitement at the arrival of the performers in a few short hours, I blurted out, "I must say, this is a fantastic job. I can't remember a more fulfilling time!"

Art leaned forward, putting his elbows on his knees, and took a sip from his drink. "Maybe so," he said, and suddenly he seemed much older than his twenty-eight years, "but thus far, you've been with me and Vanessa and Steve. Wait until it's only you, and you're all alone in a city for weeks before the circus arrives. It's a whole different story."

Chapter 7
SAFE . . . UNLESS A TIGER GETS ME DOWN

"Why do you suppose Irvin Feld made Charlie Bauman the performance director?" I asked Art, breaking the silence.

"I don't know. Maybe Irvin figured anyone who makes his living inside a cage full of temperamental tigers must be a pretty good judge of character."

Art and I sat in the car, peering quietly through the dark. Two white homes, clapboard houses, sat eerily on the other side of the tracks.

"We're to pick up Charlie Bauman and Lloyd Morgan," Art had said, and accompany them to the arena. I didn't know much about Lloyd Morgan, other than that he was the General Manager entrusted with the roustabouts and the rigging of the show. But Charlie's background, at least from the press releases, had been well recorded.

Over the years he'd been mauled by a lion four times, had claws clamped around his throat and been dragged around the ring by his neck. "But at least the cats are predictable," he rationalized to a reporter, "unlike a bear that gives no warning. You don't see anything because of a bear's thick hair. You can't see any muscle movement. A bear can sit there taking a piece of sugar from you and the next thing you know he's on top of you."

Charlie grew up in Berlin, familiar early with the life of a performer. His father had been a movie stunt man, riding horses over hedgerows and cliffs. From him, Charlie no doubt, developed his disposition for risk.

But at the outset of the war, Charlie's parents were caught helping a Jewish equestrian escape Nazi Germany for Spain. Only twelve years old, Charlie was shipped to an orphanage while his parents were transported to concentration camps. His father died several months later in the gas chambers of Bergen-Belsin while his mother endured medical experiments at Ravenebruch, leaving her permanently scarred with chronic asthma.

As soon as Charlie came of age—determined more by a shortage of men then anything chronological—he was drafted into the Germany navy, but he was captured near the end of the war by American troops. Imprisoned by the allies in an airdome, Charlie was able to escape through a gaping hole in the wall left behind by an exploding bomb. He scrambled back to Berlin where he located his mother who, widowed and sickly, was now living impoverished in a ghetto apartment. Reunited, but as an escapee with no ration cards, Charlie was forced to scavenge through trash cans in search of food for them both.

Soon thereafter, his mother, through earlier contacts, secured him a job with a small circus. A short time later he joined Circus Williams, a larger show, as an assistant horse trainer. One morning while cleaning up around the circus ring he heard a commotion coming from inside the lion cage. Several roustabouts stood frozen while inside the cage screams emanated from beneath a pile of lions. A stream of blood gushed from under their fur. Charlie grabbed a whip and a chair and in an act of supreme courage—since if no one would help the tiger trainer he could be certain no one was going to help him—he managed to force the four lions off their prey long enough to drag the trainer, Jean Michon, by his heels to safety. But with over thirty bites and claw marks it would be half a year before the lion trainer reentered the ring. Perhaps it was this early experience, his unlikely start as a lion tamer, that prompted his response to a reporter when asked if he was often in danger. "I'm safe, unless one of the tigers gets me down . . . and then the others will in all likelihood join in."

I heard it before I saw it—a waking, rumbling sound growing louder and louder—and then a single bright light shone round the bend. The train came screeching to a stop.

A thick, dark-haired man jumped off the train and began walking in our direction. "There's Charlie," Art said. He was wearing a pair of dark trousers and a weathered brown jacket. As he came closer I noticed he was carrying a large roll of masking tape. I could see the faint outline of other men in the darkness stepping off the train. One in particular, a balding man, not far from Charlie, turned to another man, a man too stunted to be viewed as normal but too tall to be labeled a midget. "I'll see you at the arena Shorty. Make sure they're careful with the spotlights."

As Charlie Baumann approached I quickly opened the door and slid into the back seat of the car.

"Welcome back to San Diego," Art said. "This is Jamie, a new trainee." Short of breath, as though he were trying to catch up with himself, Charlie glanced in my direction. The back door opened and the man who had just issued instructions to Shorty slipped in. "Hi, I'm Lloyd Morgan," he said, shaking my hand, and I wondered how much his gravelly tone was morning induced.

With an unscarred hand, Charlie Baumann reached inside his jacket and jiggled a cigarette out of a crumpled pack.

"I thought you were going to quit?" Art said.

"I'm down to two packs a day," he smiled. "Isn't that enough!"

On the way to the arena, Art and Lloyd and Charlie talked about the building and the upcoming dates, but I was too mesmerized by their presence and *how* things were being said to appreciate much about *what* they were saying. Charlie spoke with a rough German accent and while unreserved in Art's company he seemed easily distracted. Conversely, Lloyd seemed more at ease with himself, giving me the impression he was, by nature, unflappable.

Art pulled into the arena parking lot and rolled to a stop, leading us hurriedly down a back ramp and through an unmarked door.

"There are eleven dressing rooms," he said to Charlie. "The rest of the space you'll have to cordon off." Then pivoting on his heels he announced, "I'm going to show Lloyd inside the arena."

I stood there, adrift by a posse that had just split up, wondering which way to turn, when Charlie muttered something unintelligible to me, spun around and began marching up the corridor. I scurried behind as he ripped off a piece of masking tape and slapped it on a dressing room door. With a black magic marker he wrote in block letters "ELVIN BALE." "Egotists," he growled. "Give the wrong person too small a room and all hell breaks loose."

Moving up the hall, he tore off another piece of tape and scratched the name of a teeterboard act, "THE METCHKARO-FFS." "This isn't the right order, but I don't dare put the Bulgarians anywhere near the Romanians!"

While I wondered why all this had to be done at five in the morning, I followed him door to door, providing what he seemed to need most—an attentive sounding board.

Finally, he ran out of dressing rooms and we strode back down the corridor to the large open area by the back door entrance. "The performers today don't know they're in a circus anymore. If the water's not warm, if it's drafty in their dressing rooms, they start complaining."

Charlie bent down, this time stretching a long piece of tape several feet along the concrete floor, marking it in the center "CLOWN ALLEY." "I say you never worked in a circus 'til you've been in a tent with an ice storm blowing in one end!"

Art emerged alone from behind the back stage curtain.

"Would you like a ride back to the train?"

"No, I'll catch a ride later," Charlie said.

As Art and I climbed the back ramp, a flatbed truck arrived carrying several men. In the back I noticed coils of heavy rope and a stack of long aluminum pipes.

"Come on," Art said. "Let's clean up back at the hotel. The animal walk starts in two hours."

The unusual scent of diesel fuel and grease mixed with the stuffy smells of trampled hay and unwashed elephants swept through the air as Art and I stepped out of the car. I breathed in the smell, reveling in it, for no other reason than the rarity of it all.

Axel Gautier, the elephant trainer, imperious, I'd heard, even while performing, was now acting downright tyrannical. I couldn't understand his German commands, but to the elephants, horses and llamas, stumbling down the wooden ramps into the bright sunlight, they were unmistakably thinly veiled threats.

Several roustabouts, echoing Axel, shouted similar orders while the elephants were brought into line. As I watched the commotion I tried to dismiss the activists' concerns about animal cruelty, especially now that I was in the enemy camp. But I had to admit that spending hour upon hour, side by side, in the cramped confines of a train car rumbling down the tracks could hardly be a pleasant experience. I also wondered if a sharp jab in a sensitive area such as the stomach or the ear by the hooked rods some of the men were carrying didn't bring a recalcitrant elephant into instant obedience.

Art cringed as Axel, no longer the proud trainer gratefully acknowledging his elephant's performance, whacked one of the elephants on the back of the knee.

"Axel doesn't much care for the animal walks," Art grumbled. "Let's hope he calms down before the cameramen arrive."

The fact was Axel had little choice. The animals had to be transported from the train to the arena so why not capitalize on the strange sight of a herd of pachyderms plodding through the city's streets. "The problem," Art warned, "was if we made too big a deal out of it the publicity would backfire. All we'd read the next day in the paper was what a disappointment the dreary parade had been."

Art cajoled two show girls and a clown, who stood patiently by the side of the tracks, to ride along for added color, while the rest of the herd was reserved for newspaper reporters, TV personalities and anyone else who could contribute free publicity.

Cars began arriving and within a few minutes several riders stood on the curb, nervously chattering, while Art made sure they were welcomed. Fortunately, Axel Gautier had toned down his rhetoric from tyranny to simple rudeness. Anxious to proceed, he forced the lead elephant to its knees and barked at the group to send over its first rider. A lanky brunette in tan slacks stepped timidly out of the crowd. Axel told her to step on the elephant's knee. I watched as she swung a long leg over the elephant's neck and shifted her hips in position. Axel shouted a second command and the elephant struggled to its feet.

Axel loaded the riders one by one. Then with a final order, the elephants, in childlike fashion, linked their trunks around the tip of the tail in front and, bolting forward, began lumbering down the street.

"Lets go," Art said, and amidst the swirling dust I hurriedly followed him to the car.

"It's a nice crowd," I said, as we pulled in behind the police escort, bringing up the rear. Families with children, three and four people deep, lined the one-mile advertised route.

"It would be," Art said, "if the animal walk wasn't their excuse for not buying tickets to the show."

I paused for a moment, watching the bobbing reporters wave to the crowds below, and wondered for a second if indeed his statement was true.

Art and I strolled toward the back ramp, the same ramp we had escorted Lloyd and Charlie up four hours earlier. Only now the back parking lot was dotted with canvas tents, bales of hay and a scattering of portable toilets and trailers. A miniature "pie car" on wheels was dispensing donuts and hot drinks as we ambled by.

"Come on, I'll buy you a cup of coffee," Art said, "then we'll see how Lloyd and Charlie are doing."

Charlie, we were told, had already returned to the train. But inside the back stage area, a maze of blue curtains had been carefully erected. A wardrobe lady, old and heavily wrinkled, wheeled a crate full of colorful costumes by as I noticed Charlie's labels had been transplanted from the floor to the front of the curtains.

Art and I walked into the arena. "Follow me," he said, and I followed him past the first tier of seats, into the middle section, and sat beside him near the center aisle.

Lloyd Morgan stood to one side, six rows away. With megaphone in hand, he scanned the arena as two dozen men picked their way through fourteen miles of ropes and wires and metal tubing. It was all laid out in the same precise pattern in which it would be raised by cable to the ceiling.

I watched as two roustabouts, or "working men," swung their combined weight from a rope hanging from the ceiling. It was the roustabouts' job to safely secure the guy wires, move the props, rig and unrig the show and humbly shovel the elephant dung, all the while, dressed in identical blue jumpsuits, blending inconspicuously into the background. Social invisibility was something I suspected they were used to, for most of them had the defeated look of the downtrodden and destitute.

Perhaps even Feld, curiously enough, had a soft spot in his heart for them. Reportedly he and Charlie Bauman were driving through the back lot one afternoon when Charlie began complaining about a roustabout guarding the elephants, a roustabout that had been with the circus for years. "Look at him! He's half asleep, and when he's not half asleep he's half drunk. Why do we keep him?"

Feld looked over at the listless roustabout, sprawled lazily on a chair outside the elephant tent. "Have we lost any elephants?"

"No," said Charlie.

"Then he can't be doing too bad a job."

Several of the men hauled a half dozen ropes through a series of pulleys, and the rectangular framework of pipes slowly rose to the ceiling.

"How long does all this take?" I asked, spying other men in the shadows of the catwalks locking the rigging in place.

"About eight hours," Art said. "They're half way through."

Art rose to his feet and I stepped behind him to where Lloyd was standing.

"Is there anything you need?"

"Not a thing," Lloyd said, smiling as though it were an effort. "By the way, Charlie and I wanted to know if you and Rachel and Jamie would join us for dinner tonight at the train. Would barbecued chicken suit you?"

"We were filming the highlights of the two shows at winter quarters for the NBC Special," Lloyd said, as Charlie, beginning to laugh, passed him the potato salad, "when somebody made the mistake of putting Elvin Bale and Gunther in the same room. Gunther threw the first punch. Elvin somersaulted backwards. It took us twenty minutes to separate them!"

Charlie stood up, still chuckling, and placed four more pieces of raw meat on the grill, compressing them with a spatula until the blood sizzled obediently on the coals.

"How are the ligers doing?" Art interjected.

I'd read about the ligers in one of the press releases. There were two of them Charlie was now raising, a rare cross between a tiger and a lion.

"They are adorable! I just weaned them off bottled milk a few weeks ago." Charlie reached for the barbeque sauce. "People love to play with them, especially the kids, but I had to put a stop to it. They may look cute and fluffy but they're not your average kittens. People would pick them up, cuddle them in their laps, the ligers would squirm and the next thing I'd hear is someone wailing they'd been clawed. Either that or they'd try to feed them. Like all my cats, particularly my new ones, the only source of food I want them to have is from me."

Charlie's wife, Araceli, a compact, serious woman, returned from the train car with a platter of fresh onions and sliced tomatoes as the conversation drifted to Irvin Feld. They were obviously just as curious about headquarter gossip as we were about life on the train. Irvin Feld, Art explained, was embroiled in a brawl of his own. While the Blue Show was ensconced on the West Coast, the Red Show was opening next month in Washington, D.C. and apparently a newly created circus was challenging him on his home turf.

Art wasn't sure of all the details, but from what he knew it was turning into a full scale battle. Abe Pollin, the owner of Washington, D.C.'s newly built, twenty-thousand seat Capital Centre, had always expected Ringling Brothers to switch to the Capital Centre from the D.C. armory, a dingy coliseum in a crime-ridden section of the city, where Ringling Brothers had been relegated to play for years. But in a bitter denunciation of Pollin and his new arena, Irvin refused to budge. Pollin, with no shortage of ego, indignation and resources, decided to retaliate by forming a circus of his own. Christened Circus America, Pollin scheduled its run to coincide with Ringling's engagement. And to make matters worse, he put together a formidable show. Gathering a hodgepodge of acts from all over the world, he capitalized on Ringling's Achilles heel. Whereas Irvin was accused of turning the old-time circus into Las Vegas glitz, Pollin put the thrill back into the show. Ringling had superior timing and finesse but Pollin had countered with a human cannonball act, a motorcycle daredevil and a slew of splashier acts. For pure thrills, spills and bang for the buck, Art shrugged and admitted, Pollin had Irvin beat.

"But as the two circuses headed for a collision you could barely turn on the radio or television without hearing a competing spot." To pour salt into Irvin's wounds, no doubt spiraling the costs further, Pollin had even bought all the time slots to promote Circus America during Ringling's own annual televised special. Art said it was the most expensive exhibition of advertising rivalry he'd ever seen.

The bitter feud had reportedly started when Pollin, a few years earlier, had been desperately seeking a hockey franchise for his new arena. Irvin had clout with several of the owners and Pollin had asked for his help.

Allen Bloom sat in the meetings with Irvin and Pollin and according to a *Washington Post* reporter said Irvin had agreed to help in exchange for a portion of the new franchise. According to Allen, Pollin offered to sell Feld 24.5 percent of the team. "Pollin felt that was fair incentive for Feld to go out and help get him a hockey team." Irvin called five NHL franchise owners and encouraged them to support Pollin's bid. Pollin was awarded the franchise and Irvin's office was promptly flooded with calls of congratulation. "But Abe Pollin never called," Allen said. In fact, two weeks later Irvin called Pollin and Pollin apologized for his busy schedule, but according to Allen, they didn't hear from him again for months. When he did call, he denied ever making the promise. Irvin was furious.

"The press has dubbed it 'The Circus Wars' and as far as I can see," Art said, "they'll both end up losing. The ticket sales are evenly split, dividing the attendance for both of the shows, while the advertising costs are reaching astronomical levels."

As I listened to Art's tale of a bitter feud fueled by Pollin's purported greed and Irvin's sense of betrayal, I couldn't help wondering about an important missing ingredient. How did Irvin Feld, who had spent the last thirty years in a world where handshakes meant *nothing*—a world of ironclad contracts between him and his rock stars, arenas, record companies, hundreds of circus performers and a myriad of other legal relationships—how could he have attended several meetings with Abe Pollin, agreed to a one-quarter ownership of a major sports franchise and not have a written legal agreement to back up his claim?

The coals turned into ashes as Lloyd's wife, a pretty blond haired woman, removed the last of the food from the table. I noticed the smells of European spices and curry no longer drifted by from further up the tracks. She returned with an uncorked bottle of wine. The conversation meandered back to the circus as the night grew quieter around us.

I hadn't said much of anything the whole evening but finally ventured forward with a question. "Charlie, doesn't it sometimes frighten you walking into a cage full of man-eating tigers?"

Charlie looked at me with a mischievous grin. "Walking into the cage never bothers me. It's getting back out again that scares the hell out of me!"

Even his wife broke into laughter, although she'd probably heard his response five hundred times. Charlie's good humor, however, came to an abrupt end when Art casually mentioned the name Michu.

"Michu," Charlie spat. "Irvin is going to have to talk to him. I give up!"

Charlie poured forth a stream of invectives all aimed at Michu's spoiled behavior. From what Sam had told me, Michu was a known womanizer—"no doubt lustily relishing their warm embrace as women clutched this grown man in an infants body to their bosoms"—and a notorious boozer, alternating between French brandy and excessive amounts of Russian vodka. But could the "little shit," as Sam Barrett indicated one promoter had nicknamed him, be the L'enfant terrible Charlie described? Or was Charlie just frustrated that because of Michu's star status, no matter what Michu did, Charlie was left with little disciplinary recourse? How ironic, it occurred to me, the smallest man in the world stymied in some way one of the most powerful and virile men known . . . and I wondered if Michu knew it.

We talked a few more minutes, Art passing out complimentary cigars, until he slowly stood up and stretched.

"Thank you for dinner," he said as the others moved comfortably away from their chairs.

We said our goodbyes and Art and Rachel and I walked to the car and drove quietly back to the motel. Like a small child who wouldn't let go of a good movie I replayed each scene in my head. Art rolled to a stop and I exited the back seat of the car still aglow from the evening's discussion.

"Incidently," Art said, "tomorrow's your day off. But Tuesday I want you to take Michu to an opening-day interview with the *San Diego Tribune*. With luck, he'll be waiting for you at the train at eight a.m."

Chapter 8
A History Un-coated

After three weeks of absorbing Art's every word plus reading and re-reading his binders of notes he turned to me earlier in the week and asked, "How much do you know about the history of Ringling Brothers and Barnum and Bailey Circus?"

"Not much," I reluctantly admitted.

Art glanced at me indifferently, which was his way of suggesting maybe on my day off it was time I learned. The next day I returned from the library with a half dozen books. But if my research was to be worthwhile I was determined to separate fact from fiction . . . and as much as it was conceivably possible, demystify the origins of the circus.

By all accounts, the five oldest of the seven Ringling brothers first remember the inception of their idea to own a circus coming during one pre-dawn morning in 1870 along the banks of the Mississippi river, in the small Midwestern town of McGregor, Iowa. Their ages ranged from Al, eighteen, the oldest, to Gus, sixteen; Otto, twelve; Alfred, eight; Charles, six; John, four and Henry who was only one. They waited anxiously for the arrival of the circus boat, the same boat that had been stopping at little towns all along the way. Dozens of other children climbed the trees along the river bank and peered out through the leaves. Posters had been plastered by the advance men for weeks all over town and on the sides of the farmers' barns. In fact the whole town looked forward to the show's arrival.

But it wasn't just because the circus was a welcome splash of color in an otherwise monotonous landscape of long farm days and hard physical labor. This was the golden age of the circus. An age when in many ways the circus was a window to the world. Television didn't exist, nor did Hollywood movies nor for that matter modern travel with airplanes that could transport people anywhere in the world within twenty four hours.

For the average American, especially in small towns, almost everything seemed new and exotic and the circus fed off their intense curiosity. The circus was the precursor to the modern zoo. Its menagerie presented animals only seen in books and illustrations. The circus was a museum of new innovations re-shaping the country. Inventions such as the lightbulb, the phonograph and the typewriter were exhibited in the side shows. And in an age of unknown cultures the circus was a traveling National Geographic with pygmies, Australian aborigines and strange women from far off continents with stretched out lips and elongated ear lobes . . . and if the circus didn't have the real thing it wasn't beyond the imagination of the owners to fabricate it. (The wild men of Borneo, two strange looking creatures, were actually two Americans with stunted growth and intelligence). The circus wasn't just another form of entertainment. It was a fresh water river in a vast ocean of people with a thirst for knowledge.

The Ringlings watched as the puffing steamboat appeared in the distance carrying its colorful wagons, circus tents and exotic animals on a barge latched to the boat's side. Once docked, the handlers unloaded its only elephant, rolled the wagon and the rigging down the gangplank and began the all day task of erecting the tents in a nearby field. The Ringling brothers probably volunteered to help for a free ticket. Other young men were asked to stretch the canvas while the elderly watched from the sidelines in nostalgic amusement. All the shouting, commotion and strange looking people only served to heighten the expectations for the opening night's performance.

It was amidst this flurry of activity that the brothers remembered talking for the first time about building a circus of their own. In fact within just a week of the circus boat's departure the boys crafted a tent with $8.37 worth of cloth and put together an act featuring a billy goat and a trained horse, charging the grand sum of fifty cents to enter what they called the Ringling Brothers Carnival of Fun.

A few months later the boys' family resettled in Baraboo, Wisconsin and for the next several years the brothers scattered in diverse pursuits. But besides looking strikingly similar, almost like quintuplets in certain photos, with dark hair, dark eyes, identical hairlines and handlebar mustaches, the boys had one main objective in common: an insatiable desire to succeed driven by an entrepreneurial spirit that is so often possessed by first-born Americans. Their father, August Rungeling, a carriage maker, had fled Germany in 1848, bringing his parents with him a year later. He married a woman named Marie Julian who had immigrated from France only three years earlier and promptly Anglicized the name to Ringling. Once in America, August Ringling established his own business as a harness maker, and although the business was fledgling at best, he instilled in his sons a drive for independence that only business ownership can provide.

Al, the oldest and the one with the most vision, stuck to his ambition for a career in show business and roamed from traveling show to traveling show as a juggler and acrobat while learning the financial and management end of the business. Otto, Alf and Charles followed in their father's footsteps as carriage makers, while Gus worked as a carriage trimmer in small towns throughout Iowa. John, known for his brashness and eccentricities, who would become the most domineering of the brothers, was meanwhile rebelling at home. By the age of sixteen, he had already run away four times and never did complete a high school education; even though in later years, it would be he who was most responsible for the incredible growth of the business. For now, though, he was well on his way to becoming a little hellion. At the tender age of eight, his mother became alarmed at his foul language and asked the minister to speak to him. The minister told the young man that he had heard that his language had gotten quite coarse, whereupon the eight-year-old asked, "Who told you that?" The minister replied,

"A little birdie told me." The little boy then looked up in the sky and said, "I'll bet it was one of those God-damned little sparrows."

It was twelve years later, in 1882, that Al, now thirty years old, returned to Baraboo to collect his brothers to assemble their own show. Charles and Alf, easily persuaded, left their father's harness business; Otto joined as an advance man; and John was an easy recruit. Gus, however, elected to stay with his carriage business, while Henry, the youngest, proved to be a hopeless alcoholic. Although he would travel with the circus, he gradually lost the respect of his brothers and his own self esteem, even attempting suicide soon after a six-week binge.

They admitted the show they organized was woefully pathetic, with the brothers themselves providing the bulk of the entertainment. Fortunately, the sheer paucity of amusement for these small Midwest towns kept the show financially alive. But it wasn't until Al was introduced to a sage old man, Fayette Ludovic Robinson, otherwise known as Yankee Robinson, that their highly leveraged show began to take structure.

Robinson had owned shows off and on for forty years but he was now in the twilight of his career. Aging, with his energies flagging but unwilling to give up his passion, he desperately needed the spirit and ambition of the Ringling brothers, and the Ringling brothers desperately needed a mentor. A perfect combination. Together, they joined forces to create the Yankee Robinson and Ringling Brothers Great Double Show. The partnership, however, would prove to be short lived. Robinson died only two years later, in August 1884. But fortunately by then, enough of a show existed, along with the business knowledge he left behind, to begin an unstoppable drive for size and money. An intimidated competitor would later decry, "It's not so much that the Ringling brothers are so smart as much as the fact that there's so damn many of them."

A writer once said, "Anyone who concentrates on creating an all encompassing label for themselves, whether as the world's greatest lover, dancer, humorist or in P.T. Barnum's case 'showman,' risks becoming merely an animated version of themselves." Barnum was the epitome of this phenomenon, to the extent that it's difficult to see the flesh and blood through all the hype and self promotion.

Five foot ten and 170 pounds with a cherubic face, a penguin shape and a perpetual smile, Barnum was described as "constantly quick and energetic." But it was only during the last twenty years of Barnum's life that his attention would focus on the circus. For thirty years Barnum's base of operations had been a museum, albeit a highly successful museum in the heart of New York City. But although his American Museum was known worldwide Barnum's choice of professions was by no means unique. There were museum owners in dozens of big cities throughout the nation displaying a smorgasbord of curiosities and relics, some real and some contrived, from around the globe.

But where Barnum excelled he was unequaled; starting with his unrivaled mastery of multiple hyperbole, often crafting his promotional copy himself. His advance man, Tody Hamilton, a disciple of Barnum's verbal dexterity, would amusingly declare, "to state a fact in ordinary language is to permit doubt concerning the statement!" But Barnum's success was due to more than exaggeration. In an era when "other people" and comical ingenuity were the chief form of entertainment, few could match Barnum's fun-spirited practical jokes and hoaxes. Exaggeration and trickery, viewed not from the lenses of modern disdain for advertising deception, was in Barnum's time an understandable part of the landscape, applauded in fact for its cleverness.

Barnum was a businessman, unswerving in his pursuit of wealth despite the most daunting of tragedies—his home and beloved museum were destroyed by fire more than once—and although he was extravagant in almost everything he did, with his attention to detail a part of his success, he was also "the most economical man I have ever known," wrote one of his colleagues. "It made no difference who paid the expenses. If they weren't necessary he didn't want them incurred."

And perhaps most important of all, as it relates to Barnum's preparation for the work of the circus, Barnum wasn't afraid to venture out, at home and abroad, with his curiosities. For in addition to owning the American Museum and procuring with the help of others the thousands of items that filled it, Barnum was the harbinger of the Hollywood agent and present-day promoter conveniently rolled into one.

But unlike the Hollywood agent, who negotiates agreements on behalf of the performer for a small percentage of the take, leaving the promotional effort to someone else, Barnum, after footing the costs, received the lion's share of the proceeds while in turn becoming the star attraction's self-prescribed promoter and publicist.

Instead of rock stars and movie stars, and the occasional likes of a shapely Jenny Lind (the thin ankled soprano whom some say Barnum was as much enamored as the public), he more often promoted the existence of the strange and unusual . . . perhaps the strangest of all being the bizarre tale of Chang and Eng, the Chinese Siamese twins.

Chang and Eng were born in 1811 in a picturesque fishing village not far from Bangkok, in what was then known as Siam. Born to a Chinese father and half-Chinese mother, they seemed perfectly normal except for one disturbing fact. They were connected at the chest by a thick cord of cartilage a half inch long and eight inches in circumference . . . and none knew for sure what lifelines flowed through it. If cut apart it was dreadfully feared one or both would be lost. So Chang and Eng were destined to live their lives joined together in this odd yet unsolvable manner.

They grew to a full height of 5'2" and 5'1" with Eng wearing special lifts in his shoes to match his brother's height. The twins learned to run and swim and do most normal activities. They walked by maneuvering side by side and they slept face to face, changing sleeping positions by rolling over each other, which somehow they accomplished without waking.

At the age of eighteen, however, they were discovered by an unscrupulous yankee skipper who shanghaied the twins to European and North American ports, placing them on exhibit for a tidy profit. The sea captain milked them for all they were worth, deserting them a few years later, taking with him every cent they had earned.

By then, they were at least well known, and an opportunistic P.T. Barnum signed them on as part of his colorful cast at his American

Museum. Barnum's publicity preferred, of course, to present a positive spin on the twins' adjustment to everyday life—they swam, they danced, they spoke in three languages. Yet one look at an old photograph and the morose expressions on Chang and Engs' faces and the devastating reality of living attached to one another made a sham of any animated version of their lives.

Chang and Eng gradually built a comfortable estate of $60,000 and although Barnum was responsible for their financial footing neither Chang nor Eng was fond of him. In fact, both would declare they thought he was stingy.

Medically, the Siamese twins contracted illnesses such as measles and small pox concurrently and recovered simultaneously, but as adults, one went on occasional binges, while the other remained a teetotaler. Yet physically, the alcohol's effects on one brother didn't seem to affect the other.

The twins raised numerous legal questions among litigants of the time. If one committed a crime, could they both be imprisoned? Who owned what property? And is one automatically an accessory to the other's ill deeds?

Chang and Eng fell asleep and awoke in unison and even smoked and chewed tobacco in concert; however, they could not have two different discussions on two different subjects simultaneously. It was virtually impossible, no matter how hard someone tried, to engage them in such a way.

They also rarely spoke to each other, saying they both saw and experienced everything at the same time and felt the same way about it, so what was there to discuss?

The twins, astonishingly enough, met, fell in love with and married two sisters. Unfortunately, the sisters disliked one another and neither brother cared for his sister-in-law; so separate houses were constructed, three miles apart, near Mount Airy, North Carolina. Thus began a strange commute, alternating every three days from one home to the other.

The marriages lasted thirty years, and between them, they had 22 children, all normal except for a boy and a girl who were both deaf mutes. Their later years were spent quietly, tending to their two small farms and commuting in their odd yet acceptable arrangement.

In their sixty-third year, Chang caught a severe cold while presumably riding in the rain. Other reports have it that Chang's alcoholic binges finally caught up with him. Nevertheless, on Friday evening, January 23, 1874, they strolled off to bed in a small, dimly lit room by themselves. Chang couldn't sleep, and in the middle of the night, they arose and sat by a fire in a specially built chair. Eng was tired, but Chang complained that his chest hurt when he lay down; so Eng smoked his pipe until Chang agreed to go back to bed, whereupon Eng fell into a deep, restful sleep.

In the morning Eng was shaken awake by his son, to be told Chang was dead. Eng screamed out in panic, "My last hour has come!" and plunged into violent, uncontrollable spasms. Within two hours, Eng too was dead.

An autopsy was performed at the College of Physicians in Philadelphia where it was determined Chang died of a cerebral clot. No cause, however, could be found for Eng's death and it was largely believed he died of fright.

In 1870, the same year that the Ringling brothers erected a tiny tent showcasing a trained horse and billy goat, P.T. Barnum was bored. Now sixty years old, it had been two years since his second museum had burned to the ground. "I've worked enough," he had said, announcing forlornly his retirement. But in spite of his proclamation, restless and in search of something to do, he found time to finance a three-year tour for Tom Thumb and arrange a British exhibition of the Siamese Twins. It was billed as a search for an Old World surgeon skilled enough to successfully separate Chang and Eng. The Brits crowded the exhibit in fear it would be their last chance to see the twins before they were medically separated or, as some predicted, dead.

So it was with relief that Barnum accepted a proposal offered by Don Castello, an ex-clown, and William Cameron Coup, a former roustabout, to launch for his first time a circus.

But if Coup, who was undeservedly credited with producing the first two-ring circus and constructing the tents with center poles, thought the chief asset he was acquiring was Barnum's name, he was profoundly mistaken. Whether due to Barnum's "pent up" energy or his decades of "thinking big," Barnum threw himself into the creation of his new enterprise. Nothing was too large or too daring and they soon were involved in a mammoth undertaking, "Barnum's Great Traveling World's Fair," which opened in Brooklyn, New York beneath three acres of canvas tents. The show was a huge success, grossing almost a million dollars in the first six months.

Within three short years, with Coup as General Manager and Castello as Director of Amusements, a second show was set in motion, "P.T. Barnum's Great Roman Hippodrome," featuring chariot races by "Amazon" women, wild animals, clowns and "living curiosities," performing under six giant tents. But it wasn't long before Barnum was financially overextended, Coup was emotionally exhausted and a string of mishaps, capped by their star performer's fatal departure, floating over Lake Michigan in a hot air balloon, that the partnership crumbled.

Barnum took a diversion from show business, serving a term as mayor of his hometown, Bridgeport, Connecticut, before launching once again, with three new partners, an even more extravagant circus. The partnership lasted three seasons, hindered by his manager's complaints—"we do all the work with Barnum merely renting his name"—convincing Barnum to strike out on his own.

Approaching what others might consider the "frail" age of seventy, Barnum found himself facing greater and greater competition. The most noteworthy being a burgeoning circus, International Allied Shows, which was beginning to encroach on his territory. Allied had as its managing Director and one of its owners a man named James A. Bailey.

Bailey's birth name was James A. McGinnis. At the age of twelve he had run away from home and joined a small circus, Cooper and Bailey. Over the next ten years, by spotting and filling every vacuum he could, McGinnis became indispensable, so much so that when Bailey died he promptly demanded a full partnership. Cooper agreed but refused to change the name of the show. So McGinnis, perhaps in an act of defiance, placing business above lineage, simply changed his own name, becoming James A. Bailey. And within a few more years, by the age of twenty six, he succeeded in wresting from Cooper the remaining control of the show.

Six years later Bailey, along with two partners, had formed Allied International Shows and was beginning to build a reputation for himself while picking away at Barnum's following. But what caught Barnum's attention and greatly amused him was Bailey's response to an offer Barnum made by telegram for the purchase of one of Allied's newborn elephants. It was the first time an elephant from India had been born in America and the news was attracting a ton of publicity. Barnum offered Allied a purchase price of $100,000, whereupon Bailey promptly blew up the telegram to billboard size, adding the exclamation, "Look what Barnum Thinks of our Baby Elephant!"

Out maneuvered, but with new found respect for his young competitor, Barnum initiated a meeting. The result, to Barnum's delight, was the merger in August of 1880 of the two shows into what would be called the Barnum and Bailey Circus, renowned for its slogan, "The Greatest Show on Earth."

Less has been written about Bailey but he wasn't considered Barnum's alter ego. Instead, down to his high forehead, chiseled nose and neatly trimmed beard, Bailey could hardly be more opposite. Unlike Barnum, Bailey disliked personal publicity and exposure and in fact hid in his quarters when reporters were nearby. Bailey wore a derby hat to vainly cover his baldness and suffered from constant fretfulness and insomnia. Squint-eyed and perpetually nervous he was the antitheses of Barnum's charm and gregarious nature. But where Barnum was the consummate promoter, Bailey was a mechanical genius. His meticulous logistics for moving masses of men, animals and equipment by railroad cars was so admired that the quartermaster for the German army followed him around for weeks to study how he kept the whole operation together.

Bailey was a sensitive man and refused to fire performers personally; yet prone to outbursts of anger he could also dispense justice unmercifully. After one of his elephants went on a rampage in London, killing its keeper, Bailey drowned the elephant, pushing it overboard, cage and all, on the return trip to New York.

Barnum and Bailey's partnership was not without conflict, exacerbated at times by Barnum's all-consuming ego and inflamed on occasion by Bailey's habit of augmenting the staff, especially the accounting department, with personal relatives. But other than a short dissolution, the partnership would thrive and Barnum would proudly announce, "He suits me exactly—as a partner and a friend."

Following the death of their mentor, Yankee Robinson, the Ringling brothers spent the next six years in an unrelenting push to build their circus. Notwithstanding clashes and tirades among brothers with distinct personalities, they remained bonded together by adversity as much as by common goals. By 1888, the circus had twice doubled in size due to borrowing cash up to their handlebar mustaches and plowing every cent of profits back into the show. A mile long caravan of wagons hauled a circus tent one-hundred-and-forty-eight feet long by one-hundred feet wide, along with scores of animals and personnel. But throughout the Midwest, times were tough for a traveling circus, and logistics enabling them to stay on schedule were sometimes impossible. At one point midway through Iowa, they wired their banker for funds in a state of despair. Wet, cold and exhausted, they explained that the wagons were sinking to their axles in mud, and they were dead broke from paying farmers to help dislodge them. When they did get unstuck, they would find the wagons were falling apart from the strain of being pulled. The banker wired them a thousand dollars. After almost a month of rains, the sun finally broke through, enabling them to once again regroup and begin recovering their losses.

More determined than ever, the brothers continued to combine their talents and resources, and in 1889 they expanded their route. It would prove to be a year of enormous gains. With money in hand and now ample credit, they discarded their bruised caravan of wagons and in 1890, in an act that would prove to be a significant turning point, began transporting their circus by train. This change would be the beginning of a period of unrestrained growth, and within twelve months, just eight short years after Al had gathered his five siblings, the Ringling Brothers Circus had become a three-ring show carried by twenty-two railroad cars—and was now ready to challenge the big boys. Not the least of which was a giant spectacle, awesome in scope, pulled by five railroad trains four miles long, with four orchestras, twelve chariots, and one-hundred vans another three miles in length. It advertised itself as featuring over one-hundred-thousand curiosities, carrying the most elaborate and exhaustive traveling exhibition ever seen, even including a spectacular replay of Nero and the destruction of Rome. It was a show of mammoth size and national reputation, and to its two owners, the ambitious Ringling brothers didn't even exist. The show was The Barnum and Bailey Circus—"The Greatest Show on Earth."

The Ringling brothers by now had worked out a division of labor conducive to each of their strengths. Al, who originally persuaded his brothers to join him, was the Producer and Director of the show, responsible for its production. Charles headed up logistics, which included the trains, tent set up, food and repairs. Otto handled financial management. Alf was the Public Relations Director, and John managed the routing, which included arranging the schedule and negotiating with the cities and property owners for the tent sites.

Following the first law of business survival, "never pick a fight with someone more powerful," the brothers strategically routed their show to avoid clashing with Barnum and Bailey. This bought them time to strengthen their financial foundation while gradually building a following and steadily increasing the size of the show.

Much of their efforts were probably ignored, if for no other reason than during that same year, James Bailey's attention was sadly diverted. His partner and, in many ways, friend and counsel, Phineas T. Barnum, died in his home in Bridgeport, Connecticut at the age of eighty-one, thus ending a career in showmanship that would, in all likelihood, remain unmatched, if in legend alone, for years to come.

The Barnum and Bailey Circus, however, was now a national institution, and Bailey continued to manage the vast enterprise virtually alone as the preeminent showman of the circus world. He was only forty-four when Barnum died, and at the prime of his business career he was a formidable opponent.

Nevertheless, four years later the Ringling brothers, having emerged from lesser battles, bruised but victorious, decided to challenge him head on. They moved into Bailey's territory, the big towns where previously only the giants were allowed to feed.

Now the Ringlings had Bailey's attention, but the shrewd street fighter had no intention of bloodying himself in order to swat these five brothers. Instead he routed his own circus far from the Ringlings' and sent the Forepaugh-Sells circus, in which he owned fifty percent of the stock, to compete with the Ringlings and drain their resources. As Bailey's hired gun, Forepaugh-Sells clashed with Ringling in forty-five towns in that one year, but the competition took its toll on all three circuses, and with the realization they were fighting a war of attrition, Bailey and the Ringlings finally withdrew, licked their wounds and arranged their schedules to avoid one another.

The following year, Bailey decided to take his circus to Europe for a five-year tour, mistakenly believing his subsidiary, Forepaugh-Sells, could retain his audience in the states. Instead it became the beginning of the end for the Barnum and Bailey Circus. With Bailey in the background, the Ringlings could be held at bay, but without him, Forepaugh-Sells was no match for the five savvy brothers. By the time Bailey returned five years later, the Ringling brothers were firmly entrenched in his territory.

Bailey rattled his sabers for a year or two, but he was older and tired and realized he was just too outflanked for a serious challenge. The Ringlings also realized they had the upper hand and no longer considered him a serious threat. They were proven right, but for unexpected reasons. That spring, while Bailey was directing rehearsals for a new show, he was stricken with erysipelas, a contagious and infectious skin disease brought on by an insect bite, probably transmitted from one of his horses. His skin erupted in a red inflammation followed that night by high fever, nausea and delirium. James Bailey died just forty-eight hours later.

Bailey's widow inherited the management of the show, but despite an attempt to run the operations, it became obvious within a year that her inheritance would soon dwindle without her late husband's managerial skills. Accordingly when John Ringling approached her about buying her shares of stock, she justifiably agreed. So for the sum of $410,000, the Ringling brothers purchased their former adversary, the legendary Barnum and Bailey Circus.

For the next twelve years, the Ringling brothers would operate and tour both the Ringling Brothers Circus and the Barnum and Bailey Circus as two separate money making entities. By now, however, the five brothers had become enormously wealthy and were ready to reap the harvest from their efforts. They had built a financial empire, each owning considerable estates. No longer were they the poor sons of an immigrant carriage maker who as young boys had a dream of building a circus. Now they were nationally known tycoons who wielded great power and prestige. But they were also aging and realized a successor would be needed soon to carry the reins.

The seven brothers had only one sister, Ida. She was a pretty, olive-skinned woman with long, dark hair who blossomed as she matured with spunk and talent, but nevertheless, she was overshadowed and dominated by the protective instincts of her hard-driving brothers. In fact, Ida would incur their collective wrath to such an extent that they virtually disowned her for a period of several months when she fell in love with a man named Harry North, a divorcee. The family was outraged by this blow to their sense of propriety and incensed when she ignored their admonitions and married him anyway. It was only when she gave birth to a son, John Ringling North, that they buried their hurt feelings and reaccepted her back into the fold.

John Ringling North never experienced the hardships his uncles underwent. Instead he spent his childhood reveling in the reflective glories of his famous uncles, while living ostentatiously in his uncle Al's half-chateau, half-castle in Baraboo. Although connected at birth to the circus, he developed more of a reputation as a playboy and ne'er-do-well than an aspiring businessman.

Over the next fifteen years, the two circuses toured the major cities of the country virtually dominating the traveling entertainment world, but one by one, the seven brothers began to pass away; first Gus in 1907, followed by Al, Henry, Alfred and Otto, leaving by 1919 only Charles and John left of the original seven.

Perhaps it was for this reason, or perhaps it was because of the strains on business caused by World War I, or maybe it was due to the advent of motion pictures as a new form of competition, that in that same year the decision was made to combine the two shows. From that moment on, it would tour as one colossal enterprise, The Ringling Brothers and Barnum and Bailey Circus.

For the next ten years, John Ringling, the previous "little hellion," would carry on alone as the flamboyant president of the circus, earning the title as one of the richest men in the world. His reputation for self aggrandizement, even pouring a fortune into his own personal museum, was boundless. But his ego got the best of him, and when challenged in 1929 by a group of smaller circuses, he simply purchased them, an act that would have given him, for all practical purposes, a monopoly in the circus world. But he had tried to swallow too much, and when Wall Street collapsed the same year, followed by the devastating Depression, his highly leveraged position came crashing to its knees. In fact, he was in so much debt the banks installed a new administrator to run the operation, rendering John no more than a humiliated puppet. When he died in 1936, he was a broken man, and so was the institution he and his brothers had spent the last seven decades building.

He also left a legal situation that was a litigator's dream and an inheritor's nightmare. Bitter antagonisms among the brothers' children ensued in a vicious battle for control of the empire. Distrust and dislike spewed in all directions. But one of the heirs, so despised by John Ringling he'd been removed from his will, had the unexpected moxie to raise the funds of more than a million dollars the circus would now need to continue. And with the backing of the banks and now the majority of the stockholders, John Ringling North, the ne'er-do-well playboy, assumed the managerial reins of the circus.

For the next two decades, until reluctantly selling to Irvin Feld, John Ringling North, the son of the Ringling brothers' only sister, would rule as the head of the largest traveling entertainment conglomerate in the world.

I wasn't surprised to find myself riveted by one particular story during John Ringling North's reign.

Depicted in a 1938 poster, standing on the plains of Africa in a fit of rage, was what was being billed as "The World's Most Terrifying Living Creature!" Fifteen feet tall, carnivorously dripping gobs of blood from a roaring mouth, he clutched in one hand above his head the limp body of a Zulu warrior. Horrified natives ran for their lives. Eclipsing all other animal curiosities of the time, it was none other than the "Largest Gorilla Ever Exhibited"—"Gargantua!"

Gargantua was born in Cameroon, a mountainous country on the coast of Africa, nestled under the continents' great western bulge. I'd met a man once who'd been raised in Cameroon, a huge barrel-chested man, with skin the color of coal. "People don't realize how dangerous it is. Tourists park their cars, get out, go for a stroll in the jungle and they're never seen again."

"What happens?"

"Gorillas, lions, elephants . . . most of them are territorial. They can smell you, sometimes as far as fifteen miles away. Take the gorilla. Their young can be playing in a stream a mile away. They don't have to watch close. They smell something different and they're there in a minute, pounding their chests, crashing through the trees."

He stood up, pounding his chest, which made the vision all the more chilling.

"What if you have a gun?"

"A gun won't do you any good. A gorilla can bend it in half . . . and you can't run. You see one near . . . look around. They'll have surrounded you. They travel in a pack."

"You'd have to climb a tree?"

"That won't do you any good either. Half will go to eat while the other half wait for you to come down. They're highly organized."

I stared at him blankly.

"We often judge an animal's intelligence by how much he understands *our* language, when in reality they already have a complex language of their own, with nonverbal cues and messages as important as sounds."

"How do you escape?" I asked, as though I were in imminent peril.

"Back away as soon as you see one. If you start backing away immediately, they'll let you go."

In 1930, the story goes, a baby gorilla was found under a tree, cradled in its mother's arms. Normally the natives of Cameroon left the gorillas alone, but perhaps startled by an unexpected encounter, they had killed the infant's mother and father. They carried the one-month-old male gorilla back to their village.

The baby gorilla was given to a village woman who had recently lost her child. She breastfed milk to the infant for almost a year before giving the now-healthy gorilla to a local missionary couple. The missionaries, however, not realizing the havoc even a baby gorilla can wreak, gave up within a year. They sold the baby gorilla to an African trading ship captain, Arthur Phillips, for a sum of four hundred dollars and a wooden crate full of hymnals.

Along with six chimpanzees, Phillips sailed for New York intent on selling the animals for a handsome profit. But along the way, in a vengeful, cruel act, a shipmate Phillips had fired threw a jar of acid in the gorilla's face, leaving ghastly burns on his mouth and down the left side of his cheek. Conceivably it was one of the reasons the gorilla developed an angry disposition.

The captain, no doubt hiding the ape's unpredictable nature, found a willing buyer and sold the gorilla and the six chimps to a Mrs. Gertrude Lintz for a total of $2,500. Mrs. Lintz was a zoo-keeper of sorts and cared for other animals as well. But under her ownership, a houseboy further tortured the gorilla by feeding him a stomach ripping syrup saturated with disinfectant. The gorilla, now six years of age and weighing more than 400 pounds, miraculously recovered but began, unsurprisingly, to display an even more vicious temper. Up until this point, Mrs. Lintz had allowed the gorilla free run of the house, but after waking in the middle of the night with the gorilla's hands clasped around her throat—she somehow convinced the gorilla to release her with the enticement of a banana—she had the animal caged.

Becoming even more violent now that he was confined, the gorilla became an impossible boarder. So Mrs. Lintz, with some reluctance, negotiated the sale of the gorilla, accompanied by its keeper, Richard Kroener, to John Ringling North for the profitable sum of $10,000. Although Mrs. Lintz had described the gorilla as "an adorable creature with whom she used to have a cup of tea," from that moment on, the gorilla would become known as "Gargantua," destined to be displayed as "The Most Dangerous Living Creature Ever Held in Captivity!" and in a specially built cage would tour the country as the number one revenue producer for the circus.

Kroener, Gargantua's keeper, was deathly afraid of the gorilla and despite precautions during his stewardship acquired a network of stitches and scars on his arms and shoulders. One afternoon, a fellow circus employee passed too close to the cage, and as his tie fluttered in the breeze, Gargantua snatched it and slammed the man's head so hard against the bars he was knocked unconscious. North himself once accidentally got too near the cage, and the gorilla reached out, grabbed him by the arm and bit a chunk out of it.

A gorilla's strength is enormous, and with a nine-foot arm span, Gargantua could easily twist an automobile tire into a figure eight. He was also playful and loved a good game of tug of war, but each time he tossed out the rope, he would cleverly shorten the length hoping to lure his opponent, the human, closer to his grasp.

Gargantua's cage was twenty feet long by seven feet wide and consisted of a steel trapeze and a tire hanging from a chain. Gargantua often raced back and forth, jumping on the trapeze, while banging on the bars, and smacking the tire with his hand, no doubt thrilling any spectators.

North purchased a female gorilla, Toto, to keep Gargantua company, hoping a marriage partner would help calm the ape. But despite Toto's shapely sixty-two-inch waist, true love never bloomed. Both gorillas, in fact, had the same mercurial temperament. A later trainer confessed the only way he could clean their cages was to take advantage of their fear of snakes. The handler tied a fake black snake to the end of a bamboo pole and waved it at the great apes as he entered. The gorillas would then shrink back to a corner, confused and frightened.

Gargantua toured with the circus for more than fourteen years in a state of rage and captivity, until on the morning of November 25, 1949 he at last found peace. Gargantua was found dead, curled up in his cage, with his hands clasped across his head. He died at the age of twenty, exactly half the life expectancy of a gorilla allowed to live in the wild.

Chapter 9
THE SMALLEST MAN
IN THE WORLD

Gently, I knocked on Michu's door. No answer. Softly, I knocked again. Still no answer. I rapped a little harder and opened the door. A tiny figure stirred beneath the sheets, rolled over and opened both eyes. "Oh shit!"

He sat upright before clambering down one side of the bed. "I'm sorry. I'm so sorry!" he sputtered as he frantically tucked his shirt into a pair of corduroy pants fitting snugly around a protruding round belly.

The room, despite the publicity department's description of the "perfect miniaturized model befitting the 'smallest man in the world,' customized to fit his stature in every detail," was from what I could see little different from any other sleeper berth. A plain metal bed consumed half the small space, while opposite, a shrunken sink and toilet stood adjacent to a mirrored closet door.

Michu splashed water on his face, combed his brown hair to one side and, still looking apologetic, turned and extended both arms. Surprised, for some reason, at this natural expectation and surprised even further that he was practically weightless, I lifted him up. He quickly adjusted his bottom to my inside elbow, wrapping his right arm around the back of my neck. "Off we go!" I said, as though we'd been friends for years, and maneuvering out the train door I carefully placed him in the front seat of the car.

As we drove along the San Diego freeway it soon became obvious that whatever animosity Charlie Bauman held for Michu, it was doubly returned. Odious words between the two had been recently exchanged and Michu was determined to voice his opinion. Unfortunately, his tiny vocal chords produced no more than a high-pitched squeak that combined with his Hungarian accent rendered him incomprehensible. Nevertheless, I nodded in empathy at whatever he said, frowning as he did whenever he exclaimed with frequency, "Charlie Bauman no good!"

Listening intently, with limited understanding, allowed me the freedom to study his face, which contorted in anger was a mass of deep wrinkles. I wondered if the cross-hatched lines were a by-product of his miniature size or simply a deteriorating skin condition premature for his thirty five years. Regardless, his thinning hair, gapped tooth smile and a certain puffiness around his eyes gave the impression of an impish yet likeable old man. And from outward appearances, although just the size of a nine-month-old infant at 33 inches tall and 25 pounds, his body was perfectly proportioned.

According to what I'd read, Michu was a midget, preferring in fact to be called a "lilliputian," and unlike a dwarf whose cartilage has failed to develop normally, resulting in a near normal head size, a rolling gait and stunted limbs—often producing lifelong pain—lilliputians are tiny but completely proportioned. In Michu's case, it seemed logical his size was genetically induced since his parents and both his brother and sister were barely ten inches taller than he, but even Michu couldn't say for sure.

I parked along a busy street, across from a large hotel, and with Michu perched in the crook of my arm, we hurried through a break in the traffic. Thirty minutes early, we chose a table in the rear of the restaurant and each ordered coffee and pastry. Michu began to converse. I strained to hear him so rather than shout, which called further attention to himself, he climbed down from his chair, propped an elbow on my knee, looked up, and proceeded to carry on a relaxed one-sided conversation.

The reporter, a pudgy, young woman with carefully coiffed hair, arrived. She smiled, introducing herself, and with an air of alert curiosity sat down. Asking, without waiting for his response, if Michu objected, she pulled out a palm-sized tape recorder and placed it on the table between them.

She had obviously done her homework, reciting at the beginning of the interview what she had read in our press releases, while Michu, drawing on a cigarette, nodded in assent. Michu, I learned between her statements and his occasional replies, was born Mihaly Mezaros in Budapest, Hungary. His parents worked in a lilliputian theater, living with thirty others in what was advertised as "The Lilliputian House." Shows were going on constantly, Michu said. "People from all over came to see the performances. But then the war came, bombs fell," and the house along with a fairy tale existence was destroyed. And like Charlie Bauman, his arch enemy, Michu became a refugee. For fifteen years, living in a horse drawn cart, he and his family traveled the countryside, working for small Eastern European shows, performing as clowns and unicyclists while Michu danced a Hungarian jig.

Meanwhile, Irvin Feld, in his constant search for talent, had begun to hear of the little midget and by 1971, assisted by the Hungarian government, had narrowed his search to Budapest. But the government refused to report Michu's whereabouts. Instead, for days on end they paraded Hungarian acts in front of Feld until frustrated Feld blurted out, "Look, either show us this man or we pass on all Hungarian acts!"

Irvin retreated to his hotel and at ten o'clock that night a car showed up with a driver to escort Feld. It had begun to snow, the roads were terrible and the drive seemed endless. Finally, they arrived at a small village and stopped in front of a row of tenement houses. Some lights shone above and Irvin was led to the back of the houses and up a set of dark, narrow stairs. Irvin knocked. The door opened and the first thing he saw was a python slithering across the floor. The next thing he observed was a tiny figure suddenly whooshing through his legs and that, according to Irvin Feld, was how he first met Michu.

The reporter asked a few more questions, such as, "How do you purchase your clothes?" and "What do you do for entertainment?" before slipping into a slightly more personal arena. "Do you have a girlfriend?"

Michu looked away, shifting uncomfortably in his seat, without answering the question.

"Surely, like any man you must enjoy female companionship?"

she asked. "I assume *in that department* you are normal?", whereupon Michu reached over, picked up the tape recorder and punched the on/off button. He then folded his arms, stared into the distance and announced by way of his silence "the interview is now over."

After returning Michu to his train car I wondered what it was like for him and the others who were no different from me but had been given a sad twist of fate by nature. Were they bitter . . . or melancholy? Would they switch lives if they could? And more to the point, did they now feel exploited? Then I remembered a conversation a few days earlier during the barbecue. Lloyd Morgan mentioned he was flying out the next day to retrieve Prince Paul, a white-faced clown who was also a dwarf, who had been with the circus for years. It was time for Irvin Feld to renew or cancel the performers' contracts and Prince Paul had become so wrought with worry he'd been hospitalized with heart palpitations. It took Irvin's personal reassurance he still had a job to calm him back down.

It dawned on me that for people like Prince Paul and Michu, the circus was far more than a job. It was also a home. In a world of cruel jokes, rude stares and God given limitations, it was a world, for better or worse, in which they were naturally accepted.

"This is going to be your job," Art said, in a manner that led me to believe he didn't mind relinquishing it. Art picked up a large cardboard box, and with me trailing behind, we marched through the nearest portal and into the arena. Seated four rows deep to our left were several ushers and usherettes in burgundy waist coats and black bow ties. A man with glasses, the head usher, was giving last minute instructions when Art walked up. Following a short introduction, Art opened the flap of the box and took out a stack of purple foil hats, each with a pointed crown.

"There is a special number each performance just before intermission in which fifty-two children get to participate in the show. Two of the children are the 'King and Queen' of the number and have been preselected as winners of one of our promotional contests. The rest we need you to select as they come through your entrances. We need a mix of boys and girls aged five to ten." I watched as Art pulled out of his pocket a handful of circular decals. "Simply place their ticket stubs with their seating location behind these Greatest Show on Earth decals," which he demonstrated by peeling off the backing and slapping the sticker onto his chest, "while asking each child to wear a hat." As soon as the Samel Mixed Animal Act begins, which the ringmaster will announce and you'll notice by an onrush of camels, take the kids down to the Hippodrome track where show girls will be waiting to receive them. The kids will be pulled around the track in ornately designed circus wagons before completing the spec number in the center ring. As soon as it's over the show girls will bring the kids back to the bottom of the aisles." Art held up the decals again. "It's not uncommon for the kids to get lost. So please don't forget to attach their ticket stubs. Any questions?"

"What if they don't want to do it?"

"Then go on to the next kid."

Art passed out the hats and the decals while handing the head usher two red colored hats along with two ticket stubs. "These are the hats for the King and Queen, if you'd kindly take care of them yourself."

Without waiting for more questions, Art picked up the empty box and strolled out of the arena. "Your job is to bring them the hats and decals before each performance, which you'll find down in wardrobe, and then as soon as the Samel Mixed Animal Act begins, hurry inside and make sure they are actually escorting the kids! Come on," he said, glancing at his watch, "it's time for doors."

The sounds of popcorn cracking and program podiums being rolled into position quickened my pace as Art and I stepped into the empty corridor. People were already lined up behind the glass entrance door while ticket takers stood patiently beside their turnstiles. At exactly six o'clock, a man appeared and unlocked the entrance doors. At first only a few people straggled in. Then gradually dozens more began streaming in from the parking lot and nearby box office.

Every ten minutes or so Art would weave through the crowd to the next gate, stand to one side, and casually observe the ticket takers. Having been told "missing doors is a firable offense" I followed him from portal to portal, studiously imitating his watchful gaze, before finally summoning up the courage to ask, "What is it *exactly* we are looking for?"

"Letting friends in for free for one . . . collusion for another."

"Collusion? Between whom?"

"Between the box office and the ticket takers."

I glanced over at one of the middle aged, bespectacled ticket takers, harmlessly tearing the tickets.

"Each time a family walks in, they hand the ticket taker their tickets. The box office has already torn off the one inch discount stubs for any children under twelve. All the ticket taker has to do is tear off some more stubs and slip them in his pocket. Each stub is worth a dollar to the box office."

"I see," I said, not completely understanding, while finding myself now fixated on the ushers' coat pockets. "Have you ever caught anyone?"

"Not yet," he said, suppressing a slight grin, "but I may have prevented it."

Art suggested I circle to the left while he wound to the right. "After doors, feel free to watch some of the show. Just be back before intermission to help me audit the show."

Since I'd now been assigned my first major responsibility, assuring the kids were escorted into the show, I could hardly focus on the performance. Although the program indicated the Samel Mixed Animal Act didn't appear until right before intermission just leaving for the bathroom unnerved me.

How long can some of these acts last, I wondered, before finally the ring master announced, as though it was *no different then any other act*, the Samel Mixed Animal Act. Just as Art said, a dozen camels raced into the center ring. My cue had arrived.

I jumped up, scanned the arena and quickly noticed, with the exception of one usherette, none of the ushers had moved. To my horror, while a few conversed with one another, the rest stood staring in a zombie-like state at the swirling camels below.

Suddenly I was convinced the Samel Mixed Animal Act was the shortest act in the show. "Get the kids!" I screeched, sprinting from one usher to the other, glancing back, praying they were hurrying. "Shit." The show girls were already arriving at the bottom of the aisles! I tapped the last usher just as the first of the kids reached his little arm out, taking the hand of a show girl, and to my relief as the camels exited the ring, the children began gathering at the bottom of the arena floor. Nervously, I waited until the number's end and watched as the ushers led the stranded children back to their seats.

"Everything go smoothly?" Art asked, looking up from his desk. "Good," he said, sparing me a reply, "let's begin counting tickets."

Art began emptying a large cardboard box, segmenting the contents into several piles. On one end of the desk he divided the stacks into brown $6.00 tickets, blue $5.00 tickets and yellow $4.00 tickets. He then gathered in the middle, clusters of one inch brown, blue and yellow kids' stubs, each banded like the longer tickets in what he said would be groups of one hundred. Next Art fished into the box and laid out dozens of bundles of discount coupons and complimentary passes, each stapled to a hard ticket, wrapped like the others, by criss crossing rubber bands.

"What's that?" I asked, noticing a strange contraption that looked like an aluminum meat grinder sitting ominously on a nearby table.

"That's a ticket counter. When it's not broken it saves us a ton of time. Otherwise we count all these by hand." Then he stood up and stretched. "There is usually an auditor that travels with the train, but for now it's just us."

Art surveyed the table, seemingly finding order in the jumbled heaps of tickets. "Listen carefully. This is the way it works. Remember how we spread out the seating manifest in the arena and we verified that the seats matched the tickets in each of the three price categories. Well, once that was verified we now know if we sold every seat in the house what the total take would be. So now all we do is count the unsold tickets, which we call the 'deadwood,' and subtract it from the manifest. The box office must supply us with either an unsold ticket or cold, hard cash."

"The arena looked full," I said, surprised to see the mounds of unsold tickets on the table.

"It was, seventy five percent, which isn't bad for an opening night on a Tuesday. The box office helps by dressing the house, selling sections by every other row."

I nodded, thinking that was pretty clever. "It gets a little more complicated," he continued, "in that we also must subtract dollar-off kids stubs, group sales, discount coupons and any complimentary passes."

I looked slightly more confused. "This will simplify it," he said, and he handed me a form.

Auditing Form

Performance Date   _____
Time   _____

5,027 tix. at 6.00 each ($30,162)   less _____ tix. = $_____
4,820 tix. at 5.00 each ($24,100)   less _____ tix. = $_____
3,760 tix. at 4.00 each ($15,040)   less _____ tix. = $_____

                                            Subtotal $_____

      Less $1.00 kids stubs $_____

      Less _____ complimentary passes   6.00 each $_____
      Less _____ discount coupons   2.00 each $_____
      Less _____ group sales   2.00 each $_____

                  TOTAL DUE CIRCUS $_____

I studied the form. "Aren't there different priced complimentary passes?"

"No. Irvin believes if you're going to give away a ticket it should be the best seat in the house." Art reached for a stack of hard tickets. "You can start with the complimentary passes. Those have to be counted by hand. I'll feed the machine."

While I counted the complimentary passes, ascertaining each bundle was indeed one hundred, as marked, Art unwrapped the hard tickets, slid them onto a sloping tray and watched as the machine, sounding like a Gatling gun, tallied up the numbers.

"This is the way the pros used to count them," he grinned, holding a stack of yellow tickets to his ear while fanning them with his thumb.

"What happens if the box office comes up short?"

"Then they lose. It's either a ticket, a free pass or the money." And it occurred to me the box office was in a no-win situation. The best they could do, if nothing got lost, misplaced or simply unaccounted for, was break even. But before getting too sympathetic I remembered their reputation preceded them by the days of old when unscrupulous ticket sellers eagerly paid the circus owners for the chance to shortchange the customers. Not that, in all likelihood, their view of us was anything less then pickpocketing proteges of Fagin himself.

After almost two hours, counting and recounting complimentary passes and discount coupons, Art turned off the machine and scratched in the final number. "We're done," he said, confirming his total matched the box office tally. "Don't worry, there won't be as many passes to count tomorrow. We always paper the house on opening night to foster word of mouth." He reached for the phone and began dialing a number.

"Who are you calling?"

"Allen Bloom."

I looked at my watch. "But it's almost one a.m. East Coast time."

"It doesn't matter. At the end of each audit, Allen wants to know the number."

Art's fiance called him and I wandered back into the arena in time for the final few acts. Russian Cossack riders ran alongside black stallions, leaping on and off the backs of the horses, while a mustachioed man in the middle cracked a long whip. In the center ring a muzzled bear balanced on a rolling ball while in ring three a woman in a sequined blue dress bowed to the audience as a frenzied pack of miniature poodles completed a chain of hurdles.

The lights dimmed as all three acts exited the arena and then a single spotlight illuminated a clown in a blue and white suit with a bright orange wig as he wheeled out a big box. Carefully, he placed the box in the center of the Hippodrome track, brushed his hands of dust, turned and calmly re-exited the arena.

The music stopped. The spotlight shone steadily on the box. A minute passed and suddenly the lid opened. Out stepped the clown. He picked up the box and casually carried it back down the Hippodrome track.

I was dumbfounded. How the hell did he do that? I knew for a fact the floor underneath the box was solid concrete. There was no tunnel or trap door he possibly could have climbed through.

Amusingly perplexed, I noticed Art standing beside me, his briefcase in one hand and his jacket slung easily over his arm.

"How did he do that?"

"You mean you don't know?"

"I haven't the foggiest."

"Go backstage. You'll notice two clowns, each the same size, each dressed exactly alike."

I smiled, reminding myself how easy it is to be duped when you *want* to be. Art turned on his heels. "The most baffling illusions are usually the ones with the simplest explanations."

Chapter 10
TICKET COUNTER EXTRAORDINAIRE

"Excuse me. Do you think you could take me to the hospital?"

I held the office door open, looking startled at a young roust-about. He was wearing his blue uniform, his sleeves rolled up, his face pale, as he held out his left arm.

"I was pushing the lion cages. One of them got me." A deep gash from the inside of his elbow to the inside of his wrist, ugly and red, ran down his arm. Blood trickled through his fingers. This was the work of a single nail. A single swipe.

"Did you clean it?" I sputtered, remembering I'd read a lion's maul was instantly infectious due to the rotten meat caught in their V-shaped claws.

"I tried to," he said, squeezing his upper arm like a tourniquet.

"Come on!" I said. "Let's hurry," as I grabbed my keys.

"This has got to be cleaned immediately," I told the emergency room nurse. She led the man, a Polish immigrant, through a glass door and out of sight as I settled back to wait.

Earlier that morning I'd arrived at the building. The parking lot was empty and the office lights were still dark.

I didn't expect anyone to be around for several hours, but as I walked past the entrance to the inside arena, I heard the muffled sounds of a German accent echoing against the upper tiers. I peered in and saw far below, Charlie Bauman, dressed in a worn shirt and black slacks, inside a cage vigorously working with his cats. Only one other person was there, a young looking man, and he leaned against the mesh of the cage, staring in. I didn't know who he was, but I knew the trainers never went into a cage alone. Charlie had once told a reporter about a trainer in England who'd entered his cage on a Friday evening to work with his animals. No one visited the cage until Monday. When they did, all they found was a shoe with just a toe left at the tip where the lion's tongue couldn't reach. At the top of the cage, where the trainer tried to climb out, "there was just some dry, stringy bits."

On another occasion, one of the acrobats had asked Charlie if she could take close-up pictures of the tigers. She'd positioned herself where the cats exited the cage. "Kismit reached out on the way by," Charlie said "and despite the performer's thick, muscled thigh, Kismet gouged her to the bone. When I got there the tiger's claw was still embedded just above her knee."

I took a seat near the top, in a section darkened in shadow, and watched with awe as Charlie worked. He had tied a small piece of meat to the end of a long stick, and he swung the stick in a slow arc from in front of a lion perched on a pedestal to the top of an empty five-foot high stand. Accompanied by a constantly repeated German command, the lion would eventually jump to receive its reward. After weeks of repeating this exercise, Charlie would get to the point where the meat wasn't needed, nor the stick; just the German command.

As I watched Charlie, diminished in size by these frightening beasts, I was struck by the images these creatures evoked. Positioned on the Sphinx in front of the pyramids, the pharaohs had combined the body of the lion with the head of a man. Ancient Egyptians kept lions as pets, first having removed their canine teeth and blunting their claws. A famous Roman charioteer who enjoyed practical jokes would put these lions into the sleeping quarters of his drunken guests, at least one of whom awoke and died of fright.

Nor could I look at the lions without wondering what it must have been like for the early Christians and captured slaves who were thrown to the beasts for the amusement of the spectators. And then there was the mythical story of Androcles, which told the tale of an

African slave condemned to die in the arena but who was saved by a lion from whom he had removed a painful thorn years before, and now the lion wouldn't harm him. At the people's command, he was set free.

Human interest in wild animals is a powerful and universal trait. It is one in which fear and humility and control seem to accompany one another.

Charlie moved quickly around the ring for an aging man, and I sensed he could pick up movements by just a tingle in the air. Charlie finished his training and as the younger man shepherded the lions into their cages, Charlie sat down, pulled out a cigarette and inhaled deeply. I walked past him and as he looked up at me I noticed his face was dripping wet.

"Good morning," I said.

"Vot's so goddamned good about it?" he roared, and then he lowered his massive head.

The glass door opened and the roustabout walked out, his arm now swathed in a white bandage. He was carrying extra gauze and a supply of hydrogen peroxide and tape. His color had partially returned.

We drove back toward the arena. I suggested perhaps he'd rather go to the train. "No," he said, "I'll just try to be more careful."

Art was sealing a large envelope when I returned.

"Another review?" I asked, having been told we immediately mail all reviews to Irvin.

Art nodded, applying several stamps, while listening to my tale of where I'd just been. "I need you to go downstairs and see Tito," he said, making me wonder if anything surprised him anymore. "The *Los Angeles Times* wants to do a phone interview with him on Monday."

I wandered backstage, ambling past wardrobe, where two of the performers' wives were doing needlepoint, in search of Tito Gaona. Recently featured on the cover of *Sports Illustrated*, Tito was the star of the flying trapeze. Captain of the Blue Show's soccer team he was also known as one of the more congenial performers. Nevertheless I braced myself for a friendly bout of negotiations. How the sparring started, I have no idea, but I'd learned nothing was asked of the performers, outside their contractual obligations, that didn't include a bartering of favors. It had somehow become standard fare. As I approached his dressing room my imagination embraced the possibilities.

"Tito. The *Los Angeles Times* would love to do an interview with you Monday morning. Can you do it?"

"No."

"No? Why not?"

"It's my day off. We don't work on Mondays."

"I know, but this is the style editor for the *L.A. Times*! It would really help us out."

"Let me think about it," and then a pause. "By the way the show is going to be in Chicago in September. Do you think I could get some free tickets."

"Of course. How many do you need?"

"Fifteen."

"Fifteen! I couldn't get fifteen for Irvin's mother. How about five?"

"I have a lot of friends. I need ten."

"All right, I'll see what I can do. Does this mean you'll do the interview?"

As I waited outside Tito's dressing room I was also aware the system worked in reverse. It was only a matter of time before he needed something and new bargaining chips could be used or held in reserve. The curtain slid open. "Tito. The style editor for the *Los Angeles Times* saw the *Sports Illustrated* article and would love to do an interview."

Tito smiled and I noticed he had pinned the magazine cover and story to the curtains inside. Shamelessly, I stoked the flames of his ego. "We told him Monday is your day off but he insisted it had to be you!"

Tito happily agreed, letting me off easily this time with only "toadying" as my currency of exchange.

As I observed the shows and how seamlessly one act segued into another, it became apparent that a finely tuned structure had been crafted. Just like a record album in which great care is taken to facilitate mood swings by alternating fast songs with slow songs, in the case of the circus, the tensions induced by the tiger act could be relieved by lighthearted clown fare. And the performance that was spotlighted by a graceful aerialist might be followed by the high energy antics of the King Charles troupe.

But it was more than just perfect tempo that made it all work. What the audience didn't see while it was glued to the high wire act were the next three acts underneath, scurrying in the dark into position so that the minute the high wire act ended the spotlight would shift to the three rings below. And while the high wire act hurried out of view, Charlie Bauman, despite his clipped bark and intimidating glare, made sure the next act and the next act and the one after that was lined up and ready to go.

I had just finished carting the hats to the usher when I noticed a man with a beard stroll by, carrying a video camera.

"Pardon me," I said, "there is no filming allowed of the show."

"I'm a graduate student, filming for research. I've got permission".

"From whom?"

"Someone in the promoter's office."

"I'm in the promoter's office," I said, "and I'm sorry, you can't take that camera inside."

His face turned red, realizing I'd caught him in a lie, yet he became more insistent. Like any good trainee, I remained inflexible.

"Well, who else can I talk to?" he blurted out.

"Nobody!" I said, becoming annoyed at his belligerence.

"I'm as high up as you can go!"

He stared at me speechless and then turned and stormed down the corridor.

A few minutes later, watching "doors," I rounded the corner and bumped into Art.

"Can't get any higher than you?" he chortled. "Irvin will be pleased to hear that."

"I guess you ran into the film maker?" I muttered, feeling the pinch of embarrassment.

"He called me two days ago. It's a harmless project. I told him it was fine." Then he laughed again, "That is . . . if it's okay with you?"

—————

"Are you the promoter?" asked a middle-aged woman standing in the doorway. A wispy, elderly man stood behind her.

"Sort of," I said, Art's teasing still fresh in my mind.

"Good. My father would like to apply for a job."

"A job? What kind of job?"

"He's a contortionist."

"I used to work for Ringling back in the fifties," he said, "I was known as the 'Incredible Rubber Man.'"

"I'm sorry. We haven't had a side show in years."

"I can still do it," he said and suddenly he climbed onto the top of my desk.

"Sir. We really don't have any openings."

One leg moved into position behind his neck.

"I really wish you wouldn't do that."

The other leg began shifting into position.

"Sir. Please don't do that".

It was too late. I was staring at a human pretzel.

"Tell you what. Send me a resume. I'll forward it to Irvin Feld."

Michu was known to punch his fellow performers behind the knee as he walked by, to let them know he was passing, once declaring to Mohammed Ali, who had scooped him up in the palm of his hand, "I'll destroy you." For once Ali was speechless.

Michu wasn't wise cracking now, however, as I noticed Charly had picked him up and was holding him in both hands while delivering a heart to heart chat. There was no telling what Michu had done to incur his wrath.

The show had finished in San Diego, then Anaheim and had moved up the coast, and for the first time in days I decided I'd escape work early. The town of Long Beach, a narrow strip of shops and restaurants, beckoned above, a short uphill walk from the Coliseum.

"Just one," I told the maitre'd, and I was escorted to a small table in the center of an uncrowded restaurant. Only one other table was occupied, a circular booth to my left, where a woman dined with a well dressed couple.

"Lasagna," I said to the waiter, handing him back the menu, as I patiently prepared to wait.

"Would you care to join us?"

I turned my head, surprised to see the dark-haired woman in the booth looking in my direction.

"Who, me?"

"You appear to be dining alone. Why don't you join us?"

This time she smiled and her question was so direct I could hardly see a reason to waver. The other couple, startled for a moment, gave me an inquisitive glance.

"Sure . . . why not?" I said and slid into the booth beside her. The other couple re-engaged and it soon became obvious she too would have spent the evening alone.

"Don't mind them. It's my brother and his girlfriend. They're having a disagreement," she said, making light of their inattentive behavior. "My name is Susan. I'm visiting from New York."

I told her why I was here, which started a nice conversation. She was pretty, not in a girlish sort of way, more of an elegant woman sort of way. I tried to guess her age, trying to judge by the thin creases that deepened when she smiled, but it soon didn't matter. Perhaps because her manner was so polished, putting me at ease with questions and an easy laugh whenever the conversation became stilted. I noticed an expensive watch and a silver bracelet slid up and down a thin, tanned wrist and her hair, chestnut in color, had delicate streaks of auburn and red. But it was her eyes, bright and attentive, that gave her a sensuous appeal.

"How long are you here?" I asked, feeling only slightly nervous as I readied my next question.

"Only two more days," she said, as the waiter carried away the dishes.

"That's not much time . . . but I'd love to see you again. Any chance tomorrow night after the show?"

By now I'd graduated to ticket counter "extraordinaire," feeding the tickets, rapid fire, through the tabulating machine, trying to hurry Art along, without telling him I had a date.

She was waiting for me when I arrived, sitting on a bar stool at a fern draped restaurant, not far from where we had met.

"There's a pier down the hill I noticed on the way up here," I said. "It looked kind of nice. Would you mind if we took a walk?"

Shantys and shacks, some aglow under awnings, were selling snacks and ice cream, while others, deserted, reflected their age in the moonlit water below. The conversation flowed smoothly, even though as much as we talked about my life, she seemed reluctant to share much about her own. A couple passed. And then a crabber or two. And then I don't remember if it was her suggestion or mine but we drifted slowly to my room. She didn't say much and neither did I, ignoring the bright orange bedspread as I did the fact she suddenly looked older, and as I slowly lifted her shirt, past her bare breasts, her skin felt cold to the touch.

"Is there a New York number where I can reach you?" were the last words I said that evening. After hesitating for a moment, she scratched out the number on a note.

Sunday night, Art penciled in the final figures for Long Beach. I returned to the hotel room to pack for Los Angeles, the final leg of the run. Susan's presence dominated the room. Distant in one way, yet profoundly familiar in another. I knew there was no permanent connection. She lived in a world I could only imagine. But I wanted to hear her voice once again.

Perhaps I should have been surprised more than disappointed when the operator answered the phone. "I'm sorry. We have no listing at that number."

Chapter 11
THE TEMERITY TO TRY

"Ello. This is Cary Grant. I wonder if you could do me a favor?"

"Of course I . . . who did you say this was?"

"Cary Grant. I'd like to bring my kids to the matinee this afternoon but photographers can be such a nuisance. Is there any way you could lead us through a back door? I'd be forever grateful."

"No problem!" I said. "Just come through gate five. I'll alert the attendant. Look for me guarding a parking spot."

Excited, I told Art Ricker. "Guess what? Cary Grant just called!"

"So what did he want? Free tickets?"

"Free tickets?" I said, suddenly feeling indignant.

"That's what all the celebrities want."

"No. He called to avoid the photographers."

He had told me when he'd arrive and just as I had promised I stood anxiously over an empty spot on the lot. Any minute now I'll be meeting Cary Grant, the man who had so perfectly blended an agitation with the world with a self-deprecating charm. "There are others as handsome," one reviewer had said, "but not many." The same actor who had wittily replied to an exuberant fan's exclamation, "I wish I were Cary Grant!" with, "so do I."

A station wagon pulled slowly through the gate. Not quite what I expected—an Austin Healy or a Rolls Royce perhaps—but nevertheless the automobile made a direct line toward me and rolled to a stop. Two children jumped out, eight or nine years old at the most, followed by a uniformed woman—their nanny I presumed—and then out of the driver's seat a white-haired man stood up and approached. He was wearing a yellow cardigan sweater, light pleated slacks and tan loafers. "How do you do?" he said, extending his hand, and the first thing I noticed was not his age, he had to be close to seventy, nor the thick black glasses he wore, but that this was a very big man. Even from a view of six foot one, he towered over me. But it wasn't just his height, it was his frame. With broad shoulders and a very erect posture he weighed easily two hundred and twenty pounds.

"Follow me," I said, and dutifully he gathered the children and their guardian and followed me through the back door entrance. I'd made the mistake of telling our publicist, Vanessa Beal, of his impending arrival. Yet he didn't seem to mind when a flashbulb popped soon after he'd been seated. Nor did he object when a few minutes later a giggling woman, not much younger than he, ran up the aisle and kissed him on the cheek. "Tsk. Tsk," was his only reply.

During intermission I ushered him into a private suite where he regaled Tito Gaona and a few of the other performers with tales of movies made. And he quietly slipped out of his seat with his children in tow a few minutes before the end of the show.

It was early the next morning, in that pre-awake state, when sometimes distance and clarity intersect, that remembering Art's comments, I had to admit, incredulity and indignation aside . . . he had indeed gotten in for free.

Harold Ronk, the ringmaster, was in a snit, which made his sour-faced boyfriend Bob Harrison—"Rhubarb Bob," we'd nicknamed him—even snittier. Unfortunately, Bob Harrison was also the Assistant Performance Director and it didn't help that Art had unintentionally delayed the start of the show. Not that Art seemed overly concerned, at least not when it came to Bob Harrison. But Harold Ronk was another matter. Nobody wants a pouty ringmaster.

Free lodging, now that I was back at the Winner's Circle Inn, had elevated my spirts as I resisted Rhubarb Bob's icy stare. For like any new promotion, Art had said, this can have all the makings of a great success or an embarrassing flop. We all waited patiently while a monstrous BSA motorcycle rolled into view.

For weeks the radio station had been promoting a leap over nineteen cars and trucks by its foremost D. J., now billing himself as "Stevel Knievil." A ramp, eight feet high, had been wheeled into place midway up the Hippodrome track and as Harold Ronk, asking for prayers, announced the much ballyhooed spectacle, the D. J., wearing a white leather suit and a red spangled cape, revved his motorcycle engine to an ear-splitting roar. No cars or trucks, however, were in sight. The D. J., nevertheless, headed toward the ominous ramp, coming closer and closer, when, on cue, out of the back stage curtain four clowns came rushing to the spot. "Stop!" They yelled and whistled, as one dressed as a nurse and another dressed as a referee blocked the speeding D. J. Suddenly, roustabouts rolled the eight foot ramp away and in its place the clowns placed a tiny six inch ramp and a dozen toy cars and trucks.

The D.J. returned to his starting position, re-revved his engine and with little effort glided over the miniature ramp, circling the track while waving triumphantly in a parody of exalted status.

Most of the audience, chatting and moving about during the event, were indifferent at best, but the D. J., a motorcycle enthusiast, whose idea the stunt was in the first place, was beside himself with glee. "And if that's all it takes for the hundreds of free minutes of air time, who am I," Art said, "to judge its success?"

"And don't be a gawker," Art muttered.

How could he say such a thing? Had I not just befriended Cary Grant?

It was Project Hope Night at the circus, a star-bedecked benefit with Cher as the Honorary Ringmaster. My job was to greet the stars after they had walked through a cordoned off runway and entered a tunnel gate where I would then lead them to an open reception area to await the start of the show.

Was I not now a part of their world, in a fringe kind of way? An insider looking out? It certainly felt that way as I waited for the first arrivee, watching as a throng of people with cameras and eager faces pushed against the barricades. A black limousine pulled up. Out stepped Jimmy Stewart with a tall, bejeweled woman. Casually I waited as, unfazed and looking past me, he entered the tunnel gate. "Hi, Jimmy," I said. "Please follow me." Whereupon his wife, stern and imperious, looked at me and said, "That's *Mister* Stewart to you."

In an odd, transcendental way it felt better being back on the outside, *way* on the outside, and as I escorted the rest of the guests I noticed that although they didn't want to be treated like anyone else, once inside the tent and out of the limelight, like anyone else is exactly how they behaved. Kate Jackson sat alone at a picnic table looking bored out of her skull. James Brolin and Martin and Rowen sipped soft drinks, while most of the others wandered around with the same nervous self consciousness we all feel when thrust into the middle of a crowd with nothing to say.

Art motioned the stars through a back door entrance where inside Axel Gautier began helping them aboard a long line of elephants. Meanwhile, Cher had arrived, dressed in a dove-white gown with a dazzling array of peacock feathers. A phalanx of photographers circled all about. She'd also brought her daughter, seven-year-old Chastity, who, riding on the back of a baby elephant, was to accompany her mother to help start the show. The only problem was Chastity wanted no part of it. And the more people tried to cajole her on to the back of the elephant the more she proceeded to bawl her eyes out. In the interim, the celebrities all waited, mounted on the shoulders of the elephants while little Chastity was unsuccessfully soothed. Finally, to my dismay, she was led out with her mother to a sold-out crowd of twenty thousand, sniffling atop the elephant all the way.

From time to time, during afternoon shows I'd see a parent with a couple of kids sitting way up in the low priced seats, where the elephants looked like mice. They'd be virtually alone, surrounded by empty seats. It was the best they could afford. Despite Art's tough guy demeanor, he'd often invite them to move closer. "I'll tell the usher it's okay."

The matinee had ended a half hour earlier. It was the last day of shows and I watched as a dozen young women sat nervously on the boxes circling center ring. Most had donned professional dancing shoes while a few wore leotards and the others, dressed plainly, wore regular shoes or just sneakers.

But there was one girl that captured my attention. We'd met shortly after my arrival in Los Angeles. Her name was Molly and she worked in the Forum's main office. But as our friendship deepened I asked if she'd mind if I called her by her birth name, Kiyoko. No one else called her by her Japanese name and it made me feel closer.

Today was the day for show girl auditions, a publicized event held every year in Los Angeles and a few major cities. Jerry Fries, the show's assistant choreographer, had arrived the previous day. He stood relaxed in the center of the ring.

"I'm going to show you six steps," he said, "and then I'd like you to follow my directions."

The girls stood and formed two straight lines. And as I admired their innocence and enthusiasm, I remembered Sam Barrett's words way back in Norfolk. "Don't expect them to look that way in two years when their contracts run out."

"What do you mean?"

"Relationships, friendships, affairs . . . everything on the train moves at warp speed. It takes its toll."

Two of the girls, the ones in leotards, followed Jerry's moves precisely, turning in a graceful pirouette almost to perfection. The others were adequate, but no one stood out except Kiyoko, who, a half step behind, began to look confused and perplexed.

Jerry Fries showed the girls three more sequences of steps and I watched as Kiyoko's face faded from childishly alight to fragile and eventually lost. Yet I didn't feel embarrassed for her, since with little prior training, she at least had the temerity to try.

We had agreed to remeet, somewhere in one of my cities, and as

Jerry rejected all but one of the applicants, I was gladdened to see he singled out Kiyoko and, with a gentle hand on her shoulder, dismissed her with an encouraging note.

The next day Art settled with the box office and called Allen Bloom with the final numbers before walking with me to the parking lot.

"To tell you the truth, I wasn't sure at first, but I think you might make a damn good promoter. Allen told me to tell you, after returning to Washington, you'll be flying to Cleveland. It's there you'll learn the promotion business from the beginning. You'll be training under Mike Franks."

I thanked Art for all his help. After four months, four cities, thousands of tickets counted and tallied, ushers supervised and doors watched I had a much better grasp of the show. And now that I had some sense of the product it was time to learn how to sell it.

Excited, I called Sam Barrett that night, my last night in beautiful, sunny California, to tell him the news. "I'll be heading to Cleveland," I said, "where I'll be learning the marketing end under Mike Franks."

"Mike Franks?" he said. "You poor son of a bitch. Mike Franks makes mince meat out of new promoters."

PART THREE

CLEVELAND – LEARNING THE FRONT END

Chapter 12
A PICADILLY HOME

After thirty minutes of discussions with Mike Franks, I was convinced Sam Barrett was right. Although Mike, I'd heard, could be gracious to outsiders and his peers, when it came to his subordinates, as his flustered secretary could attest, it was a different cup of tea. Mike dropped several hints, none of which were overly subtle, that life had not been easy when he had first joined the circus, and he saw no particular reason to make mine any different. In fact, I had a sneaky suspicion he would go out of his way to make sure of it, at least until I'd proven myself worthy of the title *Promoter*. Fortunately, I'd been previously rattled by some of the best of them, and although proving myself to a bully was a dubious achievement I had no desire to repeat, I at least knew what I was up against, and I figured that was half the battle. Besides, Mike clearly knew his stuff, and I took refuge in the fact that I was going to be trained by one of the best of them. And from the sounds of it, we were heading into a maelstrom of unpredictable events, a proving ground not just for me, but for both of us.

Mike told me to meet him at National Airport, and as I stood at Eastern's boarding gate, dressed in my newly acquired three-piece business finest, I observed my surroundings with a tinge of bafflement. Despite the fact I stood in the nation's capital and no expense had been spared in beautifying the city's monuments and parks, the airport was in sad need of repair. The corridor was narrow and dimly lit, and businessmen, students and travelers sat in overcrowded hallways and gates; many no doubt oblivious to the fact that this was also one of the country's more dangerous airports. Situated in the middle of the Potomac River, the airport was notorious for its short runways. Ironically, pilots would claim it was one of the safest. When asked why, one replied, "because it's so damned dangerous, I have to wake up and pay attention before landing."

Nevertheless, I was eager to leave for Cleveland and I was sharpening my wits for Mike's approach. I thought back to our conversation in his office the previous afternoon. Although normally taciturn, Mike had filled me in on the storm we were flying toward.

Cleveland was the fifth largest market in the United States, with a potential circus audience of more than two million people within an hour's drive of the Coliseum. The city, I'd learned, was a fascinating mix of old and new, sitting dead-center on the south side of Lake Erie. For years a small north-central city, its growth exploded in the early 1900s when waves of European immigrants arrived by the thousands, attracted to the huge plants and factories that the nineteenth century industrialists had built along the city's waterfront and outlying areas.

Cleveland was a steel town, the home of Republic Steel, U. S. Steel and lesser giants. These huge mills were fed by iron ore and limestone hauled by mammoth lake freighters from Minnesota, where the great iron ore ranges were located; and coal, the commodity that fueled the mills, was shipped in by train from West Virginia, Kentucky and southern Ohio.

As a result, Cleveland in the 1920s rivaled Detroit in the production of automobiles. Even today, Chrysler, Ford and Chevrolet have major plants in Cleveland.

But the city had seen better days. The shift in support from manufacturing to the service sector of the economy had decimated Cleveland's old factories, idling thousands of workers, people who had worked for the same factories that their fathers had, as had their fathers before them. The city had been spiraling downward under the leadership of Mayor Ralph Perk, a short-sighted, unimaginative, yet consummate ethnic politician. Soon to follow Perk as mayor would be thirty-one-year-old Dennis Kucinich and the national humiliation brought on by default. The city went bankrupt with the banks calling in their notes, and Cleveland became the butt of the nation's jokes—the mistake on the lake. Nothing epitomized this more than the name of its tallest building, "The Terminal Tower," which cast its shadow over the Cuyahoga river, so polluted with chemicals it one day burst into flames.

But what the nation didn't see were the beautiful, old cathedrals rising above the city, the fine universities, the spectacular architecture, and most importantly, an indomitable spirit of the people to return to a past glory. The metropolis was at its lowest point, but as the city reached inside itself for its pride and stalwart resistance to decay, one colossal symbol was being built that exemplified its abandonment. "The Coliseum" was being constructed twenty-five miles south of town by Nick Mileti.

Mileti owned the city's hockey team, the city's basketball team, and was part owner of the Cleveland Indians. And now he was replacing the tiny, inner-city arena that had been the home of his sport franchises, the city's major entertainment, and the circus, for years.

The new coliseum was about to be the third largest indoor arena in the nation, with more than 20,000 seats and a concrete, outer structure surrounded by immense square columns. And it was state-of-the-art, with suspended video screens for the upper seats and elaborate loge rooms on top for VIP guests and companies.

But for years, Clevelanders, especially those inner-city ethnic enclaves, had taken their families, using easily accessible public transportation, to the tiny arena on Euclid Avenue in the center of the city. Now Mileti was saying it's the suburban population that is growing, not the city's ethnic minorities, and it is this suburban population the Coliseum must serve.

The city's preservationists were outraged, and the city's newspapers carried story after story denouncing Mileti's transfer of the arena.

But despite the controversy, Cleveland was a great circus town—always had been—because the European immigrants were fiercely devoted to their families. And even during the worst of times, when discretionary funds were at their scarcest, they would first invest in their families' happiness.

Nick Mileti was a wiry, brash, young lawyer when he made a small fortune developing houses for the elderly. It was here he had learned how to leverage large amounts of borrowed money against small amounts of his own. Through this method he financed the coliseum, but the construction wasn't leveraged enough, and newspapers were already doubting his ability to complete the project. One frustrated colleague of his even declared, "the whole damn thing is built on a foundation of marshmallows."

Mileti, Mike told me, had brought in two pros, the previous general manager of Madison Square Garden, to run the arena and Claire Rothman from the Philadelphia Spectrum to handle booking. But launching a new coliseum is a formidable undertaking, and they had one major problem . . . they were nowhere near completion. Frank Sinatra had agreed to open in just twelve short weeks with Ringling Brothers opening one week later for the start of its unchangeable, twelve-day, twenty-three-performance engagement. Irvin Feld expected revenues of more than 1.2 million dollars, and Mike had been given a budget of one hundred and fifty thousand dollars. To hit Irvin's number we would have to convince two hundred and forty thousand people to attend the show, the equivalent of one out of every four families in Cleveland. And *this* in a slowing economy that was setting new records for unemployment.

We would have to cover the town with advertising, publicity and promotions from head to toe. If we had known the chaos that would ensue, both Mike and I probably would have changed flights and headed due south, straight to the Carribean islands.

⟫⟫⟫⟫⟫⟫⟫⟩

I was standing alone in the corridor, beginning to fret, when Mike finally appeared, dressed in a sports coat and jeans, topped by a cowboy belt and black patent leather loafers. I was wearing my navy blue suit, white shirt and tie.

"Where is everybody?" he asked.

"They've already boarded," I answered.

"Let's go," he said, and feeling as though I'd mistakenly arrived too early, I picked up my bulky case and followed him aboard.

Once seated, I attempted a conversation, but he pulled out a newspaper and I realized this was a one-sided quest. So I sipped on a cup of lukewarm coffee and gazed out the window. It wasn't long before we flew above the Cuyahoga River, twisting toward Cleveland on its way to Lake Erie. And as flat, farm fields transformed into buildings and highways, we slowly descended over Terminal Tower, just blocks from Mileti's old coliseum.

"You get the luggage while I rent a car," Mike said, and he hurriedly disappeared. "I'll meet you out front."

A few minutes later I tramped out the door, suitcases hanging from each limb.

"Get in!"

"Hold on," would have been a more appropriate order as we careened into Cleveland, weaving in and out of traffic.

"Are there any hubcaps left?" I asked, as we pulled to a stop in front of a plain brick, two-story building, not far from a sign that read Baische, Blake & Gabriel.

I'd been told we always hire a local advertising agency; that even though we negotiated our own media purchases—insisting the standard fifteen percent media commission be rebated to the circus—we still needed an agency for four important reasons and would pay a modest fee to satisfy those needs. The first was a roof over our heads, along with secretarial help and the use of basic office equipment. We would work out of the agency's office until the show came to town; then we'd relocate to an office inside the arena.

Second, the advertising agency had the contacts with the local media, press, corporations and people with whom we hoped to do business and the agency cleared a path by setting up appointments with the right decision makers. Third, according to Mike, although we negotiated the media buys, the agency was billed for the purchases and there was a ton of paperwork that followed; affidavits, tearsheets, purchase orders and billing forms that the agency monitored to ensure the spots and ads actually ran and the proper accounting procedures were followed. And finally, last but not least, the agency replaced our need to leave axle nuts all over town. They were our credibility with the city officials, the local merchants and all the others with whom we came in touch during our temporary and, as some might fear, turbulent stay.

For several years, Mike had hired Baische, Blake & Gabriel, in particular their account executive Ruthy Friedman. The agency had been an old, industrial-based firm, considerably larger at one time, that had gradually shifted its focus—along with the flow of the local economy—to more consumer-oriented accounts. One of their more lucrative clients was Red Barn restaurants, a regional fast food chain with locations throughout the city, an account with natural tie-ins for the circus. At most, Mike indicated, Baische had a dozen employees, but it was still considered a solid, mid- sized agency with a few artists, writers, three active partners and, at least as far as Mike was concerned, Ruthy Friedman.

— TWELVE WEEKS OUT —

"Hello Michael. Welcome back," Ruthy said, as we arrived at the top of the stairs. Mike introduced me, and Ruthy warmly welcomed me to Cleveland.

"Have you got an office for us?"

"Of course I do," Ruthy said, and she led us across an open reception area. "I just cleaned it up for you this morning."

It was little more than a big, empty room with wood paneled walls, an old desk and a phone. We plunked our suitcases inside and followed Ruthy to the conference room. Along the way, she pointed out the office supply cabinet and introduced us to the receptionist, who would serve as our secretary.

We entered a bright, corner conference room and Mike pulled out a chair, promptly propping his feet on the table. "So what's on the schedule?"

Ruthy was short and squat and wore thick-heeled shoes. She plodded across the room with a half smile. I could tell immediately, Mike liked her. Auburn haired and matronly, somewhere in her late fifties, she had a direct, yet disarming manner. She spoke in an unhurried monotone, as though she was indicating anything you did was more likely to amuse than upset her. Later I'd learn she was something of an institution in Cleveland, a pioneer locally of women in advertising. And although she had all-around advertising expertise, she was one of the most well respected media buyers in town. She was also a great nag and could squeeze concessions out of the media even Irvin Feld could admire.

"I've set up lunch at Swingos. I told Peter Halbin I'd call him as soon as you got here. He'll meet us there."

Swingos was an Italian restaurant midway to downtown Cleveland, a popular hangout for local businessmen. "It's become an annual tradition," Ruthy said, "to hold our introductory meeting there to kick off the Cleveland campaign."

We arrived ahead of Peter and while waiting for him, Ruthy explained that he was a partner at Halbin and Bellamy, the public relations firm that Mike had hired. Like Ruthy, Halbin had handled the circus for years, implementing the publicity campaign.

We were seated in a booth amidst a clattering of plates and conversation when Peter walked in. Ruthy had said he was a celebrity in Cleveland, well known in numerous circles, and as he strode across the room, several people waved hello. He was a big man, physically imposing, with a full beard, and he exuded a well practiced warmth, the kind of warmth I suspected in which consistency was more important than sincerity. It soon became apparent he also had a great sense of humor, a twinkling, sophisticated humor, based on spotting the stark reality in an otherwise bizarre situation.

"How has Mileti been handling the negative publicity?" Mike asked.

"So far, so good," Peter said between bites, "but nothing can turn you into a raving maniac like the feeling of helpless frustration when attacked by the press. What Mileti needs is a good spokesman who knows how to listen to competing factions, calm the flames of emotion and negotiate among adversarial parties."

These were skills Peter apparently knew something about, when in earlier years, I learned, he acted as a street gang mediator on Cleveland's east side, where gangs settled their differences with lead pipes, chains and an occasional knife thrown in for good measure. "I'd spend hours shooting baskets with them on rundown school yards, communicating with them on their level. Most of their threats," he said, "were verbal posturing, but warring gangs are unpredictable."

Mike wasn't contributing much to the conversation, so following my prodding, Peter went on to explain, "This experience gave me three critical ingredients to public relations work: one, the ability to listen and gather the right information; two, the talent for diagnosing problems and coming up with solutions—while refraining from delusions of preconceived notions; and three, the ability to act as a calming strategist amidst emotionally charged issues and clients."

Peter's mastery of these principles would also come in handy when later he became the mayor's political and legislative liaison dealing directly with the city council and state legislature. In his words, he was as inside as you can get in the upper echelons of local politics.

Financially, Peter and his partner couldn't care less about the Ringling Brothers contract. In fact, Mike had budgeted a total fee of only one thousand dollars for their services; but they didn't do it for the money. They did it because it was fun, their employees loved it, it was prestigious, and most importantly, it would bring them into contact with everyone they wanted to befriend for three months out of the year. Irvin knew those were valuable fringe benefits for an agency, which was why they were offered a pittance. And although many would eventually tire of subsidizing Feld, Halbin handled the circus for years.

But beyond Peter's savvy and experience, there was another reason, a very important reason, we hired Peter Halbin. A public relations firm's ability to penetrate the media and achieve results is enhanced by far more than an engaging personality. The power a public relations firm possesses is implicitly derived from the degree of "mutual dependency" it has with the media, and here is where you have to locate the source of an agency's power. Peter was close to George Voinovich, the governor of Ohio, a relationship enabling Halbin to promote discount circus tickets throughout the city's school system and recreation centers, and most critically, Halbin was the personal representative of Bill Presser and his son, Jackie, who headed the Ohio Central Teamsters Union.

Indicted the previous year for questionable loans to the mob the Ohio Teamsters was a formidable union in a blue-collar section of the country. And politicians curried their favor for political endorsements, corporations treated them with kid gloves, and the local economy could be dramatically affected by their actions. And Peter was the primary source for information. It was not unusual for Peter to receive calls from the media in the middle of the night, "Pete, we hear the bakery union is going on strike at six a.m. and is planning to picket all the plants. Can you feed us any information?"

This is what is known as "mutual dependency." Peter never flaunted his influence, but then again he didn't have to. As an insider to men like Voinovich and Presser, he had power and he could greatly help the media, and power is a two-way street; especially when Peter would later call and say he's got a great story on the circus that he'd sure like to see printed.

Lunch at Swingos accomplished three things: a chance for Peter and Ruthy to get to know Ringling's newest "promoter," since Mike would be in and out of town, leaving me as the stationary presence; to discuss any special problems; and to provide information on this year's show and top acts.

"Mileti's Coliseum has been taking a beating," Peter interjected. "The press has been battering it daily with stories on the city's abandonment. A lot of powerful people are hoping it fails."

"How do we counter the bad press?" Mike asked.

Peter sat upright. "Let's stay the hell out of it. I'll just keep hammering home family values and flood the ethnic communities with stories on the Russian, Hungarian and Polish acts. We'll talk incessantly about how easy it is to get to the new Coliseum and try to counter the claims that inner city people won't travel that far."

We then talked about the Coliseum people, particularly their booking manager, Claire Rothman. "The Coliseum has its own in-house marketing agency," Mike said. "They'll resent any outside influence such as Baische and Halbin, so don't expect them to be any treat to work with."

Shifting the discussion, Mike asked, "What about Akron? It was never a market for the circus, but now the Coliseum is closer to Akron than it is to Cleveland."

"I've already begun gathering information on new media possibilities," Ruthy said.

Finally, we talked about the show. It was the Red Show coming this year and Mike handed Ruthy and Peter a couple of programs. We talked about Gunther Gebel Williams, the star tiger trainer, and a few of the newer acts while Peter explored preliminary publicity opportunities. Then Mike announced, "We don't have the King Charles Troupe, but we might have a black show girl that grew up in Shaker Heights. Let's take advantage of that."

Peter nodded, scribbling a few lines in his notebook.

There was a quiet pause in the conversation as we neared the end of our meeting. Mike leaned forward. "I want to make something clear." And he paused again. "The Coliseum is matching our advertising dollars one for one. This gives us more money to spend in Cleveland than we've ever had before. The Coliseum is awesome. It's one of the biggest, most impressive state-of-the-art buildings in the country, and we can make a pile of money this year. Irvin Feld is watching this town like a hawk. No one, I mean no one, three months from now should be in doubt the circus is in town. I want no stone left unturned."

It was late afternoon when Ruthy and Mike and I returned to the office. Ruthy sidled up to me. "I took the liberty of renting you a room. Mike told me to make sure it was inexpensive." She looked up at me sheepishly. "It's called the Piccadilly Inn. They've reserved you a room for a hundred dollars per week for as long as you need it."

"Come on," Mike said, and I could tell he was getting restless. "I'll drop you off."

We'd barely driven a mile when Mike pulled up in front of a tall, narrow building. A vertical marquee, chipped with age, spelled out the name Picadilly Inn. I waved goodbye to Mike and wandered in, suitcase in hand, and like entering a rundown movie theater, tried to adjust my eyes to the darkened decor. In one corner, under a dim light, sat a pool table, surrounded on the walls by fake swords and tin suits of armor. The carpet was a worn ox-blood red and from the musty smell I suspected it hadn't been cleaned for a while.

To the right, past two empty chairs and a coffee table, an overweight woman sat behind a desk, watching a small black and white television.

"I believe you have a room for me?"

"I was expecting you," she said, and she pulled out a key from a drawer. "I've put you in room 506. The couch doubles as a bed. Clean sheets and towels are delivered once a week. Call down and speak to Jerry if you have any problems." I noticed a young man staring at me from a small room to her left. The woman cracked a piece of gum with her lips and handed me the key. "The rent is due Monday mornings in cash. If you're late, we throw you out. Any questions?"

I trudged to the elevator and walked down a shadowy corridor to my room. I opened the door and immediately discovered the studio couch was bare. Stripped of its cover, there were no sheets or blankets, nor did the bathroom have towels, I noticed. I picked up the phone and called Jerry.

"Should I bring them up personally?" an effeminate voice answered.

"No," I sputtered. "I'll pick them up later," and then I noticed the window was crawling with flies so big I ducked as one flew buzzing in my direction.

Meanwhile, Mike had checked into the Holiday Inn down the street. No great shakes, perhaps, but compared to the Piccadilly Inn, it was the Taj Mahal.

A few hours later, tired, but too energized from the day's activities to sleep, I slipped on my coat and went outside for a walk. The nights had begun to turn cool. Winter was coming. And then it would be Christmas. I turned up my collar and my thoughts drifted to another place. And as I passed an abandoned store front, my throat suddenly cramped up in pain. For despite Irvin's rules, what Brad Rosenberg didn't know, what Allen Bloom didn't know, what even Sam Barrett hadn't known, was that sitting in a tiny mill town in the northern part of Maryland was . . . my wife.

Chapter 13
DANCING EVER SO GENTLY

We were married in December, December 10th, a lovely month to have a wedding, fifteen months before my meeting Brad Rosenberg.

The minute I saw her, leaning against the wooden railing, laughing with another student, I was hopelessly in love. The kind of love where all confidence is momentarily suspended. The kind of love where you can't imagine how you'd start a conversation. For days I would look for her, spying her every now and then, the sun bouncing off her light blond hair, once passing so close I noticed her eyes were robin egg blue. She smiled a knowing, wonderful smile.

It was only a few days later, standing patiently in the cafeteria line, that I managed to say hello. "Do you mind if I join you?" I asked. It was now or never. We talked over lunch and then over coffee, and then from a bench in the middle of the tree shaded campus, and from that moment on we were inseparable.

Marriage couldn't have been further from my mind. Having left home at seventeen, I'd already turned two college years into three. I could barely afford food let alone books and tuition. But scarcely two months passed before we decided to find a home. "We'll marry," we said, "as soon as we settle in."

There wasn't much available in Harrisonburg, Virginia, a tiny Shenandoah Valley town best known for its stone building campus,

Madison College, and its majestic views of the Blue Ridge mountains, with poultry farms dotting the rolling hills. But we found a perfect place almost immediately, a good omen we knew, stumbling upon a small apartment in the basement of a house, high atop a hill, overlooking the small town below.

We stared out the picture window. How can we possibly come up with the hundred and ten dollars per month plus utilities? "We'll find a way," I said, and we walked up the steps to present ourselves to the elderly couple, the owners who lived above.

"I'll turn my birth ring around so it looks like a wedding ring," she said, as we waited nervously outside their door.

Sitting together, our hips touching, in the center of a long sofa, we convinced our new landlords we'd make lovely tenants. A few minutes later we signed a short lease, said our goodbyes and strolled outside to our car, trying not to giggle before safely out of sight.

The wedding was scheduled for a Sunday night. It was a beautiful, clear, winter evening. We'd chosen a steepled, old Methodist Church. For days I had watched her sew her wedding dress, sometimes until the early hours of the morning. We took turns handwriting the invitations to our friends and family on folded pieces of paper.

The night of the wedding, our friends filled the church on both sides of the aisle. I was so nervous my legs were shaking and when my best man and I walked down the aisle and stood in front of the altar I wasn't sure I could stand. But when she suddenly appeared at the end of the long aisle, in her white homemade gown, my eyes filled with tears, and as we looked at each other I knew I'd never feel prouder or happier.

That night, after all of our guests left our home, I felt her quietly sneak out of bed. And through a crack in the door I watched her pick up her white wedding gown that lay on the floor. Slipping it on, one more time, she smiled and danced ever so gently in the soft light of the moon.

The next six months were happy months, but with both of us in school we could barely make ends meet. She soon quit her classes, taking a job as a waitress, while I drove a taxi, studying between fares, under the inside lights.

At times I wouldn't arrive home until two in the morning but she'd often be waiting up. At the end of each week we'd empty our earnings onto the kitchen table and feel fortunate to have sixty dollars between us. And although we could barely pay our bills and eat, she'd occasionally manage to bring home banana cake, my favorite dessert, from the Red Market bakery just down the street.

Christmas neared and she wanted a tree.

"We can't afford one," I said, having seen the trees advertised for ten dollars each.

I knew she was disappointed but she didn't say a word. Instead, five days before Christmas, while I sat alone in the kitchen, studying over my books, she walked in with a tree. It wasn't much more than three feet tall and it had to be the scraggliest tree I'd ever seen. Half of one side was bare.

"Where did you get that?"

"There was a man in the middle of town selling trees," she said. "I told him I only had two dollars. So I asked, 'What do you have for two dollars?' At first he said 'nothing.' And then he searched beneath the stack of trees and hauled out this one. What do you think?"

"I think it's beautiful," I said.

The next day, I gathered my business books, the books I'd intended to save, and carried them down to the campus book store. The clerk gave me seventy five cents for each book. And with the money, I bought tinsel and lights and ornaments, and before she got home, I decorated her tree.

But things didn't get any better. God knows, we tried. And gradually she became depressed and I became distant and neither of us knew what to do.

Finally, a month before my interview with Brad Rosenberg, we separated.

"I'm going home," she said, and I didn't try to stop her. The next day, after driving her home, I sat in our living room and wept.

As I turned the corner, on my way back to the Picadilly Inn, the memories came flooding back. I should have done more . . . I could have tried harder. Hadn't she wanted to come back soon after she'd left? But I was haunted by things . . . things I couldn't tell her. Things I was too ashamed to think about . . . even now.

I pulled my coat tighter round my chest and I remembered something an old woman had said. She'd been married to her husband for decades. When asked what her secret was, she replied, "It's simple. We both thought we'd married above ourselves." For a brief, shining moment I knew how she felt.

But there's nothing now I could do. I'd joined the circus, a new world, a new life, and it was all a thousand miles away.

Chapter 14

THE CAMPAIGN

I arrived at the office early and began depositing the contents of my oversized briefcase onto the top of the desk. Everything seemed to be an empty slate: blank legal pads, unfinished media schedules, my clean binder of checklists and activities, two inches of Ringling stationery, a handheld calculator and a fully loaded stapler. With a final positioning of my business cards, centered exactly on the front edge of my wooden desk, I leaned back and glowed. Let the games begin.

Mike had informed me he would be flying in and out of town over the next three months. Flying where, he didn't quite say. I simply surmised he had other places he'd rather be.

"This will be your office," he said. "I'll work out of the conference room," which I discovered thirty minutes later didn't stop him from dislodging me and my neatly placed supplies, only to cross his heels comfortably on my desk and assume his place in the pecking order.

"Listen carefully," he said, and I tried to tune out the mess he was making. "Like anything else, a campaign has a framework." He took out a piece of paper and drew three concentric circles. "Over the next few weeks I want to anchor in a triangle of three major promotions: one with a local television station, another with the city's daily newspaper, the *Cleveland Plain Dealer*, and the third with a major advertiser. This is going to be the hub of the campaign, the main engine, so to speak. Once we anchor in these," and with his pencil he extended a dozen lines, "we'll start building the spokes. The other thing we have to do this week is lock in our television schedule. This is an election year and with a November 6th opening we're already competing with the politicians for available spots."

Ruthy came in and told us an account executive from ABC was coming in to meet with us late morning. "And mid- afternoon," she continued, "we have an appointment with the Promotion Director for CBS."

"With luck," Mike said, "our first promotional break. The CBS pitch is the first of our three circles."

Ruthy handed us the Nielsen ratings. As in most major markets, there were the three TV network stations, ABC, CBS and NBC, and then usually a strong UHF station that ran movies of the week and re-runs of discarded network shows. However, often the re-runs still had a strong following, and depending on the movies the UHF station aired, they sometimes surpassed the three networks. "The other advantage to the UHF stations," Mike said, "is we can position our spots better than on the network stations, and since the costs per spot are dramatically cheaper, we can achieve far greater 'frequency' while the number of viewers, or 'reach,' can be obtained with the more expensive but popular network shows."

"By *positioning our spots*," Mike explained, "I refer to the exact placement of our thirty-second commercials within the programming time slot. Whenever possible, we want to buy in the middle of the TV show's time period and not at either end—when the viewer is more likely to change stations, leave for the bathroom or raid the refrigerator. Unfortunately, the national advertisers out of New York that place their advertising on hundreds of network stations simultaneously have first dibs on the cream filling. The local advertisers, which includes us, since we place our advertising one market at a time, are left with the less valuable end slots."

The Nielsen ratings came in a perfect bound book of sixty pages and could make the difference of millions of dollars to the networks and local stations. Based on tiny sample sizes, the Nielsen Rating

Company researched network viewing patterns and provided their results to media buyers in a concise rating format. For every hour or half-hour, day and night, the Nielsen ratings pinpointed what percentage of the viewing audience was watching what show and then further segmented the findings into children, teenagers, young adults 18–24, adults 24–35, 36–54 and over 55. Other research they provided, Mike pointed out, told us the affluence and educational levels of the audience as well.

"With this information, we can take our television dollars, thirty percent of our total budget, and begin scheduling our buys. The paid advertising should begin two weeks prior to opening night, and increase in frequency as we near opening day, gradually tapering off as word of mouth spreads during the second week. We'll, of course, saturate the Saturday morning kids' shows, pull in some of the soaps, buy some movie packages, a few programs for the senior citizens, and then zero in for reach on the popular family shows. Secondary programs—the less watched shows and re-runs—are great for frequency. The only market segment we completely ignore is the teenage market. They're too cool for the circus."

The degree of frequency required to penetrate the inner sanctums of a viewer's mind has been a much debated subject. Some research experts, I recalled in my marketing studies, claim it takes at least seven sightings of a commercial to truly plant the message, while others claim only three observations are necessary. In another opinion, neither is accurate. Their view is that the recognition factor is far more a matter of the ad's creative strength—combined with the type of product being sold—than a given frequency. Creatively, some commercials are so well crafted the consumer instantly grasps the product and is mentally and emotionally pulled in the first time they see it, while others—about ninety percent—are developed so poorly the viewer could observe the commercial a hundred times and still not be able to identify the product.

The type of product is also a huge factor. Entertainment advertising creates the most immediate receptivity, because it's exactly that, it's entertaining, and appeals to the self-indulgent side of the consumer, while more mundane products such as automobile batteries and kitchen appliances have to reach out and grab the audience by the throat to win their attention.

"Fortunately," Mike said, "as we decide how to allocate our television dollars we don't need to buy all four stations to saturate the market."

Ruthy announced that the account executive for ABC was waiting in the conference room. I was about to receive my first buying lesson, a lesson, Mike said, we'd apply to radio stations, magazines, and, almost all other media buys, with the exception of the daily newspaper. "They're usually the only game in town and as a result . . . unbargainable."

Mike gazed at the young man across the table while lingering purposefully over the Nielsen rating book.

Ruthy started the dialogue. "So what's the scoop with ABC this fall?"

"We're looking good," the salesman replied. "We've got the best Saturday morning kids line up, our news hour is a close second and ABC has Wednesday nights sewn up."

"Overall, you're running third," Mike interrupted.

The account executive stiffened, "If you mean the Nielsen's, they're never quite accurate."

"What's your thought about a promotion this year?" Mike asked, placing the book down. "We want to look at this as a package deal; a strong promotion over the air, a cash buy and a trade out for tickets."

"I'll have to talk with management. Air time is a little tight, what with the election, but I'm sure we can come up with something."

Mike listened thoughtfully, if unsympathetically, and then, allowing a pause, said, "Well here's the deal. With the new coliseum I've got a pretty big chunk to spend on television this year, but I'm only going to buy CBS and then either you or NBC. The station that comes in with the best package of buys, the best trade out and the best promotion splits the pot. The other, I'm afraid, gets nothing. So go back, talk to your people, and let me know by tomorrow."

After the account executive left I questioned why we didn't just spread our dollars among all three network stations. "Because we can capture more frequency with two, the same reach, and more importantly, given a choice of all or none, the station's willingness to *deal* increases immeasurably."

Mike and I returned to my office. "I want you to write a letter to the coliseum's Group Sales Director outlining a strategy for selling blocks of tickets to companies, groups and organizations within a sixty mile radius. We'll leave at three forty five to meet with CBS."

The coliseum, in this rare case, was in charge of group sales, but their efforts had an obvious impact on revenue and Mike wanted to make sure they did a thorough job. With a fresh perspective, I outlined a multitude of organizations to prospect, from churches to schools to the neighborhood soft ball leagues, crafting a formula for discounting tickets by the size of the group, and set a timetable to reach a list of measurable objectives. By mid-afternoon, I looked down pleased, at eight completed pages.

"Come on," Mike said, "it's time to go."

We piled into our rental car and headed downtown to CBS. Halfway there I pulled out a cigarette.

"What are you doing?"

"Lighting a cigarette."

"I hate cigarette smoke. Throw that out! If I ever smell smoke in this car I'll have it fumigated . . . with you in it!"

I slunk back in my seat. The man would make a hell of a picador if he ever left the circus.

Inside the station, we were led upstairs to a spacious office where a middle-aged man motioned us to two chairs. It was obvious from the start he was far less enthusiastic than the ABC account executive. This was for two reasons. First, we were selling *him*. He wasn't selling us. Second, since CBS was in first place in the market, they figured we'd buy them anyway so they probably didn't give a shit if we cut a promotional deal or not. Nevertheless, somewhat awkwardly, Mike placed his hands in a steeple and began a soft pitch. "What I'd like to talk about is putting together a special promotion that would benefit both the station and the circus."

The executive peered over his glasses. Mike proceeded. "We have a special promotion, a promotion we reserve for the top network station. It's called the 'underprivileged kids' promotion. The way it works is CBS announces over the air that it is hosting one thousand underprivileged kids to the Greatest Show on Earth and is soliciting requests from needy organizations for a special performance that we will call 'CBS Night at the Circus.' We'll provide the tickets and allow one of your newscasters the role of Honorary Ringmaster. He can say a few words and then blow the whistle to start the show." Mike unfolded his hands. "Of course, a certain number of spots announcing the special night would have to be guaranteed, along with mentioning the full name of the circus and its dates, but we can iron out those details later."

The CBS executive stopped fidgeting with his pen.

"I get the picture. Let me think about it. The schedule is pretty full this fall."

"I know," Mike said, "but the promotion will enhance CBS in the eyes of the community and I wanted to offer it to you first."

The executive looked at us in a manner that was more placating then reassuring. "It's got merit. We'll let you know."

The meeting seemed to be over and I was curious about one thing, "I was wondering, who decides the local time slots for each year's line up? The network or the local station?"

Mike glanced at me sideways as the CBS executive muttered a half-hearted explanation. "Well, I appreciate your time," Mike said. "Please let me know as soon as you can. I'll be in and out of the office over the next few days. You can reach me at Baische, Blake & Gabriel or the downtown Holiday Inn."

I quickly interjected, "If you can't find Mike, you can reach me at the Picadilly Inn."

Mike winced.

We pulled out of the parking lot. "That was fascinating!" I said. Mike drove away in silence. Feeling energized and searching for feedback, I asked, "By the way, how am I doing so far?"

Mike looked at me as if I'd just blown smoke in his face.

"You talk too much!"

My stomach turned. I stared at him in disbelief.

"First of all, don't ask things you ought to know. It makes you look stupid. Remember the question and ask me later." Mike turned the wheel to the left. "And secondly, don't tell people you're staying at the Picadilly Inn. Who knows what kind of reputation it has?"

As his words sunk in, actually, I had a pretty good idea.

——

The next morning, with the Nielsen book, a calculator and several media schedule forms spread out on the table, Mike was busy penciling in the TV schedule. He must have decided he needed a break and glanced up with a verbal test. "Do you know what PERT stands for?"

"You mean Program Evaluation Review Technique with an intersecting Critical Path Method?"

He looked up surprised. Thank God for small favors . . . and I felt him observing me as I exited the room.

Late afternoon I proudly presented him with my Group Sales report. It was ten pages long and polished to a well honed shine.

The next morning, the report was sitting in the middle of my desk. I picked it up and anxiously began thumbing through it. There were hardly any changes! A few small notations, but from what I could see it was largely intact. I turned to the last page. Suddenly my attention was riveted. With a red pen, he had made a huge X through my title. I was baffled. Had we been issued new titles?

I strode into his office, "It looks like the report only has minor changes?"

He looked up and nodded.

"I couldn't help noticing . . . for some reason you crossed out my title."

"That's right. You're *not* a Regional Marketing Director . . . you're *not* a promoter . . . you're a trainee!"

What a son of a bitch! I sat in my office and fumed, too pissed to tell whether it was anger or disgust that dominated my feelings.

"Incidently," Mike said, dropping by my office an hour later, as though nothing had happened. "On Monday we have a day of company meetings in Chicago. I'll meet you there."

I looked at the plane ticket he handed me, still stunned by his ability to cause pain and consternation, equaled only by his ability, such a short time later, to forget he ever had.

Chapter 15

"Ions. I Love Those Damned Ions"

"The first thing I do when I'm in a new city," Sam Barrett had said, "is hop in my car and proceed to get thoroughly lost. I don't even pay attention to the street signs. I just go. By the time I'm through, I've got a measure of the city . . . a sense of its pulse."

I turned left up Euclid Avenue, my Saturday morning cup of coffee still hot in my fingers. A siren sounded in the distance. Joe's Pizza Parlor passed on my left, as did George's Shoe Repair on my right. And soon I was driving past row upon row of sandstone houses, their wide steps separated only by wrought iron rails.

I passed an old schoolyard and the sidewalks gradually became littered. It wasn't long before I was propelled into a seedy part of town. Dilapidated buildings, liquor stores and churches. People, most of them black, sat on their stoops, while others had already begun to roam. A dog barked. A young man sprayed water on his car, and behind closed doors, I heard an argument.

This was the beguiling part of town, for despite suburbia's spurious claims of community, this was where it all spilled out. All the joy, momentary happiness, numbness and hopeless frustration was here, at any time, for anyone to see. I looked up at the sky, as if bluer, clearer air would lead me out of the slums and turned right, before my curiosity kept me frozen all day.

It was mid afternoon by the time I hit the outskirts of Parma, and as I found myself driving through pristine, white, middle class streets, I felt a sense of distance. The houses were ranch style or colonial, with an occasional stately home looking oddly out of place, but basically it was middle America, what I always heard I should aspire to. But as I looked around at the men mowing lawns, the rakes and hedge clippers hanging neatly in the organized garages, with the housewives and mothers trudging in the front doors with arms filled with groceries—even the old-fashioned barbecue in progress—I couldn't help feeling superior.

Was this really living? Safe and secure and endlessly predictable? I'd rather be dragged through thirty miles of broken glass. Give me risk, adventure, uncertainty, *anything*, but for God's sake, don't give me this.

No sooner had I checked into the Chicago Marriott than I found myself heartily greeting Sam Barrett.

"Two cokes!" he said to the bartender. "How is it going working under Mike Franks?"

"You mean Atilla the Hun?"

Sam laughed. "Well, maybe you won't be picked to be on his team."

"What do you mean?"

"That's why we're here. Allen Bloom has promoted David Rosenwasser, Art Ricker, Brad Rosenberg and Mike Franks—for their years of service or some such bullshit—to positions of Supervisor. Each of us is to be assigned to one of their permanent teams."

Permanent? This had serious ramifications. I immediately began scanning my options. Rosenwasser I didn't know. Brad Rosenberg was terrific, and after all, he'd hired me in the first place. Or perhaps Art Ricker? Hadn't he told me I'd make a damn good promoter?

"Don't ponder it," Sam said. "It's beyond our control. We'll have been traded back and forth like baseball cards by the time they're through."

Over the next several minutes I began to meet my fellow promoters. Most knew one another, while a few, like me, were relatively new.

There was studious Bobby Collins, thoughtful and kind; veteran Stan Lockridge, who seemed to be above it all; warm and wise-cracking Chris Bursky, looking for a laugh; urbane Tommy Crangle; handsome yet annoyingly arrogant Kurt Krassner; glib and lithe as a horse jockey, Tim Stinson; childishly exuberant Max Goldberg; and the calm professor, Elliott Harris.

From what I could see, not a single personality alike. So what was the common thread? Confidence. There wasn't an ounce of hesitation among us.

The meeting was about to start. We filed upstairs. "Like sheep to the slaughter house," Tim Stinson quipped.

Allen Bloom and the four anointed supervisors sat at the head table. There were the customary nods and hellos before Allen started the meeting.

"For some time, we have been looking for a system, a formula, that would provide the marketing department with some managerial depth, allow an opportunity for growth for people that have paid their dues and also create an incentive system that, based on performance, can offer some financial rewards."

The four men at the table looked on, pleased, as though a mountain had been scaled. "People need to know there is a chance to do something different . . . a reward for their years on the road." I scanned the head table, wondering who had started the pressure. "So as a result, I'm pleased to announce Mike Franks, Art Ricker, David Rosenwasser and Brad Rosenberg have been promoted to the positions of Marketing Supervisor. Each of them will be responsible for a team of promoters. This will enable more hands-on help for each of you."

I noticed some mild fidgeting in the room. "I'll be announcing the teams shortly, at which time each team can adjourn to meet as a group, but first I want to introduce the new incentive plan. Here's how it works. Just like I've always done, I will set a revenue projection based on the previous year's numbers, this year's ticket prices, economic conditions and so forth. If you exceed it, you'll receive a percentage. And whatever you receive as a bonus, your supervisor will get the same."

Allen eyed the room. "Here's the formula. If it's a two-day date you receive five percent of all revenues over the projection, a three to a nine day date, you receive three percent and if it's a ten-day date or more you earn one-and-a-half percent."

Allen grinned. "Art Ricker thought it up, so I've dubbed it the Ricker Scale."

After the laughter subsided, Tim Stinson spoke up. "What if we do less than your projection?"

"Then it works in reverse. The same percentage is deducted from any bonuses earned." The room took on a slightly more somber tone. "But I realize there are things you can't control. I reserve the right to negate the losses. Some of this will have to be subjective."

Kurt Krassner raised his hand. "Does Knoxville count? I don't close until tomorrow." Knoxville was a brand new town for the circus and Krassner was up an explosive $150,000 over his projection. . . . and it was only a six-day date.

"Knoxville counts," Allen said. We all did the math.

"There is one other thing," Allen admonished, "you only get your bonus if you serve out the calendar year. If you quit before January one, no bonus is paid."

There were a few more minutes of discussion before Allen declared, "Let's take a ten minute break. When we return, I'll announce the teams."

We reassembled in the room. There was an eerie quiet, as though we were sitting in a trench on the Somme, with some of us being selected to go home and others to go over the top. Allen began reading the names. "Chris Bursky—Rossenwasser, Sam Barrett—Ricker, Bobby Collins—Rosenberg." I was fixated on every word. "Jamie MacVicar—Mike Franks." Shit.

I always knew I'd come to a bad end . . . come back as a pack mule or something. But this was unbelievable. He couldn't stand me. *And* he wasn't exactly my idea of a Sunday school picnic.

I looked over at Tommy Crangle and Kurt Krassner, my team mates. They both seemed unaffected as Mike benignly said, "Come on, let's go meet in my room."

Glumly, I trailed behind as Mike unlocked the door.

"Take a seat anywhere," he said, acting the part of the congenial host. Mike sat down in one of two chairs while Kurt pulled out the other and Tommy and I perched on the edge of the bed.

"Gentlemen," he said, and I braced myself for a slap of cold water. "We are now a team. And I'm happy to have each of you on it."

Mike paused, glancing at each of us, and it struck me this was a different Mike Franks. Gone was the sneer, the curling lip. . . . he was almost human. Perhaps Mike was still in shock, I reminded myself, at the $4,500 he'd just earned from Kurt Krassner's efforts. Nevertheless, a cordiality settled over the room.

"The only thing I want to say is I'm here to help you, not hamper you. If you let me know of any problems I'll protect you any way I can. Just let me know early on."

Mike finished the meeting, telling Kurt and Tommy he'd be giving them their next towns in a few weeks. Befuddled, as we exited the room, it occurred to me, since Mike, due to his media expertise, still held sway over *all* the promoters when it came to their media purchases, perhaps a bit of tribal forbearance wasn't such a bad deal after all.

"Aren't you going to eat anything"? I asked Chris Bursky, who smiled back like a fat Persian cat.

"No. I've got post nasal drip. I've been swallowing mucus all week. So you see," he said, patting his plump stomach, "I'm really quite full. But eat up men. I don't want to spoil your appetites."

Sam Barrett and I and three other promoters had convened at a table in the lobby bar. A third round of beer had just been delivered as an ample helping of meat and potatoes was devoured.

One of the promoters, a blunt looking man whom I hadn't met, had come in late and was eating quietly to the left of Chris Bursky. But despite Bursky's witticism he kept glaring at Kurt Krassner. No one was paying much attention, but since I was sitting next to Kurt I couldn't help noticing the stocky man was goading him with his stare. "Why not right now?" he grunted, in little more than a whisper.

Kurt stared back, unmoved, yet he had the look of cornered quarry. "Let's go," I heard the big man say and he crooked his head toward the lobby door. Kurt slid his chair back, slowly rose, and followed him out the door.

"Where are they going?" Sam said.

"Beats the hell out of me."

Hardly five minutes passed before Kurt walked calmly back into the room, sat down, and lightly began adjusting his tie. "You'd better check on your friend," he muttered to Bursky. "The last time I saw him he was lying on the floor."

Chris didn't seem to hear. Kurt went back to his meal. I stood up and strode toward the door. As I reached the end of the bar I saw a man slumped on a stool. His shirt tail was out. His tie was askew and his white shirt was splattered with blood.

"Jesus. What happened?"

"I don't know," he mumbled, his expression uncovering confusion. "We found an empty room. I took off my jacket, put my fists up and began circling him, when—wham—he suddenly twirled on one leg and kicked me right in the face. I tried to get up and he kicked me three more times. It was all over before I knew it."

I looked over at Kurt, placidly eating his meal, and was jarred by the cold, mechanical, precision of it all, only to learn later the more belligerent of the two had mistakenly bullied a black belt in karate.

"Stick with me," Kurt boasted—a recommendation I decided I'd decline—"I'm going places in this company."

— ELEVEN WEEKS OUT —

"Ions! I love those damned ions!" Peter Halbin bellowed into the phone.

I'd called Pete at home just as he was stepping out of the shower. "What are you talking about?"

"Ions. Positive ions. They're little molecules. The spray gets them all in a tizzy. They start bouncing around, crashing into one another, and that's what makes you feel so refreshed. The little fuckers are charged with energy!"

"You're nuts!" I laughed. "Mike told me to give you a call when I returned. Do you have anything for us yet?"

"Not a thing. I've had family in and out of town and I've been up to my ass with the teamsters. Bill Presser just got indicted. I'll have a strategy for you in the next couple of weeks. Don't worry, we're still early."

"Incidently, I ordered the press kit from Washington," I said. "You should have it any day."

"Great . . . damn, I love those ions!"

Chapter 16

WHAT'S NOT TAUGHT AT HARVARD

As Mike filled in his TV schedules, I searched for signs of détente, an easing of tensions left over from Chicago . . . some change perhaps in personality. There was none. Not yet. Except for one tiny difference. For the first time, he seemed a little less intent on breaking me and a little more intent on training me.

Mike purchased CBS, even though we still didn't know if we had a promotional deal, as well as the UHF station and ABC, which had come up with the better package. By the time he was through we had locked in a tight schedule, a buy that would inundate the market the week prior to opening night, when we wanted our largest splash.

Television, Mike explained, was our biggest gun, especially promoting a visual product, and consumed a third of our advertising budget right up front. But as I listened to Mike scan the possibilities and plot out a media strategy, it gradually dawned on me that the genius in his marketing strategy was not the immense volume of advertising, nor the variety of media he planned to use, nor was it the expert scheduling—his proven metiér—nor was it even the excellent artwork headquarters would provide. The genius was how much exposure we'd obtain for free—air time and space that wouldn't cost us a dime.

It became obvious, especially having watched him maximize the deal with ABC, that by the time Mike was done, if he had spent $300,000 in cash—half of which was the Coliseum's—he'd in actuality have secured a million plus dollars in exposure . . . and that wasn't counting Peter Halbin's publicity. "And if you concentrate one million dollars worth of advertising in one marketplace, all in a thirty-day span, let me assure you," Mike said, "if people don't come to the circus, it won't be because they don't know we're here!"

Whereas Art Ricker's method of instruction had largely been by example and observation, Mike was more willing to explain in advance his intentions. "The way we accomplish this is in the use of three chips: cash, trade and promotion. The fact that we have hard cash to spend loosens up the media players. Without *that* we'd be dead in the water. The cash gives us the leverage to bargain. One crisp stack of bills on the table and everything else is open to discussion . . . and with the minor players we won't even need cash."

"The second chip,'trade,' centers around the fact that the circus and the media both have something that costs us nothing that we both want to get rid of. In our case it is unsold tickets and in the media's case it is unsold time or space. Commodities for each of us that, once passed, can never be regained."

We knew in advance we would have a healthy percentage of unsold matinee and weeknight seats, especially during the first week when building word of mouth was critical. And it was equally important to ensure that the opening night performance was packed, when the roar of a full crowd would influence the press we'd invited for the next day's reviews. The weekend tickets, Mike said, we never gave away, and it was safe to assume half of the giveaways wouldn't have come to the circus anyway. Besides that, even free ticket holders bought plenty of concessions. So Irvin's pockets, through Sells Floto, were lined either way.

"Usually the media has a surplus of unsold air time and space . . . the perfect harbinger for a beneficial swap. We want their unsold reach and frequency and we're more than willing to help them dispose of our empty seats. On occasion they'll give away our tickets as gifts to their employees and favorite clients but generally we insist, as a part of our package, on the acceptance of our third chip, a promotion—a promotion that for us means more media exposure and for them a chance to attract more listeners, strengthen their community bonds or create an advertising tie-in with one of their other advertisers."

A typical approach, Mike demonstrated, was this:

"We'd like to put together a package. The deal we are suggesting is half cash, half trade, plus a co-promotion. We will give you five thousand dollars cash for ten spots a day to run over two weeks. In addition, we will trade you six hundred tickets, our best priced seats—good for Tuesdays through Thursdays—for another ten spots a day, to air the preceding two weeks. And, third, we'd like to structure a promotion, using the six hundred trade tickets as a give-away."

"Perhaps our King and Queen promotion, whereby you announce over the air that city teachers can submit to the station the names of a particular girl or boy that has done something outstanding for the community. The station will then draw two names out of a hat for each of our twenty-three performances. At each performance, prior to the King and Queen number, the Ringmaster will announce that these winners were chosen for their community service as a special thanks from WJAY Radio."

"In order to make this work, we'll need ten spots a day, with at least a fourth in drive time, over a two-week period. Of course, we require the full name of the circus be stated, plus the dates of our engagement."

Persuaded by a highly competitive marketplace and an all or none offer, we just received $15,000 worth of advertising for $5,000 worth of cash . . . and nobody loses. "It's got to be a win-win," Mike emphasized.

"There is another type of promotion," Mike explained, "that doesn't involve negotiating with the media directly, but captures their time and space anyway. And this doesn't cost us *any* cash. This deal is done with a major store that not only has mass market outlets but also spends a ton of money with the media. For example, we'll approach the Red Barn restaurants as well as Safeway and A&P, and offer them their own special night at the circus, highlighted by an honorary ringmaster and VIP seats."

"We give them three thousand two-dollars-off discount coupons—again good for Tuesdays through Thursdays—which they stuff in the grocery bags at the checkout counters. The coupons will be printed with their logo and ours and all the dates of the show. They in turn advertise their special night, plus the discount coupons—exclusively available at their chain of stores—in all of their weekly radio, TV and newspaper advertising for a one-month period of time. In addition, we receive permission to hang circus posters in their windows and point-of-purchase easel backs by their cash registers."

"This promotion nets us more advertising than we can possibly dream . . . and everybody wins. Safeway attracts new customers. People who might not be able to afford full price tickets get a discount coupon. And we are only too happy collecting seventy percent of the full ticket price on a weekday performance. Plus," Mike added, "the huge volume of advertising sells all the other shows, our primary objective. And this promotion costs us no cash at all."

The arithmetic wasn't difficult. Combine the cash, trade, and promotions with the deluge of publicity we expected Peter Halbin to generate, and eight weeks from now we'd bombard a sixty mile radius with no less than two million dollars worth of advertising . . . all concentrated in a five-week period of time.

CBS called. They rejected our proposal. I glanced at Mike as he hung up the phone, looking for signs of disappointment. Mike gnawed for a moment on his knuckles. "That's okay. We don't need them. We'll sell it to somebody else."

Part of Mike's angst might have been relieved by the *Cleveland Plain Dealer*. They had agreed that morning to a major opening-night promotion. The *Plain Dealer* had recently established a non-profit arm to specifically direct charitable contributions to local organizations in need. Mike and I had met with Jacob Rosenheim, the newspaper's Promotion Director, the previous day. The deal was simple. Opening night would be the *Plain Dealer's* night at the circus in which ten percent of every opening night ticket sold would go to the *Plains Dealer's* list of charities. In return, beginning the day the tickets went on sale, the *Plain Dealer* would contribute two thousand column inches of space to promote the event. Furthermore, Rosenheim implied, we would receive the front page of the Friday Entertainment Supplement, just prior to opening night. Mike's first hub was now firmly in place.

The second hub came easy. Ruthy's account, the Red Barn restaurants, agreed to distribute our discount coupons, tagging a slew of radios and television spots, along with exhibiting in-store displays.

But Mike also needed promotions for Akron, now just a short distance from the new coliseum, and unlike Cleveland's politicians, we discovered the city was more than receptive. They were delighted at the idea that major forms of entertainment would now be easily accessible. As a result Mike had little difficulty locking in the *Akron Beacon Journal* for a *Beacon* Night the second week of the run while the Acme-Click grocery chain quickly snapped up our coupon give-away offer.

That left just one other deal for Cleveland to complete Mike's triangle of major promotions. And Higbee's Department store was it.

Higbee's was Cleveland's old-line department store, located in the heart of the downtown business district. As Mike deftly consummated the agreement, promising exclusivity to a long, leggy woman, the 'underprivileged kids' promotion—the same deal CBS had rejected—found a new home. In exchange for the *urchins* and a massive amount of advertising, Mike agreed Higbee's would be our sole downtown ticket outlet.

Mike's premier promotions, the hub of the campaign, were now set in motion, and other than our TV buy, we'd just received thousands of dollars in advertising for virtually nothing . . . a gigantic amount of exposure no matter what else we did.

Nevertheless, that evening Mike stared pensively out the window. And I wondered if he was thinking about the unfinished coliseum. What if, despite all our efforts, they were right? What if Clevelanders stayed away in droves? Could even a campaign with the impact of a gale force wind fill twenty three performances if Nick Mileti was wrong?

Chapter 17
RADIO IN A TIME OF BABBLEDOM

— TEN WEEKS OUT —

A small coffee shop two blocks from the Picadilly Inn did a brisk early morning business. "Eggs for .99¢," was advertised along with a hodgepodge of breakfast delights. There was the usual crowd, stodgy bankers sitting next to Italian carpenters beside elderly store-keepers, gossip mongers and a few thugs thrown in for local color. Not that I ever spoke to them, it just seemed more comfortable each morning to give them a dash of familiarity.

As I scanned the newspaper over a bagel and cream cheese a tiny article caught my attention. A comrade-in-arms had just met an untimely death. The gentleman, a circus performer, was traveling with a one-ring European show with an unusual act. Dressed in leopard skin caveman attire he stood in the ring and wrapped a large boa constrictor round and round his chest. Perhaps he'd done this for years but this time, each time he inhaled, the snake squeezed a little tighter.

The crowd's amazement soon turned to horror as his speechless, now contorted expression gave way to an abrupt and grisly end. What in God's name, I wondered, would possess a man to choose a profession with such an obvious occupational hazard?

———

I sat at my desk and perused the unfolding campaign. When Mike asked me if I knew what the term PERT meant he never explained that the Program Evaluation Review Technique was, at least informally, the basis for our marketing planning. PERT is a marketing term that describes a strategy, usually drawn in a diagram with intersecting lines, whereby a number of complementary activities converge together at a specific time to meet a specific objective. The CPM or Critical Path Method is a line within the diagram that determines the shortest, most efficient path to accomplish the objective.

The concept is basically a complicated academic term for what a cook simply does anytime he prepares a meal—timing the pouring of the coffee, the sizzling of the bacon, the pushing down of the toaster, and the frying of the eggs, so that all is ready to be served hot at the same time.

Effective marketing planning is no different, Mike indicated. All our media scheduling, from dozens of sources, would have a distinct structure designed to peak on opening night and then slowly de-escalate as word of mouth took over. Furthest out we'd begin with our on-air promotional giveaways followed by our trade advertising and then culminating two weeks out with our cash buy—where in terms of pinpointing the schedule we held the greatest control.

In order to expand our frequency, Mike said we would first plant the visual elements with a strong sixty second television commercial. But later we could just as effectively switch it to a thirty second and eventually to a ten second spot, as long as we re-captured the visual memory with the same music and opening line.

In order to facilitate the PERT method I'd been handed a training manual, a three inch thick binder, that was divided into twelve sections. Each section indicated the necessary activities that needed to be performed for each of the twelve weeks prior to opening night. Each section not only had a listing of the activities to be implemented but also contained checklists to complete and send to our supervisor to assure we were on schedule. The binder also housed a series of forms in which to pencil in our newspaper, television, outdoor, radio and all other media advertising—copies of which were to be sent to Mike Franks for his scrutiny. Finally, just as Art Ricker had done, I was to insert all our promotional deals and correspondence into the binder for ongoing reference. The twelve-week manual, in effect, was a blueprint for the PERT method of marketing.

Now that the television schedule and the promotional anchors were firmly in place, Mike began spending less and less time in Cleveland, leaving more and more of the secondary campaign to me. And having observed the master at work I was eager to begin plying the skills of my new trade.

Although television lavished the consumer with visual impact and the printed word provided the necessary practical information *it was radio*, Mike said, with its cost efficiency, that would hammer home our message with incredible frequency. Radio is the constant reminder, augmented by our television spots, publicity and promotions, that would lead the listeners to the newspapers for ticket buying information. "And over the next week, it's your job to buy it."

Radio, I'd discovered, was an extremely competitive medium with stations changing their formats from country western to rock and roll almost overnight if it meant audience share could grow. Of Cleveland's thirty or more stations, plus the stations serving the surrounding area, probably the top five stations captured seventy percent of the listening audience. But radio audiences are fickle, and a new personality from a competing station could quickly topple the most dominant player. As a result, radio was a deal maker's dream. The stations all needed cash. They were all vying for one upmanship. And they all had unsold time to trade.

There was one other aspect that whetted my chops. Radio, as an industry, moved through alternating phases—sometimes lasting years—from a heavy focus on talkative, active D.J.s with plenty of audience participation and general wackiness to periods of advertised restraint characterized by "less talk . . . more music." For my purposes the former was far more conducive to promotional creativity. In fact, the wackier the environment the better, and fortuitously, the industry had swung into high gear babbledom.

Over the next three days, Ruthy lined up the representatives of the top twenty stations. Perched on a throne in the conference room, every hour on the hour, I began to hold court.

Just as TV buyers had the *Nielsen Ratings* book as their guide, for radio I had its Biblical counterpart, the *Arbitron Rating Guide*. Arbitron provided the same rating information, allowing me to note at a glance each station's format, its total audience, the listeners by demographic segment, and the station's share of the market.

But unlike television with its prime time hours, we bought radio by drive time versus non-drive time. Drive time was, of course, the rush hour traffic, to and from work, when the audience was at its largest. That was when the stations used their lead personalities, and not surprisingly, it was when the advertising was its costliest.

Armed with my Arbitron truth serum and an arsenal of promotions, I began promulgating my three-for-one deals of cash, trade and promotion. I had enough cash to dangle to obtain an equal portion of trade and began sliding out my promotional suggestions one at a time. My best ideas I lateraled to the top ranked stations, followed by a plethora of less creative, but nevertheless frequency inducing ideas to the secondary stations.

We still had the "King and Queen" promotion, which went to the top station, a refined "easy listening" station with a sense of community spirit. The "motorcycle jump" promotion I hyped with great fanfare to the number one rock station and succeeded in locking in a deal with the station's morning D.J. He agreed he would do a buildup three times a day for a minimum of three weeks.

A country western station accepted a circus trivia contest. How many pounds of meat each day does a lion consume? Answer the multiple choice question correctly and win two tickets. Elephant jokes were also making the rounds. Call one in to the newest "oldies" station and receive two complementary passes.

As I negotiated these deals, I sat with a legal pad and meticulously recorded the details. On the left side of the pad, I carefully wrote down what they got, and on the right side, I recorded what we got. In every case, I was relentless; the full name of the circus had to be announced plus the dates of the entire engagement. Outside of this, everything was negotiable, from an honorary ringmaster to special interviews by circus personalities at the station.

Exercising Mike's dictum, a win-win situation for all, I proceeded at a dizzying pace, feeling a rare sense of power as, unlike the radio reps, I could see the whole landscape unfolding. One station had a major car dealer as a client. I suggested two free tickets for a test drive. The car dealer loved the idea. Another station had a client that was in the middle of a camera promotion and they wanted to set up a special tie-in. This one had me stumped so I called Mike in Washington. After brainstorming, we arrived at a solution. We'll bring an elephant, two show girls and three clowns to the center ring during one of the intermissions, and anyone in the audience that had brought this make of camera could stroll down and take close-up photos.

My favorite was the "Pachyderm Poo" promotion. A radio station agreed to package gobs of elephant excrement in plastic bags, silkscreened with their call letters, and announce to their eager listeners its fabulous fertilizer benefits for the lawn and garden. It must have worked, because Bursky told me people picked this stuff up like gold. "I'm almost surprised we didn't label it 'The Greatest Shit on Earth!'" he said.

Finally Friday night arrived and, smiling, I propped my feet on the desk. I began to review my copious notes. Between cash, trade and promotion, nineteen stations in Cleveland and the surrounding area, beginning four weeks in advance of opening night, would be airing seven thousand spots!

An hour later I walked out into the cool night air. The dark had flowed in like a celebratory bottle of wine. I arrived at the Picadilly Inn.

Under the hazy glow of the hanging, stained glass lamp I noticed two men playing a game of pool. One man was squinting at the table, chalking his cue stick, while the other was leaning over one corner, carefully gauging his shot. I ambled quietly over to watch from the shadowy sidelines. It was then that I noticed a third party, a beautiful woman, standing perfectly poised, just behind one of the men.

She was dressed in neatly creased ivory slacks and a matching sweater, and her complexion, an unblemished almond hue, could have belonged to an African princess. To my surprise she looked up brightly and approached.

"My name is Deborah. I haven't seen you here before."

We talked for a few nervous minutes and gradually I became relaxed in her charms. "I'm a student at the University of Ohio," she said.

Still dressed in my suit and tie—fearing she'd leave if I moved, I said, "Why don't I go up and change and I'll come back down."

"Do you mind if I join you?"

"Of course not," I said, pleasantly startled.

As we rode up the rickety elevator, I glanced over at her and struggled to conceal my excitement. For the first time in weeks, I'd made a nice friend.

I opened the door and she followed me inside. I reached in the bottom drawer, pulling out a sweater, as she casually leaned against the chair by the window.

"Would you like to make love?"

"Pardon?" I replied, my pulse beginning to race while taken aback by the suddenness of her suggestion.

"Would you like to make love?" she repeated, and this time she smiled, nodding in the direction of the bed.

"Sure . . . of course," I sputtered, realizing this wasn't a joke. She was serious.

"Good . . . but there's a small financial matter we'll have to take care of first."

"Excuse me?"

"It will be forty dollars."

A silence enveloped the room.

"I'm sorry," I announced, my anger turning to self righteousness. "I've never paid for sex before and I'm not about to start now."

"It's just a little money changing hands. What difference can it make? Believe me, none of my customers regret it."

"I'm sorry," I said, and still holding my sweater, I sank to the edge of my studio sofa. Quietly she walked past and I heard the sound of the door close softly behind her.

Chapter 18
THE ICE BEGINS TO THAW

— NINE WEEKS OUT —

Mike arrived mid-week and Ruthy and Mike and I gathered in the conference room. He hadn't been in town for several days and as we began to discuss the campaign, including a re-cap of the major promotions he had secured, it became increasingly clear he had forgotten several of the details. In fact, he began confusing some of the deals with each other.

"WTKR called yesterday," Ruthy said. "They're anxious to confirm if you're in agreement with their proposal."

Mike looked perplexed. "What was that deal again?"

Suddenly I saw a chance to prove my worth. Unlike Mike who had earlier boasted, "I keep everything in my head," I trusted nothing to memory—not even my next day's schedule—and from the very beginning I'd taken copious notes.

One by one, pretending Mike had ordered me to do so, I began parading out my records—several of which I'd already converted to formal letters of agreement—and as Mike listened approvingly, for the first time since Chicago, I felt the ice begin to melt.

"If you wish to get ahead," someone had once advised, "just look for the vacuum and fill it." I was delighted I'd finally done something right.

———

"Guess what?" said Mike, later in the afternoon, "the Holiday Inn just installed a game of Pong!"

Our campaign seemed to be pretty much on schedule and Mike was in a spirited mood, which despite my apprehension whenever he was in town, settled me as well. And now I observed another side to Mike, an unseen side masked by an unusually calm business demeanor. He was fanatically competitive. And he loved games.

"Let's go!" he said. I looked at my watch. It was only three in the afternoon.

Mike strode into the darkened lounge. "What do you want? Beginner, intermediate or advanced?"

"I'd better start with beginner."

Mike slid a quarter into the machine and with a concentration I hadn't previously witnessed began gleefully shooting an electronic ball to my side of the court. I quickly turned a knob and began angling it back and forth.

We started playing for dimes and nickels. It didn't matter to Mike if it was merely for pennies. "It makes it more interesting!" But I was no match for Mike, even when he began spotting me with handicaps. He'd obviously had hours of practice.

The next afternoon, Mike suggested the real thing. He had recently taken up tennis, a sport I had played for years. The tables were now turned. I won the first set six-one, the second set six-two and the third set six-0. I wiped my brow with my towel. We'd been sprinting for two hours.

"Good match!" I shouted and I started to stroll off the court. Suddenly I saw Mike retake his position behind the service line.

Two more sets, and exhausted, I picked up the balls. Even though he'd lost all five sets he didn't seem upset. For a minute I thought he'd goad me into one more.

Walking back to the car, I couldn't resist blurting out, "Mike, why do you love to win so much?"

Mike laughed. "It's not so much that I love to win. I just hate to lose!"

———

We had one more task to complete before the week was over: the purchase of our outdoor advertising. Mike spread out a map on the conference table and began pouring over the dots representing the available billboard locations. Earlier in the day, he'd peppered the representative with questions. "What were the traffic counts? Which billboards were lit at night? What were the neighborhood demographics?"

The circus was credited as the first industry to use billboard advertising. A hundred years ago, placards were plastered everywhere, only to be torn down at the end of the engagement and reused elsewhere or covered up by the next rival's posters. In the beginning, it was simple black and white art, but as the number of traveling shows grew so did the size of the posters and number of colors used. Gradually it reached the point one couldn't pass a roadside barn that wasn't covered in splashy advertising.

But in fact, through architecture, billboard advertising had been around for two thousand years. Centuries before the invention of the printing press enabled mass communication of the printed word, Pericles, the leader of Greece, built the spectacular Parthenon atop the Acropolis, overlooking the city of Athens, and adorned it with symbols and stories for the express purpose of communicating a message. The Parthenon was to serve as the City Treasury building, but equally important to Pericles was the constant communication of ideals for the emerging democracy—including the conduct in which the model citizen should aspire. This he expressed through the dozens of hand carved embossings surrounding the building's facade. And in the center of the Parthenon—even though Pericles was not a religious believer—was the forty-foot statue of Athena, the Greek Goddess that symbolized Athens and all of its virtues.

As we studied the map, it occurred to me, like most things garish and seemingly out of place, there is a paradoxical quality to outdoor advertising. On one hand it obscured and obliterated the natural scenery while on the other it bedazzled us with the raw, brazen commerce on which America's prosperity was built.

Yet some of the people behind outdoor advertising have historically taken advantage of those who are down on their luck. The unemployed during the Depression were easy targets—hundreds serving as sandwich board walkers since they'd do anything to earn a buck—and even now I'd occasionally see the results of an unscrupulous merchant. The most heart wrenching example I observed was a newly arrived immigrant, weather-beaten by years of hard work, walking back and forth in front of an electronics store wearing a box on his head in the shape of a television. His sad face peered through the screen. My only solace was it wasn't he that was shamed but the businessman who had exploited him.

Mike and I surveyed our options. With outdoor advertising, Mike explained, coverage was based on the purchase of a 100, 75, 50, or 25 showing. If we bought a 50 showing it meant that half the city's population would supposedly drive by our signs each day. We could also buy by demographics, pinpointing specific neighborhoods we hoped to saturate.

A rule of thumb, he said, was to stick with seven words or less if we wanted to accommodate moving traffic, and obviously use a colorful, arresting image. In our case we had an illustration of a leaping lion and a tiger on a bright yellow background. "At night," Mike said, "yellow is the most visible color one can use. Billboards come in either twenty-four sheet or thirty sheet sizes. Each sheet, measuring 28" x 42", is called a 'one sheet,' which is also the term for a large poster. Like a giant puzzle, the sheets will be pasted to the face of the billboard one piece at a time."

Mike analyzed the available outdoor spaces and negotiated a half cash-half trade deal totaling a 50 showing. But by the time we were through it wasn't just billboards that comprised our outdoor marketing. Mike purchased dozens of bus sides and scores of taxi cab tops and ordered hundreds of posters to be distributed to union halls and organizations throughout the city.

As I put the finishing touches on our Fact Sheet, which would accompany our press releases, Peter Halbin called.

"I'm ready. I've strategized a hell of a publicity campaign. Can we get together the first of next week?"

"I'll set it up with Mike," I said.

"There's one other thing."

"What's that?"

"I still don't have the press kit. Would you please call Washington and kick someone's butt?"

Chapter 19
WIND SWEPT FIELDS OF WHEAT

I peered through the frosted window of an antique store, immersed for a moment in an old tin canister, emblazoned by the blue suited Cracker Jack sailor. What was it like, I wondered, back then in America for my marketing predecessors, at the turn of the century, before modern times eradicated most diseases, discomfort and, tragically along the way, much of our sensory perceptions?

The levels of education were far more disparate. As a result the rich looked richer and the poor looked poorer. People were different. Unique. Not as conformed as today. Blind people, club feet, cleft palates and harelips were common sights. As were the harbors with dozens of tall masts, the flapping of sails and the sounds of the seamen. There were also sounds of weekend concerts in the town gazebo, the clacking of typewriters and wagon wheels noisily crossing log bridges. And most importantly there were sounds of people kibitzing in the streets. Life going on . . . not by.

Horses were everywhere, even in the 1930s. Delivery men with huge chunks of ice. Milkmen. The clopping of hooves. The tinkling of harness bells. The sight of the fire wagon racing up the street—with a Dalmatian nipping at the horses feet to make them run faster—the same Dalmatian sitting proudly with his master on the return trip home.

And what of smells? The smell of oven baked bread and the inevitable scream that followed when someone accidentally slammed the front door. Fresh baked pies. Pipe tobacco. Wood burning stoves.

And touch? The feel of hot bricks wrapped in towels placed at the foot of the bed against your cold feet . . . there was little heat in the bedrooms. The feel of oars in your hands. If you lived near a river, you rowed.

There were no grocery chains in the early 1900s. Food arrived direct from the farm or the local corner store. Hand picked berries, wild game and unpasteurized milk straight out of the bucket, warm and sweet, awakened the taste buds.

For amusement at the turn of the century there were hundreds of tent shows criss crossing the country offering otherwise unobtainable entertainment to small towns and mid-sized farm communities. Although traditionally most think of the circus when hearing the term "tent show," in fact, tent shows housed opera companies, itinerant theatrical groups, concerts and almost any form of saleable entertainment imaginable. Few of the tiny, farm belt communities had anything resembling an arena or auditorium and if they did they certainly couldn't accommodate competing shows—so the entertainment entrepreneurs simply brought their theaters with them in the form of canvas tents.

I was curious what life was like for the circus advance men of old. How was their role different from mine? In many ways I'd never know, for few, if any, left a discernible record, but I had in my earlier studies pieced together a few of the more salient differences.

For one thing the advance man usually traveled only a few weeks in advance of the show versus our two to three months of marketing preparation. And it was he who selected the fields in which to erect the tents. City and county permits had to be obtained, preferably for a site close to the center of town, and not only did the advance man negotiate the choicest site, he often planned the entire route. This was an area with which I had nothing to do. A separate department, headed by Earl Duryea, planned the schedule and negotiated the contracts. Since the arenas often received a piece of the action plus controlled their own concessions, personnel and box office operations, these negotiations involved legal wranglings and formal contracts engineered by attorneys on both sides.

There were a multitude of factors our people considered when choosing an arena but I doubt if Earl Duryea and his colleagues ever contemplated—as my earlier counterparts did—harvesting time or the schedule of pay periods for the field hands. For example, during cotton picking time in Arkansas and Texas, the workers—swollen in number by migrant laborers—were paid daily; an excellent interval to schedule the show.

All towns weren't necessarily good show towns and often there was too much competition vying for the same dates. But the competing advance men usually knew one another and there was mutual benefit over the long run by cooperating.

In addition to plastering posters all over town, advance men placed ads in the local newspapers and hired local children to distribute flyers. But the limited avenues for mass communications in the late 1800s, especially in small towns unconnected by a centralized hub, made advance ticket sales a tricky proposition—and ticket sales in advance of the show represented the bulk of the revenues. So my predecessors were dependent on attracting crowds in order to personally hawk tickets to the show. One method was the circus parade, which, as a result of the elaborately designed and often musically enhanced wagons, drew workers from the fields and offices, who lined the streets to watch the procession. To further encourage gatherings, bands accompanied the wagons, performing mini-concerts at intersections along the way.

Frequently, to garner crowds, the circus put on a promotional stunt such as the infamous "High-Diving Dog" or a tightrope balancing act strung across the center of town. And, finally, in the spirit of "motherhood" and "apple pie," the circus took advantage of America's love of baseball, forming teams out of band members and performers to compete with the local communities. In some cases, the musicians were hired more for their athletic ability than their musical talent.

The electronic media didn't exist. Transportation was still mainly by horse, bike and foot and over half the population couldn't read so ticket sales was a far more personal business. Unlike me and my fellow promoters, laboring invisibly behind the scenes, the advance man was a highly visible entity, easily found in the thick of things.

I suspect my predecessors were flamboyant, hard selling to the point of embarrassment, yet probably charming when they needed to be. And I've little doubt more than a few townspeople looked upon these itinerant and worldly peddlers with a mix of envy and amazement.

As now, there were few if any women in the game. And these men were probably adventurous types with a lust for travel and independence equaled only by a dread of predictability and self-imposed anchors. They didn't travel by plane or dine in the Hyatt Regency nor did they count their ticket sales on hand-held calculators. But I'll bet they rode slow enough over unpaved roads to wave to playing children and watch the wind send shadowed ripples through fields of wheat. And I'll bet they slept more than a few nights under the stars, and every now and then, I'll venture they shared a home cooked meal in the cozy confines of a friendly farm, the kind of home that brings a tired traveler unexpected comfort just by the sight of its window lights glowing in the distance.

Life was different in a multitude of ways—many of which were much harsher—and modern day advertising brought communication possibilities of which my predecessors could never have dreamed, but the motivation and love for communication were probably the same. And a good promoter is a highly adaptable creature, one who sees change for its opportunities, not its disruptions. Could we have adapted to each other's world? I'll never know. Would we have liked one another? Undeniably so.

— EIGHT WEEKS OUT —

Peter Halbin strolled in grinning like a Cheshire cat. He looked so pleased with himself I half expected to see feathers dangling from his beard.

"Gentlemen, I am ready!" he announced, as he plopped his large frame in one of the conference room chairs and folded his hands over his ample waist. I couldn't resist a soft jab. "Peter, you look great. Those extra pounds look nice on you."

"Oh, fuck off, my skinny Scotsman," he retorted in jest.

"So what's the scoop?" Mike asked, still amused by Peter's entrance.

"The scoop, my fine friends, is a two-pronged strategy you're going to love."

"Quit promoting the promoters," Mike parried.

"All right," Peter said. "Let me lay it out for you. We have a unique situation on our hands this year. The Coliseum is an unknown factor. All logic says it should draw like honey, but by the same token people in Cleveland are grousing about the distance and the city press has been beating up Miletti for weeks. I think the people that previously took city transportation will find a way to get there, but if I'm wrong, we're sunk, and since this is the first time we've played the Coliseum, we'd better have an insurance policy."

Mike and I listened carefully. "First of all, we do what we always do and blanket Cleveland with publicity. I'll get personal interviews with Gunther and the other circus stars set up with the major dailies. We'll capture the Friday weekend edition of *The Plain Dealer*, and I'm pretty sure I can book Gunther on ABC's nine a.m. 'Morning Exchange' talk show."

This grabs my attention. "How am I supposed to get Gunther up at eight a.m.?"

"Beats the shit out of me," Peter grinned. "That's your problem."

"In addition," Peter announced without missing a beat, "we'll see that the Hungarian teeterboard act is interviewed in a Hungarian restaurant. That ought to be good for a food section story or two. We'll saturate the black churches with weeknight discounts to drum up word of mouth, and I'll book the advance clown from here to kingdom come. The Animal Walk is out in the boonies this year, and the sight of elephants rambling down a one lane corn-fed country road can be incredibly hyped. I'll line up TV anchors and D.J.s for maximum exposure, and for Christ's sake, don't let Gunther unload the riders as soon as he's out of view of the cameras!" Peter sat up. "Finally, we'll hold clown auditions the second week of the show, which will generate a boost just as the media attention begins to wane."

"So what's new?" Mike asked, now nervously pinching his chin.

"What's *new*?" Peter echoed. "What's new is the second prong of my strategy. This year we're going to return to the days of old and give the circus back to small-town America. The people in

Cleveland who don't want the Coliseum—fuck'em! We'll give it to Chagrin Falls, Loudonville, Wooster, Strasburg, Wellington, Oberlin and a hundred other little towns we've ignored for years. There are tens of thousands of people in these little towns and we're going to tell them the circus is here for them—on their turf—the Coliseum is theirs!"

Mike's interest piqued. "How do you intend to accomplish this?"

"For starters, I've identified one-hundred-and-forty towns we want to hit within seventy-five miles of the Coliseum. Each of these towns has a weekly paper. I plan to contact every single editor by phone or personal letter and then conduct a six-week press release blitz with photos and stories going out every single week. Then I intend to invite each editor along with their families to opening night and a special press party bash with show girls, clowns and all the hoopla you can provide."

Mike looked relieved. "Think it could work?"

"I don't know, but it's worth a shot."

"All right, go full steam ahead. Jamie can assist you if help is needed."

The next day I drove to Peter's office to hear more of the details. Peter said he knew the Cleveland editors well—which editor liked animal acts; who needed to be titillated with a show girl photo; who needed to be cajoled, begged, nagged, bribed with tickets or who simply required a few chips subtly called in. But these small-town editors were an unknown commodity. They ruled over their fiefdoms with unique autonomy. Papers with names like *The Wootenville Times*, circulation 850, *The Twinburg Courier*, circulation 2,500, and the *Uniontown Messenger*, circulation 1,250, were bibles to these small-town communities. Many of these papers, Peter said, carried an American flag in the left-hand corner. Almost all of them were weeklies and they were thoroughly read. These papers reported the latest hospital admissions and the police blotter of the week—who got arrested and to what address the police were summoned for a domestic dispute. Little League baseball scores were printed, and it wasn't unusual to see wedding announcements featured on page two, not to mention bulletins such as, "Sarah Rhinehart just returned from Raleigh where she spent eight days visiting her Aunt Bertha. She had a wonderful time." Or, "Mrs. Watts held last night's annual covered dish dinner in her home for the Ladies Garden Club. She looked lovely, attired in a purple floral dress for the occasion."

These papers were rich in small-town American tradition, and for a big-city pro like Peter they obviously presented a whole new cup of tea. I asked if he had any special angles. "Yeah," he said matter of factly, "I plan to capitalize on their fear of big cities and tell them the Coliseum is now their hometown circus. You won't have to come into that drug-infested, crime-ridden, ugly city with your family. We've brought the show out to you!"

"Isn't that a little blatant?"

"Nah," he said "They're already leery of the city. We just need to drive home the point. Hell, I can't say as I blame them."

Peter proceeded to elaborate. "I know these towns. These small midwest towns that dot the countryside, east toward Buffalo, Southeast toward Akron and west toward Toledo, along Lake Erie, were originally farm towns. Each has a feed mill and a dusty railroad siding with a spur. Most have a Methodist and Presbyterian church and sometimes a Catholic church. There is almost always a downtown hardware store, an agricultural equipment store with new tractors on display, a coffee shop, and a main street barber where the old men, and aspiring old men, gossip. The Dairy Queen, with its yellow bug lights, serves as the teen hangout, just as the town swimming pool is the gathering place for the adolescents."

"Most of the villages have a pond, often near the center of town, which converts to an ice skating rink during winter. A stone enclosure usually borders one side where fires are built to warm the skaters' hands and feet. Homemade ice cream is made from fresh snow and Sunday cookouts are often synonymous with spring for extended families."

I knew from my own childhood a small town's identity is often cemented by high school sports. Everyone, old and young, rich and poor, attends the hometown football games, and the star players become local celebrities—household names—often peaking too early in life with memories of athletic heroics.

"Populations," Peter asserted, "have been dropping in these crossroad communities, especially as children grow up, leave and don't return. Many adults, consequently, put undue pressure on their kids to stay or return—regardless of the kids' potential—often at the cost of a fuller, more productive life. The self-esteem, unfortunately, of the more ambitious kids often takes a beating in the hands of small-town adults unwilling to admit their own fears and provincial limitations."

"A great many of the townspeople work in local industry in plants set up to capitalize on cheap land and cheaper labor. It isn't unusual to see a factory in the middle of a cornfield employing several hundred people. These factories make tires and light bulbs, electronic components and furniture. The jobs are often rote and mindless, prompting small-town men and women to talk wistfully of retirement while still in the prime of their lives. For many, as a result, work has little meaning in itself. It's merely time to put in between weekend family gatherings, fishing and hunting and, someday, retirement."

"There are Saturday night dances at the auction barn, and the county fair is the highlight of the year, but for our purposes, November should be an ideal month. The summer events are over and the season's holidays are yet to come. It's the perfect time to pitch the circus."

As I drove back to the office with Peter's thoughts still fresh on my mind, it occurred to me I've always had an affinity, yet ambivalently an aversion to small-town life. My father was reared in a tiny mill town of three thousand in New Brunswick, Canada and he seemed to be in an internal war with his roots all his life.

Although he later became a New York advertising executive, my father, who had grown to resent the small-town thinking of his boyhood friends, resented even more those he now held in awe—the ivy league, eastern educated men with whom he never felt he could compete. Strangely enough he eventually formed a truce with his demons. His work place became the city where he learned to look, talk and act the part. But in private, his friends, the men and women he hung around with, were the barmaids and waitresses, fishermen and mechanics, factory workers and misplaced souls . . . people in and out of hard times. My father was a handsome man by anyone's standards and next to some of his companions he looked like Clark Gable. And they held him in awe . . . the same awe in which he held those that encircled his other world.

We seldom lived longer than two years in a home, due partly to an unstable industry but exacerbated by my father's frustrations and self destructive view of the world as always greener on the other side. From New York we roamed through the deep south—Georgia to South Carolina and back again—from thriving metropolises to sleepy, southern towns, eight schools in twelve years. As a result, I never felt I belonged . . . an observer looking in . . . a behavior I didn't realize at the time was a perfect precursor to the world of communications.

But unlike my father, whose turmoil stemmed from fears of inadequacy in a world in which he never felt comfortable, for me, the tug in the pit of my stomach when I see a small town in the distance is for another reason. For me, its not the town itself but the conflict I feel that a small town evokes. My wife was from a small town. Maybe I'd hoped she'd bring a contentment that constant moving rarely had. But instead the contrast was only magnified—a conflict of rooting versus branching, the comfort of the known versus a search for the new, obligations versus selfish freedoms, spartan virtues versus roguish pleasures, family ties versus free-formed flight, old-time relations versus new found friends, a sense of community versus a sense of self, the need to belong versus the need to escape.

Moving frequently, I discovered, has its painful downsides but escape and starting over have their merits. In fact, few things can be as exhilarating as the ability to begin anew in anonymity.

Yet small towns look so peaceful, beckoning one with the promise of a simpler life . . . a slower pace and a welcome respite from daily competition and never-ending goals. But it's an illusion to think the simpler life is an easier life—a life where successes are glorified but failures are dramatized for all to see. And despite outward appearances, I've discovered small towns are far from insulated from mental illness, crime, violence, squalor and petty grievances. In fact, per capita, I am amazed at the amount of stress and strife in small-town America.

Nor are rural services as efficient as they are in large metropolitan areas. Cultural entertainment is often non-existent, libraries are smaller, intellectual stimulation is stunted, hospitals are understaffed, and employment is often precarious with one's destiny usually out of one's control, dependent at times on distant management decisions and union benevolence to save your hide from the next round of layoffs. But yet, I look at all those people talking and playing, eating lunch behind a farmhouse stoop, on two picnic tables joined together, and I wish I was there. I wish I belonged . . . but I'm glad I don't.

It was nearing the end of the week and I still had not received the press kit nor other materials I had ordered, plus I was in the mood for a little corporate gossip, so I called Nancy Pond in headquarters. Nancy transferred me to Felix Salmaggi, the head of the creative department, who assured me I'd receive everything in a few days, then sent me to Al Atkinson who confirmed that the tickets and seating manifest were on their way.

"Anything new?" I asked Nancy, now reconnected.

"Art and Rachel got married!"

"No kidding?" I said and dropped it at that, unsure if my congratulations would be welcome.

"It looks like the annual meeting will be held in the Bahamas in January."

"Fantastic! I'll need thawing out by then." The meeting, I'd heard, was designed to introduce the revamped Blue Show—the Red Show still had a second year to its tour—but was also a week of rest and relaxation for the promoters.

"What's that in the background?" I asked, thinking I'd heard Margot's raucous voice.

"They just hung up. They've been fighting again."

"Who? Margot and Brad?"

"No. Bradley and Irvin," and the way she said Bradley I could tell his full name was used not only out of respect and familiarity but out of affection.

"You mean *someone* fights with Irvin?"

"Bradley does." I hung up the phone wondering if even the golden boy was getting too close to the king.

Chapter 20
AN IMPENDING STRIKE

— SEVEN WEEKS OUT —

"I'm afraid I have to cancel our plans. Dark clouds have rolled in threatening a northeastern squall."

Disappointed, I hung up the receiver, surprised at my mood shift . . . lost for the moment.

Paul Baische had introduced us after spotting me working in the office one Saturday afternoon. "I have a friend looking for a sailing crew for Sunday races if you're interested?"

I called Paul's friend that Monday, meeting him later that week in Paul's office. He was a balding man, a stockbroker, suffering from what Paul described as the gloom of a market that over the past six months had taken the sharpest plunge since the Great Depression. The wealthy, people like Paul Baische, owned ninety percent of Wall Street's stock, and their pullback had sapped his commissions. "Why don't you lease our home in Shaker Heights," he nervously suggested at one point. "We can camp out in our apartment downtown." As much as I hated the Picadilly I graciously said no, surmising the distant confines of a posh suburbia would be even worse.

As I walked to the office it occurred to me the unexpected

weather might indeed be a factor but from the tone of his voice I suspected even the cost of auxiliary fuel was an unnecessary expense.

Feeling lonely all of a sudden, I turned up the corner, past my café—now closed for the day—wondering if this was what Art meant when he warned, "Wait until you're all alone in a city for weeks at a time before the start of the show."

A large cardboard box arrived with a bright yellow Ringling Brothers label affixed to one end. Confident it contained what I'd ordered I began slicing the nylon tape with scissors.

On top there were several white boxes housing our thirty-second and sixty-second radio commercials—with a seven-second tail for customized dubbing. The television spots were also enclosed. I promptly handed the stack to Ruthy for distribution.

There was also a slew of colorful certificates for the local personalities who would ride in the animal walk and a half dozen certificates for the honorary clowns who in full clown garb would participate in a few of the stunts. The certificates would be handed out in scrolls with the reporter's name indelibly inscribed. With any luck their gratefulness would appear the next day in the form of a positive story.

There were also ten silver whistles that came in beautiful black velvet cases. Each whistle, labeled "Honorary Ringmaster," was connected to a long blue ribbon. I particularly liked the shiny whistles, ordering a few more than were needed, never knowing when they might come in handy to soothe an upset child. Finally, there were a dozen programs along with the press kit Peter had anxiously been awaiting. Hurriedly, I threw the press kit into the back of the car and drove downtown to Peter's office.

The press kit was shoebox thick, stuffed with pre-written stories and photos that Lee Salter, our national public relations agency, prepared each year. Presumably these stories meant the local agency wouldn't have to re-invent the wheel; yet Peter asserted he often rewrote the releases. "In some cases to make them more literate and in others to simply tone down the hyperbole," said Peter. "A positive spin is one thing but the circus has elevated it to the point of nausea. Nevertheless, with modest modification we send them out by the shovelful!"

The major dailies rarely received press releases straight from the press kit. They demanded exclusives, and Peter arranged personal interviews with the performers. The same was true with the ethnic papers.

A few of the Cleveland papers had color inserts, so headquarters also included color transparencies of performers in action, but mostly there were dozens of black and white photos that came already captioned. Sometimes, Peter said, the paper skipped the release and just ran the photo and caption, plugging in the circus dates.

The press kit, in structure, was a three-ring binder color coded to match the corresponding show with either red or blue borders and was enveloped by a plastic case that snapped shut in the center. A pocket in the back held the photos and transparencies.

Inside, the kit was divided by tabs, labeling each of the sections for easy review. The first section was a general introduction of do's and don'ts—such as never abbreviate the full name of the circus and never discuss circus revenues. The second section was a brief outline of a typical public relations strategy. This was aimed at the small advertising agencies that might not have press expertise. A third section dealt with circus history followed by a list of all the performers and their hometowns—interviews with the papers were standard for any local performers. There was a schedule of all the cities the circus played—in case a reporter wished to do a preview—and then the bulk of the kit followed.

Each of the main acts had two or three releases. There was a story on costumes and their designer for the fashion pages. A story on circus transportation and general circus trivia. There was also a story on Irvin's clown college, "Med Student Switches Career to become a Clown," and releases touting the domestic side of life with pictures of Gunther and his wife cooking in their trailer or Hungarian children being tutored on the train. And finally, much to Peter's chagrin, there was a plethora of releases on Irvin Feld promoting his showmanship and business ingenuity.

"Irvin never comes to Cleveland," Peter announced, "which is fine by me. See, Cleveland is the last city played before the show returns to winter quarters in Florida for a complete revamping. This in itself is immaterial, except that Irvin chooses the town just before Cleveland to cancel or renew the performers' contracts. This he does personally, usually canning dozens of performers and show girls to make room for fresh acts."

"I witnessed this one year," Peter said, stiffening a little, "and one-by-one the performers filed out either joyous in having their contracts renewed or, more often than not, bursting into tears in the arms of comrades who had just met a similar fate."

I've got to hand it to Irvin, I thought, even though the show had to be revamped every two years it must have been tough to fire that many people in one sitting. But at least he did it personally, not handing off the dirty work to an underling. Similarly, Tom Watson, the founder of IBM, also conducted hundreds of personnel reviews each year; however, by his own admission, he handled everyone individually to avoid even a semblance of a situation that could lead to collective bargaining.

"Nevertheless," Peter added, "by the time the show hits Cleveland, the initial shock has probably worn off, replaced by an overwhelming urge to pummel the little egomaniac. Nothing like a bunch of pissed off Russian Cossacks to rattle his cage."

Consequently Irvin rarely came to Cleveland. But just because he physically avoided the city, it didn't mean he didn't want his presence felt. In fact when I handed Peter the press kit, the first words out of his mouth were, "Do I really have to send out another puff piece on Irvin?"

"If you don't, we'll send in Vanessa Beal to give you a lesson in PR."

Peter stared at my amused expression as if I'd just waved a red cape. He'd already confided in me he couldn't stand Vanessa Beal. Besides thinking she was generally useless, he resented the way she expected star treatment whenever she arrived in town. "She flies in and demands I set her up with interviews. When I don't immediately jump she can barely conceal her disdain!"

"On one occasion she came to town and I told her we desperately needed help west of Akron. I booked her in a hotel in Medina,

Ohio. I then set her up with a bunch of small town papers to impress. She fumed when she eventually realized she'd been transferred to Siberia."

Just before leaving, Peter handed me a sheet of paper. "Here, have a look at this. It's my first mailing."

Peter viewed his main task as keeping the circus fresh. He felt the entertainment editors could either see the show as a mundane repeat of an annual event or conversely as *something new*. "These editors can easily get bored with the show so I simply send an amusing letter on my stationery designed to kick start their enthusiasm."

"Once again," his release began, "the pachyderms are upon us. And again, you, our valued journalist, can take a respite from politics, scandal and mayhem and return to the joys of yesteryear. A time of fun and frolic and family values. As I write this letter, the elephants are marching on a sidewalk in Atlanta, rumbling and swaying toward the small town of Peninsula, Ohio. . . ."

Mike had arrived in town. When I returned to Baische he was reclined at my desk talking on the phone to Claire Rothman, our marketing counterpart at the Coliseum. In a schmoozing tone he smiled and glanced in my direction and I wondered if he noticed we both wore matching pairs of patent leather loafers. He seemed more relaxed than I was, which he usually *was* until I'd determined his mood, and in cordial spirits he told Claire we'd be out to the Coliseum this afternoon.

"So what's up?" he asked, his usual opening question.

I quickly gave him a re-cap of our promotions and the start of Peter's P.R. campaign. He asked me how group sales were progressing. I replied that the flyers were being mailed to two hundred organizations next week and the group sales director at the Coliseum was delivering posters personally to numerous plants and factories.

"So what else is new?" he asked, so I nervously dropped two bomb shells.

"You're not going to like this. The word on the street is Nick Miletti is running out of cash. Ruthy says he's been trading his VIP suites to contractors all over town to complete the work. He's leveraged up to his neck, and construction, I hear, is nowhere near schedule."

Mike pursed his lips. "I've heard the same thing."

"Well, we can always hand out twenty thousand hard hats opening night," I quipped.

"Anything else?" Mike asked, a little less relaxed.

"Yes. One other thing. The union that prints the *Cleveland Plain Dealer* and, for that matter, most of the other newspapers in town are pissed off about wage negotiations and are threatening to go on strike."

Mike raised his eyebrows. "Are you serious?"

"I'm afraid so."

"They're probably just rattling sabers. Why would they go on strike two months before Christmas . . . unless that's when they can most hurt the papers." Mike shrugged as though he wasn't prepared to contemplate the consequences. "C'mon, let's drive out to the Coliseum."

We sped along I77, the paucity of traffic making the drive seem longer, until off to the right the Coliseum suddenly appeared. Sitting in the middle of a corn field, the concrete structure looked huge, like a misplaced pyramid looming over the midwest.

Miletti had purchased five hundred acres surrounding the arena under the assumption the building would be so popular it would draw restaurants, hotels and other amenities, amassing an additional fortune from the increased land values. But in order to do so he was overextended, and the papers were now labeling the building, "The thirty-five million dollar Coliseum." And now, under funded and over budget, standing alone amidst the five hundred acres of flat, empty land, the whole scheme, to many, defied imagination.

We drove through the gate in a swirl of dust amidst a bedlam of construction activity. Claire Rothman, a raspy voiced, purposeful woman, was waiting in her car to greet us.

Mike introduced me. "You'll need these," she said, handing us two hard hats as we stepped over plywood and through the front door. Inside, everything was in a state of semi-completion. The walls were bare. Wires dangled from the ceiling. None of the seats had been installed, and the box office was still being gutted. Claire led us into one of the VIP suites circling above the arena. "Each suite is sixteen by sixteen feet," Claire announced, "with a living room, bathroom, bar and a dozen plush seats."

"How much are these going for?" Mike asked.

"Ten thousand dollars."

"Any selling?"

"They're going like hot cakes!"

We made our way to the front, waved goodbye and ambled back to the car, now smothered in a film of brown dust.

"So what do you think?"

Mike slowly inhaled, stared at the unfinished building, and drove away without saying a word.

Chapter 21
SECRECY

— Six Weeks Out —

"Just remember, when they finally run you out of town, step ahead of the crowd and pretend you're leading the parade!" Sam Barrett announced into the phone. I had tracked him down in Oklahoma City, having just filled him in on my activities to date. I still didn't know anyone socially in Cleveland and Sam served as a welcome relief. Other than Sam, I occasionally talked to Chris Bursky. Chris never failed to supply a joke or two. He held the keys to the corporate skeleton closet and, more importantly, he'd developed an innate bullshit detector—an uncanny ability to immediately cull out the truth, usually with a sense of irony. It wasn't a learned trait, it was a talent, I'd concluded, that he was born with, like the ability to comprehend math or play a complex musical note.

"How is it going with Mike Franks?"

"Not as bad." I said and I related my turn of events. "Now if I just didn't live in a Turkish prison."

"Pretty seedy, huh?"

"Seedy! That would be praise for this place. It passed seedy years ago. I've had flies in my room big enough to rodeo ride."

Sam laughed. "What are you laughing about?" I chided in mock anger. "You got me into this. Now get me out of here."

"Don't worry. Hang in for a year and they'll let you start trading tickets for hotel space."

"How's Oklahoma City?"

"Better. I was kind of lonesome at first but things have started to improve."

"In other words you're getting laid."

"I did meet a hairdresser last week. I've been teaching her the Texas two-step."

Sam was one of civilization's rare chameleons, mingling with high society one minute—happily seducing the mayor's daughter—while equally comfortable in a biker's bar, the kind of pub that shriveled your spine just at the thought of the possibilities. This made Sam dangerous. An evening with Sam and you never knew how the night might end. Sam's immunity was embedded in his breezy insouciance. He never gave two second's thought to where he was or who he was with.

"By the way," I said, reflecting on one of our press kit's more dramatic press release photos, "I'm curious about one thing. You know that act where Elvin Bale is swinging back and forth thirty feet above the arena floor and suddenly he lunges forward snatching the bar by his heels? How the hell does he do that twice a day? The man isn't even attached to a guy wire! Is he crazy or what?"

"Nah, he's got hooks on his feet underneath his tights that extend behind his heels. When he springs forward the hooks catch the bar."

"Are you shitting me?"

"Would I shit you about something like that?"

"Well, it still seems crazy to me," I said, unsure whether to believe him or not.

"Hell, nobody said he was sane!"

⁂

I recognized Claire Rothman's voice as soon as I picked up the receiver.

"Mike's not here," I quickly said, wondering if she'd forgotten he was out of town.

"Actually, I called to speak to you. I'm going to be downtown at noon. Can I buy you lunch?"

"Sure."

"Fine," she said. "There's a restaurant next to the Holiday Inn. I'll meet you there in an hour."

I drove downtown, surprised at the invitation, since she'd only, until now, dealt with Mike. But with Mike out of town perhaps it was a chance to get to know one another better. After all, we were all on the same team.

The restaurant wasn't what I'd expected. It was simple, with yellow formica table tops. Claire looked strangely out of place, like a set of expensive pearls amidst a tray of costume jewelry.

From what I could guess, Claire was adept at combining a cosmopolitan exterior with a tough determination. All the more reason I was gratified we shared common goals. She was surprisingly open, and I found myself liking her as she told me about her leaving the Boston Spectrum at Nick Mileti's behest.

"So how about you? How in the world did you become a part of the circus?"

Flattered, I told her of my own background, my training in California and my love for the job. "If I was any happier they'd lock me up!"

"I want to know everything!" she said, and her eyes took on a special sparkle. "I've been so busy I haven't had time to think. How are you and Mike doing? What are the promotions? How much have we spent? Where have we placed our media dollars?"

Suddenly I had a chance to spew out our marketing conquests to someone who really knew what she was doing, someone who'd spent years in the business. The more I told her the more she wanted to know. Finally, two hours later, impressed by all I'd said, she picked up the check, shook my hand and expressed her delight we'd be working together.

As I drove back to Baische, I couldn't help thinking how wrong Mike had been when he'd remarked that the Coliseum marketing people would be no picnic to work with.

Still aglow from her conciliatory spirit, I couldn't wait to tell Mike of our meeting. I quickly called Washington.

"You what?"

Sensing danger I began to repeat what I'd just said.

Mike intruded mid-sentence. "Who told you to say anything to Claire Rothman? You're to tell her nothing!" He abruptly hung up.

"Shit! I'm an idiot." Slowly it dawned on me. Why didn't I see I'd been charmed into blather! Worse, once again I fucked up just as Mike and I were getting along.

Yet despite my mistake, I still couldn't understand why, when we were supposedly co-promoting the show, he didn't want Claire to know anything. Blind sided again by Mike's wrath, I called Peter Halbin. "Beats me. Maybe Mike doesn't want her to know the deals so she can't use them to promote her other shows she's booked at the Coliseum."

The explanation was plausible, but incomplete. I was soon to learn that along with an emperor style worship of Irvin Feld, secrecy was sacrosanct. Despite an outpouring of puffery—an avalanche of information about seemingly everything connected to the circus—the fact of the matter was "outsiders" were to be told only what we wanted them to know. Gossip, dirty laundry, revenues, how it all worked was the perk of belonging—an organizational glue as ancient as the Huns.

This secretiveness was reinforced when, months later, while working out of the promoter's office in Washington, I stumbled upon a seldom used walk-in closet as I looked for supplies. The place was full of old, dusty files and broken office equipment. As I lingered over an odd assortment of sundries I noticed a stack of beautiful white binders embossed with gold print sitting high upon a shelf. I balanced myself on a chair and pulled one down. I was amazed to discover it was a detailed description of how the marketing department functioned, complete with job descriptions and formulas for most of our promotions. In short, a portrait of what I now was learning. I then noticed upon further inspection that there were dozens of these binders stored in boxes under the shelves. Fascinated by this discovery I marched upstairs to Allen Bloom to relate what I'd found. But when I showed him the guidebook he simply murmured, "Where did you get that?"

I told him where I'd found them, adding what a thorough job someone had done.

"Put it back where you found it," he muttered. "They could fall into the wrong hands."

Later I learned from Chris Bursky we had paid a small fortune to the Korn agency out of New York to print the training guides, only to have them permanently shelved upon their completion. It was simply more than Ringling ever wanted anyone to know.

Mike and I began putting the finishing touches on our media campaign. Our nights were spent strategizing while our days were spent scouring the landscape for more possibilities.

My binder was overflowing with deals we had consummated and media schedules we had bought. Three television stations, twenty radio stations, two major papers, a huge department store, dozens of grocery store outlets, and one fast-food chain—second locally only to McDonald's—were all timed to unleash their promotional campaigns two weeks from today . . . the day tickets went on sale. Our outdoor advertising was scheduled to start the very same day with a slew of billboards, buses, taxicabs and park benches as well. The Coliseum's group sales department had hung up posters in union halls and corporations throughout a sixty-mile radius and was sending out direct mail flyers to hundreds of organizations. On top of this, Peter Halbin was now in full swing, communicating his progress to us on a daily basis. Press releases and photos were already being sent to small-town papers, and Peter was beginning to schedule the advance clown.

Meanwhile we still had a few more media buys, the most important of which was our extensive newspaper advertising. Felix Salmaggi prepared the ads out of Washington, typesetting our dates and times and promotional plugs. Mike had Ruthy reserve space in the two major dailies and all the surrounding papers. The ads were scheduled to run daily beginning the day tickets went on sale.

There was one other area left to explore; any available magazine advertising. Most magazines were monthly publications, but some of the local entertainment magazines, such as "Where Magazine," were distributed to hotels on a weekly basis. These publications were excellent sources to reach visitors to the city. We compared our options by applying the CPM method of analysis. CPM stood for "cost per million," but the formula worked just the same substituting "million" for "thousand". The way it worked was simple.

For each publication, we divided the full-page rate by the number of thousands of readers they claimed in their circulation. For example, if it cost four-thousand dollars to purchase a full page in a magazine with eighty-thousand readers, then it cost fifty dollars to reach each block of one-thousand readers. If on the same token, by comparison, another magazine cost eight-thousand dollars for a full-page ad but claimed a circulation of two-hundred-and-forty thousand, then its cost per thousand was only thirty-three dollars. So what might appear on the surface to be the more expensive publication was, in actuality, cheaper and more cost effective.

There were only a few magazines that interested us. We purchased two full-page ads in each on a half-cash, half-trade basis. For positioning, we insisted on a right-hand page in the front half of the magazine—next to editorial copy. Almost all magazines charge a premium for inside covers and the back of the magazine, but personally, Mike said, he preferred an inside position next to editorial copy where the reader might be slowed long enough by an article to peruse the ad.

While Mike reviewed all of the media buys and called our major promotional partners to assure all parties were meeting their commitments, I drove out to the largest of the surrounding towns to put together a few more promotions. My bag of tricks was pretty depleted but I convinced a few of the papers to run a color-the-clown contest. But what surprised me was not the editors' receptivity but the fact that unlike the city papers that were still lambasting Mileti and his Coliseum, the small-town papers had a refreshing enthusiasm that was starting to build.

On Friday the tickets arrived. Almost a quarter of a million for all twenty three performances. Mike and I drove back to the Coliseum to go over the seating manifest with Ron Spatrino, the box office manager. But the seats had still not been installed so there was no way we could verify a ticket count, confirm the pricing levels or, for that matter, make sure no tickets had obstructed views. Nevertheless Spatrino assured us there was nothing to worry about. "Things will go smooth as butter".

That night, astir at the office, Mike leaned back in his chair. "This is going to be a hell of a campaign!" There was a look of satisfaction on his face I hadn't seen before.

I surveyed our efforts. We still had one week before tickets went on sale. I quickly ventured forth some possibilities.

"You're not going to be here next week," Mike interjected.

"I'm not?"

"You're going to be in Phoenix."

"Phoenix? Shouldn't I be focused on Cleveland next week?"

"Tommy Crangle could use some help. Besides, you've done all you can do. If it ain't done by now, it's too late. The change of scenery will do you good."

Leave Cleveland just as the campaign was about to break? It didn't make sense. I wandered back to the Picadilly. Where *is* Phoenix anyway? I stared at my map. I wasn't aware it was that far west, almost to Los Angeles. Almost, I realized, to my Japanese friend, Kiyoko.

Chapter 22
NO STONE UNTURNED

— FIVE WEEKS OUT —

Her breath on my arm was soft and sweet, as though my skin was being dusted by a feather. For the moment I didn't want to wake her.

Hours earlier, gazing out the plane window, I was fascinated by the endless miles of desert and towers of rock that ascended from the red clay in a random display of beauty. I was even more amazed when Phoenix appeared out of nowhere. A thriving, glimmering city in the middle of a vast desert. It felt almost claustrophobic, like marooning on a tiny island in the middle of a huge ocean.

I gathered my luggage, rented a car and drove to Tommy Crangle's office. He was situated in a small advertising agency that occupied a white-washed townhouse near the center of town. Despite his pleasure at seeing me, it soon became apparent he didn't really need much help, so I decided I'd drive back to my hotel, wait for Kiyoko, and revel in the next few days of rest and relaxation. Images of Kiyoko danced through my thoughts, especially the show girl audition where she'd tried so hard.

Kiyoko arrived just moments after I unpacked. Within minutes we changed into bathing suits and lay outside in the day's heat beside an uncrowded pool. Kiyoko looked beautiful. Her long, silky black hair, pretty smile and delicate figure no longer a mirage.

As we sipped on margaritas, teasing one another in a delicious game of verbal foreplay, Cleveland slipped slowly from my thoughts. The unfinished Coliseum . . . Claire Rothman . . . Mike Franks and a hundred deals all seemed to fade wonderfully away. As the sun turned from a golden yellow to a crimson red, Kiyoko and I, arm in arm, returned to our room. As she slid onto the king sized bed and turned around invitingly, I slowly peeled off the tiny bottom's to her suit, intent on prolonging the mutual pleasure as long as I could . . . and then proceeded to make love for hours. Drifting in and out of each other's arms it was as though all the tensions, all my longings, had been satisfied in that one marvelous afternoon.

I didn't wake until late in the morning. When I did, Kiyoko was curled up softly in my arms, her dark hair even prettier than usual, flowing gently against the white sheet and pillow. She had a natural beauty, one that required no makeup, and a quality some women possess that men have described as kittenish, a femininity that has nothing to do with strength and resolve but everything to do with warmth and caring. I slept longer, deeper than I had in weeks, waking to that wonderful feeling of being well rested. Kiyoko slept another thirty minutes as I lightly caressed her skin, allowing my thoughts to drift.

Kiyoko slowly stirred. I'd never been to the southwest and felt an urge to fill my senses with this new part of the country, "Why not have the café throw together some sandwiches for a lazy drive through the city."

Kioyko transitioned into a bouncy mood, and now dressed in light, summery clothes, we drove through the city's outskirts, heading in no particular direction.

Phoenix had an air of confidence emanating from its streets. A city that had found just the right pace. There was a newness to the architecture, a refreshing feeling of well being, especially as we drove through the quieter sections. The only discouragement was the irrepressible heat. Even in early October the sun was unabashedly hot. "It's not unusual," the hotel clerk had said, "to see the temperature in the summer rise to 120°. You live from air conditioner to air conditioner."

I had never seen the desert, so we drove until the city came to a stop. All of a sudden, there were no buildings, no people, no traffic, just an endless sea of red clay and stones. Kiyoko and I sat on a blanket on the hood of the car and gazed at the emptiness. It was fascinating, yet frightening, to see nature in such a state of infinity.

As the sun slowly set it became cooler, a turn from the hot midday heat, and we began to drive back to the city. On the way we passed a curving, uphill road with a sign that led to the top of a mountain of trees and large stones. We wound our way upwards, slowly, until we reached a clearing near the edge of a steep drop. We drove to the rim and stopped. The night was pitch black. Below us the entire city sparkled in tens of thousands of flickering lights. The sky above was filled with stars. It suddenly seemed as though Phoenix was a giant reflecting pool. Kiyoko and I sat mesmerized, calmed by the city's beauty, at peace in each other's company, until the early hours of the morning.

Kiyoko and I spent the next three days next to one another, while resting our minds and bodies. By the end of the week, my skin had turned a deep brown. I felt strengthened by the sun and Kiyoko's steady companionship. As I watched Kiyoko pack her clothes, I wondered how the week that lingered so long those first few days could disappear so fast in the end. As we drove to the airport, part of me desperately wanted to stay, to not let her go, but another part, now growing stronger, remembered a world in Cleveland I'd so carefully created.

I kissed Kiyoko goodbye, holding her tightly, not knowing when, if ever, I'd see her again. As I watched her board her plane back to California, I picked up my suitcase and began walking down the concourse to a different set of gates. My flight to Cleveland was leaving in less than an hour.

— Four Weeks Out —

No sooner had I stepped to the airport curb than a taxi pulled up with a bright yellow sign affixed to the roof. "Ringling Bros. and

Barnum & Bailey Circus—Coming To The Cleveland Coliseum—November 6." I looked up. Like a line of chorus girls, a dozen more stood poised, each ablaze with the Ringling logo!

I quickly shuttled to long term parking. In the thirty minutes it took to drive downtown, four huge billboards, a hundred times larger than the taxi cab tops, announced the coming of the circus. I also spied two billboards of Ol' blue eyes, Frank Sinatra, promoting the Coliseum's premiere.

I decided to bypass the Picadilly to savor my soaring spirits and drive straight to Baische.

A message was waiting. Mike Franks had called. I promptly dialed Washington.

"Where the hell have you been? I called you two hours ago!"

"I just got in from Phoenix." My euphoria began to fade.

"Well, what's going on? Have you called the box office? Did the *Plain Dealer* break with our opening night promotion? How about the TV and radio stations? Are we everywhere we're supposed to be?"

"I don't know yet."

"You don't know! Did you listen to the radio on the way in from the airport?"

"No."

"Why not? I want you listening to every station! Make sure all the promos are running. Check out Red Barn, Higbees and ABC. Call me back later. And see what Peter Halbin's lined up."

"Yes sir," I mumbled.

Ruthy strolled in and welcomed me back. Without my asking she brought in the *Plain Dealer*, gingerly placing a copy on my desk. Paper clips were attached to three pages. Just as we'd hoped, our advertisement started on the right hand page of the entertainment section. In addition, the *Plain Dealer* had devoted a half page of space to our opening night promotion and a sizable story led off the sports section featuring Mileti and the construction of his new coliseum. The story on Mileti, I noticed, was a hundred percent positive. "It appears he's been well served by his publicity department. Maybe his luck is beginning to change!"

I told Ruthy about the billboards I'd sighted on the way in, including the two announcing the Coliseum's opening night premiere with Sinatra.

"They oughta snipe Sinatra's posters with Ringling's dates," Ruthy suggested.

"Do you think Claire Rothman would?"

"I don't know. I'll ask," which, coming from Ruthy, meant, I'll figure out a way.

"Have you sent out all the insertion orders to the media for our paid advertising?" I questioned.

"They went out last week, but there's just one thing. Baische wants its money from the circus, not the Coliseum. I know Peter feels the same way."

"Why? The Coliseum is responsible for half the bills."

"Because their credit's lousy. We don't trust them."

"I see," I said. "I'll talk to Mike. But that's the first time anyone's sought refuge in the circus for their financial security. Mileti must be scrambling."

That night, perched in the Picadilly Inn, I began twirling the radio dial in search of our promotional spots. Twenty stations. Twenty deals. As soon as I heard an elephant joke or a circus trivia question I switched to another station. "Pachyderm poo being given away by the *circus*?" What happened to Ringling's full name? I made a note to lambast the account executive in the morning.

It was ten a.m. when I arrived at the office. I was anxious to hear the box office numbers for yesterday's ticket sales. So was Mike since he'd indicated, "You can often predict the size of an engagement by the first day's ticket sales."

I called Ron Spatrino. While I waited I sat ready with a sheet of paper divided into four columns that headquarters had provided. The left column featured last year's revenues, beginning thirty days out and proceeding through each of the twenty three performances. The next column was blank for Mike and me to fill in with this year's numbers. The third column was reserved for cumulative totals and the fourth was for us to record the percentage difference—up or down—from last year's totals. At the bottom of the sheet was Allen's projection: $1.2 million dollars. Double the amount of the year before, rationalized not least among other things, by an arena now twice the size.

After holding for ten minutes Spatrino returned and recited the first day's numbers. We were up forty percent.

I called Mike. I sensed he was satisfied, but also sensed he didn't want to tempt fate. "Well, all right. It appears we're off to a good start."

<hr />

Peter Halbin was now immersed in obtaining a massive amount of publicity. Nothing, Mike said, equaled the impact of press coverage. "It has a sense of newsworthiness and human interest that no single ad can generate."

The news media operated in a world of immediacy. Whereas promotion and paid advertising could be orchestrated weeks in advance we had to move closer to the arrival of the circus to grab the news media's attention. And for media interest this was a critical week for Peter Halbin.

His third press release was being mailed to the 140 small town papers he'd been blitzing each week—only this release contained the invitation to attend the opening night press party Peter was ballyhooing. Mike had lined up Gunther to appear along with a few show girls and clowns. When I arrived at Peter's office he was toying with another idea. "What would be the odds of bringing a baby elephant to the press party?"

"The press party is on the fourth tier of the Coliseum. How would we get it up there?"

"How about the freight elevator?"

"I don't know. I'll have to ask Mike."

I liked the notion but had no idea if an elephant had ever ridden in an elevator. And even though they rode endless hours in a train car, I had visions of being squashed by a panicky mastodon.

Peggy Williams, the Red Show's advance clown, was due to arrive in two weeks. Her schedule filled seven pages of a detailed publicity report. He even had her handing out balloons in the lobby of the Terminal Tower before one of the Cleveland Browns' home games.

Peter needed phone interviews for the editors of the major newspapers to whom he had promised exclusive interviews. As we ran through the list of possibilities, I suggested a few performers.

"What about Wolfgang Holzmair? He sticks his whole head in a lion's mouth, not to mention carries the beast around the cage on his shoulders."

"Can he speak English?"

"I'm not sure."

"Well, find out for God's sake. Last year I lined up an editor with a Mexican equestrian, and all she could say was 'No comprende.' The editor thought I was nuts."

We poured through the rest of the list and decided on three more phone interviews: Pio Nock, the tightrope walker who clowns around on the high wire above Wolfgang's den of lions; the circus wardrobe mistress; and Gran Picasso, a Spanish juggler who had just joined the show.

"By the way," Peter laughed, "I sold a show girl story to the *Cleveland Press*—Cleveland's afternoon paper—for a story on 'local girl joins the circus'".

"I wasn't sure we had a show girl from Cleveland?"

"We don't. Mike just thought we did. Don't worry, we found one who lived in Parma for six months. We'll fill her in on the details."

"I'm also beginning to schedule the performer interviews during the first week of the show's run with the television stations and newspapers. This will be considerably easier since the performers will at least be in town. I've got Rudy Lenz and his chimps set up for 'Morning Exchange.' It's the top-rated morning show, beating even 'The Today Show'".

"What time is the show?" I asked.

"Eight a.m."

"Well, good luck. Rudy is going to complain his chimps are cranky that hour of the morning, so don't blame me if he bites your dick off."

"Rudy or the chimp?"

After surveying Peter's advance clown schedule, the on-going press releases, all the phone interviews and now the personal interviews, I looked up and grinned. "That's nice, but is that *all*?"

"No, there's one other thing." Peter winked, dismissing my temerity. "We've sent press releases to thirty newspapers and TV stations about the pachyderm poo you're offering for fertilizer. The radio stations and the media said they'll run it as a public service announcement. I'm predicting record-breaking petunias for the spring!"

Chapter 23
ON COME THE PACHYDERMS

— THREE WEEKS OUT —

"Nick Mileti was a colorful, warm, ingratiating hustler, and people loved to be hustled," a long-time Clevelander commented. "He had enemies, but people were also enthralled by the man. Mileti was Mr. Vegas in a button-down, conservative town, and the city loved it. He would come breezing into the Pewter Mug pub in his long fur coat, turtleneck cashmere sweater and jewelry, and people were flattered just to be acknowledged by him."

At his peak, Mileti owned all or part of the Cleveland Indians, the city's baseball team; the Cleveland Crusaders, the city's hockey team; the downtown arena; WAVE radio, a 50-watt, clear channel station; and he'd founded the Cavaliers, Cleveland's basketball team. He, in fact, presided over so many major organizations that he became known among Clevelanders as "Mr. President."

Nick Mileti was the hometown boy made good. A consummate deal maker. And despite appellations by the local media of "glitter guy," "flamboyant" and "The Great Sicilian Hope of Cleveland," he preferred to view himself in less colorful terms. "I would just say I'm a hard worker," he would tell a reporter responding to his celebrity status. But Mileti knew better. Notwithstanding his attempts at modesty, he had built a sports empire worth millions and the Cleveland Coliseum was to be the "crown jewel of his kingdom."

There was no lack of ambition in this son of an immigrant family from Italy. But a kingdom built on borrowed money is a hazardous undertaking, and behind the scenes, Mileti was struggling for funds to complete his twenty-thousand-seat castle forty minutes from the city. He sold the parking rights and some of the food concession to IT&T in order to raise cash, and later, when IT&T began charging high prices, it provided fuel for the fire for those who wanted to see Mileti fail.

But if Mileti was a consummate deal maker, he was even more of a showman. And in the spirit of Errol Flynn—who believed when your luck's run out and your spirit is flagging, there's only one thing to do, and that's throw the biggest party in town—Mileti was preparing to launch Cleveland's extravaganza of the year.

On Saturday, October 26th, less than a week away, Frank Sinatra was scheduled to open Nick Mileti's Coliseum. Mileti had pulled out all the stops to book Sinatra, and the fact that Sinatra shared Mileti's Italian heritage made it a double coup. Nothing was spared in the planning of the event, and all twenty-thousand seats were expected to be filled.

Practically everyone who was anyone in Cleveland's high society had been invited. In fact, a special black-tie party of two-thousand special guests was scheduled to be hosted by Mileti and attended by Sinatra himself after the show. For the occasion, Mileti had minted gold-plated medallions three inches in diameter with a picture of Sinatra on one side and a majestic picture of the Coliseum engraved on the other. Each of the special guests would be given the medallion to wear around their necks. But even prior to the eight-thirty p.m. curtain call, Mileti had arranged an atmosphere befitting a Hollywood premiere. As ticket holders arrived, cameras would transpose their images onto two giant telescreens hanging on either wing of the Coliseum . . . and champagne bottles would be popping. Mileti had set up portable bars on the main concourse to treat Cleveland's finest.

Mike and I watched the build-up for Sinatra and Mileti's opening night with fascination, not only because we admired the gutsy determination of this Italian sports mogul, but because the success of the circus was inextricably entwined with the success of the Coliseum. And Saturday night was Mileti's chance to prove them wrong, to show the city this new state-of-the-art facility was the shiniest jewel of all, the sparkling diamond of his kingdom.

"Peter, how are you?" I said, as an introductory greeting to our almost daily phone update.

"Good," he replied. "Everyone seems to be biting on the interviews for the first week of the show, but it's a little tough this year."

"Why is that?"

"Well, with the location of the new Coliseum, I now have to add an hour-and-a-half both ways to schlepp the performers. Spontaneity is out the window. With the old arena, I could sometimes lure reporters to the building on a moment's notice if it was a slow news day."

"I see your point," I said. "I hadn't considered that. Listen, I'm getting a little concerned about these rumblings of a newspaper strike. I heard on the news last night the union is continuing to threaten a strike. What's the deal?"

"Frankly, I don't know a hell of a lot more than you. Negotiations for wage increases have been going on for several days but the Cleveland Newspaper Guild has shown little interest in the offers by management."

"Well, what are the odds for a settlement? We need a goddamn newspaper strike right now like we need a hole in the head."

"Usually these things get resolved with no disruption . . . that is, if one side clearly has more power than the other. But in this case, the union wants to test their clout and thinks they can shut the papers down. At the same time, unemployment nationally just hit six percent, the highest in three years, so the newspaper owners think the unions are bluffing. It's at an impasse right now, so it don't look good."

"One other question?"

"Shoot."

"If the Guild does go on strike, how many papers will be affected?"

"Probably all of them." Peter paused for a moment. "I'll keep you posted, but you and Mike better be thinking of a back-up plan."

"I guess you're right. By the way, are we going to see your smiling mug this week?"

"As a matter of fact, you are. I've got something to show you. Will you be in tomorrow?"

"No. I'm driving to Peninsula to check out where the train is arriving. I've got to secure permits for the animal walk, talk to the police and arrange the logistics."

"All right," Peter said, "I'll drop by on Thursday. But don't be surprised if those Peninsulites are less than receptive."

That afternoon, Mike confronted the ramifications of a newspaper strike. "If it happens it's a nightmare." All of our television and radio advertising plus the promotions and publicity are designed to generate excitement. But it's only through the newspaper advertisements that people can obtain the information they need. "It would be virtually impossible to list twenty-three performances, not to mention pricing, ticket locations and phone numbers, on the end of a TV or radio commercial. Even if we could, the listeners would never remember it. A strike could cost us a fortune."

"If they go on strike," Mike said, "the only thing I can think of is to tag all our spots with a special hotline number and have the Coliseum man a ton of phone lines to give out the information."

"Why don't I call the phone company," I suggested, "get a special number and alert Ruthy to the possibility of a new tag line . . . but good luck with the box office. They were three hours late giving me yesterday's figures and everything now is normal. Imagine thousands of callers every day for ticket information. I shudder at the thought of it."

Mike began tapping a pencil. "By the way, how much are we up over last year?"

"We're still okay I think. We've dropped a hair but we're still up 38 percent."

"That's all right. All the paid spots, TV and radio, kick in next week. If we can hold the increase until then we oughta do gangbusters."

Historically, the animal walk had been held in downtown Cleveland, but now, forty miles outside of Cleveland, the closest the railroad tracks came to the Coliseum was a tiny, picturesque village, Peninsula. Headquarters had decided to unload the animals there and then backtrack the train to Akron, where it would remain during the run.

Peninsula was exactly 2.3 miles from the Coliseum, alongside State Route 303, a winding, two-lane country road.

Downtown Peninsula consisted of a popular restaurant and bar frequented by young, urban professionals, the "Peninsula Night Club." It was situated next to the tracks where the elephants would unload. The town had one gas station, one convenience store run by the mayor, a library and the GAR Hall, a historic civil war building, which stood for the Grand Army of the Republic.

Four residential homes had been converted to antique stores. The rest of the town was composed of beautifully kept hundred-year-old homes with manicured lawns and gardens.

Before meeting with a few of the town's elders and the local police, I surveyed the drop-off point. There was about seventy feet of graveled lot next to the spot where the train would stop so there seemed to be plenty of room to unload the animals. Across from the tracks was an old wooden building that appeared to have once served as the train station. Along the front of the building was a long wooden platform that looked like an excellent place to position the press. Across the street, where the tracks intersected Route 303, was an empty field. To celebrate this "great civic event," Peter had invited a local school band from the Richfield School to play. I figured we could position them in the field a few feet from the highway. Once the animals started walking, we would turn right in front of the band, cross a small bridge over the Cuyahoga River—and then lead the elephants up a hill past the pristine houses and gardens.

All I had to do was ask the police to block off the roads and to ride escort, while convincing the town's leaders that this was an everyday event. Since I suspected they were dubious, I decided I would spare them the details of former stampedes and rampaging bull elephants terrorizing local communities, only to be shot by vigilante farmers when all else failed. I was comforted by the fact that our herd was mostly female. The bulls were just too unpredictable, especially during "must" season, when they became especially aggressive. African elephants were by nature dangerous to handle, so with few exceptions, our elephants were Asian. Fortunately, stories of "killer beasts" were none too recent; merely minor incidents such as Chris Bursky's four-hour ordeal trying to coax a herd of elephants out of a city fountain midway along the route.

The handlers took certain precautions, just to be on the safe side. For one thing, elephants and horses were natural enemies, so they walked the horses to the building either separately or at a safe distance (it was the circus parade that coined the expression "Hold your horses"), and the trainer would walk along the left side of the lead elephant with a "bull hook," which he'd use to snag the left foot of the elephant if she started to run.

Three of the town's officials and its only policeman had gathered at Fisher's General Store to await my arrival. As soon as I swung open the screen door I could tell they were nervous about the commotion they suspected would ensue. Fortunately they weren't sure what questions to ask. So I described the procession and assured them the animal walk was a harmless affair done every week of the year throughout the country. Essentially a non-event.

Unbeknownst to me, Peter had been sending out releases and advance stories to the press—"The Very First Animal Walk in Peninsula, Ohio with elephants and camels strolling along fields of corn." And the press had begun announcing the walk over the air and in newsprint to thousands of Clevelanders and townspeople living in the outlying areas. As I calmly described this tranquil event to the town's elders, bus loads of school kids from elementary schools and daycare centers, not to mention hundreds of circus fanatics and curiosity seekers, were planning to descend on the tiny town of Peninsula, Ohio.

Mike and I were sitting in Baische's conference room discussing the details of my previous day's trip to Peninsula when Peter strolled in carrying a large, bulging envelope under one arm. In contrast to my and Mike's relaxed demeanor, he was in ebullient spirits.

"Good morning, gentlemen," Peter said. "And how are you this fine, brisk October day?"

"Couldn't be better," I responded, while Mike just smiled. "By the way, what's in the envelope?" Peter stood at the head of the table crinkling his package.

"Well, I'm glad you asked," Peter said, as he moved closer to where Mike and I sat, "because this morning I come bearing great gifts," whereupon Peter opened the envelope, turned it upside down and, like confetti, out poured the contents. Hundreds of newspaper clippings fluttered to the table.

Surprised, Mike picked up a handful of newspaper stories. "What's this?"

"Those are the stories from all of the small-town newspapers I've been mailing," Peter said, as he grabbed a fistful of clippings. "It's incredible! They've been running the stories untouched. Most of the press releases haven't even been edited. The papers ran them exactly as I sent them. Shit! I've even begun getting letters from some of the editors thanking me for sending them the releases."

Mike scanned through the pile of articles. "Not only have they run the stories, it looks like a lot of them ran them on the front page, photos and all."

"Well, I don't know how we're playing in Cleveland yet, but it's obvious small town America loves us. In fact," Peter added, "I've got a ninety-percent response rate to the opening night press party and most of the editors want to bring their wives and kids."

"Hell, I don't care if they bring their long lost Aunt Bertha," Mike replied with a grin, "just give us a good review the next day and I'll be ecstatic."

"They will, my man. They will," Peter replied. "I feel it in my bones."

Chapter 24
THE SHERIFF HAD DOUBTS

— TWO WEEKS OUT —

I often felt betrayed by Saturday mornings. All week I looked forward to the approaching weekend with the anticipation of a sudden break from frenzied activity. Saturdays, I envisioned, I would wake up feeling relaxed, serene, at peace, ready to reward myself with a calm appraisal of how I intended to spend the day. So why the hell did it rarely work? Invariably, I'd wake up even antsier than I'd been the previous day with an overwhelming need to *accomplish* something. By now I realized that until I spent half the day washing my car, laundering my clothes, and performing several other productive activities, my mind and body weren't going to let me relax. Saturdays are at best a bridge to Sundays. Sunday I'll relax, I thought, as I lay under the covers half-awake trying to mentally massage my energy.

I staggered out of bed, fumbling with the electric cord that would boil a pot of water for my instant coffee, and glanced at the newspaper. Suddenly the morning's extra dose of nervous energy became crystal clear. Tonight was the opening night of the Coliseum and Nick Mileti's debut with Frank Sinatra and twenty-one thousand abiding fans. I shook off my morning fog. The wait was finally over

. . . and a ton of people had a stake in the outcome, not the least of which was Nick Mileti's publicity department.

All week, stories had been appearing in anticipation of tonight's grand opening. Sunday, the Society page of the *Plain Dealer* ran a five-column story on the Coliseum's private loges showcasing Claire Rothman and her list of buyers. Thursday, the *Plain Dealer* ran an eight-page insert devoted exclusively to the premiere, embellished with a photo of Sinatra in tuxedo and cape captioned, "The Wizard of Swoon." Mileti's face was superimposed in the background surrounded by sports paraphernalia. The story touted the grandeur of the new Coliseum—"A building so large—450 feet by 343 feet—it could swallow three football fields, seven million basketballs, thirty-seven million hockey pucks"—and traced the obstacles Mileti had overcome to bring the Coliseum to fruition. "Our lawyers, from the local board of zoning appeals to the United States Supreme Court, won twelve straight unanimous decisions . . . a fantastic record," Mileti is quoted, amidst ruminations the legal tangles cost millions, not to mention untold construction delays. Other stories during the week highlighted the advantages the new Coliseum would bring to Mileti's hockey team and basketball team. Stories within stories recounted the history of the Coliseum's construction, featuring in one case a special write up on IT&T Building Services, which through its APCOA Parking Services Division, would supervise parking. Finally, near the end of the week, two articles stressed the "easy in and easy out" plan for parking APCOA had devised. A large map of the Coliseum's location was featured with explicit directions to reach the building from a number of routes.

But even Thursday's eight-page article paled in comparison to the full, front-page cover story in the *Plain Dealer's* Friday Entertainment section. Above the headline "Second Roman Coliseum Opens" was a huge illustration of a medallion with Nick Mileti's face ghosted beside the face of Titus Flavius Vespasianus, the Roman emperor and builder of Rome's original coliseum in 79 A.D. The text compared the humble origins of each man, both from Rome, and how, through financial wizardry, fortunes were raised to build their colossal structures. "If anything, Mileti has proven to be an even greater financial wizard than his Roman counterpart," the paper proclaimed, "for he has raised millions without benefit of the power to decree tax levies, impound food imports or reclaim public lands. Our Coliseum builder had to rely on his persuasive powers and indefatigable spirit to make his dream a reality for millions of Northeastern Ohioans, who at long last will have a sports palace worthy of its name. If it weren't for Mileti, the ground on which this splendid edifice stands would still be a cow pasture."

As I scanned the morning's paper it became even more evident Mileti's publicity team had done an incredible job. The front page featured a story headlined, "Nick Mileti's Dream Comes True Tonight," followed on page four by a half-page photo of the inside of the arena with its twenty-thousand permanent seats in place. The sports section even carried a front-page story on the new sports era beginning at the Coliseum. But despite all the hype I couldn't help wondering if the Coliseum's press agents were holding their breaths in anticipation of tonight's results.

Peter and Mike and I were no less concerned. We had been touting for three months how wonderful the new Coliseum would be. And with the circus dead on the heels of Sinatra, we wanted no less than a splendid success, with living proof of the ease in which the new Coliseum now served the residents of Cleveland and the surrounding area.

Meanwhile, Jim Swingos, the eponymous owner of Mike's favorite restaurant, was nervously catering to Frank Sinatra and his entourage of bodyguards and band members. Sinatra had arrived in a private jet shortly after midnight and was whisked at noon by limousine to Swingos' establishment. Swingos said he was as nervous as the day he married. Several of Sinatra's entourage wore yellow t-shirts emblazoned with the slogan, "Ol' Blue Eyes is Back." Sinatra sat in the nearly deserted dining room, eating a steak, while Swingos kept fans and curiosity seekers away from his fabled guest.

As Sinatra rested before his evening performance, a beehive of activity was taking place at the Coliseum. Cement dust was wiped off the tables, plumbing was checked, champagne bars and food concessions were stocked and lights were tested. Because of the building's isolated location, Mileti had constructed his own sewage treatment plant, built his own water tower, and installed his own electric power substation on land adjacent to the arena. As engineers completed their final checks, ushers, ticket takers and box office personnel received final-day instructions. It seemed all was in order. Even the head of APCOA, the Coliseum's parking service, felt he had everything under control. The Coliseum had 6,700 parking places surrounding the arena and he had flown all over the United States studying parking logistics at the largest arenas.

But there was one man who had gnawing doubts. In fact, while everyone else's confidence was building, he was becoming more and more nervous. He was Howard Taylor of the Summit County Sheriff's Department and he was the officer in charge of traffic control. As Nick Mileti inspected his brown, mohair tuxedo and prepared for the triumph of his career, Taylor confided to a reporter, "I'll be very frank with you. It's going to be a mess, this being the first night of crowds at the new Coliseum. I'm anticipating problems with traffic congestion we haven't even thought of yet."

Taylor assigned twenty deputies with cruisers to help guide traffic flow, but Taylor warned, "Even the 6,700-space parking lot has a problem. Construction equipment has negated a thousand spaces."

I finished the newspaper and completed my morning chores. The urge for accomplishment gradually subsided. Looking at my options for an empty afternoon slate, I spread out a map and decided I'd drive west along the southern shore of Lake Erie toward Sandusky, then on to Marblehead, a small piece of land in the shape of a diamond that jutted into the lake.

The clouds were low, moving with the currents, with temperatures not expected to rise much above freezing. But I often found the water to be a spiritual tranquilizer, and at the very least I envisioned the sounds of seagulls and the discovery of at least one or two weatherbeaten bars with a few salty types inside to observe.

I drove past fallow fields, past signs advertising "Ice for 25¢" and "Worms for $1.95 a dozen," past locals shivering by their pickup trucks, fishing from the sides of bridges. By the time I reached Marblehead, the weather had turned worse. A northwesterly wind swept the top of the water, stopping just short of white caps, and a light drizzle dampened the grass along the water's edge, turning the brown sand into mud. I ducked into a cozy seafood restaurant that offered a view of the docks and what little activity remained. Fortunately, I brought along a novel and decided to sit near the window, and while away the afternoon. The sun didn't sink until six-thirty p.m. Having repaid the restaurant for its indulgence with a seafood dinner, I began the drive east, toward Cleveland.

As I slowly wound my way back, unshaven and a little unkempt but in a relaxed and peaceful state, I stood in marked contrast to twenty-one-thousand of Cleveland's finest dressed in tuxedos, evening gowns and sparkling jewels on their way to the eight-thirty p.m. opening of the Coliseum. Not much in the way of good news had greeted Cleveland's high society during the past year, so the urge to re-bond with their peers in a see-and-be-seen display of group identity was more powerful than usual. And Mileti was providing the perfect vehicle. If you weren't invited to this event, you hadn't *arrived*, and if you were invited, you certainly wanted to make sure everyone knew it.

As the procession of cars began driving south along I-271 and I-71 toward the Coliseum, the director of APCOA stood ready with dozens of uniformed parking attendants prepared to test the efficiency of their well-honed system. Meanwhile, Howard Taylor of the Sheriff's Department began dispatching his men to the ramps along I-271, I-303 and the Ohio Turnpike in preparation for this huge migration southward. His plan was to position his deputies along the intersecting arteries, where they would stop traffic from one direction while steadily moving the cars forward from the other lanes with the aid of bright flashlights. Taylor and a few other cruisers would scan the highway for accidents or breakdowns that could possibly impede the flow of traffic.

At seven-thirty p.m., as the first stream of early arrivals approached the parking lot, everything seemed to be under control. APCOA collected the money from the drivers and quickly dispatched the cars to waiting attendants who directed them to open spaces. Even the cars on the ramps were moving at a brisk pace as they exited I-271 and rounded the intersection at I-303 for a straight route to the Coliseum's parking gates. But about seven-forty-five, as the cars began to increase in number, converging on APCOA's parking gates from four different directions, they began to back up. As Taylor surveyed the scene, it became evident that a major problem existed. The Coliseum didn't have enough entrance gates. In fact, where it should have had gates positioned at a minimum of three entrances, the Coliseum had only opened one gate into the arena parking lot. The other two entrances were still under construction and blocked by heavy equipment. This was not a solvable problem. All the attendants in the world could only funnel so many cars into one set of gates, and the line was beginning to grow. In fact, by eight p.m., the line extended down the main artery and onto the entrance ramps, with each approaching car adding to the log jam. Within minutes, the traffic stopped, and a column of headlights extending east and west along Route I-271 and I-71 appeared to stretch forever. With only thirty minutes left until show time, Taylor frantically appealed to APCOA to move faster while radioing his deputies to streamline the traffic wherever possible.

Meantime, along Route I-271, patrons sat in their cars becoming increasingly aware that they would never make the opening curtain. But for many, the huge Coliseum glowing in the distance looked easily accessible, and besides that, there was no turning around on the interstate. Complicating matters further, cars began overheating and dropping out of the procession with steam spiraling up from their hoods. Their drivers had no choice but to abandon their cars and begin walking toward the Coliseum. As other drivers became mired behind the deserted cars, they too saw the hopelessness of their situation and began abandoning their cars by the hundreds alongside the interstate and even along the medium strip. Police officers watched the parade of tuxedoed and gowned patrons begin moving toward the arena, in ghostly fashion, with a sense of helplessness. Fearful of crossing the interstate, couples began climbing the embankments leading to a grassy field behind the building. One woman dressed in a long, formal gown tried to scramble up a bank from the highway to the Coliseum. Halfway up the hill, she slipped and fell into the weeds. She retreated toward I-271, slipped again and vanished into a ditch. A reporter from the *Cleveland Plain Dealer* abandoned his car and began his alpine climb, along with hundreds of others, slipping and sliding, grabbing at blades of grass, all the while dressed in his tuxedo and patent leather shoes. Those that did make it up the embankment still had to cross a knee-high field of brush and burrs and then blindly feel their way around heavy construction equipment until their path became lit by the arena's lights. As Taylor watched nearly a thousand people on foot crossing the interstate, he could only think, "This is absolute chaos!"

Arriving at the Picadilly I fumbled with my key in the lock. I heard my phone ringing. I grabbed it just as I thought the caller would hang up.

"Can you believe this?" Peter blurted into the phone.

"Believe what?"

"The news," Peter said. "Turn on the news. Traffic backed up for miles leading to the Coliseum. The press is announcing it as an unmitigated disaster. Hell, they're *still* trying to get the cars out of there."

I turned on the news. Film footage showed hundreds of cars abandoned along the highway, while a reporter interviewed a driver who said he was somehow re-routed all the way to Akron, and he wasn't even going to the Coliseum.

"Well, this is just *great*."

"Hell, look on the bright side," Peter retorted. "It could have been the opening night of the circus."

Fortunately, Sinatra dazzled the audience, and Sunday's papers focused on the positive aspects of the opening night. Under the headline "Champagne Flows at the Coliseum", the *Plain Dealer* down-played the traffic catastrophe, highlighting instead the glamour of Mileti's celebration. Sinatra didn't attend the special after-show party Mileti had arranged nor were there nearly the number of celebrities in attendance that were anticipated, but for the majority of Clevelanders who made it into the parking lot in time, the premiere lived up to their expectations.

By Monday, however, the impact of the traffic jam hit home and Mileti's publicity machine was in full-swing damage control. On the front page of the paper, the Coliseum's general manager apologized to the stranded motorists, offering to refund the price of the tickets to anyone who missed the performance. He also acknowledged the paucity of entrances and the lack of parking spaces caused by the construction equipment. Promises were made to prevent future occurrences, and blame was passed all around. Howard Taylor was even quoted in the article, but in an act of restraint he never stated, "I told you so."

"Well, so much for the best laid plans of mice and men," I uttered innocuously to Mike. It was Monday morning and as we sat in the agency's conference room, I scanned Mike's reaction to the Sinatra fiasco. Having reached a measure of mutual acceptance, yet still firmly under his tutelage, I was searching for his level of discomfort. Petty satisfaction on my part, but some of the learning process, I figured, was watching my supervisor under adversity.

"It's spilt milk," Mike said, shooting me an icy glance. "We've got other stuff to worry about. Have you called the box office yet for Sunday's numbers? Have you checked all the media schedules? Is everybody holding up their end of the deal? Why the hell are you late?"

I began to squirm. As I fumbled with the answers, I made a mental note to be a little less curious next time. Fortunately, just as I began to wonder how false bravado could turn so quickly into transparent cowardice, Peter Halbin strolled in with Peggy Williams, the Red Show's advance clown. She was dressed in full clown regalia and makeup. Peggy had just driven into town the night before and Peter was chauffeuring her to the first full day of activities. We had never met but I had heard from other promoters she was easy to work with. I introduced myself and offered her my chair as I politely moved down the table. As she settled her large frame into the seat next to me, I was surprised at how startled I felt by her presence. I'd been so absorbed for the past several weeks in the business of the show, I'd almost forgotten this strange and exotic group of people about to re-enter my life.

Mike's power diminished, if only temporarily, as Peggy widened the circle. Behind her red nose and two giant teardrops she was pragmatic and businesslike, questioning Mike about Cleveland and any selling points she needed to know. Mike filled her in on the Coliseum, Mileti's opening night and our marketing strategy. She listened good naturedly, offering occasional observations. It was obvious Peggy liked being in Cleveland this year, since she intended to stay through the run, allowing her to participate in the show, an opportunity she rarely had.

As I watched Peggy, noting her self assurance, I couldn't help wondering if she felt as secure on the road as she appeared. The other clowns at least have the comfort of each other. Peggy, like us, traveled alone.

I'd read her bio in the press kit and was fascinated by her resumé. She was one of the few women from outside the circus to become a clown and, in fact, was the first female clown to be hired by Irvin upon graduation from clown college. Other female clowns were often wives of circus performers who needed a job and had learned the skills from inside veterans. Peggy, however, had a degree in speech pathology and a growing passion to perform, a taste she'd developed working with children who had speech defects and adults whose speaking skills had been diminished by strokes.

In order to communicate, Peggy began developing non-verbal communication skills through pantomime, body language and hand signals. As I later watched her thread an imaginary needle and walk an invisible flight of stairs with studied perfection, I couldn't erase the image of a well dressed therapist teaching one small child how to speak. The meeting ended and Peggy and Peter began ambling toward the door. Mindful of her floppy shoes, I cleared a path to the exit telling her I was delighted she was here. She reached out and shook my hand. As she did, I thought for a moment I saw a hint of familiar vulnerability in her eyes. She wasn't much older than me.

Despite the fact that two-thousand years separated the building of Rome's Coliseum from Mileti's new arena, there was far greater complexity in the design of Titus Vespasianus's arena than Mileti's.

The primary entertainment in Rome's Coliseum was gladiator battles and animal hunts. Liberal amounts of sand were used to soak up the blood . . . unsurprisingly, the Latin word for sand was *arena*. When the gladiators weren't being forced to kill one another, they were called upon to stalk and slay wild animals. Sometimes as many as a hundred animals would be slain in a day amidst lavish set designs of mountains and wooded scenery. The sets were intricately designed to be raised and lowered by counterweights in the center of the arena.

Equally complex was a web of underground passages that housed the animals and allowed them to be released simultaneously into the main arena. The arena floor was actually a series of wooden planks covered with layers of sand. Underneath these boards were two levels of narrow passages, each containing dozens of cages. Just prior to the time the beasts were scheduled in the arena, handlers would winch the cages to the top level, releasing the animals through one side of the cage. The animals would have nowhere to go but through a trap door leading to the arena.

I can only imagine how the animals must have reacted when suddenly they were deposited into the broad daylight amidst exotic set designs and thousands of screaming spectators. As a result of the animals' immediate fear and confusion, they often had to be taunted into self defense by the gladiators. In order to protect the spectators, especially the more esteemed patrons seated in the front tiers, a safety net had been installed around the arena walls. This was capped by downward pointing elephant tusks intended to impale any beasts that attempted to scale the walls. Should either of these methods fail, Roman archers were stationed prodigiously around the arena.

Meanwhile, spectators were sprayed with perfumed water to lessen the stench of blood and mutilated organs exposed by the slaughter. Toward the end of the day, special hearses accompanied by an official dressed as Charon, the god of the underworld, collected and transported the corpses through a gate called Porta Libitinaria, named for the goddess of death, while the victors were lauded with gold and laurel wreaths.

Although the gladiator games were finally stopped in 438 A.D. and the animal hunts were abolished a short time later, there is little evidence to indicate that the human relishment of violence has abated.

Nick Mileti didn't need an intricate web of passages to support his modern day gladiators, but what he did need was frozen ice for his opening hockey game between his Cleveland Crusaders and the Toronto Toros. Unfortunately, this wasn't to be Mileti's week. Only a day after battling the publicity from the Sinatra traffic fiasco Mileti had to cancel the opening game. Despite an expected sellout of eighteen-thousand fans, one pipe that ran the length of the concrete floor became clogged, and a center patch in the arena floor wouldn't freeze. The broken pipe was discovered after the floor was flooded with water. Instead of the four layers of ice required for the necessary thickness, only two, it turned out, could be frozen.

Fortunately, the news of the hockey game's cancellation was restricted to the bottom of the sports pages, but it served as one more piece of evidence that Mileti's people were still rushing to do too much too soon.

Mike was back in Washington. In less than a week we'd be meeting the train in Peninsula. Everywhere I turned the results of our efforts were being broadcast in print and on the air. A massive blitz of publicity, promotions, cash and trade advertising, was bombarding Cleveland and the surrounding area. I was soon in constant demand by the media, the Coliseum, organizations and city officials for tickets and information. Sitting in the middle of millions of dollars worth of advertising and marketing, I was it! No sooner did I answer one line than I quickly picked up another.

My self adulation was short lived, punctured in the morning by Peter, followed by Mike for a final flattening.

"Peter, what's up?" I said into the phone.

"Nothing," Peter said. "Not a goddamn thing. Everything's wonderful, except for the fact that every time I place a conference call for an interview between an editor and a performer, the goddamn performer isn't there."

"Jesus, Peter. I'm sorry. You must feel embarrassed."

"Embarrassed! I feel like a fucking idiot. Now will you call Kansas City, talk to the promoter and tell him to get off his ass and help me line up these interviews?"

"Sure, Peter, I'll see what I can do." No sooner had I hung up the phone than Mike called.

"What's up?" Mike said dispassionately.

"About what?"

"About what? About Cleveland for Christ's sake. Why the hell do you think I'm calling?"

"Things are great," I said, frantically trying to regain ground. "The numbers are still holding. Peter is busy with the advance clown and I'm monitoring everything in progress."

Mike grunted in response, followed by a long moment of silence. "Have you called the people yet who are riding the elephants next week in the animal walk?"

"No, I haven't," I responded, not sure why I was supposed to call.

"Well, give them a call. Tell them what they're supposed to wear."

"Sure thing. I'll do it right away."

"All right. I'll see you in a few days."

"By the way, one more thing," I quickly said, feeling a tinge of panic. "What *are* they supposed to wear?"

"Gloves," Mike replied. "Gloves and blue jeans. The hair on the back of an elephant feels like barbed wire."

Chapter 25
WELL, PLAY IT AGAIN

— ONE WEEK OUT —

It was Friday, the first day of November, and I celebrated a blustery morning by arriving at the office a half hour early. I made a beeline for the coffee urn. As I settled into my chair, scanning my desk for an empty spot to rest my cup, I noticed this once barren room had taken on a whole new appearance. Posters of leaping lions now plastered the walls. Stacks of programs consumed one corner while whistles and certificates sat beside neatly arranged copies of proposals and promotional deals. Behind me, on the wall, I'd taped all the media schedules, and whatever I couldn't locate at a glance was filed by function in three-ring binders. As I quietly surveyed our accomplishments from the steaming rim of my coffee cup, Ruthy Friedman strolled in.

"Good morning, Mr. MacVicar," Ruthy said, with a slight nod of her head.

"And a good morning to you. To what do I owe this honor?"

"May I have a seat?"

"Of course," I said, thinking how calm she always seemed to be.

"Have you listened to the radio this morning?"

"No, I haven't. Did we receive some extra publicity?"

"No. But you may need some. The newspaper guild just went on strike."

"You're kidding."

"Nope."

"When did this happen?"

"They just announced it. They're setting up picket lines at six a.m, but it may not be as disastrous as it appears." Ruthy explained they've only struck the *Plain Dealer* so far, which means for the moment we can shift our ads to the afternoon paper, *The Cleveland Press*.

"That certainly helps," I said, "but I wonder how much readership we'll lose?"

"Not much. But it probably won't help your *Plain Dealer* opening night promotion."

Ruthy rose and started toward the door. "Just remember, there's only one thing predictable about advertising."

"What's that?"

"Unpredictability."

I returned her smile. "Ruthy, I'm curious. How come nothing seems to upset you?"

"Oh, I get upset," she said, "but only about things I can change, and that eliminates about ninety percent of all worries. And as far as the rest of life's problems, the faster you begin resolving them, the less time you have to worry about them. Speaking of which, I'm switching our ads to the *Cleveland Press*."

You'd think it's the bad times that make you most miss the one you love. But it's not. It's the good times you can't wait to share. So wouldn't it be better to call her when I'm happy about something . . . confident . . . not swimming in a tide of self doubt.

Rain streamed down my window that night in rivulets. For a while I was fixated by the droplets that hung motionless, watching them as other drops converged, suddenly racing unhinged to the bottom. Nightfall had rolled in a fog, shifting my gaze to the shimmering puddles below, as though my view from the Picadilly had turned into an impressionist painting.

Is it selfish to do what I want? Or is it only selfish to force another to join me? How often as children we're told, "Don't be so self-centered." No wonder we feel guilt at the thought of going against the norm, living a life of our own choosing. Only in America, with all our puritanical values, can you feel guilty about feeling good. Somewhere, some all-knowing authority figure would surely disapprove.

I reached for the phone. What if her mother answers? What if I call and discover she's not there? I'll spend the rest of the night wondering if she's with another man. My stomach turned. What if she *is* there? What the hell would I say? I'm no closer now to any answers than I was six months ago. Maybe I want my cake and eat it too—someone to share life's joys and sorrows—yet I'm unwilling to give in to a love that could destroy my freedom and independence. But is that even true? When, for God's sake, did she ever deny my freedom? I stared out the window, tapping at one of the droplets, feeling angry all of a sudden. I can't deal with it now. I'm happy for the first time in months . . . doing exactly what I want.

The rain stopped. I looked at the phone. The last time I saw her she had tears streaming down her face. Another day . . . maybe I'll know what to say.

———⟶———

The next few days passed by in a flurry of activity as I made good on my promises, dispensing tickets and logistical information to the radio stations, corporations and media. It was now or never to untangle any last minute details, especially since Mike was flying in this afternoon. Today, he said, would be our last day at Baische, Blake and Gabriel.

The train had already pulled into Akron and it was time to move our office to the Coliseum. With the animal walk tomorrow and opening night the following day, I reveled in the transformation taking place—from Cleveland businessman and wheeler dealer to fellow circus employee—not just one anymore but one of a family of two hundred. But as I packed the last of my papers into one of two black cases, leaving only dust marks on the desk as evidence of my stay, I felt a tinge of nostalgia. Ruthy appeared in the doorway, hovering, as though she wasn't sure what to do. I glanced up at the wall. "Don't worry," she said. "We'll take the posters down. What time are you picking up Mike?"

I looked at my watch. "Shit! His plane landed ten minutes ago." And I hadn't even left the office. "I am one dead son of a bitch!" I raced out of the room and leapt into the car. "Please let his plane be late."

No such luck. He was pacing the sidewalk, craning his neck for my arrival.

"Where the hell were you?"

"There was an awful accident. I've been sitting in traffic for an hour!"

Flustered, I promptly exited the airport in the wrong direction. Now what? I figured I had thirty seconds before he realized I was transporting him with thundering speed back to Washington, D.C.

Fortunately the medium strip just ahead was broken. A large white sign read "No U Turns. For emergency vehicles only."

Well, if this isn't an emergency I don't know what is. I wheeled round in the gravel, kicking up a swirl of dust.

Mike stared straight ahead, but I felt the tension dissolve. Thank God for crazy driving. We'd found a common bond.

"Where to?" I asked.

"Let's swing by Baische, pick up our stuff and then drive out to the train."

"I'm already packed."

"Good. I want to say a quick good-bye to Ruthy and then talk to the performance director to make sure we're all set up for the animal walk."

Ruthy was waiting for us much as she was the day we arrived. Dressed in her navy blue suit, she stood at the top of the landing. "So this is it. Another year."

"Almost," Mike replied. "Thanks for taking in a new promoter."

"He's welcome back anytime" she said, giving me a motherly look.

"We'll be at the Coliseum if you need us for anything. Don't hesitate to call. And keep an eye on the newspaper strike. Let me know if anything changes."

"I will Mike. And good luck. You're going to need it out there."

We picked up our leather cases and headed down the steps. As we reached the front door I could feel her still watching us from the top of the stairs.

The train sat nestled behind a warehouse in an industrial part of Akron. Stacks of old lumber and buildings with broken glass hardly befitted the eighty-six silver linked cars, yet Mike maneuvered toward the tracks as though it was a familiar setting.

Wolfgang Holzmair lounged on a lawn chair while a few Europeans shuffled around a soccer ball. "Most of the performers probably went into town. I don't see the circus bus," Mike said.

We drove slowly up the tracks. Two shapely girls sauntered beside the train. Wearing skin tight pants and light jackets, they didn't seem dressed for the weather. They smiled as Mike pulled alongside. I was certain they were show girls, thinking how different they'd look with the half-inch eyelashes and heavy mascara soon to be applied to enable their features to be seen from a distance. The short one, fair skinned, had a "girl next door" demeanor with a friendliness that came easy. But her tall, black companion looked wary and wiser than her years.

Mike rolled down the window.

"Mike, give us a ride downtown?" the pretty blond begged, as though she had just seen him yesterday.

"I can't," Mike said. "We've got to meet with Tim Holst. Have you seen him around?"

"He was in the pie car a few minutes ago," she replied, and then turned on her heels. I watched her amble away, wondering if she knew how *off limits* she was. Irvin hadn't said so directly, nor had Art or Mike, but Sam Barrett had warned, "screwing around with a show girl is grounds for immediate dismissal."

Tim Holst was in the pie car, sitting alone, sipping a cup of coffee. Unlike his management peer, Charlie Bauman, he looked boyish, with a tired, unthreatening countenance.

Mike didn't want to trouble Tim anymore than he had to on his only day off, so he got right to the point. "The animals are to be transported to Peninsula tomorrow morning at nine o'clock a.m. for the animal walk. There will be several riders plus the press."

Tim nodded. "I'll pass the information on to Gunther. Although headquarters has already informed him of the logistics."

By the time Mike and I arrived at the Coliseum, the sun was low, leaving a golden hue over the nearby fields. We parked next to the main entrance, unloaded our cases, and strolled inside.

"Is Spatrino here?" Mike asked a man behind the ticket window.

"He left a few hours ago. He was here all night."

"We're the Ringling promoters. Do you know where our office is located?"

"It's probably the last office down the corridor, by entrance three. It's the only one empty."

The room was windowless, as usual, but at least it was close to the box office. I started to unload our files. "Forget it," Mike said. "Let's call it a day. You can do that tomorrow."

As we walked to the car, the sun was just slipping behind the building. Mike stopped, hesitating for a moment, the evening glow framing his features. "You know I'm getting pretty concerned."

"About what?"

"I haven't gotten box office numbers for three days."

"Why not?" I asked, aware Mike had told the box office to now call him directly.

"I don't know. We're playing hell getting the numbers. Irvin is beginning to get pissed."

"I don't like the sounds of it either," I replied, empathizing without fully understanding the implications.

"Well, the animal walk is tomorrow. We'll locate Spatrino and find out what's going on afterwards."

"What time do you want me to pick you up in the morning?

"Seven a.m. I told Peter Halbin we'd meet him in Peninsula. By the way, we're going to stay near the Coliseum from now on, so bring all your things. I'm sure you'll be disappointed. This is your last night at the Picadilly."

I'd be surprised if the little town of Peninsula ever had more than a half-dozen visitors at any one time, and I suspected that's just how they preferred it. I'd slept restlessly, partly in nervous anticipation of the show's arrival but mostly in remembrance of my meeting with the town's elders, having assured them all would be fine. Of course, I was operating under the principle that it's easier to beg forgiveness than to receive permission. How could I predict what would or wouldn't happen?

Mike parked near the mayor's general store. The town looked just as it had before. Some of the homes lining the route had freshly painted shutters. They all had carefully landscaped lawns and gardens, some freshly cut for the day's event. It was quiet, overcast, and the only sounds I heard were our own.

Mike told Peter we would meet him at the nightclub restaurant, so we positioned ourselves on two bar stools to await his arrival. We didn't have to wait long.

"Good morning, gentlemen," Peter bellowed, nearly filling the door frame. Peter was wearing a black sweatshirt, an old pair of trousers and beaten up tennis shoes as he marched in carrying an umbrella.

"I see you dressed for the occasion," I teased.

"White bucks and elephant shit don't mix," Peter grinned. "I discovered that years ago."

"Who are you expecting this morning?" Mike asked.

"Pretty much all the media . . . newspapers and television anyway," Peter replied. "I told them to meet us here by eight forty five."

"Well, it looks like some are here early," Mike said, as we watched a gray van pull up. We saw two men slide open the door and begin unloading camera equipment. Within a short time, two other TV stations arrived followed by a dozen newspaper reporters. Peter was soon in his element, greeting and entertaining his media buddies while Mike, in the hub of things, answered questions promoting the show—each of them oblivious to outside events, unlike me.

As I glanced out the window I saw busloads of school children arriving up the street. Dozens of kids already straggled under the watchful eyes of their teachers and dozens more sat in nervous excitement in what appeared to be a caravan of incoming traffic. In addition to the buses, cars emptied scores of curiosity seekers, some with cameras and one even carried a tripod.

Peninsula's policeman was busy directing traffic as the crowd began to spill over to the parking lot across from the tracks and stand along the road leading to the small bridge over the Cuyahoga River. Spotting two of the town's elders uneasily surveying the scene, I began to smell trouble.

I sidled up to Peter, now the center of attention, and gently squeezed his elbow. He ignored me. I squeezed a little harder.

"Yes, me young lord?" he said, with a toothy grin.

"I think we've got a slight problem," I whispered. "You'd better come with me for a second."

Noting my concern, he shouted, "Drinks on the house!" slapped a husky reporter on the back and followed me to the rear. Still smiling, he looked out the window. Below us a crowd in the hundreds was now milling in the streets, and it was rapidly swelling.

"Good God. Where did all those people come from?"

"That's just what I was going to ask you."

"Shit. We'd better tell Mike before the train comes and rolls over several kids!"

"Drinks for my mates," Peter hollered again to the bartender as he quickly grabbed Mike. The three of us exited to the platform overlooking the parking lot.

"What's all this?" Mike blurted, as we looked out at the throng of people now standing dangerously close to the tracks. "Come on, we'd better help the police. Jamie, you take the right side. I'll take the left. Start moving the people back!"

Inexperienced in crowd control, I threw myself in front of a mob and began screaming, "Move back! Move back! The train is coming." This was effective except for one problem. The train wasn't coming. It was late as usual, and after ten minutes, the crowd became restless again. To aggravate matters a cold, miserable rain began pummeling the swarm of Clevelanders Peter had wittingly enticed to this civic event.

Fortunately, the Richfield High School band had now arrived. Peter spotted them grouped together across the street. Hoping they could help divert the crowd's attention, Peter sprinted across the road.

"Please, play something," Peter shouted at the band leader. As the musicians struck up a lively tune, Peter turned back to the restless reporters inside, now also growing impatient with the train's delay. Within minutes Peter returned his comrades to jovial spirits but then he noticed the band had again quit playing. He raced outside. "What happened?" he yelled at the band leader.

"We've played everything we know."

Peter started to laugh. "Well play it again!"

Meanwhile, Mike had corralled the DJ's and local celebrities waiting to ride the elephants into one corner of the lot. They were just as antsy as the reporters and crowds of people.

Finally, the train screamed round the corner. It was all we could do to move the crowd back while the roustabouts began unloading the heavy equipment, which they did with all their colorful language in front of the wide-eyed preschoolers. The band, meanwhile, started playing its repertoire for the sixth time as Gunther, recognizable only by his shock of yellow hair, began shouting in German at the handlers. They led the elephants out, and the crowd surged forward. Mike and Peter and I raced back and forth trying to keep the kids under control.

At last, the roustabouts jostled all the animals in line, loaded the celebrities, and under Gunther's command, began a brisk pace toward the town of Peninsula. No sooner did the first elephant turn the corner of the parking lot than the whole crowd broke open and began running alongside. Since there were no sidewalks, hundreds of people began trampling through the townspeople's lawns, over roses and tulips, mums, peonies and beautiful assortments of flower beds. With the ground soaked by rain, in minutes, the front lawns of little Peninsula's Victorian cottages looked like they'd just hosted a world-class polo match.

Peter, of course, didn't notice this carnage, running ahead to ensure that Gunther didn't dislodge the local celebrities halfway up the hill. Mike was far too ecstatically focused on the TV and newspaper coverage to turn around, leaving me running alone, praying "Please God, don't leave me behind!"

———

Barely did we make it to our arena office when a secretary walked in. "The mayor of Peninsula is on the line." Mike picked up the phone. The mayor was furious. "I'll never let those elephants walk through here again . . . public and private property destroyed . . . your man said it would all go smoothly. . . ."

Mike could barely get a word in edgewise, but thinking on his feet, even when soaking wet, he apologized profusely and offered the entire town free tickets to the circus.

"I'll send three hundred tickets to the librarian tomorrow morning. She can spread the word to the rest of the residents." Peter then assured the mayor we would never again publicize the animal walk in advance. Wincing, Peter hung up the phone. "Then again, perhaps we won't need to," he said, grinning at me, "We'll turn this to our advantage by telling the media, 'In the interest of public safety, we ask that you *NOT* publicize the animal walk.' Hell, that'll save Peninsula's begonias plus give an exotic twist, which should prompt even better media coverage!"

Chapter 26
TWISTING IN THE WIND

— OPENING NIGHT —

A seductive breeze blew through my window as I drove to the Coliseum, bathing me in a sense of well being. The worst was over. Opening night, despite the strike, was sold out. The parking fiasco had been solved. All our advertising was now at a fever pitch and even Mike seemed far more relaxed now that the animal walk was over and plenty of publicity had been harvested.

I arrived at the arena, noticing the once empty back lot was now covered with canvas tents to house the animals. Stacks of hay were piled everywhere to feed the horses, and several working men were scurrying about unloading the rigging, carrying equipment down the back ramp. I parked near a van where a skinny Mexican woman was handing programs and souvenirs to a young girl. I glanced at their faces expecting to see the same level of excitement I felt. But to them, it was just another town, and tonight they'd be hawking their wares to another sea of faceless people. I feigned their nonchalance as I walked down the ramp, feeling self-important and childishly giddy at the same time.

Inside the arena, miles of ropes and pipes were being hoisted in the air. Crates full of costumes and props were noisily being wheeled into place and dozens of concessionaires were hauling in their stations. I skipped up a flight of stairs and circled the mezzanine toward my new office, willfully ignoring a rancorous dispute. A wiry, tattooed Hispanic man was taking the better part of abuse from an Eastern European woman in heavy makeup. Both were shouting in their native language. I couldn't understand a word, but through their gestures, it quickly became apparent they both wanted to position their concessions at the same spot. She was staking her find but he was claiming first dibs. As I opened my office door, I was betting my money on her.

I skimmed my schedule, expecting a quiet afternoon. Mike hadn't arrived yet. The opening night press party wasn't until seven o'clock, and my primary responsibility— making sure the *Plain Dealer's* honorary ringmaster met up with the performance director—was five long hours away.

Just as I eased into my chair the phone rang.

"Is this the circus office?"

"Yes, it is," I responded. "What can I do for you?"

"I have a problem," she said, and I sensed her agitation. "I mailed in a check two weeks ago, and I still haven't received my four tickets."

"For which performance?"

"Tonight's."

"Tonight's? Give me your name and number. I'll look into it immediately. The tickets must be lost in the mail." But no sooner did I hang up then I found myself again on the end of an identical conversation, and what's more, two more lights were now blinking.

Fortunately, Mike walked in as I finished fielding a third irate caller.

"What's wrong?"

"People are calling in left and right saying they mailed in their checks but still haven't received their tickets, and we're talking about tonight's performance!"

"That doesn't make sense. Mail orders should have been processed days ago. The cut-off was last Friday. And damn it! I still haven't received any numbers. Irvin's going nuts. Let's find Spatrino and see what the hell's going on."

Mike and I marched to the box office. Several people stood anxiously in front of the windows purchasing tickets. We strode to the rear of the box office to an unmarked door. Mike rapped on the wooden surface.

The door opened. We could immediately see a bedlam of activity. Phones were ringing. Trash was all over the floor. People were sorting tickets and stuffing slots.

"Is Spatrino here?" Mike shouted.

"One minute," the seller snapped, closing the door.

We waited. Spatrino opened the door. Looking flustered, he stepped outside.

"We're getting calls from people who haven't received tickets yet for tonight's performance! What the hell is going on?"

"Mike, I'm sorry. We're hopelessly behind. With twenty-three performances and dozens of outlets calling in every day, we haven't been able to keep up with the mail orders. We're working as fast as we can. We've been telling people who haven't received their tickets, they'll just have to pick them up at the box office."

"The box office?" Mike sputtered, no longer trusting the situation. "Where are the mail orders now?"

"In here," Spatrino said. He led us across the hall and unlocked an unmarked door.

In the center of the room was a twelve-foot table. It was covered a foot high with mail orders stacked from one end to the other. And on either end, there were a half-dozen trash cans. They too were spilling over with unopened envelopes.

"Jesus Christ!" I said. No wonder Mike hadn't gotten any numbers. There's a small fortune uncounted in here.

Mike turned to Spatrino. "I want a security guard posted outside this door immediately! We're going in there to straighten this mess."

As Mike strode into the room, Spatrino opened the palm of his hand, displaying three pink message slips. "These are for you. Irvin Feld's been calling you all morning."

I could read Mike's thoughts. What am I going to tell him? We have a quarter of a million dollars of his money piled up in trash cans.

Mike and I frantically began opening envelopes, sorting ticket requests by performance. Four hours later twenty-three mounds of envelopes lay on the table. Our immediate concern was tonight's performance, now only an hour away. Mike and I put tonight's tickets in alphabetical order while Spatrino stored the tickets in the will-call window. The problem, of course, wasn't just finding the tickets. "We'll now have hundreds of people, no doubt irate," Mike cited, "crowding into the box office minutes before the performance trying to pick up their tickets." Once again, too many people in too small a space.

Late to the press party, Mike and I hurried upstairs. Normally, Peter said, under even the best of circumstances, these are dull affairs attended by entertainment editors far too jaded to be properly seduced. But when we opened the door, the room was brimming with activity. Instead of the pseudo-sophisticated, big-city editors, there were hundreds of people milling about in excitement. Whole families were swirling around the room taking pictures of one another with the show girls and clowns Mike had promised for the event. Mike was stunned. These were all the small-town editors Peter had been plying with circus hype for the past eight weeks. The same people who had run our stories, with barely a change, on the front page of their newspapers. They had shown up in droves. Small-town America at its finest. And Peter, the burly, street savvy, inner-city mediator, was putting on the corn like I couldn't believe.

"I'm so happy you could make it! This must be the missus. And are these your girls? Boy, they don't make them any prettier. You're going to love the show! We need all the help we can get. Don't forget to send me a copy of your review as soon as it's printed tomorrow. Come here, and let me introduce you to one of the performers."

"My, my. Ah do declare," I said. "Peter wouldn't say shit if he had a mouthful of it!" Mike and I watched Peter work the room. He was a natural schmoozer, mainly because he loved people and, like my friend, Sam Barrett, he had just enough chameleon in him to adapt to any situation. For us more timid souls, it was a treasure to behold.

Mike fidgeted, looking clearly out of place, and after watching Peter for a few minutes, I felt pretty inadequate myself. So I was none too disappointed when Mike suggested we head downstairs. It was time, anyway, to meet the honorary ringmaster from the *Plain Dealer*. The show was starting in thirty minutes.

As we neared the box office, our predictions had now come true. People who had been told to pick up their tickets were now crowded twenty deep behind the will-call windows. More were waiting behind the door. It looked like a giant cattle call. A steady string of cursing punctured the room. As we approached, one man in line yelled, "Who the hell is in charge here?"

I glanced instinctively in his direction. Mike quickly whispered, "Keep moving. There's nothing we can do."

We trooped toward our office, distancing ourselves from the din of the crowd. A young man and his wife were waiting. He was the *Plain Dealer* honorary ringmaster and he seemed self-possessed as he greeted us. Mike exchanged small talk with them for a few minutes before asking how the strike was unfolding. To our surprise we discovered the union and the newspaper had hours earlier reached an agreement. The paper would be back in print tomorrow.

With that dose of good news, we led the way to the backstage area through crowds of people now streaming in the doors. Safely delivered, I wished him luck and exited through the maze of curtains, strolling past performers and elephants waiting their cue. The lights had been extinguished and the arena floor was dark. I cautiously crept over cables and props, finding a place near the tumbling mats, safely hidden from view. In the shadows, I watched the ringmaster and the young man slowly position themselves in the center ring. A few seconds passed before the ringmaster, with a sweep of his hand, signaled he was ready. The two men were suddenly illuminated in a circle of light. "Ladies and gentlemen and children of all ages . . . it's the Greatest Show on Earth! Let the show begin!"

With a deafening roar twenty-thousand people suddenly shook the foundation of Nick Mileti's Coliseum. As I looked up from where I crouched, all I could see was a galaxy of people so massive in scope they seemed to stretch to infinity. I stared into the distant reaches, overwhelmed by the sheer magnitude of space now pulsating in a surge of emotion. Like me, they had come to escape to a magical land of fantasy and danger where the impossible was still possible and all that glittered was gold.

They had indeed come to see the circus, a magnificent relic of the past, so imbued in our culture to be ingrained in our souls. But I knew they also came for another reason. They came because Cleveland had been blanketed over six short weeks with a deluge of advertising, promotion and publicity, all of it carefully planned and meticulously orchestrated to leave no stone unturned. And as I gazed at the endless rows of people bonded with our world, if only for the moment, I felt as weightless as an airborne feather . . . and the feeling was wonderfully sublime.

For the next three days Mike and I occupied ourselves in the first week's activities. It was soon obvious our efforts were continuing to pay off. The box office finally caught up with itself and the numbers were running sky high compared to previous years. Allen and Irvin both seemed pleased. Our major promotions helped sell the matinee seats, and most of my time was spent watching doors and endlessly counting discount stubs and unsold tickets. After one performance, as Mike and I sat in a dingy room counting dozens of stacks by hand, I couldn't help but think how odd it was to see Mike spending hours doing such a mundane task. "Aren't you just a bit overpaid to be sitting here counting tickets all night?"

"Nope," Mike said, glancing up. "I get paid the same salary no matter what I do. This is just one of the things that has to be done."

As I watched him quietly finish counting another stack of tickets, it occurred to me this was one more axiom he had learned in order to harmonize the job's demands with his own expectations. Irvin was a master at dispensing criticism, and at Mike's supervisory level, he was no doubt rewarded with a front row seat. And I suspected Mike was paid enough to twist in the wind a hair longer than he liked. But no matter how daunting the task, he had come to display a rare certitude. A few weeks earlier, while he was out of town and I was juggling sixteen balls, wondering how I'd get it all done, I alluded to my indispensability. Mike simply interjected,

"Don't worry. If you weren't there, it would still get done. I don't know how, but I'd get it done."

⁂

Peter called just as I got to the arena.

"So Peter, how go the interviews?"

"Great," he said, "if you don't count the fact I almost got killed this morning."

"How can you get killed on an interview?"

"Well, it helps if you have a crazed monkey in your car."

My curiosity peaked. "What are you talking about?"

"I had an interview set up with Rudy Lenz and one of his chimps on Channel 4 this morning. So at seven a.m. I arrive at the train car to pick them up. Rudy comes out holding this chimp by the hand and they saunter over to my car. The chimp is wearing a diaper so as not to mess up my seat, and Rudy plunks the son-of-a-bitch between us."

"So what happens?" I ask.

"Well, we're scooting along I-77, Rudy falls asleep, and the chimp is standing between us looking out the window. I'm cruising at about seventy miles per hour, when all of a sudden the chimp decides he wants to drive the car."

"What?"

"I shit you not!" Peter says. "The chimp all of a sudden reaches over, grabs the steering wheel and begins turning it madly. I scream at this point. The goddamn monkey screams back. And meanwhile the car is swerving all over the highway. I can't believe it! I'm now flying down the highway wrestling the fucking monkey for the steering wheel."

"So what the hell happens?"

"Rudy finally wakes up, yells something at the monkey, and I get the car stopped on the side of the highway. I swear to God, I sat there and shook for ten minutes."

"Peter, I swear, it can only happen to you."

Chapter 27
A Naíve Trainee

— Week Two —

"One thing about Ringling Brothers and Barnum and Bailey Circus is it has great 'legs,'" said Mike, "which means if we fill up the seats during the first week, even with plenty of give aways, the word-of-mouth will carry us the second week. Obviously, you can't have 'legs' unless you have a good product. All the hype in the world won't sustain a lousy show."

Fortunately, the reviews had cropped up in the *Plain Dealer* and the small-town papers, and the accounts were excellent. As a result, ticket sales remained even stronger than expected. The houses weren't as full during the week-day performances but the take was now "hard cash," without the discount tickets and complimentary passes diluting the revenues. And the weekend performances were almost sold out.

We still had a dozen shows remaining and the sudden adjustment to the show's arrival had at last subsided. In fact, as I arrived daily at the arena and mingled with the performers, my office at Baische, Blake and Gabriel seemed a distant memory. So, too, did the earlier contacts I had fostered, until I heard a familiar voice call out my name. Turning around I found myself staring at the pretty face of a tall, thin woman.

"Nancy," I said, unsettled for a moment, since she was dressed far more alluringly than the last time I had seen her. "How good to see you. Are you here to see the show?"

"Absolutely. I wouldn't miss it for the world. Would you be kind enough to show me to my seat?"

"Of course," I said.

Nancy was the promotion director for Higbee's, the major department store Mike and I had persuaded to sponsor the underprivileged kids. I'd only met her twice and I was instantly attracted to her. Fumbling for small talk, I escorted her around the concourse. Fortunately, her social graces were more refined than mine, and by the time we reached her seat, my courage had found its way to my throat.

"I was kinda wondering. . . . how would you like to go out for dinner or something after the show is over?"

"Oh, that's sweet," she said. "I'm meeting a friend after the show. But thank you for asking. And again, thank you for showing me to my seat."

I mumbled a farewell appropriate to that moment of rejection when you realize you have absolutely nothing more to say. Climbing the stairs, it made me wonder what I'd have talked about if she had said yes. I was clearly out of my league with this one and what a stupid question . . . "I was kinda wondering . . . ?" If I was going to make it on the road, I'd better come up with a better approach than that. At least I could take solace in the fact that I struck out alone. Who at Ringling ever heard of Higbee's?

I returned to the front entrance, watching the ticket takers, wishing the minutes would pass faster. But the time clicked by slowly, and when finally it was time to help the ushers gather up the kids, it seemed like hours had passed. The box office gave me the deadwood shortly after intermission, and I began methodically counting the stacks of tickets. Mike was in especially good spirits as he counted the last stack and tabulated the numbers. Hoping his good mood was contagious, I asked, "Would you like to go grab a beer?"

"Not tonight," he replied. "Maybe another time. I've got a date."

"I see," I said.

"Have a good evening. I'll see you tomorrow."

I turned off the lamp, gathered my coat, and pulled the collar snugly against my neck to lessen November's cold. The building was empty, and so was the parking lot, now black and expansive, lit only by the full moon's light. All I could see was one couple walking briskly and confidently toward a distant car—Mike and the pretty promotion director from Higbee's.

It was lunch time and I was starving, so I drove around the back of the building to see if the train's portable "pie car" was serving. As I looked for an empty spot amongst the animal tents and trailers, I noticed a commotion near the elephant tent. Suburban station wagons and new model cars were pulling up, depositing several earnest looking couples. Meandering in their direction, I watched a man in an orange cardigan sweater and matching pants escort an elegant woman in a flowered dress toward two roustabouts standing just inside the flaps. One of the roustabouts, sporting a tattoo on his arm and a ring in one ear, handed the man a plastic bag. Just then I remembered this was the day radio listeners had been told they could pick up the miraculous "pachyderm poo" for their lawns and gardens.

"Here buddy. Hold this," I heard the roustabout tell the man as he opened the plastic sack. While the man in the orange sweater fumbled with the opening, the other roustabout was already plunging a shovel into a large mound of moist excrement. In a matter of seconds, the couple retreated back to their car with their bulging bag and a handful of swarming flies. As another couple marched up, I decided the roustabouts were the only sane ones in the bunch. In fact, they kept glancing at each other as if to say, "Can you actually believe this shit?"

Walking past the pie car, I noticed several hamburger patties sizzling on the grill. Suddenly lunch didn't seem as appetizing.

"Have you seen Peter Halbin around?" I asked Smiley, an amiable roustabout nicknamed for his perpetual smile.

"Yes. About fifteen minutes ago. He was headed toward clown alley."

Peter, no doubt, was already gathering a couple of clowns to help with auditions. As part of Peter's publicity plan, he had petitioned several radio stations to announce clown auditions, with the possibility of a chosen few to be selected as students for Irvin's Clown College. Unfortunately, it was a remote prospect, since thousands applied for the roughly fifty slots. And even if they were selected and then graduated, there was still no guarantee Irvin would hire them.

Nevertheless, regardless of Ringling's unlikely need for more applicants, it was another tool in our bag of tricks to secure free air time. Peter even convinced the radio stations to accept the releases as "public service announcements"—a slight stretching of the term but it worked, and Peter had scheduled the auditions for the second week when the additional publicity could help maintain our momentum.

I picked my way past rows of blue curtains, past the show girls' dressing room, smelling of perfumed air, and across the rear entrance, where a cool breeze snuck in from under the door. Clown alley was anywhere the clowns decided to locate their dressing room. Invariably, they chose an out-of-the-way place. When I arrived, I was immediately struck by their palette of rich colors. Like a splashy, gaily dancing Toulouse-Lautrec painting, the colors spilled everywhere. Baggy trousers, checkered and pinstriped, were draped over folding chairs with tubes of greasepaint scattered on the tables, all reflected from light- bulbed mirrors as a half-dozen men transformed their features. Like snowflakes, I'd heard, no two could be exactly alike. Once a clown designed his face, a moral copyright was established with rights of ownership to a new identity.

I wondered if clowns ever got bored with their appearance, how often they changed it or, for that matter, if they ever changed roles from an August to a white face.

Frosty, the boss clown, was a white face clown, which seemed appropriate. He had volunteered a few of the young clowns to accompany Peter to the audition, where twenty-some hopefuls awaited us. ABC and NBC, as well as the *Cleveland Press*, were there to cover the auditions. "A good enough turn out," Peter said.

The first contestant did an amazing rendition of the scarecrow from *The Wizard of Oz*, falling off an imaginary pole, stuffing straw back into his shirt and stumbling jello- kneed up the track singing, "I'm off to see the wizard."

"What do you think?" I asked one of the clowns.

"Actors aren't what we want," he said. "They make lousy clowns. Not spontaneous enough."

The next applicant wasn't sufficiently athletic for the required tumbling and gymnastics and several of the clowns, I was told, were obvious professionals, clowns from TV kids' shows that had been dumped into the marketplace as a result of recent FTC rulings against too much blatant advertising to children. All in all it wasn't a field day for the would-be clowns, but for us, it was a roaring success. Both stations promised to air the auditions on the six o'clock news and the *Cleveland Press* planned a full-page photo spread.

"Mike, it's almost intermission time. Are you ready to go downstairs?"

"No, you can handle this one by yourself. I'll catch up with you later."

"Suits me." It was our last promotion, and the fact that Mike was telling me to do it alone was just one more sign I'd earned his trust. I did however, feel a little squeamish explaining the details to Tim Holst, a feeling he didn't do much to diminish after reading the script. "Gunther isn't going to like this."

Nevertheless, we were already committed. Mike and I had racked our brains trying to come up with a creative promotion for the radio station with the camera tie-in. Why not some close-up photos for those who brought their XL cameras? What could be simpler than that?

Gunther was already waiting beside an elephant along with a clown and a show girl when I arrived back stage.

"Ten minutes!" Tim admonished me. "That's all the time we've got." From the scowl on Gunther's face I could tell Tim had read him correctly. "Let's go."

Gunther and his small entourage proceeded to the middle of the center ring. Like a movie with no sound track, they looked odd standing alone, while thousands in their seats fumbled with popcorn and soft drinks. I hovered near Tim. With as much enthusiasm as he could muster he raised his microphone. "In cooperation with WJLA radio, I hope you have brought your XL cameras. If you have, now is the time to join Gunther-Gebel Williams in the center ring for those close-up photos we promised."

Nobody moved. Seconds passed. Maybe a whole minute. "Announce it again," I urged.

"We've only got a few minutes! If you've brought your XL camera, now is the time," Tim echoed.

Still no one moved. This is wonderful, I thought. In front of twenty thousand people I'm making a fool out of our star performer.

Just then, midway up the mezzanine, a father stood up with two children and began ambling down the steps. I couldn't tell if he had a camera or not. Just as he reached the center ring a dozen or so others stood up. Thank God! It's not going to be a complete disaster. Then all of a sudden an entire row stood. None of them held cameras. From all sides, the seats emptied out. It suddenly looked like a Billy Graham revival.

"Shit!" Tim yells. "We've got a problem!" Not only was Gunther smothered, they were coming down in droves for a close up view of everything. "They're all over the props! There's even a kid swinging on a guy wire. Get security!"

In all three rings, the arena floor was now crawling with people.

"Do something!" I hollered at a security officer. "Get these people back in their seats!"

He immediately summoned his fellow officers. Having had nothing to do for twelve straight days they worked their way into the crowd like storm troopers. "Back! Get back!" they screamed, while one of the officers even pulled out his billy club.

I looked at Tim. There was no reason to even attempt an apology. It was forty five minutes before the show could resume. Mortified, I trudged upstairs in search of Mike.

"How did it go?" he mumbled. He was standing alone, deep in the recess of the office, quietly feeding the ticket counting machine.

"It was an utter disaster," I said. As I explained what happened,

Mike smiled sheepishly. And it suddenly dawned on me there was more than one use for a naïve trainee.

There was something disquieting about the last day's performance, as though someone you treasured was happy to be leaving you. The roustabouts backstage were already packing costumes and moving large crates up the ramp. Within a few minutes Lloyd Morgan would be supervising the dismantling of the rigging—first the high wires, then the trapeze, then the rest. The performers were moving at a faster pace, like they always did on the final day. I pretended to share in their nervous energy, nodding my goodbyes, but I was already beginning to feel empty. At least I could take solace in the company of Mike.

Mike was sitting in the box office at the end of a long table. I arrived just as Spatrino handed him a single sheet of paper. Mike scanned the numbers. He handed me the sheet. We'd done just more than 1.2 million dollars, slightly over our goal, far surpassing anything before done in Cleveland. I couldn't tell for sure but I sensed Mike was satisfied.

Mike stood up and shook hands with Spatrino, snapping his briefcase with an air of finality. We walked outdoors, past the half-collapsed tents, in view of the elephants being escorted quietly back to the train. "Take this to Peter Halbin," Mike said, withdrawing a white envelope from his inside pocket. "When you're done, meet me back at the hotel."

It was late, the streets almost deserted, as I drove downtown, with an icy wind blowing in from Lake Erie. A soft white light emanated from Peter's office just below the shades.

"Come in," Peter said. He was sitting on the corner of his desk chatting with his partner. His beard seemed to accentuate the twinkle in his eyes, and seated next to his mentor he suddenly looked younger.

"Well, did we get a bonus this year?" he asked, peeking inside the envelope. I already knew he didn't since the amount was for his fee of one thousand dollars.

"Don't worry," he said, seemingly used to Mike's penuriousness. "We don't shoot the messenger. Where are you going next?"

"I don't know. Mike hasn't told me yet. But who knows, maybe I'll be back here next year."

"Don't count on it. They never send us the same man twice." We shook hands and he walked me down to the street and stood in the cold as I walked toward my car.

As I reached for my keys, he yelled, "Hey, remember that crazy animal walk?"

"Who can forget it," I shouted back.

"Keep your knickers up."

"You too, old buddy."

I missed him already.

Mike was on the tail end of a phone conversation when I walked in his room. From the sounds of it, he was filling Allen in on the final numbers. I could see Allen leaning back in his chair with his feet propped up, savoring a cigar. Mike's tone, like Brad Rosenberg's, bordered on reverential, partly out of respect and partly out of fear. Not fear of Allen himself, but fear of Allen's power, the power to abruptly end a lifestyle far exceeding the rewards for most twenty-seven year olds. Mike must have known he'd been granted golden handcuffs and maybe it made him nervous. It would me. He who giveth can surely taketh away. But that was Mike's problem, not mine, and I was anxious to know where they'd be sending me. My first city on my own. As I listened to Mike, I knew it wouldn't be long before I'd be having similar dialogues, one on one, with Allen.

Mike hung up the phone and began emptying his dresser drawers. My brief encounter observing him with his superior was over and so was any edginess he might have had. I had to admit, with his Roman nose and wavy dark hair, he was a handsome man, and on his own level, he exuded the same charisma as Allen. With his occasional helplessness, I could see why women were enamored and I found myself wishing I didn't have such a need for his approval.

As he threw the last of his shirts in an open suitcase, he handed me an airplane ticket back to Washington. He then gave me a red

Ringling credit card for any airline or rental car, and he pulled out a corporate checkbook, tossing me that as well.

"You'll need these," he said. "The checks are for business use only, good up to two-hundred-and-fifty dollars. Let accounting know each week if you've written any. I'm heading out to the midwest for a few days. Go ahead and fly back to Washington. Take a day off. File away everything from Cleveland and then see Allen."

"Any idea where I'm going?"

"I'm not sure. Allen will tell you. Remember we're heading for the Bahamas in a few weeks where Irvin will fill us in on the new show. If I don't see you before then, I'll see you there." Mike smiled. "Don't forget. You're my protegé. Headquarters will know where I am."

"Is there anything else?"

"Good luck. You've seen the business end. You're a promoter now."

"Thank you," I said.

I turned to leave. On one hand I felt happy, but from somewhere else, somewhere I couldn't explain—a foreboding perhaps—I realized it wasn't the business end that worried me.

PART FOUR

SAVANNAH – HEADING SOUTH

Chapter 28
THE-LADY-OF-THE-HOUSE

Alongside a dozen travelers, I stood outside National Airport awaiting my turn for a taxi. An airport official motioned the cabs into
position. I advanced to the front and the attendant directed me
toward a turbaned gentleman peering at me over a steering wheel.
Too young and too cultured to be a refugee. Probably the son of a
wealthy Arab sheik, I speculated, here to attend graduate school at
G.W. or Georgetown University. I wondered if many returned home
with their education.

Washington looked crisp and beautiful this morning with its
white-washed monuments and immaculate parks. The bare trees,
backlit in the wintry air, lent an eerie stillness to the Tidal Basin,
broken only by a few tourists straggling toward the Jefferson
Memorial. It would be springtime before the onslaught of visitors
arrived again.

Traffic picked up as we entered the business district. We turned
right onto L Street for the last few blocks. Conservatively dressed
businessmen, lawyers and bureaucrats crowded the street, somehow ignoring a band of Hare Krishnas in bright orange sheets jumping up and down to an indigenous chant. Catchy tune, I thought,
but if I have to dress like that to achieve nirvana, I think I'll pass.

The driver pulled to a stop in front of Ringling's tall office building, leaving me to leapfrog two cases of Cleveland's records plus

my personal suitcase to the lobby elevator. I was anxious to see Nancy Pond, hoping a few promoters were here.

Nancy looked radiant, quickly offering to give me a hand. "Who's in town?" I asked.

"Brad Rosenberg's here and so is Bobby Collins. Allen told me to tell you to come up once you're organized."

I strode into the back room, depositing my things onto the top of an empty desk. Bobby Collins was diligently working in one corner. He and I shared a common bond having started as trainees within a few days of each other.

"Where you been?" he asked curiously.

"Cleveland. How about you?"

"Tampa Bay. I'm writing my post-date report."

We chatted a few minutes, exchanging a few stories, before he gradually returned to his task. Bob was quieter than the other promoters, almost timid, and had a reputation as the most fastidious. He'd spend hours typing his notes, assuring his records were meticulously organized. Oddly though, he was sometimes criticized for being too methodical. Personally, I'd rather follow him into town, with his carefully crafted notes, than anyone else. In fact, it wouldn't surprise me if he had a shot at supervisor should a slot ever open up. Allen and the supervisors liked him, and from my perspective he had another distinct advantage. He was Jewish.

Sam Barrett and I joked we'd have to change our names to Barrettstein and MacVicarson if we were to ever rise in the organization. A fallacy perhaps, but nevertheless, among Irvin, Allen and the four supervisors only Art Ricker was a gentile. Throw in Irvin's personal assistant and the Chief Financial Officer and the odds got worse. But from what I'd experienced it wasn't so much that non-Jews were excluded so much as fellow Jews were more naturally included. Thus far I'd been treated fairly and when it came to business they exuded an almost fanatical focus, but I also sensed a cohesiveness, perhaps ethnically based, rarely seen.

Brad Rosenberg rounded the corner just as I started upstairs. He was sporting his lopsided grin, swinging a cigarette-sized cigar in his left hand. I felt a special connection since it was he who had hired me in the first place.

"So are you learning anything?"

"I certainly am," I replied.

"Good. That's what's most important right now."

He turned and I ambled toward the elevator, elated for a moment, wondering if there was something auspicious in his comment.

Allen was on the phone. He waved me into his office.

"What do you mean you don't intend to replace them? My entire set of clubs was stolen from your locker. . . ."

"Of course I locked the door. Whoever stole them jimmied the lock."

"You don't carry insurance for theft? Those clubs cost me four-hundred dollars!" Allen's expression darkened. "Well, I don't like your goddamn attitude!" He slammed down the phone.

Oblivious to my presence, he quickly dialed a number. "Who do we know in Vegas? I had my golf clubs stolen, and the manager couldn't care less!"

"All right. See what you can do," he said, hanging up the phone.

I sat mesmerized, wondering how far his tentacles reached.

"I see you've survived your first battle."

"Well, we did have a moment or two."

"I'll tell you," he grinned, slowly recovering his composure, "I've watched Mike Franks in a lot of situations but that's the first time I've seen the rock start to crumble. How are you two getting along?"

"I think pretty good."

Allen lowered his gaze as though he understood more than I'd said. "If you ever have something you can't handle, you call me directly."

I was surprised by the unexpected ticket to bypass Mike if a dire need arose, a special chip, I decided, only to be used in emergency.

"Are you ready for your first town?"

"Yes sir."

"Good. I'm sending you to Savannah, Georgia. You'll like it there. It's a good circus town. The dates are March 10th and 11th. Two matinees and two evening performances."

"What's my projection?" I interjected, knowing I sounded eager.

"Ninety thousand. I'm giving you a nine-thousand dollar budget. Keep in touch with Mike on your progress."

We talked a few minutes longer, then he handed me last year's records and wished me luck. As I stood to leave, I looked over at the huge map of the states he'd hung on his wall. On the southeast coast of Georgia was a blue pin. Next to it, in typeset black letters, was the name MacVicar.

A light snow was dusting the city streets when I walked out of headquarters. I savored the winter's beauty, knowing for at least this year the sprinkling would probably be my last. Although the south could be bitterly cold, rarely was it greeted by winter's white comforter. I turned up the street and smiled. I could hardly complain with palm trees and magnolias beckoning me.

I hadn't seen my parents in nine months, since I'd left for California, and now on the cab drive north to the Maryland suburbs, I did so with a dose of trepidation. Invariably, no matter how much we looked forward to seeing one another, the evening would somehow derail, ruining whatever chance we might have had for a pleasant evening. I prayed my one night in town would end on a positive note.

My mother, as usual looking ten years younger than her age, wore an elegant cocktail dress. I was flattered she'd gone out of her way to look her best. Despite her softer charms, she was a lioness when it came to protecting her children. Yet she also had a unique ability to view us with objectivity, a quality that made her protective instincts that much more admirable.

My father was in jovial spirits, full of warm greetings. As he shook my hand, the ice cubes in his scotch clinked together. I sensed my well conditioned guard begin to reappear.

The evening started out innocuously enough, catching up on family news. But I found myself reticent, anxious to share in my recent activities but cautious about providing ammunition. Dad and I poked fun at each other, enjoying a game of verbal one-upmanship, and for a moment, I relaxed my guard.

"You know, I don't think I've ever been happier," I said, not sensing his mood had changed, the abrupt by-product of one drink too many. Rarely could you see it coming.

"I never thought you'd turn into a carny," he said, his cadence suddenly slowing.

"A carny? I'm an advance man for Ringling Brothers Circus."

"Same goddamn thing to me," he said with a shrug of his shoulders, sucking me in deeper.

"I don't operate a tilt-a-whirl or a ferris wheel," I retorted, my anger beginning to rise. "I work for the circus. You know exactly what I do."

"Call it whatever the hell you want," he said, leaning forward with an obvious relish. "Just know these guys are going to chew you up and spit you out."

By now I knew the conversation was futile. But the hook was too deeply imbedded. "You have no idea what you're talking about."

"Don't I?" he said, raising his eyebrows. "You'll see. My advice is to quit now while you're still ahead of the game."

"I've never quit anything . . . and I won't quit now!" I looked at my mother, trying to appear calm past the lump in my throat. "I'm calling it a night."

The next morning I arose before dawn, leaving a note of farewell, and quietly slipped out the door.

— SAVANNAH —

Cities are like people, with complex personalities, changing moods and hidden dimensions. There's an outside, I reflected, an inside and a source of power. The outside can be readily seen, the inside takes longer, and the source of power is known only to a few. I wondered how many people spend their whole lives in cities, seeing only what they want to see, learning only what they want to learn. But I didn't have a lifetime. I had only four months, and in truth just a few short weeks to size up the city. Right or wrong. It wasn't just that my judgments would help form my strategy; for me, as importantly, this was now to be my home.

I was intensely curious as I drove toward the city, past Georgia's red clay—avowed to be the blood of confederate soldiers—past beautiful magnolia trees with their unborn blossoms and past miles of indigenous kudzu vines smothering everything from trees and billboards to abandoned shacks. A sticky sweetness permeated the air evoking memories of the deep south. A place awash in contradictions, from a rich, aristocratic gentry to families living in unbelievable squalor, in unearthly conditions. From an open hospitality to a cool rejection of all outsiders . . . buttered in a distant kindness. From a Bible-belt fear of God to a segregated view of the world. For a southerner born and raised in the deep south, it was perfectly logical, but to an outsider, it didn't make sense.

I spent my boyhood years in the south, in Georgia and South Carolina. First in LaGrange, then in North Augusta, Atlanta and the Blue Ridge Mountains. It was in North Augusta that I lived along the Savannah River. The river was my means of escape. A chance to flirt with danger amidst the swirling brown water, so thick it resembled liquid caramel. And if the rapids didn't harm you, the water moccasins might, for they traveled down the river bound tightly in a knot. One bite quickly became a hundred. For these reasons, we weren't allowed to run the rapids, but we did so anyway, carefully hiding our cut-offs, sneakers and inner tubes in the woods. But it wasn't just the thrill of the fast water that pulled us to the river. It was the hours spent baking on the rocks, daydreaming about the future, that quenched our thirst for adventure. Little did I know I'd be back in this part of the world in a role I couldn't possibly imagine.

There were still a few hours of daylight left as I drove toward the outskirts of Savannah. If I had to pick a city, at least from its exterior, that was the opposite of Cleveland, this would have to be it. If downtown Cleveland was a stubble-faced, barrel-chested boxer, then Savannah was the grand dame, the lady-of-the-house hosting tea parties and afternoon carriage rides. Instead of industrial steel, she had Spanish moss draped over majestic 100-year-old live oak trees. It was art imitating life, these gray wisps of a brush so delicately decorating the city. The Spanish moss hung so lazily it disguised any signs of a restive ambience. As I turned west up Oglethorpe Avenue, the oak trees formed a tunnel, casting long shadows toward the river.

The city was originally designed around squares, twenty-four in all, and the squares were adorned with fountains and gardens amidst statues and park benches. Surrounding the squares were stately homes of differing styles. Greek revival architecture could be seen alongside British Victorian and early American Colonial. But it all blended together by a network of gaslit lamps and ornamental iron work. In fact, if anything acted as the architectural glue, it was the brilliant scrolls of black wrought iron that encased the shutters and made up the railings and balconies of these elegant homes. Iron could be seen everywhere. Iron storks served as newels, iron dolphins as waterspouts, and iron griffins as foot scrapers. An iron harbor light even guided wayward ships into port.

Just as iron originated from England to weigh down the ballasts of empty ships—the same ballasts that would return heavily laden with cotton—so too did tons of cobblestones that were put to good use paving the streets along Factors Walk and River Street.

Factors were cotton brokers, and they'd operated out of warehouses descending six stories to the river's edge. "Factors Walk" was named for the connecting bridges that enabled the brokers to walk from street level to the upper floors of their buildings. Preservationists had restored the warehouses to much of their original state, and now boutiques, restaurants and retail stores operated out of the basement floors. Construction was not yet completed but it was a start toward a vibrant tourist center along the waterfront.

Across the river, I could see shipyards, paper mills, plants and factories dotting the landscape. Savannah, I'd read, was the largest southeast port between New Orleans and Baltimore and served more than a hundred steamship lines. And with a city population of less than 120,000, the town still hosted 155 manufacturers, producing everything from food and paper to rubber and chemicals.

Oglethorpe Avenue dead-ended beside the Savannah Civic Center. Although housing only eighty-seven-hundred seats, the Civic Center occupied an entire city block. Home to the circus was to be a modern, tan, brick building with a picturesque fountain and tree shaded lawns. I was eager to see the inside of the arena but the sun was beginning to set. I needed a place to stay. I drove north toward the river, around Liberty Square, and coasted past steepled churches and storybook houses sandwiched tightly together, illuminated by the glow of gaslit lamps.

Nothing I passed was affordable, so I drove by the vacancy signs of quaint little inns and turned left on Bay Street, leading away from the town center. As I drove east, historic downtown quickly faded into fast-food joints, low-income housing and empty, abandoned lots. Finally, I spotted a small motel. It sat just past the Great Dane Trailer Park, across the street from an all-night laundromat. There were two cars out front, a rusty old Corvair and another at rest with a flattened tire. The sign read, "Alamo Plaza Motel—Welcome to Savannah—Open 24 Hours—Rooms $11.00." I slipped out of the car under the watchful eyes of two stray cats and walked toward the main office. The front of the motel had a rounded facade in the cut-out shape of a fort. I flinched from an acrid smell.

"Do you have any vacancies?"

"For the night, the week or the month?"

"The week, I guess."

"Sure do. That'll be seventy-seven dollars," he said. He reached over and searched for the key. I noticed his sunken cheeks were unshaven. "Come on, I'll show you to your room."

Behind the stucco facade, there were several small concrete buildings. Skirting some broken glass I gingerly followed. He opened the door to one of the square rooms and turned on the light.

"There you are," he said. "If you need anything give me a call."

"Before you go," I asked. "What is that awful smell?"

"That's the paper mill across the river. You'll get used to it." He left the room, closing the door behind him.

The room had a single bed on a steel frame, a broken mirror and a black phone sitting on an end table. I sat on the bed and stared at the phone, realizing there was no one I knew in the whole city. And right at that moment I'd have given anything to hear the phone ring and a friendly voice. For the first time I felt alone. I looked at the four walls, the red blinking light from the outside sign pulsating against the blinds, and all I could feel was an ache in the pit of my stomach that traveled all the way to my chest.

Chapter 29
WE LIVE IN THE ALLEYS

I was surprised there were only two advertising agencies in town, Whitson and Murlit and the Pidcock Company. Pidcock had handled our account the last two years, ever since the Savannah Civic Center opened. My notes were favorable about John Husskison, the managing partner who'd been our key link. As I parked near his office I decided if the rapport was good and he was still willing there'd be little need to call Whitson.

Pidcock was housed in a small, one-story building in the shadow of a long bridge spanning the river, a gateway to an industrial area. I rehearsed the questions I wanted to ask. Although John Husskison had been well recommended I didn't know much about his agency and even less from an insider's view about Savannah.

"Would you like a cup of coffee while John finishes his phone call?" Pidcock's receptionist asked.

"No, but please help yourself," I said, as she moved in the direction of a small kitchen. Gray haired and attractive she immediately put me at ease.

"Oh, I never touch the stuff. I just drink a Coca Cola first thing in the morning and that does me fine." How southern, I thought, as I looked at a half empty bottle of Coke on her desk, a custom I couldn't imagine adopting.

I noticed several African wildlife heads mounted along the wall. "Is someone here a big game enthusiast?"

"Not really," she said with an amused expression. "Mr. Pidcock brought those back from a safari several years ago."

"John's off the phone now. Follow me." She led me down a corridor, past the stuffed gazelles and wildebeest. I wondered if John Husskison would match my idea of a southern gentleman, patronizingly polite in pleated pants and suspenders. I was pleasantly surprised to find he was nothing of the sort. Tall and lean with thinning white hair and an angular face, he greeted me with a broad grin, quickly joining me on the visitor's side of his desk. Anxious to please he was both nervous and at ease all at the same time, somehow combining a nervous twitch with a cheerful demeanor. Just as we sat down a second man strode into the room, introducing himself as John's partner, James Ferguson. "But I go by the nickname J. Don." He had a theatrical personality that I found disconcerting, mainly because it dominated the room. "I'm on my way to an appointment," he announced, making his introduction brief.

"I've prepared a few questions if it's all right with you?" I said.

"Ask away," John replied, shifting comfortably in his seat.

I learned Mr. Pidcock, the agency founder, was independently wealthy. He had owned a successful meat packing company, Sunnyland Packing, in Thomasville, Georgia. The agency in all likelihood was a spinoff from Sunnyland's marketing department. Over time he had gradually distributed the ownership to John and J. Don.

"Did Pidcock have much background in marketing?"

John shrugged, "Pidcock had an MBA from Harvard but he never did a hell of a lot with it. But what Pidcock did do was move in the upper circles of Savannah and he is a very charming, personable fellow."

Without saying so directly, John had just confided that Pidcock was the agency "rain maker," at least initially. He had the contacts to help launch the firm.

My first impression of J. Don turned out to be accurate. He had formerly been the manager of a radio station and now personally cut several of the agency's radio spots for its clients. He also had a burning desire to be an actor, a divided focus that I detected miffed

John a little, and had already played bit parts in a couple of Burt Reynolds movies.

The agency handled several industrial accounts including Coastal Chemical Company, a maker of bleach and laundry products; Savannah Electric and Power; Robbins Packing Company and even the Georgia Ports Authority. Most of the work was print advertising with a few billboards, P.R. and some broadcast mixed in. Their client base was well suited for John's background. He had a degree, he said, in industrial management. "So naturally, I can talk the language to industrial clients." His first job, however, was with General Electric as a proofreader for a parts catalog, rewriting engineering text for laymen. "Gradually my responsibilities grew in the communications department. I ended up backing into an advertising career."

"Have you ever handled any political campaigns?"

"Yes, one."

"Did you win?"

"Nope, lost in a landslide."

"Have you handled any others?"

"No."

"Why not?"

"Nobody's ever asked us." We both cracked up laughing.

"What can you tell me about Savannah?"

"For starters, it's an extremely conservative town with a large Jewish, Greek and Irish Catholic population. Blacks comprise fifty percent of the population."

This prompted my next question.

"What is the relationship with the blacks?"

I half expected John to be hesitant but his reply was straightforward. "The blacks here are treated like second-class citizens. The elected school board is about the only public position of authority they hold. Culturally, we're very segregated. In fact, the whites are terrified that if we don't get out and vote, we'll end up with a black mayor."

"Well, then let me ask you this. What is the source of power?"

"The what?"

"The source of power," I repeated. "Who runs the city?"

"Oh. That's easy. Just follow the money. Savannah is narrow-minded, tightly controlled by a small power structure of old-line, moneyed wealth. Union Camp Paper, Dixie Crystal Sugar, the big banks in town; these companies were founded by families who still own large blocks of stock. Consequently, they influence the distribution of wealth and employment. Companies like Union Camp make sure they have people in city government, so their interests aren't adversely affected. It's the same as in any town. If you want to find the power, just follow the money."

I asked if there was anything else I should know. He added there were a couple of military bases nearby, which I jotted down in my notes.

Satisfied that with John I'd usually get a straight answer, I asked if he'd like to handle the circus again this year. "I'd be delighted," he said. "I'll carve out a space for you in the art department. You can move in tomorrow."

I got up to leave. "Where are you staying?" he asked. I cringed for a moment, remembering Mike's advice.

"The Alamo Motel."

"The Alamo Motel? You've got to be kidding. I'll make a few calls."

I liked him more already. As I strolled out to my car a picture of the city began to unfold, but there was another perspective I still didn't have and with half the population black I wanted at least one first-hand dialogue. I glanced back at the river. Tomorrow, I'll dig a little deeper.

It's strange how the oddest places can awaken some of the most pleasant memories. Feelings of peace and harmony. What could be less inviting than a laundromat; yet as I watched my clothes tumble gracefully behind the glass door while washing machines rattled on the concrete floor, I found myself serenely content. The smell of detergents and freshly cleaned clothes reminded me of the hours we'd spent together studying or preparing for a test while others folded their clothes, ignoring or sometimes scolding their children. For my wife and I, it was temporary, the owners of a kinetic energy that, someday unleashed, could easily afford a washing machine. But to the dirty-faced children and mothers dressed in five-and-dime clothes, this was their way of life. To them, it was just a part of their daily drudgery from which there was little escape. Maybe that's why I'd felt serene. For an hour or two a week, I was part of their world. But I was only observing. I knew it. They knew it. And maybe my inner peace came from knowing my poverty was at worst ephemeral no matter how distant prosperity seemed. Maybe the laundromat symbolized my rites of passage from one world to another. But as I thought back, I couldn't help feeling life was simpler then. Or maybe like now, it was simply humility I felt, that wondrous quality that pulls us down from heights too lofty.

My thoughts drifted to my father, how he had taunted me to quit. I knew there was no way I could. Yet when it came to my wife, the one relationship I truly craved, I ran. But when it came to proving myself to him, even in some daunting, impossible task, I couldn't quit if I wanted to.

In high school, I desperately wanted to play varsity football, a preposterous idea, considering at the time I weighed 119 pounds soaking wet. But the agreement was, if you made it through summer practice, you automatically made the team. The coach, it seemed to me, did everything he could to make me quit, even having me run up a jagged cliff during practice for two straight weeks, simply because I'd missed one session. By the end of each practice, my hands and knees were covered with blood, but it only made me more determined. In the end I didn't quit. I made the team. And even though I only played ten seconds during a real game, I felt in some way I'd won.

I thought about my wife. Would I even be with the circus, doing what I loved, if it hadn't been for her? "I didn't marry a taxi driver," she hollered one night. "Why don't you quit feeling sorry for yourself and get a job in your field." The next day I found the job as a layout artist, followed by other jobs in advertising, that gave me that extra edge when I later met Brad Rosenberg.

As I gathered my clothes and walked into the night I no longer felt content. I had betrayed her. And I didn't know why.

The temperature was unseasonably mild, even for Savannah, as I drove toward the Civic Center. I hoped to meet the general manager before settling in at Pidcock. The marquee announced an antique show of china and housewares in progress. I entered an expansive lobby. The arena was on my left. To my right was an auditorium, the John Mercer Theatre. Unfortunately the general manager wasn't in but an assistant indicated I was welcome to see the arena. A rotund, rumpled looking man, the antique show's promoter, nodded his approval.

Inside I was amazed at the small size of the arena, especially compared to the twenty thousand-seat Cleveland Coliseum. Although the arena floor was the same circumference, the seats only rose two tiers above the floor. How does the show make a profit, I wondered, playing in an arena this small? But I remembered what Allen once said. "Our costs are all fixed. At the start of the year we throw our expenses into one big hat and then shoot for volume to pull in our profits."

I circled the arena, anticipating my excitement a few months down the road. Next to Cleveland it ought to be a cakewalk. As I departed I was already formulating a strategy of trades, buys and promotions to saturate the city.

It was too nice a morning to race back to Pidcock so I walked west along Perry Street, picking my way past Savannah's old houses. Approaching a nearby square I spied two black men sitting peacefully on a bench. They weren't conversing. Instead they seemed satisfied to sip their lunch from brown paper bags. Perhaps this was my chance to gain a different perspective?

"Excuse me. I'm new to Savannah. I'm doing a small research project. Would you mind if I asked you a few questions?" I half expected a refusal, but the man nearest to me, in the paint-splattered pants, said, "What do you wanna know?"

I knew I was on touchy ground. I sat down and eased into my questions. "Well for starters, what's it like to live here?"

"For a white man or a black man?" So much for tiptoeing through the tulips.

"For a black man," I replied, as impassively as I could.

"Well, it's a hell of a lot better than it is in New Jersey."

"How so?"

"This is one of the best southern cities anywhere. Any black person will tell you that. We work together with white folk. Then they go their way and we go ours. Sure, some damn redneck crackers still shovel you some shit, but it's changed a lot. Back in the sixties, you couldn't even sit on the park benches."

"Are you serious?"

"No, man. That's the way it was."

"What about work? Can you make a decent living here?"

"Oh, there's plenty of work," the larger man said. "But it depends what kind of work. Some of it will kill you. My last job was unloading sacks of fishmeal down at the shipyards. That shit smells so bad it sticks with you for days."

"What is fishmeal?" I asked, at the risk of sounding ignorant.

"That's what they feed the hogs and chickens with. It's ground up fish. Comes in burlap sacks. We'd take it off the ships with big hooks. It's back breaking work. Damn dangerous too."

"Dangerous?"

"Yeah, man. Lots of people get killed. They be some crazy people work there. Say somebody thinks you're fooling around with his wife. You could be down in the hole and have something fall on your head. Or maybe a fire breaks out in the hole. You yell for help only nobody hears you."

I was glued now to his every word. This was definitely not in the tourist brochures.

"And besides that," he continued, "cables could snap, cut off your legs or throw you into the river. You a drowned rat then?"

"Can't the workers swim?"

"Don't matter. The river has a terrible current. They found one man six miles down the river. His body had been so chewed up by crabs you couldn't recognize him."

My college degree was looking better by the minute. "Driving around, it doesn't seem like blacks comprise fifty percent of the population."

"That's because whites live on the main streets. The blacks live in the alleys. You just don't see us."

"Oh," I said, sensing a tinge of resentment. We talked a few minutes more. Sometimes the two men simply started telling stories to one another. I would just listen in. They even talked about the history of the city.

"There's a tunnel under the streets where the ships would bring in the slaves at night," the older man said. "You can still see the rings in the wall where they threaded the shackles."

Before I knew it, over an hour had passed. When I finally stood up to leave, I could tell they too had lost themselves in the time.

"Being as we've given you all this information how about giving us a few bucks?"

I reached into my wallet, retrieving a ten dollar bill. "Have a drink on me," I said. They turned and wished me well. Not just for the money, I thought, but because I'd taken an interest in their lives. The money was more than I could lose. But to me it was worth every cent. In a short time I'd been shown another world. As I walked back to my car I no longer felt a stranger to the city.

⁓⁂⁓

Quail hunting was big in this part of the country. When I arrived at the office, spotting John Husskison in a red plaid shirt and hunting boots behind his desk, I wondered if that was his plan for the afternoon. I could picture him trading tales with clients as they ambled through fields of brush hoping to scare up a covey. For now, he was content to clip his fingernails into a wastepaper can between his knees. Not exactly a Madison Avenue image, but then again, New York was the least of his aspirations. In fact, he couldn't resist a jab northward as we chatted over coffee.

"Did I tell you about the New York lawyer who came down here duck hunting?"

Spotting a good joke, I smiled, "No, I don't believe you have."

"Well," John said, already starting to laugh at his own joke while exaggerating the southern vernacular, "this here lawyer comes down here. And he's hunting in a duck blind with some good ol' boys, when all of a sudden a whole flock of ducks flies by. Well, this here lawyer, he opens up with both barrels. BLAM! He knocks one right out of the sky. Well, damned if that duck don't fall on a barn roof, slide down and land on the ground. The New York lawyer leaps up, runs into the yard, and starts to retrieve the duck. Just then this Georgia farmer walks onto his porch and hollers, 'What the hell are you doing?'"

"The lawyer stops abruptly, 'I'm picking up this duck.'"

Whereupon the farmer replies, 'No you ain't. That's not your duck. It's my duck.'

The New York lawyer looks up, incredulous, and says 'What do you mean? I just shot it. It's my duck.'

'No, it ain't,' the farmer says. 'It fell on my barn, landed on my ground, and if you look over there at that mailbox, you'll see this is my property. That's *my* duck.'

Incensed, the lawyer says, 'Look. I'm an attorney from New York. If we were in New York, I'd sue your ass.'

'Well, we ain't in New York. And down here we do things differently.'

'How so?'

'Well, it's simple. Down here, we just kick each other in the balls. The one left standing keeps the duck.'

The lawyer scratches his head, looks up and says, 'Well, all right.'

The farmer says, 'Me first,' and promptly kicks him right in the nuts. The lawyer goes straight up in the air ten feet, lands on all fours, and crawls around in pain for twenty minutes. Finally, he staggers up, eyes the farmer, and says, 'Okay, it's my turn.'

The farmer looks at him and says, 'Fuck it. You can have the duck.'"

⊰≫⊱

"Come on. Let me show you your new digs," John said, still chuckling as he led me across the hall. John had partitioned the room in half. One side was the art department outfitted with a drafting table, Pantone ink books and several colored markers carefully positioned. The other side contained an empty desk and filing cabinet he had prepared for me. I placed my briefcase on the desk.

"Is there anything else you need?"

"I'm leaving for the Bahamas tomorrow. If you could gather all the media rate cards for me while I'm gone, I'd appreciate it." He said he would. Then to my surprise he added, "Incidentally, when you get back, I've worked out a deal with the Downtowner Inn across from the Civic Center. You can move over there for the same price as the Alamo."

"You're serious?"

"Just don't flash your Rolex around."

"What do you mean?" I asked, glancing at my nineteen-dollar Timex.

"Last year's promoter checked into the Desoto Inn, one of our pricier hotels and promptly did an interview the next day with the morning newspaper. The reporter thought he was arrogant and wrote about him flashing around his fancy jewelry."

Irvin must have loved that, I thought, since I'd heard he didn't like self aggrandizing promoters, let alone negative publicity.

"Well, it's nice to know I'm following a class act."

"Don't worry," John said with a grin. "I'll tell them you're a hell of a duck hunter."

"By the way. How did you get the deal at the Downtowner?"

"Chris Barberi, the sales manager at WJCL TV, set it up." My expression showed I was still curious. "The TV station is owned by J. Curtis Lewis. Lewis also owns the Downtowner Inn. He was the mayor of Savannah when the Civic Center was built across the street from the hotel. At any rate, we've been a friend of the station several years."

John returned to his office. A few minutes later the graphic artist with whom I'd be sharing my office strolled in. He introduced himself as Harry. A strange looking man, he walked with a limp, whispering conspiratorially out of one side of his mouth. After listening to him a few minutes, it became apparent he didn't feel the agency had enough work to keep him busy. He had taken the job a few months earlier, leaving his wife, for the time being, alone in Florida. "I don't think I'll be here long," he said. "I don't plan to settle in. In fact, I'm not even going to buy a television. If there's something good I want to watch, I just go see it at the K-Mart." I wondered if the television salesmen were on to him.

I spent the rest of the day getting used to my new surroundings, filing away forms and office supplies. It was hard to focus on Savannah knowing I was leaving for the Bahamas the next morning. It was my first trip to the islands. I was particularly curious to meet Irvin Feld. Everywhere I went his name sent shivers up the corporate spine. Why was this man so revered or, better still, feared? But there had to be more than fear. The man after all had made millions.

Chapter 30
IRVIN'S GRANDIOSE PLAN

"A Man's Wealth is Measured by What He Doesn't Need."
— HENRY THOREAU

Irvin Feld was a deeply troubled man, a fact his personality refused to conceal. Despite the smooth delivery of a natural-born salesman—and when Irvin wished to persuade you, no one could be smoother—he was incapable of suppressing an inner rage so explosive and so spontaneous and so unpredictable that even those closest to him gave him a wide, wary berth. To compound matters further, few people realized Irvin had no peripheral vision. An operation several years earlier to remove cataracts prevented him from going blind but had left him with only straight-ahead vision. Consequently, standing to either side of Irvin, it would seem as though he were ignoring your presence completely. If "eyes are the windows to your soul," then between Irvin's thick glasses that magnified and blurred the shape of his eyes, the tunnel vision that obliterated the outside world, and his violent emotional outbursts, he was indeed a man hard to fathom.

The start of any great fortune often begins with the acts of a simple peddler like John Ringling and P.T. Barnum. Albeit a "hell of a simple peddler" with the gift of salesmanship . . . pure unadulterated persuasion in whatever form it takes. For some it's sincerity, for a few it's the gift of language, for others it's fear and intimidation and for many like Irvin Feld it's just dogged perseverance inspired by good old capitalistic greed. But whatever the combination, the belief is the same. These people knew that no matter how big and complicated business gets or how theoretical the Harvard MBAs try to make it, business still boils down to one simple fact: somebody has to *sell* somebody something. But Irvin this time might have bitten off more than he could chew.

Some would say metaphorically his lack of peripheral vision had caused him finally to overreach his talents and business acumen. For immediately after Irvin sold the circus to Mattel, he began drawing up plans for a grandiose seven-hundred-and-fifty-acre theme park that would furnish Ringling Brothers and Barnum and Bailey Circus with a permanent, stationary money-making machine. The theme park would not only be a symbol for all the circus exemplified in America, but would be a testament to the genius of Irvin Feld, a business venture that would secure his rightful place alongside Barnum, Bailey and the seven Ringling brothers.

The theme park would be named "Circus World," and Irvin's vision offered the public a wondrous view of the circus. Every day the park would feature old-time circus parades, elephant rides, animal acts, and a permanent tent with holes in the canvas to allow children to sneak in under the big top. People could even attach themselves to guy wires and experience the thrill of the flying trapeze. And to top it all off, towering over the park would be a giant replica of Jumbo, two-hundred-feet high, with a dazzling restaurant on top. So persuasive was Irvin, and so convinced was Mattel of his vision, that the company spent millions developing the land and constructing the park to bring it to fruition. They also bought, hook, line and sinker, Irvin's theory that by purchasing the land and constructing the complex in Orlando, Florida, right next to Disney World, tourists would now flock to both attractions. Irvin even boasted, "I have great respect for the Disney organization, but it's all animation. It's not real. We're live, real people, real animals performing. . . ." But Irvin had miscalculated. Families that came to Orlando were there for one reason, to see Disney World, and when Circus World opened, the crowds were a minuscule three or four hundred a day, barely enough to pay for the personnel, let alone the construction of a giant elephant and revolving restaurant. Shocked at the early failure of the park, Mattel shut it down and began a three-million dollar renovation to try to save its investment. And in a devastating blow to Irvin's ego, Mattel rescinded his authority and substituted a group of theme park experts to salvage the complex.

Surely, as Irvin flew to the Bahamas, the failure of his vision must have caused him great anxiety. But Irvin was not the type of man that would allow a setback, even of this magnitude, to stop him. He was a driven man. But what was behind this drive? What caused an almost maniacal drive to obtain power and wealth? Was it the persecution he surely must have felt as a child of Jewish immigrants in a small town barely over the Mason-Dixon Line? Was it watching his father descend ignominiously into bankruptcy during the depression years? Was it his tiny stature, barely over five feet tall, even as an adult? Perhaps it was all three, for Irvin, above all else, demanded control. Even the smallest of details would have to be seen by Irvin for his approval. But the drive for power and money was more easily explained. What wasn't so obvious was what was behind the inner conflict that manifested itself in such tempestuous outbursts. Much of the inner turmoil must have come from the view that Irvin was living a double life. On one hand, he was driven to publicize his accomplishments and prominence, unabashedly turning the spotlight on himself, while on the other hand, some said, harboring secrets that would horrify him should they someday be exposed. As an icon of family values and family entertainment, not only did Irvin have to contend with a wife who committed suicide over feelings of neglect, but even more devastating might be another secret, a secret his ego would never allow revealed, especially for a man achieving maturity in the 1940s. For Irvin Feld there was no such thing as coming out, and surely if the spreading rumors were true he must have spent many a night lying awake wondering if the world would discover he was gay.

A steady breeze drifted through my room causing the gentle sway of an indoor palm. Past white louvered doors I could see glimpses of turquoise water. With time to spare before this evening's meeting

I quickly changed into my bathing suit. I must have been one of the first to arrive for I didn't see any of my fellow promoters. But what I did notice was Allen Bloom's wife and Shirley Feld, Irvin's late brother Izzy's widow, reclining on two chaises not far from the pool. I decided I'd ignore them, a tricky proposition pretending you don't know someone when you do; but they looked a little too aloof and influential for my own good.

It was clear to me the minute I arrived in the Bahamas that Irvin had spared no expense. Ever the promoter himself, Irvin had a special affinity for the advance men, I'd heard, and despite the frequency in which he'd haggle over minute costs it was rumored he had budgeted more than twenty-thousand dollars for the gathering. Nevertheless, I was surprised to see a bowl of fresh fruit and a bottle of red wine along with a welcome note awaiting me in my room.

One by one, the promoters began to appear. First Tim Stinson, then Chris Bursky, Max Goldberg and Eliott Harris. Sam Barrett was one of the last to arrive. For the first time, he and I looked more in tune with our surroundings. With our waspy light hair and complexion we were practically sun worshipers compared to our comrades, seemingly more at ease inside a New York deli.

Greetings were followed by a litany of cities we'd just promoted, were promoting or would soon promote. Now that I'd graduated from the ranks of trainee to full-fledged promoter I felt comfortably talkative, confident . . . a blissfulness bordering on perfection. That is, until I was rattled by the presence of a woman strolling casually toward us. Perhaps it was the way her hips moved or a certain seductiveness she possessed that contrasted with her wholesome looks, but as soon as she sat down my energies refocused. Apparently, she'd accompanied a gentleman from our national P.R. agency, a man I barely knew. She had flown in to join him for the week. I could only assume they shared an intimate relationship, but when she turned and introduced herself neither of us could hide an irresistible curiosity.

A change of scenery, I decided, before my infatuation became obvious, might settle my nerves. I excused myself and ambled along the beach toward a fleet of catamarans half out of the water, their sails fluttering in the wind.

"Hello mate. Want to rent a sailboat?"

"No thanks. Not today. I just got here," I said.

He was leaning back in a beach chair. About my age, I guessed, only he wore a short pony tail and a day's growth of beard.

"Where are you from?" I asked.

"England."

"England? How did you get here?"

"I was driving lorries to the south of Spain. Saved a few quid and hitched a ride on a ketch about three weeks ago. Bloody broke now, but what the hell, I got here all right."

"How long are you planning to stay in the islands?"

"I don't really know," he said, with an unconcerned shrug. "Six months . . . a year. I'll see how things go."

Here he sat, dead broke, no concrete future, and he couldn't care less. One of those types who follow the trade winds. An adventurous, roguish sort with a thirst to see the world. Not much different from me I suppose, but unlike him why was I so hellbent on climbing some mythical corporate ladder? Maybe some day I'd kick back and do it his way.

"You know I could have made a bloody killing on a boat a few months back. The owner had tax problems. He would have taken three-thousand pounds easy. I could have sold it for eight. That's the way to make a fortune. Spot these old wrecks, fix them up, and sell them for a healthy profit." He lowered his gaze and looked out to sea, absorbed for the moment in his missed opportunity. Perhaps we weren't that different after all.

I headed back to my room to change for Irvin's dinner. Everyone had left the beach, including the woman with the long, wavy hair.

I searched for the meeting room in nervous anticipation. Despite Irvin's occasional benevolence, notwithstanding the basket of fresh fruit and bottle of wine, it was clearly a monarchy for whom we worked. We all served at our boss's pleasure. Everyone knew it. And it didn't take a judge and jury to be banished from the kingdom. Perform or you were out. And by all accounts, if you were accidentally in the wrong place at the wrong time when Irvin was in a foul mood, you could just as easily hasten your exit. Simple rules we all accepted. There were no unions, no government agencies nor regulations to protect you. And despite flutterings and protests at the periodic injustices, one didn't solicit one's colleagues to act as a shield.

The hotel had placed us in a large room off the main courtyard. When I arrived promoters were still filtering into the room. In fact, a small bottleneck had stopped us at the entrance when suddenly a young man burst through the door, grabbing the elbow of a nearby waiter. "We've got to find some chocolate syrup!" he yelled. "Irvin needs some for his ice cream!" The waiter looked at him like he was crazy so the young man repeated the plea to another waiter rushing by.

"Who the hell is that?" I asked Sam Barrett, observing the scene beside me.

"Oh, that's Stanley Wynowski, Irvin's personal assistant. Irvin must have muttered he wanted syrup for his ice cream, so Stanley's going nuts."

"Does he have a title?"

"Yeah, vice president of something or other, but he's really Irvin's personal valet. Pretty harmless, but I'd watch what you say around him just the same. We ought to screw him up and tell him we just heard Irvin say he'd rather have butterscotch."

A head table had been positioned near the far wall in front of a number of round tables for the promoters and a few of the headquarters staff. Irvin sat at the center of the long table looking tinier than I'd expected. His thin arms protruded from a light green, tropical shirt. If it wasn't for the large cigar he held confidently in his fingers he'd have looked almost frail. The other men at the table conversed freely with one another, making Irvin look uncomfortably isolated, especially since the chair to his left was vacant while Stanley searched frantically for chocolate syrup.

Next to Irvin sat Allen Bloom, followed left and right by the four supervisors, Brad Rosenberg, David Rosenwasser, Art Ricker and at the end of the table Mike Franks. Like Irvin, each of the supervisors wore a casual sport shirt and like Irvin, each was smoking a fat cigar, including, to my amazement, Mike Franks. I was tempted to rush up and fumigate him but it was far more enjoyable watching him succumb to one of Irvin's big stogies.

The smoke clouded the room and so did the noisy chatter as the promoters took the head table's cue and conversed across the tables. Chris Bursky cracked jokes while Sam Barrett filled me in on Oklahoma City, oblivious for the moment to Allen Bloom's clinking of his glass. Brad Rosenberg joined in, banging his glass on the table, and the room suddenly quieted.

Allen paused for a second, flicking his ashes. "First of all I want to thank Mr. Feld for hosting this meeting. I'm sure you'll all enjoy the balmy weather and there will be plenty of time for rest and relaxation. But for right now I'd like to turn the meeting over to Mr. Feld."

All eyes shifted to Irvin. "Good evening gentlemen. I'm delighted to see so many familiar faces. Chris Bursky, I see, continues to grace us with his presence, as does Max Goldberg." Irvin scanned the head table. "I'm also delighted to see our new management team. Together they bring a wealth of experience."

"We've had a good season this past year but next year is going to be magnificent!" Irvin spoke in a measured tone, reminiscent of a Middle Eastern merchant, focused, reassuring and deliberate. "We've got some exciting new acts for next year. Gunther, for the first time ever, is going to circle the arena astride an uncaged tiger on the back of an elephant, two natural-born enemies brought together. I've also found an incredible twelve-year-old kid that can ride a three inch bicycle. And as a final coup we've signed Philip Petite, the french tightrope walker who just made international headlines promenading between the two world trade center towers. Allen will fill you in on the rest of the new acts tomorrow."

Irvin's demeanor changed, suddenly looking somber. "Unfortunately, I'll be leaving in the morning and won't be here the rest of the week. A few of you may have heard. The day before yesterday a fire broke out on the train en-route to the mid-west. Three people were killed. Smiley, whom most of you know, was one of them. All we know is it started in wardrobe."

While we digested the news of the tragedy Stanley Wynowski whispered something in Irvin's ear. "Before I leave for the memorial services there is one issue I want to discuss." Irvin took a puff on his cigar. "Lately we've had several trademark infringements. This is a matter I don't take lightly. When I bought the circus I paid big money for the rights to the slogan 'The Greatest Show on Earth.' It's 100 years old and anytime someone uses even a facsimile of our slogan it's a violation of our trademark. So the next time you're in a town and someone wants to ride on our advertising coattails with 'The Greatest Carpet Sale on Earth,' I want to be called personally. Is that understood?"

I had the distinct impression that Irvin's attorneys intended to batter any infringers, at least if they didn't immediately cease and desist.

Ringling Brothers didn't have a logo to protect per se, a special mark or illustration to identify itself. Instead, it was the slogan that had become our trademark. As the meeting progressed, I couldn't help reflecting how much time and energy corporations invest in their logos, especially since the original purpose for a logo had long since disappeared. The fact of the matter was that at the turn of the century, when mass production naturally led to mass marketing, more than fifty percent of the population was still illiterate. They simply couldn't read. So companies went to elaborate lengths to have marks or illustrations emblazoned on their packaging to help consumers identify their products.

Protecting the heritage and value of "The Greatest Show on Earth" certainly made sense, but I remembered when NBC decided to dump their famous "peacock." After nonsensically paying a New York advertising agency a reported sum of $750,000 to design a new logo (which became a graphic treatment of the letter "N") they were promptly sued by the Nebraska Educational Television Network, who was already using an identical logo they had just paid an artist a fee of $100 to produce.

This was after—in a modern-day version of "Look, the emperor has no clothes"—the president of NBC, Herbert Schlosser, having seen the New York agency's new logo, had proudly proclaimed, "It will be the thread that's woven through all of NBC's public appearances."

NBC settled out of court, giving the Nebraska network $500,000 worth of equipment, plus $25,000 in which to design a new logo. The small station then promptly replaced their capital "N" with a lowercase "n" and announced, "Everybody here likes our new logo, but if some other network just loves this one, we'll be happy to negotiate. There's still some equipment we can use."

The president of NBC, I suspect, was not amused, nor was Irvin Feld as the meeting came to a close. Allen thanked Irvin again, announcing we'd reconvene in the morning followed by lunch and a free afternoon.

The next morning we filed once again into the sunlit meeting room. Without Irvin Feld's overpowering presence Allen Bloom now dominated the room. But unlike Irvin, with his precise, unwavering enunciation, Allen spoke haltingly, thoughtfully, as though he were pushing his words through. Yet it somehow added to his charisma, for it's one thing to fear a man, as most of us did Irvin, but quite another to trust a man, as most of us did Allen.

Brad Rosenberg sat close to Allen, removing any doubt, at least in his own view, he was first among equals amid the three other supervisors. Yet Allen and Bradley, side by side, were a study in opposites. Whereas Allen's comments were short and terse, Brad's remarks, like Irvin's, were smooth and verbose. Their looks even sharpened their differences, Allen's swarthy toughness standing in contrast to Brad's polished wardrobe and self-conscious mannerisms. But what Allen may have lacked in outward graces, he gained in wisdom and longevity, learning over time how to survive alongside Irvin's overbearing ego. Watching Bradley tread fearlessly toward Allen's terrain, I wondered if Allen would intercede when the clash between Irvin and Bradley finally came or whether the seasoned lion would step aside and let the young cub self-destruct.

Allen asked Bradley to read the descriptions of the remaining new acts. A few of the promoters, in Irvin's absence, now felt emboldened. "What we need is a human cannonball act," Tim Stinson declared. "Like Circus America has. I hear all the time we've gotten too tinselly."

Allen nodded his head, reminding Tim that for thrills we had Elvin Bale's high wire motorcycle act. A few others agreed with Tim before Chris Bursky shifted the discussion to advance publicity.

"What I want to know is can the advance clown have a beer during lunch?"

"Hell no," Allen grinned, "There's nothing worse than a lethargic clown!"

The laughter subsided when a female voice spoke up from the back of the room. "Excuse me, Mr. Bloom. Can I ask you a question?"

We turned to stare at a young black woman. She was the daughter of a prominent governor. Allen, probably as a favor to the politician, had hired her at the beginning of the year to work with the King Charles Troupe to help garnish sales and support from the black community.

"Yes, Pamela. What is it?" Allen replied.

"I'm confused," she sputtered, "I have no idea what I'm supposed to be doing."

The room turned uncomfortably quiet as we collectively wondered how Allen planned to hurdle this unexpected embarrassment. Whatever she wasn't doing she'd been doing it for the past nine months. Allen lowered his voice to an audible whisper, "We'll talk about that later Pamela . . . in my office."

The rest of the meeting stayed on a serious course. Sam Barrett asked, "How do you handle tensions in the middle of media negotiations?"

"You've gotta know when to push and when to pull," Allen volunteered. Brad Rosenberg elaborated, "When disagreements get heated, the louder they yell, the softer I speak." Mike Franks, who had remained silent until now, said, "Nobody wins by taking home all the marbles. It's only good if both parties win. Spend as much time thinking about their needs, not just yours, and you'll succeed every time."

"Amen!" exclaimed Allen.

The topic switched to group sales. "I haven't had much luck," said one of the promoters. "I question whether the time is worth the effort."

Since I'd just completed a successful group sales campaign in Cleveland, I suddenly found myself in the spotlight. At Mike's prompting, I briefly outlined the strategy I'd employed to ensure most of the corporations and organizations in the city had been contacted. "Sometimes not knowing why something can't be done can be your best ally. You just stumble forward and who knows? The results might surprise you."

The meeting continued thirty minutes more to adjournment. As we exited down the hotel corridor I suddenly felt a hand on my shoulder. "I just wanted to tell you I was impressed with what you said."

"You were?"

"Damn right," Allen said. "Too many people focus on why something can't be done instead of just doing it. We need more of your kind of attitude." I clung to his words as he disappeared around the corner.

I had the whole afternoon free as I approached my British friend.

"This one will do," I said, pointing to a fourteen-footer with white pontoons and a thin, blue stripe.

"Right mate," he said, rolling the words as only the British can do. "There's a bit of a breeze kicking up. Do you know what you're doing?" He slid the bow into the water.

"Yeah, I'm fine. Just help me get it past the breakers."

We waded up to our chests, keeping the sail pointed toward the wind so it wouldn't take off alone. Each swell lifted the gunnels to our shoulders. Past the foam, the waves hit a trough. I scrambled onto the top of the canvas, grabbed the tiller, yanked on the main sheet, and sailed over an oncoming wave.

"You're off!" he yelled, and I watched him stand still in the surf, growing rapidly smaller.

Once clear of the breakers, I quickly acclimated myself to the boat. Catamarans are the fastest sailboats made and the sloop-rigged sail had quickly filled with air. I hauled in the line attached to the mainsail. The tiller was connected to two rudders each trailing behind a pontoon, and the boat's stern quivered, light and agile to the touch. Now I could feel the wind and sun against my face. The son-of-a-bitch was beginning to purr. "I'll bet I can plane this bastard," I thought, as the boat began riding the tops of the waves. Wrapping my ankles around the hiking strap, I leaned over the side, revealing a washboard stomach from years of boyhood sailing. My upper body stretched over the water, the tiller in my left hand, the main sheet straining against my right.

"Come on, you bastard," I taunted. "Get that pontoon up!" Slowly the starboard pontoon rose from the water.

"That's it, baby. Now we're sailing." I felt a rush of adrenalin as I peered down eight feet at the only pontoon in the water. "Go, you son-of-a-bitch, go!" And suddenly I was catapulted back in time. Just my father and me, heading for the starting line. Thirty sailboats keeled over in the wind, water spraying over the gunnels, all trying to reach the starting line first. The ten-minute gun goes off. "All right, time me," my father says, as we head away from the starting line. "Let me know when we hit three minutes."

"Okay, three minutes," I yell.

"All right, coming about!" he screams. I snap the jib sheet out of the cleat.

"Clock me back to the starting line." I stare at the stopwatch, glancing at the committee boats on either side of the imaginary line. "Two minutes!" I cry, just as we cross the starting line.

The five-minute gun goes off. Smoke spirals into the air. "Let's do it again," he says, salt water dripping from our faces. We tack once again until we hear the three-minute gun, then the one-minute gun, then the thirty-second gun. There we are, thirty boats streaming for the starting line. Now it has to be perfect. Speed and efficiency are everything. The language all comes back to me. "We're jibing. Watch the boom. Pull in the sheet. Three more inches. Come on. Come on. Come on!"

"How much time is left? Shit! We're going to cross too soon. No we're not. Wench it in. We're flying, baby! Watch that other boat. The bastard's going to ram us . . . starboard! Good. Okay. Let's stay windward. We're there. 10, 9, 8, 7, 6, 5, 4, 3, 2, 1. Boom. We're over!"

I let out a rebel yell. The catamaran was planing, surging on top of the water. Freedom! Unadulterated freedom. Just me and the wind. "It doesn't get better than this!" I held the tack as long as I could. Then the wind calmed to a gentle breeze. I turned the boat away from the wind, letting the sail out as far as it would go, gliding with the sun, the wind to my back. I noticed that a lone seagull was soaring overhead, flying with the currents, keeping me company.

I felt myself relax. The boat in my control. One moment having tested its limits, daring it to throw me, the next moment gliding me home.

Control . . . freedom. Can the two co-exist?

My thoughts drifted to my wife. We'd go through such wonderful periods of harmony, only to lose it, unsure how to regain it. With love, so often comes control, possessiveness. Some would say we humans are simply territorial . . . possessiveness leading to jealousy. The word rolls off your tongue, as though it weren't jagged and rough, a state of mind I detest for it defies all I value. How can one truly love without giving the other complete freedom? Freedom to spend time with others, those of their choosing. Freedom to be. Sure, boundaries must exist. But birds with clipped wings never soar.

Can one ever love purely? Giving freedom completely. Now you're planing, surging forward together on the tops of the waves.

How did we lose it? God knows, we had it in the beginning. Maybe if I'd told her more often I truly, deeply loved her, that I accepted her for exactly who she was, that I was there to stand and applaud, not change and resist . . . maybe if I'd heard the same. Someone once said, "To love because of things is one kind of love but to love in spite of things is a lasting kind of love."

Well, it doesn't matter now. What's done is done. I've got my freedom back and there's a wide open sea ahead of me. Perhaps its best to shed all the shackles, I thought. "Just you and me," I confided to the seagull.

The sun had begun to turn orange, reflecting off the white sail, as I headed in for shore.

The salt spray and open air workout tired and energized me all at the same time. I lay on my bed, cooled by the afternoon shade and slept, the kind of sleep that feels warm and cozy, slipping out of consciousness to awake with no recollection of having thoughts or moved a muscle. I looked at my watch and realized I'd slept through dinner. Yet I suddenly had an urge to be around people.

Refreshed and changed, I strolled through the lobby in the direction of laughter emanating from the bar. Inside a dimly lit room, smelling tropically fragrant, Sam Barrett sat at one end of a table, Chris Bursky at the other and across from an empty chair sat our New York publicity agent along with the light-haired woman I'd met earlier on the beach. I felt my breathing shorten. I exchanged pleasantries with the men, but the glance she gave me when our eyes re-met revealed the intensity hadn't changed. My gestures didn't show it but she riveted my attention. I didn't want to know anything about her, nothing that could detract from the infatuation I felt. A mole, to the left of her lower lip, gave her a special beauty, hinting at playfulness. But I think it was her eyes, that direct gaze she offered that was so instantly seductive.

I noticed her breasts underneath her white silk blouse were large against a narrow frame. The kind of breasts that were round on the bottom and then gravitated upwards to where the nipples began. I didn't imagine her nipples as small and pink but large and brown, circling the front of her breasts.

Sam was laughing. Chris was pouring drinks. And her companion was trying to capture her attention. They didn't seem a match, and I sensed he knew it. Drinks rounded the table, and everyone, including me, seemed to relax even more. For a moment, I almost forgot how much I wanted her, when suddenly I felt her toe ever so softly brush against my ankle. At first I thought it was accidental, but I caught her eyes and she stared back without wavering. Then I noticed the tiniest trace of a smile, as though she alone possessed a secret, and I felt her toe rest lightly on my foot. I was frozen to the spot. Then slowly, tantalizingly, she began moving her foot up my leg. Her foot reached my knee, and then she moved her toes to the inside of my thigh, pressing steadily forward, all the while laughing and talking yet glancing over in darting flashes. I tried my best to act nonchalant, normal, oblivious to this beautiful woman's slow climb toward my crotch.

For a fleeting second, I thought of her friend sitting beside her, and how many men, in an act of male solidarity, might reject her advances. I obviously wasn't one of them. During her next mischievous glance, I shot my eyes to the left, just once, as discreetly as possible. Following my cue, she announced she was feeling a bit lightheaded and would possibly return a little later. I watched her walk past, her hips curved against her tight, dark skirt. I waited an agonizing couple of minutes before proclaiming I too was calling it a night.

She was leaning against the wall in the corridor. I met her smile as I slid my hand into hers. Not a word was exchanged. I led her to my room and slowly began unbuttoning her blouse. Her breasts flowed freely over the top of her bra.

At one in the morning, empty and full from every form of lovemaking we knew, reality finally hit. What were we going to do now? And more specifically what was to be the explanation for her disappearance the last two hours? Passion, barely tempered, drove our thinking.

We decided, at least for this evening she'd tell her companion she had gone for a walk and fallen asleep along the beach. Beyond that, all we knew was we shouldn't be seen together. Even though she had lessened my guilt by implying that her relationship with her host was purely platonic, my instinct for survival told me deception was the better part of discretion.

The next morning she informed me she'd told her friend she was going home. The situation just wasn't right. But instead of leaving the island she checked into a white stone hotel perched high atop a cliff, only a short stroll away, hidden safely behind a bend.

Mornings I spent in meetings but afternoons and evenings we spent together. When we weren't making love we sometimes swung gently on a hammock overlooking the sea. I discovered she was part American Indian. She had grown up in Montana where two generations of European ancestors had mixed with Indian blood. Her grandmother, she said, was a full-blooded Sioux. That explained, I thought, her smooth dark complexion and prominent, high cheekbones. She was majoring in journalism at New York University, having worked part time at the P.R. firm. Her goal, she cited, was to work for a travel magazine and someday perhaps write a serious book. We talked of writing. Oscar Wilde and minimalist poets. Why the classics were so hard to read in today's fast-paced world. Why Hemingway blew his brains out and Faulkner became a rummy.

"Faulkner loved the south though, didn't he?" she said. "Not necessarily," I mused. "He once told an interviewer it was simply what he knew. And there wasn't time in one life to both write and learn someplace new."

Our interests merged while our passions grew inside our veil of secrecy, but there was little doubt we were living in the present. She had a degree to finish and a career to launch and I could barely afford a dilapidated hotel let alone airfare to New York.

Mike Franks cornered me near the end of the week. "There's not much yet to report," I informed him, "other than the fact that last year's promoter left town with a few bruised feelings!"

"No big deal," Mike grinned. "Just tell them he's no longer with us. It's a whole new year . . . it always is."

Saturday I packed my bags and made one last walk to her hotel. She was waiting outside alone. "Thank you," we said, which was different than goodbye, for we both knew we wouldn't see each other again. I walked back by way of the beach, grateful just the same for the gods of unpredictability. Perhaps now I'd return to Savannah, cleansed for a time of the feelings of loneliness.

Chapter 31
RAZZLE DAZZLE

"So, how was your trip?" John Huskisson asked, brightening with a wink.

"Fine," I replied, filling him in while sparing him the more lascivious details. You never know with southerners. Even possessed of a bawdy sense of humor it's hard separating the Christian fundamentalists from the fundamentally rakish. They all go to church—whether they want to or not—because southern pressure for moral one-upmanship would surely bring social and business ostracism if they didn't. But personally, hypocrisy in any form churned my stomach. And when it came to doing business in the south, I found myself suspicious. "Don't be fooled by that southern charm," Sam Barrett warned. "They're raised that way. But push 'em to the wall and they're tough as nails."

I could hardly disagree, having been chased home from school as a "damn yankee" on more than one occasion. I should have known I was in trouble when, at the age of nine, I arrived in the deep south to find the confederate flag proudly flying *above* the U.S. flag. But yankee prejudice was mild compared to the black-and-white water fountains and segregated restrooms that indignantly separated the whites from the blacks.

But if anyone on the receiving end rivaled the southerners'

distaste for blacks it was the "poor white trash," so labeled by the middle and upper classes. For the uneducated whites living on the fringe, the abuse was even worse, for they, above all else, distorted the myth of white superiority. I couldn't help wondering if the need to belittle any group in order to lift one's self esteem spoke of nothing less than a massive sense of inferiority. Maybe it was the civil war. God knows they were still fighting it, and someone had to pay for the lingering blow to their stalwart pride. But for the victims, how deep the abusers' resentments went and for whom it was all just psychic compensation had little bearing on the effect.

I glanced at John Huskisson, though, with his affable manners and silver-haired courtliness, and felt at ease. His open revelations about how the city worked, and even its racial attitude, brought a comfortable harmony. I trusted him . . . even though the south just naturally made me edgy. I'd learned years earlier I wasn't one of them, and I certainly had no illusions I was one of them now.

I sensed John hadn't invested a lot of time thinking about the circus while I was gone. But then again, I wasn't sure what to expect from him outside of a sounding board and some influential introductions. Fortunately I'd been mulling over the possibilities during the past week and had hatched a general strategy, an approach I'd gradually adopted, preferring to input data, then allow time for it to crystalize.

Outside of my media buys and publicity possibilities, I decided I'd pitch the "underprivileged kids" to one of the TV stations, see if I could persuade the *Savannah Morning News* to run a promotional contest, and then parlay my bag of tricks to the radio stations. There was a major car dealer in town that flooded the air waves. I figured he might be open to a ticket give-away for a free test drive. But none of these ideas targeted the black population, and it was here I decided to focus some special attention. "We live in the back alley behind the main streets," the man on the park bench had said. Now I just needed to figure out how to reach them. Perhaps Ringling had a built-in solution, provided I could sell them into doing it. "Why not, opening day, have the King Charles Troup unicycle through the alleys, handing out discount coupons to the kids, while picking up a basketball game or two?" John Huskisson liked it, suggesting, "It might even snare a last minute walk-up crowd to help supplement the major promotions."

⟶⟶⟶

The Downtowner Inn was pretty from the outside. Five stories high with ornamental railings circling each floor, it was clearly a hotel with a *local* flair. I'd been given a room on the second floor, over-looking the parking lot across from the Savannah Civic Center mar-quee. To the west, I could see traffic exiting to the suburbs on Oglethorpe Avenue. The room was color coordinated with an amber bedspread and prints of boats along the bayou. And above the TV, a picture of an antebellum home and an oak tree draped in Spanish moss graced a white wooden frame.

Thanks to John Huskisson, this was to be my home for the next several weeks and though barely larger than an average sized bed-room, it was nice not to see plaster peeling from the ceiling or smell stale cigarette smoke embedded in the carpet.

The room felt clean. I folded away my belongings, feeling again as though I'd passed my initiation from Picadilly trainee to full-fledged promoter.

⟶⟶⟶

"Sam, how are you?"

"Not bad, but I'd rather be back in the Bahamas."

"I know what you mean," I echoed.

It was 9:00 a.m., Salt Lake City time, where I'd tracked him down and even though the islands seemed far away, I wasn't ready to distance myself any sooner than I had to.

"I'd still like to know where the hell you were most of the time," Sam sputtered.

"I'd met someone," I answered vaguely, feeling a little guilty that I hadn't told him in the first place.

"I figured as much," Sam said. "Have you met anyone in Savan-nah yet?"

"No, not a soul. But I've only been here a short time. Have you heard anything new?"

"Not much. Just that Elvin Bale has a new act."

It didn't surprise me. As soon as their contracts were signed the performers had better be coming up with something innovative if they had any hope for a renewal from Irvin.

"This one's simple," Sam said. "He plans to run round and round the outside of a giant spinning cage. He's calling it the 'Wheel of Death.'"

"Sounds prophetic."

"It is when you consider he plans to do it forty feet up with no guy wire, blindfolded."

Remembering Sam told me Elvin wore hooks on his heels when he lurched from his swinging perch, I quipped, "What does he plan to do, wear magnets on his feet?"

"No, I think they're in his head this time."

"Yeah, well see if you can borrow them," I bantered. "We're up for renewal ourselves this year."

The weekend had arrived and I was intrigued by a poster advertising a tent show forty-five miles southwest of town. The circus had invented negative advertising more than a hundred years ago, blasting its competitors with claims of fraudulent advertising. And the poster carried forth the tradition with a swipe at "the modern day indoor glitz" and a return to the "authentic circus of old." The show didn't pose any threat to my efforts, but I was curious to experience one of the tiny "mud shows."

Once out of Savannah I switched to the back roads, where the highway became a two-lane asphalt road marked in the middle only intermittently. The people moved slowly, a habit of preservation from living in energy sapping heat in the summer, a byproduct of which people often called the southerners lazy. A falsity compounded from earlier days, when rural people often contracted hookworms that entered through their shoeless feet, further draining their energy. I passed three teenage girls walking along the road wearing pink curlers in their hair. They stared at me as I passed, as did the coatless children playing on the wooden porches. I half expected them to point at me and scream, "Whitey!" But maybe they were simply gazing at me because I was staring at them.

What amazed me the most were the sharecropper homes. There weren't as many now as when I'd first moved south, but the impact of the lonely shacks had not lessened. Perhaps it was because their naked impoverishment was so utterly exposed, so unhidden from public view, that the houses seemed so foreign. For the shacks weren't sheltered in the trees. Instead they invariably sat in the middle of a dusty, barren field without even shrubs or bushes for foundation dressing. It seemed inexplicable to center these dwellings in the middle of the fields, especially as I gazed at their sloping tin roofs, half-rusted but still blinding in the sun. Tin was waterproof, available, cheap and labor-free, but, my God, what must it be like in the summertime? My fingers burned at the thought.

Most of these homes had windows, but some did not. Few had indoor plumbing, so frigid showers were pumped from a well, and wooden planked outhouses served as the communal toilet. I wondered why these shacks were still here. Laws that once made it illegal for sharecroppers to leave while in debt, had been abolished for years. And surely northward migration offered a better way of life, but I suspected their world was all they knew, and as bleak as it was, it at least brought survival.

As I drove past these strange houses, as weird and as fascinating to me as ancient ruins, only to find nothing had really changed, I remembered more vividly my earlier life in the south.

My father had been promoted to Director of Advertising for Callaway Mills, a textile firm in a sleepy town in the Bible belt of Georgia. Callaway Mills built the Community Center, churches and even sponsored a network of little league football teams. They virtually owned the city. And for us, fresh from New York, and now settled in a redwood home west of the city, we were practically a part of the landed gentry.

On the outskirts of town, poor whites lived in what were called "shotgun homes," small, rectangular houses, so called because they had no angles. You could shoot a bullet straight through them. Children strolled barefoot to school and little girls were often seen walking down unpaved roads, literally wearing flour sacks. Flour came in twenty-five pound sacks made of pretty floral patterns. Their mothers had discovered two of the sacks made a thin, cotton dress.

For the poor, rural black families, life was equally different. I came to know a young black woman who lived nearby, and she painted a portrait of a life fascinating in its simplicity yet spellbinding in its emotional complexity. She grew up one of nine, her birth certificate beside her name having listed her as "colored." Her father was a maintenance man for a local company. She and her siblings had a strict upbringing and their life, as so often happened in small southern towns, centered around the Baptist Church. It was the local gathering place for country folk that seldom saw neighbors during the week. But just as importantly the church was the great equalizer. From choir master to deacon, even the lowly farm hand could assume positions of importance.

"We weren't allowed to dance or listen to rock and roll. It had to be bible music," she said. "We could only listen to gospel music on the radio. And all nine kids, six girls and three boys, behaved! If we didn't, we'd have to select our own switches from the dogwood or mulberry trees, and our mother did the lickings."

But even though her father retired from the same company in which he'd been employed for years, her family was enormously self sufficient. "We had to be. We could never trust our security to the white world."

"My mother made quilts and all the kids' clothes. And we'd can during the summer . . . anything that could go in a jar went in a jar—pears, peaches, tomatoes, string beans, squash, pickled cucumbers. With the lid tightly on, the food could last for months. We even made jelly out of berries and apples. We had some chickens and pigs so we didn't have to go to the store much. We'd even take homegrown corn and have it ground up into cornmeal, then store it in big, heavy sacks. There was lots of sugar cane around and we'd suck on the sweet fiber during summer, sometimes taking it to a nearby mill to be made into molasses. The white folks could fire us but we weren't going to starve to death."

"There was a pond nearby for swimming and fishing, and with as many brothers and sisters as we had, you were seldom lonely. But despite a certain insular existence, the fact that I was black was driven home in pounding blows at an early age. I'd look out the bus window each morning and pass an all-white school only ten minutes from where I lived—and then proceed for another forty-five minutes to a school for us black children."

Perhaps it was best, I thought. She would have been mortified to witness the Friday morning pep rallies, climaxed each week by a rousing rendition of "Dixie," Confederate flag and all!

"I remember, downtown, there was a hot dog stand where the white people could go inside, sit down and eat underneath whirling fans, but we couldn't go in. Instead, there was a tiny window marked 'Colored,' and if we wanted anything to eat, we'd have to twist our heads to order and then wait there for them to slide the food out."

"On Saturday nights, the Klansmen would come out and do their 'serenading'—that's what they called it. It would be pitch dark, and they'd drive through our neighborhoods in long processions honking their horns and flashing their headlights. It used to scare us children to death when Daddy told us who they were and what they would do. But I think the worst memory I have, worse than the Klan, worse than the hot dog stand, the one I'll never forget is the time I had a terrible toothache. I was only twelve and I was in horrible pain. We didn't have a car, so my mother called Mrs. Green, who she did cleaning for, and asked her if she'd take me to the dentist. When Mrs. Green arrived, I was so relieved I jumped into the front seat and sidled up next to her, whereupon, she looked down at me and said, 'No, child, you're going to have to sit in the back seat. You're colored.' I don't think I'll ever forget that incident. I was just so hurt."

Her words came back to me as I drove toward the tent show, past pine trees and dark gray limbs left bare for the coming winter.

I spotted the tent show a few miles past what could only be described as a crossroads, a feed store and a railroad track comprising the center of a small town. The show was set up in the middle of a large cornfield. Fifty or so pick-up trucks and old cars were parked in front of an entrance gate where a ticket seller in a booth was selling admission tickets for two dollars.

It was mostly farmers, some with their families and some alone, that were wandering the grounds. From what I could see, the admission fee was just the beginning. Eager children tugged at their fathers' overalls for money to play the games or catch the rides. In fact, it was more of a carnival than a circus, with the only real link to the circus being a few freak shows, which most of the reputable circuses had discontinued years ago. Nevertheless, a sheep with five legs and a horse with six toes were on display for the enticing price of fifty cents. An outside poster showed the sheep bounding gracefully on all five legs, but in actuality, the fifth leg hung uselessly from a rear hip, and the horse, I discovered, had only partially developed its hoof, giving the appearance of six small toes. It occurred to me the value of admission was far more to witness the disparity between reality and the advertising than it was to see the freak of nature itself. The main attraction, a show that didn't start until the evening, was the "wall of death." A colorful billboard illustrated a man going round and round the inside of a huge wooden cylinder on a big—probably mufflerless—motorcycle.

But it was the games of chance that captivated me. Obviously, there was no way the rubes could win. The best they could often do would be to take home a trinket that was worth a fraction of the cost to play, but it didn't seem to stop them from trying to beat the odds. I was curious about the games, but even more curious about how the carnies pinched the locals with seemingly little guilt. As I strolled past a milk can toss and a farmer's kid trying to pitch pennies onto a plate, I spotted a man sitting alone near one of the tents. "A little out of season for a tent show," I said, as I approached him. He looked up at me and nodded, clearly not wishing to be drawn into conversation.

"I'm with Ringling Brothers and Barnum and Bailey," I said, "working out of Savannah doing the advance work."

He took a second glance. "No kidding. I used to work for the Ringlings back in the fifties. Sold tickets to the menagerie, fed the animals, did a bunch of stuff. Does North still run the show?"

"No. He sold out to the Felds about six years ago."

He blushed a bit, unable to hide he'd lost touch with the big shows. Like many carnies, he had a double look. Weather-beaten and ruggedly handsome on one hand, but with some obvious flaw on the other. Because of his well manicured mustache and piercing, blue eyes, I mentally imagined him in a Wall Street suit, but then just as quickly discarded the notion, as I noticed the broken blood vessels on his nose and cheeks from too much drink. Carnivals seemed to be full of the also-rans. Charming enough to con your socks off, but seedy enough to look painfully deficient, even inside their own surroundings.

"Are these games real money makers?" I asked.

"Aw, this is chicken shit stuff," he said, unfastening his jacket to reveal a hole in his sweater. "Penny ante crap. But it's legal."

"Is that an issue?" I said, trying to balance my naivete with my curiosity while hoping to win his trust.

"Yeah, the FBI's been tough this year. They've closed three shows that I know of, for fraud. See, the local jurisdictions will allow games of chance, but if it looks like the customer doesn't have a chance in hell, then you get busted for fraud. Razzle Dazzle is a good example."

"Razzle Dazzle?"

"Yeah. It's also known as 'Roll Down.' I heard a doctor in South Carolina lost $76,000 playing it. Hell, the FBI even gave one of their agents five-hundred dollars for shake-down money. The guy got so caught up in the game, he spent the five hundred and then a thousand of his own!"

He smiled. "It's called Razzle Dazzle because we make them think they can win big money, but then we razzle dazzle their money away. The way it works is we have a playing surface shaped like a football field with a bunch of holes and either numbers or letters next to the holes. The numbers correspond to a conversion chart that equals yardage gained. If the player gets a hundred yards, he wins a ton of money. The player gets eight marbles, and after paying for each throw he tosses the marbles onto the board."

"So what's the problem?"

"The problem is he can't win."

"Why not?"

"It's simple, cause we keep changing the rules. First of all, the numbers on the board never correspond to the conversion chart. We cheat in his favor in the beginning to get him hooked. Then when he's up around eighty yards, we start playing it straight. To make matters worse, we change the meaning of the letters beside the holes to suit our purpose. Say it says HP beside the hole. That could be half a point or house prize, in which case, we give him a stuffed dog and end the game. Believe me, we'll get him to ninety-nine yards and drain his savings before he ever wins that last yard."

I looked at the farmers, living from crop to crop, and was amazed at the pride in which the carny told me how easily people were swindled. It struck me that to him this was a craft, no less worthy than any other, and if you became good enough at it, you were just as deserving of the spoils. He took a special delight in telling me about the games that exploited science in their perfidy. One was the "Pendulum," which the carny would adjust every now and then to let somebody win, but otherwise, it was simply a matter of physics. A bowling pin was propped on a table, and in order to win, you had to hit it from behind with a weight on the end of a string that you released, but from the angle it was set up, if you missed the pin by only a fraction of an inch on the right, you would miss the pin on the return by the exact same amount on the left.

The carny said he liked the simple cons, deflated balloons a dart couldn't pop, and anything metal that rolled or dropped could easily be influenced by magnets, but he reserved his true appreciation for the games requiring legerdemain, *sleight-of-hand*, for these required a practical skill, and of course, there was always the element of risk. "You could get caught."

"The best known of the sleight-of-hand cons is the shell game," he said.

I told him as much as I'd seen it, I didn't have the foggiest idea how it worked.

"I'll demonstrate," he said, enjoying letting me in on the secret. "Pretend there's three shells on the table, and I put a pea under one of the shells." He lifted a small stone from the dirt under his chair and placed it on his thigh. "Now while the rube is watching the shells slide rapidly around, the carny has got the pea under his thumb the whole time."

"I don't get it."

"It's easy. Watch as I show you." He placed the small stone under the first knuckle of his thumb. "See, as I slide my thumb backwards, the pea moves forward and, conversely, as I slide my thumb forward, the pea moves backward. If I was moving a shell, I could slide it in and out of the shell at will." He grinned as he moved a soiled hand through his dark hair.

"That's incredible," I said. We talked a few more minutes, then he said he had to go back to work, so I said goodbye. I strolled across the dusty field to my car, repelled by this occupational cousin of mine, while at the same time enjoying a strange fascination, a privilege he'd taken me into his confidence. But despite what my father had said, I was no carny. Once in Cleveland I'd bargained with the owner of a small radio station for far more than I'd given in return and it wasn't a feeling I liked.

Chapter 32
A LONELY BENCH

I was worried I was wrong, that Savannah might be tougher to promote than a major market, the businessmen reluctant to experiment outside the advertising mainstream. But I was surprised how easy the first few promotions fell into place.

My first break came with the CBS television station. I'd pitched the "underprivileged kids" promotion, part-cash, part-trade, to the station sales manager. "I very much doubt it," he said, citing their commanding ratings. But the next morning, in a far more conciliatory tone, he asked if I'd come in and meet the General Manager. Unbeknownst to him, the General Manager had a need to win community points.

I was ushered into a formal reception area, then led down a long corridor and into a shaded office. "Sit down, please, Mr. MacVicar." I was startled to see a man half hidden in shadow, pudgy, almost albino looking, with a queasy smile. Warner Brothers, I thought, couldn't have cast this better. Any second I expected him to begin stroking a Persian cat while calmly describing his intent to blow up the globe. "Ah'm told you have an interesting proposition," he said.

I filled him in on the details. He listened patiently, then clasped his hands together, smiling. "Ah believe, Mr. MacVicar, this is a grand idea. Ah'm sure our sales manager will be most happy to work out the particulars."

With less theatrical flair, the *Savannah Morning News* agreed to a color-the-clown contest, the top radio station accepted the king and queen promotion, and the car dealer bought the test-drive ticket give-away. Savannah was turning out easier than I thought. Partly due, I suspected, to Mike Frank's secondary advice. "When negotiating, don't forget there are stated, obvious needs and then there are hidden but no less important needs. For example, the radio salesman has to sell air time but he may also be bucking for a promotion. The details of the deal may solve the first need but it's positive reinforcement that serves the second."

So far I was well ahead of schedule and I sent Mike media reports, letters of agreement and strategy thoughts daily. It wasn't enough to be good. I was determined to show Mike I'd be one of the best.

A luxury I didn't have in Savannah was Peter Halbin—a public relations guru—and after four months of observing him, I'd come to the conclusion that public relations was considerably more than sending out press releases. For one thing, P.R. firms were often called in for crisis management. A prominent client is the subject of a newspaper article that rips him apart, a national hockey team suddenly has four players accused of gang rape, a public company commits a major environmental disaster. There's no end to unexpected catastrophes, and the participants, in the moment, are in no state of emotion to know how to handle the onslaught.

"Sometimes," Peter said, "no response is better than an immediate response. I knew a man whose organization was subject to particularly bad press, but in my view, it was outrageously unbelievable, and besides that, it was a one-day story. I strongly advised he ignore it. Instead, he wrote a detailed letter defending every accusation and mailed it to his clients. The sheer amount of response led the recipients to suspect he had something to hide, and in effect, he threw fuel on a fire that would otherwise have quickly burned out. The dumb schmuck!"

I also watched Peter's staff write speeches for clients, help direct their clients into the right clubs, coach their clients on how to speak and how to appear before television. They rounded up celebrity endorsements, organized press kits, created photo opportunities and occasionally produced audio-visual shows.

Most P.R. pros are exceptional writers (although Peter Halbin, to my amazement, could barely spell, but he made up for it in the shmooze department), and often wrote and edited their clients' magazines and newsletters. They frequently influenced and lobbied legislators and, furthermore, organized, promoted and directed annual meetings, conferences and fund raising events, not to mention press conferences, open houses, award dinners, workshops, international business symposiums and charity balls. "A really good P.R. pro," Peter indicated, "not only makes sure the client attends the right functions, he may even sweet talk the host into assuring the right seating mates. Hell, we'll even rescue a client from a bore on the right cue. One client simply tugged her right earlobe and we'd tactfully whisk her away."

I slipped in a press release about lions and tigers and carefully sealed the envelope. For a moment, I was tempted to embellish it with a few lesser known facts. Earlier one afternoon, I'd stumbled on a water stained book written in the 1930s. The author, Tyrwhitt Drake, would have earned the enmity of Edgar Rice Burroughs' protagonist. He captured wild animals, held them in captivity, then sold them to traveling European circuses.

"Animals are no less subject to the law of supply and demand," Drake said, "than any other product. And the more available a particular species, the less it commands in price. The weather," he cited, "is also a factor. The warmer seasons, when the shows are traveling, produce the highest price. Partly because most of the animals are captured in Africa and their chances for survival are far greater when they can slowly acclimate to the colder climates."

"Male animals are especially untrustworthy," he went on to say. "Sooner or later, sometime in their life, they'll prove dangerous. Lion cubs only weigh two-and-a-half pounds when born, despite the fact they'll grow to five-hundred pounds as adults, consuming as much as sixteen-pounds of meat a day. Yet it's a mistake to think they're anything but wild, even as babies." But the author reserved his strongest reproach to the docile, yet underestimated bear.

"Keeping one in captivity is impossible. They can easily rip the floorboards out of the bottom of a cage and bend one-inch iron bars with their powerful arms. It's also a myth they kill their prey by suffocating them with a bear hug. What's more likely is they'll pull you toward them and then rip you to shreds with their claws. And forget fending them off with a whip or a chair. That may work with a lion but it only makes a bear madder. He won't even stop for a breath."

I was fascinated by the grisly details but his arguments for animal captivity were selfishly callous at best—excepting perhaps one. A menagerie owner took pity on a small herd of caged bison, so he constructed a two-acre, fenced-in field instead. Unfortunately, the bison mysteriously began dying, with no explanation in sight, until it was discovered they were soiling the grass, then eating their own waste. The more open yet still confined space provided more freedom, but in the end wound up killing the herd.

I sealed another envelope, deciding these factoids were better left undisclosed. I glanced out the window. The sky had turned dark. And at the moment I was consumed by another thought. It was Friday night, the weekend had arrived and I was dreading it. It was a three-day weekend and as I watched the last of the agency's staff head out the door for home, I felt an uneasiness grow in my stomach. The Bahamas trip had worn off and as Savannah's winter emptied the streets, casting a gray veil over the city, I felt a sense of loneliness return. I fiddled with the handle on my briefcase. Where's that steely resolve? I'll just have to fight it, I chastised myself, and slowly stood up and exited through the glass door.

※

Maybe it's living out of a hotel room, I lamented, as I flopped down on my bed. The four walls just seem to close in around me. Someday, I won't give a shit *what* the house looks like, I just want a never-ending series of rooms. As I lay there, gazing at the ceiling, I found myself suddenly struggling for a sense of purpose. Most of the important work had been done, yet it was still weeks before tickets went on sale. I was in the great Serengeti of the campaign. For the moment, I couldn't even feel a sense of accomplishment.

Maybe I had too much time on my hands. Time to reflect. Time I didn't have in Cleveland to dwell on the notion that most of my life was now wrapped in the circus. Maybe if I keep busy it will pass, I thought. I wandered into the bathroom and stared in the mirror. "Come on, let's get the hell out of here."

Savannah's tourist literature boasted of being home to four forts built in the 1800s. I was no buff on military history, but it might be fun, I thought, to see what an old fort looks like. Fort Pulaski appeared to be the largest, so I drove east, meandering past marshlands, until I reached a square, gray stronghold on a grassy plain, jutting toward the Atlantic Ocean. Built to guard a sea-approach to Savannah, two moats had to be crossed before entering the fort over a wide, wooden drawbridge. Unfortunately, a cold drizzle, reflecting my mood, had begun to fall. Saturday afternoon or not, it was still the dead of winter. The fort was almost deserted. Two small children clung to their father's coat, braced against the wind, and a young couple's laughter echoed across the parade grounds, toward where I stood by a large, black cannon pointing out to sea. I could barely see them. A wisp of blond hair and a black leather jacket swung playfully between a row of brick arches. How I wish it were me, I thought, whisking her back to a cozy, crackling fire. I smiled at the thought, then watched her friend guide her away by the waist. I ran my hand along the top of the cannon's barrel where the water from the drizzle formed a thousand tiny puddles. My hand turned red and hurt from the cold. Suddenly, the fort didn't seem such a good idea. As the wind whipped across my face, my throat began to tighten, and I walked toward my car.

I left and headed back to Savannah. The sun hung low as I stepped into a windowed cafeteria that I sometimes visited when my pockets were light and my stomach empty. For $3.95, the sign said, you could eat as much of the basics as your taste buds could handle. Hot gravy was glopped over green beans, mashed potatoes and southern cooked chicken. Usually, the place was filled with businessmen and storekeepers, but today I was the only patron. I wondered why they had bothered to open.

By Sunday, the drizzle had turned into a downpour, so I stayed in the room, spending my time between television and trying to draw the old house with the live oak tree. Artistic talent was genetic, and I was lucky to have inherited enough of it to lose myself in a sketch pad and a number two pencil. There was always a sense of accomplishment duplicating another artist's work, even if it was just a copy. Between the steadily falling rain and my hours of drawing, I fell asleep early and slept soundly until the following morning.

When I awoke, I was struck by the stillness of the day. The errand runners of Saturday and church goers of Sunday had returned to their homes for the Monday holiday. It was a cold morning. But it had stopped raining. I dressed warmly and left the hotel. I walked northward, and in the quiet of the morning, I realized that other than to say, "May I please have another cup of coffee," I hadn't talked to another human being for the past three days. There wasn't a soul out, just the gray skies. An abandoned paper bag lifted by the wind, was transported to my feet. "If only you could talk," I said. What I'd give to have someone, just for a moment, to share a thought.

I walked for a while and finally came to one of the city's little squares and sat down on a park bench. I thought of John Huskisson and how he'd left on Friday with a smile on his face. He had a full house for the weekend, he said, and a feast to prepare. I thought of the Cleveland suburbs and the families I'd so easily scorned, derided for their sense of structure, their escape from adventure and excitement. And then I thought of my wife . . . her wispy, blond hair . . . what they all might be doing right now . . . and I started to cry.

Chapter 33
ASHAMED

The start of the week is not normally what most people cherish. But as I walked into the agency's office, it couldn't have come soon enough. Even Henry, the kooky artist with whom I shared an office, was a welcome respite from three days of solitude. But as I watched the others resettle into their work week it was obvious they were centered and I was not. I wondered if they noticed a slight desperation in my demeanor. I opened my briefcase. The weekend was over and I was again surrounded by colleagues and co-workers. Surely any lingering despair would soon dissipate.

But as the week droned on I focused more and more inward, not so much on what was causing my loneliness but instead on what could bring it to an end. The solution seemed painfully obvious. I needed the companionship of a woman. Not just any woman, a bonding relationship, a spiritual blending of two souls each caring deeply for the other. Just the thought of it enlivened my senses. Someone to make me feel whole again instead of this emotional cripple I was rapidly becoming. The vision of her consumed my thoughts, but the solution was nowhere in the offing. I opened my binder and reviewed my schedule. Maybe if I threw myself into work I wouldn't think about it.

Perhaps I could have picked a better task for the week than group sales. Cold calling organizations wasn't the most uplifting of activities. But it helped fill the void. Sales were light, but I consoled myself with the hope I'd sell plenty of tickets at full price once the bulk of my campaign got underway.

Fortunately, the final day of the week, a young lady, Sarah, from the box office called to say our tickets had arrived. It was a good enough excuse to call a halt to my sales prospecting. Late afternoon, I marched over to the Civic Center to review the seating manifest. Preparations inside were being made for a revival that evening and the box office was busy selling tickets. Sarah hollered out she would be my daily contact once tickets went on sale. She handed me the manifest to sign, pointing to a large chart of the arena's seating configuration on a nearby wall. It struck me she was far more hospitable than most box office personnel, who generally preferred to keep seating locations obscured from the public's view. From the vantage point of the box office I'm sure it limited dickering, especially the night of the event when lines were long. Confirming the seating manifest's accuracy, I waved goodbye to Sarah and departed for the weekend.

The day had turned colder as I walked across the parking lot. I wondered how many northerners knew how cold the temperatures in the south can get. Then again, I wasn't sure the southerners knew either. The hotel bedspread and blankets were as thin as wafers.

It looked just as cold when I awoke Saturday morning. I gazed out the window. The sun was hidden behind overcast skies. I watched a squirrel scamper along a limb. The streets would once again be devoid of sound and human activity, as though the weather had declared itself a silent victor. It was winter mornings like these, in the redwood home in La Grange, that I remembered my father lacing his hunting boots, stuffing packs of cigarettes inside his canvas jacket. Unshaven, dressed comfortably, in contrast to the three-piece suit he'd hung up the night before, he seemed drawn to another world, eschewing the tidy attire the business world required.

I felt flattered when he'd ask me to join him, wanting to hunt for something. I dared not ask him what. I just wanted to watch him. To study his every move.

My father's personality was so strong it would cling to my

thoughts long after we parted. But he was an elusive, mysterious figure with interests so intense, diverse and fleeting that by the time I ventured forth with a mutual interest, he'd long passed the initial enthusiasm I still embraced. Nor could I predict how he'd respond to an interest of mine. But to me, he could do no wrong. And little was more important to me than to earn his approval. He had the power of Zeus, the power to make Apollos of his sons, golden-haired charioteers able to steer white stallions across the sky. And for a time, I was made to feel as though I, too, could do no wrong. But that was soon to change, for like Zeus, my father had a darker side.

I wish Sam Barrett was around, I reflected, as the morning slipped into afternoon. Sam's self-deprecating humor always made light of any situation. Nancy Pond had said he was in between towns. There was no way of reaching him. A chat with Sam at a dismal moment could be a bridge through a long weekend.

Some people, I heard, had mastered inner peace and harmony without the company of others for years. I wish I knew their technique. What did they know that I didn't? It was baffling. I'd always been so sure of myself. Why had I now become so dependent on the affirmation of others? I dreamed again of the beautiful lady whose heart I'd steal, if only I could find her, of sunlit picnics and gentle conversations. There was a purity in my vision, a reflection of all that was good and serene.

Dusk had come slowly. It was Saturday night. Once again I felt the room closing in around me. Perhaps Savannah's river front could offer some solace. Maybe I might even meet someone. I pulled on a nice sweater, ambled downstairs, crossed Oglethorpe Avenue and headed east toward the Savannah River. It was almost four blocks to the historic section, where the cotton factors once worked.

Shrouded in fog, the stone warehouses loomed above the upper city's streets. A flock of white pigeons, cast in light, swirled around an old church spire. Carefully I descended down the narrow steps, feeling water trickle along the rocks over soft moss. The clatter of busy merchants echoed in my imagination as I felt my way down the dark corridor. At the bottom an abandoned railroad track ran down the middle of the road. The streets were so quiet many of the establishments had closed, but one, the Bull's Horn, still had a yellow light glowing outside its door.

I walked in. Like an English pub, the interior had stained glass windows, whitewashed walls and rich, wooden paneling. Ship models and artifacts from the sea were scattered around the nooks and corners. I noticed only one man sat at the bar on the far left side. He was a black man dressed fancy in a white linen suit. I chose a seat two stools down and ordered a beer. Expecting to nurse my drink in silence, I was surprised when he turned, greeting me with a warm look.

"Are you a traveling salesman?" he asked, showing genuine interest.

"No, I'm in advertising," I said.

"No kidding," he said, now shifting his whole body toward me, displaying a pair of two-toned shoes. "I'm a photographer."

"Wow, that's great," I said. "What kind of photography do you do?"

"I'm a fashion photographer," he said. We talked openly about how liberating it was to work in the arts. "Can I buy you a drink?" he asked. He was as smooth as ice, gliding effortlessly through the conversation, not saying anything particularly profound, but somehow making me feel important, as thought I was being praised for something I didn't know I did.

"Do you have a girlfriend?" he asked.

"No, I'm kind of new in the city." And then I said, "Actually, to be honest, it's been kind of tough. I really haven't met anybody."

"Yeah man," he said, with a sigh, "being alone can be a drag." The bartender handed me a second beer. "But I'll tell you what. Since I'm a fashion photographer it just so happens I have one of my models traveling with me. How would you like to meet her?"

"Pardon?" I replied, unsure I'd heard him correctly.

"She's not that far from here. She's really beautiful! But like I told her, if you're going to be a model you know you've got to pay some dues."

For a moment I couldn't speak. He wasn't a photographer. He was a pimp. Who was this woman? Was she a prostitute or did she really believe this was the kind of dues you had to pay to become a model?

My mind raced with all the reasons why I should get up and leave. But I couldn't move. In some primitive way it was a glass of cool water being offered in the midst of a parched, barren desert.

"How much?" I asked nervously.

"Thirty dollars," he said. His smile was now slick and beckoning. He was the one in control. Suddenly I felt I'd become a duplicitous member of this threesome, but as captured prey.

"I don't have it in cash. Will you take a check?" I said, hating myself for the sounds of pleading, wondering what happened to my staunch refusal in Cleveland.

"Sure man," he said. "I'll give her a call. Where you staying?"

"The Downtowner Inn."

"That's great. She ain't but a few blocks from there. I'll tell her to wait across the street." He returned from the phone booth. "Okay," he said.

"It was nice meeting you," I said, and I immediately regretted it.

She was standing near a tree, partly hidden in the shadows yet close enough to a street lamp to reveal her features. I'm not sure what I expected, but this frail, young woman wasn't it. Dressed in plain white shoes, a dress with a collar and a light wool overcoat, she looked more like she was going to church than to give her body to a stranger. She acted nervous, almost as nervous as me. So I just smiled a little sheepishly.

"Hello," I said and touched her on the arm.

She followed me without saying a word. I opened the door to my room, inviting her inside. Taking off her coat, she unveiled a dress far too thin for the winter's cold.

"My name is Wanda. What's yours?"

"Jamie," I replied and then clumsily asked, "How long have you been doing this?"

"Only three days," she said timidly. "I'm going to be a model." She paused, "Leon said I needed to pay my dues first."

Shit. She believes him.

"How is it going so far?" I said, weighting curiosity with concern.

"I don't know," she mumbled. "Last night Leon fixed me up with two men. It was awful. They were both drunk." She moved toward the bed. "Do you want me to take off my clothes?"

"I'd really just like to talk."

"Leon will kill me if you don't pay me!" she said, suddenly alarmed.

"No, no, I'll pay you," I quickly replied. "It's just that what I'd really like is some company."

"Okay," she said, still not sure she was doing the right thing.

We talked for awhile, mostly about her dreams of being a fashion model in New York. She said Leon had told her she had what it takes. I was torn. She wasn't even particularly attractive. Anyone could see she didn't have a chance in hell of becoming a model. But how was I to tell her that? When she talked of becoming a model, it was the only time she seemed happy. The dream was all she had. I listened to her, trying to give her a sense of understanding. It was what she needed, and it was something I could give.

I thought I could just talk, just listen . . . but I couldn't. "Would you come over here?" I asked quietly, wanting to hold her.

She nodded and moved from the edge of the bed to where I was sitting. "Am I too heavy?" she asked. "No, you're perfect," I said. Her body was light, her skin soft. I touched her face, breathing in her smells, hoping maybe she alone could cure the pain and emptiness I'd been feeling. I wanted her. But even more desperately, I needed her. I looked into her eyes and slowly unbuttoned the top of her dress, revealing a white laced bra that only covered her partly. I reached in and gently pulled out her breasts. Her nipples were long and soft. I placed one in my mouth and suckled her, much as a baby would seek nourishment from its mother. Afterwards, we had sex. I didn't want to, for her sake. But I did.

She left the room by herself. I wanted to drive her, but she wouldn't let me. Instead, she folded my check, placed it into a small pocketbook and walked out into the frozen air, leaving her smells behind to linger on my sheets.

Instead of feeling full, I felt ashamed. Shitty. Why didn't I just tell her the truth? Who was I kidding? I might not have changed anything. But I could have tried. Maybe I could have at least planted a thought about what was happening before it was too late. Instead, my own needs overrode simple human caring. And worst of all, she was being fed an illusion. Thanks to that son-of-a-bitch, Leon, her ultimate downfall would be far worse.

Why would anyone abuse someone like that? What did she do to deserve it? Suddenly, I was angry. I was angry at myself. And I was angry at Leon. I hated his guts. And slowly, just as surely, I felt another rage, a rage that had festered for years. I was angry at my father. He, too, knew what he was doing. But he did it anyway. What possibly could he gain? The memories came rushing back, nights I'd hidden deep inside. I thought of Wanda and Leon. She feared him, yet revered him. She would do anything to win his approval, even debasing her body and soul. What was most important to her? To be a model. The paragon of physical beauty. Yet even that which she most coveted would she destroy to gain his love. I knew too well what she had done. For I too had done it to myself.

My father seemed to have everything going for him. I'm not even sure how it started. My mother said it was the New York crowd. Cocktails and drinking were the Madison Avenue way of doing business. But after we moved south, the drinking intensified. It brought out a mean streak. At the start it was moments of biting sarcasm, but the verbal abuse got worse. It could last for hours, three or four at a time, seldom less than two or three nights a week. I can still remember the words, the look of disgust on his face when his demeanor would suddenly change. "You know, son. You know what's become clear to me. Your mother has finally won. She's turned you into a mama's boy, a goddamn namby pamby."

Invariably his drink would spill on the floor. Then he'd switch to my sister, sitting expressionless beside me, neither of us allowed to move. "As for Buddha, she thinks she can get through life on her good looks. Well, let me advise you, young lady, you can sit there and glare at me all night, but with your lazy attitude you're heading for a trailer park and a mill worker for a husband." We'd watch the ash on his cigarette grow longer as he became fixated on his own words, hoping when it fell, maybe it would divert his attention.

Then as I grew older, the dialogue would change. He seemed to know how to strike at the core of your self perception. "You're not a people person, are you, son? I know you don't want to hear this, but you're a cold fish. And don't think my friends don't see it." Ironically, I'd fight back tears as he denounced my insensitivity.

Finally, the booze and endless diatribes would wear him out. He'd storm off to bed. I'd lay awake, telling myself he didn't mean what he said, it was only the drink.

I prayed some morning he'd take me aside and say, "I'm sorry, son. I didn't mean what I said last night," but he didn't. I wanted to cry out and shake him, but I never did. For like a Jekyll and Hyde, he was also kind and caring, seductively immersing himself in self pity. As a result, I was punished twice, once for absorbing my own pain and again for absorbing his.

I had tried not to think about how worthless I felt, but even now, it penetrated my life. The affection from others had been my emotional lifeline, but in a twisted way, even that he sometimes thwarted. While he lauded his own friends it became apparent that not only was I worthless, so too was anyone who held me in regard.

It wasn't long before my anger turned inward. And it didn't help any that I was on the verge of deserting my wife, a shame that was tearing me apart. After two years of struggles, I earned my degree. But with no job on the horizon, and not a dime to our name, we were at our wit's end. I had to find shelter somehow, a place for my wife and me to live, if only for a short while. With nowhere else to turn I approached my mother. "Could you help, just for a month or two, until I find a job?"

"Of course," she said," And your wife, where will she live?"

My body sagged under the weight of her words. Even if, unaccountably, her intentions were good, without saying so, it was obvious that as a couple we weren't welcome. It was the final blow to my already fragile marriage.

Escape was my only option. Now as I tried to understand my actions, I realized I was caught in an impossible conflict. To earn the love and affection of my parents I sought desperately their approval, yet in the very face of that quest, I destroyed the one thing, my marriage, that was providing the only love and emotional support I had. There were other options. Options I should have taken, but it was as though the size of the sacrifice was in direct proportion to the love and acceptance I craved, especially in the face of contempt I so often experienced. I ended the marriage with a callous determination, numbing myself to my wife's feelings. And for that, I could not forgive myself. I was ashamed, ashamed to have betrayed my wife's love in a futile attempt to win the love of my parents and ashamed to have harbored the secret inside, never telling my wife what drove me away . . . a shame that now tore at me with disgust for my cowardly retreat. All I could remember were the tears running down her face as I did what I didn't want to do, but felt compelled to do nonetheless. Now, as I remember her sitting on her bed pleading with me not to leave, I despised my parents, but even more, I hated myself.

I walked out onto the hotel balcony, gripped the black iron railing and stared down at the pavement below. Tears welled up in my eyes as I once again remembered the joy I felt when she walked down the aisle. I grabbed the railing tightly, wondering what it would be like to dive off, my arms held firmly to my sides as my brains splattered on the asphalt below. Maybe then I could punish myself for the suffering I had caused my wife. It would be so simple. I'd lost all faith in family and walked away from. . . .

"Are you okay buddy?" I looked over to see a man standing outside his room a few doors down. I hadn't even heard him come out. Jarred, I hollered back, "Yes. I'm all right," and then watched him return inside.

I looked down at my knuckles, white from gripping the iron railing, sucked in the frigid air and suddenly felt angry. God damn it. That's it. I'm tired of the pain. . They can't hurt me anymore. And I can't hurt her. I refuse to think about it, any of it. Somewhere there's light-haired women, orange sunsets and lone seagulls following in my wake. Fuck 'em! Fuck all of 'em! And I noticed the marquee off in the distance, brightly lit against the darkened sky, boldly announcing the coming of the circus. I haven't lost everything. Not yet. Not by a long shot. I've still got the circus. I'll call Mike tomorrow. I'll tell him I want more to do. And when that place is filled with people and they know who did it, nobody, nobody can take that away. I'm going to be the best. I don't care if it kills me. I'm going to be the best they ever had.

Chapter 34
MY SAVING GRACE

My new attitude gave me an almost magical strength. The more I focused on the circus and what I could achieve, the less pain I felt. It was as though I'd taken a powerful drug, turning feelings of guilt and rejection into a newfound sense of worth. I doubled my efforts, visiting the nearby Army base, newspapers and small towns, promulgating promotional deals. I even crafted a speech on marketing the circus, asking John Huskisson to generate a few speaking engagements. But as busy as I became, I wasn't taking chances. "Things are fine," I said, when Mike called for his weekly update, "but in the future, please give me more to do. Four months to promote one small town is just too much."

"I'll see what I can do," Mike said, sounding empathetic to my request.

Two other events radically changed my outlook. The first was the fact that tickets finally went on sale. Now I could chart daily the results of my efforts. Each evening, I'd anxiously call the box office for the day's results, comparing each day's sales to the year before, then studying the cumulative totals. Thus far I was ahead by ten percent. My hard work was paying off. But there was another reason for my change of spirit. It was Sarah. Each day, I found myself looking forward to not only the numbers, but to hearing her voice.

At first she was strictly business, but then she began teasing me. "I swear," she said, "you're the hardest working promoter I know."

It was sometimes slow in the box office late afternoons when I phoned and gradually we began chatting about things other than ticket sales. She was divorced, she said, had one small son and had lived most her life on a farm. She'd worked at the Civic Center for the past three years but had ambitions to return to college. She wanted to be a teacher. Finally, late one afternoon, I asked her if she'd join me for a cup of coffee. "I'd love to," she said, her voice pleasantly rising. "I thought you'd never ask."

Suddenly, I had it all. The numbers were way ahead of last year's. I wasn't just stumbling anymore, I was racing at the top, and now I had a woman in my life, someone who cared. The circus was only two short weeks away. I marveled at how I'd finally found happiness, even if there was little time left. I looked back at where I'd been and vowed I'd never go through such misery again.

The first signs of light broke through the pine trees as the train rolled round the bend. I quickly finished my last gulp of coffee. Working men leapt off the train, keeping noise to a minimum so as not to waken the passengers. Charlie Bauman acknowledged my wave. Lloyd Morgan sauntered close behind.

"So how are ticket sales?" Charlie asked.

"We're up ten percent over last year!"

"Good! Irvin will like that. Maybe for a few days he'll get off my ass."

Lloyd chose not to comment, seemingly content to ride to the Civic Center in silence. He didn't seem concerned about the rigging of the show either. "This one's pretty standard," he shrugged.

I pointed out the location of my office and quickly returned to the train. Sitting in the pie car, I anxiously awaited Charlie King. We'd only spoken twice, but even from a distance I admired him. Only twenty two, he had already developed a knack for relaxing those around him, helped no doubt by an easy gait and natural smile. Certainly an asset in first coaxing, then keeping, ten ambitious kids from the ghetto glued purposefully together.

"I'd like to, but I can't. What I do for one promoter I'm afraid I have to do for the others," he explained. "Cycling into unpredictable neighborhoods sets an uncomfortable precedent."

I wasn't quite sure what was so uncomfortable about it but I trusted his reluctance. "Well, could I at least have Keywash and a few others for an early morning television studio appearance?"

"Absolutely! What time do you need them?"

"Seven thirty tomorrow morning, here at the pie car."

The animal walk succeeded without a hitch. Thanking the reporters I dashed around to the front of the Civic Center. Long lines were formed outside the box office windows. Sarah saw me and smiled. "It looks like you've sold out the opening night performance!" Excited, I walked inside the arena, remembering the black and white photo hanging in Brad Rosenberg's office.

Axel Gautier stood near the center ring, watching a woman inside the cage. Another man stood calmly by, keeping an eye on a black puma being led across a tightrope. I sidled up next to him. "Is that a hard trick?"

"We don't teach tricks," he said, not minding the intrusion, "we only get them to do what they already do instinctively, only to do it on cue." I hadn't really thought about it like that. "Take the seal. To a human being, bouncing and balancing a ball on your nose is very difficult, but to a seal, it's a skill they already have. It's neck is very flexible. And it can turn it's head almost 360 degrees. In its arctic environment, it can naturally bounce fish from its nose to its mouth. It's a skill they already have. The same principal works for all the animal acts. You can only teach them to do what they already do instinctively." I wasn't sure whether he was over simplifying or not, but it certainly sounded logical to me.

As I strolled back toward the dressing rooms I tried to think of what natural talent we homo-sapiens deployed. Complaining, I suppose.

Only a few performers were milling around so I was surprised to see Michu sitting on a box outside clown alley, looking sullen.

"Anything wrong?" I asked, concerned by his look of consternation. He wanted to go into town, he said, but his chaperone was nowhere to be found. A Yugoslavian performer, I'd heard, accompanied Michu whenever he ventured out in public, not because of his celebrity, but rather because he might be trampled by large dogs or ebullient children. Even inside the arena he was in danger. He was once knocked down by an acrobat rushing to make cue and spent a painful week recovering. "I haven't seen him," I said, "but if I do, I'll let him know you're looking for him."

I observed a few dirty icicles still clinging to the train's windows as I waited outside the pie car. Feeling cold, I glanced at my watch. Seven thirty-five. Where the hell were the men from the King Charles troupe? Ten minutes passed. Then five more. Frantic, I asked a roustabout to show me Charlie King's cabin.

Charlie answered the door, groggily. "Where are they?" I stammered, "The interview starts in twenty minutes!"

"They didn't show up? Damn!" Charlie pulled on a shirt and rushed down the narrow corridor, banging on metal doors. Keywash, the troupe's designated comic, stuck his head out his door. "I'm sorry man. We played poker half the night. Give us just a second!"

Keywash and two others stumbled down the steps, shoving three unicycles into the car trunk, apologizing all the way to the station. With only a minute to spare we raced inside. The studio was dark. The show's host, fastidiously dressed, sat in his office. "We're ready!" I said.

"It's too late," he spat, too disgusted to look up. "I canceled the show. The first time in twenty years."

I slowly drove back to the train. The only consolation I had was the performers felt worse than I did, and at least I'd have a chip to cash in for the next town.

By late afternoon the arena was bristling with pre-show activity. I could barely get to my office, as wardrobe mistresses noisily wheeled crates of costumes to the dressing rooms. When it came to the costumes, I had to admire Irvin. Like David Selznik in his production of *Gone with the Wind*, Feld spared no cost on quality, all the way down to the lace. "Even if the audience can't see it," Irvin said, "the performers can feel it and will project it in their stride and self esteem."

With twenty minutes remaining, families streamed through the turnstiles; the sounds of cotton candy spinning and popcorn popping permeating the air. Shouts of concessions being sold and programs hawked rose above the clamor. It was organized confusion, the unruly sounds and smells penetrating my senses.

The last of the crowd scurried in, and from the inside upper tier I could see the lights dim and hear the horns start the show. I skipped down a level, then hurried to the bottom of the arena floor. Charlie King winked as he paraded by, Michu waved, and several show girls smiled, reveling in a sold out house. I smiled back, aglow in a wave of euphoria.

Great news followed good news. Mike Franks called the next morning to congratulate me. But even more importantly, he had my next assignment. "This ought to be all the challenge you can handle," he said. "You're going to Indiana. You'll be promoting Terre Haute and Evansville. The towns are a hundred miles apart, two totally separate markets. The circus will arrive early June, playing each town back-to-back, nine days and seventeen shows in Terre Haute, followed by two days and four shows in Evansville."

"What are my projections?"

"Three hundred and sixty thousand for Terre Haute, eighty thousand for Evansville."

Fantastic, I thought, two towns, not one, and even less time to promote them. "What did we do in each town last year?" I asked.

"Nothing. We haven't played either town in twenty years. It's a brand new game."

I finished the last show in a state of excitement. Not even the building superintendent who undeservedly walked into my office asking to have his palm greased could shake my sense of destiny. And even though I wouldn't see the cash until the end of the year, Savannah had finished $10,000 over projection. With a five percent bonus on a two-day date, I had just earned five hundred dollars!

I could barely sleep that night, tossing and turning, thinking of Indiana, two towns, just three months away. I kept thinking about what Mike had said. The circus hadn't played there in twenty years. Did anyone really know what the numbers could be? They knew I was good, but I'd show them I was great. I'd not only hit their numbers, I'd double them! I smiled at the thought, almost giddy in nervous anticipation.

PART FIVE

INDIANA

Chapter 35
THE DARK, RICH SOIL

"What do you mean Brad Rosenberg quit?" I blurted into the phone. I had just arrived in Terre Haute and called headquarters, expecting to speak to Nancy Pond. Instead, Chris Burskey picked up the phone.

"What the hell happened?" I asked in disbelief.

"He quit. Nancy Pond and Margot are also gone."

"Are you serious?"

"I was shocked too. It all came apart at Madison Square Garden. Nancy and Margot were there helping him. I don't know what happened, but Irvin got pissed off at Nancy and Margot about something, and he fired them. Rosenberg was outraged. He demanded Irvin rehire them on the spot. Irvin refused. So Brad turned around and told him he quit."

"Christ, Rosenberg had to be making fifty grand a year!"

"At least," Burskey agreed. "But he ain't coming back. Allen drove out to his house, I heard, to try to talk him out of it, but Bradley said that was it. He was through."

"What's he going to do?"

"Beats me," Chris replied.

I hung up, called information for Brad's home number and dialed the phone. I let it ring a dozen times, but there was no answer. I picked up my coat. I had to go into town, but I'd try again tonight.

Still stunned, I drove into the center of Terre Haute. Bradley was Irvin's golden-haired boy, his prince among courtiers. How could he resign? I knew tensions had been building, but somehow I felt they needed each other too much to implode. Surely Brad would artfully dodge Irvin's wrath. I tried to focus on the road. I still couldn't imagine him gone. I remembered once in Cleveland, when I didn't think I could stand Mike Franks another minute, I called Rosenberg and grumbled. He listened patiently. Then he asked, "What percentage of your job do you deal with Mike Franks?"

"About ten percent," I replied.

"Well, there you have it," he exclaimed, and I could feel his grin over the phone. "Where else will you find a job that you love ninety percent of the time?"

It was vintage Rosenberg. If he couldn't find a positive spin, nobody could. But his impact on the company didn't come from his sterling salesmanship nor his position as Irvin's chief recruiter. For me, he represented balance, a link to normalcy. Irvin was ragingly unpredictable. Allen was up to his neck in work and Mike Franks could run from hot to cold in a New York minute. Even though I spoke to Rosenberg rarely, just knowing he was there was an island in the storm.

As I drove downtown, trying to become less consumed by my thoughts of Rosenberg, I was dismayed by my new surroundings. Terre Haute was dull. Boring. The buildings all looked stark. Even Indiana State University seemed, from my limited view, a collection of plain brick buildings amidst barren concrete sidewalks. Maybe it was Savannah, I reflected. Had its stately antebellum beauty spoiled me to a normal city?

Carl Bruce indicated his advertising agency was in the Sycamore Building, between Wabash and Ohio streets, five blocks southwest of the Civic Center. "There's nothing fancy about the offices," he said. I turned right at the light. I'd already eliminated two advertising agencies over the phone, but I liked Carl's tone of voice, quiet yet seemingly self-assured. I could also tell he was enthusiastic, which was worth ten points in my book. "Are you kidding?" he replied, "I'd be like a kid in a candy store!"

I climbed three flights of wooden stairs and knocked on the door marked C. M. Bruce Advertising. Carl was eagerly awaiting my arrival. My first impression was that he was about thirty-five years old. Solidly built, wearing thick, unstylish glasses, he had the look of a scholar. But I also sensed a positive energy. This wasn't someone easily defeated.

"Let me tell you about the agency," he exclaimed, leading me back to his office.

"Before you do," I replied, I'd first like to hear about you."

Carl eased back in his chair, pleasantly surprised. He told me he had graduated from Indiana State, just down the street, with a masters degree in television and radio. He'd worked for CBS TV while attending college, starting out in production before switching to media sales. "Leaving television, I became the advertising manager for Smith-Alsop Paint Company, a huge retail operation with sixty stores in ten states. This meant I'd now been on both sides of the fence, as a media seller and now a media buyer, but I also knew the retail business. My father spent his career as a salesman for a wholesale hardware firm. I'd grown up in it. Two years ago," Carl said, "I spotted a void in the market. Terre Haute is the retail hub of a region 150 miles in circumference. There is nowhere else to go. The surrounding area is rolling farmland and the rural families from the outlying villages come to Terre Haute from miles away to do their shopping." Carl smiled. "An appliance store owner who appeared on television commercials once told me with amazement, 'People come into my store just to meet someone who's been on TV.'"

"The city is filled with retail stores—Sears, Roots Department Store, electronics stores—everything the small towns don't have. And with my retail experience, combined with my media background, it only seemed natural to start my own agency. In two short years, even though I only have a staff of four, my agency has grown to one-and-a-half million in billings."

"Well, what do you know about promoting entertainment?"

"Nothing," he replied, and there was a moment of awkward silence, "but no one else in town knows anything about it either."

"Well then," I laughed. "I guess you're hired." I figured he was right, and besides that, he had the local chain of Pizza Huts as an account not to mention several retail stores, all promotional possibilities. "We're going to tear this town up," I declared. "The fee is three-thousand-dollars, guaranteed, plus a five-hundred dollar bonus depending on ticket sales. Do you want it?"

"Just tell me what to do!"

"Good," I said. "For starters, tell me about Terre Haute."

Carl and I talked for the next two hours. He filled me in on the demographics, the media, and the key advertisers I needed to know, but what stood out most was his view of the people. "There is a tiny black population," he said, "no major ethnic groups; predominantly blue-collar families mixed in with a college-town atmosphere. But, I tell you what," he said proudly, "You'll never find nicer, warmer, gentler people. They'll give you the shirts off their backs. This region has strong family values with a healthy spiritual air. Softball, bowling, picnics, everything is centered around the family."

He talked further about his own upbringing, his interests, his wife and four kids. As he went on, it became clear to me, when it came to midwest family values, Carl was the epitome of all he spoke.

It was odd speaking with Brad Rosenberg at his home. Even late at night, on what few times I needed to reach him, I'd always found him at the headquarters office or some distant city. It was even stranger that he seemed so relaxed, at peace with himself.

"Is it true?" I asked, sounding overly plaintive.

"I'm afraid so," he replied.

"Surely, differences can be worked out. I can't believe Irvin would want to lose you."

"I don't know, but I'm afraid there's no going back. Not this time. This has been building for months."

"Any idea what you're going to do?"

"Not right now . . . but I've got a few ideas."

"Well, even though you weren't my direct supervisor," I said, feeling an urgency to maintain ties, "I had enormous respect for you. Once you decide what you're going to do, I hope you'll let me know."

Instead of a quick response his reply was warm and genuine. "You're feelings are certainly appreciated. Feel free to stay in touch. I'll be sure and keep you posted."

I hung up the receiver, feeling on one hand a sudden emptiness but on the other a certain excitement. Anyone who was making the money Brad was raking in yet still had the courage to tell Irvin to shove it was not going to sit on the sidelines for long. I couldn't imagine my leaving the circus, but it was strangely exhilarating to think Brad Rosenberg might include me in his plans. I carefully filed away his number, deciding I'll call him back in a week or two. What harm is there in finding out?

I moved my records, what little I had, into Carl Bruce's office the next day. I could tell he was anxious to get started. "Why don't you line up the TV stations, the Pizza Hut contact and a few popular department stores. I'll be back in a few days to pitch the major promotions."

I didn't share my enthusiasm with Carl but I was curious to see Evansville, my second back-to-back town, a hundred miles down the road. I closed up my desk, grabbed my suitcase, and drove toward the interstate.

U.S. 41 curved southward, straight by comparison to the twisting Wabash River, flowing east of the highway in the same direction. The Wabash Valley was the name of the region, an Indian name conjuring up images of green, fertile farmland and gently rolling fields. Terre Haute, I learned, was a westward crossroads where settlers once converged. The name is French, meaning "highland," and was labeled such by French traders who'd discovered that the elevated forest was the highest point on the Wabash River. As I drove out of town through Vigo County, I could see the results of modern progress. Manufacturing and industrial plants dotted the landscape, producing everything from plastics and paint to aluminum, oil and asphalt. To the east, in Clay County, coal and iron ore were mined, and Terre Haute harbored a network of railroads for shipping the minerals northward. But as I drove south along the interstate, the urban landscape gradually transformed into rural tranquility, and I began to see the Indiana I had hoped to find.

I had asked the hotel desk clerk what was unique about Indiana. He thought for a minute, then said, "There *is* one thing that sets us apart from anywhere else. It's the dark, rich soil."

His description reverberated in my mind as I drove toward Evansville for he said it with such passion. And thirty minutes down the road I began to be served an array of delights, desserts from heaven to cleanse the soul. Thick, rich, black dirt recently plowed, stretching row upon row as far as the eye can see. Children riding bicycles along a lazy country road ending peacefully near a farm- house porch. Steeples rising gracefully, unobtrusively in the distance as if to announce, "We're here if you need us." An old red barn, antique signs plastered on its rotting wood. And a yellow school bus, as shiny and clean as a new spring day, rolling along beside me. I thought of the circus children. There were twenty-five living on the train, a traveling city that had three full-time tutors. I won- dered what the youngsters thought when they witnessed yellow buses whisking children to country farmhouses at the end of a tire- less day.

Corn was Indiana's main crop, but now that winter was over, farmers in the fields were preparing the soil for wheat and oats, soybeans and rye. Rarely, I noticed, did I see more than one farmer in the field at a time. I wondered if they were loners by nature, sitting on a tractor all day in the middle of a vast, empty expanse. I wondered what they dreamed about.

It was dusk when the tousled hills began sprouting traces of civili- zation. A sign read ten miles to Evansville, and my pulse quickened in anticipation. It always did when a brand new city appeared on the horizon, especially one in which I was about to be immersed.

I don't know what it was, but as I drove through the city streets, into the center of town, I could feel a vibrancy, a life-giving force that contrasted sharply with the dullness I felt in Terre Haute. There was almost a sinfulness in the air that teased my senses. Sometimes these things can be subtle. Maybe it was the traffic, a bit more noisy. Maybe it was the people. They seemed to move a little brisker. Or maybe it wasn't so mysterious. Maybe it was the two girls I watched walking down the street, hips undulating unabashedly.

The Harrington Hotel loomed unexpectedly, an inviting presence. A white neon sign announced rooms starting at $28.00. That was more than twice the amount I'd paid in Savannah. But my raise had thankfully come through, and I remembered what Sam Barrett had advised, "Always check into the best hotel in the city the first night. That way you start out with a good first impression." Besides, the sign also said, "Live entertainment-every Thursday, Friday and Saturday." I could hear the upbeat tempo of a band drifting into the street.

Inside, to the right of the lobby, the same nightclub boasted well-known celebrity acts. Four dark-haired men in matching green sports coats were featured on a poster as tonight's entertainment. Regulars perhaps, "Rock and roll with a mix of oldies and Elvis impersonations." I finished filling in the hotel form and strolled across the lobby. As I did, a member of the band, one of the men on the poster, appeared around the corner with a giggling, young woman clinging to his arm. He didn't notice me but she glanced in my direction. She smiled. I smiled back and walked toward the elevator. I liked this town. This was my kind of town.

I rose early the next morning, selected my favorite tie, gathered my notepad and headed down to the restaurant.

"May I have a quiet table?" I asked the hostess. "I'm meeting several people this morning."

My waitress came over. "I'm Lee Ann," she said, and asked for my order. I told her I wasn't hungry, "But I'll be here for a couple of hours, if you could keep the coffee flowing."

I'd set up three interviews, eager now that I'd hired Carl Bruce in Terre Haute, to hire an advertising agency in Evansville.

The first agency scheduled was the biggest one in town. "McDonald's is our anchor account along with the city's largest bank." Their representative, a prissy man in his forties, proceeded to belittle the other local agencies. He himself was an import of sorts from Chicago, a connoisseur he told me, so to speak, of the fine art of advertising.

The second agency representative was a much more humble soul. I could tell he'd love the account, but he almost choked on his danish when I told him the total fee was two-thousand dollars. "Our rates," he said, "are seventy dollars per hour and the owner charges the client if we so much as break a pencil on his behalf."

I was beginning to worry when the hostess indicated Rick Johnson was waiting in the lobby. Rick was the owner of Johnson Productions. Unlike the others, he wasn't the emissary of an advertising agency. Rick was a rock promoter. I had decided to interview him somewhat on a lark. He had heard through the trade papers we were coming to Evansville and had sent a letter of introduction to headquarters. Nancy Pond had forwarded it to me, and I figured, what the hell, he'd at least made an effort.

The hostess ushered him in. I was surprised he wasn't wearing a business suit. Instead, outfitted in blue jeans, a denim jacket and boots, he walked toward me with a quiet assurance, not an arrogance, just the walk of someone accustomed to flying untethered.

"Sorry about the informal clothes," he said. "I quit wearing a suit years ago."

As we talked over coffee and toast, I studied him intensely. He had a face that was anything but simple. Pock marked from childhood acne he was nevertheless ruggedly handsome with brown, wavy hair and a dark complexion. Athletically built, he had a magnetic quality. Thirty-three, thirty-four I figured at tops, he projected a persona that he was sociable when he wanted to be but not to be trifled with.

"I promote concerts along with a few Broadway shows around the tri-state region," he said, "but I heard you were coming and I've never worked with Ringling. It sounded like it might be fun." It seemed like a stretch, I thought, he certainly wasn't the typical agency.

"Do you have any office space?" I asked, fearing he was a one-man show. "I usually work out of the agency."

"Sure," he said sipping his coffee. "It's not just me. I've got a staff of three others. My offices are in an old house. There's a room next to mine you can use."

We talked a bit longer. It was clear he was savvy and knew the entertainment business. Finally I revealed, "the fee is only two-thousand dollars." Expecting a rejection if not a forceful debate, I was surprised when he simply replied, "Fine." The more we talked, the more I found myself drawn to him. A free spirit, without a doubt, and he obviously knew the game. A far cry from Carl Bruce, I thought, but nonetheless still a cousin of sorts. After all, was Ringling Brothers not owned by a former rock promoter? Was there really much difference promoting rock shows than the circus? At any rate, cousin or not, he was anything but boring.

I called Mike Franks in the afternoon and told him I'd hired my two agencies. I told him all about Carl Bruce in Terre Haute, and then I told him I'd hired Rick Johnson. There was a long pause on the other end. Concerned, I reluctantly asked, "Is there anything wrong?

"No," he said. "It's your town. Just be careful."

I hung up, digesting Mike's uneasiness and wondered if I'd made the right decision.

Butler Area Public Library
218 North McKean Street
Butler PA 16001

Chapter 36

MONEY. IT'S PURE AND SIMPLE

I awoke early and wandered downstairs for breakfast. The hotel was quiet and the restaurant was empty, except for Lee Ann busy filling coffee creamers and sugar baskets. She'd spent so long attending to my guests the previous morning I felt as though I knew her. One day in Evansville and already I connected with a familiar face. She saw me and smiled so I was careful to choose the same table, figuring it was her regular station.

"Are others joining you again this morning?" she asked.

"No, just me," I answered. "By the way, thanks for all the attention yesterday."

"Ain't nothing to it," she said, with a noticeable country twang. She was older than me by at least ten years, petite, with a brassy flirtatiousness, almost as if to say, "I may not be a rocket scientist, but then again I don't have to be to attract your curiosity." As I followed her with my eyes, I decided there was something about a country woman I liked. If they were interested in you, they just didn't hide it. Not that it meant she was yours for the taking, but at least you didn't have to wonder if there was a fancy. I noticed a wedding ring on her finger when she returned with my eggs and found myself picturing a man who could break men in two.

"How long are you here for?"

"Actually," I said. "I'll be in and out for the next three months."

"Are you going to stay at the Harrington Hotel?" she asked, leaning over to refill my cup.

"I'm not sure," I replied, wondering if I could afford it.

"Aw, stay here," she said in mock begging, her eyes twinkling just a bit. "And remember, be sure and ask for my station."

I finished my breakfast, strolled toward the lobby and marveled at how quickly my financial judgement could be altered by morning lust.

Rick had penned directions to his office the previous afternoon. With no time to waste, I told him I'd be moving in the next morning. His office, he reminded me, wasn't an office in the traditional sense of the word. In fact, as I drove off the main highway, I soon found myself in a tree-lined neighborhood of old homes. I followed his instructions, driving past Dutch colonials built in the years when families were large, houses that had seen their better days but celebrated their past with sixty-year-old maples and elms towering on either side of the slate sidewalks. It seemed strange to be looking for a rock promoter's office in the midst of such tranquility. Yet somehow, instinctively, I knew when I found his address, there would be something different. And there was. The house looked like all the others. But in front of the house, sat a sleek, black, stretch limousine.

I walked inside. Rick greeted me.

"What's with the limousine? I can't resist asking."

"Oh, that," he said, glancing out the front window. "I bought it second hand a few years ago. The rock stars love it. We meet them at the airport, sometimes right on the tarmac, then shuttle them around to the hotel, arena, wherever they want to go. Come on, I'll show you around."

Rick gave me a brief tour, pointing out some of the obvious reconfigurations. The front room had been turned into a reception area. What once was a den was now filled with records and tapes. The back of the house had a kitchen and Rick operated out of a large room in-between where he'd positioned a desk and chair in the center of the room.

"This is your area," he said, "I hope it will do." He showed me to a small office directly behind his, occupied by an old desk and filing cabinet.

"I ordered you a phone with a separate line," he said. "It should be in tomorrow. Make yourself at home."

I began sorting out my things, my binders and forms and schedules, generally becoming organized. And, one by one, his staff arrived and introduced themselves. His receptionist was a plain-looking woman who appeared very efficient. She also seemed quiet. I gathered Rick kept her busy so I made a mental note to consider hiring a part-time secretary for my own needs. A rotund man in a well groomed Norwegian beard came in mid-morning, introducing himself as Stan. I nicknamed him "Captain Whitehead" since he instantly reminded me of the salty squire in the Dewar's scotch ads.

"What do you do?" I asked politely.

"I'm Rick's assistant," he replied. "I'm also the limo driver."

I decided immediately I liked him, down to earth and centered with a carefree manner. Finally, the last of the staff appeared. I was talking to Rick when he arrived; a bony-faced man looking slightly disheveled who suddenly appeared at Rick's desk.

"Did you do what I asked?" Rick inquired.

The man nodded.

Rick then proceeded to give him a list of menial tasks. I watched the man concentrate as Rick carefully explained what he wanted him to do. Then, as Rick neared the end of the roster, the man suddenly blurted out, "All right, but I've got to go home and change my pants first!"

He turned on his heels and left. Rick sputtered, sympathetically, "He's probably been thinking about changing his pants all morning." Without confirming my suspicions, I surmised the man just wasn't all there.

I decided I'd stay a few days and accomplish as much as I could before returning to Terre Haute. It helped that I was also irresistibly drawn to my new surroundings. Evansville had more of a manufacturing base than Terre Haute, which attracted a diversified brand of business. This naturally led to a greater number of ad agencies and people in communications, which gave the city, from my point of view, a lively bounce to its step. But one comparison baffled me.

Evansville, I noted, had a population actually greater than Terre Haute, which made me wonder why Evansville had been given only four Ringling performances while Terre Haute had been scheduled for seventeen with projections that were five times as great? On the surface it seemed odd but I trusted headquarters knew what they were doing.

As I worked behind Rick's office, I couldn't help overhearing his conversations. Like us, Rick lived on the phone. But his style and mannerisms were mesmerizing, one minute charming and cajoling, the next minute outraged and threatening. He could change so fast, I couldn't tell if his reactions were real or just simply an act. Either way I was thankful I was the client and not the stunned recipient.

Captain Whitehead wandered in from time to time, unpretentiously curious about what I was doing. Unlike Rick, his gestures and speech were unhurried, which coming from someone else might have made little difference, but from him made everything he said seem more important. Gradually I got a much better sense of Rick's world.

Rick was what was known as a local promoter, one of dozens around the country, territorial creatures who were a vital link to the music industry food chain, sandwiched strategically between the talent, the talent manager, the booking agency and the arena. Concerts, Stan said, all started with the booking house, or talent agency as they were often called. The talent agency, usually located in New York or Los Angeles, owns the act, he told me, which means they have bought the rights to the tour. "The risks are huge. A given rock star can sell out a hundred-thousand seat stadium one year, then barely fill an auditorium the next. There's mammoth money to be made, but the losses can be just as great. Once the rights to the tour have been bought, the talent agency negotiates with the rock star's manager for a certain set of dates, essentially tying up the act. The agency next calls the local promoters like Rick throughout the country giving each a piece of the pie. 'You've got four dates in June,' they might say. 'Here's what they are. What can you do?' The local promoter then calls the arenas and concert halls in his area to see what's open and sets up his deals. The talent agency usually demands a large advance, often up to twenty-five percent of the estimated gate up-front and a percentage of the balance. The local promoter then haggles with the arenas. It's all in the contract," Stan emphasized. "And a percentage point or two either direction can mean the difference of thousands of dollars!"

"There must be a ton of competition," I said, thinking every rock enthusiast in town must dream of a big score.

"There is in the beginning, but once you're established, it quickly becomes very limited," he said. "Say you've bought the rights to a tour and want to play in Baltimore, you'd better go through the local promoter."

"Why?"

"The buildings require it," Stan said. "They want to deal with someone they know, someone who can follow through with an audience, not a crackpot who promises one thing but then can't deliver. Over time, though, the buildings rue the day," Stan paused and smiled. "Because the local promoters gain power with the talent agency and begin wielding it, playing one building against the other, and essentially end up calling the shots. A conversation between the promoter and the building might go like this, 'I've got the 20th of June open. Are you ready for Aerosmith?'"

"Can't do," the building employee replies. "We've got the mayor that night. It's an annual awards gala."

"Fuck the mayor. Put him in a back room."

"I can't do that!" the building representative says, alarmed.

"If you don't do that, you ain't getting the Moody Blues in September. Don't screw me up on this!"

I listened to the dialogue seeing how quickly tables turned.

"Well, who owns the buildings?" I wondered.

"The cities usually do," Stan replied. "They're often run by some bureaucrat."

Having some idea of the nonsense that happens at these concerts, I pressed further. "Why in the world does the city want to get involved in the rock concert business in the first place?"

"Money," Stan blurted. "It's pure and simple. Money. They take ten percent right off the top, which goes to the city as an entertainment tax, plus they get a percentage of the gate. Why else would they put up with this crap?"

"Like what?" I asked, fanning the flames.

"You name it. Drugs, stampedes, arrests, overdosed kids. Hell, some of these arenas even have holding cells in their basements. I'm talking serious stuff; knifings intermittently, kids throwing up blood, passed out in the halls, disoriented, people suffocated from heat exhaustion or being squashed by the crowds."

"Hardly sounds like a worthy civic affair," I said.

"Like I said, it's money. Pure and simple as that."

The next day, Stan and I talked again. Rick was busy and so was I for that matter, but my curiosity got the better of me whenever he was willing to chat.

"What about the marijuana during the concerts?" I asked.

"The buildings don't even attempt to control that," he said. "There would be chaos if they did. Once," he said, bemusedly, "we were counting tickets in our office. The building had turned the air conditioning way up to counter the heat. We didn't know it, but the smoke from the concert began infiltrating the office through the ventilation system. By the time we were finished counting tickets we were stoned out of our minds."

There was one other thing, something I'd heard about and wanted to know. "How about the perks given to the stars?" I asked, "Limos are one thing, but what else is there?"

"You name it," he said. "You wouldn't believe the riders on these contracts the buildings sometimes have to provide. Hot meals—no pizzas or sandwiches—a case of Jack Daniels, parties after the show. If you don't do it, the rock stars get pissed off. And if they get pissed off, they don't come back. But it isn't just the rock stars," he added. "I saw a rider on a date for Frank Sinatra that included twelve rolls of cherry Lifesavers, three cans of Campbell's chicken soup, two egg salad sandwiches, a carton of unfiltered Camel cigarettes, two bars of Ivory soap, six boxes of Kleenex, one bag of miniature Tootsie Rolls, several brands of booze . . . my God, the rider went on for twenty-three pages."

—————

I was pinning a make-shift calendar to the wall when Rick strolled in. "Do you think you've set up enough appointments?" he asked in amazement. Three days had passed and Rick couldn't believe the number of contacts I'd made.

"Not yet," I laughed. "Remember, your entire audience is eighteen to twenty-four. Two radio stations and you're covered. I've got everyone from two to ninety to reach."

I started to tell him I was heading back to Terre Haute when he interjected, "What do you say we hit the town tonight? We'll take the limo, stop by some bars. Have some fun."

"Sure! What time?"

"I'll meet you in your lobby at eight o'clock."

I drove to the Harrington Hotel feeling full of good spirits, delighted when the desk clerk handed me a pink message slip. "You had a call from Washington, a Mr. Franks."

Anxious to give Mike an update I quickly dialed the number.

"Where are you?" I asked.

"Springfield," he said. "What's up?"

I rapidly filled him in. There was a moment's pause before he said, "I have some bad news for you."

Again there was a second of silence.

"Your friend Sam Barrett's been fired."

"What?"

"I thought you'd want to know."

"When did this happen?"

"Yesterday," Mike said. "He left a number where you can reach him. Said he'd be there and asked me to give it to you."

"What the hell did he do?"

"I don't know. I heard he screwed up in Greensboro. Irvin had it in for him. But let's face it, this wasn't Sam's schtick."

I thanked Mike for letting me know, hung up, and dialed the number. Sam came on the line. I could tell he was still in shock.

"So what happened?"

"I don't know. I kept asking Allen the same question but the only thing he said was I didn't have the killer instinct."

"Killer instinct? What the hell does that mean?"

"I don't know. That's all he'd say."

I paused, searching for something to say, for I knew what Allen had meant. This was Allen's way of letting him down easy. Sam was too nice a guy. He'd probably hung himself, made a mistake somewhere in Greensboro, but they'd waited until he'd finished the date to can him. Sam loved the job but from our previous conversations I could tell he was struggling. It just didn't come naturally to him.

"What are you going to do?"

"Beats the hell out of me."

"Have you called Brad Rosenberg?"

"Yes, but he doesn't even know what he's going to do yet."

"What about another circus? You've got plenty of experience now."

"I don't know," he said. "Once you've been with the biggest anything else would be downhill." There was an awkward moment of silence. Then he said softly, "I think I'll go home for a while, back to Texas . . . it's been a long time."

"Damn, Sam. If it wasn't for you I'd have blown my brains out, sitting in Cleveland or Savannah in some dingy hotel without a soul to talk to for three straight days."

"Yeah," he laughed, "I know what you mean. Listen, you'll do great. And don't worry about me. I'll land on my feet. As soon as I know where I end up I'll give you a call."

I clung to the phone a few seconds longer. Neither of us knew what to say.

"I'll miss you, Sam."

"I'll miss you, too. Take care of yourself out there."

Rick Johnson arrived shortly after eight. It occurred to me he always seemed to have a trace of a smile, as though he'd just been amused by something or thought he was about to be.

"Ready?" he asked, broadening his expression to a grin.

"You lead, I'll follow."

As we turned to leave the lobby a young woman suddenly appeared. She had the same sprightly step I'd noticed the night I'd first arrived when, arm-in-arm beside the band member, she'd strolled past me down the corridor.

I could tell she recognized me, or at least I thought she did by the way she focused on me rather than Rick.

"This is Sheri," he said, introducing us. He proceeded to tell her why I was in town. "I hope to see you around," she said, and she said it in a way that sounded sincere, and then she disappeared as light and airy as she arrived.

"So who is that?" I asked, with no preconceptions, other than an obvious flirtatious interest.

"She's nothing. Just a groupie," he said, dismissively.

"Groupie?"

"Yeah. She hangs out with the local bands that come into town."

I felt like defending her, for some reason, but decided not to pursue it, wondering what she'd done to deserve his obvious disdain.

"Come on. There's a bar in the hotel. Let's have a drink in here and then we can go from there."

The bar was dark and crowded. Music blared from a lighted jukebox in the corner. Waitresses in white blouses and short black skirts jostled between the tables balancing trays of popcorn and beer. Rick recognized a few people and smiled as we wove our way to a quieter table in the back of the room. Even disengaged, Rick had a persona he was somehow more at ease than anyone else in the room, above it all. We sat surveying the scene.

"You know, I don't believe I've met those two ladies," he said, nodding toward a table against the wall where a blond, busty woman sat with a short-haired friend, her hair cut in a chic style.

"Well then, I have been remiss. Follow me," I said, as I got up from the table, wondering where my sudden bravery was taking me.

"Excuse me," I said, relaxed in the gracious impersonation of an overly polite host. "I'm embarrassed. There is no other way to put it. I hope you'll forgive me, but I've somehow forgotten to introduce you to my friend." The two young ladies looked up, a bit startled but amused. "This is Rick Johnson. Rick, my apologies, this is. . . ."

"Ann," the blond woman replied, now smiling at the ease with which she was introduced.

"Of course you are, and my apologies again. This is. . . ."

"Linda," her short-haired friend replied. We sat down at their table and Rick picked up where I left off.

"You know, I have an uncanny ability in guessing the occupations of total strangers," he exclaimed.

"No!" Ann replied, in mock amazement.

"Yes. It's true," he said, without missing a beat. "In fact, I'll bet you're a nurse."

"How did you know?" Ann replied, suddenly impressed with his self-proclaimed gift, forgetting perhaps, she was wearing a nurses' graduation ring.

"And I'm not sure," Rick said, squinting at her friend, "but I believe you work in an office. Wait, I have it. You're an office manager."

"Exactly!" she said. "Now it's your turn. What do you do?"

"Well, Jamie here is a ball bearing salesman and as for me, I'm also in sales. In fact, believe it or not, I'm a lingerie salesman."

"You're kidding," they said, almost in unison.

"No, that's right. In fact, this year I'm introducing a whole new line of transparent tops."

I sat up, wondering where he was going with this.

"Yes, it's a brand new line. Do you two wear lingerie?"

"Occasionally," Ann said.

"I thought so," he professed. "Well, then, do you mind if I ask you a couple of questions?"

They looked at each other.

"Come on. We're adults. This is serious," he said, pleafully defensive. "This is how I make my living. There's nothing to be embarrassed about. Okay, here's my question. Do you prefer silk or double-crotch panties?"

I tried to suppress a grin, realizing we were on dangerous ground, as both women looked at him in dead silence. Rick never broke role, looking from Ann to Linda in earnest need of a reply. Suddenly, Linda burst out, "You're full of shit!" and we all broke-up laughing.

"Follow me. Our carriage is waiting," Rick announced. "Let's go for a ride!" And as though it was the most natural thing to do we trailed behind him to the entrance. Rick raised his left arm and the limousine suddenly appeared with Captain Whitehead at the wheel.

"Ladies, please," Stan said, jumping out and opening the rear door. I thought their eyes would fall out. Rick reached for a bottle. We rounded the corner and Rick popped the champagne. "We'll take a dozen," he said, embellishing the ladies with a dozen roses from a street corner peddler. And suddenly, we were all caught up in the fantasy of the evening.

As we careened around town, I remembered only weeks earlier I could barely spell the word "date" let alone acquire one. Now suddenly there were women all around. And in Rick's company, I wondered how I ever doubted my prowess.

By the end of the evening only Stan could walk a straight line. He pulled up in front of the Harrington Hotel. Rick smiled, waving goodbye and I sensed he couldn't care less if he ever saw them again, but I liked Linda. She had an innocence in her attitude that along with her short hair made her that much more enchanting. "Call me if you like," she said, timidly slipping me her number, and I told her I would as soon as I returned from Terre Haute.

As I started to walk inside, Rick leaned out the car window. "When you come back I'll show you the rock-world from behind the scenes. I've got back-to-back concerts with Alice Cooper and the Eagles."

I came down for breakfast, already accustomed to starting my day off with Lee Ann. She looked up from behind her station, "A late start I see. So how's everything so far?"

"Couldn't be better," I said. And I meant it. Never before had I been so enamored by a new city. Rick Johnson, Sheri, carousing through town in a limo, romancing Linda . . . it all seemed unreal. I almost hated going back to Terre Haute.

I finished my coffee and toast, no longer in doubt it was here at the Harrington Hotel that I wanted to stay. "I'm with Ringling Brothers and Barnum and Bailey Circus," I said to the hotel manager. "I'll be in and out of Evansville for the next three months. Could there be any sort of a financial arrangement?"

"We stay pretty booked," he said, seemingly uninterested.

"I'll also advise the ringmaster and a few of the others who often stay in hotels to reserve their rooms here."

"I suppose I could offer you a ten percent discount," he relented.

"I'll take it."

I threw my bags into the trunk. It was mid-afternoon by the time

I drove out of Evansville. With its familiar roadside attractions U.S. 41 reminded me how different my world had become in one short week. Not only had my personal life taken a dramatic turn for the better, but my business dealings were all falling into place. I'd already lined up major promotions in Evansville with the top television station, the daily newspaper and the biggest shopping mall in town. Everyone I spoke to was thrilled about working with the circus. Why headquarters had projected only $80,000 for Evansville was beyond me. With the promotions I'd arranged and the campaign I planned to implement I'd sail past that with flying colors. And, what's more, it was a five-percent commission date. If I hit the target I had set I'd be bathing in money.

Gradually the outskirts of Evansville turned into rolling farm fields once again. My thoughts drifted to Linda, my auburn haired friend. In a way she reminded me of my wife, not in appearance or mannerisms, but in her kindness, an ember glow that once enveloped us. Maybe love is but a fleeting glimpse of that marvelous, transcendental feeling we're told that someday lifts your soul to the heavens. But that's just it. It's a taste, as though God were saying this could be the one. But now it's up to you. The garden must be tended.

As I drove northward the sun began to set, casting a gentle glow over distant barns and cattle, and slowly a spectacle began to unfold. I pulled over to the side of the road. Brilliant reds became violent orange, yellows turned into golds, blacks into blues, each color stretching across the sky as the sun descended toward the horizon. "Go God, Go!" I shouted in a spontaneous burst of ecstacy.

I stood still, watching the display evaporate, the last sliver of sun dipping beneath the crest. Slowly, I drove away, wondering if I had just been sacrilegious? Who am I to cheer on God? Yet had I not been dragged to church a hundred times and in all those times had I ever felt the way I just did, God and me, connected?

My thoughts shifted to college classes, time and space, infinity—backwards and forwards—how the whole bloody thing started and I wondered, if God in all his wisdom, created such a thing, then who created Him?

Darkness had fallen by the time I drove into Terre Haute and just as the day had disappeared into night my thoughts transitioned into what lay ahead. I was sure I'd break all records but there was one thing about Terre Haute that unnerved me. It was more than just an irritant. It was downright insane. I drove off the highway. I'll tell Carl Bruce about it tomorrow. It's just something we'll have to deal with.

Chapter 37
I REALLY DON'T LIKE THIS TOWN

"You're not serious?" Carl said. For the first time I saw him flustered.

"I'm afraid so. It's in the contract."

"What are we supposed to do, stand on the sidelines and wait?"

I shifted uncomfortably in my seat.

"We can't even compete?"

"Listen," I said, trying to placate myself as much as him. "It's no big deal. We'll put all our guns into position, then unload our barrage the minute they leave town. We'll have less time but when the townspeople hear it's Ringling Brothers and Barnum and Bailey Circus coming, they'll be back in droves."

I tried to dismiss his annoyance, but frankly, I couldn't believe it myself. How could Earl Duryea, our contract negotiator, have agreed to such a stipulation? The contract spelled it out. Every year the Hulman Civic Center hosted the Shriner's Circus and this year was to be no exception. They were coming full-force in three weeks.

Obviously the Shriner's Circus wasn't in the same league as Ringling, but according to the contract I couldn't even utter we were coming until the end of their last performance. And the Shriner's Circus didn't end until April 15th, two weeks before our tickets went on sale, leaving me with half the time to advertise. "And the

Shriner's," Carl warned, "many of whom are local merchants, distribute discount coupons and promote the hell out of it."

Dumbfounded, I'd pointed out the constraint to Allen. "Don't worry," he said. "There's plenty of entertainment dollars to go around." I took his comment to mean there was no way a rinky-dink circus like the Shriners' could hurt us. But more importantly, I told Carl, I took solace in the fact that despite layoffs at Indiana University and some of the local plants and even though a nationwide recession still swept the country, unemployment statistics for the region held steady. In fact, to look at local economic reports, one wouldn't know Terre Haute was part of the same country. Carl frowned. "I hope those economic indicators are factoring in the young people that have been leaving the state to find work."

"Look," I said, deflecting his concern, "there's no sense dwelling on the negatives. What matters is that this town isn't going to know what hit them when we get through. Did you line up the TV stations, Pizza Hut and a major department store for me to talk to?"

Carl nodded, handing me a sheet of paper.

"Good," I said, and I quickly glanced at the appointments. "We'll review these later. I'm going over to the arena to see the building and meet the general manager."

Located in the middle of town the Hulman Civic Center was owned by Indiana State University. At a glance I wondered if it was designed by the same architect. The building was only three years old, red brick, round and surprisingly bland. But with a seating capacity of twelve thousand it was probably well appreciated in a city of fanatical basketball fans.

I walked inside. Compared to Savannah's Civic Center, it was huge. Once again, I was awestruck by the phalanx of empty seats, floor to ceiling. I stopped and gazed for a moment, imagining the arena full of people, then walked around the upper tiers until I came to a door marked Administrative Offices. A matronly woman greeted me, ushering me into the spacious office of the general manager.

"I'm Robert Hanley," the general manager said, rising from his desk. "This is my assistant." A short, stocky man rose part way up from his chair. For the next several minutes we talked about the seating manifest and the box office procedures. Hanley was calmly efficient, almost coldly so, which I expected a city bureaucrat to be. But beyond his attempt to convince me that he knew how to run an arena, there was something oddly amiss. As we spoke I realized what it was. His excitement about the coming of Ringling Brothers was almost nil. Personal enthusiasm on the part of the general manager isn't a necessary requirement, I reflected, but considering the last time we played Terre Haute we were still under a canvas tent, his lack of zeal was strange. "I'll be back in touch when the tickets arrive," I said.

"Don't worry," he answered. "We'll be ready."

I had plenty of work to do, but I decided I'd return to the hotel early. I'd been gone for over a week and I suddenly had an urge to call Brad Rosenberg. I was curious about what had transpired.

"Your timing couldn't be better," Brad said, his effusiveness back in his voice. "I've just accepted an offer."

"What is it?"

"I can't tell you now but what I can tell you is I'm looking for advance men, only the creme-de-la-creme. I've got a hell of a package for the right men. Are you interested?"

"Of course," I said, having no idea what he was talking about but excited just the same.

"Great. Fly into Washington next week and I'll tell you all about it."

I hung up and looked at my calendar. I'd have to fly from Terre Haute to Washington and then straight back to Evansville. Delighted but apprehensive with so much to do, I eased my conscience by deciding I'd work on the plane both ways.

The next two days were a flurry of activity. Carl and I met with the major promotional prospects. One by one, the deals fell into place. CBS, the number one station, took opening night with the underprivileged kids promotion. Pizza Hut, Carl's retail chain account, offered to do a ton of tie-in advertising in exchange for a mid-week night, some complimentary passes and a special clown appearance. Even a local speedway, a home to Indiana's favorite sport, jumped at a chance for a promotion. Carl watched in wonderment as we wielded every trick in the book. "I've never seen anything like it!" he said. "We're going to hit this town like a ton of bricks." But our crowning achievement—the coup d'etat—came at the end of the week.

NBC was trailing the other stations in the ratings, badly, and in a mid-sized town like Terre Haute, a weakened prey could be bled to death in a hurry. It wasn't necessarily the station's fault; they had to live with the programming they got. At first, I'd ruled them out of my buy, until Carl ushered in a tall, thin, red-faced man with a nervous smile. He sat down, feigning an air of confidence, but I watched him fiddle anxiously with his pencil. The more we talked, the more it became evident he was desperate. He'd give anything to be in on the buy. It wasn't that he didn't have viewership, it was just that he was solidly third. I held all the cards so I threw out a bold idea.

"I'll tell you what. I'm interested in beefing up the crowds for the second week's performances, specifically the Tuesday through Friday matinees. If you could give me fifteen spots a day for four straight weeks promoting those four days, I'll give you ten cents on every dollar of revenue for those four shows, along with a bonus if you sell them out! Hell, if you fill up even three quarters of the seats, you'll make out like a bandit. And don't forget, Ringling hasn't played here in twenty years!"

He nodded, a little weakly. "I'll talk it over with my general manager." When we shook hands, I noticed the redness in his face came from hundreds of broken corpuscles.

Carl and I spent the rest of the afternoon filling out the newspaper schedules while strategizing our press releases. As I started to leave the phone rang. I listened for a minute, then smiled at Carl. "That's it. They took it! I can't believe it. Between CBS, the daily newspaper, Pizza Hut, the major radio stations, and now NBC, we have more advertising about to hit one city in a six-week period than few towns have ever experienced before."

<hr />

I decided I'd celebrate my good fortune. It was Friday night and Carl had left the office. The last thing I wanted to do was to return to an empty hotel room.

The streets were quiet as I drove through town, past a few college nightclubs and a hotel bar, none of which looked too inviting. They weren't what I was searching for. I was more in need of a working class hangout, a place where people were having fun just being themselves, a place I'd probably find outside the city. I headed west, past the Vigo County fairgrounds, past the Maple Leaf Motel, meandering past homes that looked too little for their inhabitants. I wasn't sure of my direction but I knew my destination. I wanted a tavern where people had simple dreams and simple pleasures.

It was almost ten o'clock when by luck I spotted the perfect lounge. People were milling out front. Inside, I could see shadows dancing to country western music. The building was plain, just white boards over a concrete foundation with a blue neon sign flashing out front. I parked next to a spruced-up Fairlane and ambled inside. It was just what I was looking for. I ordered a beer and stood by the bar. Everyone seemed to know one another but I didn't feel out of place. The music sounded more Cajun than country with a catchy backwoods charm. The beat was strong, so strong that a girl in a wheelchair couldn't resist. She rolled out to the middle of the floor, titled her wheelchair, and wildly pivoted to the sound of the music.

I stood at the bar for what seemed like hours watching the people mingle, content to stare and share in their spirit, drenching myself in their comraderie. Finally, it was almost midnight. I left, closing the door behind me and strolled toward the parking lot. My skin felt clammy as the cool night air hit the perspiration on my face. A dog barked in the distance, disguising for an instant an altercation going on a few cars down. I recognized the couple. They'd been dancing together earlier. She had been drinking freely. I tried to ignore them but he was yelling at her. All she was doing was standing in front of him sobbing. Suddenly he pushed her aside, screaming, "I don't give a shit what you do," and stormed back inside. She fell on her hands and knees, still sobbing uncontrollably. I hurried over, unsure what I was going to do, and helped her to her feet. Her mascara had smeared down her cheeks. Her lips were trembling too much to speak. She braced herself against me. It was obvious she was too drunk to drive and I couldn't send her back inside. I noticed her knees were scraped and beginning to bleed. I walked her toward my car. "Come on. I'm going to take you home." She lived in Terre

Haute, she said. As I drove away I tried to soothe her. "Everything's going to be fine," I kept saying.

I wondered if he'd care when he noticed she was gone. She let on this was not an infrequent occurrence. She said she was worried about a little girl she had left at home with a babysitter. I eased in front of a small, white house. A light was on in a bedroom. I could see a teddy bear in the windowsill. I gave her a number where she could reach me, just in case, and then watched and waited until she was safely inside.

I drove home feeling sad. I really didn't like this goddamn town. I was tired when I got to my room. I lay on my bed and found myself doing what I vowed I wouldn't. For some unavoidable reason I suddenly wanted to re-live every detail, the last time I saw my wife.

How could I tell her she wasn't welcome, that there was room in my parents' house but not in their hearts? I simply told her I'd take her home. Our last morning, we piled what little we owned into our old car, a Buick in need of repair, and drove north toward her parents' home. Her clothing filled the back seat. The dishes we'd been given as wedding gifts rattled in the trunk. Her parents' home was five hours away. Neither of us said much as I drove up the highway. When she did speak, she simply said she didn't understand why we still couldn't be together. "Because you have to eat," I said, sounding irritated, but inside fighting back tears.

Her mother was waiting for us when we arrived, a simple house in a tiny town. My wife and I carried the clothes up the stairs to her bedroom. She was silent until we'd hung up the last of her dresses. Then she sat on her bed and, clutching a teddy bear, began to shake. "I don't know why I can't be with you," she said between sobs.

"Because you can't," I said.

"Please don't leave," she pleaded. Tears streamed down her cheeks.

"I can't. I wish I could stay but I can't." I hugged her tight one last time, and then turned and walked away.

I stared at the ceiling remembering every word. What had she done to deserve such pain? Her only request was that I stay . . . and I couldn't even do that.

I turned off the light and tried to focus on other things. Monday I'll be meeting with Brad Rosenberg. Try to think about that. I closed my eyes and uneasily the past slowly gave way to sleep.

Carl handed me the Nielsen rating guide. I was determined to complete as much as I could before flying to Washington. Between penciling in my TV schedule and jotting down notes about my promotional agreements I'd forgotten all about the earlier evening.

"There's a phone call for you," Carl's receptionist said.

"Who is it?"

"I don't know," she replied. "She said she's an acquaintance from Friday night."

A noticeably different tone but familiar voice came on the line. "Thank you," she said. "You were very kind. I'm sorry I put you out of your way."

"It was no trouble," I said, trying to sound reassuring. "I'm glad I was able to help."

"Will you at least let me buy you dinner for your good deed?"

"How nice," I said. "But I'm afraid I won't be back for a week or so. Can I take you up on it when I return?"

I hung up feeling surprised, relieved. She sounded much better than the last time I saw her. I muttered something to Carl about shared adversity. He looked at me sort of strange. I gave him my Evansville phone number, gathered my bags, and headed happily for the airport.

Brad Rosenberg looked handsome, standing between two white columns, as I drove up his driveway. Dressed in a yellow sweater, he already sported a deep tan.

"I've got some errands to do," he said, and he grabbed two pairs of trousers, motioning me toward his car. Our conversation was light as first we stopped at a drug store and then pulled up in front of a tailor. "Follow me," he said.

I wandered into the tailor's. An old man was waiting. Neither he nor Brad seemed in a hurry. By now more than an hour had passed since we'd left Brad's house. I was beginning to feel annoyed. If this was his way of building curiosity, it wasn't working. I hadn't traveled all the way from Indiana to watch his seams be measured. Be patient, I told myself, as Brad finally finished.

"My new office is in Tysons Corner," he said. Brad's office had a panoramic view of northern Virginia but nothing in sight offered me a clue to his new position. He sat down behind his desk and began questioning me about my recent towns. I told him about Savannah and all about Indiana and the more we talked, the more I became anxious to impress him. After listening attentively, he leaned forward and, as if to end the questioning, asked, "So, all in all, have you learned the promotion business?"

"I've done more than learn it. I could tell you what's on every page of the promoter's manual!"

"Is that so?" he said. "What's on page fourteen?"

Suddenly I felt like a fool. He was calling my boast. "I think it's a checklist on group sales."

"You think? You don't know?"

"Not exactly," I said, feeling embarrassed.

Brad stared at me. "It's all right. I'm sure you know the manual, but why overstate your credentials? It isn't necessary and you only lose credibility when you do."

I felt silly but at least I began to unwind in his company.

"Have you heard of the Freedom Train?"

"I believe I've read something about it," I said.

He began to fill me in. "It's the bicentennial celebration coming up, and the government, along with several private institutions, has funded the creation of a special museum, the Freedom Train, to carry the nation's heritage into the hinterlands. It will be brimming with American relics. Its purpose," Brad stressed, "is not to bring our history to the big cities but to deliver it instead to small and mid-sized towns across America."

"Sounds fascinating," I said.

"I need advance men to promote it and I don't have the time to train them. Right now I've got some Congressmen's kids, Yaley and Princeton types, but what I need are pros, guys that know what they're doing, guys like you."

It was interesting, mostly because Brad Rosenberg was heading it up. But a traveling museum, wonderful as it may be, isn't the Greatest Show on Earth. Besides that, I pointed out, "the bicentennial only runs two years. Then we're all out of a job. What then?"

"You're right," Brad said. "That's why I'm going to pay you five-hundred dollars a week—net." My interest peaked. That was twice what I was making, even with my raise. "And to sweeten the deal," Brad said, "we'll pay all your expenses."

"Hotel and food?"

"We'll even pay for your toothpaste."

Now the offer was quadruple what I was earning. But there was something else that interested me. "Let me ask you this? Would I have a base somewhere. A home I could return to on weekends?"

"As long as you get the job done, I don't care where you live."

It seemed too good to be true—four times the money I was making and now an escape on the weekends. I began to think it over. "There is no way I can leave Ringling in the middle of a date," I said. "Indiana would have to be finished first."

"Of course," Brad said. "It's only good business." We talked a few more minutes and I said, "I'll let you know in a few days."

I boarded the plane to Evansville, dazzled by Brad's offer, overwhelmed to think I'd be making four times the money plus having the chance to work with Brad Rosenberg. The Freedom Train wasn't Ringling, and the idea of quitting still seemed inconceivable, but he'd said I could pick a city, maybe in southern California, make friends, and fly home on the weekends. If I said yes, I could leave the four walls behind.

Suddenly I remembered Jack Sullivan and me sipping margaritas as the sun set slowly over Port-o-Fino. "You know Jamie," he drawled, "we're all going to end up in the same place. It's how we get there that makes all the difference."

I gazed out the window and stared down below. There was nothing but darkness. I'd made up my mind. Tomorrow I'd call Mike Franks.

Chapter 38
KEEP AN OPEN MIND

It took me until late afternoon to summon up the courage to call Mike Franks.

"I don't know how to tell you this."

"Tell me what?"

"I'm leaving the circus."

"You're what!"

"Don't worry, I won't leave you in a bind. I'll finish Indiana first." I searched for the right words. "I've got a job offer I don't know how to refuse."

"But you love the job."

I felt guilty enough telling him I was leaving so I told him all about Rosenberg's offer. He was silent on the other end.

"Are you sure?"

"Mike, the last thing I want to do is leave Ringling, but I'm starving out here. Even with my raise, by the time I pay for my hotel and meals I'm broke by Wednesday. I know you want to weed out the good promoters from the bad but this is impossible."

"I understand," he said. "Let me talk to Allen. I'll get back to you."

"Okay," I said, "but I've made my decision."

I hung up feeling rotten. Leaving Ringling was the last thing I wanted to do but Brad's offer was just too good to resist.

The next morning I arrived at Rick's house early. My plan was to drive to the arena, a few miles south of Evansville, and introduce myself to the key personnel. I'd already been told I was in for a shock. "To say the arena is behind the times is a euphemism," Rick hollered in, adding, "Wait till you meet ol' man Strausel." A radio executive had warned, "The senile old bastard is as mad as a hatter." The general manager in Terre Haute was beginning to sound like a dream. Just as I started to leave, Rick's secretary stepped in.

"You've got a message," she said. "He called last night. Allen Bloom."

"Allen Bloom?"

I stared at the message. I expected a response from Mike, but not from Allen, and nothing this soon. I slowly dialed the number.

I was surprised how easily I got through. "Jamie?" he said, and he sounded so pleased to hear from me for a moment I wondered if Mike had told him. "Mike tells me you've turned into a damn good promoter."

"Well, I've given it my best, sir," I said, feeling my way forward.

"Well, I'm not surprised. I knew you had what it takes when I met you." He paused for a moment. "Mike told me about your conversation yesterday."

"I figured he had," I said. "I feel bad. It's not something I want to do."

"I understand. But will you at least do me one favor?"

"Sure," I said.

"I want you to come to Washington. Delay your decision for two days. I'll wipe out my schedule for the afternoon. We'll have lunch, spend some time together. Can you grant me that one favor? Come in with an open mind."

I wasn't sure what to say.

"What's two days for a major decision?"

"When would you like me to come?" I asked. "I hate to disrupt your schedule."

"What's more important than this?"

"Yes, sir," I conceded. "I'll take the first plane tomorrow." I hung up feeling as though I'd just entered a whirlwind. Barely had I unpacked and here I was flying back to Washington. I called the airlines securing a ten a.m. boarding. I glanced at my watch. At least I still had plenty of time to see the arena and meet ol' man Strausel. That ought to divert my attention for the rest of the day.

Painted blue and white over cinder block walls, the arena looked more like a worn, circular, one-story pillbox than an indoor coliseum. I gazed at the structure, wondering just how the circus was going to fit inside. My concern was exacerbated when I went into the building. It must be the shallowest arena ever built. The ceiling was barely thirty feet above the floor, which was fine for basketball games and rock concerts but clearly not suited for a circus. The flying trapeze artists will be hitting the rafters. And Elvin Bale could forget about rigging his wheel of death. The swinging pendulum would crash through the ceiling. But aside from the problems Lloyd Morgan would face rigging the show, I was even more amazed at the seats. The top-priced seats were bright yellow chairs circling the bottom of the arena. The next section up were blue middle-priced seats and then the top third of the arena, which comprised thousands of seats, was nothing but old wooden bleachers. I wandered up to the top tier for a closer inspection. A faded black number, spaced a foot apart on the bleachers, had been sequentially stenciled in place.

Between Rick's warning and now the sight of the dilapidated building, I should have been prepared for ol' man Strausel. I wasn't. Inside a shabby office with government-issued furniture sat an odd looking man with thinning white hair. He was dressed in a suit and tie belonging to the 1940s. He looked up at me full of energy. The problem was, I quickly discovered, it was energy that was scattered like marbles.

"Hi, I'm with Ringling Brothers Circus. Are you Mr. Strausel?"

"Sure am. It's a pretty day outside."

"Yes, it is. We're certainly anxious to play here."

"We've got a rock concert this weekend right after a basketball game."

I nodded. "I saw the arena, sir. It looks like we might have a rigging problem."

"Ain't never had one before."

"We've never played here before."

Suddenly I was rescued by a gray-haired, stern-mannered woman only a few years younger than he.

"May I help you?" she said, suspiciously.

"Says he's with the circus," Strausel piped in.

Christ almighty, I'm in a nightmare. Fortunately, although she was as ill-mannered as he was loony, she was at least lucid. We talked for several minutes while Strausel looked on, fidgeted, and occasionally interjected his unrelated thoughts. Gradually, I managed to convey most of what was necessary. I was beginning to feel a little more at ease when I remarked, "I'd like to meet with your box office manager."

"We don't have a box office manager."

"Nope," Strausel joined in. "Don't need one either."

"What are you talking about?"

"Each show sells its own tickets," his colleague said.

"You mean there's no box office, no outlets, no nothing?"

"That's right," she said, looking at me as though I'd just lost my hearing.

I drove back to Rick's office, stunned. Forty-thousand tickets were about to arrive in boxes to go on sale in less than a month. How was I supposed to create a box office and a chain of outlets in the next three weeks? I didn't even know where to start.

Rick was on the phone when I marched into his office.

"Well, I met Strausel," I said. "Tell me. How the hell does he do his job?"

Rick laughed. "He doesn't really. His assistant, Betty, runs the place. She's been with him for years."

"I met her. If they need a cover, why don't they just get rid of him?"

"Beats the hell out of me," he said. "Maybe they know he's sick. They plan to condemn the building in a couple of years anyway."

I quickly informed him of the problem with ticket sales. He swiveled around in his chair. "I thought you knew they had no box office."

"Hell, no," I said. "And this is no rock concert. I can't just sell tickets out of a record store."

Rick pinched the bridge of his nose. "I'm up to my ass in concerts this weekend, but I know a guy who can set up a box office. I'll give him a call if you like."

"That would be great," I said, "I'd appreciate it! I've got to return to Washington tomorrow but I'll be back on Thursday."

As I turned to leave, he changed the subject. "What are you doing this weekend?"

"Nothing," I said.

"Good. You know those two concerts I mentioned last week? We pick up Alice Cooper Saturday morning at the airport. He plays Saturday night in Evansville. After that, it's the Eagles in Terre Haute, nonstop 'til Sunday morning. You want to come along?"

"Sure!" I said.

"Good. Stick with me. You're in for a treat."

A little less troubled, I drove home to the Harrington Hotel. The nightclub sounded livelier than usual. I resisted a peek inside. It was late and before packing for Washington there was an important call to make. I reached in my wallet and slipped out a piece of paper. Linda Browning, I'd written. The name sounded so American despite her lovely European flair.

"No limousine rides this time," I said, teasingly. "But would you like to join me for dinner Friday evening?"

"I'd love to," she said.

I hung up and smiled, pulled out my suit and began shining my shoes for tomorrow.

Nervously, I waited outside Allen's office. Maureen told me he was on the phone but should be off any minute. Maureen was extremely efficient, almost stoic, unlike Nancy Pond, who had always seemed flustered. She even looked officious with her conservative suits and perfectly coiffed hair pulled tightly back in a bun. While I waited, I wondered if Maureen ever had a crush on Allen or could it be the other way around? Other than the theory opposites attract, I had no basis whatsoever for my mental wanderings, but the thought of it amused me. Why wouldn't she be attracted to his physical charm and power? I remembered Brad Rosenberg once telling me, "If the struggle ever comes down to it and you can't endure Mike Franks, tell Allen Bloom about it. He's the one person who can breathe the fear of God into him."

It had been twenty minutes since I'd taken a chair in the reception area, and my thoughts had shifted to how I would quit, while thanking him graciously just the same. As I started to rehearse my reasoning for the fifteenth time, Maureen stepped in. "He's off the phone. You can go in now."

"Jamie," he said, grinning. "Don't sit down. I've made lunch reservations at Duke's."

He slipped on a tan jacket over a turtleneck sweater, slid three cigars into his coat pocket, and guided me out the door.

"I don't know when we'll be back," he said to Maureen, as we strolled toward the elevator.

Duke Ziebert's was one of those establishments most Washingtonians didn't frequent, unless they were important. "Mr. Bloom," the refined yet pompous maitre d' greeted him. "I have a nice table reserved for you."

We took our seats and I watched Allen settle comfortably into a brown leather chair. He was the only man in the restaurant not wearing a tie, yet I could tell he couldn't care less. He wasn't flouting convention—he just never accepted it in the first place.

I felt awkward now that we were face to face, but there was something about his demeanor, something I'd begun to remember, that was wonderfully relaxing. At first, I thought it was his leisurely attitude. "We're in no hurry," he'd told the waiter. "Give us plenty of time." But gradually I recalled it wasn't his pace. He just naturally exuded warmth.

I didn't know quite what to say so I plunged in. "Well, I guess Mike filled you in on my resigning."

"Yes, he did," Allen replied, carefully lighting a cigar. "But I'm really not interested in talking about that. I'd rather talk about you." He paused, then followed with a question. "When did you first decide you wanted to be in advertising?"

I was caught off guard since his interest seemed so genuine. I told him about my father's influence, our family's sojourn through the deep south and my own leanings toward advertising, especially the creative end. "I can remember helping my father brainstorm ideas for Calloway Mills when I was only ten." Allen listened attentively, occasionally asking a question, nodding frequently, and often just indicating his approval.

Appetizers were followed by the main course and the main course by dessert and coffee. Before I knew it, I'd been talking for two hours. I apologized but Allen quickly said he was intrigued by what I had to say. "At forty, I need all the youthful opinions I can get!" I smiled. He was only three years younger than my father.

I asked about his own start in the business and I laughed when he told me he was just a kid when he boldly told Irvin, "You're going to make me a rich man someday."

Allen lit a second cigar. "You know Jamie, this management system we've created is brand new. But we're already talking about future supervisors. Your name has come up more than once."

"You're kidding?"

"No. I'm serious. You're well thought of around here. It's men like you that form a nucleus. I've often thought, give me three or four good men and I can accomplish anything. Others can come and go, a revolving door, but the nucleus, the family, that's what's important."

Suddenly we were on the same page—the opportunity to be a part of an exclusive group—a group that knew no boundaries. Simultaneously, I felt a wondrous sense of acceptance. Allen was offering me his coattails, just as Irvin had once offered him his. What's more, Allen knew about the benefits of Brad Rosenberg's offer. For me to decline it, to spurn that kind of offer would be something he'd never forget.

We talked a little longer, mainly about the circus and his thoughts of the future. It was obvious I was already a part of his inner circle. Finally, as though it was the most natural thing in the world, I said, "I'll stay." A look of satisfaction swept across his face.

"Amen!" he exclaimed, and with that definitive word, I felt as though a heavy yoke had been lifted from my shoulders. Now I could concentrate full steam ahead on setting new records in Indiana. The money could wait, even a new title, and as far as loneliness was concerned, between Rick, the work I had to do and the women I'd met, I couldn't imagine much more of that.

I filled him in on Terre Haute and Evansville. Then I added, "There's one thing you may not have known. Unbelievably, there's no box office in Evansville. But I've lined up someone who can handle it through my agency Rick Johnson."

"How much does he want?"

"I'm not sure. I meet with him on Friday."

Allen frowned. I could tell he didn't like it. "I guess we don't have much choice," he said. "But watch him."

That night, I called Brad Rosenberg. I might as well get it over with.

"Brad, I'm sorry," I said. "I changed my mind."

There was a moment of silence. "He got to you, didn't he?"

"Who?"

"Allen," he said. "He got to you."

Chapter 39
BILL SWEENEY

"Your ten o'clock appointment is here," Rick's secretary announced. I decided I'd go for broke—all or none, as Mike had taught me in Cleveland—quickly beginning anew in Evansville. I'd already lined up my major promotions but I still hadn't finalized my radio buys. The largest two stations I'd saved for last. But I had already parted with my "King and Queen" promotion as well as the "street urchins" and "Evel Knievel." What in proper magnitude was left? On the way back from Washington it hit me. Let them decide. I'll simply tell each account executive I'm buying the station that comes up with the best package. The only condition is their focus has to be on the matinees.

"We don't give away air time," the first account executive said, his smile in an instant evaporating. "We're the number one country station in town."

"Maybe so," I replied. "But your biggest competitor's not far behind. It's winner take all." I didn't like his attitude so I leaned a little harder. "I also don't have much time. I need an answer this afternoon." He exited in a hurry, leaving me with the impression he didn't much care for my airs either.

Just before noon, Jill Bolaro, from the number two station stepped in. Her demeanor couldn't have been more different—nor for that matter—her appearance. "I'll pitch it to the general manager the minute I get back," she said. "I'm sure we'll come up with something!" I turned and wished her luck. There was something, I had to admit, about a shapely full-bodied woman, especially a bit of a flirt, that skewed my objectivity.

Rick was preoccupied with his upcoming concerts and acting ill-tempered, I noticed, as he issued orders to his staff. Nevertheless, I asked, "Did you have a chance to line up the meeting with your box office contact?" I knew he didn't need any distractions. "No problem," he said. "He'll be here tomorrow at three o'clock."

It was mid-afternoon and I was putting the finishing touches on my newspaper schedule when the phone rang. It was Jill Bolaro. "We'd love to do it," she said. "We'd like to offer you ten spots a day for two weeks plus we'll discount our rate card by twenty percent for the cash buy. We're calling it 'Family days at the circus.' Our only request is that we want to collect for our air time during the second matinee."

"Okay," I said. "As soon as I hear from the other station I'll let you know."

An hour later the man from the leading station called. "We've decided to make an exception," he said. "Our morning DJ will promote the matinees as a ticket give-away. He'll mention a free drawing every thirty minutes for the next two weeks. We'll, of course, need a few hundred tickets."

His level of commitment was just as good but with a two-day date I wasn't interested in giving away tickets. "I'm sorry," I said. "But I'm afraid I'm going with the other offer."

I quickly called Jill.

"We got it?"

"You sure did," I said.

"Fantastic, can I buy you a drink after work to celebrate?"

"Sounds like fun. I'm staying at the Harrington Hotel. Why don't I meet you in the lounge at six?"

I hung up and tried to re-focus but I couldn't. With this latest deal, I'd now structured a hell of a package—a four show sell-out for sure.

———

I arrived at the hotel bar just before six. It was dark inside. A dozen tables were spread around, each with red flickering candlelight. I chose one a discreet distance from the center, wondering if my thoughts were getting carried away. Does her invitation have to be anything but business?

She walked in a few minutes later and I watched her adjust her eyes to the dark. She was tall and curvaceous, just as I'd remembered. The only difference was she had unfurled her hair. No longer tightly bound, her hair flowed loosely, brushing against her shoulders.

"Congratulations," I said, extending my hand.

"You made my day," she exclaimed, still gushing with the same enthusiasm she'd earlier displayed.

"I'll have a gin and tonic," she said.

I told the waiter to make it two.

"So tell me all about the circus. Your life must be full of excitement!"

I couldn't resist painting a colorful picture. She plied me with questions until finally I asked, "How about you? Are you married, divorced, single? How long have you been selling radio time?"

"I've been with the station for three years, divorced for two. And I've lived in Evansville all my life," she said, sounding slightly exasperated. "How long have you known Rick Johnson?" she said, changing the subject.

"I barely know him. I just recently hired him. Why? Do you know much about him?"

"He's well known around here, sort of a strange duck for this town."

"Is he well liked?"

"I'd say he's liked by some, not by others."

The lounge had gradually become occupied with people but other than the steady hubbub of noise, I failed to notice their comings and goings—perhaps because our conversation had returned to our personal lives and our curiosity was now undeniable. Our earlier exchange had been replaced by side glances and light conversation. "My mother was Korean, which explains the shape of my eyes," she said. I was starting to feel guilty. We'd just met over business and now, three hours later, we were dancing around the obvious. I started to touch her hand as she laughed at one of my observations, when the waiter appeared with a tray and two drinks.

"Excuse me," he said. "I'm sorry to interrupt. The gentleman over there ordered these for you."

"Who?" I said, wondering who I knew well enough to buy us a pair of drinks. The waiter pointed to a table with a group of people. At first I didn't recognize anyone but then a man in a blue suit raised his hand and slowly waved. He had an all-knowing look on his face. I waved back feeling self conscious, like a man without an alibi. It was her competitor, the man from the other station.

——›››

Lee Ann didn't seem herself, especially for a Friday morning, when I expected her spirits to be more bubbly than usual. I watched her go about her tasks, waiting on her customers, but her smile vanished as quickly as it came, as though it was an effort to be momentarily friendly. It occurred to me, if her sincerity could be measured in the time it takes a smile to disappear, then she was failing this morning miserably. She finally noticed me sitting at my table and strolled over. Without prying into her personal business, I adopted a caring tone. "It's a beautiful morning," I said, trying to resonate cheerfulness. "I hope you've planned a lovely weekend."

"Nope, I haven't planned a thing," she said.

"Well if anyone deserves a nice weekend, you do," I said. "You're the friendliest waitress in town." For the first time, a natural, more relaxed smile passed her lips.

"I'm sorry," she said. "I'm in a pretty piss-poor mood this morning."

"I noticed."

"Well, I'm just sick of it," she said. "One of these days I'm going to leave him."

"Who?"

"My husband. He got home last night from some stock car race at three o'clock in the morning, a stock car race that ended at ten. Am I supposed to believe he was out with the boys? I woke him up at seven. He hadn't seen the kids all week. Then we got into it in front of the kids. I told him, 'You wait and see! What's good for the goose is good for the gander.' That made him furious. I walked out and I swear, I thought he was going to hit me. I don't give a shit. He's screwed around once too often and one of these days he's going to see how it feels."

I could imagine her flaunting away as she walked out the door just to provoke him further.

"These things sort themselves out," I said. "I'm sure he'll realize what a wonderful wife he has and make amends," I explained, not believing a word I was saying.

I could see she didn't believe me either. But at least her confidence, or maybe her defiance, had returned. By the time I left, her amiable nature was back in full swing.

My anticipation was racing ahead of the day's events as I drove to Rick's office. My day was full, tonight I had a date with Linda Browning and tomorrow it was off with Rick for a weekend of concerts. "It doesn't get better than this."

"There's a young lady named Lisa Hollings waiting for you," Rick's secretary said, as soon as I opened the door. "She said she's here for an interview."

"Interview?" Of course, how had I forgotten? Did I not write it down? "How long has she been here?"

"Almost an hour."

I hurried into my office. "I'm so sorry. I don't have an excuse in the world."

She smiled and when she did, I noticed on the right side of her face the corners of her lips and her cheek barely moved. It was so contrasting to what otherwise was such a pretty face.

"It was a car accident," she said, shyly. "It severed the nerves in my right cheek. It's okay, everyone notices."

I sure hoped she could type, because as far as I was concerned, she already had the job. We talked for several minutes. She said she was living with her parents, out of money and saving to go back to college. I told her my needs were mostly clerical, typing proposals, following up on the media and generally staying on top of things, especially when I was out of town in Terre Haute. "It's strictly part time, two or three days a week, three or four hours a day, but its yours if you want it."

"Could I bring my boyfriend to the circus?"

"You can bring your whole family. Front row seats, I promise."

"I can't believe I'm working for the circus."

"You'll believe it next week," I laughed. "Bring a rented type-writer and come back Monday afternoon. I'll have plenty for you to do."

I couldn't have Lisa type my agreements until they'd been converted from my notes to letter form, an informal recap with hopefully a binding close. I was crafting my fifth letter when Rick walked in, side-by-side with a muscular man who was carrying a motorcycle helmet under his arm.

"Hi, Bill Sweeney," he said, shaking my hand.

"Please, sit down," I said. "I appreciate your coming in."

"Anything for a friend," he said, glancing at Rick.

I looked at Rick trying to gauge his reaction. "I understand you have quite a bit of experience selling tickets."

"I've been doing it for years."

"Is this something you do for a living?"

"No. It's something I do to pick up some extra cash."

"What kind of shows do you do?"

"Musical concerts, that sort of thing."

"Well Ringling's a little more complicated than a concert, what with complimentary passes, kids' stubs, discount coupons and per-formances back-to-back."

"Nothing I can't handle," he shrugged. "Just tell me what you need and I'm sure you and the powers-that-be will be happy."

I didn't mind self confidence, but his answers were a little too pat for my taste.

"I just want you to understand that we require an accounting down to every last penny or you make up the difference. Are you clear on that?"

"Of course. Just give me your procedures."

I saw no point in antagonizing him, especially since I'd driven home my point, plus our auditing procedures would catch any discrepancies. So I proceeded to inform him, "We start counting dead wood by intermission but by the end of each show I need a financial accounting, along with all unsold tickets. I either have an unsold ticket in my hand or the price of admission. It's as simple as that."

He nodded affirmatively. I told him I'd be setting up a Ringling bank account locally for all deposits. I'd give him the account number in a few days.

"No problem," he said. I switched the discussion to ticket outlets. He said he had a few he'd used for years, drug stores and department stores that would be glad to host a booth at no charge in exchange for the free advertising and walk-in business.

"What about your fee?" I asked.

"My charge is twenty cents for each ticket sold."

I did a quick calculation. It was roughly four percent of our top ticket price. Headquarters probably wouldn't like it, but it seemed reasonable to me. I also didn't see that we had much choice. Nevertheless, I hesitated for just a minute, searching for any reason I might have missed not to hire him.

"Well I guess we're in business," I said, ending the momentary silence. "Why don't you proceed ahead securing the outlets. I'll call you as soon as the tickets arrive."

"Wonderful," he said and as he rose he winked at me, this time offering a thumbs-up instead of a handshake.

I watched Rick escort him out the door. He certainly seemed competent enough. But I still felt uneasy. He was just a little too slick. Then again, that didn't make him dishonest. Maybe as a result of Allen's warning I was just being paranoid. After all, he'd come with Rick's recommendation. Besides, he was probably the only game in town and with tickets going on sale in less than four weeks and me in Terre Haute half the time, who had the occasion to look for an alternative? He'll do fine, I quickly reassured myself.

———※———

"Mister Franks," I said, playfully emphasizing the word mister.

"How's my protegé?" he said.

"I couldn't be better. By the way, it looks like you're stuck with me."

Mike laughed. "I know. Allen told me. That's terrific. You made the right decision."

I filled him in on my week's events telling him in the end about Bill Sweeney. He listened but didn't offer any objections.

"So what about Terre Haute?" he asked.

"There won't be a stone unturned. I'm positive we'll do great!"

"Good work. Incidentally, how's your tennis game?"

"I'm not sure. I haven't lifted a racket since you and I played in Cleveland."

"Good. I just signed up for a two-week tennis camp in Arizona. I plan to trounce you while you're in Washington."

"Washington? When will I be in Washington? I just got back."

"Oh, didn't I tell you?" he said, and by the tone of his voice I could tell he was feigning innocence. "It's your next town. You're promoting it this year."

"I'm what?" I said, not sure I was hearing him correctly.

"It's your town. Allen told me yesterday."

"Are you serious?"

"It's yours," he said. "But don't feast on it now. Just focus on Indiana. Washington will come soon enough."

I hung up, astounded. This was incredible. Washington, D.C. was Irvin's home turf, second only to New York in prestige. Suddenly, it was obvious. This was Allen's way of saying thank you. It was also his way of saying, "You're on the way up!" Wait until Bursky and the other promoters find out. I floated out the door. Do gangbusters in Indiana, then it's on to the nation's capital.

"You look beautiful," I said, as she opened the door, silhouetted against the light. I'd been looking forward to seeing Linda Browning all week, an excitement mixed with nervous anticipation, a nervousness that I feared would spoil the first half of the evening. But now, as I stood in front of her, a relaxation born of good news, took affect.

"Please, come in," she said softly, and she guided me toward a comfortable sofa. In fact, the whole room was comfortable with an organized sense of clutter she'd clearly taken care to arrange. Dried flowers accented loosely thrown pillows while pottery lamps and braided rugs blended with prints of wooded countryside. To the right of the living room in a small nook surrounded by green plants and candlelight, sat a table with a bottle of wine. Two glasses sparkled among neatly laid silverware.

She ventured, "You know this may be crazy, but even though you invited me out to dinner, I just thought, I'll bet it's been ages since you've had a home cooked meal. So, I've baked a lasagna, a home cooked recipe I might add. How would you like to kick off your shoes, loosen your tie, and have dinner right here?"

"I can't remember the last time I've had a home cooked meal."

"Good," she said. "Why don't you pick out some music while I stir the sauce."

I selected a tape called "Holiday in Italy," which seemed perfect for the occasion, and then did as she suggested. I took off my shoes and loosened my tie.

I could see her from the living room as she prepared the salads. The smell of tomato sauce, rich with spices, wafted into the room. Her hair, I now noticed, had even more of an auburn tinge. But it was her smile that dominated her presence. She radiated warmth. Eyes may be the window to the soul, I thought, but it's a woman's smile that brightens the way.

"Dinner's served!" she announced, and with a ready compliance, we positioned ourselves at the tiny table.

"I hope you like it," she said. "The recipe has been handed down through my family for generations."

"I'm sure I will," I said, as I poured the wine.

Between the lovely Italian music, her dark brown eyes and now the dinner and wine, I couldn't imagine how the evening could improve. I told her all about my conversation with Mike Franks, trying to sound excited without the sudden vanity I felt. We talked about the circus, life on the road, and periods of loneliness. "But right now," I said, "I've never felt happier."

"I'm not as content with my job," she said. "It's an office job that isn't very challenging. But I'm taking the foreign service exam, hoping to work for the State Department and perhaps receive an overseas assignment." She lived in France, she said, as a child, and when she spoke of growing up her spirit was as light as the music.

"Well, if we were in Europe and you were my date, do you know what we'd be doing at exactly this moment?" I asked.

"No, what would we be doing?"

"We'd be dancing?"

"Yes!" she said. "But I'm a terrible dancer."

I got up, moved the coffee table and cleared a space. Bowing just slightly, I said, "Madam, may I have this dance?"

It was an elegant Italian waltz. As I took the first step, I said, "Feel my hand against your waist? If it presses you gently to the left, then glide ever so easily to the left. If my palm pushes you gently backward, then you'll know that's the way I'll be moving. All you have to do is follow me."

I was no Fred Astaire, but she was so soft and so feathery light, any mistakes I made seemed utterly irrelevant. The more we danced, the closer we got, and the closer we got, the less we moved. The evening drifted effortlessly away. It was one in the morning when we noticed the time. How had six hours passed? She walked me to the door and with a promise to see each other next week I drove home, holding on to her embrace.

Rick had told me to meet him behind-stage at eight o'clock. "I'm here to meet Rick Johnson," I informed the guard outside the door. He quickly made a phone call, telling me someone would be out to get me. I pinned a pass with my name on it to my shirt pocket. Within a few minutes Stan appeared at the door.

"Captain Whitehead!"

"At your service," he replied with a grin.

"How goes the day so far?"

"Great. We picked Alice up at ten this morning and took him straight to the golf course."

"Alice Cooper plays golf?"

"He's a fanatic. Eight handicap. In fact we just got here half-an-hour ago."

I'd never seen a rock star up close and this one, from everything

I'd heard, was as crazy as they came. While most of the touring bands were leftovers from the sixties, singing love ballads in bell bottoms, Alice Cooper was in a class by himself. Everywhere he performed, people were up-in-arms over his outrageous behavior, including everything from mock masturbation to strutting on stage with a snake draped round his neck to allegedly pulling the head off a live chicken. How deranged could an Arizonian minister's son get?

We stepped behind the stage, a monstrous platform abuzz with electricians and stage hands making final adjustments, and turned up a narrow corridor. Up ahead I could see a group of people milling outside a door. "There's Rick," Stan said, "standing near Alice's dressing room."

Rick was conversing with an attractive middle-aged man dressed elegantly in a suit.

"Jamie, I'm glad you could make it. Let me introduce you to the mayor. I was just telling him about Ringling Brothers coming to town."

"It's a pleasure to meet you," I said, shaking his hand. He had one of those interesting faces that made you want him to like you. I was searching for words to continue the conversation when suddenly the door swung open. We all stared, askance. It was Alice Cooper himself. Cadaverously thin, he was dressed in a torn red leotard with a silver chain wrapped around his waist. His hair, black and curly, cascaded down his shoulders. Black teardrops descended from his eyes while long dark spikes drooped from the corners of his lips, accentuating a chiseled jaw and grotesquely pointed nose. On closer look, he was also no adolescent.

"Can you believe I actually make a living dressed like this?" he said, breaking into a grin. The tension broke and we all cracked up laughing.

"Come on in," he said, as gracious as a country gentlemen. "There's plenty of soft drinks and sandwiches on the table. Make yourselves at home."

Gradually the room filled up with other members of the band including two female back-up singers. I overheard one of his assistants tell a reporter, "We are only twelve cities into a forty-city tour. That's why Alice runs three miles a day in preparation." Alice

A Look Back
AN EARLY GALLLERY

While deeply grieving over the loss of Charity, his wife of 44 years, Phineas Barnum fell in love with the talented 22 year old daughter of an English friend, Nancy Fish. Posed happily soon after their wedding in 1874, Nancy, like Charity, gradually became reclusive as a result of Barnum's energetic absences.

It was late in life that Barnum started his circus career. For years he owned the American Museum, south of City Hall in New York City, and traveled the world in search of treasures, including the famous likes of Chang and Eng, Tom Thumb and Jenny Lind.

Following the ruin by fire of his third museum, the indestructible Barnum rises from the ashes and proclaims the start of a grand exposition, a circus. Advertising posters like these were widely distributed, and today are considered works of art.

THE GEAUGA REPUBLICAN.

JULIUS O. CONVERSE, Editor.

CHARDON, O., WEDNESDAY, MARCH 6, 1872.

REPUBLICAN STATE CONVENTION

BARNUM'S CANNIBALS.—The four cannibals (three men and one woman)
which Barnum proposes to place on exhibition, were obtained from the king of
one of the Cannibal Islands, where they
were captives taken in war, and, by the
laws of Cannibal warfare, were doomed
to death. Barnum was obliged to give
heavy bonds that, at the expiration of
their three years' reprieve, he would return them. In the operation, he claims
double credit as a humanitarian; first,
he does not furnish them with their
regular diet of roast missionary; and,
second, he proposes to forget his bond,
and not return them to tickle the palates of their epicurean captors. He
considers this breach of contract justifia-
ble, as he is willing to pay the amount
nominated in the bond, especially if the
investment proves a profitable one.

FIGI CANNIBALS.
Imported by P. T. BARNUM for his Great Show.
KI NA BOSE YACO,   KO RATU MASI MOA,
RA BIAN, the Dwarf.   OTAVAH.

If Barnum and other showmen couldn't
present the real thing, they weren't afraid
to fabricate it. Exhibited with verbal
dexterity in the Fiji tradition of "flesh
eating cannibals," their exploits were
questionable since the Princess was a
former house maid from Virginia.

One wonders how these
albino children, exhibited by
Barnum, must have felt. Or
for that matter, The Wild Men
of Borneo, advertised as "wild
and ferocious, captured off the
shores of Borneo" – who were
actually retarded brothers,
Hiram and Barney Davis, raised
on an Ohio farm.

Shanghaied from Siam by a Yankee skipper, Chang and Eng
would later become one of Barnum's most profitable ventures.

Chang and Eng with their wives and two of their
children. Strangely enough, the Siamese twins married
two sisters, fathered 22 children, and having built two
houses three miles apart, they commuted from one
home to the other, alternating every three days.

A farm house built in view of a
spring in 1843 by Chang and Eng.
In the evenings they would stroll
along a nearby hill.

Shy and reserved, a rare photo of James Bailey. Impressed by Bailey's logistics for moving masses of men, animals and equipment, a German Quartermaster followed him around for weeks to study his ingenious methods. "He suits me exactly as a partner and a friend," said Barnum.

The home of James Bailey in Harlem, New York.

An 1876 photo of the Cooper and Bailey Circus. Born James McGinnis, when Bailey died and Cooper wouldn't change the name of the show, Cooper's ambitious new partner, James McGinnis, simply changed his, becoming James A. Bailey.

A 1908 photo of the Barnum and Bailey band. Members were often chosen as much for their athletic skills as their musical talents.

"To state a fact in ordinary language is to permit doubt concerning the statement!" Amusingly declared by Tody Hamilton, Barnum's advance man.

The advance men had introduced the art of co-promotion in this early 1900s circus parade in Wisconsin.

1895, Marion, Ohio

The circus was always about children. They would eagerly volunteer to pass out fliers and help stretch the canvas for a free ticket or two.

The Ringling family, 1895 – front row, left to right: John, Marie Salome and August (parents), Ida, and Henry. Back row: Al, Alf. T., Gus, Charles, and Otto. A competitor would declare, "it's not that they're so smart, it's that there's so damned many of them."

In a pre-television era when crowds easily mingled, little could be more enticing than the salesmanship of the sideshow barker.

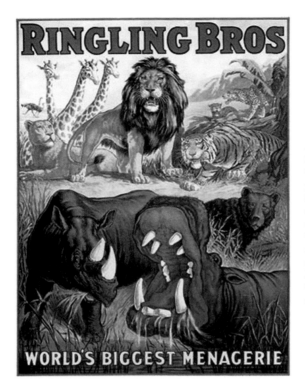

As depicted in the art from this early poster the circus was the precursor to the modern zoo, presenting animals only seen in books and illustrations. It also was a traveling fair and museum displaying inventions such as the lightbulb and exotic visitors from far-off cultures.

The happy and sad visages of `white-face` and `August` clowns when clown alley was more often than not outdoors.

Advance men rarely removed the old posters. It was easier to plaster the new advertising on top. If not paid a fee, the barn owners were assuredly treated to every new show in town.

"Early tents used a simple umbrella shape. But by adding support poles the center could be left free, which led to the three-ring circus. At the turn of the century these giant circus tents took up two acres and could hold over ten thousand people."

– Red Sky Shelters

In 1885 Barnum was having breakfast in New York when the news was delivered. One of his great sensations, Jumbo, was accidently killed by an unscheduled train while being led down the tracks after a show.

A photo of P.T. Barnum a few years before his death, which ended a career in show business heralded to this day. If the industrial revolution belongs to Europe, some might say the art of mass communications belongs to America, excelled unmatched by Phineas Taylor Barnum.

James Bailey, still in his prime, carried on alone until stricken by a fatal skin infection a dozen years later. For the sum of $410,000 the Ringling brothers purchased the circus from Bailey's widow. From this point on, the show would tour as the colossal Ringling Brothers and Barnum and Bailey Circus, The Greatest Show on Earth.

One by one, the Ringling Brothers passed away until the youngest, John Ringling, remained singularly in control. But John overspent – including the construction of a 32-room Venetian, Gothic mansion – and over-risked, and in the end, he left the circus in financial shambles.

It was John Ringling North, the ne'er-do-well nephew, who had the moxie to raise more than a million dollars, which the circus would need to continue.

Neither the tiger nor the horse look very happy.

THE TERROR

Tremendous New Educational Feature Awes Al G. Barnes and Sells-Floto Spectators

Continued

With a smirk of cruel calculation and a sadistic scowl of challenge on his huge bestial face, Gargantua The Great now defies civilization from behind the heavy, chilled steel bars of the strongest cage ever built.

Of triple reinforcement throughout, the twenty-foot cell-like prison on wheels in which he may be viewed with perfect safety, is an interesting and unusual exhibit in itself, combining all the known scientific devices for air conditioning and insulation.

Two outer enclosures of heavy, shatter-proof plate-glass surround the massive barred cage, the germ-filtered air of which is kept at an even temperature of 70 degrees Fahrenheit, providing protection against colds and pneumonia, which almost invariably have been the cause of death among these awesome anthropoid apes.

The country's leading experts have reproduced in the construction of the cage of The Big Show's dangerous captive, as far as humanly possible, the actual atmospheric conditions of far-off Belgian Congo's coastal region, the native habitat of Gargantua The Great and his mighty forebears.

STRIKING CONTRAST

So much like a horrifying nightmare vision of what man might have been, Gargantua The Great offers the most pernicious portrait study ever recorded by a camera lens.

Gargantuan news clipping. Orphaned as a baby gorilla and nurtured by a village woman, the infant ape was sold to Mrs. Gertrude Lintz, whom she described as gentle enough to have a "cup of tea."

Under Ringling's later ownership Gargantua would tour with the circus for fourteen years. With a justified mercurial temperament he could easily twist a tire into a figure eight.

The impact from the 1944 Hartford circus fire dealt the Ringling heir a final blow. Sadly, 168 people – many of them children – died as they tried to escape. Financially crippled from the ensuing lawsuits, the circus limped along, until sold in 1967 to the savvy entrepreneur, Irvin Feld.

A circus clown rushes with a bucket of water.

chimed in, "If Alice didn't," he said, referring oddly to his rock persona in the third person, "it would quickly cease to be fun."

Just then a stage manager opened the door. "It's time to go on."

Rick, Stan and the mayor and I followed the crowd out of the room, wound our way down the hallway and positioned ourselves to the right of the stage. Like a swarm of locusts, kids were everywhere, thousands of them lighting up the darkness with matches, stomping their feet in anticipation, in unison.

Suddenly white smoke began filling the stage, green lights began flickering and a noose dropped from the rafters. The kids roared. The mayor and I looked at each other, caught up in the excitement as much as the crowd. In the meantime Alice Cooper crawled through the smoke like a reptile before he leapt to his feet, stared lewdly at the throng and then broke into his number one hit "School's Out."

I drew up to the mayor after the third song. "Would you be interested in being an honorary ringmaster for our opening night performance?" I shouted, spontaneously figuring there was certainly no harm ingratiating myself with the mayor.

"I'd be delighted," he smiled. "Just send a formal invitation to my office."

"I'm heading up to the administrative offices," Rick announced. "Feel free to join me later."

I stayed with the mayor, enjoying the show, until he said he had to go and then I began maneuvering my way through the crowd. The stale smell of marijuana permeated the air. Some of the kids already looked dazed. I opened the door to the main office. A young girl was lying on the floor. Vomit splattered her shirt. She looked as though she was hardly breathing. A man with a crew cut, wearing a trench coat approached, "Who the hell are you?"

"I'm with the circus," I replied, sounding apologetic.

He eyed me warily while Rick hollered in, "He's okay detective. He's with me."

Rick was sitting in the middle of the room at a long table counting unsold tickets, seemingly oblivious to everything around him. Suddenly the door banged open and a stocky man in his thirties, wearing jeans and a sweatshirt, shoved a tall kid into the room. The kid was handcuffed and sobbing uncontrollably.

"Up against the wall, you fuckhead!" the man screamed, slamming the teenager against the wall. The boy's voice was so choked with tears he could hardly speak.

"I didn't do anything," he sobbed. "Why did you hit me?"

"I didn't hit you! If I'd hit you, you'd be in the hospital. I tackled you from behind."

"What did I do?" the boy blubbered, now shaking in spasms.

"You were scalping tickets. That's what you fucking did."

"No, I wasn't. I was just selling mine. I swear it."

"Who the fuck are you kidding?" the cop yelled back.

The boy kept crying, pleading with the cop to take off the cuffs. Finally, the policeman realized he was telling the truth but after taking off the cuffs he grabbed the kid by the throat and drove his head back into the wall, "If you ever, if you ever tell anybody what I look like, I'll have your balls. Do you understand?"

The boy nodded, wiping at his tears. While this was going on, ol' man Strausel kept sticking his head in and out of the room. To my amazement Rick never missed a beat. He just calmly drew on his cigarette while finishing his count.

"That's it," Rick said, completing his last stack of tickets. "Not bad. What would you say the attendance was?"

I tried to collect my thoughts, still shaken by the hysterical teenage boy. I knew how many seats were in the arena, plus I needed to account for the crowd watching from the arena floor. "I don't know. About fifteen thousand," I said.

"Good guess," he replied with a smile.

Just then, ol' man Strausel again stuck his head in the door.

"Now if you really want an astute observation, the man to go to is Mr. Strausel," Rick said.

Rick looked at me and winked. Strausel blinked. Rick was ridiculing him right in front of his face. "So, how about it, Mr. Strausel, what's your guess? How many tickets were sold?"

Strausel stared at him, expressionless. For a minute, it seemed like he wasn't going to answer. Then all of a sudden he blurted out, "Eight thousand."

Rick clapped his hands. "See, I told you he was an astute observer!"

Rick spent another hour wrapping up loose ends. He finally summoned Stan to fetch the limo. Rick and I piled into the back seat while Stan drove a steady course toward the interstate, then north toward Terre Haute.

"If the Eagles' take tomorrow night is this good, I'm set for the month!" It was well past midnight but we were all wide awake. "Stop here," Rick said, spotting an all-night diner beside the highway.

"Stan," he said, "pull the limo right up to the front door. Jamie, you sit in the back seat. Stan and I will jump out and open the door for you. They'll think you're a fucking rock star!"

I leapt out, sauntered through the front door and found myself standing in front of three waitresses, staring at me from behind the counter. So this is what it's like to be famous. I averted my eyes, suddenly feeling removed from the whole human race.

Rick later led the way out of the restaurant, darting ahead to again hold the door of the limousine. We flew up the highway, laughing. I was feeling as high as could be. We finally arrived at the Terre Haute Holiday Inn. "Sleep tight," Rick said, turning up the corridor. "But not too late. We have a meeting with the manager of the Eagles at seven a.m. over breakfast."

Chapter 40
DON'T WORRY. JUST SIGN IT.

It was no secret, among rock-and-roll historians, that Bruce Spring-steen, and Bob Dylan before him, and Elvis Presley before him, had a rocky, destructive relationship with their fathers, replaced by an all-consuming bond with their surrogate fathers who catapulted them into international acclaim. In the case of Elvis Presley, the substitute took the form of an older, wiser, shrewder Colonel Parker. For Bob Dylan, the surrogate was Albert Grossman, and in the case of Bruce Springsteen, it was Mike Appel. Parker, Grossman and Appel shared a predominant skill in common—the ability to recognize raw, undeveloped, musical genius, and then massage that talent into a lasting, almost unbreakable, dependency—physically, emotionally and financially.

Just as Irvin Feld sought out new talent, other managers signed their willing prey to long-term contracts, at a time when, as small nightclub acts, they'd sign almost anything. The manager would buy them new equipment, new instruments, put them into recording studios and, if need be, even break up their band—separating the wheat from the chaff—sometimes keeping only the lead singer, if he was really the source of talent and future earnings. Later, they would personally manage all the money, handle the recordings, book all the dates, schedule all the interviews and pay all the bills—

including the cost of plastic surgery, as Irvin Feld engineered with Paul Anka, if they thought an improved appearance might generate sales.

I thought of Irvin Feld with his hunger for fame and fortune. As brutal as he could be, I could also envision him as a paternal figure. But with the exception of Colonel Parker, these relationships never lasted. Just as Paul Anka eventually broke from Irvin Feld, so too did Bob Dylan from Albert Grossman and Bruce Springsteen from Mike Appel. Perhaps the reason was greed. The rock stars no longer needed their mentors. Or maybe it was a traumatic disillusionment when reality finally struck, for fathers are rarely propelled by such blatant manipulation. Maybe the sudden acknowledgment that the emotional bridge was built of money was simply too hard to take. Either way, like spurned lovers, the endings were acrimonious and bitter, for the basis of any natural love is genuineness and that was the one quality, the most important quality, that was missing.

Rick and I had been seated only a few minutes when the manager of the Eagles ambled in. He wasn't what I expected. Dressed in blue jeans and a white T-shirt with "The Eagles—Tour of the Century" silk screened on the front, he was fortyish, fat, and, surprisingly for seven a.m., jovial. I was expecting someone hardened, and if not attractive, at least not a man half-bald, with a flat nose and mirthful chubby cheeks.

"So, how's the tour so far?" Rick asked.

"Great. The kids are really great! They've never played so well," he gushed. "We killed them at the Spectrum and we're already sold out at the Forum."

"You're damn near sold out here as well," Rick told him.

"Good. They'll love to hear it. We didn't get in until three in the morning but I'll let them know as soon as they stumble out of bed."

Rick and the manager talked for several minutes, running down a checklist of things that had to be arranged—what had been taken care of and what hadn't. Rick was obviously efficient for few things hadn't been done. The discussion branched off about the competition. "I understand The Moody Blues are doing very well," the large man said. The room was hot and he kept wiping perspiration off his face, but he never lost his spirit, especially when Rick said, "The Eagles are my highest grossing concert."

The manager helped himself to a second serving of eggs and toast and then, satisfied all had been accomplished, bid us goodbye and meandered off with a smile.

"I'm amazed," I turned and said to Rick. "What a decent guy."

"What does that mean?" Rick said, a little confused.

"He seems so warm and caring."

"He probably is," Rick agreed, "considering he is the man who founded and launched the group. They wouldn't be where they are today if it wasn't for him, but he isn't their only backer. There's others and all they care about is money. That's the name of the game." Rick was silent for a moment. "It used to kill me back in the sixties. These guys with love beads and flannel shirts singing about peace and harmony. Shit, they were worse than any of them. Greed, man, fucking greed, that's what it was all about."

I was too keyed up from the morning's meeting to go back to sleep so while Rick rested in his room I reviewed my strategies and analyzed the numbers. Surely Evansville ought to sell out. And here in Terre Haute, with the Shriner's Circus almost done and my advertising about to start, there was still no reason I shouldn't double my $360,000 projection. $720,000 had a wonderful ring. And why not? I had more damn stuff about to hit this one-horse town than it had ever seen. All I had to do was sell out the evening shows while filling up seventy percent of the matinees. I could see Allen's face when I reel off the number. He'd be ecstatic!

Just then I heard a knock on my door. I looked up, startled to discover it was almost noon.

"Come on. You going to sleep all day? We've got to get down to the arena," Rick yelled from outside the door.

"I'm coming," I shouted back. "I'll be right there."

There was a bedlam of activity going on as Rick and I took a seat ten rows up in the stands. Forklifts were pushing the stage together. Carpenters were hammering brackets in place while wires were still being routed. Huge lights were being wheeled to the floor on small tractors. No one person appeared to be in charge. Instead each group seemed to be acting independently. It was fascinating to watch, especially since most of the workers looked sadly out of shape. But long hair and cigarettes aside, they clearly knew what they were doing. Occasionally, I noticed, someone would crack a joke or rib one of their fellow workers but mostly it was all pretty serious.

"Who are they?" I asked, pointing in the direction of a half-dozen girls milling around the floor.

"Groupies probably, hangers-on the stage hands picked up somewhere last night."

"That one's cute," I said, nodding toward one of the girls with slender hips.

"Yeah," he said. "A bearded clam. I love those bearded clams."

It took me a minute to figure out what he was talking about. "Where'd you hear that?"

"I made it up. Or how about cracked valise?" he laughed. This particularly amused him and he repeated it again more loudly. For the first time I realized he, like me and most other men, was unsure of himself around women, attracted to them on one hand but fearing or distrusting them on the other. Maybe his uneasiness stemmed from control. Most aspects of his life he had managed to control, but women were an entity he couldn't. Although I'd seen him quite charming and women clearly liked him he was reticent to put his ego at risk. Odd, I thought, as I watched him rise confidently from his seat.

"I'm going to the box office," he said. "Hang out here as long as you like."

I watched the workers for the rest of the afternoon as lights were clamped into position, earphones were tested for sound and quality and the microphones were put into place. Gradually, as more and more was completed, the workers grew fewer. Even the girls disappeared, and although I was inside the arena I felt the darkness coming on.

Rick and Stan finally appeared from one of the upper tier entrances. "Why don't we all get something to eat," Rick called out. "The concert doesn't start until eight p.m., which gives us a few hours to kill."

Stan suggested a small café around the corner. It was a well-lit family oriented restaurant. I hadn't showered since the previous morning and now felt out of place as well- dressed parents and children filtered in for Sunday dinner.

"We look like a trio of desperados," I said, managing a grin as I glanced about.

"Who knows?" Rick said, enjoying the fact we stood out. "Maybe we'll all end up in suburbia yet."

It was quarter-til-eight when we arrived back at the arena. The halls were full of kids and more were streaming through the doors. We positioned ourselves near the stage and once again, in ritualistic fashion, the kids began stomping their feet. The concert stalled. By now I was certain it was part of the manager's plan. Make them wait. Build their anticipation. And then hurl out the band when the crowd hit a fevered pitch, just before they turned ugly. The manager of the Eagles must have done this a hundred times. I watched him now as he opened the stage door. I could see his full frame patiently blocking the entrance. Finally, he stood aside, his belly bounced, his arms waved frantically, and the band raced past him onto the stage. The timing was perfect. For the next three hours, the Eagles played hit after hit. When the band members put down their instruments and descended the stage, the kids kept screaming at the top of their lungs. The manager was beside himself. "They love you! They love you!" he shouted and waved the band back on stage for two encores.

Rick joined me downstairs a few minutes before the last of the crowd had left. "Come on, the band is gathering at the bar at the Holiday Inn. Then there's a party afterwards."

We arrived at the Holiday Inn and the Eagles were already in the lounge, sitting around a long table sipping beers. At the head of the table sat the leader of the band, wearing a mustache, trimmed goatee and a black beret. Next to him sat the lead singer, a wholesome looking man with long, blonde hair and strikingly boyish features. The others, to me, looked a little odd, almost vacant in their expressions. I sat down at the other end of the table opposite one of the guitarists. He was a strange fellow with curly hair and jerky mannerisms. In fact, he was so clearly on edge, he made me feel at ease.

"Great concert!" I said, trying to initiate a conversation.

"Thank you," he mumbled, shakily lighting a cigarette, before taking a long drink.

"That must be awesome," I said. "I can't imagine what it must be like to play in front of fifteen-thousand screaming kids."

He smiled faintly, nodding in agreement.

"What are you going to do when it ends?" I asked.

"When what ends?"

I had no idea, other than intense curiosity, what was leading me down this track. The others at the table were actively engaged in conversation while I seemingly had his attention. But just as I started to continue the dialogue two men entered the room with purposeful expressions and began circulating among the members. These must have been the backers Rick had been talking about. One of them approached the man I'd been speaking to. He was moving at a rapid pace. "Sign this," he said, placing a white document on the table in front of him.

"What is it?" the band member said, looking up.

"Don't worry. Just sign it," he said, smiling while placing a pen in front of him. I watched in disbelief. Within minutes, each of the band members had signed some kind of contract and not one of them had taken the time to read it.

After the two men departed, I picked up where I'd left off. "The screaming kids, the adulation. What are you going to do when it stops? I mean it can't last forever."

I was searching to see if he had it all in perspective. He looked at me and his face suddenly turned red.

"Who are you? Are you some kind of goddamn reporter?"

"I'm sorry," I said, and I noticed a few others glanced in our direction. I'd egged him on without anticipating the consequences. "I'm not a reporter. I was just trying to make conversation."

Fortunately, the band member in the black beret exclaimed, "What are we doing down here? There's booze and food on the fifth floor."

The floor was already crowded when we arrived upstairs. I recognized several of the people. A few were the stage hands I'd earlier watched. I also spotted some of the girls that had been hanging around. One of the girls was noticeably older now that I saw her up close. She was only in her mid-thirties but her skin was pasty and her eyes had dark pouches. The lines around her eyes gave her a sad look, and I couldn't help feeling sorry for her. She didn't seem to be with anyone in particular, and I wondered how she got here.

The party, or at least some of it, moved from the corridor and into one of the large bedrooms. The lead guitarist, still wearing his beret, reclined on a double bed while two attractive young women in halter tops sat at the foot. The lead singer, the one with the boyish face, walked by. One of the girls moved over and patted the bed. She was stunning but he barely acknowledged her, declining her invitation with a shake of his head.

Jesus, I thought, so that's what it's like.

Rick and I stood on the fringe while the room got stuffier and noisier. People moved in and out. The air got thicker with smoke and some of the people began to look dazed. I was curious to see if any of the band members scored—who was pairing with whom—when suddenly I saw one of the stage hands, a burly man, shoving a woman toward the bathroom door. She wasn't resisting yet she wasn't moving voluntarily either. She just looked sort of wasted. I wasn't sure if Rick noticed it too. I watched the man open the bathroom door and push her in. Just before the door closed, she turned and I saw her face. It was the older woman with the dark, sad eyes. My breathing quickened when I turned to Rick.

"What's going on?"

"I don't know. But I don't like it."

Everyone else seemed oblivious. They probably didn't notice anything unusual but I stared at the white bathroom door. Finally the door opened. The tall, seedy looking man walked out, quickly shutting the door behind him. He snatched a fellow worker by the arm. "Come on. Let's get the hell out of here."

"Why?" I heard his friend say.

"Just go," he replied nervously, and he dashed out of the room.

"Come on," Rick said. "We're out of here too," and he grabbed me by the elbow.

"What about the girl?" I said and I looked back at the bathroom door.

"What about her?" he shouted. "Let's just get out of here."

He clasped his briefcase, telling a woman to go check the bathroom, and was halfway down the corridor by the time I caught up with him. I felt guilty not knowing if anything had happened to her. I was sure the stage hand didn't even know her. She was just easy prey. He was probably already speeding out of town.

Stan was sleeping behind the wheel of the limo. Rick threw his thick briefcase into the back and we piled into the seat. "To Evansville," he said, and Stan quickly pulled away toward the highway.

Within a few short minutes it was clear to me Rick had already forgotten about the incident. I rationalized that he'd probably seen worse a hundred times.

"How about celebrating?" he said, and he poured us each a glass of wine. "A toast to success," he said, "good old fashioned success." And then he opened his briefcase. It was brimming with cash, huge wads of twenty dollar bills.

"Here, want to play catch," he said, and he tossed me a stack in the air. I caught it, spilling wine all over my shirt.

"Where did this come from?" I said, my eyes gaping wide open.

"It's my take of the gross," he said. "What do you think it is?" Then he grabbed another stack and tossed it toward me. I grabbed the pack and threw it back.

"Hey, Stan, here's one for you," and he tossed a stack to the front seat. Stan laughed. I laughed. And the limo sped down the highway. I wondered what the farmers would think, the ones toiling in the dark, fertile soil, as we drove down the interstate, tossing back and forth, thick, rich wads of cash.

Lisa came in lugging a rental typewriter. I quickly grabbed it from her and wrestled it onto a space I'd just cleared.

"Well, welcome aboard," I said.

I could tell she was happy to begin.

"Are there any forms I need to fill out before I get started?"

"No. Just keep track of your hours and I'll settle up with you each week." I had asked Mike about a formal hiring process but he had said to just pay her out of the Ringling checkbook he had given me.

"You're in luck," I said. "I've got plenty for you to do and you get to do it in peace and quiet. I'm heading up to Terre Haute. Don't worry," I said, noticing a slight look of alarm. "I'll be back on Wednesday or Thursday. I'll call you from Terre Haute. You can easily reach me if you need me."

I gave her the stack of promotional agreements to type as well as the letter formally inviting the mayor to be honorary ringmaster.

"Where's Rick?" I said, as I passed his secretary on my way out the door. "It's almost noon."

"Oh, I don't expect him in," she said. "He rarely comes in the day after a concert."

I could see why, I thought, feeling tired, but I had too much to do and too little time to do it. Sleep could come later. Besides that, I was anxious to get to Terre Haute. The tickets were in. I hadn't seen Carl Bruce in days. And even though it seemed like years, it was only a week since I'd been invited out to dinner by a rescued damsel in distress.

Chapter 41

OBLIVIOUS

Sin city? It was hard to believe but true. At least that's how Terre Haute was vilified twenty years earlier. Terre Haute had indeed come a long way from the sight of corn-fattened pigs being herded through the city's streets toward the numerous slaughterhouses along the Wabash River before a future proliferation of railroads, brickyards and breweries in the early 1900s. But as manufacturing spread, along with progress, so too did an assortment of vices. Political corruption, prostitution and gambling certainly weren't unusual at the turn of the twentieth century, but for some reason, Terre Haute attracted more than its share. In fact, the city at one time was so colorful, that in addition to "Sin City," the town had been labeled the "Paris of Indiana."

But even though it had been thirty-five years since the mayor and twenty officials had been sent to Leavenworth prison for election fraud, national magazines as late as the 1950s still described Terre Haute as a bastion of crime and debauchery. Some people blamed the Chicago mobs. Others said it was the influence of labor unions. But whatever the cause, a 1957 discovery that Terre Haute was home to a large gambling syndicate only added fuel to the flames.

Meanwhile, as residents and merchants fled to the suburbs, the city structure was aesthetically crumbling as well. Fire and decay had left gutted buildings along some of the city's once prosperous streets and the town, more and more, grew shabby in appearance. No doubt, the city would have continued its steady decline had not the concerns of several civic groups as well as the timely expansion of Indiana State University in the early 1960s finally reversed the course.

Now as I drove off 41 and into the center of town, past the ornate city courthouse with its tall, domed roof and past the newly renovated Greyhound bus station, I could see plenty of signs of urban renewal. Shopping centers and modern buildings replenished the once dilapidated downtown streets, and any signs of vice had long since disappeared. But so too had the vibrancy of the city, it seemed to me. Where, after all, was its pulse?

I turned right onto Cherry Street and headed toward Sixth Avenue. It was a good city, a decent city, full of civic virtue. But I couldn't help thinking a vice or two might add a little character. I drove toward the Hulman Center, slowly circling the arena. Maybe it wasn't the city. Maybe it was me. Maybe I just hadn't given it a chance. What the hell. The same goes for the arena manager, Robert Hanley. Maybe I was just in a bad mood the first time I met him.

I strolled into the arena. Cleaning crews were sweeping between the seats. The stage had already been disassembled and folding chairs were being quietly placed on the concrete floor. It all seemed surreal. Less than twelve hours ago, the Eagles were performing in front of fifteen-thousand screaming fans and now all you could hear were paper cups being swept along the arena floor.

Hanley was seated behind his desk wearing a cardigan sweater. He glanced up at me as he calmly lit a straight stemmed pipe.

"Mr. MacVicar," he said, lighting another match. "Sit down."

"I understand the tickets are in," I said, as I sat in one of the chairs in front of his desk.

"Yup," he said, puffing a little harder on his pipe.

"Well," I proceeded to explain, "since you haven't experienced Ringling Brothers before and tickets are going on sale in less than three weeks, I wanted to make sure you have plenty of ticket sellers on hand."

"I'm sure our usual two sellers during the day will more than suffice."

"I'm not sure you understand. I am about to bombard this town with advertising and promotion to the likes it's never seen."

"I hope you do," he said, calmly. "But you just do your job and I'll do mine."

"Look," I said, unable to control my agitation. "I'm planning to sell out several performances and I don't need people walking away because the lines are too long."

"Don't worry," he said, unfazed by my insistence yet sounding slightly angered. "We'll handle it."

I turned and walked away, hoping I'd made my point, but now no longer doubting my reasons. "That man just irritates the shit out of me."

The thing I liked about Carl Bruce was that whatever he lacked in charisma he more than made up in enthusiasm. He beamed when he saw me. "It's about time you got here. I was beginning to think you'd deserted us!"

"No such luck," I said. "Besides, who would promote this town if we didn't do it?"

"Not to mention tying up three-thousand loose ends," Carl retorted, still grinning.

"We've got a lot to accomplish," I said. "Are you free to work alongside me?"

"I'm all yours," he replied.

My office was just as I had left it. A poster of two leaping tigers hung on the wall near a stack of agreements neatly typed on my desk. Thankfully I was organized. Trying to juggle two cities in my head would be a nightmare.

"Get me the Nielsen and Arbitron reports," I said. "We've only got three days to close out our media buys."

I flipped through the stack of agreements while Carl retrieved the ratings books. All my promotions were scheduled to kick in on Monday, one day after the Shriners left town. Normally I'd let the promotional spots do the front-end lifting while my publicity and paid advertising followed in behind, but with my marketing time cut in half I had no choice but to start my paid advertising sooner.

At least this way, I consoled myself, tickets will go on sale with a bang.

Carl and I sat at his conference table and for the next six hours we scratched out the media schedules. First the primary newspapers, then the dozens of surrounding papers, then a few local magazines, and then we wrestled with our outdoor options. It was seven o'clock before we turned to the television schedule.

"I don't know about you, but I'm getting cross-eyed," Carl said.

"I know. I'm feeling tired too. But let's work another hour before we call it a night. Don't forget, we have all of our radio buys to do tomorrow and I want to make sure all our promotions are still set in stone. I have a phone call to make," I said, "so let's take a break." It wasn't much notice I was giving her but the idea of dinner for two tonight or tomorrow was now even more enticing.

"Hi, is your mommy there?" I asked a squeaky voice, the owner I envisioned of the teddy bear I had seen in the window.

"No," she replied. "But my grandma is here."

A pleasant voice came on the line. After introducing myself, I said, "I'm only at the office for another hour or so and then I can be reached at the Holiday Inn." I hung up the receiver, wishing a hotel address didn't sound so unseemly.

"All right Carl, that's it for today," I finally said, having penciled in the bulk of the TV schedule. "Your family will start thinking I'm a bad influence."

Unfortunately, the Holiday Inn was just as I'd remembered it. Dimly lit, the room was decorated in shades of burgundy. I was beginning to wonder if they went out of their way to make it depressing when the phone rang.

"How are you?" I said, my mood suddenly lifted.

"Great," she said. "Except I have some bad news. My little girl is sick. I'm stuck at home for the next few days. Can we take a rain check on dinner?"

"Of course we can," I replied, trying to sound undiscouraged. "I'll be back fairly often. I'll try you again in a week or two."

I said goodbye and ambled toward the window, surprised at my downward change of spirit. In the distance I saw the bright golden arches of McDonalds. Next to it was a Burger King. I was hungry and tired. At least a burger was a burger, even in Sin City.

Carl arrived just minutes before me.

"Let's get started," I said. "I'm driving back to Evansville tomorrow and we've got a lot to finish."

We worked all day and into the night. As I watched Carl feverishly filling in the TV schedule while I selected the radio buys, I could tell he was just as excited as I was. "There's nothing like a sold-out house," I said, "especially when you know it was your hard work that did it."

It was almost ten by the time we finished. Carl looked drained but he also had a look of shared satisfaction.

"We're going to do it, aren't we?"

"You'd better believe it," I said.

The next morning I reconfirmed all the major promotions—Pizza Hut, CBS, the major radio stations—all were ready to go. Even Ralph Finley, the nervous man from NBC, was clearly excited. His was the biggest promotion of all. "You're going to make a fortune," I said, reminding him of his cut of the matinees. Carl overheard and smiled.

"So what's next?" Carl asked, eager for more to do.

"What's next," I said, "is I'm heading back to Evansville. But you're going to be busy lining up activities for Steve Smith. He'll be here next Wednesday. By then we'll be in the thick of things."

"Who is Steve Smith?"

"The advance clown. Didn't I tell you?"

As I drove toward Evansville, I couldn't believe that what used to take me two weeks to accomplish, I'd now completed in three days, partly because I did what I had to do in the time I had to do it, but mostly because I now knew what I was doing. The decisions I used to ponder had become instinctual, second nature. Maybe that's when you know you're good. You no longer think, you just act. "What malarkey," I laughed. All I do is think. How big will ticket sales be? How am I going to get everything done in Evansville?

What about Bill Sweeney, my freelance ticket seller? Can I trust the son-of-a-bitch? And what is Robert Hanley's problem? I would think he'd be delirious we were coming yet he still acts like he couldn't give a shit. I rubbed my eyes, straining to see past the headlights. Who cares? It wouldn't be long before they'd all be asking what hit them.

I wondered what my secretary was doing. She sure was cute. So was Lee Ann for that matter, not to mention Sheri and the sexy radio rep Jill Bolaro. And what about Linda Browning? Our second date was Friday night. Jesus, how could we possibly top the first?

And promoting Washington, D.C.—Mike had said don't think about it. How could I not? Imagine my parents' reaction. What kind of budget would Irvin give me? Half a million at least. I'll blanket the airways! No one will be able to turn on the TV without seeing an advertisement. It doesn't get sweeter than this!

I turned on the radio but my mind kept bouncing, reviewing all the details. God, there was a ton of them. Yet never had I felt in such control. This was one ball I wasn't going to drop.

Suddenly I saw a sign for Evansville shining in the dark. That's impossible. I'd just left Terre Haute. And all of a sudden I realized I couldn't remember the road for the last sixty miles, not even a single curve. I couldn't even remember steering the car.

Chapter 42
A POWDER BLUE SUIT

Lisa's eyes lit up when she handed me the stack of promotional agreements, all neatly typed. Perhaps it was her eagerness to please, but something about her delighted me to see her happy.

"Great job," I said, a bit more effusively than the amount of work merited.

"I forgot to tell you, I'm not that fast a typist, but I'm accurate!" she exclaimed, relieved I was satisfied.

I looked at her beaming face and decided I'd reward her with something more interesting to do. "Do you know anything about publicity?"

"No. But I'm willing to learn."

"Good," I said, and I pulled out the press kit. "I need you to go to the library and find out the name of every small-town newspaper within sixty miles of Evansville. Then I want you to select a story, retype it on our stationery, attach a matching photo and mail it. You're to do this each week for the next five weeks. In fact, from here on in, I consider you my Ringling Publicity Director. Do you think you can handle it?"

"Absolutely!" she said, and I smiled as she bounced out of the office. I planned to review her story selections but I wasn't too concerned. I knew the small-town papers would run the stories just as they did in Cleveland. As for the Evansville paper, I planned to handle the entertainment editor myself. Rick could help by arranging several interviews for the performers.

Elated, I scanned our promotional agreements. In scale and scope, the number of promotional spots were staggering. Hundreds of spots were scheduled to break on radio and TV in just a few days. It was amazing what a "no stone unturned" approach could accomplish, or was it more like "divide and conquer," I thought, as I came to the letter I'd written Jill Bolaro.

My pulse quickened as I dialed her number. Even her name sounded sexy.

"Good morning," I said, "Is Jill Bolaro there?"

"One moment," a voice replied. "May I tell her who's calling?"

I held my breath for a moment wondering if her interest was still just as strong.

"Well, hello," she said with a coquettish inflection that removed all doubt. "Welcome back."

"It's good to be back," I said, in a flirtatious tone that mimicked her own. "I've been thinking about you."

"You've crossed my mind a time or two as well," she said. "In fact, when it comes to negotiating I've decided I could learn a tad from you."

"Well then, I wouldn't want to disappoint you, would I?" I parried, enjoying the lascivious repartee we'd quickly fallen into.

"Absolutely not," she laughed. "But to be fair to our busy schedules shouldn't we hold our instructions during non-office hours?"

"I can't imagine it any other way. Perhaps you should give me your home number."

"Why of course. It would only be appropriate."

"You're trouble."

"God, I hope so!"

I hung up wondering why I didn't ask her out on the spot but the anticipation was simply too delirious.

Proofing Lisa's stack of promotional letters gradually released my nervous energy. Between correcting a few misspellings and adding several paragraphs for further clarity it was early afternoon by the time I was finished, time to place a call I'd been reluctantly avoiding.

I reached for Bill Sweeney's number. Surely he'd secured the ticket outlets by now and clearly the man knew what he was doing, but the more I thought about him the more I disliked him. Beneath his smooth exterior I detected a sharp edge, a meanness perhaps, that he wouldn't think twice about deploying. Fortunately, I reassured myself as I dialed his number, none of this has anything to do with ticket sales.

"Jamie!" A deep voice resonated over the line, reminding me of his firmer than necessary handshake.

"Hi, Bill. Are we all set?"

"Of course we are," he said. "Weinbachs East and Airway North Park are both going to sell the tickets."

"Only two locations?"

"Hey, this isn't exactly Manhattan. Besides, they're not going to go out of their way if they think everyone in town is hustling tickets."

"You have a point, I suppose," I said, unsure whether he really believed this or was just being lazy. "As long as you're sure we're covered."

"Like I told you, I've been doing this for years. Trust me."

I hung up, feeling relieved our outlets were secured, but no more comfortable about him. A little positive reinforcement, I figured, wouldn't hurt.

"Rick," I said, as I ambled into his office. "Are you sure about this guy, Sweeney?"

Rick looked up and smiled. "Of course I'm not sure. He's an asshole. But he's the only choice in town."

"Great, I'm much relieved."

"At least he's our asshole, so quit fretting. You young Turks are worry warts. Now on to more important things. When are we going to hit the town again?"

"How about tonight?" I said.

"I can't tonight. How about tomorrow night?"

"I can't. I've got a date."

"A date? With whom?"

"Linda Browning, the short-haired woman we met the other night."

Rick grinned. "Well aren't you the swordsman. It just so happens

I'll be at the Harrington Hotel tomorrow night. Maybe we'll run into each other."

"Maybe so," I said, and I was amazed how charming he could be when he wanted. No sooner had I been worrying about Bill Sweeney than I found myself back at ease, trading barbs with an alley cat. If there was one thing I liked about Rick, it was his insouciance . . . at least when it came to Ringling.

"How goes it in Terre Haute?" I asked, understating my sense of anticipation.

"Great! We've got Steve Smith booked solid. It was a piece of cake." Carl almost sputtered in his excitement on the phone.

"Well, don't forget to have plenty of press around. It's the media coverage we need."

"It's already taken care of," he said. "By the way, my wife and I would love to have you over for dinner the next time you're up."

"I'd love to," I said. "But I won't be there until Tuesday and then just for a few days."

"I'm beginning to think you don't like it up here."

"No, it's nothing like that," I said, realizing he was feeling slighted. "It just seemed to make sense to base myself here in Evansville." There was an awkward moment of silence. "Think of it this way," I said, trying to find a positive spin. "You won't have to share the glory when we sell out all the shows!"

Outside I could see the late afternoon had turned into a tranquil summer evening. "Good night," I said, as I strolled past Rick's desk.

"See you in the morning," he said busily, barely acknowledging my departure.

"By the way," I said, "things are going to start getting crazier and I can't be in both places at once. You're going to have to start checking our spots on the air. And if you don't mind, you're going to need to start setting up interviews for the performers."

"Sure. Whatever you say," he said, and I noticed a hint of irritation. At first, I was a little surprised, but I figured he wasn't used to being told what to do.

"Well, good night," I repeated and stepped out into the still evening air.

As I drove toward the office the next morning, visions of a quiet romantic evening with Linda Browning danced in my thoughts. I couldn't wait to be even closer to her. Perhaps dinner out, and afterwards, an endless night of lovemaking. Lord knows we could barely restrain ourselves the last time together.

Lisa presented me with her list of newspapers as soon as I walked in the office. She had done her research and now couldn't wait to start picking out the stories. I advised her to alter the tempo, mailing out a high-action article one week followed by a family-interest story the next. Within minutes, she had covered the floor with glossies. She was having so much fun holding up the photos and pumping me with questions I readily gave up any thoughts of serious work.

To enliven matters further, Rick walked in a few hours later, turned on his tape deck and blasted up the volume. "Thank God it's Friday!"

"Are you crazy?" I hollered over the music.

"Hell no! It's Friday. Let's have some fun."

Lisa started laughing. The rhythm was wild. First I heard only drums, then a sax kicked in. Lisa and I looked into his office. The son-of-a-bitch was dancing. Not only was he dancing, he was singing with the lyrics.

Rick's hands shot over his head and his hips began gyrating in perfect rhythm, bumping against his desk as he glided to the center of the room.

"Man, you can dance for a white boy!" Lisa shouted, clapping her hands. "You're certifiable!" I hollered. Rick grinned, swinging his hips, singing to the music.

"I'm outta here," he yelled, and without missing a beat he snatched his briefcase and began sliding out the door. "See you tonight, circus man."

"That's it," I said, smiling at Lisa. "It's definite, the inmates have taken over the asylum."

Between Rick's spontaneous performance and Lisa's playful choice of press photos, the rest of the day was useless. And why not? Rick was right. It was Friday and two hours from now, I'd be dancing with Linda Browning.

※

I drove downtown and marched into a men's store a block from the Harrington Hotel. A powder blue suit was hanging in the window. I'd noticed it for several days, every time I drove home. The color was the prettiest blue I'd ever seen, the color of robin's eggs. The material, I now felt, was a soft linen, soothing to the touch. A dark blue thread circled the lapels.

"I don't suppose I could get the pants tailored by tonight?" I asked, hopefully. "The jacket fits perfectly."

The owner looked at me surprised. "I'm afraid not," he said and then turned round with a thought, "but the jacket is cut just like a sports coat. Why don't you wear the jacket with a pair of dark slacks. You'll look like a million dollars."

"Great idea," I said. "If you don't mind, I think I'll wear the jacket now."

"Of course," he said, and I stood again, admiring myself, in front of the three-way mirror. When I come to Washington, I proudly thought, this is what I'll wear.

※

"I swear, is it possible for you to not look beautiful?"

"Oh, come on. I'm plain and I know it. I've been told that all my life."

"Well, whoever told you that should have their heads examined. You're one of the prettiest women I've ever met. How many women can go out without an ounce of makeup, just enter and light up the room."

"More! More!" Linda said teasingly as she moved closer, nestling her face against my chest. Not only were her features wholesome but her scent was as natural as a tropical breeze.

"What is that you're wearing? You even smell wonderful."

"I'm not wearing anything. It's probably cocoa butter. I use it for my skin."

"No wonder I felt I was back in the Bahamas. Come here. Give me one more deep whiff!"

"Enough!" she said laughing. "You're taking me to dinner."

"I certainly am," I said, "and I'm determined to top our first date. I know just the right restaurant, a quiet dinner for two, candlelight and dancing. What do you think?"

"Actually," she said and she acted a little uneasy, "I sort of thought it would be fun to be around people. I guess I should have said something but I told some friends we'd meet them for dinner."

"I see," I said, trying to hide my disappointment. "That's fine. I'm sure they're a nice group of people."

"Let me get my coat," she said. As she walked to the closet I tried desperately to switch gears. It's no big deal. Who says the second date has to be the same as the first? If I act disappointed I'll only look like a jerk. If she wants to have a fun evening with friends then that's what we'll do.

She directed me to a pizza parlor a few miles away. Her friends were waiting when we arrived, two men and a woman. The woman truly was plain and the men looked like computer nerds, or at least the one with the black rimmed glasses did. A fun bunch, I thought.

Linda introduced us. I could tell their friendship was longstanding. They were delighted to see her. Why not, I thought, she was clearly out of their league. Make the best of it, I told myself, and I searched for common interests.

The only thing I discovered was one of the men had a brother who thought he might be interested in advertising. As the evening dragged on, the more I looked at Linda the more disgruntled I became. If we're not going to have a romantic evening at least let's have a fun evening. These had to be the most boring people I'd ever met.

Finally they announced they had to leave. Thank God. Half the evening was ruined but the other half can certainly be salvaged.

"Would you like to go back and have a drink at the hotel?" I asked.

"Okay, if you want," she said hesitantly, and I could tell I hadn't done a very good job hiding my feelings.

She didn't say much on the way to the hotel. She seemed a bit sullen and I wasn't sure how to turn the evening around. Thankfully as we walked in the hotel and strolled across the lobby, I spotted Rick Johnson talking with friends near the bar.

"Look! There's Rick Johnson. Now we can have some fun."

She stopped and turned. "What did you say?"

"I said, 'There's Rick Johnson. Now we can have a good time.'"

"You didn't like my friends?"

"Your friends are fine. But you have to admit they were a bit dry."

"You mean boring?"

"I didn't say that."

"You didn't have to."

"What do you mean?"

"You couldn't have been ruder. You didn't even try to get to know them."

"What's there to know?"

"Screw you!"

I stared back defensively.

"It doesn't matter. You're only here for six more weeks. What's the point anyway? Take me home."

I drove her home, frustrated and angry. Who needs this crap?

"Good night," she said, and she closed the door.

I awoke and sat up in bed, slowly adjusting to the light. My shoes sat on the floor. My gaze drifted upward and focused on my wallet resting on top of the dresser. Nearby was a scattering of loose change. Everything was just as I'd left it but none of it seemed connected, as though my personal affects had become isolated. What the hell was I thinking? I never acted like this before. Do I know how to mess up an evening or what? And what's more, I liked her. I liked her a lot. What right did I have to criticize her friends? At least she has friends. My eyes fixed on my briefcase. Maybe if I called her right away and told her I was sorry. I looked in the mirror, frozen. And what would be my explanation? I'm a thoughtless idiot. From the disgust on her face that was already evident. What's the use? She was right. I'm only here for six more weeks, hardly time for anything serious. Sunlight flooded the room. I glanced at my watch. It was only eight o'clock. My stomach knotted at the thought of another night with no plans. Suddenly I thought of Jill Bolaro. I got up and reached for her number.

"Hello, Jill. It's me, Jamie."

"Jamie? Good morning. I didn't expect to hear from you so soon."

"I know it's kind of early but the weekend snuck up on me and I awoke with a crushing desire to see you tonight."

"You did, did you? I suppose that could be arranged."

"Fantastic! I know just the restaurant."

"Why don't we meet at my house at seven o'clock. I'm sure we'll come up with something delectable."

Rejuvenated by thoughts of Jill I drove up the sun dappled street leading to Rick's office. The neighborhood was quieter than usual, much as I would have expected for an early Saturday morning. I turned on the copier machine, breaking the silence with a gentle humming sound, and clattered through the kitchen in search of a cup for coffee. My two binders, I noticed, were bulging with notes and promotional deals, schedules and agreements I'd been so busy orchestrating that I hadn't had time to keep Mike abreast of my weekly activities. If I was to be the best promoter I'd also have to be the most thorough. Today was the perfect day. No one in the office. No one to disturb me.

Between Terre Haute and Evansville the binders stretched two hundred pages, but surprisingly, the mundane task of copying the pertinent pages quickly became enjoyable as I thought of Mike's approval. Unfortunately the media schedules were too big to fit on Rick's copier. I'd already seen how other promoters had sloppily taped the pieces together. Instead I sat down and carefully recopied the TV, radio and newspaper schedules.

The day flew by and by the time I was through I had two neat heaps of promotional announcements and a fresh stack of media schedules. I'd also written Mike an executive summary highlighting all the campaign's important points. How many promoters do that, I wondered, as I sauntered out of the office.

Maybe Jill was right. Maybe there were a few things she could learn from me. There were certainly a few things I could learn from her and with less than an hour to go I was anxious to find out. I hurried back to my room, showered, shaved and changed shirts three times in anticipation.

Music emanated from behind Jill Bolaro's apartment door. A saxophone moaned seductively. My heart began beating rapidly.

I knocked on the door, softly, then twice more. When she opened the door I could barely move. Jill was standing in the doorway, three feet away, wearing nothing but a black negligee. Her shapely figure was no longer concealed by a business suit.

In each hand she held a wine glass, her arms open wide. "I hope I didn't overdress."

"I think you're dressed perfectly. But you're standing so far away."

"Am I?" she said, stepping toward me.

"That's better," I said. "Do you have any idea how sexy you are?"

"I'm happy you approve."

"But actions speak louder than words."

"Do they?" she said, and laughing she handed me a glass of wine and took me by my free hand. She led me through her dining room, past her kitchen, down a dark corridor and into a candlelit bedroom. She released my hand, walked away, just far enough, then crossed her arms, grabbed the silky material and slowly pulled it up and over her beautiful breasts.

The hotel restaurant was hopping when I went downstairs for breakfast. Lee Ann looked as saucy as ever, dashing from table to table, but she smiled sweetly when she saw me sit down.

"When are you going to let me take you away from all this?" I said.

"Is that a proposal? You know I'm a married woman."

"Yes, but he won't appreciate you the way I will." I said, winking with a teasing tone. "Perhaps you would like to accompany me to Terre Haute?"

"Well, I'm afraid it's a little short notice," she said, with a wicked grin, "but you never know. Ask me the next time. I just might forget I'm married."

I grabbed my suitcase, waved goodbye, and headed out the door.

Chapter 43
THE GREATEST SALE ON EARTH

"I wasn't expecting you until tomorrow," Carl Bruce said, happily surprised.

"How could I resist? After all, this is the day it starts!" It was Monday morning and I'd arrived late Sunday afternoon. The Shriners had come and now finally gone. I smiled at Carl. "I don't want to know how they did. I've purposefully avoided the arena. Even remnants of their departure might shift my focus."

This was the week I'd been waiting for. The culmination of all our hard work. All the promotions and advertising, television, radio and newspapers, had leapt from the starting gate just hours ago. Steve Smith was due in town Wednesday for non-stop publicity events and on Friday, only four days from today I told Carl, "Tickets go on sale!"

"Well, don't just stand there," Carl said with a grin, "help us stuff envelopes." Carl and his secretary stood behind a table lined with envelopes, press releases and black-and-white photos, all ready to be collated and stuffed.

"Sorry Carl. You're on your own. I'm checking out our billboards today."

It was a beautiful day. I grabbed a map of the city along with the billboard locations and hastily retreated before traces of guilt emerged.

Cottony clouds drifted above and with each passing billboard I became more excited. Lions and tigers jumped out from beneath banners of copy. "For The First Time In Twenty Years! Ringling Brothers and Barnum and Bailey Circus returns to Terre Haute." Where else, I thought, can one receive such instant gratification, forgetting for just a moment I'd spent the last six weeks laying all the groundwork. I tried to slow down. This was no day to hurry. While savoring each billboard, I scanned the airwaves. Every time I heard one radio spot I'd tune to the next station for another. By mid-afternoon I'd heard several spots, each of them accompanied by this morning's newspaper, lying open beside me, to our full-page, two-color ad. The perfect start.

I pulled into the Holiday Inn and sprinted upstairs. CBS and ABC each had a prime time spot on the local news. But it was NBC with its lagging ratings that kicked off its promotion with a bang. In the space of one hour I watched two spots promoting the matinees. Who knows? Maybe I'd even sell out the matinees!

"Are they all up?" Carl asked, strolling in bright and early.

"Every last one of them," I said. "It's a sight to behold."

Carl grinned, "I saw several spots on TV last night." He opened his briefcase and handed me a clipboard. "Here's a copy of Steve Smith's schedule".

"Good God. Are you sure you didn't over book him?"

"You said to keep him busy."

"Steve will love you. If there's anything he hates it's waiting around."

Pleased, I handed him back the clipboard. Suddenly the sight of Steve was no longer a marketing abstract. After weeks of not having seen them, he and Robin would be arriving this afternoon.

I called the office in Evansville. Lisa was hard at work on her publicity mailings. "Give Bill Sweeney a call and see if he needs any help," I said, "if you run out of things to do."

Rick was out of the office. Everything seemed calm, at least compared to Terre Haute.

"You have a call," Carl said. It was Ralph Finley, the nervous account executive from NBC.

"Have you seen any of our spots yet?" Ralph asked, excitedly.

"I sure have. You're going to make a fortune. Keep up the good work!"

No sooner had I hung up than I was told a reporter from the Terre Haute *Tribune-Star* was on the line. "He wants to do a story on the circus. Can he come over and meet with you right away?" Carl hollered in.

"Of course!" I said. "This is just what we want. The whole town is in a frenzy."

I quickly pulled out our press release about the history of the circus, highlighting what the show was like the last time we were here, and waited for his arrival. He was young and bright and we instantly connected. "I'll take anything of interest you've got," he said. I told him all about the animal walk, handed him a program and made certain he was attending opening night.

"What a coup!" Carl declared. "I knew they'd be interested but I didn't expect them to rush over the first day we announced we were coming."

Carl's secretary walked in. "While you were meeting with the reporter a Steve Smith called. He said he and Robin were at the hotel."

"Fantastic!" I said, and I grabbed my briefcase and darted out the door.

The orange and white trailer was sitting beneath a shade tree in the back of the Holiday Inn parking lot. I knocked on the door, listening to the pleasant rattling of dishes inside.

"So how's the handsomest promoter in town?" a voice boomed out from the window.

"Quit flirting with the promoters," Steve chimed in and suddenly they both appeared in the doorway.

"Is it ever great to see you two!"

"It's great to be here," Steve blurted out. "Ten more minutes of dusty road and I'd have shot myself."

"Well, I've got the perfect cure. The hotel's got an outdoor pool with, believe it or not, a Jacuzzi."

"We'll be there in ten minutes!"

I quickly changed, ordered three drinks from the bar and slipped into the swirling water. Within minutes, Steve and Robin appeared and, unwrapping two white towels, immersed themselves in the bubbles.

"So catch me up on everything," I said, anxious to hear any news.

"We're as isolated as you are," Steve exclaimed, reaching for his drink. "We haven't heard a thing."

"Which may not be bad," Robin said.

"It's like Allen told me, I guess," recalling his sparring bout with the company's accountant, "you can't beat an enemy that can't be seen."

"Thanks for the tight scheduling," Steve said, after studying Carl's calendar. "I'd rather be too busy than too slow."

I ordered sandwiches from the waiter, refilled our drinks and thanked Steve in advance, knowing as we parted he'd be up at the crack of dawn.

While Carl Bruce was personally chauffeuring Steve around, I busied myself sketching the outline for a group sales strategy. This was brand new to Carl and he at least deserved a day of fun without me. By late afternoon I was anxious to find out how the activities went. I drove back to the hotel and as I turned into the lot, I spotted Robin and Steve. He had already changed into street clothes and as soon as they saw me, they began running in my direction.

"How did it go?" I hollered.

"Wonderful," Steve replied. "But wait till you hear what we have to tell you."

"What?" I said, and Robin seemed even more excited than Steve.

"Guess who is having 'The Greatest *Sale* on Earth?'"

"What are you talking about?"

"Sears," Steve said. "Robin went shopping this afternoon and there in the mall is a huge banner hanging from their store. 'The Greatest Sale on Earth.'"

"You're kidding? That's trademark infringement. Irvin will go bananas." Then I laughed. "By the same token he'll love it! As Allen once said, 'It's money in the til.' This is Sears, of all places, a national chain. Do either of you have a camera?"

"I do," Robin said.

"Fantastic, we've got to take pictures! There's probably all kinds of circus signage inside. But you've got to do it. Someone might recognize me."

"You bet," Robin said and she quickly grabbed her camera. We arrived at the shopping center and sure enough, a huge banner stretched across the second floor of the building. "The Greatest Sale On Earth." They'd even illustrated circus wheels on either side of the letters.

"My God. You'd think they'd know better."

"Think of it this way," Robin said, "your advertising must be working."

"I'll wait here," I said. "See what you can get."

Robin and Steve jumped out and raced toward the store. Within minutes they ran back.

"It's incredible," Steve said, grinning. "The whole store is covered with signage and circus paraphernalia. We took a ton of shots. We were practically running up and down the aisles."

"Did anyone see you?"

Steve stooped to catch his breath. "One of the managers saw us and threatened to throw us out. I guess we were a little too obvious!"

I quickly drove to a one-hour photo center. Steve and Robin were right. Circus signs were everywhere. They even had cut-outs of clowns holding up balloons. Allen will love this! The photos spoke for themselves. Just before I stuffed them in an envelope I added a one-sentence note. "You can't beat an enemy that can't be seen!"

I picked up the phone to call Allen when suddenly I remembered Irvin's directive in the Bahamas. "I want to be called personally."

My hands all of a sudden felt clammy. I'd never even talked to Irvin.

"I'd like to speak to Irvin Feld," I told the receptionist.

"I'll transfer your call."

"Irvin Feld's office," a formal sounding voice replied. Office, I thought, it feels more like I'm calling Versailles.

"This is Jamie MacVicar," I said, "one of the promoters. I'm here in Terre Haute, Indiana, and there is a trademark infringement taking place. I thought Mr. Feld might like to know."

"I'll see if he's in."

My heart started pounding.

"Hi, Jamie. This is Irvin."

"Mr. Feld?"

"Yes, Jamie, what can I do for you?"

"Well, sir, I hate to bother you, but I'm in Terre Haute. . . ."

"Yes, I know," he interjected.

" . . . and I just found out Sears is running a huge promotion. The Greatest Sale on Earth."

"You're kidding me! Hold on, I'll get our corporate attorney, Jerry Sowalsky, on the line. Jamie, tell Jerry what you just told me."

I told him everything I knew. Then I said, "I took the liberty of taking photos. Would you like me to send them to Allen?"

"No, send them directly to Jerry," Irvin replied.

"Yes sir," I said.

"Thanks for letting me know. By the way, Allen tells me you're doing a great job. I'm looking forward to working with you in Washington."

"Thank you, sir. I'm anxious to work with you too."

I hung up. I couldn't believe it. Irvin knew who I was. He even knew I was doing Washington. I sealed the envelope, walked briskly to the post office, and dropped it in the mail.

I spent the next day with Carl and Steve. It was a joy watching Steve perform again. I still couldn't get over my conversation with Irvin. I told Steve all about it. I sensed he knew I was moving up fast. And I relished the thought he'd be spreading the news.

It was dark by the time we were finished. I suggested dinner but Steve said he and Robin would be leaving early. I shook Steve's hand and hugged Robin goodbye. "Thank you," I said, "for the much needed company."

I wandered back to my hotel room, surprised this time to discover there wasn't a lump in my throat. Life was churning too fast. I didn't have time to be sad. Besides, I thought, as I turned down the sheets, the moment I've been waiting for has finally arrived. Tomorrow, tickets go on sale.

I awoke Friday morning with a start. Suddenly I remembered I had sealed the envelope of photos and in all the excitement I had forgotten to pull out the note I'd written Allen, "You can't beat an enemy that can't be seen!" Jesus Christ, Irvin will think I'm nuts. What the hell, I consoled myself, who cares if I sound a little crazed, as long as ticket sales today go bonkers!

I polished my shoes, grabbed my coat and hurried into the office. It would be the end of the day before I knew the first day's box office results. The waiting was killing me. No matter how hard I tried, I couldn't get my mind off the numbers. What if we sold out one of the performances—all fourteen-thousand seats—on the first day of ticket sales? Imagine crossing out the date on the newspaper ads with a big "Sold Out" in diagonal type. Just think what it would do for sales. Irvin would be ecstatic.

Finally my watch read six o'clock. I swore I'd wait one more minute.

"May I speak to the box office manager, please?"

"This is she."

"Hi, this is the promoter for Ringling Brothers. May I please have today's numbers."

"Yes, of course you can. It is three-hundred-and-seventy dollars."

"I beg your pardon?"

"Three-hundred-and-seventy dollars," she replied.

"That can't be," I said. "How many tickets is that?"

"Fifty-eight," she said, matter-of-factly.

"Fifty-eight?"

I hung up the phone and stared at the receiver. Fifty-eight tickets? What in the hell had happened?

Chapter 44
WHAT?

Fifty-eight tickets? That's impossible. Maybe I didn't hear her right. Maybe she gave me the wrong number. Maybe she confused me with a rock show or something. What if I called her back? Maybe it's some kind of weird joke. I stared at the phone, unable to move. My thoughts were spinning but my body was paralyzed. Slowly the number sank in. Fifty-eight. Not fourteen-thousand. Not ten-thousand. Not even five-hundred. Fifty eight.

Gradually, panic turned into confusion. Okay, so I didn't sell out a whole show the first day tickets went on sale. What the hell does it mean? We haven't played Terre Haute in twenty years. Maybe there's a buying pattern I don't know. It's Friday. People are busy thinking about the weekend. Maybe that's it . . . the weekend. Carl said that's when everyone comes into town, all the farmers, all the small-town folks. Of course, why not? I'm in the midwest for God's sake. Nobody does anything here quickly.

But what do I do about tomorrow? I'd planned to head back to Evansville. The last thing I wanted to do was stay all weekend in Terre Haute. But there was no way I could leave now. Evansville would just have to wait until Monday.

———

I woke up Saturday morning wondering how long I'd been rehashing the what-ifs. What if sales took off today? What if they didn't? It seemed like I'd been thinking about it all night. I stared at the ceiling, immobilized, knowing as long as I lay there I'd stay caught in the whirlpool. I swung myself up and within seconds the swirling stopped. Where was my resolve? How could I allow such thinking? Since when was failure an option? The word wasn't even in my lexicon. I just had to work harder.

The more I thought about my decision to remain in Terre Haute the more I was glad I stayed. There was plenty of work to do, especially in group sales. All morning and into the afternoon I poured through the yellow pages, writing letters to every group listed. By four o'clock I had a stack half-an-inch high. I wandered over to the hotel window. Bleary eyed, I'd had enough.

From my window I could see the spot just vacated by Steve and Robin's trailer. How odd, I thought, to go from such an easy warmth to a sudden longing for human contact. I started to turn on the TV when I thought of my housebound friend. Why not try her again? By now her daughter should be better. Maybe we could all do something together?

I dialed her number hoping she was home.

"Oh, hi," she said, sounding a little startled.

"I'm back in town for a few days. How would you like to get together tonight? We can bring your daughter along if you like."

"I'd love to, really I would . . . but I can't, not tonight."

My spirits sank. "Well, how about tomorrow? I'm here all weekend."

There was an awkward silence. "I can't. I wish I could. Give me a call next time. I'll try to get free."

I hung up feeling baffled, wondering if it was me. But reuniting was her suggestion all along. Then I remembered how she sounded, hesitant, almost as though she was hiding something. I'll bet it was him. It had to be. I walked across the room. Well if she's that damn stupid she gets what she deserves. I stared out at the empty parking lot, feeling more helpless than angry.

I looked at my watch. Ticket sales still had two long hours to go. Never had time moved so slowly. Even then I waited five more minutes just so the box office manager wouldn't think I was crazy.

"Jamie, here," I said, trying to sound as if I'd fallen into a routine. "How did we do today?"

"Pretty good," she said. "Two thousand and forty dollars."

"How many tickets is that?"

"Three hundred and twenty. It was nice and steady all day."

"Great," I said. That was more like it.

The next morning I threw myself again into group sales. By the end of the day, I had another fresh stack of letters. Nothing like hard work, I reminded myself, to assure success. Anxiously I reached for the phone. Despite rain all day and shorter Sunday box office hours we'd still sold two hundred tickets! Now all I had to do was see a steady increase over the next thirty days, then a strong "walk up," and it would be all downhill from there. Once again I made a mental note to remind Robert Hanley to have plenty of ticket sellers on hand.

As soon as I arrived at the office I called Mike Franks and gave him the weekend's numbers. He didn't say a word, which coming from Mike was an excellent sign. "No news is good news," he always said. I handed Carl Bruce the stack of letters. "Here's a good start. If you can have these typed and call a few more groups over the next few days I'd be grateful. We need every organization within sixty miles to receive a group discount offer."

"Consider it done," he said. And on that encouraging note, I hurried out the door on my way back to Evansville.

I was disappointed Lisa wasn't there when I strolled into the office.

"Anybody seen my secretary?" I shouted to no one in particular.

"She called and said she'd be in this afternoon," Rick's secretary responded.

"I see," I said, realizing I'd begun to miss her.

Rick was standing up talking on the phone when I'd walked through his office. I couldn't help noticing his jeans had a crease.

Shirking suits was one thing, I mused, but that didn't mean he didn't have his standards. My desk was neat and organized, just as I'd left it. The only difference was a note Lisa had taped to the front indicating she'd be in at two o'clock.

I heard Rick hang up so I trooped in before he became distracted again.

"How is everything going?"

"Fine," he said, eyeing me with his familiar look of amusement. He started to return to his work. "By the way, I spoke with Bill Sweeney."

"You did?" I said, a little surprised.

"I wanted to check up on him. After all, I did recommend him. He seems to have everything under control."

I returned to my office and reached for Sweeney's number. Tickets went on sale in just four days and despite Rick's comment I was still nervous about Sweeney and his insistence on only two outlets. He picked up on the first ring.

"Don't worry about a thing. We're all set up," he reassured me. "I sent our seating manifest to Strausel yesterday along with instructions for the ticket takers."

I hung up and debated whether to call ol' man Strausel now that he had the seating manifest. It was standard procedure but I shuddered at the thought. I was having enough trouble focusing today without adding a scatterbrained conversation with him. I quickly glanced through my notes. I still hadn't hired the ushers nor, for-that-matter, the musicians, something I should have done days ago. This had to be the only arena in the country where I had to line up our own ushers. "That's your problem," Strausel had said. Fortunately, a local union was only too happy to oblige. I called the foreman, a husky sounding man named Jerry, who told me he'd supply the workers. I told him I expected sell-out crowds. "No problem," he said. "Nineteen ushers ought to do it. I'll collect my fee after the last show, union wages plus ten percent for myself."

That could have been worse, I thought. On to the musicians. I dialed the local musicians' union. The phone rang several times. Finally an old man answered. He kept saying "what?" and within minutes, I realized he was hard-of- hearing. "Trombones!" I hollered. "I need to have two trombones, one oboe, one violin . . ." and I repeated the rest of the roster for a third time.

I told him the circus had an orchestra leader, Bill Pruyn, who was also a trumpeter. One drummer and an organist also traveled with the show. The rest we were obligated to hire from the local unions. If we didn't, the unions could shut us down, or at least the musical part of the show. To compound matters, each performance required over two-hundred compositions and the acrobats and animal trainers naturally timed their stunts to the music. The slightest miscue could be dangerous. Allen Bloom hated the situation and vowed he'd change it, but for now, there was nothing we could do. We were under the thumbs of the unions. And to exacerbate the problem, the unions often featherbedded. They required a minimum number of musicians to match the size of the show, and we had to hire them whether or not they were on Bill Pruyn's list. Sometimes we could argue with the union but most times not. I did my best. But after shouting for ten more minutes, I was happy to get by with only two more musicians than we needed.

By the time I finished it was almost noon. Luckily I caught Jill Bolaro just before she left for lunch.

"Hi. I just got in. Feel like company tonight?"

"I'd love it," she said, "but company's just what I've got, friends in town for the week. I'm stuck until Saturday."

"I see," I said, disappointed. "Well, I guess Saturday night it is."

It was three o'clock before Lisa showed up. I didn't know why but she wasn't her jubilant self. We reviewed her publicity strategy. I gave her the media schedule to be typed and then told her I'd be here through Wednesday, in Terre Haute on Thursday, and then back in time for the weekend. She nodded saying while I was gone Bill Sweeney had dropped by, and she quietly returned to her work. But a few minutes later she said, "Would you mind if I didn't work here on Thursday, if maybe I worked out of my home?"

"Sure, that's fine by me," I said, glancing over at her, "Is there something wrong?"

"I'd just rather not be here when you're not around, if that's okay."

"Sure," I said. "I don't want you to feel uncomfortable."

I walked her to the door that night, puzzled. I realized she wasn't going to tell me her reasons, but I still wondered what had happened that had upset her so.

The next two days I called the media, setting up performer interviews with radio stations, TV stations and the newspaper. Rick said he was too busy this week to help. Each evening I anxiously called the Terre Haute box office. Ticket sales were still holding steady, about two hundred a day, neither moving up nor down. I was at a loss not knowing if the results were good or bad, with no recent past to compare.

Thursday morning arrived, the day tickets finally went on sale in Evansville. I grabbed my car keys. "I'll be damned if I'm going to sit around here all day on edge," I told Rick. "I can just as easily call Sweeney from Terre Haute." As I started to walk out the door, Rick's secretary hollered in, "Mike Franks is on the phone."

"I was beginning to think you'd forgotten about me!" I said. "Where are you?"

"Washington, D.C.," he said, and I could tell by the tone of his voice this wasn't a supportive call.

"Is there something wrong?"

"Yeah. Irvin's pissed. What's with the news story in the Evansville paper about Rick Johnson bringing the circus to Evansville?"

"What are you talking about?"

"Don't you read the paper? Our clipping service just sent us the article."

"I'm sorry, I haven't seen today's paper. But I'll get right to the bottom of it."

I hung up and quickly grabbed a copy of today's paper. Sure enough, on page seven a two-column headline jumped from the page. "The Greatest Show on Earth comes to Evansville." I quickly began reading. "Ladies and Gentleman! Boys and girls! Children of all ages! A splendiferous splash of superb sensation comes to Evansville. . . ." I kept reading. There it was, paragraph four, "Ringling Brothers and Barnum and Bailey Circus returns to Evansville for the first time in twenty years, bringing with it the thrills and excitement long associated with the circus. Booked here by Johnson Productions. . . ."

I couldn't believe it! How the hell did that get printed? I strode into Rick's office.

"What's this?" I said, pointing to the article. "Since when did you bring The Greatest Show on Earth to Evansville?"

Rick shrugged. "They write whatever they want to write."

"That's crap! You obviously talked to the reporter. You must have told them you booked the show or why else would they print it?"

"So what? Who gives a shit?"

"Irvin gives a shit! You're paid to be our advertising agency, not our booking agent."

Rick rose from his desk. "Do you think I give a damn about the fucking circus?" Suddenly the anger, the rage I'd seen, out-of-the-blue, directed at others, was now aimed at me.

"I think you give a damn about the two-thousand dollars I'm paying you!"

"You can take the two-thousand dollars and shove it up your ass!"

We stood frozen, glaring at each other, my heart was pounding so fast I thought it would break a rib. I hoped he couldn't see my hand trembling with rage.

"Fuck you, Rick! You're an asshole," I said and I stormed out of the office, slamming the door behind me.

How dare that son-of-a-bitch scream at me about only earning two-thousand dollars. He hasn't done shit! The only thing he's done is introduce me to Bill Sweeney who's probably so crooked he couldn't walk a straight line. I spun out of the driveway and set off for the interstate.

As if I didn't have enough goddamn troubles, with a building manager so senile I can't even talk to him, an arena so derelict it ought to be condemned and a head musician who's damn near deaf. Plus I was busting my ass in Terre Haute and I didn't have the foggiest idea what the numbers meant. To top it all off Jill Bolaro was having friends in all week and it didn't even occur to her to invite me over. Not once! And now I had to put up with this bull-shit? The more I thought about it, the angrier I got. Angry at Rick, angry at Strausel, angry at the whole situation. Screw it! Who needs him? He could shove it up his ass for all I cared. I had a job to do and nobody was going to stop me. As for Terre Haute's advance ticket sales, I had three more weeks to go. They hadn't seen anything yet. By the time I'm through I'd have walk-up business they won't believe.

I arrived in Terre Haute energized into action.

"What's next?" Carl asked.

"Come on. We've got work to do." For the next three hours, we pored over maps, strategizing promotions with small-town papers I hadn't even considered.

Finally it was six o'clock, the moment I'd been waiting for. I picked up the phone and called Bill Sweeney.

"Jamie, here," I said. "How did it go?"

"Great. First day's sales were two-thousand-three-hundred-and-sixty dollars."

"You're kidding!"

"Nope."

I hung up the phone. Thank God. That was ten times Terre Haute's opening-day numbers. And Evansville was only a two-day date! All I had to do was not lose focus. Don't let this other shit get in the way. Concentrate on Terre Haute—work even harder—sell out Evansville, and then ride into Washington, D.C. on a golden, winged chariot.

Chapter 45

A GENTLE RAIN

The first thing I did when I arrived in Evansville was request the same room.

"Two-thirty-three? Yes sir, it's still open," the desk clerk replied. If I had to stare at four walls, at least they could be the same four walls. A little familiarity never hurt. From the lobby I heard voices coming from the restaurant. Lee Ann spotted me strolling down the hall before I even passed the hostess desk.

"Well, hello stranger," she said. "Did you miss me?"

"Why do you think I'm back?" Just as I'd hoped, our relationship had subtly changed. I could tell by her slightly more tentative teasing and I could tell by the flutter in my stomach whenever she caught me glancing in her direction. Somewhere in our last conversation we had crossed a line and now a tension sparkled between us.

"Are you still going to rescue me from all this?" she asked, brightening with a smile.

"I'm counting the minutes."

I slowly drank a second cup of coffee and asked for my check. "I'll see you again tomorrow."

Terre Haute's change of scenery had only delayed my confronting Rick, without easing any of my foreboding. As I drove to the office, I replayed our fight over and over. Now what was I supposed to do? I certainly couldn't fire him, not with the show coming in three short weeks, me in Terre Haute half the time, and all the media and promotions at full tilt. Then again, maybe he was going to fire me. It was, after all, his office.

I pulled up in front of the house, having little idea what to expect. The limousine was parked in his driveway. I grabbed my briefcase, walked nervously up the porch steps, said hello to his secretary, and marched into his office. He was sitting behind his desk, his feet propped up, reading the paper. Our eyes met. I clenched the handle of my briefcase, not sure what to say, and suddenly he smiled, at first a tiny smile, then a great, big, shit-eating grin. I couldn't help it, I smiled back. He laughed. I laughed. And in an instant, the tension was broken.

"I thought you were gonna whip my butt last week," he said.

"I would have if you weren't so big! How do I go from hating your ass one minute to tolerating you the next?"

"It's easy. I'm a lovable guy. How about a few beers tonight? I'll buy."

"You're on!"

"Good. Meet me at Dusty's at eight o'clock. It's a good old country-western bar. You'll like it."

I resettled into my office, surrounded by papers, almost giddy with excitement. Welcome back to Evansville. I had just arrived and already the weekend was full. Tonight, out with Rick and tomorrow with Jill.

***

Sycamore and Ninth was the address Rick had given me for Dusty's. The tavern was certainly in the right location, situated over an old set of tracks between an industrial yard and an abandoned factory. Nevertheless, I could see a revolving red light inside. The parking lot was already full.

I chose a table near the back and watched several couples dance the Texas two-step while I waited for Rick. He arrived a few minutes later. And as usual, he knew several people.

"Two Buds," he said to the waitress as she ambled over toward us. "How come you haven't picked up any women yet?" he chided me with a grin.

"I was waiting for you," I retorted.

"Well, how about those two over there?"

"Which two?"

"Those two," he said, pointing to two women sitting up front.

"I don't know. They look pretty rough to me."

"They'd probably turn you every which way but loose," he laughed. "They're just waiting for someone to talk to them."

"Well, all right," I said, "if you insist. Let's go."

"No, you go."

"Pardon?"

"I'm serious. I can't do it, not like you. You're incredible at this. It's really fun to watch. You're amazing. Go talk to them. I'll come over in a minute."

"Suit yourself," I said, not sure I warranted his praise. I got up, wound my way through the tables and calmly pulled out a chair.

"Mind if I join you?" I said.

They stared at me blankly.

I proceeded forward. "My name is Jamie. This seems like a nice place."

They still said nothing.

I looked over at Rick. He smiled and waved at me from the corner.

"Where are you from?" I asked.

"Evansville," the taller of the two responded.

"What brings you here?"

"The band."

"The band?" I echoed. "Are you a fan of their music?"

"You might say that. We date the guitar player and the drummer."

"Back so soon?" Rick said.

"You son-of-a-bitch, you knew they were with the band."

"I didn't, I swear I didn't," he said between bursts of laughter. "Well, maybe I had a hunch . . . but that's all! Come on," he said.

"I'll make it up to you." And for the next four hours, he introduced me to a slew of people. Some he knew. Some he didn't. He couldn't care less. Finally he said, "I'm going home."

"Going home?" I snapped back. "It's only two in the morning. I'm just getting a second wind!"

I drove back to the hotel too charged up to sleep. What a ball it was being out with Rick. The man was incredible. I must have danced with six different women and talked to twenty different people. And to think the crazy bastard had set me up. I finally drifted off to sleep, not waking until mid-morning. It was almost ten-thirty. I swung my feet out of bed. Just enough time to shower and shave, and hit the office. Then before I knew it, it would be time to pick up Jill Bolaro. I sure hoped she had a quiet evening planned.

I called Mike Franks late afternoon.

"So how's it going?" he said.

"Great! Ticket sales are still holding steady in Terre Haute and opening day sales were spectacular in Evansville. And I've got more women in my life than I know how to handle!"

"Well just remember one thing."

"What's that?"

"Beauty may be only skin deep, but ugly goes right to the bone."

I worked for two more hours, reminding myself that on Monday I had several permits to obtain. Water tanks were needed for the elephants, electrical hook-ups for the trailers, off-duty policemen for security, and I still hadn't even mapped out the animal walk. I looked at the calendar. It was only two and a half weeks and the show would be arriving in Terre Haute. I still had a ton to do here in Evansville. I couldn't be in both places at once, but I could sure be in each more frequently. From here on in, I decided, I'd rotate two days in one town and two days in the next. And to maximize my time, I'd leave at dawn and return after dusk.

I looked at my watch. It was almost time to meet Jill. I had just enough time to map out the animal walk. The train would be stopping only two miles from the building. But why not make it a huge splash? After all, when was the last time Evansville had experienced an animal walk? I took out a red marker and began routing the walk, first to the west, then through the northeast and finally right through the center of town. Eight miles.

Axel Gautier, the elephant trainer, wouldn't be happy, but the publicity would be fabulous. I could imagine the crowds lining the streets.

Jill looked beautiful stepping outside her door.

"You ready?" she said.

"Where to?" I asked, as she handed me her coat.

"Dancing!" she announced. "My house guests just left. Let's have some fun!"

"Where did you have in mind?"

"Everywhere," she said. "I'll drive!"

For the next five hours we hit every nightclub in town. The only one we missed was the one Rick and I just left. I couldn't understand where all my energy was coming from but just the sight of Jill's long legs in her short, black dress kept me in a state of frenzy. It was almost midnight when we burst through her door. Our clothes peeled off, piece by piece, on the dash to her bedroom, before laughing and giggling, we slipped beneath the covers.

Laughter turned into craving before all that remained, two hours later, was tenderness. And then she fell asleep in my arms, her brown hair spilling over my chest, and through an open window, amidst the sound of her breathing, I listened to a gentle rain fall quietly on the street. I could smell the leaves, and occasionally, I could hear a car pass by. And for the first time in weeks, secure in Jill's arms, I fell peacefully, deeply asleep.

Chapter 46
PANIC

A stack of messages was waiting for me when I walked in the door, organizations wanting free tickets, local Terre Haute papers with questions, circus fans from out of the woodwork. I looked at the pile and grinned at Carl. "Hold on to your seat. "This is only the beginning!"

I figured I'd return the media calls, while letting Carl handle the circus fans and ticket requests. With group sales already at a discount and expectations of sell-out crowds, "I have no intention of giving out freebies," I told Carl. "Besides that, we already have the urchin promotion."

I shifted my feet uncomfortably. "I drove by the arena on the way in. How's my friend Robert Hanley?"

"Funny you should mention him. He called here yesterday morning wondering when you'd be back."

"Well, I guess that's the closest I'll ever get to an endorsement," I conceded. "Hanley had to acknowledge us sooner or later."

I told Carl I'd be back shortly and drove across town to the Hulman Civic Center hoping again I could re-convince Hanley to have more ticket sellers on hand. Hanley was standing outside his office smoking his ubiquitous pipe.

"I'm glad you could come over," he said. For a change he

sounded more cordial. "I thought I'd show you the backstage area behind the arena."

I followed him downstairs, neither of us saying anything. We strolled along the arena floor before passing through the backstage entrance. Hanley paused, nodding ahead. "This is where the circus can spread out." It was easy to be impressed. All of the walls were freshly painted a two-toned yellow and white. The floors were shiny, recently waxed, and on either side of a long corridor were rows of dressing rooms with full-length mirrors and double-door closets.

"Charlie Bauman will be delighted," I exclaimed. Hanley smiled, tapping his pipe, clearly proud of his fashionable arena.

"Don't forget, we'll need plenty of ticket sellers," I said, hoping his generous spirit might elicit even more of a response.

"Don't worry," he demurred. "I'll provide whatever we need."

I was gladdened to see Carl had followed through with the group sales mailing while I was in Evansville. All of the letters, including several new ones, were neatly typed and ready to go. I also noticed that a large box of posters and three cartons of direct mail flyers had arrived.

"How long are you here this time?" Carl asked.

"Just today and tomorrow. From here on in I'll be shuttling back and forth. There's a ton to do."

I glanced at the posters, knowing he would help me any way he could. "Why don't we start with those posters and flyers? Do you know any kids that could give us a hand for a few bucks and front-row seats?"

"My son's a Boy Scout. I'm sure we can round up a crew."

On the drive up from Evansville I'd thought about all the things we'd done and all the things we now could do. For starters I decided I'd call all the people with whom we'd arranged promotions. There must have been forty names. There wasn't anything new to report but by the time I was through I'd again hyped most the media.

All the next day I returned calls. Just as I'd hoped, many of the small papers and radio stations wanted performer interviews. But I only had a handful of English speaking performers. So between calls I pitched the TV and larger radio stations. By nightfall I leaned back in my chair and scanned the results. "Guess what, Carl? There is no longer a day the first week without at least one interview!" I rose from my desk. "Another day without seeing the sun."

I grabbed my suitcase and set off back for Evansville. Too excited to eat I settled for a Coke and a pack of peanut butter crackers. It was eleven o'clock when I arrived at the Harrington Hotel.

I reached for the phone. "Jill, it's me. Any chance of getting together? I just got back in town."

"Sure," she mumbled, drowsily. "Why don't you come over tomorrow night?"

I hung up, surprised she was in bed so early. I quickly unpacked my things. Well, at least one of us was still wide awake.

I arrived at Rick's office before anyone else. I sat down at my desk and surveyed all I still needed to do. I gazed at the calendar mentally counting off the days and suddenly I realized with the interviews and all I'd arranged, once the show came to Terre Haute, there was no way I'd be thinking about Evansville. I'd be totally preoccupied. I stared again at the calendar. Damn. I had less time to devote to Evansville than I'd thought. Everything that still had to be done had to be completed in the next eight days. I hadn't even lined up the riders for the animal walk yet. And to make matters worse how much help would Rick really be? We may have made peace but he still wasn't any assistance.

Time was too precious to waste. I'd avoided it long enough. I picked up the phone and called ol' man Strausel. "If you don't mind I'd like to come out and have a tour of the backstage area."

"What for?"

"Well . . . it's my job. The circus will be here in no time at all and I need to know what facilities you have."

"What we have is damn good enough for the rock shows, country western shows, antique shows. . . ."

"I realize that, sir, but you see, we have two-hundred performers and eighty-seven animals. It's a little more complicated."

"Suit yourself!" he said, and hung up the phone.

Exasperated, I jumped in the car. Whatever he had on the mayor had to be something.

Strausel and his assistant Betty were waiting impatiently. I followed them downstairs. It was worse than I imagined. The building had only three dressing rooms, barely enough toilets for ten people let alone two-hundred and just one central area hardly big enough for the show girls.

"This is totally inadequate!" I blurted, wondering again what headquarters was thinking. "We'll need to rent dozens of port-a-johns and extra generators, and most of the performers will have to camp outside in make-shift tents. God help us if it storms! And in addition," I said, shuddering at the memory of the cops he had hired, "we'll now need tons of extra security!"

"Well, the contract said no such thing!" Betty spat.

Speechless, I drove back to the office and called Earl Duryea, our contract negotiator. "Are you aware what a disaster this arena is? I'm talking three shabby dressing rooms, that's all." Earl sputtered an apology but was still little help. "You'll just have to manage the best you can."

The rest of the day I called security agencies, port-a-john companies, tent suppliers and electrical firms. "What a nightmare," was all I could think.

When I showed up at Jill's I was relieved to discover she'd made dinner and purchased two bottles of red wine. Exhausted, I thought I'd be too tired to talk but somehow I couldn't stop. "Doesn't anyone in this city know this man shouldn't be running an arena?" We talked late into the night, finishing both bottles of wine before finally falling asleep.

The next morning I commandeered the elephant riders, twelve in all, being careful to choose the most lively media personalities in town. "It's going to be eight bumpy miles," I warned, but none dropped out. I made a note to send tickets to the riders, relishing the thought of the publicity.

Late in the afternoon Lisa arrived. For a warm pleasant moment I gladly put my worries aside. It was reassuring just having her near.

"Is there anything else I can be doing to assist," she asked, "besides mailing out the press releases?"

"Not just now," I said. "Although you can send our animal walk riders opening night tickets." And suddenly I remembered the mayor. I'd mailed out his invitation but had forgotten to confirm the arrangements. "Could you send the mayor a note, asking him to meet me in Strausel's office, seven-thirty opening night, thirty minutes before showtime?"

It was late when I returned to the hotel and my thoughts were still swirling. Ticket sales in Evansville still outpaced Terre Haute but even in Evansville I couldn't take any chances, not if I wanted a four-show sell-out.

I pulled off my clothes and crawled under the sheets hoping I'd fall asleep quickly. But my thoughts kept turning. I sat up and clicked on the TV. It didn't help. I kept thinking of all I still had to do and how I was going to get it all done. Finally, I drifted off to sleep, but I awoke in the middle of the night. In the dark my thoughts were still spinning. The exact same thoughts kept coming, round and round, and nothing I could do would make it stop. I turned on the light, sat up and stared at the wall but my mind kept racing. Frustrated, I stumbled up. My hair, I saw in the mirror, was matted against my forehead. My shirt was wringing wet.

I staggered over and sat by the table in front of the hotel window, keeping a distance from the bed. Outside the night was still. My head had begun to throb. Slowly I let it drop. It was seven a.m., jolted by the sounds of traffic, that I awoke again with a start.

I showered and shaved and ambled downstairs for a cup of hot coffee to go. Lee Ann spotted me as soon as I sat down.

"You're not staying?" she asked, almost imploringly.

"I'm afraid not," I said. "I'm driving back up to Terre Haute. But I'll be back in a few days."

She handed me the styrofoam cup, brushing my hand, and for a moment, I didn't want to go.

I still couldn't tolerate Terre Haute but I did like Carl. In fact, the more we worked together the more I admired him. All day long we went over details—Pizza Hut, CBS, NBC's cut of the matinees, ABC and the small-town papers. I made notes of all the follow through needed and then asked Carl to phone Ralph Finley at NBC. "He's a jittery guy to begin with. By now he must be apoplectic. Tell him advance sales are a little flat but not to worry. We'll have a hell of a walk-up!"

For the first time in days it was early when I left the office. I returned to my room but one look at the four walls and I had to escape. I climbed back in my car and drove south toward the seedier side of town, in the direction I'd encountered the drunken woman. I had no idea where I was going, so I turned up any street that appeared interesting. Finally, I saw a small sign, "Jesse's Bar—Topless Dancers," and I parked the car. Inside, a woman was dancing on a platform in the center of the room. She was tall with long blond hair, the kind of girl I'd remembered in high school that looked as though she belonged in another world, the type you fantasized about, just wondering what she looked like naked. I sat not far from the stage. She danced to the music, provocatively swaying, in nothing but jeans and a white cowboy hat.

It was midnight when I meandered out and drove back to my room. I'd had several beers and fell hard asleep but I awoke again with a jolt. Goddamn it! It was doing it again. My mind was racing. I turned on the light. It was five in the morning. Over and over, like a gatling gun, I was counting the numbers. If my projection was $360,000 and I needed to do $720,000, and only twenty percent was sold in advance, how many tickets at the windows would I have to sell? The numbers kept firing, round and round, and all I could see were lines of people, with only one seller, Robert Hanley, standing behind the box office window.

I gave up trying to sleep, rose to my feet, dressed and packed my bags for my trip back to Evansville.

The hotel was quiet when I pulled into the parking lot. I wandered inside, renewed by the dawning of a new day. Lee Ann was all alone in the restaurant.

She peered out from behind the steel coffee maker and at first I thought I saw a look of hurt and anger, but a smile lit across her face.

"Table for one?" she said.

"Two would be nicer."

She smiled again, more warmly this time, and there was something about her this morning that was especially nice.

"One of these days," I said. "I'd like to take you out for a beautiful, romantic dinner, just you and me and a bottle of red wine. What would you say to that?"

There was a moment of silence, a long comfortable moment. "I'd like that," she said. "I'd like that a lot. How about tonight?"

Chapter 47
LEE ANN

All day long I'd waited for this moment, to touch her, to hold her, to take her tiny body with her round, firm breasts, then curl up next to her, her light, silky body pressed softly against mine. Surely, she'd hold me and care for me in ways she couldn't for her husband.

When I saw her waiting in the restaurant all I could think was what an idiot he must be. How could he possibly neglect a woman like this?

I'd never seen Lee Ann dressed in anything but her waitress uniform, but tonight she wore a V-neck red sweater, pulled tightly over breasts that were larger and fuller than I'd imagined. She was wearing plaid slacks, and her fingernails were freshly painted a bright red to match her sweater.

"I never noticed you had such nice fingernails," I said, sliding in next to her on the same side of the table.

"That's because they're fake," she said with a nervous laugh. "My cousin put them on for me today. I thought you might like them."

The restaurant wasn't quite what I'd hoped for. It was noisy but Lee Ann had chosen a booth way back in the corner. I had said it was best for her to decide where to meet.

We chatted for several minutes. I looked for signs of hesitation but all I could detect was a calm determination. I wondered for a moment if she'd ever done this before. We ordered dinner and a bottle of red wine and talked about her kids. There were three, two girls and a boy, the oldest one twelve, and then we talked about her childhood growing up in Evansville. She'd married young, straight out of high school. She was proud at the time, she said, to be the first of her friends married.

"It seems like I've been married all my life."

"Well, you wouldn't know it," I said. "You've got the spirits of a twenty-year-old."

"How sweet," she said. "Come on, let's get out of here." Outside, the summer air was warm. The traffic was sparse.

"Where are you parked?" she asked.

"Over there," I said, pointing to a car in a darkened corner of the lot. She stuck her hand inside my elbow and we marched toward the car. I opened the door. When I slipped into the driver's side, she was already near. Without saying a word, she looked up and kissed me. I could smell her hair and feel her breasts brushing against my chest.

"Are you going to make love to me?" she whispered.

I turned the key in the ignition and drove out of the parking lot. She snuggled against me. I could feel her warmth. I wanted to take her in my arms right then.

I passed a couple of hotels that didn't seem right, then pulled up slowly to a white, wooden building spotted in green light. I sensed the desk clerk knew why I was there. Lee Ann waited outside in the car.

We drove around the building to a room in the back. I opened the door. Inside, standing beside the bed, we kissed again and I touched the side of her face, content to caress, as long as she'd let me, her lips, her cheeks, her beautiful smooth skin. We sat down on the edge of the bed and I slipped off my shoes, peeling off my shirt. My hand held hers as she rose. "I don't need these," she said and she lifted her sweater. Next came her bra, then her slacks, and finally the rest. She eased into bed, her small body finding my arms. She moaned and her fingers dug into my back, but all the while her eyes stayed closed, her head turned blindly to the side. I rolled her on top, maneuvering her upright, but her gaze tilted to the ceiling.

"Open your eyes," I said. "Look at me."

"What?"

"Look at me. I want to see your eyes."

"Sure," she replied, but it wasn't what I needed.

Finally we both lay back. I held her in my arms but it wasn't for very long. "I've got to go," she said, and on the way to her clothes she stopped and stared in the mirror. "Not too bad," she said, looking over her shoulder, "for a woman with three children."

I got up and held her close, hoping for a warm embrace. Instead we made love again. Afterwards, she seemed satisfied, but almost as if it had little to do with me. I tried to understand. I'd wanted more but maybe this had to come first. Maybe next time she could think of me, I thought, as I drove her back to the restaurant.

I was tired when I stepped into my room. My red message light was blinking. I called the desk clerk. It was a message from Mike Franks. Maybe it was important. I quickly dialed the number, having no idea where he was. After several rings, a sleepy voice answered.

"Hi, Mike, it's me returning your call."

"What time is it?"

I looked at my alarm clock. It was four a.m.

"It's a little late. I'm sorry," I said. "I thought it might be important."

"It's okay," he said, sounding more alert. "I was just calling to check up on you, to see if everything's all right."

"Thanks, I appreciate it," I said. "Things are fine, I'll call you later in the week."

I felt the bright summer sun warming the side of my face. I opened my eyes. Ten a.m. Shit! How did it get so late? Damn it, I had told the front desk to wake me at eight-thirty. I grabbed the phone. "This is Room 233. Didn't I tell you to give me a wake-up call at eight-thirty?"

"Yes, sir, you did," a composed voice answered. "We did call you. You must have gone back to sleep."

"Oh, I see," I said, and I hung up the receiver. Agitated, I jumped out of bed. There was too much to do to waste any time. I quickly dressed, packed my suitcase and headed downstairs to the lobby. There was only silence emanating from the restaurant, despite the lingering smells of breakfast, and for a second I was tempted to duck in to say hello to Lee Ann. But I didn't. For some reason, right at the moment, I just didn't know what to say. Besides, she must be as tired as me. I'll see her when I get back. Maybe then we could pick up just where we left off. I couldn't help smiling at the thought as I opened the glass door.

Before heading up to Terre Haute I wanted to check Sweeney's ticket outlets. Weinbach's East and Ayrbach's North Park were on opposite ends of town. Traffic was busy when I pulled into Weinbach's. Clean and orderly, the drug store sat in the middle of a strip of retail stores. Inside, I was given directions to the back of the store. A colorful booth had been erected, decorated with circus posters and small flyers. A freckle-faced teenager was helping a customer. I didn't introduce myself, instead waiting and watching long enough to be satisfied he knew what he was doing.

I found my way to the second outlet. Ayrbach's, judging from its merchandise, was chosen to cater to the blue collar family. Situated to the right of a large intersection, the store was already crowded.

"Excuse me," I asked the clerk. "How do I buy tickets for the circus?"

"There's a booth in the corner," he courteously replied.

The wooden structure was dark and empty.

"Oh, he must be late. Just hang around," the clerk reassured me. "He should come in shortly."

Shortly? Since when does shortly sell tickets! I strode over to a pay phone.

"Why are you getting so upset?" Bill Sweeney said. "It's only a few minutes after nine."

"Bill, we said the tickets were on sale promptly at nine! If there isn't anybody there, how do we know the customers will return?"

"Look, it's no sweat man. I know what you want. I'll take care of it."

I turned onto the interstate thinking it was a damn good thing I'd decided to check. It seemed like he'd gotten the message but I still didn't feel right. Every answer he gave me always sounded so flip. I pulled off the highway and called Rick.

"Listen. I just got off the phone with Bill Sweeney. You gotta keep an eye on this guy."

"Jamie. I've got other things to do than follow Bill Sweeney around!"

"Jesus, you can piss me off! Does everything have to be a fight with you? I stopped by Ayrbach's and no one was there. Could you please give me a little help?"

"Look, Jamie, I'm sorry I'm irritable, but there's other things in my life besides Ringling. Go to Terre Haute. I'll talk to Sweeney. I'm sure the man knows what he's doing."

"Sometimes, Carl, I swear you're a breath of fresh air," I said, little calmed by the long drive to Terre Haute.

"Have you eaten anything yet?" he asked.

"No. I'm not hungry. I'll grab a sandwich later. How are things going?"

"Good," he said. "I've got a whole troop of Boy Scouts hanging up posters. The mailers went out and I think we sold three blocks of tickets."

"Terrific!" I said. "I'm going to enjoy handing you your bonus!"

For the next two hours we reviewed the affidavits the radio stations had sent confirming their schedules thus far. Unexpectedly weary as we neared the end of the batch, I said "I'm sorry Carl. My mind is going dead."

"No problem," he said. "I'll finish up."

I drove to the Holiday Inn and trudged upstairs to my room. After stripping to my shorts I splashed cold water on my face and flopped on the bed. I wondered if my friend, the one I had rescued, was home. Her mother answered the phone. "I'm sorry," she said. "She's out of town for the week."

That's it. I give up. I curled up against the pillow, rolled over on my side and drifted off to sleep. For the next ten hours, I couldn't recall moving a muscle.

———

The next day I worked on group sales. There weren't many takers but several said they'd get back to me. "Group sales means group decisions," I lamented to Carl. Nevertheless, I felt a positive current in the air. "Now's the time to turn up the heat. Keep monitoring the promotional spots," I told Carl. "I'll be back in a few days."

Perhaps it was my full night's sleep or maybe just clearer thinking but all the way to Evansville I felt grounded in good cheer. It won't be long before the circus arrives, I reminded myself, just don't slow down now.

It was dark by the time I arrived. It was good to be back. After all, in the morning I'd be seeing Lee Ann. Who knows, maybe she'd be available after work?

———

It had been three days since I'd seen her and now as I strolled down to the restaurant I was anxious again to hold her, to smell her, to touch her sweet face. Perhaps even this weekend she could escape for a day. After double checking myself in the mirror I scanned the large room. I didn't see her so I sat at my customary table in the middle of her station. I thought I heard her voice but it wasn't her usual laughter. From behind me I heard a waitress say, "Lee Ann, you have a customer." I pretended not to notice when she walked up beside me.

"Good morning, good looking!" I said, and I glanced up with a smile. My heart immediately sank. "My God, what happened?" Her right eye was swollen shut, it was purple and red and painfully raw.

"You should have seen it the other day. I guess makeup doesn't help much."

"Oh, Lee Ann. I'm sorry. I'm so sorry."

"It's not your fault," she whispered. "I knew what I was doing."

My stomach churned. "What can I do? Is there anything I can do? Do you want to talk later on?"

She looked at me and suddenly her eyes filled with tears. "I can't," she said. "I can't. Please don't see me anymore."

Chapter 48
ADRIFT

I walked into the office. Rick was red faced and fuming. "The damn phones have been ringing off the hook. Everyone from the City Council to any needy group within fifty miles wants free tickets. The circus is all-consuming!"

"You know Rick, I'm really not in the mood for this." I stepped into my office and closed the door.

I sat down and suddenly felt overwhelmed. I couldn't cope with this. I felt like shit and Rick was in one of his moods. I stared at my desk, at the stack of messages, but all I could think about was who could I call? A friendly voice. Someone to talk to. Anyone. And suddenly I had the urge to call Linda Browning. I wanted to reach out, to say I was sorry. There was no hesitation. I picked up the phone and dialed as though nothing had ever happened.

"Jamie," she said. "What a surprise. I've been thinking about you. I've been hearing radio spots about the circus all over town."

"It's almost here. I've been pretty busy." I paused for a minute. "The reason I called is I want to apologize. I really acted like a jerk among your friends. I just wanted to say I'm sorry."

"It's okay. It was a bad night. It happens to us all." She hesitated for a minute and I didn't know what to say. Finally she broke the silence. "It was good of you to call. Maybe I'll see you at the circus."

"Maybe so," I said, a little awkwardly. "That would be nice. You take care of yourself." I hung up feeling relieved, yet all day long I couldn't shake a heavy lump in my throat. The least little thing and I was afraid I might cry.

It was late when I drove back to my room. I didn't eat. I didn't want to be around anyone. My gaze settled on the black phone. Why did it always stand out from everything else in the room? I wished Sam Barrett were around. What I'd give to hear his voice. Why did he have to go and get his ass fired? I didn't even know how to reach him. The pain I'd felt all day welled up in my chest. And suddenly I felt worthless. What the hell am I even doing here? My father was right. I'm in over my head. I stared out the window and my thoughts drifted back and I found myself thinking about Jack Sullivan. How long ago it now seemed, the sight of his friendly face, his wiping his hands as I stepped on his boat. Just him and me, sitting in the white California sun, sipping margaritas. I opened my briefcase, searched through my address book and quickly dialed the phone. It rang several times.

"Hello," a man's voice said.

"Jack, is that you?"

"I'm sorry. You have the wrong number."

"I'm calling Jack Sullivan. Is this an old whaling barge in Portofino?"

"Yes it is. But the previous tenant left months ago. I'm sorry."

The room smelled musty when I awoke the next morning. I got up and wandered over to look at the calendar. Five more days. Thank God, only five more days. The circus would be here. I could sense my mood start to lift. And once again I remembered what it was like in Savannah, in Cleveland, and California. The pride, the feeling of accomplishment, the euphoria I felt. Wait until the performers see the crowds. They'd be ecstatic.

⚡

I drove up the highway, reminding myself two more days in Terre Haute and then a final two in Evansville and that would be it. I'd be driving back to Terre Haute for the last time. The sun streamed through the window. I tightened my seat belt another notch. I'd just have to eat nonstop when this was all over.

My first call from Carl's office was to the box office. Opening night and the first weekend was doing pretty good but with seventeen shows we still had a long way to go. I glanced at Carl. "All our advertising is coming to a peak. Fill up the first few days and word-of-mouth should take care of the rest."

"Where is the newspaper story the reporter promised us?" Carl asked. I quickly dialed the young reporter at the Terre Haute *Tribune-Star*. It was understandable when he said he was waiting for the show to arrive. "Don't forget about the animal walk," I reminded him.

"Don't you worry," he said. "I wouldn't miss it for the world."

"A story on opening day is just as good," I reassured Carl. "By the way, be sure and send tickets to the king and queen contest winners."

Carl asked about the clowns for his client's Pizza Hut promotion. "No problem," I said, putting his mind at ease. "I'll have at least two. What about the small-town papers?" I asked. "Have we invited all the editors to opening night?"

"Not yet."

"Not yet? What do you mean not yet? Get on the phone. This is the fun part! Incidentally, did you call Ralph Finley?"

"Yes, and you were right. He's a nervous wreck. He promised he's been running twenty spots a day. That ought to sell out a few matinees."

I almost forgot and quickly called the Holiday Inn, reserving three rooms for Harold Ronk, Bob Harrison and two couples who normally requested a local hotel. I reminded myself to do the same in Evansville. All the next day Carl and I checked and re-checked our efforts until finally we ran out of time.

"I'm drained," Carl said, "totally drained. Is there anything else we can do?"

"If there is I'll be dammed if I can think of it. We've run hundreds of spots, placed tons of publicity, and done every promotion I know." I stood up and gently squeezed his shoulder. "I can feel it, Carl. Believe me, it doesn't get better than this!"

"This is it!" I hollered out the window. My last drive to Evansville, the last trip down this highway before the circus comes to town. Country farms and shaded fields passed by as I flew down the road. If they could harness my energy they wouldn't need horses. "There's nothing to stop me now. To hell with Rick. To hell with Strausel. To hell with them all. There's not going to be an unsold seat left in the house."

Rick was just leaving when I pulled into the driveway. "Where are you going?"

"I'm a walking zombie. I just did two concerts back-to-back."

"Well, come on. I just got here. Let me buy you a beer."

"I can't. I'm exhausted."

"Come on. One beer?"

"All right, but just one."

We drove separate cars, parked at the Harrington Hotel, and walked to a nightclub a block away.

"Look at this place. It's crawling with women."

Rick sipped his beer and just smiled. "I swear to God. I'm so tired I can't even think fucking straight."

"One more," I said, egging him on.

"You're fucking crazy," he said, and I ordered two more beers. The more I tried to liven him up the more faded he looked. Even introducing two women didn't help. All he could do was complain how exhausted he was.

"I'm going home," he finally announced. "I don't give a shit what you do."

"All right, I give up!" I exclaimed. We walked out into the street. It had rained and lights shimmered on the wet pavement.

"Don't you ever get tired?" he shouted.

"Tired? How can I get tired? I'm invincible!"

"Invincible?" he said, and then he started to laugh and he couldn't stop. He just kept laughing all the way to his car.

I awoke the next morning feeling anything but invincible. What the hell was I so batty about last night? Rick must think I'm a nut. I got up and picked up my clothes. Two more days to go and then that would be it. I drove to the office trying to stay focused but Terre Haute was still fresh on my mind. I kept becoming confused. Just when I thought I'd completed something in Evansville I remembered it was something I'd done in Terre Haute. When I arrived at the office dozens of message slips were waiting. I could hardly believe it! Rick had ignored every call. He hadn't even tried.

I began returning the calls, one by one. Most were requests for free tickets or special appearances, which I declined as politely as I could. Except for one. He had called three times, an elderly man who indicated he managed a hospital for the mentally ill. "Is there any way you could bring over a few performers? It would mean so much to the patients." My schedule was cram-packed but he was already so grateful I couldn't refuse. I agreed to bring three clowns the morning the train arrived. I was nearing the end of the stack but by six o'clock I was running out of steam. I strolled into Rick's office. "Did you talk to Sweeney?"

"Of course I did. He's fine. Would I steer you wrong?"

I walked back to my desk hoping I could focus on all that remained to be done.

The moon was slipping between darkened clouds when I finally left the office. Stepping inside the hotel lobby, a familiar hit was blaring out from the nightclub.

It couldn't be true. Sure enough, a huge poster announcing Blood, Sweat and Tears hung outside the lounge. Amazed, I peeked inside. There they were, bathed in light and perspiration, belting out their biggest song to a room of little more than thirty people. My God, they had filled concert halls of thousands not five years earlier. I gazed inside the room, reminded of my conversation with the musician from the Eagles. So this is the end of the road. This is how it all ends. Singing songs you've sung a thousand times to a tiny audience in a tiny town in the middle of nowhere.

Tired, I retreated to the lobby when a voice called out. "Jamie, I haven't seen you in ages."

I turned and it was Sheri, Rick's so-called groupie. She seemed a little tipsy.

"Hi," I said. "I've been up in Terre Haute."

"Well, we never got a chance to know one another."

"I know," I replied, instinctively liking her no matter what Rick had said.

"How long are you here for?"

"Only until tomorrow," I said. "And then I'm back on the tenth when the show comes to town."

"Well, it was nice to see you," she smiled. I nodded and said goodnight and trudged upstairs.

On Wednesday I felt strange all day, as though I was letting go of something I never really had. It was my last day in Evansville and the next time I'd be here would be the day of the animal walk. I called the mid-town police precinct to verify the route and then I called Bill Sweeney. "I'll be in Terre Haute from here on in. I'll be calling you each evening for the numbers."

"You don't need to worry about a thing," he said. "I'll be right here until the ninth. Then I'll be closing the outlets and moving the box office to the arena."

I hung up and noticed the rental typewriter was missing and remembered in all the activity I'd neglected to check in with Lisa. "I'm sorry," I said. "I've been so busy I've barely had time to think."

"That's okay," she said, and then she paused. "If you need anything, please don't hesitate to call."

I drove back to the Harrington Hotel and flopped down on the bed. Uneasily, I began wrestling with my thoughts, trying to think of anything I might have forgotten. I was tired, too tired to think. I kept replaying my activities in hopes it would lead to something, anything, I still hadn't done.

My thoughts grew thicker, merging with my need to rest. But barely had I spiraled into sleep when I awoke again drenched in sweat. I turned on the light, nervously fumbling for my watch. But even sitting up wouldn't calm my nerves as I noticed, with alarm, both my hands were shaking.

Numbly, I waited out the night, clutching a plea as my means of consolation. It was less frightening to stay awake than attempt to fall back to sleep. At the first sign of light I'll call Mike.

"Mike, it's me, Jamie. I'm sorry to wake you."

"It's all right," he said, sleepily. "What's up?"

"Everything's fine, really, but with everything going on I could sure use some help. Is there anyone you could send me that could give me a hand?"

There was a moment of silence. "Let me see what I can do. Where are you going to be tomorrow night?"

"I'll be in Terre Haute."

"Okay. Give me a call tomorrow. I'll be at home."

I drove up to Terre Haute and tried not to think about twelve days of shows. It was dark when I returned to my room. I hurriedly dialed Mike.

"Mike, it's me."

"I've got good news," he said. "I'm sending down Rich Green."

"Who's he?"

"He's a trainee. We just hired him last week."

"A trainee? I need help, not someone to train."

"I'm sorry. That's all I've got."

I searched for a way to respond, to not show my dismay. "Thanks anyway," I said. "I know you tried."

"Look," he said, hesitating for a moment. "Maybe I could come in and help."

"Could you? Man, that would be great!" Relieved, I hung up the phone. I knew I could count on Mike.

Chapter 49
THE NUMBERS

Wake up you rotten ass town! Don't you know the circus is here? I leapt out of bed. I was so excited I could barely drive.

I turned right on Seventh Street, anxious to get to the arena to see if anyone had arrived. I rounded the corner. Just as I'd hoped, two trailers were parked on the far side of the lot. They must have gotten in during the middle of the night. The trailers looked like Elvin Bale's and Wolfgang Holzmair's. I drove by, close enough to hear the soft purring of their generators. Beyond, beside the ramp, sat a huge stack of hay. Cut and squared into bales, it stood more than twenty feet high. For me, it glistened in the early morning sun. I rolled down the window and took a deep breath. Never had dirt and dust and dried-out grass smelled so good.

I pulled to a stop near the station, restlessly awaiting the train's arrival. The station stood in contrast to the city's newly built arena, its arched wooden frame holding a lonely vigil over a curve in the tracks.

My coffee had grown cold as I glanced at the list of performer interviews I'd soon be handing Charlie Bauman. I could hear him bellowing now. "How am I going to get all deze people to do dees?"

And I tried to take solace in Chris Burskey's encouragement. "Don't worry. He'll at least respect your efforts."

Minutes passed like hours when just then a green and red light began to blink madly. I sat up and peered down the tracks, willing the train forward, when suddenly it appeared, rolling round the corner, a magnificent steel animal screeching and sliding to a stop.

Charlie was the first man off the train. He jumped out between two cars while yelling at the roustabouts to be careful with the rigging. Lloyd Morgan emerged from behind, sauntering toward me, seemingly oblivious to all the commotion.

"So vat do you think? Maybe I should become a promoter," Charlie exclaimed, sliding into the front seat.

"You're way too nice a guy," I immediately teased back.

"Lloyd, how are you?" I asked, shaking his hand. I noticed his hair had grown thinner.

"I'm fine," he murmured in his typically unruffled fashion.

"Well, we're on our way to a state-of-the-art building," I said, turning the ignition key. "But you'd better enjoy it while you can. After this we'll be heading down to Evansville and you can't imagine what you'll be up against. By the way Charlie, here's my list of performer interviews." I figured I might as well get it over with.

Charlie leafed through the list, registering little reaction, until reaching the bottom. "I see I'm being interviewed by CBS TV."

This had to be done deftly. "They're the biggest station in town. I needed someone of your stature. I hope you don't mind."

Four more trailers had pulled into the back lot by the time we reached the arena. I quickly escorted Charlie and Lloyd down the ramp and into the backstage area. Roust-abouts on tractors piled high with rigging followed us.

"I'd like to stay longer," I said, after a brief tour of the dressing rooms, "but I've got to hurry back to the train. Axel Gautier is probably already unloading the elephants and the press should be arriving any minute."

I pulled out of the parking lot, delighted to see families with kids gathering along the curb. Sure enough, half the elephants were already off. Axel pretended not to notice me, screaming in German at the elephants and anyone standing nearby.

Carl arrived. I asked him to keep the press and the riders bunched together while I made sure the kids stood away. The last of the elephants finally stumbled down the ramp. I decided it was safe to approach Axel. "The walk is short, less than a mile," I said, and I pointed to a nearby group of riders. "Bring them here," he snorted, "one at a time," and he whacked the lead elephant behind the knee. For the next twenty minutes he loaded the anxious reporters onto the back of the elephants' necks. Then with a jolt, surprising even the police, he took off, striding alongside the lead elephant.

I motored along behind, watching the riders wave to the crowds. Hundreds of people lined the streets and even the weather worked in our favor. There wasn't a dark cloud in the sky.

Axel brought the elephants to a halt in front of the building and the riders stepped cautiously from the elephants' necks to an upturned knee. I thanked the reporters for their participation, making sure they each had tickets to tomorrow's opening night. Then I lingered for a moment, watching as Axel and his herd of Asian elephants, off in the distance, disappeared behind the building.

"No time to rest," I hollered over to Carl. "We've got to pick up the clowns and a show girl for your Pizza Hut promotion. They're meeting us back at the train."

A tall, leggy show girl and two clowns were already waiting at the pie car. I thanked them profusely in advance and then escorted the two clowns in my car while Carl chauffeured the show girl in his. The Pizza Hut was brimming with families and kids. I watched as the show girl and two clowns waded into the fray while I shouted my thanks again.

I remained for a moment but I was anxious to get back to the arena. "Would you mind returning the performers to the train?" I asked Carl. "I'm to be there with all the rigging going up. I'll catch up with you in the morning."

Several tractors were now in the lot. Tents were being erected and working men were wheeling wooden crates up and down the ramp. Inside the building miles of rope and aluminum pipes stretched across the floor. Lloyd stood in the center with a walkie talkie and megaphone, directing the actions of two dozen men. He was so self-assured it almost looked easy as pulleys and ropes raised the intricate steel web to the ceiling.

I watched for several minutes and then noticed it was almost four o'clock. Lloyd announced over his megaphone they would finish up tomorrow. I waited until the last of the workers had left. Then I walked quietly up the ramp, past the tents and trailers and crates filled with costumes and props. At the top of the ramp I paused, soaking in the sights, before grabbing my briefcase and hurriedly returning inside. The box office was closing in just a few minutes.

When I arrived back at the Holiday Inn, I poured over the day's box office numbers. It was the best day yet. Forty-three hundred dollars. The box office manager implied there were lines all day. Not long lines. Four or five people deep at two different windows, but they were steady. Clearly it was starting. Including today's numbers, my total advance was now $83,000.00 in regular sales and $12,000.00 in group sales. At an average ticket price of $5.65, factoring in the group discounts, I'd now sold 16,800 tickets. Tomorrow's opening day sales, I figured, ought to be fantastic, especially since the event was falling on a Friday. And if we sold out Saturday and Sunday, then the word of mouth for Tuesday through Sunday should be incredible. I took out my calculator. Seventeen shows in all, a Friday night opening, two on Saturday, two on Sunday, closed on Monday, and then two each day Tuesday through Sunday, with a twelve-thousand seat arena to fill. All I had to do was sell six-thousand tickets per show, and by Thursday's matinee I'd sail past the company's $360,000.00 projection. That would leave Thursday night, Friday and all day Saturday and Sunday to double the figures. I felt a chill as I looked at the number. $720,000.00. What a lovely sound. My commission alone would be nine-thousand dollars. I added the numbers again. Then I turned off the calculator and climbed into bed. Get some sleep, I told myself. All the excitement in the world won't make tomorrow arrive any sooner.

Chapter 50

STUNNED

"Is this a beautiful day or what? How did the Pizza Hut gala go?" I hollered to Carl as I streamed into the office.

Carl grinned a little sheepishly. "Great in one sense, the parents and kids loved it. But my client was a little peeved. Some of my staff brought along their kids and he felt they spent more time with their families than helping out with the promotion. I warned them but they wouldn't listen."

"It's no big deal," I said. "Wednesday is Pizza Hut's night at the circus and your client is the honorary ringmaster. I'll make sure he has front row seats and the red carpet treatment. The important thing is, did we get any publicity?"

"We sure did. WHIR came by as well as two other stations."

"Fantastic! Have you heard anything over the air about the animal walk?"

"Not yet. But I'm sure the DJ's have been talking it up."

"Well, I hope our newspaper reporter was there. It would be great to have a story break this afternoon in the *Tribune-Star*."

I began gathering my papers. Carl watched as I stuffed my files and binders into two black leather cases.

"I guess this is it?" he murmured.

"Only if you mean *it's* the eye of the storm," I laughed, aware of what lay ahead.

"Is there anything I can be doing while you're at the arena?"

"Just keep monitoring our spots. Make sure we receive what we're paying for." I snapped my briefcase shut, regretting I sounded brusque. "Tonight is the urchin promotion. CBS will be bringing twenty-five hundred underprivileged kids. They're also sending a crew to interview Tito Gaona followed by an interview with Charlie Bauman during intermission."

I perused the rest of the weekend schedule. Tomorrow morning I had to escort two clowns to Terre Haute Speedway while at the same time Michu had to be chauffeured to ABC. In the afternoon there was a radio interview with Elvin Bale. "On Sunday morning," I said, "Harold Ronk, our ringmaster, is being interviewed by an evangelical TV station. I hope they don't squirm at the obvious. Harold is so light in his shoes he makes Tinkerbell look like a brute."

"There is one thing you can help me with since I can't be in two places at once. Could you escort Michu to ABC tomorrow morning while I'm at the speedway?"

"Sure, I'd love to."

"Great. Doors open tonight at six o'clock. Meet me at the entrance at five forty-five and I'll take you backstage and introduce you."

I seized the weathered leather cases and started for the door. "Thank you," I said, stopping as Carl reached for the knob. "Thank you for everything. Next Sunday night, when it's all over, we'll celebrate with a bottle of champagne!"

I expected to hear sounds of working men noisily hoisting the rigging, but the arena was strangely quiet. Instinctively, I marched straight ahead into a tunnel marked Concourse E through a pair of heavy dark curtains. Twenty feet further I stood at the railing and looked down. It had all been done. Lloyd and his crew must have arrived before sunrise. I plunked down my cases and stared out in renewed awe. Three rings embossed the floor surrounded by the clean canvas path of the hippodrome track. And above each ring hung the looped ropes. Over ring one, swings were suspended for Tito's flying trapeze. Miles of aluminum pipes sparkled, even in the dusty light. And amidst the tumbling mats and teeter boards, and

ladders that climbed to the rafters, was a huge red logo in the middle of the center ring. "Ringling Brothers and Barnum and Bailey
Circus—The Greatest Show on Earth."

I strolled past Robert Hanley's office, knowing he was probably
there. Whatever was the cause of his recalcitrant attitude, I didn't
need it on opening day. All I cared about was that he had enough
ticket sellers to handle the crowds. I opened the door to my office
and was surprised to see a nice maple desk, filing cabinet and
matching credenza. Half of one wall was a window looking out
onto the concourse. I hung up a poster of three clowns, spread out
my files, and stacked my boxes of honorary whistles. All I needed
were the hats for the kids each show and I was set. Billy Williams,
the new auditor for the Blue Show, would be bringing the hats from
the train, I was told, along with the rackety ticket-tabulating
machine. Billy and I hadn't met but I couldn't imagine an accountant living aboard a circus train. Maybe we'll hit it off, especially
if we don't have much dead wood to count, I mused, smiling to
myself.

The phone on my desk rang, startling me for an instant. It was
Carl. "You're not going to believe this."

"Believe what?"

"The newspaper. They ran a front-page story on the animal
walk."

"That's great!"

"Maybe you'd better wait until you see it."

"I'll get a copy," I said and hung up the receiver. I strode out the
front door to the street where a bright orange newspaper rack
stood. I slipped in a quarter and pulled out a copy, quickly finding
the front-page story. My legs almost buckled. In the middle of the
page was a photo of a little boy sitting on a curb looking forlorn.
Above the photo blared the caption, "Ringling Animal Walk a
Bust!" story on page A3. I quickly turned the page. Beneath another
photo of elephants parading down the street was a second headline.
"Animal Walk Disappoints Crowd." The copy continued. "The
people of Terre Haute were sorely disappointed. Gone are the days

of circus wagons and calliopes, replaced instead by a herd of dirty, gray elephants straggling down the street."

I couldn't believe it. Sure, there were always a few old-timers who missed the elaborate parades of yesteryear. But why focus on that? Everyone else loves the event. How often do kids see elephants and camels rumbling down their street? Who the hell wrote this? I searched for the byline. That bastard! It was the solicitous reporter I had liked so much. Stunned, I marched back to my office. "How could he?" I shouted into the phone, throwing the paper down on my desk. "And to think I liked that guy!"

"I couldn't believe it either," Carl said. "But what can we do?"

"Well probably not a damn thing," I fumed. "But it pisses me off!"

I hung up and stormed out of the office, strolling toward the box office. Facing the sun, I stood watching people buy tickets, hoping my anger would soon subside, but I couldn't help feeling betrayed. And for what? What kind of a jerk would do something like that?

I was determined not to let the story ruin my opening day. I wandered out back behind the arena. It was still pretty quiet, yet it wouldn't be long before the hawkers erected their stations and the performers began to arrive. It was late in the afternoon when I left for a quick sandwich. When I returned, I noticed the blue circus bus had parked near the back ramp. I was anxious to see the performers. Even if I didn't know all their names, I knew most of their faces. I even looked forward to seeing Harold Ronk and rhubarb Bob Harrison, but most of all, I was looking forward to seeing Charlie King. Ever since his inner-city unicyclists had overslept in Savannah and he and I had panicked and later laughed I felt some kind of bond. Perhaps it was because he was a promoter himself. He was the one with the moxie to gather these men and give them a way out. Or perhaps I was drawn to his natural warmth, a genuine concern for the feelings of others.

Just after five o'clock a studious looking man with a squeaky voice appeared at my office. He was carrying two boxes of hats and trailing the ticket-counting machine behind.

"You must be Jamie. I'm Billy Williams," he said, extending his hand.

We chatted for a few minutes, then I showed him the room behind the box office where we'd be counting the dead wood. "Hopefully not a lot," I grinned. He seemed pleasant and we agreed before parting to meet shortly after intermission each show to audit the results.

Thirty minutes later I toted a stack of hats out to Section C where two dozen ushers dressed in red braided sport coats were sitting in a bunch. Several were silver-haired retirees plopped along a cadre of young men and women. I told them how important it was to the future of the circus, and especially to Irvin Feld, that in each show, fifty-two children have a chance to participate in the circus. "Marvelous wagons have been built to transport the kids around the hippodrome track." I passed out the hats until I reached fifty-two and then delivered their instructions. "If you see King Charles and his group of unicyclists racing madly around the track, you're already too late. At the end of the spec all you have to do is get the kids back to their seats. Are there any questions?"

"No? Then good." I looked at my watch. It was five forty-five, only fifteen minutes until doors, and I remembered Carl was meeting me at the front entrance. I raced upstairs.

"Come on," I said, motioning him toward me, and we hurried downstairs to the backstage area. Wardrobe mistresses were unloading costumes while performers, still dressed in street clothes, ambled past us down the corridor. Back door Jack was already seated in his chair by the rear door.

"Have you seen Michu?" I asked.

Without raising his portly frame, he pointed a stubby arm toward clown alley where Michu was sitting on top of a wooden crate.

"This is Carl," I said. Michu twinkled as he'd trained himself to do. "Carl will be picking you up at eight in the morning for your interview with ABC TV."

Michu nodded in agreement while Carl smiled warmly. "If there's anything you need," I said, emphasizing the word *anything,* "just let Carl know."

"Well, I've got to run up and do doors. Someone's got to keep an eye on the ticket takers," I said. Michu nodded again, his countenance mimicking my serious tone.

"Well, you're on your own," I said to Carl. "Who knows? By the time we're through you may be a part of the flying Wallendas. I'd escort you out but I've got to bolt."

Billy Williams was standing at the front entrance while people anxiously waited to be admitted. The ticket takers were all at their turnstiles. And then with a shrill whistle the doors were unlocked. Billy and I watched for a few minutes and then I turned and headed off alone around the concourse. There were eight gates in all and I was eager to cover all of them at least two or three times. At first there was only a trickle of people. And I watched as some of the ticket takers stood idly by. But gradually the doors began filling. I hung back, several feet, enjoying the sight as kids and families, older people and couples crowded their way in. As I darted from one entrance to another it occurred to me that it wasn't just seeing the results of my efforts that enlivened me, it was reveling in the energy of the people. If you didn't see it in their smiles you saw it in their stride and you saw it in their eyes. They were all delighted to be here.

I noticed an adult stroll in with several children and I watched as he handed the ticket taker a packet of complimentary passes. I wondered if he was an employee of CBS or more likely a volunteer from a local social agency. These weren't your typical kids. No matter how excited they were I couldn't help noticing there was something amiss. A sadness perhaps they just couldn't hide. I watched as a little boy and girl waited patiently in line. She was about eight years old. He was about five. They were holding each other's hand. A brother and his older sister, I presumed, not because of similar traits but because of how protective she seemed. I wondered if she ever got to feel like a child. I followed their small group into the arena and watched them being led upstairs. Afterwards, when the usher returned, I pointed to their row of seats. "Do you see that little boy and girl up there?"

"Yes," he replied.

"Do me a favor. Give them each a hat."

———

I weaved around the concourse now teeming with people as those that had entered and crowded the concessions mingled with those still streaming in the doors. The shouts of the barkers were winning over the sounds of the children. "Program! Program! Only two dollars. Life-sized picture of Michu. Come and get your program!"

I circled once more and started walking rapidly back to my office to meet the guest CBS ringmaster. Past entrance E and F, I weaved in and out of the crowd until, to my surprise, off to my right, leaning against a column, I recognized a young man talking to two others. I was so shocked to see him, I stopped dead in my tracks. It was the young reporter from the *Tribune-Star*. I refused to budge until he acknowledged my stare. I wanted, if nothing else, to see his expression when he met my gaze. I didn't have to wait very long. But when he did suddenly notice me, there was none of the arrogance or belligerence I expected. There was simply embarrassment. He smiled timidly as if to say, "I'm sorry. I was just doing my job."

I moved on, losing myself in the crowd. There wasn't much point in talking to him. There was nothing to say.

It was easy to spot my honorary ringmaster. Who else but a TV anchor could be so perfectly coiffed standing outside my office? A cameraman hovered nearby.

"How do you do?" I said. "Are you ready to interview Tito Gaona?"

"Yes," he said, adding politely. "The results will be on the eleven o'clock news. And tomorrow we'll air the interview with Charlie Bauman."

"Great, come on downstairs," I said and I presented him his honorary whistle.

Tito was outfitted in his costume of yellow leotards and white platform shoes when we arrived. The cameraman hung a portable light on a nearby post while Tito perched on the corner of a table. I waited until the interview began before announcing I'd be back for the opening of the show. I circled the concourse again, savoring the last minute stragglers, before hurrying back downstairs to introduce the anchor to Harold Ronk.

Harold was already standing in the darkened wings of the backstage arena. I thanked the newsman for all of his help, citing in particular the underprivileged kids, and then I made my way to a section of seats near center ring. I climbed up the aisle and sat on the third step as I'd done many times in the past. But somehow tonight it felt special.

As I watched Harold Ronk and the CBS anchor navigate their way to center ring, amidst the clamor of the crowd and the excitement that permeated the air, I could see show girls fidgeting behind the curtain. They wore tiaras of ostrich feathers and plumes, nearly a dozen to a headdress, accented by elaborate costumes. Outfits that more than a hundred tailors and seamstresses had spent nearly a year fabricating, with upwards of fifty thousand sequins on each, so perfectly designed that even the feathers were dyed to match the colors of the fabric. And as the first of the show girls stepped onto the hippodrome track, my skin prickled at the source of her pride. For no one, not Harold Ronk, not the performers, not even Irvin Feld could know of the work I had done. But the results—the thousands of people now in their seats and the joy on the faces of the performers as they marched out to a packed house—that they could see. I beamed as I scanned the crowd, occasionally spotting the upturned face of an underprivileged child, and suddenly I felt so proud I could feel a warm knot in my throat. Oblivious to the people around me, my eyes began misting. And as the performers marched by and waved to the crowds, I waved back, sometimes catching their eye. And when Charlie King passed by his eyes lit up, and saluting the audience that stretched out before him he gave me a thumbs up. I extended my fist and my thumb shot out, and at that moment I was so filled with emotion I didn't know whether to laugh or cry. I just sat on the step, still clinging to the feeling of euphoria until the last of the performers had left. Then I headed upstairs. During intermission I had the interview with Charlie Bauman and then all I'd have to do is wait to see what the numbers totaled.

Chapter 51

RENEWED

Charlie Bauman was toweling his face when we arrived. "It will have to be quick!" he announced, flattered he was being interviewed but annoyed it was during intermission.

"I'm sorry," I replied. "It was the only way I could make the eleven o'clock news."

Considering Charlie and his Bengal tigers were the first act of the second half I couldn't blame him for wondering what I was thinking when I'd scheduled it.

"Let's hold it to three or four minutes," I pronounced and anxiously glanced at my watch. Fortunately, Charlie transformed into a gracious performer as soon as the interview commenced, and although it was brief they were satisfied they got what they wanted.

I thanked Charlie again, escorted the interviewers back to their seats, and scurried back to my office to meet Billy Williams.

"Let's see what we did," Billy hollered, tilting his ticket counting machine on one end. "The box office ought to be ready by now."

Billy and I strolled down the concourse, wheeling his aluminum contraption behind. I knocked on the box office door. A congenial looking woman greeted us. No sooner had we positioned ourselves at the table and plugged in the machine than she returned with the "dead wood," a cardboard box filled to the top with the unsold tickets, kids' stubs and complimentary passes. Billy emptied the box on the table. There were only a few dozen yellow tickets, the highest priced seats, eight stacks of blue tickets, the mid-priced seats and about thirty stacks of red tickets, the lowest priced seats. Billy fed the hard tickets into the ticket counting machine while I began counting the kids' stubs.

"That's it," Billy announced twenty minutes later. He slipped a rubber band around the last stack of tickets and penciled in the number, subtracting the total from the twelve thousand seat manifest. "Eighty three hundred seats were filled."

We next subtracted a dollar each for more than four thousand kids' stubs and then began counting the complimentary passes, one by one, by hand. Between the underprivileged kids, the press and CBS, there were thirty-two hundred tickets attached to the complimentary passes. We subtracted these from the total and tallied up our numbers. "Twenty-three thousand eight hundred and twenty dollars," Billy said. "We match the box office exactly."

"Agreed," I said.

I threw the dead wood back into the box, initialed Billy's sheet, and hurried down the concourse, anxious to call Allen Bloom.

"He's playing poker downstairs," his wife replied. "I'll get him."

I suddenly remembered Chris Bursky had mentioned that Allen and Irvin and a few others got together on Friday nights and played poker. They'd been doing it for years.

"Are you winning?" I asked.

"I don't know yet, are you?"

"I sure am," I clamored. "We did $23,820.00."

There was a moment of silence as he jotted down the number. "Okay", he said. "I'll talk to you tomorrow."

I hung up the phone and smiled. With tonight's take of $23,800.00 plus $88,000.00 still remaining in pre-sold tickets that was $112,000.00 already in. Sixteen more shows and I was already a seventh of the way there!

The show was nearly over by the time Billy and I had finished. I grabbed a cold hot dog, and walked into the arena, taking a seat in the highest tier. Not much of a dinner but tonight it tasted like a feast. The flying trapeze was the closing act and I watched Tito and his sister Chelo climb carefully up the narrow rungs and then step off onto a tiny plank. Perhaps it was the music, an elegant Viennese waltz, or the grace in which they smoothly glided, but as I watched Tito hold the swing for Chelo and then release her to the hanging arms of their catcher, I was again enchanted. The perfect end to a perfect night. After all the noise and excitement, it was like watching a swan drift lazily home.

Tito capped off the act by performing his triple, then bouncing off the net while flailing for the catcher's empty swing. The crowd, as usual, roared. Finally, he grabbed the side of the net and flipped his legs over to the arena floor where Chelo was waiting. No sooner had they donned their capes, bowing to the audience, than Axel Gautier and his herd of elephants thundered out, followed by two-hundred performers walking in single-file, waving goodnight.

I arrived downstairs just as the elephants came rushing in. Show girls and clowns were hurrying to their dressing rooms, pulling off hats and peeling off jackets on the way. I passed clown alley, nodding to three men as they sat in front of lighted mirrors already rubbing off their makeup.

"Do you know where I'd find the King Charles Troupe?" I shouted.

"They're over that way," Prince Paul hollered back, pointing to a long row of curtains.

I meandered down the corridor, glancing at the name tags taped on the front of the material. Just as I reached the end of the row, King Charles came ambling out.

"Great crowd! I've always told Mike Franks you're the best promoter."

"I learned it all from you," I said and he broke into a toothy grin.

"Listen," I said. "Now that you're here in town, why don't we go out for a beer one night?"

"Terrific," he replied. "How about Monday night? It's our first day off."

"You're on," I said. "Where do I meet you?"

"Can you pick me up at the train? I'm in car 112."

We shook hands again and I watched for a minute while he sauntered up the ramp. Then I walked back to my office, through the empty arena, past the sweepers cleaning between the seats. I wasn't used to the concrete floor and I noticed my feet had begun to ache as I trooped out to my car. It was almost midnight. I was tired. But I couldn't help feeling we were off to a hell of a start. Tomorrow was Saturday, the biggest day of the week.

I awoke envisioning all I needed to do. There wasn't any time for breakfast. I had promised the Terre Haute Speedway two clowns for this morning's race and tonight was their night at the circus. They'd been promoting it for weeks.

I drove by the box office on the way to the train, just in case people were already lining up to buy tickets. I stared out at the vacant parking lot. A bit presumptuous, I laughed, since the box office doesn't open for two hours. That son-of-a-bitch Hanley better have plenty of ticket sellers on hand.

"Ah yes," the chubby clown said when I stepped into the pie car. "The smell of gasoline and burning rubber. How well it blends with my morning coffee!"

"Just think," I teased back, "you're riding in the rear car."

The taller clown, the one wearing a bright orange wig, puckered his lips. "And they told me I'd never be racey."

"Come on you two, grab your coffee. We're going to be late."

We pulled up to the Speedway, thirty miles south of town, and I could see why they called it a mud track. It was nothing but a huge circle engulfed and banked on all sides by a dusty, dirt raceway. The cars were already warming up while a few began circling the track. The noise was deafening.

"Is this macho or what!" the chunky clown hollered.

"I can hardly hear you," I yelled.

"This is nothing," the other said. "Wait till they all take off around the track."

There were three officials standing near a stage so I drove in their direction.

"Hi," I said. "We're with Ringling Brothers. We're supposed to kick off the race."

"Good," one of them said. "Follow me."

In a nearby hut we were introduced to his promotion director who choreographed it on the spot. "One of the clowns," he said, "should announce the start of the race while the other clown waves the checkered flag."

Of course, there was no way the two clowns could make it that simple.

As the portly clown attempted to start the race, the other clown began fouling up his efforts. He frantically waved the flag before his cue, then paraded down the track with two giggling girls from the audience, his pants falling down on the way. Meanwhile, his cohort took out a mirror and began preening on the hood of the lead car. With impeccable timing, they finally relinquished their hold, turning the proceedings back over to the announcer.

"They loved it," I cried. "Thanks a million."

"Nothing to it," they smiled, just as naturally as another day's work.

The arena doors would be opening soon. I dropped them off and raced back to the arena.

Hot damn! There were plenty of people lined up at the box office windows. There must be ten or more waiting in each line. So why the hell doesn't Hanley have a third window open? That's it. I've had it with this guy. I've worked too hard to let this idiot screw it up. I pulled to a stop and strode into the building. Hanley was inside his office calmly lighting his pipe.

"For Christ's sake! It's a Saturday! Why do you have only two windows open?"

He looked at me and his eyes began to narrow. "If we need a third window," he countered, carefully controlling his tone, "I'll open one."

I marched into my office and sat down. The phone rang. It was Carl. His voice was a soothing contrast to my sudden consternation.

"Anything wrong?" he asked.

"No, I'm just fighting with Hanley," I blurted, trying to suppress my anger.

"Well, other than that, how goes your morning?"

"Great," I said, regaining my composure at the memory of the clowns' silly antics.

"How was Michu?" I asked, almost forgetting his interview with ABC.

"He's a bit of a handful."

"Literally and figuratively," I joked.

"How do you understand him?"

"You don't. You just feed him vodka and hope he doesn't look up the receptionist's skirt."

I hung up the receiver and noticed people were now streaming past my window. Shit. They've already opened the doors. I ran out and began circling the concourse. It looked like a sizeable crowd. I dashed toward the box office. It was busy, twenty people deep. Hanley had finally opened a third window. Cars, I could see, were backed up, winding their way into the parking lot. Damn, what a pretty sight!

I raced to another entrance. Families were coming in droves. Finally my hard work was paying off. Billy Williams, I noticed, was standing by concourse D. I smiled and waved as I sprang by. I was having fun striding from entrance to entrance.

I heard the orchestra strike its opening chord and I scurried inside the arena. Surprisingly, it was only half-full, about five or six thousand people. Certainly respectable, but from the looks of the crowds surging in, I'd easily expected more. Well, it was only the first show and a Saturday matinee at that. Tonight would no doubt be a sell-out.

I ambled toward my office, reviewing my list of activities, reminding myself of the interview with Elvin Bale during intermission. Casually, I opened the door. Two feet were propped on my desk.

"Mike Franks!"

I'd forgotten how handsome he was. He was leaning back in my chair. He looked relaxed, more relaxed than I'd recently seen him. He smiled back warmly.

"When did you get in?"

"Only about a half-hour ago."

"You should have told me when you were coming. I'd have booked you at the Holiday Inn."

"It's no problem. Allen's secretary made all the arrangements."

"Well, it's really great to see you!" I said, and for the first time in weeks I felt awash in relief. The circus was one thing, but with Mike, it felt as though family had arrived.

Mike rose from his chair. "I'm going to head down and check with Charlie Bauman and say hello to a few people. I'll circle back at intermission and give you a hand with the dead wood."

"Sure, Mike," I said, feeling another wave of assurance. "Thank you. Thanks again for coming!"

I replayed the numbers in my mind, knowing Mike would be pleased with the results thus far, and then watched as the ushers gathered the kids for the show. With Mike in town I wanted there to be no mistakes. One by one, I watched the ushers walk down the aisles with the kids in tow. And then I hurried downstairs to make sure Elvin Bale hadn't forgotten the radio interview. I knocked on Elvin's dressing room door, then knocked again. He opened the door and behind him I observed his wife, Jeanette, sitting in front of a mirror carefully applying her makeup.

"I'm here for your interview," I announced. "I hope you didn't forget."

"Of course I didn't," he said with a smile. "Where do I go?"

"Just follow me," I said. "There's a phone reserved around the corner. It's a live interview. He'll be calling any minute."

I opened the door to a small room, inside were two chairs and a phone. We sat down and waited for the phone to ring. I was tempted to ask him questions, beginning of course with the obvious. Why would anybody in the prime of life risk life and limb twice a day while lunging from a swing in hopes of catching a bar by his heels, only to later in the show run blindfolded round and round a giant hamster cage spinning fifty feet in the air? Instead I said, "If you don't mind, I'd be most appreciative if you mentioned the show will be here through next weekend."

Then the phone rang, thankfully breaking the silence. I listened as he spoke. "Yes," he said, "I understand the risk but this is what I do . . . sure I'm scared, I'd be a fool not to be. But when the crowd responds in a thunderous roar it all seems worthwhile . . . I know I look like an all-American college boy but the truth is I grew up in the circus. My great-grandfather was a juggler and my father was a tiger trainer. It was my father who made me confront my fears."

Elvin paused and I sensed what he was about to say wasn't something he normally revealed. "I was rehearsing catching the swing with my heels when one morning my father walked in. 'Now do it with no safety harness,' he demanded. "Terrified, I did. And I've never used a safety line since. What's next? I'm not sure, but I'm working on an act for next year's show Irvin Feld ought to love . . . Don't forget the show will be here all week long, right through Sunday."

Delighted, I strolled back to my office. "Elvin was great," I said. Mike was sitting at my desk, leafing through my binder.

"The dead wood ought to be here any minute."

Mike looked up and gestured, glancing over my right shoulder. "It appears there's someone here to see you."

I turned and standing in the open door was a woman holding the hand of a young girl. Outfitted in a white dress, the little girl was smiling, but her mother's expression was tentative, almost sad.

"Hi, Jamie."

I didn't respond.

"I was wondering if you'd like to go out after the show," she said softly.

I looked at her and suddenly felt angry, frustrated at the times, when alone, I'd tried more than once to connect. Where was she when I needed her? "I'm sorry. Three times and you're out."

Her shoulders slumped. For a moment, I thought she might cry. Then she turned and walked away with her little girl.

"What was that all about?" Mike asked.

"Nothing," I replied, and I could see from his look he was puzzled. "She was just somebody I once knew."

Billy Williams walked in and the three of us retreated to the room behind the box office. With few complimentary passes for a Saturday show it was simply a matter of feeding the hard tickets into the machine. I watched while Billy separated the stacks, handing them in bunches to Mike.

"Fifty-two hundred attendance," Billy Williams pronounced.

"Great!" I said, and I looked at Mike for a reaction, but Mike had been in too many battles to register any emotion.

"Well, I'm exhausted," Mike announced. "I'm going back to my room and take a nap. Why don't I meet you back here later and we'll grab a bite to eat?"

"Sounds good," I said. "I'm not going anywhere. That's for sure. I'll see you back here when you're ready."

I'd hardly thought about Evansville since I'd arrived three nights ago in Terre Haute, but suddenly I was intensely curious to see how we were doing. I picked up the phone and called Bill Sweeney.

"Thirty-seven hundred dollars," he said.

"Today alone?"

"That's right," he confirmed. "And the top price tickets for opening night are almost gone."

"That's fantastic!" I said, and I hung up the phone. I'll let Mike know over dinner.

It was late when Mike returned, well past the evening's intermission. I was cautiously excited. It wasn't the Saturday night sell-out I'd hoped for, but at least we'd had 8,200 attendance, 2,200 more than the 6,000 average I needed.

"How'd we do?" Mike asked.

"Pretty good," I said and I told him the numbers.

He swirled the numbers around but still offered no comment.

"So what do you think?"

"We'll just have to see."

"Well, I think the word-of-mouth will start paying off soon," I said.

"C'mon, let's get something to eat."

We drove to a nearby restaurant, a plain looking place with yellow tables. An eager-to-please waitress flounced over. She was young with a friendly demeanor and pretty face.

"May I take your order please?"

"You certainly can," I replied, noticing the curve of her hips. "Have you worked here long?"

"Just a few weeks," she said, blushing slightly.

"It's a shame. It would have been nice to have met you sooner. But I'm still here for another week."

"I see," she said, fumbling for her pad while completing the rest of our order.

As she walked away I said to Mike, "Now that's a sexy woman."

Mike glanced over quietly, proffering the same puzzled look I'd seen earlier. "You remind me," he said, "more and more every day of Neal Kessler."

I awoke Sunday morning wondering if my blood had been replaced with lead. I didn't want to move. But if Saturday was a busy day, I reminded myself, Sunday was often better. And with a one o'clock followed by a five o'clock show I'd at least be finishing up earlier. If I could get through today, tomorrow I'd have all day to rest.

I owed Harold Ronk for this one. The religious station wanted to do a live feed, which meant Harold had to be dressed in his top hat and coattails at nine o'clock in the morning. I slipped on my socks and squeezed into my shoes, noticing a blister had formed on my little toe.

He was already waiting in the lobby. We drove out to the arena. A white van marked Christian Network was waiting by the ramp. I suggested to two well groomed men that we shoot near the elephants. A foul wind was blowing. That ought to keep the interview short, I mused, stifling a grin. Harold was not nearly so amused.

Harold and I drove back to the hotel. I trudged upstairs. Though it was only ten-thirty I suddenly felt weary. The thought of one more hour's sleep was tantalizing. I stepped out of my clothes and slipped in between the cool cotton sheets. Even the bright morning sun sneaking through a crack in the curtains couldn't smother the joy I felt. I only hoped this morning's coffee wouldn't keep me from falling into a deep, solid sleep.

The alarm clock jarred me awake. I jumped up, still tired but mentally refreshed. A cup of coffee "to go" tasted better than the first and a stop at a drugstore for Band-aids took the sting out of my toe. Sundays were often the busiest, perhaps because Saturdays were reserved for errands. On Sundays the family could finally relax. Cars were already slipping into the parking lot and I felt a nervous anticipation. Thank goodness Mike was here. Maybe he could start helping with the interviews while I watched the doors and handled the promotions. That alone would take a load off my back. Maybe he could call and check on Sweeney. I barely had time to think about Evansville.

I pulled into my parking space and hurried into the front entrance. The doors were just being opened. Neither Billy nor Mike were anywhere in sight so I began my stroll around the concourse. By now the ticket takers recognized me and nodded as I walked by. Through the glass entrance doors I noticed the sky had suddenly turned overcast. A light drizzle began dampening the sidewalk while a gusty wind flapped at the women's skirts.

I watched as the people filed in, expecting the crowd to grow thicker. But it didn't. Instead it remained a slow, steady stream. Just my luck. Sunday afternoon and it was a dark, dreary day. Finally an hour passed and I peeked inside the arena. Most of the high priced seats were filled, the second tier was spotty, and almost no one sat in the upper tiers. Four thousand people at most. My stomach fluttered. Even with the rain the house ought to be nearly full. Maybe word-of-mouth takes a little longer here? I wandered back to my office, curious to hear what Mike was thinking. If anyone knew, it was him. Together we'd figure it out. I opened the door but he still wasn't there. I sat down at my desk, knowing I'd soon have to happily relinquish my chair, when the door suddenly opened and Mike strode in. He was carrying a small suitcase.

"Did you finally decide to move over to the Holiday Inn?" I asked with a smile.

"Not exactly," he said.

"Well, I guess it wasn't a sell out crowd."

"You can't win them all," he shrugged.

"Oh, I'm just getting started," I interjected, not wanting to sound discouraged. "We've been running promotional spots for next week's matinees for weeks!"

"All you can do is the best you can," he said. "Well, I guess I'll be heading on. I've got a plane to catch in less than an hour."

"You mean you're leaving?"

"You'll be fine," he said. "Walk me out."

I got up and ambled beside him, out the entrance toward a rental car parked by a puddle by the curb.

"I was hoping you'd be staying a little longer," I said.

"I'm sorry," he said, placing his suitcase in the trunk. "I would but I've got to get back." He closed the trunk, slipped into the driver's side and waved goodbye. I nodded and then watched as he pulled away, rounding the corner, before disappearing from view.

I stood there just watching the street and then turned and walked slowly back to the building. I wandered down the corridor and turned and walked into the arena. I climbed up and sat in one of the empty seats and stared out at the circus below.

My thoughts all of a sudden seemed jumbled. Nothing seemed to make any sense, except for a feeling I couldn't shake. Suddenly I felt cut adrift, utterly alone.

Chapter 52
NUMB

I awoke and strained to hear a sound, any sound, but the hotel, as always, was quiet. The silence accentuated the stillness of the room, broken only by a shaft of light that illuminated millions of dancing dust particles otherwise invisible to the naked eye. I lay there mesmerized by the sight, struck by the contrast between the seen and the unseen.

I couldn't get over how alone I felt. Even after waiting all these weeks for the circus to come I felt strangely disconnected. I was part of their world, yet I wasn't. They at least had each other. Over and over I saw Mike walking out of the arena and me following along like a pathetic puppy dog. Why did I feel so abandoned, so full of despair? He wasn't my father, for Christ's sake. He wasn't even my friend. He was my boss. So why did my chest hurt when I watched his car pull away? Why does it hurt even now?

I wondered what the performers would be doing all day. Probably as little as possible. I stared at the dust particles, watching them move in slow motion. Part of me wanted to get up, but part of me didn't want to move. I couldn't decide what to do with myself. It was the only day of rest I would have, but I desperately wanted to be busy. The last thing I needed was to be alone.

I sat up in bed, shocked to feel how stiff my body felt. Those damn concrete floors are going to kill me. I slowly stood up, grabbed the back of a chair and stretched my legs. I've got to eat something this morning, I reminded myself, noticing in the mirror how hollow my stomach was beginning to look. I opened the curtains and stared outside, surprised to see the streets were as lifeless as my room. But at least the evening rain had cleared away the hot summer haze that had been lingering the last few days, leaving behind a cool, clear morning with a hint of a breeze to sweep away the puddles.

As I gazed out the window, I remembered tonight was the night I was to pick up Charlie King at the train, and my mood began to shift. Suddenly things didn't seem so bleak and hopeless, especially when I remembered how excited he was at the idea. We'll hit a few nightclubs, have a few beers, I thought, and I was amazed at how my spirits began to lift.

I stood in the shower longer than usual, letting the water re-energize my body, while a torrent of thoughts raced freely through my brain. The more I focused on the goals I'd set, the more secure and connected I felt. My mission, surpassing all projections, was what mattered most, and the more I went over the numbers, the more I felt a sense of certainty. I reached for a towel. I'll give Carl a call. He needs to know this is only the beginning. Every waking minute must be spent figuring out how to get people in those seats.

I dried off, slipped on a pair of gym shorts, and grabbed my briefcase and calculator. Once again, I added up the numbers and factored them into the remaining shows. Sunday night was weaker than I'd hoped, but I still only had to average 6,200 tickets per show. I thought about Ralph Finley, the fidgety salesman from NBC and the countless promotional spots he'd been running for weeks for a cut of the matinees. I'll bet these midwesterners, with their thrifty ways, have been holding back. There is a recession in the country, after all, and with farm folks it doesn't matter when they come. And with the matinee discounts NBC has been promoting, what better way for them to spend a sweltry afternoon? And even if I don't hit a matinee crowd of 6,200 a show, we'll probably fill all 12,000 seats next weekend after nine straight days of word of mouth.

What an intoxicating feeling! I played out the numbers, each with a slightly different twist, each geared to hit that magical number of $720,000.00 I remembered what Mike once said, "One way or the other, it'll all get done." He was right. There was no point in worrying about what had to be done. I'd just have to do it! There'll be plenty of time for rest later on.

I looked out the window and was surprised to see that the streets were now filled with the hustle and bustle of late-morning traffic. It was after eleven, and I'd already spent three hours lost in my thoughts. Only the afternoon to go, and then I'd be picking up Charlie. It appeared I was finally back to my old self.

"Where's Mike Franks?" Carl asked.

"He had to go . . . left town," I said, "but there's nothing you and I can't handle."

"I thought this was your day off."

"It is for the performers," I said, "but I figured there were things you and I could do. You wouldn't have Ralph Finley's number handy, would you?"

I phoned Finley and reminded him to meet me tomorrow afternoon in front of my office along with his general manager, the honorary ringmaster, just before the show.

"What do you think?" he asked nervously.

"About what?"

"Attendance," he said. "I've heard it's been a little slow."

"Relax," I said, trying to put him at ease. "We're going to do gangbusters!"

I called the box office. Thirty-eight hundred fresh dollars had come in during the day, bringing my total to $159,300.00 Five hundred and sixty-one thousand to go. The best was yet to come.

It was almost six-thirty when I left the office, just enough time to grab a fast dinner, return to the hotel, change and pick up Charlie at eight o'clock. On a Monday night, there couldn't be much activity at most of the well-known taverns in town, but there was one place on the outskirts I'd seen, the Roadside Grill, that always seemed to be busy. At least their sign, "Live Music Seven Nights a Week," indicated so. Some shit-kicking country music was probably their forte, but I figured Charlie, if anyone, was adaptable.

The sun was low on the horizon when I arrived at the train, leaving the cars in a dusky shadow. Car 112 was what Charlie had said. Unfortunately, 98 was the number emblazoned on the car directly in front of me, the closest I could park. I turned to the right and began walking along the gravel, noticing weeds had grown tall between the stones. For some reason—perhaps for the performers' privacy or perhaps for my own—I found myself trying to be quiet, but I might as well have been wearing a cow bell for all the good it did me. There must be an art to walking on loose stones, I lamented, kicking out a small avalanche every ten feet or so. Finally, seven cars down the track, I turned and climbed up a pair of steel steps and opened the door.

Bright lights and rock music blaring from an open room instantly hit me. So did thick cigarette smoke and a locker room odor from people living too close together. All of a sudden I realized why reporters were never allowed on the train.

"Care for a drink?" was the next sound I heard, and I looked up to see one of the show girls swaying next to an open door. I recognized her instantly. Sam Barrett had introduced us way back in Norfolk before I'd even joined the show. I could hear other voices in the background, people laughing and partying in adjacent rooms.

Before I could answer, she slid up next to me. She was barefoot and wore black hip-hugger slacks, exposing a thin, toned midriff underneath a white, knotted blouse. "We're having a party," she said, slurring her words, and before I knew it she had pulled me toward her and was pressing her hips against mine. Her breath reeked of liquor, and all I could think was, "Shit! I'm not even supposed to be here, let alone be screwing around with a show girl! Any second someone else could come through one of those doors." Thank God it was Charlie.

"We've been known to start a little early on Mondays," he said with a grin, and I quickly extricated myself from her grasp.

"Come on. Let's go," I said, feeling strangely relieved to be bounding out the door. "Do you have any idea what Irvin would do to me if he knew I even touched a show girl?"

"Don't worry, I'm not telling him," Charlie laughed, "and she's too bombed to remember!"

"You think it's funny, don't you?" I said, unable to resist a grin.

"Where are you taking me?" he asked.

"Don't worry. I found the perfect place, just your kind of music."

As we drove across town, I wondered if I was making a mistake. Perhaps this was amusing to me, but how many black men could be found in a country western bar, in Indiana of all places.

"Listen," I said, feeling a little guilty. "The place is called the Roadside Grill. It's a country western bar. It was the only place on a Monday night that advertised a live band. We don't have to go there."

"Hell, don't sweat it. I've been accused of being too white all my life."

"By whom?"

"Everyone in the troupe, for one."

"Why? Just because you're so articulate?"

"Perhaps, but more likely because I get along with whites as well as I do blacks."

I let his words sink in for a minute or two, realizing as absurd as it sounded, it probably wasn't absurd to him.

"This is it," I said, as we pulled into a parking lot already half-full of cars. "You can sure hear the crickets out here in the country."

"Just think," he said, "ten thousand years ago it was nighttime that ruled the earth."

"You're right," I said. "Now who in their white mind would know that! Come on, I'll buy you a beer."

I opened the door, leading the way, and I was right about one thing. There wasn't a black man in sight. But if Charlie was anything, he was comfortably disarming. With his perpetual smile and easy gait, any glances we got were benign.

"Too many years in the deep South," I shrugged.

"Times do change," he said, and instead of feeling self-conscious, I felt proud, as though status had been conferred on us for standing out from the crowd.

We stood with our backs to the bar, sipping on our beers, and I was reminded of the afternoon with Jack Sullivan. That wonderful feeling of sharing time with a friend and not even having to speak, relaxed in the tranquil notion we both thought in the same way, having no rush to explore and uncover. The bar stretched long and easy and was filled with people standing and sitting. In front of us, tables were filled with couples, and some with women enjoying a night out. I scanned the crowd, seeing if anyone interested me, while the band began tuning its instruments.

"Something tells me we're not going to be able to hear ourselves think in a few minutes," I hollered above the din of the crowd. Charlie nodded, and as he did, I caught the eye of a woman sitting next to the stage with two others. I felt the self-assuredness to which I'd recently grown accustomed, and when I smiled at her, she didn't act coy. She didn't avert her gaze. She just smiled back.

"I think she likes you," Charlie said.

"I think you might be right," I said, surprised as she stood and walked onto the stage taking her place behind the microphone.

She was wearing a light blue vest and a fringed country skirt cut four or five inches above her knee. Her face was wide with a warm smile, but I couldn't take my eyes off her legs. They were smooth and tanned with small ankles and the roundest calves I'd ever seen. I felt strangely nervous waiting for her to sing. Was she any good? Would her voice match her confidence? As soon as the sax sounded, she began to sway to the music, glancing sideways at her fellow musicians. Then she approached the mike and placed her mouth only inches away. The rhythm picked up, and as she shifted her weight from side to side, I watched her thigh muscles become taut, leading me to imagine how round and inviting her body must be. When she started to sing, out came a deep and beautiful sound sung with an intensity of feeling and concentration that gave me a chill.

"She's incredible," I said to Charlie.

"She's good," he said appreciatively, as I stared, mesmerized by her voice and the gentle swaying of her hips. Finally, the lead guitarist, after a series of songs, announced they'd be taking a break. As she descended the stage, I applauded, smiling as though she and I were the only ones in the room, and to my surprise, she walked calmly toward us.

"You were fantastic!" I told her. "Seriously, there are a lot of nice voices out there, but yours is distinct. What a beautiful sound!"

"Thank you," she said. "Where are you guys from? Somehow I have the impression you're not from around here."

"We're with the circus," I said, "Ringling Brothers. I'm the advance man, and Charlie's a performer."

"No kidding!" she said, and suddenly there was a kinship, a commonality she hadn't counted on.

We chatted comfortably, and I made no attempt to hide my fascination. I was deliciously attracted to her. But as tender as her voice was, there was a hardness about her. Like us, she'd chosen a life on the road, and perhaps like us, the novelty was wearing off. For all the confidence it took to lead the life she was living, I could also sense an insecurity, a need for deeper acceptance. As I watched her walk back to the stage, I couldn't resist feeling flush with excitement, flattered she'd chosen to spend time with us.

"What's with me tonight?" I said to Charlie.

"You're in the biz," he said nonchalantly, as though it should be obvious. "There's a connection." And as I stood there in my corduroy jacket and jeans, I felt strangely sublime. In that moment, as I looked over at Charlie and again at the singer, I felt connected to something, a family perhaps. Something I couldn't define, but I could taste it and touch it and feel it. And it felt good. I wasn't simply alone.

In between sets, she returned to join us, and the more we talked, the more comfortable we became. And in between stories and in between laughs, she was content to be quiet yet stay by our side. Her body would occasionally lean into mine, and perhaps out of deference to a feeling we both shared, she told me her boyfriend was picking her up at the end of the evening.

"He's young, but he's damn good in bed," she whispered awkwardly, and I knew they didn't have much in common. But then she said all I needed to hear, "I wish I were going home with you."

She announced they were packing up tonight for a gig across the state, and we talked for a few minutes more. Then she said it was her last set and wandered back toward the band.

I looked at my watch. It was long after midnight. "Come on," I said. "I've got a big day tomorrow. We'd better call it a night."

Charlie drank the last few sips of his beer and placed the bottle on the bar. As we walked toward the door, I caught her eye one more time, smiled and waved wistfully goodbye.

Perhaps another time, I thought, as Charlie and I stepped out into the cool night air.

"To the train," he said with a grin.

As we drove along the deserted streets, past the white, wooden houses—some still illuminated by soft, yellow porch lights—it occurred to me, he might know something I'd been wondering about.

"By the way, Charlie, did you ever hear of a man named Neal Kessler?"

"Yes, he was a promoter," he said, with no hesitation.

"Did you know him?"

"Yeah. He was sort of a crazy character."

"How so?"

"Well, he was quite the ladies' man, for one thing. Every time you'd see him he'd have some gorgeous woman around. Sometimes in a bar he'd have two or three."

"Why? Was he particularly handsome?"

"Not really. He was kind of average. Actually, he was even a little overweight."

"Then what was his magic?" I asked, now obsessively curious.

"It was his intensity. He was incredibly lonely on the road, and as a result, when he met a woman, he focused all of his energy, all of his charm, on pulling her in."

"What ever happened to him?"

"I don't know. He left the show a couple of years ago. Somebody said he'd turned into an alcoholic. When he wasn't charming women, he was hanging out at a bar. I haven't heard anything about him since. Why do you ask?"

"Nothing important," I said. "Mike Franks mentioned his name a few days ago. I was just curious."

All the lights were off on the train when we pulled up. Any signs of a party had long been extinguished. Only the loud chirping of the crickets and the moonlight casting an outline on the silver cars gave any life to the train at all.

"Sorry I can't get any closer to your car," I noted.

"No sweat," Charlie said. "I've walked it a dozen times. Hey, thanks for a hell of an evening!"

"No, thank *you*," I said. "It was a great time. I needed that."

I waited and watched him turn down the side of the tracks until I could no longer distinguish him from the darkness. I pulled the car out and reflected back on the evening, the first normal evening I'd had in weeks. When was the last time I'd been out with someone I knew, someone with whom I had something in common, someone fun yet calm and relaxed in manner? And then I thought about Neal Kessler, alone on a bar stool, unable to cope with life on the road. Is that who I reminded Mike of? I didn't even like bars, and I barely drank. Sure, there were similarities, but that's all they were, similarities. As I drove the rest of the way home, I tried not to think about it, but I couldn't stop. There was just something about him that struck me as sad.

Chapter 53

THE MATINEES

I rose from bed and felt a flutter in my stomach. It was Tuesday, the beginning of the matinees. My evening with Charlie King suddenly seemed eons away. I dressed and strode downstairs to the restaurant. But the thought of food was preposterous. I was far too excited about the day's numbers to eat.

Between the weekend's word of mouth, the interviews thus far and NBC's hammering away at the matinees, I was anxious to leave for the arena. I finished my coffee and reviewed my notes. Another radio interview before the show, this time with Charlie King, then a rendevous with Ralph Finley and his general manager for the start of the show, a two hour break—the evening performance—and then that was it. An easy day for a change.

I drove to the building, deposited my briefcase and walked inside the arena. Jeanette Williams stood in the middle of the center ring waving a long rod, shouting demands to a dozen black stallions swirling around. Absent her heavy mascara and now dressed in faded jeans and a T-shirt, I hardly recognized her. Elvin Bale sat in the first row keeping a watchful eye. He too looked oddly out of place, sipping coffee and wearing a sweatsuit instead of his acrobatic cape and white leotards. To their right, a teeterboard act was inducting its newest member. An ox-like man with a handlebar mustache stood in the center of the ring barking orders to two teenage boys, who promptly jumped from a tall platform to the end of a seesaw, catapulting a tiny girl to his thickly muscled shoulders. I surmised she couldn't be more than five or six. Fortunately, she was attached to a guy wire, because half of the time she missed completely and the other times she landed on his head. It might have been amusing if she wasn't so disappointed.

I waved to Elvin, who gestured back and I smiled at the teeterboard act as I strolled back stage. It was quiet, no one else had arrived, and as I ambled past the dressing rooms, there was something about the stillness that was strangely calming, as if I were walking by old familiar homes. And in the process the nervous fluttering in my stomach stopped. I walked toward the back ramp. Drawn by the bright sunlight, I meandered up the incline and peacefully looked around. The portable pie car, behind the tent, was serving hot coffee and doughnuts, and suddenly I was hungry. Fortified by two doughnuts and a large, creamy coffee, I sat in the sun, warming the side of my face. Even the smell of the elephants and an occasional horse's snort couldn't disturb my thoughts. What a wonderful evening I'd just had with Charlie. Perhaps, I decided, it took a few days—a few days to settle down and feel a part of their world. I sipped the rest of my coffee, then stood up and stretched, beginning a stroll around the lot, content to wander past the tents and smile hello to the roustabouts. It felt so serene I hated to leave, but as performers began to arrive, I could feel a worried energy return. I wondered if Robert Hanley had opened any more box office windows.

Elvin Bale and Jeanette had relinquished the ring to a tumbling act while the teeterboard troupe was still hard at work. I hurried along, heading up the steps. At the top of the stairs I darted outside. Just one box office window was open, although there were only a few people in line. Nevertheless, I still didn't trust Hanley and knocked on the box office door. "I just wanted to be sure you had plenty of ticket sellers on hand," I exclaimed.

"Don't worry," the ticket seller said, trying to placate me. "Whatever happens, we're ready."

Slightly more assured, I walked back to my office and settled in to wait. There wasn't much I could do until the doors finally opened. An hour later Billy Williams strolled in. He always appeared so calm and it was beginning to irritate me. Then again, all he had to do was *count* the numbers. Today he seemed a little more smug than usual, which made me refrain from conversation, so I was doubly relieved when he looked at his watch and announced that the doors were about to open.

"I'll go to the right," I pronounced and exited out the door. As I walked around the corridor, past the gates and ticket takers, I was surprised to see the halls looked cavernous. They'll soon be full, I told myself, as I watched a few families straggle in. I passed Billy Williams when I rounded the front entrance. He was chatting and laughing about something with one of the ticket takers. I nodded but kept moving, anxious to see the activity at all of the entrances. As I circled a second time, I could see the hubbub begin to increase. It always does, as each minute passes, but most of the crowd, I noticed, was coming in through the main gate. The side entrances were still pretty quiet. It won't be long, I speculated, before the front lot is full—and that's when the cars are directed to either side. As I turned on my heels, three buses pulled up. I watched as a swarm of kids followed by a busload of senior citizens began climbing out.

"Get ready," I said to one of the ticket takers. "You're about to be busy."

I departed and headed back to the main entrance, noticing parents and kids were now spreading out in front of the concessions. There were lines at each of three windows buying tickets. Not long lines. But there was still thirty minutes to go. And from what I could see, the main entrance had a growing stream of people. If this keeps up, I'll easily have six-thousand attendance, maybe even seven or eight! I looked around to locate Billy Williams and spied him talking with one of the concessionaires.

"Billy," I shouted. "I've got a radio interview to do with Charlie King. I'll see you at intermission."

I scurried around the concourse, absorbing the din of people strolling in, and ran down to Charlie's dressing room. He had already changed, and seeing me, grinned from ear to ear. "Thanks again, man, for last night. That was really fun!"

"It's you I should thank," I said. "Follow me. The D.J. should be calling any minute."

We weaved our way past performers congregating in and out of their dressing rooms. Sporadic drums and horns sounded as Bill Pruyn noisily tuned the band and Charlie Bauman screamed that there was twenty minutes to go. The clamor was even louder by the time we reached the phone room and closed the door. Then all of a sudden it was quiet. We only had to wait a minute or two and the phone rang. Someone told Charlie to "stand by." I listened for a moment as Charlie began to respond but all I could think about were the people streaming in upstairs. I was tempted to walk outside and steal a glance at the audience, but I waited, knowing the interview would be over any minute. Finally I looked at my watch. Only eight minutes to curtain and I still had to retrieve Ralph Finley and his general manager. I signaled Charlie to cut it short and bolted out the door. Fortunately Harold Ronk was standing nearby. "I've still got to get the honorary ringmaster," I hollered. "Don't start without us."

Harold nodded, obviously perturbed, and I raced down the corridor. I scurried by a column of elephants and burst through the curtains and onto the arena floor. I stopped in my tracks. All of a sudden it felt as though someone had punched me in the chest. Where the hell was everybody? There couldn't be more than two-thousand people in the seats. I scanned the arena, eyeing the crowd scattered amidst the thousands of glaringly empty seats. Suddenly it dawned on me. I told them to open more windows! The box office probably has lines stretching out to the street. I raced up the stairs, hitting two at a time, and noticed the main corridor was empty. Out of the corner of my eye I saw Ralph Finley and a gentleman in a suit standing outside my office. I pivoted and ran outside to the box office. There was no one in line. I turned to a ticket taker inside. "Is that it? Is that everybody?"

"Yeah, I guess so," he said. "It looked like it was going to be busy for a little while and then it just dwindled."

Dwindled? What does he mean it just dwindled? What the hell happened? My mind went blank. Numbly I turned and saw Ralph Finley and his boss staring at me. I've got to get them downstairs, but what do I say? They've been promoting these matinees for weeks. I expected the crowds to be hanging off the rafters. I stumbled in their direction. Just get it over with. Get them downstairs. I can't let them see that I'm worried. Christ almighty, how can they not? I marched up and presented my hand. "How do you do?" I said, trying to mirror the General Manager's composure while ignoring Ralph Finley's glances. "The attendance is a little light today but it's only the first matinee." I tried to sound reassuring.

They followed me down to the arena floor where Harold was impatiently waiting. "Right this way," Harold said, barely disguising his annoyance. I listened as the General Manager thanked the audience for coming, then I scanned the seats again for a delayed perspective. In the broad light of day, with no darkened sections to skew reality, the audience was undeniably small, but at least it was dispersed. I studied the expression on Charlie Bauman's face while trying to read Harold Ronk's reaction, searching for signs of disappointment. Then I looked at the faces of the performers as they waited behind, ready to suddenly appear. No one but me seemed alarmed. It was business as usual, a lighter than normal crowd, but nothing they hadn't seen before. I stood to the side, not knowing how I was supposed to feel, other than a pressing desire to escape, to be alone, to sit in my office and think. As soon as the General Manager exited the ring, I motioned he and Finley toward the stairs. Thanking them both, I told them I'd be in touch and then lied and said I had an interview backstage. I watched as they disappeared up the aisle, then followed their steps, intentionally muting my thoughts until I reached my office and pulled the door softly shut.

I sank behind my desk hoping solitude in a familiar place could bring clarity to my thoughts. But focus was no match for fear. I could barely think. It didn't make sense. It's the middle of summer and there's no school in session. The coliseum ought to be packed. Maybe it was NBC. They'd run hundreds of spots but their ratings are dismal, a distant third at best. Maybe nobody's watching. Suddenly hope seemed to win over doubt. Maybe I'm overreacting? Two thousand people for the first matinee isn't a disaster. Hell, if this were Savannah, the arena would be a third of the way full.

I picked up a pencil and twirled it between my fingers, staring at the spinning black type, then picked up the phone and called Carl.

"How's it going?" he inquired.

"It's pretty light," I said, refusing to hide my disappointment. "What do I have to do in this town?"

Carl and I took another look at the schedule. Tonight was the king and queen promotion so I knew I had plenty of promotional spots running all day. "Our newspaper ads are prominent, but our TV I have to admit, peaked as it should, Sunday night. Even our radio I'm afraid is beginning to trail off. But none of this is unusual. By now the word-of-mouth should be taking over. Is there anything left in the media budget?"

"Not a penny," Carl responded.

"Well, keep thinking. There must be something we still haven't done. Let's spread the word around Michu's retiring. It's the last time you'll ever get to see him!"

Carl laughed and somehow I felt better, bolstered by a fresh determination. "Maybe Allen will want to up the ante and throw some more bucks into the budget?" I hung up and wandered out into the arena and watched as the ushers began gathering the kids. Then I strolled over to the room next to the box office where Billy Williams was waiting.

"The dead wood is here," Billy said. I began counting the complimentary passes while he fed the hard tickets into the machine. Neither of us felt like talking and nearly two hours passed by the time ten-thousand unsold tickets had been tallied. Billy penciled in the numbers. "Seventeen-hundred and ninety-two paid attendance."

"Okay," I said, as he handed me the slip of paper. "I'll go give Allen a call." I headed back down the corridor and again my concentration went numb. "Seventeen-hundred and ninety-two attendance?" I closed the door and plunked down. I picked up the phone, feeling my stomach begin to tighten.

"Hello. Allen Bloom's office," Maureen said into the phone.

"Hi, it's me, Jamie. I've got today's numbers. Is Allen in?"

"He stepped out of the office for a few minutes. Do you want to give the numbers to me?"

"All right," I said, feeling slightly relieved. "Ten thousand eight-hundred and thirty-two dollars."

"And what's the fresh money?" she said, and I was surprised she knew what it meant.

"Not much," I replied. "It was a pretty light walk-up. Eight hundred and twenty-six dollars."

"I've got it," she said. "I'll let Allen know."

"Okay," I said. "Tell him I'll call him at home tonight with this evening's figures."

I left the arena and drove back to the hotel, more out of restlessness than necessity. I changed shirts and motored across the parking lot to a 24-hour diner. I wasn't hungry but I hoped if I filled my stomach, it might stop the panicky feeling that was churning around. At least it had worked before. I ordered fries and a fish filet and sat by the window, washing the food down with a tall orange soda. The evening performance should be busy and that in itself should have a calming effect. But what if tomorrow wasn't any better? What if the matinee was worse? The more I pondered the imaginables the more difficult it was to eat. I forced down one last bite, leaving half a bag of fries, and headed back to the arena. I was ready to see this evening's results, starting with people streaming in. Maybe, with a little luck, tonight's attendance will be so fabulous it'll negate the matinee.

I purposefully waited until doors had been opened a few minutes and then strode out onto the concourse. It was busy. No Saturday night, but it was at least much brisker than this afternoon. I could feel a renewed buoyancy as I passed the box office, observing a dozen people waiting outside for tickets. The noise began to accelerate as the concessionaires, in broken English, shouted out their pitch.

I circled back to the front entrance and then hurried over to the head usher. "Tonight is the king and queen promotion. Be sure the boy and girl sitting in these two seats are taken to the ringmaster." I handed him a piece of paper with their seat numbers jotted down.

"No problem," he said. "I'll take care of it myself."

I peeked inside. The lights were dim but it appeared as if the arena was at least a third full. I didn't want to guess at the numbers. All I knew was it was a hell of a lot better than this afternoon.

Just before intermission there was a knock on my office door. It was the head usher. I couldn't tell if he was angry or frustrated. "They weren't in those seats!"

"Who?"

"The king and queen."

"Well, what did you do?"

"I ran out of time. I just handed the ringmaster two kids I picked out of the audience."

"That's the only thing you could do," I assured him. I closed the door. That was strange. Maybe the contest winners had gotten the right seats but had come to the wrong show.

Billy Williams walked in. I anxiously waited for a call from the box office. Finally the box office manager buzzed. "The dead wood is ready." In less than an hour we arrived at the numbers. Four-thousand one-hundred and twelve paid attendance bringing in a total of $23,600.00 But almost all of it, I noted, had been sold in advance. The box office walk-up was only $2,174.00, which meant my total cash in to date was only $161,000.00. I reached for the phone and called Allen.

"I've got the numbers."

"Give me the total and give me the fresh," he said.

I gave him the figures. There was dead silence. I wasn't sure how to respond. He hadn't hung up so in a moment I said, "What do you think?"

There was a long pause, then he took a deep breath. "It don't look too good."

I held on, searching for words of encouragement to offer. "Tomorrow will be better."

We disconnected and suddenly I felt the full weight of his words. It wasn't what he'd said, it was *how* he'd said it, almost with resignation. I replayed his voice, hoping I'd find some consolation. Maybe he's just tired, I thought, I can't get discouraged. Somehow, by the time I'm through, I'm sure he'll be ecstatic.

I drove home and stripped off my clothes. Tired, I collapsed on the bed, not even pulling down the covers. I just lay there, fixated on the ceiling, trying to ease my concerns, but then out of nowhere, in the middle of a positive thought, a heaviness rolled over my chest. My throat tightened as I reached over and turned off the light. How am I going to turn this around if I can't even control my emotions?

———

I woke up at daybreak and lifted my head, feeling as though someone had placed a ten-pound stone on the back of my skull. I reached
around and massaged the base of my neck. I squeezed as hard as I
could, trying to knead the tension, feeling the weight in my head
grow lighter. When I rose, my body felt weightless as I tried to walk
firmly on the floor. But just as the tension in my neck would subside,
the flutter in my stomach would return. Moving forward, doing
something, I knew would ground my feet. But what could I still do?
I needed a plan. I needed to think clearly, to stop my thoughts from
just tumbling. I pressed my fingers against my forehead and took a
long, slow breath. I had to get to the arena, throw myself into the
fray. It was the only way through. And slowly I felt a tingling in my
feet. My weight began to shift.

On the way to the building I racked my brain for something I hadn't
done—a promotion, a publicity stunt, anything I hadn't considered.
Maybe Robert Hanley would have an idea. The thought of asking
him anything chilled me to the bone but it *is* his town, after all, and
the success of the circus has a direct affect on his arena revenues.

"Have you seen Robert Hanley around?" I asked his secretary.

"The last time I saw him he was with the operations manager.
You might check down in the maintenance office."

I nodded and began wandering around to the far end of the building, wishing I didn't have that headachy feeling from waking so
edgy this morning. A small sign pointed down a darkened set of
stairs. At the bottom of the steps I could see a light emanating from
a small room. I opened the door slowly. Hanley was sitting on a
steel-legged chair across the desk from a heavyset man. He was
wearing an olive sweater and for a change wasn't smoking his pipe.

The operations manager smiled. He at least made an attempt at
being friendly. Yet I was confident he was indelibly connected to
Hanley. Papers were scattered on his desk and behind him sat the
remnants of an old popcorn machine.

"What can we do for you?" Hanley asked, looking up.

"I'm not sure," I said. "As you know I've been promoting this town for three months. In fact, I can't think of a promotion I haven't done."

Hanley glanced at his operations manager, then back at me.

"Anyway, I'm not sure what I'm asking, but the numbers are not what I'd hoped for. We've still got today, tomorrow and all weekend to go. Is there anything, knowing this town as you do, you can suggest?"

The operations manager looked at Hanley and Hanley sat up. Without even hearing his answer I knew I'd made a mistake. Why was I humiliating myself in front of this man? He hadn't done a damn thing to help me so far.

"Ringling knows pretty much all there is to know about marketing," Hanley muttered, and then he looked over at his operations manager. "All I know is by now I'd have made more money on concessions with the Shriner's than I'll make on ticket sales with Ringling for your entire engagement."

Hanley leaned back and the chubby man behind the desk shifted, averting his gaze.

"I see," I said, and I realized the conversation had ended. "Thanks for your help."

"Anytime."

So that was it. The son-of-a-bitch had been pissed from day one. No wonder he didn't give a damn about Ringling. Unlike us, with the Shriner's, the arena received a take on the concessions. I wondered what Allen would say when I told him.

Chapter 54
HOPE

I sat in my office, still stunned by my conversation with Hanley, but I had little time for wasted agitation. The sun was out and it was a beautiful day. That could mean a hell of a walk-up. I quickly reviewed my notes. WNUR was interviewing Jeanette Williams shortly before the show. I hoped the reporter would ask Jeanette what she thought about Elvin's stunts. What could it be like to be married to a man who risked his neck twice a day? Another interview was scheduled for tonight with a show girl, and at the same time I had promised I'd take care of Carl's client, the Pizza Hut owner—front row seats, honorary ringmaster—the whole bit. I started to fret, then figured I'd worry about juggling it all later.

I stepped outside to check the lines at the box office. It was still quiet, and the afternoon had turned hot. Terre Haute on a steamy summer's day reminded me of the deep south, and I wondered if the heat would help or hinder today's sales. Surely there were thousands of children simmering on farmhouse porches tugging at their grandmothers' sleeves to take them to the circus.

I watched as a few people bought tickets and then ambled back inside. Billy Williams was already standing by the entrance. Cars, I noticed, had begun to pull up, and I crossed my fingers. I waited and watched for another few minutes as the doors finally opened, then decided I'd walk backstage. I needed that feeling of home again, that comfortable feeling of family that calmed my nerves. I glanced around, thinking I'd see a few people, but most of the performers still hadn't arrived. I walked past the King Charles Troupe dressing room hoping Charlie might be there, but the room was still empty, so I wandered over to clown alley thinking I might find some activity there. Just as I'd hoped, there were four or five clowns in various stages of makeup. I waved to Prince Paul and two of the others as they sat with their chins up, busily occupied, then I headed down a long hallway of heavy, blue curtains. As I rounded the corner, a little girl caught my eye. She sat on the concrete floor playing with a small doll. I didn't recognize her at first. Her brown hair was twisted in a long braid, almost to the small of her back, and her tiny frame protruded from a sparkling blue sequined costume. I wondered why she was dressed so soon and then realized this was her debut, her first time in front of an arena full of spectators. I smiled as I passed by, thinking she might recognize me, hoping this time she'd land squarely on her father's shoulders. I turned around after I'd passed and looked at her again, remembering how hard she had tried, not quitting no matter how many times she had missed, and for an instant, a brief instant, I again felt that lump in my throat. My mouth went dry and then it was gone as quickly as it came. I headed purposefully back up the stairs.

From deep down in my stomach I sensed something was wrong before I even hit the concourse. Where was the sound of the barkers, the men and women standing behind the counters selling cotton candy, posters and popcorn? I walked through a darkened tunnel and into the wide, sunlit hallway. A Mexican woman was standing behind her stall quietly folding T-shirts while her husband stood idly by with pennants strung over both arms. There was no one else around. I nodded at them, feeling the nervousness in my stomach start to grow into an undefinable fear. I was anxious to get to the main entrance. That was where all the activity would be. I hurried along, feeling a little winded, refusing to analyze the long, empty corridor until I could see what was happening. Finally I rounded the last corner and stopped. Billy Williams was leaning against the wall, his arms folded casually across his chest. A ticket taker, dressed in a burgundy coat, was tearing tickets for an elderly couple, while another ticket taker waited for a young family to enter.

"What's going on?" I asked Billy, and I knew he could sense my fear.

"It's pretty quiet."

"How quiet?" I said, and before he could answer I asked, "Is it quieter than yesterday?"

"I'm afraid so."

I stood there for a moment, suddenly drained of all energy, not knowing what to say.

"I see," I mumbled.

"What did you say?" Billy asked.

"Nothing," I said, and I turned and walked toward the arena, not looking left or right. I was no longer even thinking.

I strode through the entrance, into the well lit arena and stood at the railing, looking out at the tiers below. Thousands upon thousands of empty upholstered seats rose to the ceiling. A scattering of a few hundred people, a drop in the bucket, were spread throughout the arena. Entire sections of six hundred seats held only a family or two. I stood and watched, unable to focus, as a few more people trickled in.

Finally, when the last of the stragglers had entered, I turned and walked back to the front entrance doors.

"By the way," Billy said, and he handed me a piece of paper, "somebody from WNUR called. Something came up. They won't be able to interview Jeanette."

"Okay," I said quietly. "I'll tell her." And without reading it, I folded the note and placed it in my pocket.

Some of the concessionaires were already collapsing their stalls as I walked slowly past. I needed to inform Jeanette, but inexplicably I turned before reaching the back stairs and stepped into the last portal to the arena. I stood again at the top of the aisle and watched as Charlie Bauman stood stoically by, waiting to summon the performers to render their grand entrance. The sticky floors plucked at my feet as I descended the long stairs to the spot where I'd proudly stood. Harold sang out the start of the show and I gazed at the sparse arena. I watched as the curtains opened and the elephants rumbled in with a dozen dazzling show girls atop their necks, followed by an endless stream of performers smiling and waving to row upon row of empty seats.

Shame kept me glued to the spot. I looked over as though I was reaching out to the heavens, and as each performer passed, by my presence alone, I tried to say I was sorry. But nothing I could say, no look I could give, no thought I could think could replace the shocking awareness, a realization too deep to feel, that no matter how much I'd hoped, no matter how much I'd done, no matter how hard I'd tried . . . I had failed.

The last of the performers exited the arena, and I stepped out onto the hippodrome track and followed them backstage. Jeanette's dressing room was the first room on the left. I knocked on her door. "I'm sorry," I said. "I should have told you sooner, but the interview was cancelled."

Numbly, I turned and headed up a long corridor of curtains searching for Charlie King, hoping for a glance, an exchange that might reassure me. I knew Charlie would understand. When I arrived at his dressing room, a room full of men were noisily changing clothes. I slipped through the curtains to see if he was there. "He's not here," one of the men said, pulling on his shirt. Others in his troupe glanced my way, and I turned and started to leave when I heard my name shouted out.

I swung round and standing behind me was one of the clowns. "Jamie," he repeated, glaring at me with a look of disdain. "Where are all the people?"

Suddenly I no longer felt so numb. I looked back into the dressing room. All motion had stopped. Two of Charlie's friends just peered at me blankly. Silently, I turned and walked away. I walked back down the long corridor, turned right at the end and marched up the ramp. Everything seemed to be a blur. When I reached the top, I strode past the roustabouts, past the tents and the horses, and hopped into my car. Almost blindly, I turned on the ignition, with one goal in mind; I had to get out of there. I spun out of the lot. I had to get back to my hotel.

I drove down busy streets, oblivious to the traffic, and pulled into the hotel parking lot. I entered through the side of the building. As I did, I heard voices coming from the bar. One loud voice was particularly familiar. I walked in. Sitting on a barstool, half inebriated, was Ralph Finley.

"That damned circus. I should never have trusted those bastards!" he shouted to anyone who would listen.

I couldn't believe it. That son of a bitch!

"Finley," I spat. "Could you please come with me?"

He swiveled around, and I watched as his eyes slowly came into focus. Suddenly his angry demeanor took on a look of fear. He slid off his stool and followed behind as I trooped down the hall and got on the elevator to my room.

"Come in!" I demanded, and I slammed the door.

"How could you?" I stammered, as he stood ashen faced in front of me. "How could you sit down there and lambast me and the circus to everybody and their brother?" Suddenly I found myself choking back tears. "Is this what I get from you? No one knows more than you how hard we've tried, how much effort went into this town!"

"I'm sorry," he stammered.

"You ought to be sorry!" I screamed, cutting him off, and I felt my face redden. "Goddamn sorry!" And suddenly I could see the look on his face wasn't just fear. He was in a state of abject shock, stunned by my outburst.

"Get the hell out of here!" I exploded, and I watched as he stumbled to the elevator, pausing to glance back at me.

I closed the door and as I heard the elevator open, I trembled with rage. Suddenly I felt sick. I stood in the middle of the room, at the foot of the bed, and all I could hear were the words, "Where are all the people?" Over and over I heard the words, seeing again the vacant looks on the performers faces and, as he said it, the expression of disdain on his lips. I began to shake. I could no longer hold it inside. My hands covered my face and pressed against my flesh as tears sprang to my eyes. Through blurred vision I stared at the ceiling as the anguish came spilling out. "I tried! God knows, I tried! I did everything, everything I know. I don't know what else I could do." I repeated the words over and over until I backed against the wall and slowly slid to the floor. My chest throbbed as a noose tightened around my throat, and I pressed my fingers against my forehead trying to hold back the tears. I cried until there was nothing left. Then I sat there, too drained, too exhausted to feel anything but the empty sense of failure. I rose and sat down on the bed and looked around the room. It reeked of that sun blanched feeling of loneliness. Slowly I stood and staggered into the bathroom and turned on the cold water. My eyes were red and my face was flush with dried tears. The cold water stung my eyes, clinging to my chin in droplets, until I smothered my face in a thin cotton towel. Still drained, I took a deep breath and looked at my watch. My God, almost two hours had passed. I had to get back to the arena. I tucked in my shirt, headed down the hall and hurried out to the car. I drove up the street, desperately trying to collect myself before easing to a stop behind the building.

Intermission was ending as I dashed through the corridor and into the room beside the box office. "I'm sorry I'm late," I blurted. "Are you ready to start?" Then I noticed the dead wood was stacked neatly in the box.

"Don't sweat it," Billy said. "I'm already done. Here are the numbers." He handed me the sheet.

"Really, I'm sorry," I repeated and I sat down and looked at the numbers.

"See you tonight," Billy said as he exited the room.

I studied the sheet. Only 345 people had attended. Less than $2,000.00 total with only $336.00 in fresh money.

Somberly I stared at the numbers and then stepped down the hall to my office and nervously picked up the phone. I was immediately transferred to Allen.

"It's not very good." I said and then told him the numbers.

There was a moment of silence. "Not very good?" His voice slowly rose. "Not very good? It's a financial disaster!"

For a moment I couldn't respond. Startled, I searched for an answer. "I was hoping maybe we could put more money into radio?"

"What for? What would be the point of throwing good money after bad?"

"I guess you're right," I mumbled. Quietly I hung up the phone. I slumped and stared at the wall, shaken by his outburst. What had

I expected? He was right. It was a disaster, a shameful financial disaster.

An hour later I called Carl and told him I'd spoken with Allen. "There won't be any more money," I said. Carl understood but shared my sense of frustration.

"Keep thinking," I implored, still clinging to hope. "We've still got four days to go."

I swallowed half a tuna fish sandwich and anxiously waited. It was almost time for doors for the evening performance. Once again I double checked my schedule. Logistically I'd have to shuttle back and forth between the radio interview with the show girl and Carl's unhappy Pizza Hut manager.

I glanced around and noticed the incoming crowd seemed a bit brisker. Several of the ticket takers were tearing off discount coupons available only through the Pizza Huts. Suddenly my sagging spirits began to lift. I paced around the concourse, peeking inside, and noticed the lower sections had a sizeable number of people, two or three thousand so far, and I wondered if maybe the tide was beginning to turn. If I could have a good showing tonight, then a strong crowd this weekend, I could still surpass the company's projection. By how much, who knows?

The radio reporter interviewing the show girl arrived and said he'd record her comments and air them later in the week.

"Could you air them tomorrow?" I exclaimed. "I could use a push now."

"I'll try," he said and with that reassurance I escorted him downstairs, introducing him to the head wardrobe mistress. "Just show your ticket to an usher when you're done," I said, and I hurried back upstairs.

The Pizza Hut owner, along with his family, was waiting by the front door. "I'm sorry I'm a few minutes late," I said, trying not to be overly apologetic. I showed him and his family to their center-row seats. I could see how Carl could be easily intimidated. The owner was a big man with the gruff manner of a long-time taskmaster.

"We've only had a few honorary tiger trainers," I said. "But don't worry. Just stand behind Charlie Bauman and crack your whip whenever he does."

His face began to lose color. "Just kidding," I chuckled, and I handed him his honorary ringmaster's whistle. I remained long enough to watch the start of the show and then escorted him back to his seat.

In less than an hour, Billy Williams and I had tallied the dead wood. Twenty three hundred in attendance with only a little over $1,200.00 in walk-up. I totaled my numbers, retotaling them again. I stared at the figure in disbelief. Halfway through and I only had $160,545.00 in the till with just Thursday, Friday and the weekend to go.

Just after eleven o'clock I called in the numbers to Allen. "How are you doing?" he asked, and his voice no longer sounded angry. He seemed as though he was genuinely concerned.

"I'm okay," I said. "Don't worry, we're still going to hit the numbers." Then I added, as positively as I could, "I'm no quitter."

"I know you're not," he said, and suddenly I felt the same as I had in the restaurant when he'd convinced me to stay.

"There's something else I wanted to tell you," I said. "I had a conversation with Robert Hanley this morning that was odd."

"How so?"

"Well, I think I'd mentioned to you how cold he's been. Even the slightest concern and I felt as if I was practically ignored. Well, this morning I was talking to him and his assistant and all of a sudden he lamented, 'By now I'd have made more money from the Shriners on concessions alone.' Pretty strange talk from somebody who wants us back?"

There was a pause on the other end and then Allen said, as though it had become indelibly etched, "Maybe he doesn't want us back."

Tired, I tried desperately to fall back asleep. A midwestern storm pelted rain in sheets against my window. The wind and the rhythmic pounding against the pane kept my thoughts swirling around. I couldn't get the numbers out of my head. Finally, I gave up and sat by the window, watching the rain splatter against the darkened city until dawn finally broke.

I drove toward the arena, acutely aware of the wet leaves strewn across the street. It was as though autumn had violently arrived. A branch snapped underneath my tires, and I wondered how long it had been since I'd had a full night's sleep.

Low lying, gray, puffy clouds lent an air of serenity to the city as I drove toward the building. The streets seemed quieter than usual. Uncommonly for June there was a cool chill in the air.

I turned right on Severn Street, past an abandoned apartment building. Broken glass lay on the ground amidst weeds growing through cracks in the sidewalk. I kept driving south, away from the arena, deeper into the poorer neighborhoods, somehow gaining comfort in their rickety conditions. Rain sprinkled my windshield as I drove past row-houses in sad need of repair, past cars that were faded and rusty. I drove past an old elementary school built like they used to be, tall and square and foreboding in dark red brick. No wonder it was often depressing to go to school. I spotted an elderly man shuffling along the sidewalk and stopped and asked directions, just to talk to someone about something other than the circus. He pointed me toward the arena and I began to drive back. The show had arrived just seven days ago, yet, it occurred to me, I could barely remember what it was like before.

I turned left and began driving through the center of town, prolonging my hold on the calm. As soon as I thought about the circus, flashes of bright colors and blackness from quickly dimmed spotlights mingled with the reverberating sounds of the music. And suddenly I remembered it was the sounds of the trumpets that had woken me during the storm. Over and over, the music pounded against the windowpane. Even now, I couldn't seem to get it out of my mind.

I pulled into the parking lot. A few of the men from the King Charles Troupe were practicing on their unicycles, tossing a basketball back and forth. Elvin Bale was toweling wet dust off his trailer. And Charlie Bauman, in an exceptionably good mood, was smiling at one of the show girls stepping off the bus.

I walked down the ramp and entered the backstage area. Several performers were milling about. One of the show girls was sitting on the lap of her boyfriend while three others walked by, laughing and nodding hello. There was a gaiety in the air, or seemed to be, or maybe my awareness was just heightened today.

I saluted a few members of the King Charles Troupe who smiled and waved back, and then I walked into the arena and up the long flight of stairs to the main entrance. Billy Williams had some errands he said he had to do so I positioned myself where he normally stood at the doors. As soon as they opened I began my stroll around the concourse. It was quiet as I circled to the rear of the building. Only one ticket taker had been stationed at the back entrance. He looked uncomfortably bored so I stopped and began a conversation. He was temporarily between jobs and this gave him a few bucks. His uncle, he told me, had worked for a circus. We talked for several minutes, then I heard Bill Pruyn's familiar warming up of the band. I strolled back toward the front, stopping long enough in my office to see that there weren't any messages, and then slowly walked back to the front entrance. There was nobody coming in.

I waited a few minutes and then heard the band strike its opening chords. I crossed my fingers and walked toward the entrance, hoping there were seated at least several hundred if not one or two thousand people. I looked down at the arena floor. The opening procession had begun. All two hundred performers and dozens of animals along with their handlers had paraded out onto the hippodrome track to begin their three-hour performance, and then a wave of nausea swept over me. I stared out in shock and then turned and walked slowly away, back to my office, stopping involuntarily, bending over, fighting the urge to throw up.

I opened the door and sat down, listening to the band play the opening number to a father and mother and three little children sitting halfway up on the other side of the arena. Other than them, there was nobody there.

Chapter 55
How?

Five people. Five people in the middle of 11,995 empty seats. And that was it? This was beyond believability. Had it ever happened before? And yet all three rings of performers played on. Somehow, it never occurred to them not to. But what must they think? What must the ushers think or the box office for that matter? And for Christ's sake, what must the five people think? They must feel ridiculous! Should I ask them to leave? Come back for another performance? What would happen then? Would the performers just stop? Horrified, I shuddered at the vision of two hundred performers milling backstage with nothing to do because there wasn't one single person in the audience. At least with five people there was pride in, "The show must go on!"

But when does this nightmare end? This was only Thursday afternoon. I still had tonight and Friday, Saturday and Sunday to go. This wasn't a wrong turn or misdirection. This wasn't just a disaster. It was a complete and utter catastrophe. I was standing alone on the helm of the sinking *Titanic*.

I didn't move for two straight hours. I couldn't call in the numbers to Allen. How do I tell him we only did $27.50 for an entire performance?

The phone rang twice. I just let it ring. The noise sounded so hollow. Everything seemed distant. Evansville, Washington, D.C., even Allen Bloom seemed light years away.

I was amazed as I sat there, too stunned to think, that I could feel anything at all. I was numb, numb to the bone, as though every last worry and emotion had been wrung. If there was any sensation at all, it was fear, a discernible anxiety that the lack of sensation might end.

I wandered through the rest of the afternoon dead to any heightened awareness. Even the interview with Axel Gautier just before the evening performance seemed mindless. I heard him speak in clipped authoritative tones but I couldn't remember a word he said.

Shortly after the interview I again stood watch by the doors. For all practical purposes the evening performance was just as pathetic. Only eight hundred people attended. "I'll call in the numbers to Allen," Billy said.

"Thank you," I responded, too devastated to pick up the phone.

I drove back to the hotel and braced myself against the back of the bed, too weary to think, too exhausted to try to sleep.

The phone rang. Who would be calling me at midnight?

"Jamie. It's Al Atkinson."

"Al Atkinson?" I replied, wondering why he would be calling. Al Atkinson was Allen's right hand man, a gentle man in his fifties whom I'd met a few times in the beginning. An ex-promoter, he worked in the main office and handled the company's printing.

"We're a little worried about you," he said. "I heard you had a pretty rough day."

That's a bit of an understatement I started to say and suddenly the lump in my throat returned and I could barely speak into the phone.

"Look, it happens to the best of us," he said.

"I just don't know what to do, Al. I've done all I can."

"Hey, we know that, Jamie. That's all we've ever asked. You're one of Allen's favorites, you know."

"I am?"

"Yeah. You and Bobby Collins."

"That's nice to hear," I said.

"Is there anything I can do from here, anything at all?" Al asked.

"No," I said. "Just let Allen know I'm sorry I didn't call tonight. Let him know I'm doing everything I can."

"Okay," he said. "Just remember I'm here if you need me."

I hung up the phone and slid back on the bed, feeling the soft cotton bedspread against my skin. I closed my eyes, clinging for a moment to Al's soothing words. I thought of the performers, the entire cast playing to a tiny audience of five. I'd seen it with my own eyes and I knew if there had only been one, one small child with a ragged ticket, the show would have played on.

I lay there, my mind adrift, caught in a misty pride that I was part of a family that just didn't quit. Never had, never would. They'd risk their lives rather than turn away one paying customer. Then slowly, gradually, I drifted off to sleep.

It was early in the morning, half awake, that an idea lit across my mind. Why hadn't I thought of it before? I sat up and turned on the light. I'd figured it out. I finally knew what was going on. What seemed so incredibly complex was actually incredibly simple! When Earl Duryea had orchestrated the routing of the show at the beginning of the year there must have been a gap he couldn't fill. Maybe it was a building's negotiation that fell through at the last minute, or maybe it was simply travel logistics, and suddenly he couldn't get the schedule tightened up. And now he had the entire show on his hands with nowhere to go. What were they going to do? Let them sit on the side of the tracks for five straight days with nothing to do? That explains it! This was always just a three-day date. They stretched it to nine hoping it would fill the gap. There was no other explanation. I glanced at my watch. I could hardly wait to call Allen to confirm my discovery.

I staggered up, somehow reenergized. I pulled on my jeans, buttoned up a white dress shirt, and went downstairs and ate breakfast, the first full meal I'd eaten in two days. Allen wouldn't be in his office until at least ten o'clock. I lingered at the breakfast table, scanning the newspaper headlines, thinking how nice it was to be interested in something other than the circus, feeling liberated that maybe the disaster wasn't entirely my fault.

———

Allen was on the phone when I called. Maureen said he'd call me right back. I nervously waited.

"Jamie, how are you doing?" he said, and I again heard a tone of concern.

"I'm fine," I replied, realizing as I said it I sounded too ebullient for the circumstances.

We talked for a few moments, each of us purposefully avoiding the debacle at hand. Then eager to confirm my theory, I pronounced, "Allen, I figured it out!"

"Figured what out?"

I proceeded to tell him what I knew. That in the middle of the night I had solved the mystery. It was all just logistics.

"I could see where that would be possible," Allen said, and I could tell by the gravity in his voice he was being truthful, "And I guess I can see how it could look that way . . . but it simply isn't the case."

"I see," I said, feeling not only deflated but embarrassed to be grabbing at straws, and I quietly hung up the phone. At least it's Friday, I lamented, the weekend is bound to be better.

Each day, no matter how tired I felt, I figured that if I could just push through a positive thought, I could somehow replenish the well. The epitome of mind over body. But this morning as I drove to the arena, past shoppers strolling along the sidewalk, beside motorists busily about their day, I felt even more drained than usual. It suddenly seemed an enormous effort just to string two thoughts together. I couldn't afford to be tired, not this spent, not yet. I knew I was only getting three or four hours of sleep, but no matter how hard I tried, I'd wake up and my mind would be churning, and I couldn't fall back asleep. I'd be thinking about the same things over and over again.

Wary as well that I hadn't been eating enough, I stopped on the way and picked up a milkshake. I'd always been told I was skinny. I hated being thin, as though it was a slight on my masculinity. I glanced down at my waist, feeling better as the milkshake bloated my stomach.

———

I walked into my arena office and picked up the phone. I was anxious to speak to Bill Sweeney now that he'd moved the outlets to the Evansville arena. He picked up right away. I could hear sounds of people in the background.

"How's it going?"

"Great," Sweeney said. "We've had long lines ever since we opened today!"

"How's the building?" I asked nervously, then added not waiting for an answer. "Do you see ol' man Strausel?"

"Yeah, he pops his head in every now and then. I tell him we're fine and he leaves us alone."

"What about Rick Johnson?" I asked. "Has he been checking in with you?"

"I haven't heard from him in awhile. But don't worry, like I said, I'm on top of everything."

"All right," I said, feeling pissed again at Rick. "Keep up the good work and I'll see you this Monday." I hung up, beginning to feel excited, and thought about my secretary Lisa. I hadn't talked to her in days. Surely she must be proud of all the Evansville publicity she had helped to engineer. I reached in my wallet and dialed the number she had given me, hoping to hear her voice, but nobody answered the phone.

With my spirits still aloft from my call to Bill Sweeney I picked up the phone and dialed Carl Bruce. "I guess we'd better be settling up our invoices pretty soon," I said.

"You've already seen all the media affidavits," he assured me.

"I know, but you still haven't been paid your agency fee."

"When would you like to see me?"

"How about this evening shortly before the performance?"

"I'll be there," he said. "Is there anything else I can do?"

"I wish there was," I said. "You've already done more than I could have asked."

I hung up and reflected back on the late nights he and I had worked together perusing all of our options, looking at every angle. Somehow I was determined to give him the five hundred dollar bonus I had proffered. I didn't care, even if we didn't meet our projections no one had tried harder than Carl.

Seven hundred people attended the afternoon show. It wasn't much but it was a triumph compared to the previous day, a sign that the weekend had at last arrived. Billy and I tallied the numbers. Thirty-five hundred and twelve dollars, giving me a total of $168,000.00 now in the till. I called Allen and related the numbers. "Carl Bruce," I informed him, "is coming by tonight for his agency fee. I'd like to give him the $500.00 bonus I'd proposed. His fee doesn't come close to the work he's done."

"That's crazy," Allen said.

"I know, but he deserves it!" I felt myself becoming angry.

"Jamie. A deal is a deal."

Frustrated, I stammered, "What if you give him the $500.00 bonus I earned in Savannah?"

"You're being emotional," Allen said. "This is business!"

I hung up and stared at the phone, feeling somehow I'd betrayed Carl, holding out a carrot beyond his reach. Unlike Rick Johnson in Evansville, he'd never lost focus.

That night the sky had turned overcast and the wind had picked up, a warm balmy breeze. I was reminded of the Bahamas, gathered in the restaurant with Allen and the promoters, talking noisily, while big leafy palm trees flapped in the shadows.

I stood alone on the curb outside the arena waiting for the cars to begin pulling up. It was Friday night. The first night of the weekend. Something told me it wasn't too late. There was still word of mouth. Fill up the weekend and we could still hit the numbers.

The first of the cars eased around the corner and turned into the main parking lot. Before long several other cars began turning the corner, a slow, steady column, and I noticed a slight back-up had formed at the parking lot entrance. I began to pace back and forth feeling an excitement start to build. Then I heard my name called out. It was Carl. He had walked up and was standing behind me.

"They're coming!" I shouted. "They're coming!"

"Who?"

"The crowds!" I said. "I knew we shouldn't have given up hope!" Carl looked out.

"The parking lot's starting to fill up," I hollered. "It's the weekend. It's starting to turn around! I knew it was just a matter of time."

Carl stood by my side and we waited and watched until the cars began to come more sporadically, no longer a steady stream, a few at a time. A third of the parking lot had filled.

Slowly it dawned on me, that was all there was going to be. I didn't say anything for a few moments, nor did Carl. Then I quietly reached into my pocket and pulled out his check.

"I'm sorry about the bonus I'd offered. I wish I could give it to you. If I had any money I'd pay it myself."

"That's all right," Carl said. "I'm just glad I got the chance."

"Me too," I said, and then we stood there for a moment, awkwardly, not knowing what to say, not knowing how to say goodbye.

He turned and started to walk away. "Carl," I shouted after him. He turned and I noticed his face was drawn. His eyes were misty with tears. I pointed up at the big marquee with its gold lights sparkling out, "Ringling Brothers and Barnum and Bailey Circus—Terre Haute, Indiana."

"Thanks," I hollered, trying to smile, trying not to cry.

He nodded, his eyes still rimmed with tears. Then he waved goodbye and walked away. I stood near the curb for a few minutes longer, feeling the breeze against my face, wishing he hadn't left, then slowly walked back to the building.

I found Billy Williams back stage talking with one of the show girls. By the comfortable look on her face I was pretty sure she was his girlfriend. She was between numbers. It seemed strange to see her wearing eyeglasses while dressed in her costume of ostrich feathers.

"I hate to break this up," I said as politely as I could, "but I need you to write me another check. My company checkbook is too limited to cover what we owe Finley."

"Let's go," he said, and we headed upstairs to my office. I told him about the deal with NBC. "In exchange for a ton of advertising, I'd agreed to pay ten percent of the matinees."

As we walked in silence, I remembered my encounter with Finley, as though it had happened only minutes ago. I could still see him frozen to the carpet, red faced and disheveled, while I madly stormed on in rage. I fought the compulsion to feel sorry for him—to be manipulated by a drunk who could alternately be cruel and obnoxious—only later to somehow feel pity. I was angry for having been angry but I'd be angrier still if I allowed him to make me regret it.

I pulled out the letter of agreement and showed it to Billy as he plugged in the adding machine. The four matinees, Tuesday through Friday, less discounts and complimentary passes, added up to $22,500.00. "We owe NBC $2,250.00," I said, "a fraction of what we'd received in advertising."

"Not a bad deal," Billy said as he made out the check.

"Well, the result wasn't what I intended," I said, and I handed him back the check. "You're the keeper of the stamps. Would you mind mailing it for me?"

I waited until I returned to my room to call Allen. Even when he was frustrated his voice had begun to have a calming effect. It was almost as though he was the only one that mattered. Regardless of who I encountered, or what had transpired during the day, it was Allen's opinion that counted. In the beginning, when I'd called in the numbers, the dialogue had seemed routine, but now it seemed as if Allen awaited my calls. His voice was immediately familiar and he was never the first to hang up. He lingered for a moment or two to see if there was anything else I wanted to say.

I told him we did a little over two thousand tonight in attendance and I gave him the numbers. "But I still have high hopes for Saturday and Sunday." He asked how I was doing. I told him I was a little tired, then not wanting him to worry, I said, "I'll try to rest Monday, after the animal walk, while the show is setting up in Evansville."

I hung up feeling a little better, undressed and climbed between the cool sheets, wishing the maid hadn't tucked them in so tightly.

Now if I could just get the sounds of the circus music out of my head. I tried not to think about Evansville nor the final two days in Terre Haute. I just wanted to sleep. If I could go back in time, when I was a little boy, it would sometimes help. The weeks in Canada during summer vacations, visiting my grandparents and combing through the woods. Seeing my grandmother's sweet smile and my grandfather's look of approval. I thought about my mother and father moving further away to the deep south. How different it was from the big city. Then I found myself remembering the day my father first took me hunting. The colors of the season came back as rich and vivid as if I were there. I was nine years old. My father had bought me a 22 caliber rifle. I could still see its barrel and thin tipped sight and feel the hard wooden stock against my shoulder. I'd watched him all winter hand carve the wooden parts of an old Lee Enfield he'd bought, sanding and staining the grain until the clunky rifle was a slim, sleek version of itself. I could still smell the linseed oil he used to protect the wood and hear the steel rods sliding noisily down the barrel as cotton swabs cleaned out the grease. He was as proud of that rifle as anything he had ever owned. It was practically an antique, the infantry weapon of the British during World War I. And now, thanks to his efforts, it was a modern-day deer rifle. "One of the best rifles ever made!" he'd say. "Accurate to three hundred yards."

My father had bought a used Morris Minor truck that winter, a miniaturized pickup truck, and he built a wooden platform on the back. To the platform he bolted an old chair, an armchair with the stuffing falling out.

I'd been practicing with the new 22 he'd given me, shooting cans he'd strung on twine between two trees. Every now and then, I'd hit one and the can would spin and tumble in the air, but mostly I'd just miss. One morning, he drove up in his Morris Minor truck with the chair bolted on the back, leaned out of the window and asked, "Are you ready to go hunting?"

"Sure," I said. He handed me a box of shells, "hollow points," he called them. I followed his directive and clamored up onto the chair.

"Load up," he said, "and put on the safety," and I carefully placed a bullet in the chamber and snapped it shut.

We took off through the woods down an overgrown dirt road half bouncing out of the seat. Weeds as tall as the window flew by in a blur. Occasionally he'd look back with a grin just to make sure I was still there. I waved back at him, not caring if I shot anything or not, I was just happy to be with him.

It seemed like we'd driven for an hour over ruts and stones and holes in the road when we entered a small clearing. I'd almost forgotten why we were there when a beautiful, white rabbit ran in front of the truck and stopped to my right, standing still in the tall grass. I could see it perfectly. It couldn't have been more than ten feet away. Its fur was the color of snow and the rabbit stood erect on its back haunches, its front paws bent in the air. There was no way it was going to stir. It was hoping it couldn't be seen.

Everything was terribly quiet as my father turned in his seat and looked at me through the rear view window. I knew how proud he'd be of me. I turned slowly toward the rabbit, careful not to make a sound, and placed the rifle butt against my shoulder, feeling the cold barrel against my cheek. The rabbit remained motionless. It was so close I knew I couldn't miss. I looked down the barrel, positioning the site right below the rabbit's shoulder, right in the middle of its chest where I knew its heart was beating, breathed in slowly, held my breath just as my father had taught me, and pulled the trigger.

The shot "cracked" in the air, and the rabbit leapt straight up and began to run. My father quickly motioned at me to follow. I jumped off the chair and ran in the direction I'd seen it go. I'd only gone thirty or so feet when I stopped and there it lay. I dropped to my knees and looked at it. It lay on its side, its chest gasping for air, its fur still snow white, as white as it was only seconds ago, except now, below its right shoulder, a bright red patch of blood, still wet and oozing, blotted its fur.

I looked on in horror as the rabbit quit breathing. I picked it up, still warm in my hands, and carried it to the truck.

We drove back to the house and my father laid the rabbit on a stone near our back porch. "You can clean it later," he said. "Good shot!"

I looked once more at the rabbit, lifeless, far away from its habitat. Then I opened the screen door, walked upstairs to my room, closed the door, and promptly sat down and cried. For the next two nights, I cried myself to sleep. My father insisted I clean the rabbit, but I refused. "If he shot it, he cleans it!" he shouted at one point to my mother.

"Can't you see he's upset? He's not like you!" my mother shouted back.

Finally he gave the rabbit away to an old man who lived nearby. He gladly carried it away. My father never took me hunting again after that. I wish I'd never gone that day. I wish I hadn't killed that rabbit. But more than anything I wish I hadn't let him down.

I woke up at the first sign of light, bone tired. I knew I'd slept a few hours more soundly than usual, but as I stood up, I felt dizzy. Every joint in my body ached. I limped stiffly into the bathroom, methodically avoiding the mirror.

I went to the closet and looked at my clothes. Except for my powder blue suit I was saving for my trip home to Washington, there was nothing I hadn't worn at least three times since the last time cleaned. I pulled out a shirt, one that seemed a little better than the others, and tucked it into a pair of jeans. I finished dressing, grabbed my briefcase, and trudged down the hotel corridor. Everything I did had now become routine.

When I arrived at the arena and walked out onto the concourse I was surprised to see several fresh faces. I'd gotten used to the retirees as ushers and ticket takers all week and it was almost disorienting to see school kids fill up the jobs for the weekend. Most of them didn't know who I was, even though I recognized a few of the faces from the weekend before. I watched as their supervisors instructed them about the parts of the tickets to tear, and I looked on as the ushers were handed the hats for the fifty-two kids in the show. Not taking chances, I asked one of the girls holding several silver hats if she knew what to do. She nodded and said her supervisor would remind her when the time came to gather the kids.

Now, as I wandered around the concourse watching the ticket takers more carefully, the numbers again began swirling in my head.

As of last night, I had $172,000.00 in the bank, with just four shows to go. But at least they were Saturday and Sunday shows. I urgently tried to calculate what I'd have to do to meet Allen's numbers. If only I could hit $360,000.00, the company's projections, Allen I knew would be pleased. I again multiplied out the seats by the average ticket price. Factoring in the four remaining shows, there were forty-eight thousand seats left to sell. At an average price of $5.50 a ticket, that meant there was still a potential of $264,000.00. All I needed was $188,000.00 to make up the difference—a good matinee, a great Saturday night and then a hell of a finale on Sunday.

My pace picked up as I strolled around the concourse. The Saturday afternoon crowd was now pouring in. Just the thought that I could still hit Allen's numbers and suddenly I didn't feel as depleted. I watched as the sunlight bounced off the crowd's bright colors, shirts and dresses of yellows and greens. I waved at Billy as I hurried by, then peeked inside and smiled at the usherette I'd earlier questioned. I could feel my pulse start to quicken. I tried not to deceive myself but I noticed even the concessionaires seemed to be coming back to life. A Mexican woman with a gold tooth held up a flashing toy and smiled as I scurried by. I smiled back and remembered all of a sudden how great it felt to feel like a success, to not feel as though I'd let everyone down.

I glanced inside the arena. There had to be at least two thousand people. It wasn't as many as I needed but I could feel a glimmer of hope. I sat in one of the empty seats and for the first time in days I watched some of the show, biding my time while I waited for the dead wood to count.

"The box office is early this afternoon," I said, entering the room as I noticed Billy Williams had already begun sorting the tickets.

"I guess they're getting better at it," he said.

I elected to feed the machine while Billy counted the kids stubs and carefully recorded the numbers. An hour later, Billy penciled in the results. Twenty three hundred attendance. "A little over ten thousand dollars," he said. But it was the fresh money that mattered. I quickly scanned to the bottom of the sheet. Under fresh money, Billy had written in $2,900.00. "Is that all?" I asked. Billy just looked at me. I handed him back the sheet, too exhausted to say anything else. With only three shows to go my total had barely moved.

I carried the box of tickets back to the box office and wandered backstage in search of Charlie Bauman. I was tired, so fatigued I could barely think, but before the evening performance I had to tell him about Evansville. I knocked on his dressing room door.

"Come in!" he bellowed in his thick German accent. I opened the door. He was sitting behind a makeshift desk, his costumes and tuxedos hanging on a rod behind.

"I thought I'd better tell you a little bit about Evansville," I said.

"What is it?" he grumbled, impatiently running a huge hand through his dark hair.

"Well frankly, it's a mess," I said, looking over at him warily. "I understand the train will be arriving early Monday morning. I have the animal walk to do and won't be able to take you and Lloyd to the building." I handed him a map in which I'd circled the location of the arena.

"So what's the problem?"

"Everything. To start with, the building must be a hundred years old. The top section of seats, believe it or not, are all wooden bleachers. The ceiling is only thirty feet off the ground. I've got no idea how Lloyd is going to rig the trapeze, let alone Elvin Bale's wheel of death."

I glanced up at him feeling even more uncomfortable. "I'm afraid there's more. There are no dressing rooms either."

"No dressing rooms?"

"Well, I think there's two or three, but most of the performers will have to change outdoors. I ordered a dozen tents and portable toilets for the rear of the building."

"Christ almighty! Who arranged all this?"

"I don't know but there's one other thing. You'd better warn Lloyd Morgan that the building manager won't be much help. He's a senile old bastard. The best thing we can do is stay out of his way."

———

Later that night, Saturday night, only 2,200 people attended the show. Billy and I counted the unsold tickets and factored out the fresh. Holding my breath, I stared at the number. My total was now just $178,000.00. I gazed at the number, too stunned to analyze it. All I knew was I only had one day to go and I wasn't even close to the company's projection. I called in the numbers to Allen and then wandered out to my car. I tried to find the ignition but lamely I kept missing the slot. When I arrived at the hotel I just sat there in a stupor. Finally I climbed up the stairs, unlocked the door, and lay down on the bed. I didn't even bother untying my shoes. I shut my eyes and the room started to spin. I didn't want to think about the numbers. Whatever I did tomorrow, it wouldn't make any difference. One more day . . . and then Evansville. And then I can go home. No more four walls. But now I needed to sleep. I needed to stop thinking about it, just get through another day.

I woke early still wearing the same rumpled clothes. In the distance I heard the faint sound of church bells, then spasmodically my body lurched to the side. I caught myself, as if I was falling. My heart began racing and for one terrifying moment I didn't know where I was, and slowly it dawned on me, partly in apprehension and partly in relief, it was Sunday morning, my last day in Terre Haute.

I tried to concentrate, trying to focus my thoughts. I'd have to check out of the hotel. There wasn't much point in returning. A one o'clock show, then a five o'clock show, and then I could settle up the numbers with Hanley. By eight or eight-thirty, I could be on the road to Evansville. I felt a stinging sensation as I stood and pulled off my sock. A new blister had formed on my little toe, my left foot this time. I carefully unwrapped a fresh band-aid, feeling proud of my attention to the basics. I pulled out my checkbook and wandered down to the front desk. My bill for the week came to $273.00. I only had $308.00, which included the company's most recent deposit, and a five dollar bill in my wallet.

"I'm a little embarrassed," I said to the desk clerk, knowing I'd need cash for gas and I'd be left with barely enough for my hotel room in Evansville. "Could I make this out for twenty dollars more? It's Sunday and I'm a little short of cash."

I mumbled my thanks and returned upstairs and slowly gathered my clothes. Surprised at how weak I felt, I hauled my things down to the car. Placing my shirts as neatly as I could in the trunk I closed the lid, then leaned heavily against the side, taken aback by how hard I was breathing.

I took one more deep breath, slipped into the seat and drove out of the Holiday Inn parking lot. It was quiet, a typical Sunday morning with very few stores open and very little activity in the street. There was no other day like a Sunday to give you that sense of aloneness on a strangely deserted street. Even an old, mangy dog sleeping on the sidewalk in front of some wooden steps seemed peacefully abandoned.

I pulled into a gas station, an independent station, one of a few that was still around, and asked a young boy in a T-shirt to please fill it up. Next door to the station was a small hardware store that had propped its front door open. Some rakes and a wheelbarrow were sitting out front. I wandered over while the boy cleaned my windshield and I looked in the window. Sale tags scrawled in bright red magic marker were prominently displayed in front of hammers and saws and a few other tools. But what caught my attention was a tiny, black grill sitting atop three aluminum legs about eight inches long. The sign on the grill read $6.94. I stared at the grill and suddenly it occurred to me. I could cook my own food. Why not? This way I could stretch out my money. I still had four days to go and who needed restaurants? I walked inside, purchased a frying pan, a small bag of charcoal, a tin can of lighter fluid and was handed the grill right out of the window. Now all I needed was some eggs and some bacon and tomorrow morning I'd cook my own breakfast. As I walked back to the car, I unexpectedly felt a new sense of power. There was something about cooking your own food, taking care of your own needs, that suddenly made everything else seem less significant. I drove a few blocks down the street, stopped in a convenience store, and then placed a small bag of groceries in the back seat next to the grill and sack of charcoal.

The arena was silent with the exception of a few roustabouts in the back lot sweeping up some stray hay and shoveling some horse dung into large plastic bags. A truck pulled up and I watched three men begin to load empty water canisters into the back of the bed. It was early in the day, but slowly the tear-down had begun. I watched for a few minutes, sadly aware that shortly after the last show ended, there would barely be a trace we had been here.

I entered the building through the one glass door I knew was unlocked and then turned and walked down the empty corridor and into my office. My Terre Haute three-ring binders were stacked on top of one another by the side of my desk. An empty, thick, black briefcase sat on the floor and beside it sat another one filled with my binders and notes for Evansville. I resisted the urge to open it, to begin pouring through Evansville's schedules and activities, not wanting to change focus, still hoping against hope this would be the best day yet.

I drifted back outside, buying a cup of hot coffee, then sat and waited, feeling the hot summer sun notch up. More and more roustabouts began to show up and finally the blue circus bus rolled in, letting off the first round of performers. A few of the performers nodded in my direction as they straggled toward the arena, but several paid no attention at all. There was one person in particular I was looking for, and finally I spotted him,

"Hey, Charlie! Charlie King!" I shouted, at first not recognizing him half-hidden in a low-slung black leather hat.

"Jamie," he replied, suddenly looking up and turning toward me. "Where have you been? I've been looking for you."

"It's good to see you," I said, warmly clasping his hand, embarrassed to admit how ashamed I'd been. "I've been up in my office, keeping a low profile I guess."

"I see," he said with that look of intensity that made him so likable. "Are you holding up okay?"

I nodded, not knowing quite what to say, then blurted out excitedly, "Evansville is looking great. The last time I talked to the box office it looked like we'd have pretty big crowds!"

"That's great, man! If I can do anything to help, just holler."

"Thanks Charlie," I said. "I may need it." And I shook his hand once again.

I walked back inside and waved hello to a few of the ticket takers while once again the doors were pushed open. Hanley had only two ticket takers stationed at each door and even the number of ushers seemed lighter than usual. I began my circle around the concourse praying he was wrong, still clinging to one last hope, that if only today, the last day in Terre Haute, we could end with a bang.

The concrete floor seemed less forgiving than usual as I made my way around the concourse, nodding to the concessionaires whenever I could catch their eye, not wanting them to give up the ship. A few small children came running past ahead of their parents, and I watched as people slowly filtered in through the turnstiles. But I could already tell, it no longer took long, there would barely be a crowd at all. I finished watching the doors, then stepped inside one of the entrances. There were only three or four hundred people at most.

Silently I sat in my office, unable to feel anything but the weight of the catastrophe, waiting for the dead wood to arrive. As I calculated the numbers, realizing how disastrous it was—that even with tonight's performance I wouldn't come close to the company's projections—I suddenly realized that even my five hundred dollar bonus from Savannah, the money I'd been counting on, was gone. Just as I'd earned five percent for exceeding projections, I remembered Allen's words, "We deduct the same percentage for not making the projections," and I was nowhere close.

I told Billy I'd count the dead wood. "Are you sure?" he said, looking askance at the huge stacks of unsold tickets.

"I'm sure," I said. "It will give me something to do between now and the evening performance." I didn't want to tell him I wanted to be alone. "I'll see you tonight," I said, grabbing the first stack of tickets.

I began feeding the machine, knowing it would take me twice as long, deluding myself I was now earning my keep. Frustrated, I started again. I kept losing count. Concentrate, I reprimanded myself, before I become more tired. Finally I subtracted the last of the tickets from the manifest and wrote in the numbers. Only 412 people attended the show, bringing in barely two thousand dollars and only half of it fresh.

There's no point in calling Allen, I conceded. I'll wait until this evening's performance and then give him the final numbers. Besides, it won't be that long now to wait.

I carried the dead wood back to the box office, then grabbed a hot salted pretzel and coke and sat in the arena, watching the sweepers clean the debris.

The band members were always the first to show up. My cue as they tuned up their instruments that the doors for the evening performance were soon to reopen. For the last time I stood guard by the front entrance. There were fewer people coming in now than there were this afternoon. The minutes stood still as I went through the motions one final time. At intermission Billy brought in the dead wood, and with little conversation, we counted the unsold tickets and tallied the final numbers. Two hundred and twenty six people, he noted, had attended the last show. Billy wrote in the final numbers with a red pen into a separate box and handed me the sheet. My goal of $720,000.00 reverberated in my head as did the company's goal of $360,000.00. I looked at the numbers. In bright red ink the figure diminished the page. My total for all seventeen shows, the entire Terre Haute engagement, was $181,000.00. Mortified, I stared at the number, and then picked up the phone and called Allen.

I delivered him the final figures and then asked if there was anything I could do. "Could I try to negotiate a better deal with Hanley?"

"You can try if you want to," he said, "but it probably won't do you much good."

I turned and thanked Billy, telling him I'd see him on Tuesday in Evansville, then picked up the sheet and walked slowly to Hanley's office. It was after nine o'clock but he said he'd be waiting to settle up. When I arrived he was sitting behind his desk with a matching sheet of paper from the box office and a check for the full amount. We agreed on the number, then I said, "As you can see, this has been a disaster for the circus."

Hanley nodded, not bothering to take his pipe out of his mouth.

I proceeded ahead, trusting I could eek out a concession. "Given the circumstances, I was hoping you might discount the rent to the circus?"

Hanley took out his pipe and leaned forward with a look of astonishment. "Why would I do that?"

"Because it's not unheard of," I retorted, trying to defend my position. "I've heard you've done it for a few rock shows that didn't do well . . . local promoters."

Hanley glared at me. I glared back. And there was no way we could hide it. We couldn't abide one another.

"It's been a pleasure doing business with you," he said with an air of finality.

I shook his hand, wanting, if nothing else, to have the final word. "Likewise," I said, and I turned and exited the room.

As I took one last walk to my office, trying hard to erase Hanley from my mind, I heard sounds of voices coming from the arena floor. I stepped over and looked inside. Lloyd Morgan was standing in the middle with his bullhorn, surrounded by aluminum pipes and ropes coiled neatly all over the floor. Working men were carrying tubing to a waiting truck, while a forklift retrieved the hippodrome track now rolled into a huge green cylinder

I watched for a minute, then walked into my office and gathered my two black briefcases, stuffing the empty one with the last of my Terre Haute files. Then I turned off the light and walked into the warm summer night, strolling past the empty parking spaces to my car sitting alone under a tall yellow light. I lifted the briefcases into the back seat, looked one more time at the huge empty lot, and then, devoid of all energy, drove out of the front gate. I turned right on Seventh Street, past the small homes, past the small businesses, past the green Holiday Inn sign blinking in the distance, refusing to think about Terre Haute anymore. It was over, done with . . . a disaster of epic proportions. There was nothing anymore I could do. And as I headed down the highway toward Evansville, remembering Sweeney's last words—"There were long lines all day!"—I knew as much as I'd ever known anything, that whatever it took, no matter how tired I was, even if I was so tired I could barely remember my name, all of my strength, everything I'd ever wanted to be had to be focused on only one thing. Nothing else mattered. Evansville.

Chapter 56

EVANSVILLE

The Evansville Arena took on an almost ghostly appearance as I drove through the front gate, past the marquee proudly announcing our arrival, and across the parking lot's vast expanse. It was now past midnight, and as I drove closer to the building, the pale cinder block walls seemed strangely ethereal, their cracks and peeling paint hidden by the night's blackness. Somehow, before anything else, even before checking into the Harrington Hotel, I'd been inexorably drawn to the building. Charlie Bauman and Lloyd Morgan would be arriving first thing in the morning, and I had to make sure everything that I had ordered had arrived. But there was another connection, a deeper connection I needed.

I drove up to the front entrance where ol' man Strausel or Bill Sweeney had hung a sign that read, "Box Office—Tickets for Sale," and I counted eight narrow windows, waist high. Then I drove slowly around the curve of the building, refamiliarizing myself with its shape. Like a giant, white one-story pillbox it still struck me as the oddest building I'd ever seen. I drove past the entrance where the undercover cop had tackled the teenage boy, cuffing him and dragging him into Strausel's office, berating him until he was a sobbing, hysterical mess. I drove past the third and fourth entrances and finally arrived at the rear of the building. I was relieved to see several huge rolls of green canvas mat sitting next to a pile of wooden tent poles and then off to the right, near the ramp, the portable toilets I had ordered had been lined up all in a row. I wondered for a moment if Charlie Bauman would slap tape over the doors marking them male versus female.

A stack of hay sat next to a septic tank and on the far end of the parking lot, barely visible, I spotted the performers' trailers. There were five of them, families that preferred living separately from the train, or at least I thought they were families. Maybe a few were simply performers who wanted more space. I couldn't help noticing how far apart they had parked. Each had selected a site several yards away from the others. I drove once more, slowly around the arena, needing somehow to reclaim it. Then I returned again to the back of the building. I peered through the darkness at the trailers off in the distance, and then in an instant it hit me. Why even check into a hotel at this time of night? Why not stay here and just sleep in the car?

I drove to a secluded, darkened spot and rolled to a stop, then turned off the ignition and, feeling a strange contentment, pulled out a shirt from the trunk, rolled it into a pillow and squeezed my long frame into the front seat of the car. But each time I turned I bumped into the steering wheel or the door handle, and the air, I noticed, had turned cold and sticky on my skin. It was impossible to sleep. But for some strange yet pleasurable reason, I was determined to try, to wake up in the parking lot next to the building alongside the other performers.

Finally, feeling as though I'd spent the night on a rumbling train, I sensed the darkness changing to gray, the nighttime turning to dawn, and I opened my eyes and sat up. Apprehensive, yet nervously excited, I slid out of the passenger side of the car. The air felt cool. I pulled on the crumpled shirt I'd used as a pillow and looked around. A light glowed in the trailer nearest to me though it was still a good distance away, and it felt good to know that I wasn't the first one awake. A moment later, I watched a young man, shirtless with dark curly hair, open the trailer door, walk outside and flick a cigarette out onto the pavement. He was holding a cup of coffee and seemed unfazed by his new surroundings. There was something oddly impressive about his nonchalance, his lack of concern, as he sauntered back inside.

I looked at my watch. It was barely six in the morning, and as I watched another light go on in a trailer I felt almost giddy. I opened the back door and slid out the charcoal and grill along with the pan and the food I'd just bought. I shook the charcoal into the grill, sprinkled it with lighter fluid and lit a match, instantly feeling the grill's heat dissipate the morning chill. As the flames died down, I squatted next to the grill and blew gently on the red coals, watching them slowly turn white, and in that moment, I was profoundly aware that I'd attained a new and even higher transformation. Everything else was insignificant. I was now focused on the basics, my own survival. And compared to that, what else could possibly matter? All else in the moment seemed strangely unimportant. It was odd, as I sat there, warmed by a gentle breeze, how secure and superior I suddenly felt. How many human beings caught up in the goals of others, absorbed by modern civilization's barrage of complex means to survive could even remember what it felt like to return to the basics? Alone, independent of all others, out in the open air.

I reached into the grocery bag and pulled out three eggs, cracking them on the side of the pan. I'd forgotten to buy a spatula. Instead I grabbed a plastic spoon and began scraping it along the bottom. But it seemed like forever before the yellow yolk hardened into something edible. I decided not to attempt the bacon, but there was something satisfying about finally devouring the eggs while gulping down a warm cup of orange juice. Now all I had to do was clean up the mess. But in the middle of a parking lot the best I could do was dump out the coals and remove what I could of the eggs with a dry paper napkin. A moment later, feeling more soiled than superior, I piled the dusty grill and dirty pan and plates into the back seat of the car and slid slowly into the driver's seat, switching on the engine. My skin felt clammy and gritty and my legs I noticed were stiff from a long sleepless night. What I desperately needed was a hot soothing shower and, just as urgently, some time to pore through my binder of notes. All night, by trying not to think about all I had to do I instead could think of nothing else—an eight-mile animal walk in a few short hours, the follow through of a myriad of promotions, performer interviews, dead wood to count, Sweeney, Strausel and Rick Johnson—all floated through my thoughts while I tried to sleep. And instead of a clear-cut list of all that awaited me, my mind darted back and forth. All of it started coming back to me but I couldn't remember what went first and who joined with what. I had to get to the hotel before the onset of the animal walk, before I met with an angry Axel Gautier, the press and a dozen frenzied riders. I needed a quiet, peaceful hour to somehow sort things through.

The Harrington Hotel was as imposing as I remembered it, jutting into the edge of a busy street. A sign out front announced its latest entertainment. Jerry Reeves, a tall country western singer and good ol' boy sidekick of Burt Reynolds, was playing three nights in the hotel lounge. I parked in the back lot, grabbed my binder of notes, and entered through the rear door, hoping my old room was available. Just the sight of the familiar lobby began to enliven me.

"That room is available, Mr. MacVicar. Welcome back." The desk clerk handed me the key. "By the way, I believe there are a few other people from Ringling having breakfast right now in the dining room."

"Wonderful," I said, and anxious to see who they were I marched down the corridor.

I'd barely entered the dining room when I was greeted by an unexpected scowl from Harold Ronk and his sour-faced companion, Bob Harrison. I pulled out a chair and sat down, beginning uneasily, "I trust you like your accommodations?"

"What accommodations?" Harrison spat. "We arrived last night to discover there were no reservations!"

"What are you talking about?"

Harold Ronk jumped in. "You told us you were making reservations. We got in last night and there were no reservations. We had to settle for a double bed instead of a king!"

I couldn't believe it. I knew Harold Ronk was a prima donna but I didn't need this crap right now. Especially coming from not only him—even if he was the ringmaster—but from his asinine buddy,

Bob Harrison. I sprang up from the table almost knocking the chair over.

"What makes you think I need this shit? I made the reservations a week ago. So what. The hotel screwed up!" Harold's expression changed to one of pained shock while Harrison continued to glower. "I'll straighten this out with the hotel right now but I'd goddamn well appreciate it if you realized there are other things in my life besides you two!"

I stormed out of the restaurant suddenly fighting back tears and flounced into the hotel office. "Why did my people from the circus not have reservations?" I demanded, as three people abruptly stopped what they were doing. A white-haired lady replied, "Because there were no reservations?"

"Look again at your records!"

"I'm sorry, Mr. MacVicar. Perhaps you forgot to call. We simply didn't have any reservations."

Awkwardly I stood in the center of the room, still furious, yet unable to prove that I'd phoned. Feeling frustrated that the day had started out so miserable, I sputtered, "For God's sake, don't screw anything else up!" and I exited the room.

As I unloaded my suitcase from the car and carried my clothes up the stairs I couldn't decide who enraged me the most, Harold Ronk, Bob Harrison, the hotel staff . . . or myself. I knew I'd intended to call. That I remembered. But for the life of me, now that I reflected back, I couldn't remember doing it. Maybe in the midst of the Terre Haute commotion, as much as it baffled me to admit it, I'd simply forgotten to call.

I plunked my clothes and my suitcase on the bed, trying to calm down and sat at the desk with my Evansville binder. There would be no time to shower and shave. I looked at my watch. It was already past nine and the animal walk was scheduled to start at ten-thirty.

I flipped through the letters of agreement, struggling to concentrate, scanning the details as fast as I could. Jill Bolaro's station was holding a special family day promotion. Tuesday afternoon was the urchin promotion. Tuesday night was opening night, the night the mayor had agreed to be honorary ringmaster. Wednesday afternoon was the hyped-up motorcycle jump, and the final show Wednesday night was reserved for the newspaper's king and queen promotion.

I quickly turned the binder tab to "Performer Interviews." There were two Tuesday afternoon, one before the show with Elvin Bale, then an interview with Tito Gaona during intermission, and a third I'd arranged just before the evening performance with Michu.

I rubbed my eyes, reminding myself I only had to think about one thing at a time. Today was the animal walk. That was all I had to do. I turned to the page that counted the most. On the top of the form was Allen's $80,000.00 projection. Two days, four shows and only $80,000.00 to achieve. Normally, I faithfully filled in the thirty blanks preceding opening day with my daily totals, but my calls to Sweeney had been sporadic. Nevertheless, it was yesterday's cumulative total that now mattered. By yesterday's close of day I'd already taken in $46,000.00, and this in a city with a population greater than Terre Haute. Sweeney had said the Tuesday matinee was going strong. Tuesday night could be selling out and he still wasn't sure about Wednesday. Evansville's advance sales, I noted, were across the board better than Terre Haute's. I pulled out my calculator. There were 7,500 seats in the arena, 2,500 at $5.50, 2,000 at $4.50, and the remaining 3,000 seats—the rows of wooden bleachers that circled the upper tiers—were selling for $3.50 each. Minus group sales, complimentary passes and dollar-off children's tickets, I quickly determined if I sold out all four shows I could easily surpass a hundred thousand dollars, twenty thousand over projection.

I turned off the calculator, glanced at my watch and ruffled through the pages for the directions to the train. Finally I found them, placed the map neatly in my pocket and quickly glanced again at my watch. It was almost time. I got up and hurried into the bathroom, splashed cold water on my face and patted my shirt pocket once more, before dashing out to the car.

An eight-mile parade, perhaps the longest animal walk recently schemed, was now only minutes away. Suddenly, as I drove toward the train, I felt my heart start to flutter and the tension began to give way to a renewed excitement, much as a wearied fighter must feel when hearing the bell for the final round.

Chapter 57

SLEEP . . . PRECIOUS SLEEP

I followed the directions, twisting through some of Evansville's older, working-class neighborhoods as I made my way to the train. Somehow it didn't feel like a midsummer's morning. Instead it felt as though fall was approaching. A moody, gray sky cloaked the houses and old trees in an unusual stillness. A few children, I noticed, even wore sweaters as they played on the stoop of a wide veranda.

I turned right and drove a few more miles until I came over a rise. Peering ahead I saw the blue flashing lights of police cars and what appeared to be at least two or three hundred people milling around. The train had stopped in the middle of the road, sandwiched between two white crossing gates with red blinking lights. I quickly sped up, bringing the car to a halt by the side of the road. I nervously darted into the crowd. The roustabouts had already unloaded the elephants along with the camels and llamas and horses. Fifteen riders, the city's leading media personalities, were sequestered off to the right.

"Where is Axel?" I shouted to the nearest roustabout. He pointed to one of the train cars. I hurried over and scrambled up the steps. The door was open and the inside of the car looked like a war room. Two heavyset policemen wearing leather jackets and motorcycle boots stood over a map spread out on a table in the center of the room. Axel Gautier was standing at the end of the table shaking his head in disbelief. "Eight miles?" he muttered furiously. "Who planned such a thing?"

He looked up at me, knowing full well it was me, but he was too angry to acknowledge my presence. He knew there was nothing he could do about it. The route had been promoted for weeks. In a flourish, he turned on his heels and brushed past me, pretending I didn't exist.

"I'm the promoter," I said to the two policemen now staring at me bewildered. "As soon as the elephants are mounted we can start."

More people were still arriving when I stepped off the train, and as I gazed down the street I noticed families with young children were beginning to stand along the curb.

I watched as Axel's roustabouts helped hoist the last of the riders, then I walked over to the edge of the tracks and waited for the police car to pull into position at the front of the column. I looked down the road, watching more and more people stroll out of their homes, and while I waited for Axel and the lead elephant to start, I felt a cool mist begin to moisten the air. As I stood, watching the roustabouts shuffle into place, I remembered tracing the eight miles on the map with a red magic marker, making sure we would wind through the right neighborhoods, the shopping district and into the heart of the city before walking the final three miles to the arena. It seemed like a good plan at the time, garnishing, I had hoped, a ton of publicity. But now as I waited, looking at the roustabouts, most of whom seemed down on their luck, suddenly it didn't seem like such a good idea. How the hell could I make them march eight miles and not be willing to do it myself? I edged my way through the crowd and took my place, four elephants back from the front.

Axel shouted something in German and the elephants lurched forward at a far faster pace than I'd imagined. All of a sudden I began to have second thoughts. How was I possibly going to walk eight miles? My legs already felt like concrete slabs and a dull ache from a sleepless night had now settled into the back of my skull. I scurried to catch up, glancing over at one of the roustabouts, a misplaced California surfer type with long blond hair and a lean muscled body. But instead of feeling a camaraderie, his gentle lope reminded me of how tired I was.

Just keep putting one foot in front of the other, I kept repeating, try to get into some kind of rhythm. We rounded a corner and the sweet smell of freshly cut grass wafted through the air, and for a moment I felt buoyed, strengthened by boyhood memories.

I glanced up at the newscasters, bobbing and weaving on the necks of the elephants, excitedly waving to the crowds below, while families stood watching from the sidewalks in front of their homes. I scanned the children's faces looking for signs of disappointment, the kind of resentment so harshly reported in Terre Haute, but instead all I witnessed was a wide-eyed innocence as they looked up in awe from the backs of their fathers' shoulders while grandparents looked on in anxious anticipation. One woman standing on a street corner shouted, "They're coming. They're coming!" and I watched as she raced down the street to a waiting group of friends.

We trooped forward and I began to wonder how many miles I'd charted for the suburbs when suddenly the manicured lawns gave way to a long row of shops and small businesses. Storekeepers and employees and late-morning shoppers lined the curb, waving and smiling to the riders. All of a sudden I forgot how tired I was and began to feel an electricity in the air. The police car made a sharp turn onto a narrow, tree-lined promenade leading to City Hall.

Suddenly, as far as I could see, there were throngs of people, seven and eight feet deep pressing eagerly along the curb, straining to get a better view. Onlookers stood on park benches while others perched from street lamp bases. As we approached we were surrounded by people surging all around to gain a closer look. This was unbelievable! Where the hell did they all come from? All of a sudden I felt like the conquering hero, Caesar himself, or better still Hannibal, as the surrounding masses cheered his return.

Aloft in the feeling of triumph I looked up and twenty feet in front of me a woman in a black dress darted out from the curb. She was running alongside the elephants busily snapping pictures. Christ almighty, what the hell is she doing?

"Hey, lady!" I shouted, trying to catch up to her. "Get away from the elephants!"

She turned and to my surprise it was Jill Bolaro. I hadn't seen her since the night we'd fallen asleep in each other's arms and the rain fell gently outside her window.

"I just wanted some pictures," she exclaimed, smiling apologetically.

"I know, but you'll have to get back!" I said, noticing the hips that had so easily seduced me.

"When will we be settling up?" she shouted as she retreated, referring to her station's media fee for the family day matinee.

"Find me at the arena, right after Wednesday's matinee," I hollered, then watched her lose herself in the crowd as quickly as she had suddenly appeared.

The elephants reached the end of the promenade directly in front of the mammoth, gray City Hall and the police car came to a stop, our cue we could unload the fifteen now tired riders. I noticed spectators peering down at us from a third-story balcony while Axel helped the riders dismount and I pleaded with them to please give us coverage. As the last of the riders stumbled off an elephant's knee, I peered over at the waiting police car. It looked so inviting. And suddenly I was tempted to crawl into the front seat to ride out the final three miles. I'd made it this far but the hot summer sun had broken through the clouds and for the past thirty minutes my vision was blurred. I'm sure the strange spots were from the sun but what if they weren't? What if I suddenly couldn't see? What if I collapsed? What would Axel think then? In that moment Axel lurched forward again and my legs felt even heavier. What if I stopped? What if I rested by the side of the road? But then how would that look, with me trying frantically to catch up? I reminded myself this was all I had to do today. Then I thought about Sweeney's projections. If I focused on the numbers I wouldn't worry as much. There were only a couple more miles to go.

A cloud temporarily blocked the hot sun as we rounded the last curve in the road. The entrance to the building was less than a hundred yards away. I strained to see past the elephants, past the overgrown grass and wildflowers that accompanied the highway, to make out any sign of activity. There appeared to be several cars, ten or twelve at least, in front of the building and I could see people, I couldn't tell how many, standing in front of the box office.

We passed through the front gate and as Axel and the elephants turned to the left and circled behind the building, I headed off alone across the parking lot, moving my legs as fast as I could. There were eight or nine people at each of five windows. And suddenly I felt like I'd just spotted a beautiful flower in the midst of a wind swept desert. I paused for a second to savor the sight as ticket sellers shouted, "It's the best seats we've got." The people were waiting in line patiently and as cars pulled out of the lot more cars were pulling in. I darted through the front entrance and knocked on the door to the box office. Sweeney opened the door. "Jamie, come in," he shouted, almost in a panic amidst the clamor of the sellers and the phones blinking lights.

"This is chaos!" he yelled, grabbing one of the phones. "You didn't tell me it would be like this."

I quickly glanced at the wall of blinking phones, observing they weren't all being answered. "I'll help," I said, "before we start losing more sales!"

I quickly punched one of the lines. "Yes, there's plenty of great seats in the house!" Then I turned to Sweeney and smiled. "I told you this was no one-night rock show!"

"Come on down!" I repeated, glancing at the rack of yellow, blue and brown tickets hanging on the wall. "Every seat's a good seat!"

Sweeney mashed out a cigarette in an already overflowing ashtray and helped the sellers while I raced from one blinking light to another. As I repeated my mantra of "plenty of good seats," I stared at the backs of the sellers, perched comfortably on stools behind the windows. One of them, a fat man, exchanged tickets and money without even removing the cigar from his mouth. These were no longer the kids I'd seen staffing the booths at Ayrbach's Northpark and Weinbach's. Instead, like Sweeney, they were a burly bunch with an impregnable air one wouldn't want to aggravate. Sweeney hurriedly handed them tickets while quickly refilling the racks as I made sure none of the lines were left unanswered.

"Did you eat?" Sweeney hollered over and I looked up at the clock, startled to discover I'd been answering the phones for three hours.

"No, nothing yet."

"Why don't you go eat? I think we can handle it from here."

"Are you sure?"

"No sweat," Sweeney said, looking relieved that the onslaught was slowing. "Don't worry about tomorrow. I'll have plenty of ticket sellers on hand."

"That's good," I said, almost too spent to add the obvious. "You're going to need every one of them."

Inside the building, with the exception of faint noises coming from the arena floor, the corridor was quiet and still. I could see ol' man Strausel's office to the right and for a brief second I was tempted to announce my arrival. But listening to some off-the-wall diatribe was the last thing I needed right now, nor was I in any mood to run into his surly assistant, Betty. Besides, I wondered, would he even remember who I was?

I headed off to the left, turning right through the first portal. Lloyd Morgan stood in the middle of the arena floor surrounded by ropes and tubing while dozens of working men awaited his instructions. But instead of his usual take-charge demeanor, Lloyd looked frustrated and confused. No doubt he was wondering how he was going to hang the rigging from a ceiling barely thirty feet high. I glanced around at the rest of the arena. It was just as I remembered. Hundreds of bright yellow chairs, the highest priced seats, ascended for several rows from the arena floor, followed by numerous sections of blue middle-priced seats, then row upon row of old wooden bleachers. As I gazed at the bleachers, I remembered the black numbers, barely a foot apart, and how faded the imprints had become. Surely Strausel could have sprung for the money to at least make the seat numbers readable. Lloyd had begun to confer with Shorty, his diminutive assistant, when just then I spotted Strausel striding in from the other side of the arena.

"Shit! Just what Lloyd needs."

Strausel made a beeline for Lloyd, and despite the old man's frail features I could see a familiar snarl.

Lloyd looked befuddled by whatever Srausel was saying and I could tell he was starting to get irritated. Then to my relief, Strausel shut up and turned and disappeared through one of the gates.

As I stood there wondering what bizarre concerns he might have been ranting, I suddenly remembered I'd left my car at the start of the animal walk. Now what was I going to do? I barely had enough money for dinner let alone a taxi. I wandered back to the box office and rapped on the door.

"I thought you left?" Sweeney said, with a look of surprise.

"Almost," I replied. "I forgot that my car is parked back at the train. Is anyone leaving in that direction?"

Sweeney began to inquire when abruptly the fat man, the one with the cigar, looked over in my direction. "I'll give you a lift," he said.

"How long have you known Bill Sweeney?" I asked, as we walked toward a large Buick.

"Not long, three or four years," he said. "But he pays well. He's even been known to slide in a good tip."

"Do you know Rick Johnson?"

"Yeah, Sweeney and he work together from time to time."

I sat in silence as we drove to the train. Was I becoming overly suspicious? Had Rick said they'd actually worked together? I thought he'd said he just knew of him.

"Thanks for the ride," I said, and I slid into my car, parked on the side of the street.

It seemed like weeks since I'd seen Rick and in some weird way I missed him. I just hoped to hell he wasn't in a volatile mood. I was too damned drained today for that.

I kneaded the back of my neck as I drove up next to the familiar black limousine and tried to pull myself back into focus.

"I'm back," I said cheerfully to his secretary, attempting to start out confidently. "Is Rick here?"

"He's in his office," she said with an unreadable expression.

I strolled into his office. He glanced up from his desk and immediately I could tell he was agitated.

"Did you see the animal walk?" I asked curiously, trying to mitigate whatever was irritating him.

"Do you mean the animal walk where the elephants dumped in front of the City Hall, right in front of the mayor?"

For a moment I just stared at him incredulously before blurting out, "Are you serious? Thousands of people lined the streets and all you can talk about is the elephants taking a dump?"

"Well, who's going to clean up the mess?"

"Jesus, you're unbelievable! The city, that's who's going to clean it up!"

I turned and started to retreat into my office, infuriated at how fast he could enrage me, when he stood and handed me a note. "Here, this guy called you this morning. He was pretty upset. Something about you bringing clowns out to his hospital this morning?"

I stared at the note. It was the elderly man from the mental hospital. "Shit, I forgot all about that!"

I hastened into my office, reached for the phone, and instantly recognized his voice. "I am so sorry! I've never forgotten something like this before. I hope I didn't disappoint anyone."

"Well, we have about four hundred patients and we'd brought them all into the auditorium. We'd been talking about it for days."

"I'm very sorry," I reiterated, picturing the disappointed faces while finding myself grasping for a solution. "What if we come tomorrow morning?"

"What time?"

"Eight a.m.," I suggested.

"Great," he exclaimed. "That would be wonderful." I took down the directions again and hung up the receiver. Then I stared at the phone in disbelief. Am I losing my mind? How am I going to find four clowns willing to get up at the crack of dawn with barely a night's notice?

It was almost five o'clock and I'd have to return to the train, but I couldn't leave before retrieving the day's numbers from Sweeney. On my desk was a huge stack of messages, calls that had arrived while I'd been in Terre Haute. Wearily, I leafed through the stack. There must have been thirty or more messages. There was no way I could even start. Whatever they wanted it was too late now.

I glanced around at the rest of the office. Papers and notes were neatly piled up and in one corner was a batch of publicity photos, now coated with a thin film of dust, photos Lisa and I had selected, sitting on the floor before laughing at Rick's dancing. Media affidavits were heaped on one corner of the desk and near the window I noticed the honorary ringmaster whistles and certificates. Anything I didn't need I began throwing away while anything I thought I might need I stuffed into my binders.

Just as I'd packed the last of the papers Rick wandered in. "I'm leaving," he announced. "I'll see you tomorrow night at the arena."

"Yes, thanks for everything," I said, not sure what I was thanking him for.

I picked up the phone and called the box office. "How did we end up?"

"Fifty-six hundred," Sweeney said. "A damn good day!"

I added up the numbers. We now had $52,000.00 in the till. Not bad, especially considering we'd sold at least 1,200 tickets today. But what did the figures mean? Mentally I tried to calculate what kind of walk-up we needed to hit $80,000.00, or for that matter to top one hundred. I found myself lost in thought, trying to decipher a formula, but I was too tired to make any sense of it.

I picked up the briefcase, grabbed the ringmaster whistles and ambled out to the car. I slipped into the driver's seat and began the drive back to the train. It was pitch dark when I pulled up next to the tracks. I didn't see signs of life anywhere let alone three or four clowns I could corral for tomorrow. I was starting to feel hopeless when I spotted one of the roustabouts walking alongside the tracks.

"Excuse me," I yelled. "Can you tell me where the pie car is?"

"Number three," he hollered back, pointing around a curve.

I got out and began stumbling down the tracks trying to make out the numbers in the dark. Finally, I located the number, half hidden by dirt, and climbed up the metal steps. Reality had begun to set in. What are the odds of finding four clowns at this time of night? The lights were dim when I opened the door. Behind the counter was a short-order cook and only one of the tables was occupied. Three working men were having cups of coffee sitting next to Prince Paul. Prince Paul? All three feet of him sat there in silence. Maybe he'd be willing to help? Had he not been in a hospital himself not too long ago, sickened by fear Irvin wouldn't be renewing his contract?

"Prince Paul, I'm sorry to disturb you but could I talk to you for just a minute?"

"Sure," he said in his aging gravelly voice, looking up as I hovered nearby.

I knew he could be irritable and I held out little hope, but I was desperate, and he was the only option I had. "Prince Paul, I know this is an impossible request but I've gotten myself in a bind."

To my surprise he listened sympathetically. "How many clowns do you need?" he asked.

"Three or four," I blurted out. "If there's any way at all you can help?"

He hesitated for a minute, then said in a reflective yet kindly tone. "All right, let me see what I can do. Be back here in the morning at 7:00 a.m."

I walked back to the car, relieved, but now so tired I could barely think. I slowly pulled away from the train and began driving back toward the hotel. The charcoal grill and dirty plates rattled noisily in the back seat. I tried to focus, trying desperately not to make any wrong turns. Each mile now seemed excruciatingly long. But all I could think about was getting back to the hotel to sleep . . . precious sleep. Even the words sounded lovely.

I pulled into the Harrington Hotel's parking lot and made my way up the stairs, repeating over and over again not to forget to set my alarm clock. I had to be up at six a.m. I opened the door, turned on the light and stepped inside. Everything was just as I had left it. Except on the center of the bed was a long white box. I walked over and opened it. Inside, wrapped in white tissue, were a dozen long-stemmed red roses.

I couldn't believe it. How thoughtful of Jill Bolaro. I fumbled through the wrapping. At the bottom of the box I found a small white card.

"Welcome back," the card announced. "Call me when you get in. I'd love to see you." Then next to the phone number it simply read, "Your admirer, Sheri."

Sheri, the "groupie" as Rick had called her? She must have been at the animal walk. Then I remembered I had spoken to her the night before I'd left and told her I'd be back on the tenth.

I lay down on the bed, shutting my eyes, awash in the scent of roses, recalling no matter what Rick had said, how kind I had found her to be. How far away does she live? Could I even find her home at this time of night? This doesn't make any sense, I don't have the energy to move. Maybe if she just let me sleep. Maybe if I could just curl up in her arms. She'd have to wake me at the break of dawn. I picked up the card and read it for the fifth time, then no longer thinking, reached over and picked up the phone.

Chapter 58
DON'T YOU END UP THERE

Sheri was waiting for me in the doorway when I arrived.

"You look tired," she said.

"I am. I'm exhausted."

"Come with me," she said and she led me through her living room to a bedroom in yellow and white in the back of the house.

"I'll be back in a minute," she said.

While Sheri walked out of the room, I slowly peeled off my clothes and flopped down on her bed and then stared at my body. Horrified, I noticed my hip bones protruded upward like two wings on either side of a caved-in, hollowed-out stomach, and I now noticed my ribs were a series of bumps barely covered by a thin layer of skin. Ashamed, I reached for the light, when Sheri walked out of the bathroom, naked, toward me.

"I'm sorry," I muttered. "I guess I haven't been sleeping or eating too well."

She didn't say a word. She simply slid her body onto the top of mine and turned off the light.

"Can we just sleep?"

"Of course," she said gently and slid to my side, holding me close with one arm.

The sound of the alarm clock came crashing through the dark. I sat bolt upright.

"I've got to go. I promised an old man at the hospital I'd have four clowns to him this morning."

I quickly pulled on my jeans, an old flannel shirt, and my tennis shoes over my bare feet, throwing my socks into the back seat of the car.

"Dammit, I've got to make room!" I opened the door and pitched the charcoal grill and the dirty plates into the trunk of the car.

The four clowns were waiting for me outside the pie car in their baggy clothes and floppy shoes when I screeched to a stop.

Thirty minutes later, we pulled up in front of a large, red brick building, plain and depressing, and wandered through the front door.

"This way," a tall, thin man, not as old as I'd envisioned, said with a smile, and we followed him down a corridor to a gymnasium surrounded by wooden bleachers. As the clowns waited in an adjacent room, hidden from view, I sat erect on a metal chair, feeling awkwardly unkempt next to the dignified senior director.

I'd never seen a mental patient before and now I watched them file into the makeshift auditorium, hollow-eyed and stiff. They looked more like they were going to a funeral than a fun fest. Emotional zombies.

After the last of the inmates had taken their seats I waved to the clowns waiting in the room to the right, their cue to burst into the auditorium, tumbling and cartwheeling and spraying one another with water. But they might as well have been performing to a cold, empty room. Four hundred patients stared out, almost all in stony silence. It was eerie. I scanned the faces of the counselors, who in contrast were smiling at the clowns' antics, yet none seemed surprised at the multitude of vacant expressions. I felt my stomach begin to tighten. What could possibly have happened to make these people so lifeless? I focused on the clowns, hoping it would all soon come to an end.

Finally, after a half-dozen routines, they raced back toward us, honking and waving to the muted audience.

"Come on!" I yelled. "Let's go." I was anxious to get out of there.

"Thanks again," the director hollered as we piled into the car.

Small stones crunched underneath the tires. "I'm sorry about that," I mumbled.

No one said anything, and I drove back to the train in silence as quickly as I could.

I sank down in the chair in my hotel room, trying to remember what I had to do next. I picked up my notes. Elvin Bale, there was an interview with Elvin before the first show. I shut my eyes, trying to rest if only for a few seconds. Like I did before the animal walk, I had to just think about one thing at a time. The doors, Elvin Bale and then counting the deadwood. That's all I had to do. I dropped my head, feeling the blood rush to my scalp, attempting not to think about anything else, but inside, swirling around, I kept seeing thousands of people swarming about, waiting outside the arena.

I rubbed the back of my neck, unable to stop my visions from spinning, until finally I stood up, changed clothes and headed out the door.

When I pulled into the lot, people were already lined up at all eight of the box office windows. I watched for a minute, feeling a flood of new hope, already sensing this was no Terre Haute, then hurried around to the back of the building. Several performers were executing stretches while others were doing somersaults and knee bends on mats spread among the tents. Charlie Bauman had erected an outdoor village with narrow streets and corridors amidst row upon row of curtains. I rounded a canvas corner and gazed at a young woman in white leotards helping a small boy dismount from a practice swing. Then I spotted several program sellers walking purposefully down the ramp and I hurried inside.

Other program sellers had already begun arranging their stations, opening boxes and piling programs on top of their podiums, a sign that the doors were soon to be opened. I darted past the concessionaires, past several gates, until finally I reached the box office. People were crowded outside the main entrance waiting to get in and the lines at the box office were now easily ten people deep. I raced outside and glanced in both directions. People from all sides were converging on the building. Watching the doors would just have to wait. What I needed now was to immerse myself in the incoming crowd, to be swallowed up in the excitement! I scurried alongside the building.

"Jamie!"

I turned, startled for a moment, and suddenly I spied Lisa coming toward me. She looked beautiful, fresh and tidy in pink slacks and a white blouse.

"Jamie, where have you been? I haven't heard from you in days."

"Lisa," I exclaimed as I tried to quickly comb my hair with my hands, "What are you doing here?"

"I'm here with my family. You gave us great tickets! What can I do to help?" I could hardly hear her over the noise of the crowd.

"Nothing," I hollered. "You've already done a great job. I'll look for you during the show!"

She waved and I lingered for a moment watching her bounce through the crowd. Then I turned and began weaving my way to the front entrance.

I arrived at the box office and discovered people were now jostling one another for position, some of them shouting angrily as the time before the show dwindled. I stared helplessly, then noticed a ticket taker pointing his finger toward me. A young man in a suit came running over.

"Are you the promoter?" he asked, trying to catch his breath. Then without waiting for an answer he stammered, "I've been looking all over for you. I'm with the newspaper. I'm here to interview Elvin Bale."

"Oh shit!" I sputtered. "Come on, follow me. We don't have much time. The show is about to start!"

We rounded the building. "Has anyone seen Elvin?" I shouted. Someone replied, "His dressing room is over there," and I ran up and hollered inside. Elvin came out appearing calm and composed. I nervously reminded him of the interview I'd scheduled while I introduced him to the waiting reporter. He looked at me blankly, then beckoned the reporter inside. Relieved, I left them alone, then scampered down the ramp to where dozens of performers had gathered behind the backstage curtain, awaiting Charlie Bauman's signal for the start of the show. I glanced over at Charlie. He was annoyed about something. Then I heard one of the show girls exclaim, "Harold Ronk is refusing to sing."

I sidled up to Charlie. "Is there anything wrong?"

"You should ask Bill Pruyn!"

Alarmed, I peered inside. Bill Pruyn, baton in hand, was standing on a platform in front of a dozen musicians, looking exasperated. Suddenly I saw why. Most of the musicians he'd been sent were so old and feeble they could barely stand, let-alone play their instruments. A few of them looked almost eighty! I quickly glanced over at Harold Ronk. He was standing in the center ring, seething as the orchestra tried to pluck out the opening number. All of a sudden Charlie opened the curtain and the performers paraded out onto the hippodrome track. I watched in consternation as Harold Ronk recited the lyrics, refusing to sing. Then numbly I turned and headed up the stairs to my office.

I opened the door and through a haze of cigarette smoke, I was taken aback by seven or eight people milling around, people I didn't even know.

"Who are you?" I asked a man standing idly by.

"I'm with the box office," he said. Then another told me he was an usher and another a ticket taker. I started to shout, "What the hell are you doing in here?" when all of a sudden the door flew open. Lloyd Morgan burst in pursued by ol' man Strausel. Suddenly Lloyd whirled around, clenching his fist, "Look old man, I know you're sick, but if you don't get out of my way. . . ." Then Lloyd abruptly stormed out of the room.

I had to get out of there. Everything seemed to be tumbling in a blur. I opened the door and stepped out into the arena. All of a sudden I heard a familiar voice. I looked up to my left. Billy Williams had gathered the ushers and was standing on the steps with a box of hats, explaining about the kids in the show. How could I have forgotten such a thing? I raced up the stairs. "I'm sorry!" I stammered.

"Don't worry," he said. "I've got it." And he glanced at me as if to ask, "What in the hell is wrong with you?"

I wandered back to the office and plopped down in a chair and tried to collect myself. What must Billy Williams be thinking? For

Christ's sake I've got to start paying attention. I have to stop making so many mistakes.

Billy Williams strolled in and without saying a word he set up the ticket-counting machine. "I'm sorry," I repeated and we waited in silence as Bill Sweeney tabulated the numbers.

Ten minutes later, Sweeney walked in with a brown box. He dumped the dead wood on the table in front of us. "Not bad," he said, "for an opening matinee." Billy began separating the stacks of yellow tickets from the blue tickets and the lower priced brown.

"Let me know when you're done," Sweeney said. "And by the way, you probably won't have many tickets to count tonight. It looks like a sell-out."

Billy and I began counting the unsold tickets, but it was all I could do to not think about tonight's sold-out performance. "Forty-one hundred and sixty seats sold," Billy said, "of which a thousand were bought during walk-up." He handed me the results. My total was now $57,140.00. Suddenly I didn't care what Billy Williams thought. The numbers were coming in.

I reached for the phone to call Allen.

"He's gone for the day," Maureen replied.

"Is he reachable?"

"I have no idea where he is."

"Okay," I said, disappointed. "I'll call him at his home tonight with both sets of figures."

I got up and strolled out of the office, savoring the sounds from the arena floor, turned right and drifted around the concourse, carried along by the beat of the music and the aroma of sweet-scented cotton candy. For once, I didn't care about the details. It was the numbers that counted. Today, tonight and then tomorrow and I'd be done. All I had to do was just keep putting one foot in front of the other.

The music came to an end, signaling intermission, and people began streaming into the concourse. I hurriedly wound my way down to the arena floor in search of the reporter who'd be interviewing Tito Gaona. She was standing near center ring with a cameraman. "This way!" I shouted and they followed behind me backstage. Tito was still changing costumes so I began feeding her information about Ringling as fast as I could. I was amazed how much history I knew. I was beginning to regale her about Irvin Feld when Tito stepped out. Her attention shifted and for a moment I felt awkward, embarrassed at how much I'd been rambling. Tito deftly took over. I stammered goodbye and worked my way back to the office.

I opened the door and was disturbed to find Billy Williams fending off two frustrated men. One was an elderly man and the other was a thickset man dressed in casual slacks and a sport shirt.

"You told these men to meet you here at intermission," Billy said, quickly eyeing me. "This man hired the musicians," Billy said, pointing to the old man. "And this other gentleman is the union foreman for the ushers."

I sat down at my desk. The elderly man leaned forward. "I've been waiting for twenty minutes," he spat, and he handed me an invoice. I examined the invoice, scanning to the bottom where he'd added ten percent for himself and promptly told Billy to pay everything but his ten percent.

"What are you doing? You can't do that!" the old man exclaimed, his face starting to redden.

"I sure as hell can. The musicians stink! You don't deserve a penny!"

"We'll see about that!" he said and he snatched the check from Billy and stormed out of the room. I looked up at the union foreman who had been watching from the back of the room.

"I'm here to collect for the ushers," he said.

"How many did we hire?"

"Nineteen."

"How many are here?"

"Nineteen."

"Count them," I said, turning to Billy.

"Count them?" Billy replied, looking at me surprised.

"Yes, count them!" I repeated. "Make sure nineteen are here."

The foreman inhaled a deep breath. Billy looked at me oddly as he opened the door and meandered out of the room.

I waited patiently, wondering if indeed there would be nineteen, strangely suspecting there wouldn't, when fifteen minutes later Billy and the foreman returned.

"How many did you count?"

"There were nineteen," Billy said.

"Okay, go ahead and pay him." Still satisfied I'd done the right thing I watched the foreman march out.

I sat on a step behind the arena, watching as the Ringling bus pulled up near the back ramp, letting off three performers who had gone back to the train between shows. It was almost dark. Doors for the evening performance would be opening any minute. Stiffly, I rose from my perch where an hour had passed quickly and shuffled toward the box office. The souls of my feet from the hard concrete floor had begun to ache.

"I'm sorry, that section is sold out. How about a lower-priced seat?" I heard a ticket seller tell a buyer. I quickly glanced at the parking lot. People were meandering in from all directions. And the ticket sellers were swamped at each window. I prayed the ticket sellers wouldn't let anybody leave. "Make sure they buy tickets for tomorrow!" I shouted, as a couple started to walk away.

I watched more cars pull into the parking lot, rapidly filling it up. Then I hovered near the ticket takers, reveling in the chaos, as they tried to rush people through the turnstiles. "Programs! Programs! Get your programs!" a concessionaire barked while a fat woman wove through the crowd holding pennants and a blue flashing toy above her head.

I glanced at my watch. It was thirty minutes before curtains, time for the interview with Michu. I pushed through the crowd and hurried downstairs. Back door Jack had already escorted the camera crew to Michu's dressing room. As I rounded the corner, Michu, all aglow in artificial light, sat atop a box, entertaining the crew.

I watched for several minutes, electrified by the commotion as performers shuttled back and forth, then I marched past an old wooden crate and into the men's room. It was brightly lit but private. And for the first time in weeks I wanted to burst out laughing! I leaned over the sink, gripping the white porcelain on either side, and gazed into the mirror. Then suddenly I did what I had wanted to do for ages but never had the guts. I turned on the faucet, immersed my hands in water, and with several strokes slicked my hair straight back from my forehead. I looked up and grinned. "There, now you look like a man!"

I strode out of the men's room, past the backstage entrance and onto the arena floor. I could feel droplets of cold water slide down my forehead and prickle the back of my neck.

"Jamie! Where the fuck have you been?"

I looked up. It was Rick Johnson. He was suddenly looming over me like a raging bull.

"Backstage," I sputtered, feeling instantly agitated. "What the hell is the problem?"

"The mayor has been waiting upstairs in Strausel's office for an hour!"

"So what? I'll get there when I get there!"

"Jamie, it's the goddamn mayor!"

"I'm going," I said and I turned and began scrambling up the stairs.

"Where's the mayor?" I blurted as I swung open Strausel's door.

"He's already gone downstairs," said a young woman.

I shut the door and ran back down the steps, scanning the arena floor. The mayor, standing out in a three-piece suit, stood quietly in the dark, not far from the center ring. I raced to his side while he waited for Harold Ronk's introduction. "I'm sorry!" I said, apologizing profusely. "I got caught up doing other things!" Then realizing this was my chance, I exclaimed, "There is something I need to tell you. Maybe nobody's told you this. Maybe it's easier because I'm from out of town, but it's something you need to know. This building is run by a very sick man. He's old. He's senile. He has no business running a building like this. Why does the city keep him on? Why isn't he fired? This building's a mess!" Harold Ronk began belting out his introduction, "Please welcome as honorary ringmaster for tonight's performance, the honorable mayor of Evansville. . . ."

"Do you know what I'm trying to say," I said, as the mayor strode toward the roar of the crowd. He said a few words, then handed the microphone back to Ronk and began stepping across the arena floor. I caught up with him as he picked up his pace, beginning again where I'd left off. We reached the bottom of the stairs, surrounded by sections of people, and he took off up the center aisle, first sprinting then bounding two steps at a time. Lamely, I raced up the steps behind him trying desperately to catch up until instinctively, suddenly I stopped . . . and it hit me. What he was running from was me.

I looked up and watched him disappear, then wandered down to the bottom of the steps and sat down. My God, the man was embarrased to be seen with me. It's no wonder, I realized, I couldn't quit talking. I was practically ranting and raving.

I watched the show for a few minutes, trying to re-center, hoping my uneasiness would subside, then quietly headed back up to the office to join Billy Williams.

Just as I'd hoped, we didn't have to wait long for the tickets. Sweeney strolled in with the dead wood. There was a smattering of yellow tickets—a few hundred at most—two or three stacks of blue, about two hundred complimentary passes and maybe three hundred brown bleacher tickets. We quickly added them up and subtracted the totals from the seating manifest. Almost a complete sell-out! Sixty-seven hundred paid attendance with a total of $8,862.00 in fresh. "You now have a gate of $66,002.00," Billy said.

"That's all I need to hear!" I took Billy's sheet and announced I was going home, back to the Harrington Hotel. It was late but I wanted to call Allen from the solitude of my own room. I was anxious to hear his reaction.

"Allen, we did fantastic!"

"Good," he said. "Give me the numbers."

I told him the figures for both shows, the matinee and evening performances. I again visualized him jotting down the numbers by his night stand. "Good," he said. Then he paused and asked, "How are you doing?"

"I'm fine . . . but it's been a long day. It started at six a.m." Then I found myself talking about the mental hospital. "I took four clowns to a mental institution this morning. I'd never been to one before. Just seeing those poor people . . . it was frightening."

"Well, just don't you end up there!" he blurted. I hung up the phone feeling puzzled. It seemed like such a strange thing to say.

———

I crawled under the covers and tried to sleep but the numbers kept swirling around. Not knowing if I'd lain there ten minutes or two hours, I finally got up and wandered over to the dresser. It was ten after one. The coffee shop at least was open all night. I pulled on my jeans and looked in my wallet. I only had two dollars. And to make matters worse, I hardly had a penny in my checking account.

I glanced up, and in my briefcase I saw the black Ringling checkbook Mike Franks had given me. I opened the cover. Wells Fargo Bank glared out in type on the top of each check. I tore one off, feeling suddenly queasy. What was I doing? I'd never stolen anything in my life and now I was stealing from my own company. But what was I going to do? I had one day left and not even enough money for food. I wrote the check out to myself for twenty dollars, walked downstairs and nervously handed it to the desk clerk. He gave me a twenty and vowing under my breath I'd repay it as soon as I got back to Washington I ambled into the coffee shop.

A few of the vinyl booths were torn. I picked one of the worse ones. Somehow it made me feel more comfortable. There were two waitresses but only one other diner. He was sitting with his back to the wall, facing me, about ten feet away, hungrily eating a full plate of bacon and eggs. I ordered a glass of milk and a slice of lemon meringue pie, though I didn't feel much like eating. The waitress brought me the pie, then timidly approached the other diner. "Can I have your autograph," she asked, almost giggling.

"You sure can," he said in an obvious twang and I was surprised to see it was Jerry Reeves, the country western singer who was performing in the hotel lounge. He smiled at the waitress and handed her back the slip of paper. Then he eagerly went back to devouring his breakfast. I asked for my check, then stared at him for a moment, thinking how rare it was to see a famous performer so happily alone in the middle of the night.

I sat up, having tossed and turned all night, and swung my feet out of bed. Everything hurt. I tried to focus. The harder I tried to think, to push some thought past some dull impenetrable wall, the more the back of my head ached.

Just don't quit now, I reminded myself. This is it . . . the last day.

I stood up and wandered into the bathroom and splashed cold water on my face, then showered and slicked my hair back tight again. I walked over to the closet to the left and there, on the far right, still in the cellophane, was my powder blue suit I'd saved for today.

I pulled it out of the closet and laid the suit on the bed, admiring it once more before slipping it on, its beauty and freshness reversing how tired I felt.

I drove to the arena and parked in the empty lot, aware that I had hours before the matinee started. But they were hours I suddenly looked forward to, empty hours I could fill wandering from the arena to the backstage area and back, basking in the delicious smell of success.

The concourse and deserted arena were enchantingly still as I marched backstage and hiked up the back ramp. Nearly gloating I walked past two roustabouts standing guard over a tent full of horses, then I smiled warmly in their direction. They nodded back lackadaisically. Who cares? For the first time in weeks I felt wonderful!

It was shortly before noon and I was sitting at my desk, going over the numbers again, when the arena doors finally opened. I stepped outside and watched the first few cars pulling in, then hurried downstairs to see if the D.J. and his motorcycle had arrived. I noticed the fake ramp had been pushed onto the hippodrome track. I hastened around to clown alley. Frosty, the boss clown, was still applying his makeup. I quickly told him the D.J. should be here any minute. "Can you take care of everything?" I asked. "I've got to get back to the doors!"

"Okay," he said, and I retreated without waiting to see if he was nettled.

The trickle of cars had grown to a steady stream by the time I returned upstairs. I dashed outside to witness the people in line buying tickets. I waited for a few minutes and then started around the side of the building. Suddenly I saw Rick Johnson ushering two ladies and four small kids through a side entrance door. One of the ladies had short brown hair. She turned and I was startled to see it was Linda Browning. Then I recognized the other woman. She was the blonde-haired friend of Linda's, the same woman Rick and I had met in the bar.

"Look who's here!" Rick shouted and he gestured toward Linda and her friend.

"What are you doing?"

"I'm letting them in."

"Where are their tickets?"

"They don't have any."

"Then they better go buy them," I said.

"You're kidding me?" Rick replied, as Linda began fumbling in her purse.

"Every dollar counts," I blurted. "You ought to know."

Rick looked at me in disbelief. "Forget it, I'll buy their tickets myself."

I circled the concourse and then glanced inside the arena. It was easily two-thirds full. I was just in time to see the D.J. cycle over the tiny ramp. Then I hurried back to the office to wait for the dead wood. An usher stuck his head in the door. "A woman named Jill Bolaro has come by twice in search of you."

"Tell her if you see her again to wait outside. I don't have the check for her invoice yet."

Billy Williams sat down and we waited for the dead wood. A few minutes later Sweeney walked in looking delighted and placed the box on the table.

Billy began feeding the machine as I handed him the stacks of tickets. "It's better than yesterday," he said. "Forty-three hundred and sixty-three paid attendance with a fresh take of $6,400.00." I glanced at the numbers. My total was now $72,402.00.

"We owe WTOL $1,350.00," I said, pulling out Jill's media bill. Billy made out the check as I reached for the phone to call Allen. He wasn't in so I gave the numbers to Maureen.

I took the check from Billy. "While you're at it, I'll need a check for my agency, Rick Johnson. Make it out to Johnson Productions for $2,000.00."

I wandered outside in search of Jill. A bedlam of people noisily filled the hallway as I glanced in both directions. Then I spotted her about ten yards away strolling up the concourse.

"Jill," I shouted. She swiveled and walked over.

"Tell your station thanks for the good work," I said as I handed her the check.

"I will," she said, taking it, and then with nothing said of anything shared, she turned and walked briskly away.

I swung around and swept past my office to the box office and glanced inside one of the windows. There were still plenty of tickets to sell for tonight's final performance. But I couldn't see any reason why they wouldn't all sell. And if they did, I quickly calculated, I'd easily surpass one hundred thousand dollars, twenty grand over projection, a record for sure for a two-day date.

The show was almost over when I spotted Rick Johnson walking out of one of the entrance doors. I reached in my pocket and pulled out his check. He looked at the amount, and accepted it with the tiniest of smiles. "I'll see you tonight," he said, and I was surprised to be spared a snide comment or two.

Wearily, I drove back to the Harrington Hotel where my suitcase, I noticed, lay open, its contents pouring out in disarray. I sat down on the bed and called the airport. There were only two flights in the morning back to Washington, one at seven a.m. and one at ten-thirty.

I shut my eyes, praying the time between now and the evening performance would pass quickly, half trying to rest and half trying to stay awake. Repeatedly I glanced at my watch as the gray afternoon sky gradually turned dark. Finally, as though I was willing the minutes forward, my watch read six forty-five. I rolled out of bed and staggered to the bathroom. I had fifteen minutes until doors.

It had begun to rain. The car was wet when I slid into the driver's seat and drove toward the arena. People huddling under umbrellas were already standing outside the box office.

I limped inside, taking my place near the front entrance and watched as a long line of headlights snaked steadily into the parking lot. Anxiously, I started around the concourse.

The distance between the gates seemed longer than usual as I hobbled along as fast as I could. People were swarming all around me, jostling, sweeping me along, and suddenly in the midst of their rushing to and fro and the clamor of hundreds of children . . . suddenly I realized it was over. This was all I had to think about. No more promotions. No more interviews. This was it!

I floated downstairs, immersing myself in the performers' energy, knowing it might be months before I saw them again, watching as they lined up behind the backstage curtain. Then I hurried up the steps as the lights went out and the ringmaster announced the start of the show.

The corridor was empty now, only the concessionaires' straightening-up remained, as I walked anxiously toward the box office. I peered outside. There were only a few people still buying tickets. I waited for a moment to see if any more cars arrived and I walked back inside. I nodded to the ticket takers, then feeling my mouth go dry, I marched into the nearest portal. I stared out, looking in all directions, scanning the arena from floor to ceiling. My chest began pounding. The arena was full. Jammed to the rafters! I took off running, checking every row, every seat, every section. There was hardly an empty seat. A few dozen at most. I stood there mesmerized. I did it. A sell-out! Over one-hundred-thousand dollars for a two-day date!

I ran downstairs. "Where is Harold Ronk?" I hollered, trying to catch my breath.

"He's not performing tonight. His assistant is," one of the show girls replied.

Just then a young man in a red sequined coat and top hat appeared from outside the curtain.

"I've got an announcement to make!" I stammered.

"What announcement?"

"We've just broken all records. I need you to say, 'Thank you Evansville! With your attendance tonight we've just broken all records for a two-day date!'"

He stared at me blankly. "I can't say that."

"Why not?"

"I can't announce anything unless Irvin Feld personally approves it."

I pleaded with him again but I could tell it was no use. "All right, I understand," I relented. What did it matter? In a few minutes I'd settle up with Bill Sweeney and then everyone would know!

I walked inside the arena and sat down, swimming momentarily in the sold-out crowd. Then, unable to wait another second, I scurried upstairs and opened the door to the office. To my surprise, Bill Sweeney stood waiting behind his table with the box of dead wood. To his right, Rick Johnson stood smiling, and behind him were three of the ticket sellers. I even saw Captain Whitehead standing off to the left.

"Well, here it is. This is it," Sweeney said, and he dumped the contents on the table. Out rolled eight or ten stacks of yellow tickets, several stacks of blue tickets and one stack of brown tickets. I stared at the tickets and then looked at Rick and Sweeney. "Where did all these unsold tickets come from? There isn't a section, a row, hardly a seat that doesn't have someone sitting in it." On the top of one of the stacks, I noticed the ticket even read, Seat 1 -Row F, the start of a whole row! My mind began racing. They both looked at me as I gazed at the hundreds of tickets.

"What are the numbers?" I blurted.

"Fifty-seven hundred and twenty paid attendance," Sweeney said. "Your total for the date is $80,802.00."

Rick smiled. "You should be proud. You beat your projections!"

I stared at Rick and Sweeney and the sellers standing behind the table, then I looked again at the tickets. Fifty-seven hundred attendance in a 7,600 seat arena. How can that be? Every seat was filled. I began backing out of the room. "No. This is impossible. Something is terribly wrong."

I ran out the front door. A security guard was standing beside the entrance. "Was the parking lot full?" I cried.

"Yeah, I guess so," he stammered. "It looked like it to me."

Just then I saw Charlie King walk out of the building toward one of the concessionaires. "Charlie, you've got to help me. Follow me!" I took off running around the parking lot.

"What are we doing?" Charlie said, sprinting along beside me.

"Count!" I shouted. "Help me count the parking spaces!"

I ran through puddles, shouting out sums of numbers. "There must be two-thousand spaces! How many people to a car? What's the average sized family? Three-point-three people? That's seven thousand seats. Charlie, the box office is telling me only fifty-seven hundred people attended the show! That can't be. The seats were all full!" Then suddenly I stopped dead in my tracks. Like a bolt of lightning it hit me. They had printed a set of duplicate tickets.

Charlie stopped and bent over, clutching his knees, trying to catch his breath.

"Charlie, the tickets are counterfeit!"

"What?"

"The tickets are counterfeit. They printed a duplicate set of tickets. Where else could they get hundreds of unsold tickets?"

"Are you serious?"

"Charlie, we've got to go back and get the tickets!"

We waited for several minutes for everyone to leave, then we piled into my car and drove slowly back to the front entrance. The lights in my office were out as I walked nervously back into the building. The office was deserted, everyone had left. I looked around the room. Two huge boxes of ticket stubs sat on the floor next to the dead wood. I threw the unsold tickets into one of the cartons, then whispered to Charlie, "Help me grab these two boxes."

We each lifted a box and stumbled outside. As we were shoving them into the trunk a shrill voice hollered out. "What the hell are you doing?"

It was Betty, ol' man Strausel's assistant.

"We're taking these tickets!"

"What for?"

"I need them!" I wailed, and I jumped behind the wheel and sped out of the parking lot.

"I've got to find Billy Williams," I stammered. "We've got to get over to the train!"

I raced up the street and turned in the direction of the train. Then suddenly I heard a screeching of tires and a car swerved to our left, nearly hitting us.

"Jesus!" Charlie hollered. "You just ran a red light. We almost got killed. Why don't you let me drive."

"I'm sorry," I said, noticing my hands had begun to shake. "I'll try to calm down."

The train soon appeared out of the dark. "Pull in here," Charlie said. I pulled into a gravel lot near one of the train cars. Charlie pointed ahead. "That's Lloyd Morgan's car. He'll know where to find Billy. I've got to go back to my room for a minute."

I sprang out and hopped between two cars and knocked on the door. The door opened and Lloyd Morgan stood groggily in his pajamas.

"The tickets are counterfeit! I've got to find Billy Williams. Can you tell me where his train car is?"

"Two doors up," he mumbled. "By the way, there were two men looking for you here earlier."

Shit. That had to be Rick and Sweeney. I raced up the tracks and sprang up the steps to Billy's car. The lights were on and I could hear him talking on the phone. I pounded on the door. Nobody answered. I hollered inside, "Billy, the tickets are counterfeit!"

The door finally opened. "What are you doing here?"

"Billy, the tickets are counterfeit!"

"What are you talking about?"

"They're counterfeit. I'll show you!" And he pulled on a jacket and followed me outside. I hurried over to the car and opened the trunk.

"What are these?" he asked, staring at the two boxes of ticket stubs.

"They're the tickets. They're counterfeit!"

"What makes you think so?"

"Because, goddamn it, they are!" and I reached inside one of the boxes, grabbed a handful of tickets and threw them in the air. "They're counterfeit," I screeched, "and you should have uncovered it!"

Billy looked at me stunned, then turned and began walking slowly back to the train.

"Where are you going?" I hollered. "Come back here! You're going with me to Washington!"

He stopped and looked back at me. "I'm not going anywhere."

Frantically, I crouched down and began scooping up the tickets from the mud. Suddenly Charlie King reappeared.

"Charlie," I cried, relieved he was back. "I need your help. I need you to come to Washington with me."

"Washington?"

"Charlie, it's an emergency. Is there any way you can go?"

"I guess so. I suppose I could leave for a few days. Let me tell some guys in the troupe and get a few things."

Waiting for Charlie I suddenly realized everything I owned was back at the hotel. There was no way I could grab my clothes now. That's the first place Rick and Sweeney would be looking for me.

Charlie marched back carrying a shirt rolled up in a pair of pants. "Where are we going?" he asked, as he quickly slipped into the car.

"I don't know. There isn't a flight out until seven in the morning. But we can't stay here."

I pulled away from the train, trying desperately to gather my thoughts, but everything was muddled. My mind just kept racing. Over and over I saw Rick and Sweeney smiling behind the stacks of unsold tickets. No wonder Rick had accepted his check so easily. He was stealing a fortune from the back end! I turned the steering wheel to the left, at midnight the streets were empty but the rain splattering on the windshield made everything look blurry.

"I've got to call Allen," I said, and I drove across several streets looking urgently for a pay phone. Finally, off to the side, next to a darkened field, I spotted a telephone booth. I stumbled through some tall grass and closed the sliding door behind.

"I want to make a collect call," I said to the operator and gave her Allen's number.

"Where are you calling from?" Allen inquired as soon as the operator hung up.

"I'm calling from a pay phone. Charlie King is with me. Allen, the tickets are counterfeit!"

"What?"

"The arena was full. There was hardly an empty seat. Yet Sweeney handed me almost two thousand unsold tickets! There had to be a set of duplicate tickets. I've got the stubs in the trunk of my car."

"I told Mike Franks to watch that guy!" Allen blurted.

"Allen, I'm scared. They know that I know. I think they're looking for me."

"Jamie, theft is one thing. Murder is another. Let me talk to Charlie King."

I sat inside the car and waited as Charlie talked, and I watched as he listened and talked some more. What could they be talking about for so long? Could there be a problem with Charlie coming with me? Finally Charlie walked toward the car. "Allen wants to talk to you."

"Allen, yes?"

"I want you to bring me the tickets."

"Bring you the tickets?"

"Yes, Charlie is going to come with you. I want you to bring the tickets to Washington."

Chapter 59

IT SOON BECAME CLEAR

I sat back down in the car next to Charlie. "Allen wants us to bring him the tickets." It was raining even harder as I backed up, turning the car toward the street.

"Where are we going?" he asked.

"I don't know."

"We can't just drive around for the next six hours!"

A pair of headlights suddenly appeared and began moving slowly toward us. I stared at the approaching car, frozen to the seat. What if it was Rick and Sweeney? The car slid past. Inside was a young couple. My heart started pounding. Charlie was right. It's too small a town. We had to get off the streets. I pulled back into the field and switched off the lights, having no idea what to do next.

"Are you all right?" Charlie asked.

"I'm okay," I said, trying to slow down my breathing. "I've just got to think." I sat paralyzed, staring at the phone booth, trying to figure out what to do, when suddenly I thought of Lisa. "If there's anything you need, anything at all," she had said. I pulled out my wallet, and inside, crumpled on a piece of paper, was the number she had given me. I rushed back to the phone booth and dialed the number.

A man answered the phone.

"Is Lisa there?"

"It's awfully late," he grumbled.

"I know it is but this is her boss from the circus. It's an emergency. Can I please talk to her?"

"Hello, Jamie?" she said, sounding surprised.

"Lisa, I know it's the middle of the night, but I need your help. It's Rick Johnson and Sweeney. They've been stealing from the circus. Can I stay at your house for a few hours?"

"Where are you?"

"I'm at a pay booth outside a field. There's a sign behind me that says Stanley Wright Ballpark."

"That's near where I went to high school," she said. I quickly pulled out my pen. "Turn left and go to the third street, turn right on Franklin, right on Davidson, and I'm the fourth house on the left."

"Where are we going?" Charlie asked as I wheeled out of the lot.

"To a friend's house. She was my secretary and she knows Sweeney and Rick Johnson. We can stay there for a few hours."

Minutes later we parked outside a small, white wooden house. A porch light was turned on. I knocked softly on the door. Lisa, barefoot in jeans and a sweater, opened the door and led us into a small den. Charlie and I sat on the sofa as I quickly told her the whole story. A few moments later her father walked in. He was a large muscular man. I told him what I'd just told Lisa. "I'm sorry to disturb you," I mumbled, "We're probably in no danger. . . ."

"I wouldn't be so sure," he said. "This is a strange town. There's no telling what can happen here. Come on, Lisa. You'd better leave these gentlemen alone."

"Okay," Lisa said, looking worried. "Is there anything I can do?"

"Thanks, no. You've already done enough."

Charlie turned and pulled out one of the pillows. "Why don't you get some sleep?"

"You go ahead. I'm going to stay awake."

Charlie lay down on the sofa, curling up his knees, and quickly fell asleep.

I sat fixed in a chair and stared out the window, trying to think things through. The more I thought about Rick and Sweeney, the more it began to fit. No wonder they were looking for me. This theft wasn't just confined to the circus. Who knew how big it was? Or how many people were involved? It had to cross state lines. Rick was no doubt the leader. Sweeney wasn't smart enough. He was probably just one of the key henchmen. How many years? How many rock shows? This wasn't small time, this was big time! Over and over, the more I thought about it, the more it soon became clear. Ol' man Strausel, no wonder they wanted him there. He was too demented to suspect anything. Maybe the mayor even knew. Hell, he was probably getting a cut. No wonder Rick kept excusing Sweeney. He couldn't have anybody else in there. It all began to make sense.

I stared out the window, transfixed, amazed at how all the pieces were coming together. Finally, a glimmer of light broke through the dark. I looked at my watch. It was almost six. I shook Charlie by the shoulder. "Come on. It's time. We've got to hurry to the airport."

It was cold and damp when we walked out to the car. I checked to make sure the two boxes of tickets were still in the trunk, then following Lisa's directions, we drove to the main highway and turned north. A few minutes later a green sign emerged from the fog. "Hulman Regional Airport, sixteen miles."

The sun had begun to creep up and the airport windows shimmered as I pulled into the parking lot. Two men in white shirts and navy blue ties stood behind the counter as Charlie and I strode in, carrying the two large boxes of tickets, and dropped them on the floor.

"I'd like to purchase two one-way tickets to Washington, D.C.," I said. "And I need to bring these two boxes with me."

"What's in them?" one of the men asked. They looked at me quizzically and then at the boxes.

"Ticket stubs," I said, opening one of the boxes. I started to feel myself panic. "I'm with Ringling Brothers Circus. We just finished the date and I have to bring these ticket stubs with me."

I handed him my red Ringling credit card.

"Just a minute," he said, studying the card, then both men disappeared through a door behind a luggage conveyer belt.

"I've got to go back to the car and get my pants," Charlie said.

"No!" I implored, grabbing him by the arm, feeling suddenly frightened to be left alone. "Why bother with them?"

"Jamie, I'm going to get my pants," he repeated, and he ambled out the glass doors.

I stood alone, scanning the other passengers, looking for any signs of Rick and Sweeney, wondering what was taking the two counter men so long.

Finally, they both reappeared.

"All right," the tall, thin one said, still eyeing me suspiciously. "But you'll have to buy a seat for each of the two boxes." Then while the other man watched he wrote out four tickets.

Nervously, I looked back at the two boxes of ticket stubs sitting behind the counter as Charlie and I made our way to the gate. Everyone I passed seemed to be glancing at me and I realized any one of them could be working for Rick Johnson or Sweeney. I began watching their slightest movements, knowing in an instant someone could reach out and grab me.

"Let's sit in the corner," I whispered, "where we won't be so easily seen." We sat down and the minutes passed like hours. I kept staring at the flight attendant, hoping she would hurry and board the plane. Finally she called rows 23 through 37. Charlie and I stood up. We were the first to board. And as we walked up the narrow aisle toward the back of the plane, I was surprised to see, two-thirds of the way up, the two huge cardboard boxes strapped tightly to the seats. They looked bizarre, looming above the window, strapped in as though they were about to be executed. We took our assigned seats one row in front of the boxes, Charlie chose the window seat while I hunched near the aisle.

Businessmen in crisp, white shirts and dark suits boarded the plane. Several of them looked at me as they passed by. One man, a middle-aged banker type, sat across from me. He glanced over and began working out of his briefcase on his lap.

"Please fasten your seatbelts and make sure your seats are in an upright position," the flight attendant announced before taking her seat. The plane began rumbling down the runway. The pace picked up and the metal framework vibrated as the plane in a deafening roar reached maximum ground speed. I watched as the flaps on the wings slid open and suddenly, instead of my usual nervousness, I felt a surge of relief as we lifted slowly off the ground.

We banked to the left. A ray of sunshine pierced through the window and I watched as the last remnants of Evansville turned into patches of farmland. Charlie breathed heavily, shifting position, closed his eyes and leaned his head against the window.

"Would you care for coffee?"

I looked up and a stewardess stood over me holding a pot in one hand and a tray in the other.

"Yes," I said, pouring in my own milk and sugar, wishing the cup wasn't so hot that I could warm my hands.

"I'll be back with breakfast."

I took a sip of coffee. What made Rick Johnson think he could get away with it? My God, there were hundreds of unsold tickets on the table. Did he think I was stupid? Or had he just been doing it for so long he got greedy? That had to be it. The bastards got too greedy. What must they be thinking now?

"Would you care for eggs or French toast?"

"Eggs," I said as she refilled my cup and slid me the tray.

How much money was involved? How much money had they stolen? For how many years? My head began to swim. I could see the headlines now: "Midwest counterfeit ring broken by Ringling promoter!" It will probably be on the front page news with pictures of Rick and Sweeney and maybe even ol' man Strausel. Who knows? Maybe it will be on the national news. Perhaps the story has already broken. By now Allen has probably called the papers. I wonder if photographers are waiting in his office? This is unbelievable!

I noticed the banker type across the aisle was staring at me. What the hell? Little does he know he'll be reading about me tomorrow in the papers.

The plane began to bounce. I tried to shovel in bites of food while keeping my coffee from spilling. My mind was swirling, thinking about the commotion that awaited me, while the stewardess returned and removed my tray.

I got up and staggered into the bathroom, splashing cold water on my face and slicking back my hair, trying to make myself presentable. I snapped open the door and noticed the stewardess had taken a seat across from the galley. I sat down beside her.

"I guess you're wondering what's in those boxes," I said, pointing diagonally across the aisle. "Well, this is just between you and me but I'm with the F.B.I. and those are counterfeit tickets."

She looked at me curiously without uttering a word. I couldn't tell if she was impressed or not.

"I just thought you should know," I said, and I got up and sat back down in my seat, wondering what made me tell her I was with the F.B.I.

The sun was no longer coming in the window and the plane had turned gray and cold. No one else seemed uncomfortable but suddenly I felt very chilled. I turned up the collar of my suit and sank lower in my seat, trying to keep warm. Hearing footsteps, I looked up. The stewardess handed me a package.

"I thought you might need this."

I nodded, realizing I was shivering, and unfolded the blanket, letting it drape over my shoes, clutching it under my chin. My mind kept spinning while the plane slowly, gradually descended into Washington.

"Wake up, Charlie, we're here!" Charlie stirred as I stood up and began untying the straps around the boxes.

"We'll get those," the stewardess announced.

"I need them!"

"Don't worry, we'll bring them out. You need to exit the plane."

"Okay," I said, realizing I had no choice, then suddenly caught in a line of businessmen I found myself standing at the gate looking back at a long, empty corridor. Where were the tickets? And where is Charlie? I began heading back onto the plane.

"Where are you going?"

A silver-haired security officer in a starched, white shirt stood in front of me, blocking my way.

"I'm going back on the plane."

"No you're not."

"My friend is on the plane. I have to find him!"

"You are not going back on the plane."

"I've got to!" And just then I noticed two men peering at me through a small window in a nearby door. The gate was jammed with people. Several, I noticed, were now watching me.

"Who do you work for?" the security officer demanded to know.

"Who do I work for?" I echoed, and I started again to panic. Do I tell him the F.B.I., corroborating what he must have heard from the stewardess, or do I tell him the truth, which sounds even more preposterous? He stood steady, staring at me.

"I work for the circus, Ringling Brothers and Barnum and Bailey Circus."

"All right," he said and he suddenly seemed satisfied. He looked up the chute, then stepped to one side. Charlie was walking down the ramp, followed by a flight assistant pushing a hand cart with two boxes of tickets.

"Where were you?" I cried, not waiting for an answer. "Come on, we've got to find a taxi!"

"Ten-fifteen 18th Street," I told the cab driver as Charlie and I squeezed into the front seat. "Can you see out the back window?"

"I'm okay," the cab driver muttered, straining to see past the two boxes. I gazed out the window, watching the Potomac river, brown and swollen, flow rapidly by. Rush hour had ended and traffic sped along the George Washington Parkway toward the city. We drove under the 14th Street Bridge, past the Pentagon, and turned up the ramp onto Memorial Bridge. The business district was just over the hill. Any minute and we'd be there.

The driver twisted toward L Street, drove several blocks and turned left on Eighteenth, pulling up in front of the tall glass building.

"That will be seventeen dollars."

I looked in my wallet. I was two dollars short. "Can you loan me three dollars?"

"Sure," Charlie said. I handed the driver the rest of my money. I wrestled with the first of the two boxes while Charlie pulled out the second. We hurried across the sidewalk, then entered through the glass doors and scurried along the marble lobby. I hit the elevator button and impatiently awaited its arrival. The doors swung open and we plopped the boxes inside. A bunch of ticket stubs spilled all over the floor. I punched the eleventh floor button and dropped to my knees, gathering up the tickets as fast as I could. The elevator jerked to a stop and the doors slid open.

Ten feet away, behind the circular white desk, the receptionist sat up, her mouth gaped open. Charlie held the elevator door while I crawled on the floor scooping up the tickets, then suddenly Maureen, Allen's secretary, appeared.

"Don't worry. I'll get those," she said calmly. "They're waiting inside for you."

"Okay," I said and I picked up the box and with Charlie behind me, I flew past the startled receptionist. Turning, I strode into Allen's office.

"Where do you want these?" I blurted.

"Over there is fine," Allen said. He was seated at his desk. I was surprised by his somber expression and the stillness of the room. In front of him Al Atkinson sat in one of the swivel chairs and next to him sat Joe Kastner from the accounting office.

I plunked the box on the floor behind them while Charlie placed his next to mine and slipped quietly out of the room.

"Would you like a cup of coffee?" Maureen asked.

"Yes," I said, leaning against a side table, facing Allen and the two men. I looked around the room wondering if photographers would be coming any minute. "Don't you want to look at the tickets?"

Maureen came in and handed me a cup of coffee. My hands were shaky and I spilled some on my jacket.

"I'll get you a napkin."

"Don't you want to look at the tickets?" I asked again.

"Thank you for bringing them," Allen said. "We'll look at them later."

"I think you'll see that they're counterfeit."

Al Atkinson stood up and opened one of the boxes. "We don't know that for sure."

"What do you mean you don't know that for sure? The place was sold out. Seventy-five hundred people. There are two thousand unsold tickets in the box. Some stacks are whole rows, starting with the first seat in the section."

"There weren't seventy-five hundred people there," Allen asserted.

"What do you mean?"

"We have another system in place. The program sellers counted a number well short of that."

"Are you telling me you don't think the tickets are counterfeit?"

"I'm saying that we don't estimate that there were seven thousand people there."

"Do you think I'm making this up? The arena was full!"

"No, I don't think that at all."

Al Atkinson stepped forward flipping through a stack of yellow tickets. "Jamie, these are all just random tickets. The first ticket in the row just happens to be the one on top." He walked over and showed me, fanning the tickets with his thumb.

"I don't care," I stammered. "The place was sold out!"

Allen stared at the floor as though it were painful to look at me. "We called the arena. After the show starts, people from the bleachers often rush down and fill up the seats below, then the others spread out on the bleacher seats. That's why the arena looked full."

I rubbed my forehead. "What are you telling me? I made this all up?" I looked at Allen. "You think I'm crazy don't you?"

Allen's chin dropped. "I don't think you're crazy. I think that you're tired. You need to get some rest."

I looked over at Al Atkinson and Joe Kastner. They stared at me benumbed. "You think I'm crazy too!" The room was suddenly quiet.

"I've called your father," Allen said. "He's on his way here."

"You what? You called my father? Why would you call my father?" I started to turn. "Allen, what I did was over and beyond!"

"I know it was," he said softly. Tears welled up in my eyes. I burst from the room, racing past the receptionist. Just then the doors to the elevator opened. Maureen stood inside. Next to her, in a navy blue suit stood my father.

"Hello," he said.

Maureen stepped out and I walked in. Enraged, I rode the elevator down in silence. I'll get a hotel. As soon as the elevator stops, I'll find a hotel.

I stormed through the lobby, out onto the crowded sidewalk. My father walked briskly beside me.

"Where are you going?" he asked.

"To a hotel!"

"Well can I buy you a beer first?"

The light turned green and I began walking across the street. "No, I don't want a beer!"

Traffic swirled all around us. The sun suddenly blinded me when someone from behind hollered my name. I whirled around. "Jamie," Charlie shouted. "You did the best you could!" I didn't know what to say. I just stood there in the middle of the street, defeated, and watched as he slowly disappeared into the crowd.

"I'll get a taxi," I heard my father say and then I saw him standing next to a yellow cab, beside an open door. I wandered over and got in. He sat down near to me and closed the door as the taxi slid into the morning traffic.

I glanced over at my father. He tried to smile. Then I looked down at my powder-blue suit, the suit I'd saved for this day. My pant legs were caked in mud and my jacket and shirt were crumpled and covered with stains. My throat began to tighten and I looked at my father. Tears rimmed my eyes. He pretended not to notice. He simply said with a kindness and a sadness I'd never heard before, "Let's go home."

Chapter 60
TOO LATE

My father took off his jacket, loosening his tie, and sat on the end of the sofa. "What happened? Tell me all about it."

I told him everything. He listened patiently, allowing me to talk straight through. "They think I'm crazy. What I did was over and beyond the call of duty!"

"It's not what you did, it's *how* you did it," he said slowly. "Stress is something everyone faces. It's how you handle it that makes one man different from another. The truly successful ones work hard but they also play hard."

I stared at him numbly.

"Why don't you go shave and clean up and then get some sleep."

"Okay," I said, "but I'm not crazy."

I stumbled down the hallway, suddenly frightened of being alone, scared of my own thoughts. I flipped on the light switch and for the first time in days I beheld myself in the mirror. My cheeks were gone and my eyes were sunk deep in my head. I was staring in horror at the face of a concentration camp victim. My lips began trembling and tears sprang again to my eyes. My God, what have I done to myself?

I turned off the faucet and staggered into my sister's bedroom, peeled off my clothes and crawled under the sheets. But as soon as

I closed my eyes, the sounds of the circus music came back. Around and around, louder and louder, the music swirled in my head. Suddenly I was still there, limping around the concourse, wandering in and out of the crowd, smiling at the ticket takers. I lay still trying to sleep, but over and over as I circled the arena, the music kept blaring in my ears.

I awoke to find my mother was sitting on the side of the bed, not saying anything, just watching over me. "I'll be okay," I whispered.

She got up, brushing my forehead with her hand. "I didn't mean to wake you." As she started to leave she turned and said, "Earlier this afternoon you had a call. She was the nicest lady. She was concerned about you. Her name was Sheri."

Sheri, of all people? Wouldn't you know. I thought of the roses she'd sent, trying to remember the hours we'd just spent together. Then I heard my parents talking in the living room in hushed tones, my mother sounding alarmed, my father somehow trying to soothe her, and then somewhere in his words I heard him say, "Despite everything, he finished the job. He got the job done. He never quit."

I rose and began searching for my suit pants. I couldn't find them anywhere. "Has anyone seen my clothes?"

"I put them in the clothes hamper," my mother hollered back.

"I'll get you some of mine," my father said. I heard him opening his closet doors and shuffling through his chest of drawers. He handed me a shirt and a pair of khaki pants. I put them on, feeling awkward, trying to keep them up by tightening my belt around my waist.

"I've made you something to eat," my mother said. I took the plate and sat on the sofa. I could see they were trying to act like everything was normal. A man on the TV was talking. I stared at him, unable to understand what he was saying. My mind kept wandering. Nothing he said made any sense but I couldn't stop staring at him.

"Are you all right?"

I turned and my parents were looking at me.

I nodded and took a few bites of food. "What is he talking about? Is he talking to me?"

"It's the news. You're listening to the news."

The phone rang. My mother picked it up. "It's for you, a woman named Jill Bolaro."

"Jill?"

"How are you doing?" Jill said, sounding concerned. "I was just talking to Rick Johnson."

"I'm fine. I'm a little tired . . . I just need some rest. What did Rick tell you?"

"Not very much. He just said you had reached the end of your rope."

"I see," I said. I thanked her for calling and hung up the phone.

"Who was that?" my mother asked.

"A friend. Someone I once knew."

"Why don't you try to get some more sleep?"

"All right," I said, and I stumbled back up the hallway and sank down on the bed. I tried not to think about anything. But once again the circus music came back. I could hear every sound, so clear, so distinct, so loud. Then suddenly I was rocked to one side of the bed. I sat up. It felt as though a wrecking ball had swung from one side of my head to the other, slamming against my skull. I stared at the darkness, my head was pounding, then suddenly it stopped. What in the hell was that? I sat there frozen, letting some time pass, and then slowly my eyes became heavy. And I slipped back under the sheets.

I awoke, sensing early morning light and paddled barefoot into the living room. The house was still. My father was dressed. He sat on the sofa reading the paper. Just then the door swung open and my mother burst in the room carrying two bags of groceries. "You'll never believe what happened! I accidentally picked up the wrong bag of groceries. I've never done that before in my life! Look at all this stuff. Turnip greens, broccoli, cauliflower. Well at least we'll eat healthy for a while!"

I looked at her, dazed. Why was she telling me this? Why was she lying to me? It was obvious she bought all those vegetables for me. Can't anybody just tell me the truth?

"I'll get some money," I said and then I remembered my wallet was empty. I suddenly felt ashamed. "I'm sorry. I don't have any money to contribute."

"Don't be silly," my mother said.

My father stood up and a moment later returned from his bedroom. "I put twenty dollars in your wallet."

"You did?" I said, and I didn't know quite what to say. "Thank you."

After breakfast I wandered outside and sat alone on the patio. I turned on a radio and as I listened it seemed that every song, every verse, all of a sudden was heightened. I started listening to every word, reaching out for answers. The songs seemed so calming. The Eagles came on and I listened even closer . . . the words were rich.

"Oh, and it's a hollow feelin' . . . It's another Tequila sunrise . . . Take another shot of courage. . . ." It was all about me . . . they were singing to me.

I sat in the chair mesmerized, unable to move, until the afternoon sun settled slowly behind the building.

At dinner I couldn't eat very much. The TV was on but it just sounded muddled. "It's late," my father said. "We're going to bed. Why don't you do the same?"

"I will later," I said, and I turned off the TV and clicked the radio ck on. I sat in the dark anxious to hear something soothing. A man was talking with a man and a woman. The woman spoke hen laughed. There was something about the sound of her nd suddenly I realized it was her. My heart started pounding. new I'd be listening. I perched on the sofa waiting for the call letters and then I heard the announcer say goodnight. the kitchen and dialed information. Frantically I phoned "Is that woman still there?"

n who was just on the show." I pictured her blond nd gentle smile.

"I'm sorry, there's nobody here but me. Everyone's left the studio."

I placed the receiver down and looked up. My father was standing in the hallway.

"Who are you talking to?"

"Nobody."

"It's after midnight."

"I know."

"I want you to get some sleep."

"No."

"No?"

"I'm not sleeping until somebody tells me the truth!"

"What are you talking about?"

"I want the truth. Everybody keeps lying to me."

Suddenly my mother appeared. "What's going on?"

"He refuses to sleep."

I glared at my father.

"Okay, stay up," he said, and wearily they retreated back to their bedroom.

I poured a glass of wine and sat back down on the sofa, forcing myself to stay awake. I didn't trust anyone anymore. I had to stay awake and think things through. I lay down, closing my eyes, feeling myself go drowsy, feeling if only I stayed awake I could figure things out.

I awoke and my mother and father were sitting at the dining room table. My mother was still in her bathrobe but my father was dressed in pressed slacks and a sport shirt.

"Anything wrong?" I asked, and just then I found myself thinking more clearly, but I was worried by their expressions.

"We think you should see a doctor."

"I'm sorry about last night."

"We just think it wouldn't hurt."

"I'm fine, but if you think it's a good idea," I murmured.

"Just to be sure," my father said.

I got up and dressed, feeling embarrassed again in my father's oversized clothes and followed him out the door.

Thirty minutes later we were waiting in a small room with only a chair and an examining table. A young black man came in and said he'd like to ask me a few questions.

I spoke very slowly, being careful to answer him correctly.

"I'm through," he said. "The doctor will be in in a few minutes."

My father and I looked at each other, silently waiting, and then suddenly the door swung open. The black man walked in, followed by a thin, harried man with a clipboard.

"I told him I'm tired. I just need some rest," I assured the man with the clipboard.

He looked at me observantly. "I agree. Go home and get some rest."

My father and I walked slowly down the corridor. He didn't say anything until we got to the car. Then he spoke softly. "Well it helps to be sure."

It was late in the afternoon when I called the Ringling office. The receptionist answered. She seemed surprised to hear my voice. "Everyone's asking about you! All the promoters, Steve and Robin. . . ."

"I'm doing okay. I'm trying to get some rest. Have you heard from Mike Franks?"

"He's in Tulsa with the show but he was here the afternoon after you arrived. He was devastated when we told him what happened. He just keep saying, 'I shouldn't have left. I should have stayed.'"

I hung up the phone. Tulsa? And suddenly I realized the show was no longer in Evansville. In fact, it hadn't been there in days.

"What is today?" I asked my mother.

"Saturday."

"I think I'll go to the pool."

"The pool? Sure . . . if that's what you would like to do."

My father got up. "I'll get you a bathing suit."

I slipped it over my bony frame. I knew I needed to be around people, to do something normal. The pool was surrounded by tall, brick apartment buildings. It was crowded when I walked through the front gate. The weather was sunny and hot and children were shouting and splashing in the water. I chose a white chaise by the edge of the pool and sat down on my towel, gazing at all the activity.

A skinny boy with black hair was jumping in and out of the water while a little girl was floating in a small yellow tube. A teenage girl came out of the pool, dripping wet, and lay down on a chaise beside me. The air was now filled with the clamor of children, and suddenly I realized these could easily be Allen's children or someday, Mike Franks'. And I realized it was children just like these that had died in the Holocaust, murdered while they clung terrified to their mothers' laps. I stared at the children and all of a sudden I could feel their horrible suffering. Tears began rolling down my cheeks. The girl lying beside me looked over and quietly returned to the pool. It didn't matter. Nothing mattered. It was all just so tragic. All of these beautiful children taken away and as they played all around me, I sat there and sobbed.

At dinner everybody was especially quiet. Finally my mother spoke.
"Why were you crying this afternoon at the pool?"
"I don't know. I just felt sad."
"Sad about what?"
"I don't know."
That night, my mind kept swirling. I couldn't focus on anything. I didn't know what to believe anymore. Something was wrong, terribly wrong, and I didn't know how to fix it.
I turned to my mother. "I'm frightened. I can't sleep. I can't think. My thoughts just keep shifting. What's wrong with me?"

The next morning I awoke having slept for a few quiet hours. Both of my parents were dressed.
"We laid out some clean clothes for you," my mother said.
"Are we going somewhere?"
"We called someone else, someone a friend recommended."
"This is ridiculous. I don't need to see anyone else. I feel great this morning."

"It's already arranged."

I strode into their bedroom. Another set of khaki pants and a sport shirt were laid out on the bed.

"Can I wear a white shirt?"

My father hesitated.

"Of course you can. He wants to wear a dress shirt," my mother said, and she reached into his closet and pulled out a freshly starched shirt.

I sat in the back seat of the car feeling strangely spirited. For some reason, everything seemed funny. We entered the back door of what looked like a medical facility and I was directed into a small room. My parents waited outside. I sat on an examining table again waiting for the doctor to come in. Wouldn't it be funny if I played a trick on him? What if I stood behind the door and pretended the door hit my knee? I began giggling at the thought of it, me sprawled all over the floor. I didn't have much time to waste. I had to get in position. I hopped off the table. Just then the door opened.

"Hi, I'm Dr. Schweitzer."

"Schweitzer? And I'm Livingstone, I presume."

"Do you want to tell me what's going on?"

"I'd rather not," I laughed. "Why don't you tell me?"

He smiled, looked at me for a moment, and replied, "I'll be back shortly."

"Not if you're returning to Africa," I hollered.

I sat on the table, dangling my feet over the edge, trying to think of a joke I could play on ol' Schweitzer.

The door opened and my parents stood outside along with Dr. Schweitzer.

"Why so glum? We're all going to Africa."

"We can leave now," my father said, holding a piece of paper.

"Home?"

"Actually, no. The doctor recommended another stop."

"Well good for ol' Schweitzer," I said, glancing over at him as he said goodbye to my parents, thinking how much he reminded me of Carl Bruce in Terre Haute.

I slid into the back seat of the car and lay down on the seat, gazing up at the phone lines and tree limbs and clouds as the car swept along the street.

"What's he doing?" I heard my father ask.

"He's lying down," my mother said.

We pulled into an underground parking lot and took an elevator up several floors. "This way," my father said and he knocked on a heavy green door at the end of a short hallway. The door opened and a young woman greeted my parents. We were standing in a huge reception area. Several people were milling around. While the young woman talked with my parents I noticed a poster hanging on a column in front of me. Under a blue sky with white puffy clouds it read, "Neurotics dream about castles in the sky. Psychotics live in them."

Various people in jeans and casual clothes were sitting off to the left in front of a TV and from somewhere in the back, I could hear a radio playing. Something was very strange about all this. Every now and then someone would look at me and then quickly avert their eyes. Slowly it dawned on me, this was some kind of a set up, and my parents were in on it. Irvin could arrange this. He had the resources. He could rent a whole building if he wanted to, hire professional actors, arrange all the props, everything down to the last detail. Any minute there is probably going to be some huge surprise.

"Follow me," the young woman said and we walked down a hallway and entered a small room with a sofa and three chairs. We sat down and she began asking questions. My mother tried to answer but suddenly burst into tears.

"What are you crying for?" I snapped, starting to feel angry.

The young woman asked a few more questions and then we all stood up.

"You're going to stay here a little while," my mother said. Tears were still streaming down her cheeks.

"Whatever you say."

"I'll bring clothes and pack a few things for you," my father whispered. The young woman led them out to the front door while I waited and watched, anxious to find out what happened next.

"Come this way," she said patiently, and she led me down a corridor, opening one of the doors. Inside were two twin beds and a couple of dressers. Clothes were scattered all over the place.

"This will be your room. Make yourself comfortable. We'll be back shortly," she said, closing the door.

I sat down on one of the beds and looked around. The room was a mess. Whoever lived there wasn't very tidy. On the end table, I noticed, between the two beds, was a plastic container with yellow frosting and crumbs inside. I picked it up and took a deep smell. It was banana cake, my favorite dessert. I took another deep whiff and began licking the sides, tasting it, reveling in the sweet smell. The door opened and a young man in a sweater walked in.

"What are you doing?"

I just looked at him. He walked back out of the room.

I began searching the room. What else is in here? What other clues have they placed? I opened the drawer to the nightstand and began rummaging through pens and paper. The door suddenly opened. A kindly man in a suit stood looking in.

"I'm Dr. Gray. Are you okay?"

"I'm fine," I said, and he closed the door quietly.

She's here. That's the surprise. She's here somewhere. Any minute she's going to appear. I've got to find her. I stood up and rushed out of the room, turned right and began opening all the doors. I couldn't find her anywhere. I ran down the hall, turned left, and suddenly found myself in front of the reception area. The young woman who had earlier greeted us stood behind a long, rectangular counter. On top of the counter was a tray filled with dozens of small cups.

"Here, Jamie, we'd like you to take two of these."

"What are they?"

"Pills," she said, and I noticed two men standing nearby, observing me.

"I'm not taking those."

"You have to."

"No. I'm not taking anything."

The two men, a tall black man and a young, smaller man came around the counter. Two others suddenly appeared. I went into a crouch. This was going to be fun. One of them said, "Grab him," and suddenly I was lifted off the floor. I began kicking and punching while they carried me down a hallway. Someone from the TV room screamed, "Take him to isolation!" I freed one foot and kicked out. One of the men, the young one, groaned. We turned down a narrow corridor. It was dark. Someone yelled, "Get the door!" I could see it at the end of the hallway. "No!" I cried, "No!" I tried to grab onto it but they pried off my fingers and wrestled me to the floor, holding me down. "Get his clothes!" someone yelled, and my shoes came off and then my pants and shirt. "Hold him," the young woman said gently, and I noticed she had followed them into the room. She was squatting beside me clenching a long needle. They held me tighter while she rubbed a spot on my hip and then inserted the needle, slowly releasing the fluid.

They held me for a few moments longer, and then they got up. I lay there, and behind me I heard voices and shuffling of feet, and then I heard the door close and the sound of it locking. The room was suddenly still. Slowly my body became lifeless, unable to move. My naked flesh pressed against the cold concrete floor and then I began to shiver and shake. I stared at the steel door and four walls and grabbed my knees and curled up into a ball trying to keep warm. "Those bastards! Those sons-of-bitches!" I screamed, and then I looked at my naked body and I knew no one cared. There was no one to hear me. I had nothing now. I'd lost it all. Not even the clothes on my back. And I started to cry. And as my consciousness, the only thing that I had left, flowed out of my body like a madly rushing, swollen, dark river, from deep inside me, from a place of unbearable pain and anguish and failure, a place I never wanted to go, I cried out, "I'm sorry. I'm so sorry. Please help me. I love you. I love you so," and then I arched my back and through streams of tears, I screamed out one final word. "Christine." The only word that ever mattered. The name of my wife, my beautiful, beautiful, beautiful wife.

PART SIX

GOING HOME

Chapter 61

WHY?

"Oh God, Christine, forgive me. How could I have been so cruel? I'm sorry. I am so sorry!" Tears flowed like torrents falling on the cement floor. I curled up my knees, shaking, sobbing, feeling as though ten tons of bricks weighed on my chest. And then I saw her sitting on her bed, the bed she'd slept in as a little girl, clutching her stuffed bear, unable to look up at me, as tears streamed down her cheeks and I told her I was leaving. "Oh God, Christine. I love you. I'm so sorry. I never wanted to leave you. I didn't know what else to do!" Tears dripped down the side of my nose. I sat up on one elbow trying to breathe. "If only I could start over. If only I'd been different." I lay back down and cried, sobbing until all that remained was a hollow, dried-out feeling.

I looked up at the ceiling, rubbing my eyes. How long had I been in here? It felt like I'd been blacked-out for days. I looked around the room. It was empty, nothing but a concrete floor, cinder block walls and a yellow steel door with a small window. The only item in the room was a paper nightgown someone had left in the middle of the floor. Was that supposed to protect me from myself? What if I stood up and smashed my head against the wall?

I crawled over and picked up the paper nightgown, tearing it in half. I wrapped it like a towel around my waist and then sat against the wall, near the corner, across from the steel door. What was I doing in here?

"Someone let me out of here!" I yelled. I sat there leaning against the wall waiting for someone to open the door, but nobody came. "Goddamn it! Let me out of here!" I screamed again. Still no one came. I picked up what remained of the nightgown and began tearing it into little pieces, laying the tiny bits in an ever widening circle on the floor. I was mesmerized by the intricate pattern I was forming, when out of the corner of my eye I spotted a face peering in at me. It was the black man's face, one of the men who had carried me in here. "Let me out of here!" I screamed. He was wearing glasses. He just stared at me blankly. And then he disappeared. "That son of a bitch!"

I leaned back against the wall thinking of all the ways I could kill myself. What if I balled up the paper and shoved it down my throat? I could choke myself to death. The ceiling was acoustical tile sitting on a metal frame. What if I ripped out one of the metal ribs and stabbed myself to death? "That would show them."

More time passed. This time it seemed like hours. His face reappeared in the window. I jumped to my feet. "Open the door! Let me out of here!" I demanded. He waited and watched and then once again vanished from sight. "Damn that son of a bitch! How long do they think they can keep me in here?"

I sat back down, so angry I could spit, and stared at the four walls. Tears welled up in my eyes. A few minutes later he turned up again at the window. I looked up through blurry eyes. "Please let me out of here." He disappeared again and my shoulders slumped. "What do I have to do to get out of here?"

The room felt hot and suffocating. I stared at the window in the door waiting for him to come back again, hoping it would be soon. Finally someone appeared. It was the woman, the pretty woman, the one who'd given me the shot. She looked in for a minute and then I saw his face again peering through the window. I got up and walked slowly toward the door, placing my face only inches away. "Please open the door. Please let me out. I'll do whatever you say."

The door cracked open. "Please," I said, "please." He opened the door wide. The woman was holding my pants. "Here, you can put these on and follow us."

I followed them up a long corridor, holding my pants up with one hand. We turned left and passed several rooms, most had their doors open, some had people sitting inside, until we got to a room near the end of the hall.

"This room will be your room," she said matter of factly. I walked inside. There was a small bed, a white sink against the wall, a nightstand and a double closet. At the foot of the bed was my suitcase.

"Your father brought over some clothes."

It was my suitcase from Indiana. Somehow they'd retrieved it.

Just then a large man walked in carrying a tray. "We figured you'd probably be pretty hungry." I reached out but before I could grab the tray he said, "You'll have to take these first," and he handed me a white cup with two pills and a drink of water. I swallowed the pills as he stood observing me.

"Eat, and I'll be back to get you in a few minutes so you can meet your group," the young woman said. "By the way, my name is Nancy."

I started to devour the food but suddenly my whole body felt sluggish. I was awake yet my body began to feel heavy. It must be those pills. Even my thoughts began to slow down. It felt as though the words in my head were moving in slow motion. I picked at the carrots and peas and potatoes, finding myself staring vacantly at the plate.

"Come with me," she said. I looked up and it was Nancy in the doorway. "It's time to meet your group."

I shuffled down the hallway behind her. All the bedrooms now were empty. We passed the reception desk, and I heard voices coming from one of the rooms. She opened the door and ushered me inside, taking a seat herself.

"Welcome," said a balding, middle-aged man with a pleasant face. "Please take a seat."

I sat down and looked around the room. Who *were* these people? One of them looked like a teenaged neighbor I used to know. What was he doing in here? I stared at him but he didn't seem to recognize me. Almost everybody was young. There was a black girl wearing short cutoffs, a pale faced boy in a baseball cap who was staring down at his lap, a fat woman with fake red nails, and an older man who was tall and ruffled. He was fidgeting with his hands.

"My name is Harold," the balding man said. "Would you care to introduce yourself?"

"Why? You already know who I am."

He looked surprised. "How would we know who you are?" Then he asked, "Do you know who we are?"

"You're all actors. Irvin Feld hired you."

"Actors?" he said with a grin and then he made a funny face, cocking one eyebrow. "Yes, and I'm Sean Connery!"

He introduced the rest of the group and then he announced that he worked with Dr. Gray. "I'm a counselor. You'll meet with us each day and then you'll meet with Dr. Gray alone twice a week. But I'll be going on vacation next week so Dr. Gray will be taking over the group."

Twice a week? How long was this charade supposed to go on? I watched for several minutes as Harold interacted with the group, sometimes listening, sometimes talking, sometimes goading someone to speak. They were good. They clearly all knew their parts. Irvin had done a great job.

Finally Harold interjected, "That will be all for today," and everyone noisily dispersed. I wandered out into the main room. Several people were watching TV while some looked like they were meeting with visitors. On one of the side tables there were several magazines. Almost all of the covers showed faces of celebrities, movie actors and actresses. Suddenly it dawned on me, gazing at the cover of a handsome face, maybe my father was a famous actor, my mother too. They were certainly attractive enough. Maybe they never wanted to tell me for fear I wouldn't live a normal life. Maybe this was their way of telling me. I felt a chill of excitement . . . their way of introducing me to a family of performers.

I heard music again coming from behind the TV room, soft rhythmic music. I wandered in the direction of the melody and found myself standing behind double swinging doors. I walked inside. There were people dancing to the music, swaying gently to the tune. An old lady, half-toothless, in an old cotton dress moved dreamily around the room. When she saw me she looked up and smiled. I noticed the two girls from my group dancing with each other. I stood and watched, amazed at how smooth even the heaviest people moved.

After three or four songs the music stopped and people gradually began leaving the room. I walked up three steps to a platform in front of a large window and sat down in one of two chairs. I stared outside at several large office buildings surrounding a vacant lot. In the middle of the lot, way down below, sat a small wooden house with a rotating sign that read, "Ed's Barber Shop." I gazed out the window trying to figure out where I was. It didn't look like any city I'd ever been in, except maybe Los Angeles. Was I somehow back in L.A.? How the hell did that happen?

I sat in the chair the rest of the afternoon just staring out the window. Finally someone announced dinner, and I wandered back to the main reception area. Trays of food along with pills and water were lined up along the counter. I was handed my pills and was watched again to make sure I swallowed them whole. Then I took my tray and sat by myself in the corner.

I sat there until a lady behind the counter announced in a loud voice. "Lights out in thirty minutes." I got up and shuffled down a long hallway back to my room. I sat on the side of the bed. I was staring at my clothes scattered about the room when suddenly the tall, thin man from our group, the man that was fidgeting with his hands, burst in.

"Hi, I'm Albert," he pronounced, and he plopped down next to me taking a gulp from a can of Sprite.

"I pace a lot," he stammered, taking another slug. "I saw you when you came in. I thought they were going to take you to St. Elizabeth's. Several patients said that's where they should take you."

"St. Elizabeth's? What's that?" I asked, noticing his two front teeth were broken and he had a fresh cut on his forehead.

"It's the state mental institution. I've been there. You get put in there you may never get out. Hey, you want some Sprite?"

"Sure," I said, and I took a big gulp.

"Well, I gotta go pace. I've only got twenty minutes." Then he stood up and bolted back out of the room.

"Lights out," another woman yelled, and suddenly the corridor went dark. Exhausted, I reached up and switched off the light by my headboard. I crawled under the sheets, feeling myself drift into a deep, heavy sleep, only to be awakened a few hours later by a sharp, nagging pain in my groin. I sat up. My stomach was aching. I had to go to the bathroom. I stood up, losing my balance. Everything in the room looked hazy. Where the hell am I? Where is the bathroom? I stumbled around the room, tripping over my suitcase, until the pain became unbearable. I couldn't hold it in any longer. I staggered toward the wall, stood on my toes and helplessly urinated into the white porcelain sink.

I was perched on the edge of my bed, wondering how long this one act play was going to continue, when my father, dressed in a business suit, strode into the room.

"Hi," he said, looking starkly out of place. "How are you doing?"

"I'm fine," I said, feeling agitated.

He reached over and touched my knee. "When you're all better we'll go fishing. Just you and me."

What a stupid thing to say, I thought. "You know I hate fishing!"

He looked a little bewildered, smiled, and quietly rose and left the room.

A few minutes later, I walked out into the main room. Albert brushed past me flailing his arms. He was pacing up and down the hall, breathing heavily, muttering to himself. I stared at him as he turned around and marched in my direction. He was exactly my father's build. Suddenly, frighteningly, it dawned on me. Albert *was* my father. A quick change, make-up and false teeth. What acting! What great character acting!

"It's time to take your pills," the man behind the counter announced. I swallowed the two white pills, feeling my thoughts slow down again to a crawl. Suddenly I could barely think. What in the world were they giving me?

"I want to see a doctor," I sputtered.

"Pardon?" the man behind the counter said.

"I demand to see a doctor!"

"Dr. Gray is your doctor."

"No, I want to see a real doctor."

"We'll see what we can do."

Nancy walked up. "You're late for your group."

I followed her down the hallway and sat quietly in the one empty chair. Albert looked winded from all of his pacing. I studied him carefully. Behind his glasses those could easily be my father's eyes. He was there watching me, looking after me all this time. As I stared at him it suddenly occurred to me, my God, maybe I'm not even who I think I am. Maybe I'm an actor myself and I've been being filmed for years.

The hour passed quickly. The group disappeared. I wandered back to the main recreation area, lost happily in my thoughts, and sat down again in the upholstered chair. I stared out the window. Down below was Ed's Barber Shop. There was something about the view that made me feel secure. I could sit there all day and just think, not talking to anybody, and nobody would bother me. After lunch I returned again to the chair, wondering if I'd ever actually starred in a movie. The overcast sky slowly turned to dusk and the traffic crept forward in a river of red lights.

I woke up the next morning to a man standing over my bed.

"You wanted to see a doctor?"

"Yes," I said groggily.

"Well, he's here. You'd better hurry up if you want to see him."

I stumbled down the hallway, in the moment not caring if I saw the doctor or not, and was shown into a room with a table and chair. A young, serious looking man with a stethoscope around his neck stood in the middle of the room.

"Sit up here," he said brusquely, and I sat on the covered table.

He quickly took my blood pressure. "Here, step up on the scale," he said. He seemed impatient. I took off my shoes and stepped up.

553

He slid the bar over. "One hundred and twenty-nine pounds. How tall are you?"

"Six foot-one."

He didn't say anything.

"I guess I've got some weight to put back on," I muttered.

"Yes, you do," he said, and he quickly returned his instruments to his black bag and left the room.

I got up, no longer sure why I'd asked to see him, and shuffled out of the room.

That afternoon I wandered toward my chair by the window, and I saw one of the girls I knew speaking with the more talkative boy in our group. They were both gesturing to each other and when they saw me, they suddenly stopped. I approached them hoping to have a conversation. "Hi," I said. "Don't stop on my account."

"That's okay," she said, and they both looked flustered. "We were told not to do any role playing around you."

Later that night, when I went to bed, my thoughts kept turning over and over. Suddenly nothing was making any sense. A daily routine had formed. If there was some surprise to be sprung on me why hadn't it been sprung by now? I fell into a deep sleep and awoke in the middle of the night. I had to go to the bathroom again. This time I got up and wandered past the bedroom door. There were bathrooms down the hallway to the left.

"Who's up?" a voice with a thick accent shouted down the corridor. I looked to the right. A black woman sat on a chair at the far end of the hall monitoring the passage.

"I have to go to the bathroom," I said. "Can I go to the bathroom?"

"Yes," she hollered. "And then get back to bed! It's the middle of the night!"

Her words and her tone resounded in my ears. She didn't know me at all. And I didn't know her. She was simply doing her job. And then suddenly, as though a foggy mist had just lifted, I knew where I was. This wasn't Los Angeles. These people were not actors and I was nobody special. This was a mental hospital and I was one of the patients.

I sat up in bed, clinging to the realization I'd been crazy, while terrified I could suddenly turn crazy again. I had to see Harold. I had to tell him as soon as he got in that I now knew who I was!

Chapter 62

WHEN CAN I LEAVE?

I waited outside Harold's office until I saw him round the corner, slipping out his keys.

"Harold, I know who I am!"

He turned the key in the lock and smiled. "Harold. I know who I am! I'm Jamie MacVicar. I'm in a mental hospital. No one is acting. Last night everything suddenly became clear."

He sat down and shook my hand. "Welcome back," he said. "You'll have to tell the group all about it."

"When can I leave?" I stammered.

"Not so fast," he responded, starting to laugh. "This afternoon you'll see Dr. Gray. We'll take it one day at a time."

"This afternoon? Christ almighty, that's an eternity!"

Harold's gaze returned to some papers on his desk. I backed away from his door and headed for the public phones.

"Mom! I snapped out of it. I don't know what happened but somewhere in the middle of the night I realized where I was. I've got to get out of here. Can you quickly call Dr. Gray?"

I hung up the phone, trying to breathe easier and wandered past the TV room to my bedroom. The place was a mess. My clothes were scattered all over the chairs and floor. I bent down and began folding my t-shirts, neatly placing them in my suitcase at the foot of the bed, when Nancy stuck her head in the room.

"Cleaning up your room? That's a good sign."

"I snapped out of it," I proclaimed. "Last night."

"That's wonderful," she said. "I'll see you at the group meeting."

I finished folding my clothes, tidied the bed and walked back out to the main area. I wanted to stay busy, to be around other people. The last thing I needed was to be all alone. Nancy was working behind the counter alongside a man and a woman dispensing pills. Other patients were now wandering around the halls. Some were watching TV. Some were still eating breakfast and others were just standing alone. I took the white cup and swallowed the two tablets. I looked around the room and suddenly it felt as though I was seeing it for the first time.

Unlike the gleaming white, frightening walls of an insane asylum I'd so often seen depicted in the movies, it looked instead like I was standing in an airport lobby surrounded by bland plastic seating and scattered stacks of magazines. Branching in three directions, the passageways to the rooms were not much different than a college dormitory.

In the center of the room was the nursing station where meals were served along with the cups of pills. The attendants I noticed all wore casual clothes, and other than the outdated vinyl seating the room was disarmingly plain. But there was one feature that kept me transfixed. The front door. It wasn't your typical door. It was an ugly, green steel door firmly locked in place. Despite what I'd heard—"Anyone can leave anytime they want"—it was painfully obvious that without permission no one was going anywhere.

I was starting to feel jittery when one of the attendants I'd seen talking with Nancy walked up. "Hi, I'm Robert," he said. "I'm a graduate student. Would you like to talk?"

"Sure," I replied, grateful to have something to do. I followed him down a hallway to a small office with a desk and two chairs. I noticed he was overweight, wore glasses and acted studious.

"Have a seat," he said, and he sat down and picked up a pad of paper and a pen. "So what's going on?"

He looked so earnest and it was such a relief to be asked I started talking, blurting out everything from the beginning that had happened. He listened patiently, occasionally giving a nod or taking down a note. "How long do we have?" I interjected, nervously aware I was taking up much of his time.

"As long as you like. It's why I'm here," he replied. I burbled on for a few more minutes and then ran out of things to say.

"Is there anything else? Anything at all you want to talk about?"

"There is one thing," I said, a little hesitantly.

"It's my upper lip. It keeps curling up. It feels as though someone is tugging on the left side with a piece of string. I've been wondering if it has something to do with mustaches. Irvin Feld never would allow us to wear one."

"Now that's the kind of thinking that got you in here. It's simply an adverse reaction to the medicine."

"I see," I said, startled, and I warned myself to ignore my imagination.

"I'm here Monday through Friday. We can talk again tomorrow," he said.

I rose and thanked him, heartened I'd had someone to talk to, and hurried back to the phones.

"Mom, did you talk to Dr. Gray?"

"Yes," she said, but this time she sounded subdued.

"What did he say? When can I leave?"

"He said there is no point in pressuring him," and then she paused for a long while. "He said this didn't happen overnight and you're not going to be cured overnight. He said you needed to stay off the circuit for awhile."

I hung up the phone and glanced at the clock. It was only an hour until the group meeting. I decided I'd talk to him myself.

Dr. Gray hardly said a word to the group, content to let Harold set the pace of the dialogue. As Harold chided the shy boy with the baseball cap to say something, anything, Dr. Gray, dressed in a plaid suit, just sat in his chair with his chin tucked into his chest, gazing up at whoever was talking. I was beginning to wonder what could possibly change his cow-eyed expression when Albert suddenly jumped to his feet and asked if anyone minded if he paced around the room.

"Jesus Christ," I blurted out. "If you're not crazy when you arrive here, you sure as hell will be by the time you leave!"

Harold laughed. "Sit down," he told Albert.

Dr. Gray finally smiled. "A good sense of humor is the first sign of good health."

"Great, so when can I get out of here?"

Dr. Gray fixed his gaze again. "Why don't we talk about that after the group meeting? I believe today is our individual session anyway."

I was anxious to see Dr. Gray yet nervous about how I'd sound. Could I convince him I was okay enough to go home? Shortly after lunch I told Nancy it was time. She said Dr. Gray's office was on the fourth floor. She unlocked the heavy green door. I walked out into the hallway and approached a set of elevator doors. It felt strange to suddenly be on my own. The elevator descended to the next floor and two men in business suits got on. I wondered if they knew I was a patient. I looked at the piece of paper Nancy had given me. Room 413. It was a wooden door and Dr. Gray's name was stenciled on the outside. I knocked and walked in. He was sitting behind an open desk in front of a rectangular piece of carpeting that hung soothingly on his wall. The threads, I noticed, had strong earthy colors.

"Sit down," he said politely, and he promptly resumed the exact expression he had displayed for the group, gazing up at me silently. I could tell he wasn't going to do much talking. So I told him everything I'd just told Robert, only more. I told him I'd always had a lot of drive and ambition but how this time it had gotten out of control, and how under the same circumstances it could have happened to anyone. It had all been a logical progression.

"Yes, but a healthy person would have stopped. They would have backed away before self-destructing. You didn't. We have to find out why."

"How do we do that?" I said, looking up at him.

"By the time you're ready to leave, you'll know what you need to know."

"How long will that take?"

"I don't know. Maybe a few months, maybe sooner. It depends on you." Then he smiled. "From what you've just told me you'll no doubt break all the records!"

I sat there not knowing what else to say. A few minutes later he looked at his clock. "Time's up," he said quietly.

I stood on my feet feeling confused. He got up from behind his desk and walked me to the door. As he opened the door I hesitated. "Dr. Gray, just tell me one thing. What do you think happened to me?"

He paused for a moment. "I don't know but I do know one thing. Your marriage threw you for a loop."

The rest of the day I was more befuddled than ever. I thought I had found a few of the answers but now all I had were questions. How long would I be in here? What really happened and why? And how do I know it can't happen any minute again?

That night, lying in bed, I heard the steel door swing open. Then I heard the scuffling of feet and a petrified woman scream out. It was the screams of an animal, out of control, terrified. "Put me down!" she cried and amidst the muffled sounds of feet and voices I could hear her being carried down the hall. Then a door slammed shut and the noise abruptly stopped. Frightened, I clutched the pillow, and I could feel her tormented soul reverberate in my chest.

The next morning I awoke with a vision of Christine going over and over in my mind. It felt like she'd been with me all night. I knew now I had to see her. I couldn't run from it any longer.

I quickly dressed. Nancy was standing behind the nurses' station. "I've got to see Dr. Gray!"

She glanced at me suspiciously. "You just saw him yesterday afternoon."

"I know but this is important. I've got to see him again right away."

She hesitated for a second, looked at her watch and nodded okay.

"Thank you!" I said as she let me out the front door. I rode the elevator down three floors, knocked on his door and entered the office. He looked up surprised.

"Dr. Gray, I need to see my wife. She's working now in Washington, D.C. and I need to see her."

To my astonishment he said, "I think that's a good idea. I'll let Nancy know."

Standing by the phone, I unfolded her number, noticing my hands had begun to tremble. I clutched the receiver in my palm. Suddenly, for the first time in months, I heard her voice.

"Christine MacVicar. Adden and Lockwood Incorporated."

"Christine, it's me, Jamie."

"Jamie?"

"Christine, I need to see you."

"Where are you?"

"I'm here in D.C."

"When did you want to see me?"

"Now."

Chapter 63

EMOTIONS

My clothes smelled musty. I quickly shaved, tucked in my shirt and tried to make myself as presentable as possible. She'd said "meet me in an hour" in the lobby of her building.

I stepped out onto the sidewalk. The sun stung my eyes. I wasn't used to all the noise and swirling traffic. I hailed a cab and gave him the address, 1100 Connecticut Avenue, then sat in the back seat rehearsing what I was going to say, excited I'd be seeing her any minute. Maybe we'll hug each other. I'll tell her how much I love her . . . how wrong I'd been.

The taxi pulled to a stop. I jumped out, walked through a bustling crowd, and opened the glass doors to a huge, empty lobby. She was sitting quietly on a marble planter, holding a brown envelope. Her hair was different, cut shorter, more business-like, I noticed.

"Christine!"

"Jamie?" she replied, not rising up. "You look emaciated!"

"I know. I wasn't eating very well for a while," I said, trying to soften the startled look on her face. I sat down next to her and started to speak.

"Before you say anything," she interrupted, "several weeks ago I filed for divorce. I've been waiting to hear from you to give you the papers." She glanced down at the brown envelope in her lap.

I looked down at the envelope clasped between her hands.

"I'm sorry," she whispered.

I started to tell her what I'd come to say, but I could see from her resolved expression it wasn't any use. "Could you do me one favor?" I asked. "Could you hold onto the papers for a week or two more, then mail them to me? It's been a little rough these past few weeks."

I wandered back into the busy street and hailed another taxi. Sitting in the back seat I stared out the window, unable to focus, not sad, not angry, not anything, just stunned.

Nancy was standing behind the counter when I walked in. "How did it go?"

"Not too good. Have you seen Robert around?"

I searched the hallways until I found him speaking with another student. "Can we talk for a few minutes?"

I sat down in his office and told him what had just happened. I don't know what I expected him to say.

"Well, you faced it," he said. "At least now you know."

We sat in silence for a few moments. Then he asked, "Isn't it time for your group?"

"You're right," I said, glancing at my watch, and I hurried out of his office.

The group was already in session when I stepped into the room. "I'm sorry I'm late," I said, and I quickly plopped down in my chair.

The room was silent. No one was talking. "Do you want to tell us why you're late?" Harold asked. Dr. Gray was slouched in his chair, his legs stretched out before him.

I told the group about Christine and where I'd been. No one said anything, including Dr. Gray, but somehow I sensed their approval.

The room became silent again. Dr. Gray didn't move. He appeared content to let the stillness pressure someone to speak. I looked around at the group. Vera, the black girl with the cut-off jeans looked agitated. The boy with the baseball cap just sat there, quietly sad. The young man who looked like my ex-neighbor seemed alert and at ease, but I'd begun to suspect he'd gotten in trouble and his parents no longer wanted him around. And Albert, as usual, was fidgeting in his seat in the corner.

Vera broke the silence. "I don't like how men around here have been looking at me."

"What do you mean?" Nancy asked.

"I don't like how some of them eye me."

Nancy turned to the group, reminding us that at one time a rape had indeed occurred. Albert grew excited and said something about an inmate who had been caught having sex with another patient.

The room grew silent again.

"Perhaps," I said, trying to suggest a solution, "you shouldn't dress so provocatively."

"Who says I dress provocatively?" Vera spat, and she glanced at me coldly.

Nancy quickly broke in. "Perhaps it's a good idea that we all be careful how we dress . . . just to avoid any problems."

The group dispersed, and I wandered over to the main area. A woman, I noticed, in a dark dress, was standing alone at the far end of the room. She was pale and looked tired. I stared at her for a few moments, helpless to assist, knowing she was the woman the previous night who'd been dragged down the hall.

"Hello, my name is Marty." I turned and saw a middle-aged man, handsome and neatly groomed, standing to my left.

"Are you one of the attendants?" I asked.

"No," he said, seemingly amused at the question. "I'm one of the patients."

"Well, you certainly don't look like it," I said. I was surprised to meet a patient who reminded me of the people I often associated with on the outside. "What are you doing here?"

"I was a teacher . . . I guess I still am. I've been depressed for awhile. It's a long story."

"Don't worry, you're in good company," I said, pointing to an old man sweeping the floor. "He was a psychology professor before he landed here."

Marty smiled and, feeling encouraged, I cracked a few jokes. He laughed and we talked for a few minutes before he said he had to go. We shook hands, and I stepped up to the rec room to my favorite chair, delighted I'd finally made a friend.

After dinner, I noticed Marty sitting in the TV room with a well dressed, attractive woman. "I told my wife about you," he volunteered after she'd left. "I told her it was the first time in months someone had made me laugh."

The next morning I awoke feeling refreshed. I was anxious to talk to the group. I was determined to work hard, ask questions, talk incessantly if need be, to try to understand what happened and why.

I walked into the session with a renewed sense of purpose, but no one said anything, regardless of what I uttered. How, I wondered, was this going to work?

After lunch I located Robert in his office and we talked again. We talked about Christine. I told him all about our relationship. It felt different knowing that it was over. An uncertain anguish had disappeared. But I still felt a failure, a feeling that I'd shamelessly abandoned her, someone I'd loved, someone who needed my help.

"Perhaps," Robert said, "abandonment is a word you know well. Maybe it's no longer for her, but for you that you need to grieve."

My mother arrived mid-morning. I could tell she was trying to act cheery. We sat in two chairs, away from the TV room and all the noise. She looked worried. "Why does your upper lip keep twitching?" I told her it was the medicine. "He'll be taking me off it over the next two weeks." Then we talked about my brother and sisters as I searched for a way to feel normal. "There's a hike scheduled for ten AM this Saturday morning. The attendants are taking us. Do you want to come along?"

"I don't think so," she said, sheepishly.

"I hope I won't be here much longer," I said, as I hugged her goodbye. A little while later I realized how absurd it must have seemed to her, as absurd as it had begun to seem to me. My mother and I and a long line of inmates hobbling through Washington, D.C.

————

Vera looked upset during the group session. Nancy kept asking her what was wrong but she refused to speak. There were long periods of silence. I could hear Albert breathing heavily next to me. Finally Vera muttered, "I don't know what's wrong with me. I feel like I'm separated from my vagina." She was quiet again. Dr. Gray sat motionless in his chair. Finally he looked at his watch and said softly, "time's up."

Robert approached while I was standing near the front desk. "Would you like to go downstairs?"

"Downstairs?"

"There's a little café with outdoor seating. Why don't we talk outside today?"

I followed him to the elevator and down to the main lobby. A glass door at the rear was marked Deli. We ordered two cups of coffee and then walked past the counter and turned to the left into a small courtyard. Two wrought iron tables and chairs sat atop irregular squares of gray flagstones. Nestled nearby were two potted plants. We sat down and for the first time in days I felt a hint of what it would be like to feel normal. It felt as though I was miles away from the hospital. I looked around. A light breeze tugged at my napkin. "It wasn't that long ago that I was wearing a three-piece suit," I said.

"I know," Robert replied. And he took out his notepad. "What would you like to talk about today?"

Calmed by my new surroundings, yet terrified by the notion that by anyone's description I'd gone stark raving mad I abruptly blurted out, "What pushed me over the edge? Why was I so delusional?"

"That's easy. Lack of sleep and sheer mental and physical exhaustion. Three days and three nights without sleep under tumultuous conditions and we'd all be psychotic, hallucinating with the best of them. The question that's more important is why you drove yourself to such a destructive state."

"It sure as hell wasn't my plan. I was trying to navigate myself through the chaos as unemotionally as I could."

"Unemotionally?"

"Yes, without getting mixed up in all the negative emotions."

"Is that what you've always done?"

"I suppose."

"Well, what worked for you in the past, shutting yourself off from your emotions as a self defense, is not going to work for you as an adult."

"Who wants to experience bad emotions?" I scoffed.

"Anyone who wants to feel joy. Only when you learn that it's healthy to feel painful emotions will you also allow yourself to feel the full impact of pleasurable emotions." Robert leaned forward as if to emphasize his point. "Let's understand that there are no bad emotions. All emotions are good." He paused for a moment. "Take anger. What does anger do?"

I stared at him unsure.

"Anger propels you to take action. What about happiness? Happiness tells you you're doing the right thing. What about fear?"

"Fear tells you that there is danger."

"Exactly. And what about sadness? Sadness tells you there is something to grieve. Ninety percent of depression is simply bottled up grief."

I looked at him, frowning. "What about pain? What possible good can come from pain?"

"That's simple," he said. "It's from pain that we learn and grow."

It was late in the evening when I ran into Marty. He seemed unusually quiet. I told him I'd spent all afternoon talking with Robert. I tried to tell him some of the things Robert had said, hoping it might help. "You can't run from your feelings," I said. "They'll only fester and manifest themselves down the road in ways that are ten times worse."

He still looked depressed. "Do you want to talk?" I said, sensing some of the healing power Robert must feel, while wondering what was causing his depression.

"Sure, why not?" he mumbled. "I was just going to call it a

night." I followed him to his room. He stretched out on the bed, and I sat on a chair near the foot of his bed.

"So what happened?" I asked, trying to sound comforting. "How did you end up here?"

Marty sighed, shifting his position. "The judge gave me two choices, prison or here. In ninety days I go back before him."

"Prison?" I echoed, knowing I'd heard him correctly.

"I was in Germany," he cited, "working on a special research assignment. I got involved with a young German girl. I didn't know anyone. She suddenly became my whole world. All my eggs were in one basket."

"Just like me," I said.

"She was crazy. I didn't realize it at the time. I just got sucked in. I was madly in love with her. At least I thought I was . . . and then everything got insane. She had a boyfriend. He'd abused her. She'd led me to believe he was evil. She talked about him endlessly. It was sick. I just kept spiraling downward. We came up with a plan . . . we decided to castrate him."

"Jesus," I said. Suddenly I couldn't absorb another word. "I'm sorry," I sputtered, and I bolted from the room. My God, how crazy can you get? I sat on the edge of my bed, terrified, reminded of how fragile the mind can be, remembering how only a few days ago I thought I was the center of the universe. What if back at the airport someone had approached me? What if, as Marty might have done, I'd hurt someone? How does a mind even operate? Muscle and bone I can understand. I can touch them, feel them, see them, but how am I supposed to heal my mind? What in the hell is a "mind" anyway? Every minute, twenty-four hours a day, it never goes away. I can never shut it off. And then, as I discovered, bizarre thinking can happen. You can literally go insane. How can I be sure it won't happen again, especially when I don't even know how it works, where my thoughts even come from? What if in the middle of the night, in the middle of my sleep, I go crazy again?

I awoke the next morning feeling restless, feeling as though I'd been awake most of the night. But I knew where I was. I reminded myself, I know who I am. It's Saturday. My thoughts, for the moment, are clear. Then suddenly I wished Robert were around.

There'd be no group session today either. For that I was glad. There was only so much craziness I could take. I stayed by myself most of the day, avoiding Marty, feeling guilty I'd run out on him. By night-fall I'd begun to regain my balance. I'd gone all day without going bonkers. I saw Marty standing by himself in the lobby. He saun-tered toward me. "I'm sorry," he volunteered. "I shouldn't have said anything."

"No, it's not your fault. I'm just not as strong as I thought I was."

By Monday, I was looking forward to the weekday routine, Robert and Dr. Gray and even the group sessions. The weekend, I reflected, had been achingly long.

I filed into the group meeting and took my usual seat. Albert was particularly edgy. He kept jumping up from his chair. Frustrated, Nancy finally yelled out, "Albert, sit down or you're going to be confined to your room!"

Albert suddenly lurched forward, raising his fist, and snarled like an uncaged animal. Instinctively, I stood up, blocking his path to Nancy. "Put your fist down!" I shouted. Albert stood still, not sure what to do, and then slowly returned to his seat. He sat quietly for the rest of the session.

After the meeting, I lingered behind, wondering for a moment about my actions, when I overheard Dr. Gray ask Nancy, "Were you scared in there, before Jamie came to your defense?"

"Yes," she said, looking over at him. "I was."

I meandered out of the room, feeling gallant, as though I'd finally done something worthwhile.

It was two o'clock in the afternoon—time for my alone session with Dr. Gray. I was hoping for an insight, something, anything, a nugget that might prevent this from happening to me again.

Dr. Gray inquired about my mother and father, listening carefully while I talked. "I could never please my father," I said, "or myself, I suppose, for that matter."

"Is that why you set such impossible goals?"

He spoke so rarely that I focused on his question.

"I guess so," I said.

He was silent again. I knew the time was almost up.

"Even certain relationship goals can be unachievable," he said. "And it's okay to quit trying."

After dinner I went searching for Marty. We were starting to talk when the teenaged boy in my group ran up excited.

"Did you hear about Albert?"

"No."

"He escaped."

"Escaped?"

"Yes. He left the hospital."

"How the hell did he do that?"

"He dashed out the front door when somebody was coming in."

"What are they going to do?"

"I don't know. Call the police, I guess."

I thought about Albert, wondering what in the world he was doing. He could barely tie his own shoelaces let alone rummage aimlessly around Washington, D.C.

The next afternoon I met again with Robert. It had now become a daily occurrence. Without his help I realized I'd never get out of here, certainly not living on Dr. Gray's insight or two a week. We were lingering downstairs in the outdoor café when I said, "Why have you spent so much time with me?"

"I'm doing a case study for graduate school. I thought I'd use you. Is that okay?"

"I think so," I said, feeling uneasy.

"Don't worry. Your name won't be used."

Monday finally arrived. I walked into the group meeting. Everyone was there, including to my surprise —sitting quietly, dolefully in the corner—Albert. His hair had been cropped and he was wearing fresh clothes.

"What happened?"

"They caught me. I was trying to crawl into the back seat of a car and they caught me."

"Almost a month has passed since I arrived at the hospital. Dr. Gray, I think I'm ready to leave. What do you think?"

"It's what you think that matters."

"I'd like to go home."

"You can leave with my blessing under one condition. I'd like you to attend my group sessions Tuesdays and Thursdays at four o'clock. I'd like you to be an out-patient for a while."

"All right," I said. "But just tell me one thing. How can I assure this won't ever happen again?"

"Just watch for the warning signals."

"Warning signals, what are those?"

"You'll know what they are," he said.

I got up uneasily from my chair and headed back to the elevator. "Watch for the warning signals . . . you'll know what they are." What is that supposed to mean? Does it mean becoming too emotional, jumping to the wrong conclusions, not getting enough sleep, beginning to feel tired? I'd fallen apart, gone nuts, bonkers, over the edge, cuckoo. And now when I ask how to prevent it from happening again this is what I'm told?

I reached for the phone. "Mom, I can go! He said I can leave."

"When?"

"Tomorrow," I said. "I'll give you a call."

I entered the last in-group session. Harold looked particularly rested. "You look healthy today," I said, ignoring his oversized paunch.

"So do you. It looks like you've put on some weight."

"About half of it," I said. "Today's my last session."

"I heard," he replied, settling into his chair. "Let's begin. Where's Albert?"

Everyone looked around.

"I'll find him," Harold said, rising up.

We waited. Five minutes later Harold walked back into the room, laughing.

"What happened?" Nancy asked.

"I found him. He was pacing up and down the hall so I began walking beside him. 'What are you doing?' Albert asked. 'I'm pacing,' I said. He then promptly stopped and sat down. 'Well, if you're going to pace,' he said, 'then there's no point in both of us doing it.'"

After the group meeting I wandered back to my room and began packing my suitcase. Reaching for a piece of paper, I wrote down what I'd learned. Like a mantra, a psychological safety net, I'd have to keep reminding myself what I'd discovered . . . don't run from your feelings. They'll just come back later much worse. Set realistic goals. Maintain a balance. Don't put all your eggs in one basket. Deal only in reality. Over and over, I'd just have to remind myself.

I marched out to the telephone. "I'm ready, Mom. I can go now."

"Good, we'll see you when you get here."

"You're not picking me up?"

"No, you'll be fine. Just take the bus."

"The bus?"

"Yes. There's a stop in front of your building. There'll be one marked Silver Spring."

"Okay," I said, a bit nervous, and I made sure I had a few quarters.

I strolled out to the lobby in search of Marty, knowing I wouldn't see him again. There was a house rule, one I didn't understand, that required patients never to contact one another once they got out. I found him alone in his bedroom.

"I'll be thinking about you," I said. "I know I'll never forget you." I hugged him goodbye. Then I proceeded up the hallway in search of Robert, smiling and waving goodbye to Nancy along the way. Dr. Gray breezed past. "I'll see you next week," I said. "Thank you for everything."

He turned and shrugged. "It's my job."

Robert was sitting at his desk cleaning his glasses. He looked up. It occurred to me he was one of those people that looked better, more complete, in spectacles. "I don't know what to say. I don't know how to thank you."

"Sit down for one more moment," he said. I pulled out a chair and found myself searching for signs of a personal attachment.

"I've been thinking a lot about this and there's one final thing I want to tell you." He paused for a second. "It slowly dawned on me that for you not quitting was a matter of your very survival, your whole sense of self. You'd programmed yourself into thinking that not quitting in the face of failure was the next best thing to success. If you couldn't succeed you could at least kill yourself trying and somehow salvage your self worth. Your self esteem was so low that achievement at any cost had become a matter of life and death." He paused again, allowing his words to sink in. "It's only through repetition, telling yourself you are worthy, that you can gradually erase all the times you were told you weren't. Ten times a day I want you to tell yourself, 'I am a good and loveable person,' until slowly, eventually, you believe it."

"I'll try," I said. As I turned and walked down the corridor I reflected on what he'd just said.

I hauled my suitcase outdoors and stood in the hot August sun, waiting for the bus. Finally, I was free . . . broke, unemployed and unsure of myself, but at least I was free.

Chapter 64

WHAT NOW?

"I'll try not to stay too long. I just need a few weeks to get back on my feet."

"Don't be silly. This is your home," my mother said. "We've opened up the den for you. We want you to stay here as long as you like."

My father nodded.

"Thank you," I said.

The next morning my parents went to work, and I stepped out to the pool. I thought I'd have more energy but instead I discovered just making breakfast was exhausting. I tried not to think about how depleted I felt, yet the least amount of activity made me feel drained. "It will take time. You still need to rest," my mother had said, but three more days by the pool and I was already beginning to feel restless. I had to find a job. But who is going to hire me now? And what am I going to write on the application when they ask if I have any history of mental illness? If I tell the truth I'll never get hired and if I lie they'll surely find out from Ringling. And what if I do find a job and I can't take the pressure? What in the world will I do then?

I still remembered Kaufman Advertising. Their president, Fred Edelson, had liked me. He was planning to place me in their management program. I reached for the phone. "Is Mr. Edelson in?"

"One moment, please."

"Mr. Edelson? I don't know if you remember me but a couple of years ago I applied for a position with your firm. We talked about a management training program. I was hoping there might still be an opening."

"Yes, I do remember you. But I'm sorry, with this fragile economy we're not hiring right now."

I opened the phone book, encouraged he'd at least given me his time, and quickly scanned the list of advertising agencies. There were only six on the page but no one, I was told, was even interviewing. Discouraged, I shuffled out to the pool and skimmed through the classifieds. At least there were plenty of manual labor jobs listed. If worse came to worst, I could always wield a shovel. Even at $3.50 an hour I could make ends meet.

"How was your day?" my mother asked.

"It was all right, I guess. But I have to find work."

"Why?"

"Why? Because I don't have a job."

"Who said?"

"What do you mean, who said? I was fired."

"Did someone tell you that?"

"Do you mean I wasn't?"

"Unless someone said you no longer work for the circus then I assume you still do."

"You're kidding! How can I find out?"

"I don't know, why don't you give them a call?"

I hurriedly reached for the phone. "Allen, it's me, Jamie. I'm finally out of the hospital."

"Great. How are you feeling?"

"I'm fine, a little tired, but almost like new. My mother just told me I may not have been fired. I still might have a job. Is that true?"

"Of course you still have a job. We simply put you on leave of absence."

"When can I start?"

"Why don't you give me a call next week. We'll set up a time to talk. There's no need to rush."

"What will I do? I'm not sure I'm ready to go back on the road."

"That won't be necessary. You can help me here in the office. We'll discuss that when we meet."

"Fantastic! I'll call you next week." I couldn't believe it. I still worked for Ringling. And now I'd be working directly with Allen.

———

It was almost four o'clock. I looked up at the brown, brick face of the building, trying to distinguish which window I'd gazed through for so many hours. I wasn't quite sure. I glanced over at the outdoor café, half expecting to see Robert sitting with a new case study. But the tables were empty, accompanied only by a few tiny sparrows.

I pushed the elevator button for the fourth floor, wondering what to expect from Dr. Gray's out-patient group. I opened the door. Everyone was already seated. Dr. Gray calmly introduced me to the group, which included a tall, matronly looking woman he indicated was his assistant.

A thin, blond-haired woman, somewhere in her twenties, sat across from me. She was seated next to a grim faced woman, outfitted neatly in a business suit. To my right an anxious looking man wore a white shirt and tie. He was sitting a few feet apart from a plump man with glasses. I wondered if any of them had spent time in the hospital and quickly surmised none had. They didn't seem frightened enough.

Dr. Gray's assistant turned to the young woman. "You were attracted to Jamie when he came in, weren't you?"

The young woman frowned. I felt uncomfortable.

"Well, weren't you?" she repeated, baiting her for some reason.

"Not really," she said. "Well, I suppose I noticed him."

This seemed to pacify the assistant. I began to wonder who needed the most help. The discussion among the group started with little prodding. The man in the white shirt couldn't understand why he was feeling so much anger while the fat man fretted about his failure to keep a girlfriend. The up-tight woman reported she was looking again for another job and the young girl my age didn't say much of anything. She was probably still steaming from the assistant's assault. Well, at least the dialogue will be far more intelligent, I reflected. Dr. Gray's timer went off. He turned to me and asked, "What do you think?"

"I think this is great," I said. "You're neurotically nervous," I declared to the man on my right. "You're painfully insecure," I said to the heavy set man. "Your job expectations are unrealistic," I exclaimed to the businesswoman. "And you're obviously confused," I said to the young, blonde girl. "I'm sure I'll fit right in."

Everyone looked at me, stunned.

"That's it for today," Dr. Gray whispered.

I exited the room, aware I'd just been incredibly rude, yet pleased for some reason with my instant analysis.

***

Mid-morning I heard a knock on the door. A policeman was holding a clipboard in one hand and a brown envelope in the other.

"Are you Jamie MacVicar?"

"Yes," I said.

"Could you please sign here?"

He left and I opened the envelope.

It was official. I was now divorced. I took a deep breath, allowing the finality to wash over me, then placed it in the bottom of my dresser drawer.

***

It was Tuesday when I called Allen, still early in the week, but I was anxious to see him.

"How about three o'clock Friday?" he said, and I could tell he was stalling, making sure I had even more time to mend.

"I'll be there," I replied.

I was a few minutes late to Dr. Gray's out-patient session. The group had already arrived. I sat back, hoping to learn from everyone's problems, when the wiry woman grumbled that I was dead wrong. She certainly didn't have a problem holding onto a job. The thin man wanted to know why I'd spent a month in the hospital and the fat man demanded to know why I thought he was so insecure. Even the young woman, who supposedly liked me, said, "Where do you get off telling me I'm confused?"

"How did I get to be the focus?" I asked.

"What did you expect," Dr. Gray interjected, "after you lambasted everyone at the end of the last session?"

I quickly ate lunch. It was Friday afternoon and I'd finally be meeting with Allen. Apprehensively, I rode the bus downtown, wondering what type of reception I'd receive.

"How are you?" he asked, rising tentatively from behind his desk.

"I'm fine," I said. "It's good to be here. I guess I was in pretty bad shape the last time you saw me."

"Have a seat," he said, still smiling, and he motioned me to one of the chairs. Mike Franks strode into the room. We shook hands and he promptly sat down.

"Just Jamie and me for now, if you don't mind," Allen said. "Of course," Mike replied, and he quickly exited the office.

A momentary silence filled the room so I began telling Allen what I'd learned, how my self worth, I discovered, had been tied to a sense of accomplishment. How meeting his goals had unwittingly taken on such importance.

"Yes, but you doubled the goals I gave you," Allen said.

"I know," I replied. And then I couldn't help asking, "Why didn't you stop me?"

"I didn't want to stifle your drive."

"I see," I said, hesitantly, wondering if I'd have even listened. I mentioned a few other insights I'd learned. To my surprise, he mumbled, "I had some problems growing up myself. As a kid I was constantly getting into fights."

He paused for a minute so I asked, "Have other promoters had problems on the road? Should the structure perhaps be examined?"

"We've had a few other situations, but I can't change the corporate structure over two or three incidents."

I nodded, passing over his answer, yet I felt disappointed that what had happened hadn't made more impact. "What can I do for the company now?"

"Actually, there are two things. We could use a Director of Promotions, a gatherer of materials for any promoter who wants to know what the other promoters are doing. And secondly, I need to improve our marketing manual for the new trainees."

"Great," I said. "But don't we have a pretty effective manual?"

"Yes, but it's outdated. The supervisors want you to tinker with something new."

"I'll do my best. When can I start?"

"How about next week?"

I strolled excitedly out of the office. Director of Promotions while single handedly improving our manual? What an opportunity! I pushed the elevator button to the fifth floor, stepped out and walked into Mike Franks' office.

Mike came around from his desk. "There's a restaurant on the corner. Can I buy you a cup of coffee?"

We ambled across the street. I told him about my discussion with Allen, all about the manual, and the task of gathering up the promotional materials.

"That's great," he said. "What else did Allen say?" And he seemed a little worried.

The waitress brought over two cups of coffee. "That's about it," I replied.

Mike looked up. "I should have stayed in Terre Haute," he began, and I sensed he wasn't just trying to cover his rear. "You looked tired, but I thought you were going to be all right. As for your drive, I knew you were ambitious, but just like we'd played tennis, I thought you were being competitive."

"It's not your fault," I said, relieving if I could his concern. "What happened to me was probably going to happen sooner or later anyway."

We talked a few more minutes, mainly about his ideas for the manual. "If there is anything I can do to help", Mike said, "just let me know."

~~~

It was a sunny, Saturday morning. I grabbed a legal pad and walked out to the pool. Propping the pad on my knees I began to sketch out the manual, drawing how the binder cover might appear. I penciled in a title and began illustrating a series of tabs.

"What are you doing?"

I glanced up. My father was hovering nearby.

"I'm working on the manual."

"It's Saturday. Why don't you put that away. There will be plenty of time to start on Monday."

Reluctantly, I put it down. "You're right," I said. "Monday will get here soon enough."

Later that evening a familiar song came on the radio. I quickly reached over and turned it off.

"Why did you do that?" my mother asked.

"I just don't care for it," I said, feeling a wave of fear churn in my stomach. It seemed like only yesterday that I opened the doors and watched as the patients danced gently to its rhythm.

The first thing I did when I arrived at the office was pull out an old, steel desk from one of the promoter's cubicles and place it at the head of the room so I wouldn't feel so hidden. I was arranging a pad on the top of my desk when Al Atkinson walked in.

"Welcome back," he announced.

"Thank you," I replied.

"How about lunch today? I'll get you acquainted with company headquarters."

I accepted, reflecting how calm he behaved, considering how deranged I appeared when I burst into Allen's office. "I'll see you at noon."

I strolled down to Felix Salmaggi's creative department to see what samples he had before stretching out the existing promotional materials along the wall.

"It's good to see you," Felix said, "You look good." Then he shook his head. "I don't know about those guys upstairs. They hire these kids, send them out into the middle of nowhere, and then a year or two later they're shocked when someone comes back on a stretcher."

I told him what I was looking for, feeling as though I'd just received absolution. He opened an old file cabinet drawer.

"This is it," he said. "Other than one or two promoters nobody sends me anything."

I took what he had—two yellowed newspaper clippings that touted a color-the-clown contest—and told him the promoters will just have to start sending me new materials.

Al Atkinson and I walked up to Gusti's and chose a covered table outside. "What exactly do you do these days?" I asked, knowing that years ago he too had been a promoter.

"I'm sort of Allen's trouble shooter. Occasionally I'll go into a town and help out a promoter. But lately I've been assigned to ticket orders, that, and negotiating the price of our printed materials."

Listening to him describe his role I had the impression he was beginning to feel underused, but not yet enough to go anywhere else.

"There's something I want to tell you," he said, and I wondered if this was the purpose of our luncheon. "You guys out on the road think of headquarters as this organized, efficient support system. Well, it's not. I just want to warn you not to expect something that it isn't."

I returned from lunch and shuffled hesitantly down to the accounting department. I had committed a fireable offense. And even if it cost me my job I knew I had to confess. Joe Kastner was sitting behind his desk. "Joe, I did a terrible thing."

He gave me a look of concern.

"I literally didn't have money to eat. I've never stolen anything in my life. I'm sorry, but I wrote a check to myself for twenty dollars in Evansville. I'll pay it back as soon as I can."

"Don't worry," he said. "We'll just chalk it up to extenuating circumstances."

Mike Franks seemed preoccupied when I entered his office. His feet were propped up on his desk. "Here," he said, "you'll need to take care of this," and he handed me a newspaper clipping. "Send them a couple of T-shirts or something."

I stared at the paper. It was the front page of the *Terre Haute Times*. Above a picture of a forlorn girl and boy, the headline read, "King and Queen Dethroned." The article went on to report how the two children had sat patiently and then dejectedly as the ushers swept past while they watched a set of imposters take their rightful place. I remembered the usher panting at my office door, panicked that he couldn't find the winners. I turned to Mike, "I'll take care of it," I said, and regretfully I glanced again at their photos.

For the next four days I worked on the manual, combining a few forms, lessening the paperwork and improving the overall clarity. I showed the results to Mike Franks. He was impressed. "It's exactly what we needed," he said.

The phone on my desk rang. It was Allen's secretary. "Allen would like to see you," Maureen said. "There's something he'd like to discuss."

"I'll be right up," I replied, excited he had something he might want me to do. I could also advise him on the progress of the manual.

"What's this all about?" he said. Glumly, he handed me a letter. It was written by an attorney on union stationery, Local 127, Evansville, Indiana. I quickly read it. The letter was on behalf of the musicians' foreman in Evansville. He was suing the circus, stating he'd been stiffed out of his commission.

"It's true, I'm afraid. I didn't pay him his commission. He gave me a group of decrepit musicians that could barely play. I thought Bill Pruyn would have a fit."

"Okay," Allen interrupted. I handed him back the letter. "I needed to know the facts."

On the way back I stopped by Al Atkinson's office. "Don't worry," he said. "Allen's just sensitive on this issue. He's been conducting a lengthy negotiation with the national musician's union to limit the number of locals we're required to hire."

It was Friday, the end of the week, and I was busily completing the manual when Bobby Collins marched in, depositing his briefcase in one of the cubicles.

"Where have you been?" I asked, anxious to hear some news from the front.

"Cincinnati," he said. "How are you doing?"

"I'm fine," I said, trying to sound cheerful, and I filled him in on the preparation of the manual plus the need for more promotional samples.

Bobby spent the day filing away his notes and typing an appraisal for the next promoter. "Have you heard anything from your friend, Sam Barrett?" he asked. I told him the last thing I'd heard, he'd gone back to Texas. Then he asked about Brad Rosenburg.

"He's still promoting the Freedom Train as far as I know," I said. "Rumor has it, now that he's divorced, he's dating Nancy Pond, our former secretary."

"So I've heard. Speaking of dating," Bobby said, "are you seeing anyone?"

"No," I said, the idea of seeing someone having been far from my thoughts.

"Good," he said. "There's a friend of mine who lives here in town. Her name is Charlene. I think she'd like to meet you."

Chapter 65
AFRAID

"Hi, this is Charlene. I'm a friend of Bobby Collins'."

"How are you?" I said, a little surprised by the phone call.

"I understand you're a promoter like Bobby."

"Yes . . . well, at least I was. I'm here in the office for a while."

"Bobby told me." She hesitated for a moment. "I thought you might need a friend . . . we've met, you know."

"We have?"

"I was visiting Bobby in Cleveland. You left me a ticket in the will-call window. I thanked you. You were busy at the time."

"I think I remember," I said, and I tried to recall her face. We talked for a few minutes. Her voice was kind, and I was grateful for her efforts to connect. Finally, I sputtered clumsily, "Perhaps you'd like to get together? Maybe have a pizza or something?"

"Sure, I'd like that."

"I'm staying with my parents right now. I don't have a car."

"That's no problem. I'll pick you up. Would tomorrow night be okay?"

The next morning I showed Mike Franks the final manual. I'd placed the reorganized pages in a three-ring binder for his review. He leafed carefully through the tabs. "This is good. Have you shown it to Allen yet?"

"No, I'm going upstairs right now."

Allen was talking on the phone when Maureen motioned me in. He was laughing about something and I overheard him say a word about Datsun automobiles. Finally he hung up the receiver. "Damn, I could sell ice to the Eskimos!"

He sat up, still grinning. "I just closed a deal with Datsun. In exchange for the inside cover of the program plus free tickets in several cities they're going to feature us in their national advertising."

"Great!" I said, sharing in his excitement. "You make a hell of a promoter."

"That I can do. I can't do anything else but that I can do." He smiled, reaching for a cigar. "If my wife wants me to do something around the house, I tell her, 'If you so much as need a light bulb changed go to the Yellow Pages. I wouldn't even know which way to turn it. But if you need a city promoted, if that's what you need? Don't go anywhere else. Come directly to me. I'm your man!'"

I handed him the manual, taking advantage of his good spirits, and carefully pointed out the changes I'd made.

"This looks good. Be sure and show it to the three supervisors."

I started to leave, but he began again, this time in a more serious tone. "You know, this is the best I've felt in weeks. I've been in a real slump, emotionally lethargic. I think it was the agreement I negotiated with the musicians' union. The transaction took me over a year. People said it couldn't be done. And then when I did it, when I'd conquered the mountain, I suddenly felt empty. Now what am I supposed to do? Everything else seemed insignificant. You know what I mean?"

He was silent for a moment, reflective. Then he stood up and shook my hand. "Good job on the manual."

I stood in the parking lot waiting for Charlene. It had begun to drizzle, giving the air a balmy aroma. Suddenly a small, tan Nova pulled up and a blond-haired woman stuck her head out the window. "Jamie. Hi, I'm Charlene. Get in."

I climbed inside, still not recognizing her. But she had a beautiful face and an easy manner.

"I know a nice restaurant" she said.

We ordered a pizza, and I soon found myself telling her what had happened, figuring Bobby Collins had already told her something.

I sensed a non-judgmental tone in her voice. She told me she was from a village in Pennsylvania. "Population three hundred," she said. "And when I told my parents I was leaving to get medical training my father bawled out, 'Who do you think you are?'"

"That must have been hard," I said.

"The pressure was enormous. You just weren't expected to leave."

She drove me home. There was something strong and stable about her. I leaned over and kissed her good night.

"Can we see each other again?"

"I'd like that," she said.

I mailed a copy of the manual to Ricker and Rosenwasser, requesting their comments, then returned to the few newspaper promotions I had laid out on the floor. I puzzled over why only Chris Bursky had responded to my memo asking for samples. Nor apparently were any of the promoters interested in what I might already have. I guess they're just busy, I surmised, and I wondered why even Allen hadn't called in days.

My father was grilling steaks on the back porch. I wandered out and watched him stand guard over the coals. Like most evenings, other than when I was visiting Charlene, I felt the safest staying close to home.

"Where does Charlene live?" he inquired, putting down his barbeque fork.

"She lives in a house, kind of a group house, with three other roommates."

He tightened his coat, seemingly studying the steaks. "Do you know what you need? What you need is to be alone, to go away somewhere all by yourself." He paused for a moment. "Go out in the woods, camping or something, for a few days."

"Why?"

"To lessen your fears. To prove to yourself you'll be fine."

He was right. Other than in my cavernous office I hadn't spent much time by myself. It seemed as though being alone was how it all started. I couldn't tell him that at times I was still scared of my own thoughts, that sometimes driving alone in their car, I'd ask myself, what if I went crazy again? What if some voice inside my head told me to veer off the side of the road, right into a tree? Then I'd test myself, "One . . . two . . . three . . . do it! . . . four . . . five . . . six. . . ." I'd get to ten and breathe a sigh of relief, proving momentarily that even if I demanded I do something crazy, I still wouldn't do it.

"You're right," I said, as he stepped back from the smoke. "I guess for now I just still feel a little uneasy."

—————

I sat in the office and stared out at the empty space in front of me, glancing at my watch for the five hundredth time, remembering how busy I used to be. It was Thursday, almost three o'clock. Thank God I at least had my group session to attend.

Dr. Gray was being unusually participative and the group was actively engaged, but for some reason today I felt frustrated. How was this truly going to work? "Doctor Gray, are two hours a week really going to lead us to the insights we need?"

"It will," he said, speaking softly, "if you understand the time in between is as important as the time in session. It's the time you need, consciously and unconsciously, to process what you've heard."

—————

"My talent is comfort," Charlene said, teasingly, and I found myself spending more and more time in her home. Her room was near the back porch, a snug room with ruffled curtains and fluffy pillows. Whatever we were missing in intensity, I decided, we seemed to gain in stability. "I get lonely alone," she said, and I sensed she enjoyed being needed. Late one evening she whispered, "You could move in here with me you know."

"What would your roommates say?"

"I'll talk to them," she said. "I'm sure they'll be fine."

Her suggestion for now was the perfect solution. I wasn't ready to move out on my own, but it was time I broke away from my parents.

"I think I'm going to move in with Charlene," I announced at the dinner table.

"Are you sure?" my mother asked.

"Not completely," I said, wavering a little, "but I can't stay here forever. I guess it's the right thing to do."

"When?"

"Friday," I said, "sometime late afternoon."

Friday afternoon I was packing my suitcase when I heard the front door ease open. "I thought I'd come home early to see you off," my father said, and he walked slowly past the bedroom.

A moment later I heard the back door swing open. I folded my clothes, being careful to pack everything, what little I had. I squeezed the lids shut and carted the suitcase down the hallway, past the kitchen and dining room and turned left out the screen door. My father was sitting quietly on the back stoop, holding a beer, looking off in the distance.

"Well, I guess it's time to give it another try," I said.

He glanced up and his eyes were misty. He tried to say goodbye but he was too upset to say anything at all.

Chapter 66
FREE

Winter was coming on and the days in the office seemed interminably long. Each morning I'd call my father and we'd chat for a few minutes. Then for the rest of the day I'd pretend I had something to do. I couldn't stand this much longer, even if I did need the insurance to pay for Dr. Gray's group sessions. Maybe Allen was just being kind, allowing me to get back on my feet. Maybe he just didn't know what to do with me. But this was the death of a thousand cuts. I'd rather do anything than just stare at the same walls all day.

Charlene strolled into the bedroom. "Hi, hon, how was your day?"

"All right," I replied, too embarrassed to tell her I'd spent it with little to do. She stood near the closet and suddenly I felt queasy, never knowing what stupid reminder would unsettle me. If I told her she'd probably think I was still crazy. What am I going to say? Please don't wear your nurse's uniform around me. It reminds me of a month I'm trying to forget.

"What are we having for dinner tonight?" she asked, changing to a pair of jeans.

"Anything you like," I said, relieved to see her closet door close.

The phone on my desk rang. It was Allen. "I'm looking for a give-away item, something kids can take home with them and keep. How about seeing if you can come up with something?"

"You bet!" I said. "I'll get right on it."

For the rest of the week I scoured my brain for ideas, researching catalogues and advertising specialty shops, eager for a solution. Finally I prepared a list of items and hurried upstairs to see Allen. He scanned the list. "Everything looks too expensive. I don't want to spend more than ten cents apiece." Then he looked up and mumbled, "Just leave me the list." I walked back downstairs empty handed. For the next few days I tried to think of something new, offering a few ideas, but it was obvious Allen's interest had waned.

The young blonde girl announced that she would no longer be coming to the group sessions. The way she told us it sounded as though she was reading from a script. She was moving to another city, she said, but added that she felt she had made progress. Everyone said goodbye and murmured encouragement, but I sensed no one felt that for her they'd had much affect.

The manual arrived. Thirty brand new copies. I proudly touched it, luxuriating in the textured contours of the cover, feeling as though I'd accomplished something important, applying a talent for detail and structure to an instructor's manual for future trainees.

I drove home, still ebullient, and strode into the bedroom. I was surprised to see Charlene sitting pensively on the side of the bed. "Anything wrong?" I asked.

"My house mates, actually one in particular, have begun to complain. It's not you. She hardly knows you, but just having a man in the house makes her feel awkward. I'll try to talk to her some more."

"Maybe it would be better if I found my own place," I said.

"We could get a place together?" she said, and she began to bite her fingernails.

"No," I said, not wanting to hurt her feelings. "Perhaps I should try some time on my own."

The next day I looked in the newspaper under furnished apartments and spotted an affordable efficiency. "At least I won't need furniture," I said. "And the advertisement boasts of dramatic views."

Charlene and I drove out to the apartment. It was a high-rise, a red brick building perched on a Virginia hillside overlooking the airport and the city. We rode the elevator to the eleventh floor where a well dressed woman was waiting. As soon as she opened the door a beautiful nighttime view of the city twinkled before us. Red car lights shone through the window and streamed past the Pentagon, over the river toward the Lincoln Memorial and white domed Capitol.

"I'll take it," I said, glancing at a sofa bed and a tiny kitchen all encapsulated into one single room.

The next day I moved in. It only took a few minutes to unpack my belongings. I was anxious to experience the friendly ambiance of a high-rise apartment that I'd so often heard advertised. But other than muffled conversations from behind closed doors, I didn't see a soul. I returned to my apartment feeling strangely isolated. Maybe it's the season, I reflected, and I glanced out the window, grateful Charlene would soon be over.

For the hundredth time I sat at my desk feeling useless, any feelings of accomplishment having long since vanished, but today for some reason I felt particularly exasperated. As long as I stay here, I reflected, I won't look for another job, but if I quit, at least then I'll be *forced* to find another job. With a full scale effort I ought to be employed in a matter of weeks. Whatever I do, I have to do something. Who knows? Maybe publishing? Books have always interested me. I reached for the phone and called Maureen. "Do you think I could see Allen?"

I walked to the elevator, propelled more by impulse than rational thought, still hoping there might be another outcome. I took a seat outside his office and waited for Maureen to escort me in.

"Allen," I said, blurting my thoughts before I changed my mind. "I've made a decision. I've decided to resign. As much as I appreciate what you've done for me, I feel as though it's time to move on."

Allen appeared unsurprised, maybe even a little relieved. "I support your decision," he said. I felt myself start to weaken. "I've often worried," he said, "what if something should happen to me? Who would explain your position?"

His words sounded hollow. I could tell he was trying to solidify my decision. But I couldn't go back on the road and I couldn't go on like this. "Did you mean what you said about the Savannah bonus?"

"No problem," he said. "We'll mail the check to you next week."

"If you hear of anything I'd be grateful if you'd let me know."

"I will," he said. "In fact, I'll make a few calls."

"Thank you," I said, feeling amazed I'd actually done it. I returned to my office and called Charlene. Then I rode the elevator down to the lobby and exited the front door, inhaling a deep breath of cool, crisp air. I did it. I quit. What I was going to do now I didn't have the foggiest idea. But I knew one thing for sure, the days of feeling useless were over!

Chapter 67
UNEMPLOYED

I looked out my apartment window. The days had begun to turn gray. People below scurried to the bus stop, joining others already waiting in overcoats, huddled within themselves.

Well, at least they had somewhere to go, I thought. Perhaps my decision to quit wasn't so smart after all. True, now I was forced to find a job, but at least then I had an identity. Now, barely a week later, I wasn't sure what I was qualified to do. Sure, there was a litany of things I used to do, but now they seemed disconnected, unnecessary in the real world.

I reached for the newspaper. It was far too early to be discouraged, even if the country was still in a recession. Unemployment was high and so was inflation but my father had said, "there's always a good job for a good man." He also warned there won't be much hiring until after the holidays.

I opened the classifieds to the heading marked advertising. A local ad agency was searching for an account executive but having a "following" was a stated prerequisite. An association was in need of an art director, and lastly a small suburban paper was looking for a space salesman, paying only a straight commission. I turned to the management section hoping a company might be hunting for a marketing director, trying carefully to flush out the marketing management ads from those that were just looking for salesmen. One ad in particular caught my attention: "International company looking for marketing managers. Fast growth. 20K plus a year. Only marketing professionals need apply."

I quickly dialed the number, spilling out my qualifications to a young woman who answered the phone.

"You sound perfect," she said. "Could you be here tomorrow at one o'clock?"

"Of course!" I said, having been told I'd be meeting with the Vice President himself, Mr. Williams.

That afternoon the phone rang. To my surprise it was Allen Bloom.

"Jamie, I think I've found a job for you! The only catch," he said, "is the job is in St. Louis. The arena is looking for a promotion director."

"I see," I said, disappointed. "I'm afraid for now I'm going to stay closer to home." I hung up, thanking him again, grateful he'd done what he'd said he would do.

Charlene walked in carrying a lovely green house plant. "I thought this might cheer you up. How did your day go?"

"Wonderful," I said. "Allen Bloom called. There's a job in St. Louis." Sensing her alarm, I quickly added, "I told him it was too far away. Other than that, still no calls yet to any of the resumes I've mailed, but I've got my first interview tomorrow."

"You do?" she said, returning from the kitchen with water for the plant. "What's the job?"

"I'm not really sure. I was so excited I forgot to ask."

I'd read somewhere that the best way to look for a job is to treat the hunt itself as a job. Be up and dressed and sitting at the table prepared to spend the next eight hours selling a worthy product. The phone sat ready on the table along with a legal pad, pen and an orderly row of newspaper clippings. I'm a one-man business, I told myself, the boss, the employee and a hell of a product.

Feeling emboldened, I picked up the phone. This was a bit of a stretch but what harm could it cause? The ad read, "Senior Executives. Top management and marketing positions. 40K plus. Executive Recruiters. Call Mr. Levine."

"Levine here," a man snapped. Instantly I detected a sharp nasal tone.

"Good morning, sir. I saw your ad, and though I've not served in senior management I've had considerable responsibility."

"How old are you?"

"Twenty-four."

Click. The line went dead.

I looked at the receiver. Was there something wrong with the phone or did he just hang up on me? I quickly re-dialed the number.

"Levine here."

"We were just speaking. Did you hang up on me?"

"That's right. I've got no interest in speaking to a twenty-four-year-old."

Click.

An hour had passed by the time I returned from my irate walk. What an obnoxious bastard! How rude can you get? I could still hear his voice and the sound of the phone go dead. I hopped in the shower determined to not let him ruin my day, especially the day of my first interview. Gradually my focus shifted. I wondered what Mr. Williams would look like, no doubt a distinguished looking man. They had said that the firm was an international company, so surely they'll see my travel as an asset. Maybe there will even be travel overseas?

I parked behind a mid-rise white office building and checked my tie in the rear view mirror one more time. "Suite 100," she had said. I noticed the lobby looked surprisingly plain. I walked past the elevators and peered down a corridor. Midway on the left, a sign had been posted on an open door, "Cooper Industries, Suite 100." I looked in. Two men and a woman were seated amidst twenty or so empty chairs while a man holding a pipe relaxed in front, leaning against a dark wooden desk. He looked up and smiled, "Come in," he said.

"I'm here for a one o'clock meeting with Mr. Williams."

"Have a seat," he said, smiling again.

I sat down feeling uneasy. Whatever was going on, this wasn't what I'd expected. I studied the man at the front of the room. Weathered and grandfatherly, he was dressed in a sweater and tweed sports coat. And in between puffs on his pipe he glanced warmly at a large dog sleeping at his feet. "This is Molly, my retriever," he exclaimed to the room. "She follows me everywhere."

I sat in silence as a half-dozen other people filed into the room and were told to take a seat. Most of them looked as confused as I was, even though a few of them looked on in eager anticipation.

Finally the man moved away from the desk, steadied his voice and began to speak. "I'm here to tell you about a new career, one in which through the dint of your drive and perseverance you can have success beyond your wildest imagination." The dog began to stir. "This isn't a career for everyone, but for those that succeed, not only are there financial rewards, but one day you might even rise to a position of sales management. But first, like anything else, you have to prove yourself." Then he reached behind the desk and pulled out a vacuum cleaner. "Cooper," he said. "How many of you have heard the name Cooper?"

I couldn't believe it. This was the international management job? Resume in hand, I was sitting in a group interview learning how to become a vacuum cleaner salesman? I listened in a state of morbid curiosity while he talked about how to get referrals from friends and family. Then he said, "Sitting in the office adjacent to me is Mr. Williams, the Vice President of Sales. Those of you that don't have it in you to be a Cooper salesman are free to go. But for those of you that would like to stay, Mr. Williams will now gladly interview you one at a time."

Quietly, along with three others, I exited the room. We didn't say a word to one another. It was one of those moments, I thought, when the act of leaving was more than enough to suffice.

"How was the interview?" Charlene asked that night.

"It wasn't quite what I expected," I said. And in an act of kindness, she left it at that.

＊

"Sometimes when there's nothing going on, when there aren't any interviews scheduled for the day, you can always just drop in on a company's personnel office and hand off your resume," my father said, trying to be helpful.

"Have you ever gotten a job that way?"

"No, but what have you got to lose?"

Another week had gone by without a single nibble. What the hell? Maybe he was right. So dressed in my best suit, accented by my brown leather briefcase, I took the Metro bus to Farragut Square. All around me people walked briskly by with important places to be. Pretending I was one of them, I marched alongside for three city blocks, then bravely entered the lobby of a tall glass building. But as I stared at the registry of companies, reading and rereading the roster, I was suddenly back to myself. Unemployed. This was a stupid, depressing idea . . . but I was here. I might as well give it a try.

The receptionist glanced at me blankly. "I'm afraid we don't have any employment applications to fill out."

"No, of course not," I said, awkwardly. "I was hoping I could leave a resume . . . just in case."

She took the resume and I backed out hastily. I took a deep breath, beholding a long hallway and a row of other offices. Slowly I walked past several glass doors, nervously smiling at a few of the secretaries. This was ridiculous. This wasn't a minimum wage position I was applying for. How can I possibly get a job this way? Scolding myself for my lack of resolve, I stepped into the last office.

"Do you mind if I drop off a resume?" I asked, and without waiting for an answer I did so and retreated. Then feeling as though the size of the accomplishment was in direct proportion to the discomfort I felt, I promptly boarded a bus back home.

"This may take longer than I thought," I said to Charlene. I paused, feeling sorry for myself, "Christmas may be pretty bleak this year. I'm already a third of the way through my savings."

"Have you thought about applying for unemployment?"

"What do you mean?" I asked, not telling her I viewed such an act as a last resort . . . for people who had given up all hope.

"You paid into it. Why not take it? It *is* your money and that's what it's there for."

I couldn't argue with her logic, even if emotionally I still felt like I was stealing from the system.

The unemployment office was located at 500 C Street. "May I see your last pay stub?" the administrator asked. Then confirming my address, she said, "A check will be mailed each week." I simply had to fill out a card indicating at least three jobs I'd applied for the prior week and mail it back in.

"You mean I don't have to come back?"

"Not unless you want to," she said. She took out a calculator. "You'll be receiving $93.00 per week."

"Thank you," I said, and I got up and stepped out, past the long line of registrants, hoping, whether the money was rightfully mine or not, I'd never have to do this again.

Despite my crushing need for something to do, I was tempted to skip the session at Dr. Gray's. Perhaps, I reasoned, this was the beginning of my ability to let go. But then as I walked down the street, I found myself obsessing again, wondering if I'd ever have a tranquil day or even an hour when I wasn't acutely aware of what had happened. I passed others and I studied their faces, and it seemed obvious they'd never had a like experience. I was envious that the daily, terrifying fear of the loss of self, even their own sanity probably never even crossed their minds. I opened the lobby door, suddenly relieved that for the next hour I wouldn't be alone.

It was the young business woman's turn to be the focus. Sitting upright, poised and well dressed as usual, she'd been complaining for several minutes about her parents' permissiveness, how their lack of discipline had led to her inability to stick to anything, from jobs to relationships to a bit of everything, when Dr. Gray's assistant broke in. "How long are you going to be a victim?"

She looked up surprised. "What do you mean?"

"I mean, when are you going to take control of your life? That was then. This is now. Nothing good will come from staying a victim."

After my experience with Levine I was gun-shy of employment agencies, but Snyder and Snyder was everywhere.

I soon found myself sitting in a cubicle in front of a pudgy faced man. And suddenly it was as though we had never spoken.

"What ad was that?" he asked. And I fished out the clipping from my wallet.

"I think that job was filled," he said. "But let's see what else we've got."

He opened a tin box, and I watched as his stubby fingers began leafing through a series of index cards.

"Here's one," he said. "An automotive parts company." It quickly became clear to me that he had no intention of matching my experience to a position. Frustrated, I watched as he fumbled through the box, occasionally picking up the phone and leaving a message behind.

"Aren't there any management trainee positions?" I asked, more to clarify my stated goals than to elicit a response.

He closed the box and looked up at me. I could tell he hated what he did for a living. "No, I'm afraid not," he said, eking out a smile. "Why don't you give me a call in a few weeks?"

I got up and left, feeling misled from the beginning, but somehow feeling sorrier for him than I did for myself.

It was a little after five o'clock. I stared out the window, watching as the first round of government workers stepped off the bus. It felt strangely comforting watching them return home, as though the end of their day gave me permission to quit worrying about mine. In fact, for the next three days, there was fortunately nothing more I could do. Christmas was Sunday, and Charlene had asked me to join her and her family in Pennsylvania.

We drove up I-270, north toward Harrisburg, past rolling hills and farms, arriving at a house on a small hill overlooking the tiny hamlet of McEvansville. Smoke spiraled from a chimney, and like in a storybook, two pies sat cooling on a window sill.

Charlene's mother greeted us warmly while her father, a giant bullfrog of a man, pondered me from a living room chair. Finally, after a few minutes of silence, he shook his head. "I don't know about my daughter. She used to bring home such big, strapping fellows."

For the next three days, we mingled with aunts and uncles and cousins. I was amazed at their self-sufficiency. They chopped their own wood, canned their own vegetables and when deer season started, they gratefully packed their outdoor freezers with venison. I was further surprised by how much food preoccupied their thoughts. When they weren't cooking it, they were talking about it. "What do you think of this?" her father asked me one morning at seven a.m., handing me a slab of frozen meat.

"It's nice," I said, handing it back.

"We're having it for dinner," he said, proudly placing it on the counter to thaw.

Christmas afternoon I followed Charlene's cousin and his son through frozen fields, looking for rabbits in the hedgerows. I declined their offer to shoot. Instead, crunching through snow and rotting corn stalks, I reveled in the peacefulness that comes from such wide open places.

The next morning, feeling refreshed, well-fed and surprisingly renewed, Charlene and I packed the car. Her father strolled out with two bags of groceries. We said our goodbyes, turned south and headed slowly back to Washington.

Jerry's Restaurants, a national chain of twenty-four hour-a-day restaurants, was looking for management trainees. "Long hours—holidays and weekends," the ad read. Just what I need. Well, at least they were honest. The ad went on to tout, "excellent benefits and rapid advancement."

I dialed the number, pretending I was just what they were looking for. I'd had my fill of the restaurant business working my way through school, but at least it was an interview. And even if I didn't take the job, it sure would be nice to get an offer.

"Howard Johnson's Motel, Route 50 in Fairfax," I was told. "Room 312." I walked up an outside set of stairs and knocked on the door.

"Come in," said a man, wearing a white shirt and navy blue tie, motioning me to a chair by the window. A second man stood in the middle of the room. He too wore the same shirt and tie. If it wasn't for the fact that his skin was black, they could have been twins.

I looked around the room, surprised they hadn't converted it to a makeshift office. It was simply the standard hotel room with two double beds and a dresser consuming most of the space.

"I'll be the person conducting the interview," the man who had opened the door said. "We have a suite of two rooms. We're both conducting interviews all day." The black man nodded in agreement and then disappeared into the adjacent room.

We exchanged a few pleasantries. Then I couldn't resist asking, "Why does the job require such long hours? Doesn't that simply burn out your trainees?"

"That's exactly the point. The training is meant to be grueling. We want to see who will make it and who won't."

Now I was certain I didn't want the job. "I see," I said.

"The first thing I want you to do is fill out this application," he said, handing me three pages with a series of questions and blank lines. "I'll be back in a few minutes and we'll review it together." I settled more deeply into the chair and pulled out my pen.

The first page asked the standard information. The second page was an essay question, which I filled out diligently, telling them just what I thought they wanted to hear about why I wanted a career with Jerry's, and the third page was a litany of personal history questions.

I was midway through the third page when I suddenly stopped. There it was, vibrating off the page, "Have you had any history of mental illness in the past five years?" I stared at the question. This was my chance. What would happen if I told the truth? I'd always assumed I'd be immediately rejected but did I really know how they'd react? Why not find out with a job I didn't want? Carefully, methodically, I wrote, "Yes, I recently had a nervous breakdown."

A moment later, the door to the other room opened. "Are you done?" the man in the white shirt asked. He took the application and sat on the corner of the bed. I watched him as his eyes read the first page . . . the second . . . and then shifted to the third. Suddenly, as though he'd lodged something in his windpipe, his eyes fixated on the page. His lips turned into a frown. Without looking up he said, "I'll be back in a minute," and application in hand, he retreated into the adjacent room, closing the door behind.

Well, I'd certainly gotten my money's worth. I sat up. I expected a reaction, but this was more than I'd bargained for. Becoming more amused than shocked, I couldn't wait to see what happened next.

I waited for several minutes. Then the door finally opened. Both men walked into the room, only now it was the black man who was carrying my application. Still standing, he loomed over me and, with a look of gravity and a voice that was incredulous, he opened the application, placing his finger on the dubious question. "Would you care to explain this?"

As calmly as I could, observing that their expressions remained perplexed, I gave them a condensed version. Leaving out the unnecessary details, I focused on overwork as the chief culprit. "But I've learned my lesson," I said. "And in certain ways, perhaps I'm better off than those that never have."

They both looked at me in silence, solemnly, and then almost in unison said, "Thank you for coming in. We'll let you know."

I shook their hands and walked back down the steps to my car, safe and secure in one thing. Now I knew. And I'd never do that again.

Two days later a form letter arrived from Jerry's. I'd at least hoped for something more personal. "I'm sorry we can't at this time accept your application."

Surprised only by the speed of the response, I calmly walked over and placed it in the trash can.

~~~~***~~~~

Why was I so stupid to quit a job without having a job? I opened my checkbook. Three and a half months had passed. My Savannah bonus had long been spent and the unemployment checks barely covered the rent. Just as I was spiraling into despair the phone rang. "Good morning," my father said. "I was thinking," he said. "You've always mentioned publishing. There is a man I once knew, an executive for National Geographic. He's probably nearing retirement but here's his number. His name is Paul Oesur."

"Thank you," I said, and before I could find a reason to hesitate I dialed the number.

I could tell Mr. Oesur was elderly by the strain in his voice. "I know you probably don't personally have an opening," I said, "but I was wondering if I could just stop by and ask your advice." He paused, and perhaps sensing my desperation, murmured all right.

Mr. Oesur, I could easily see, was a dignified man. He was also very old. But he listened patiently as I described my search. Then shakily he reached for a pad of paper. "This man owns a printing company, Colortone Press, but he also owns a small publishing company, Acropolis Books."

I looked at the paper and next to a phone number he'd written, "Al Hackl."

"Thank you," I said, as effusively as I could. As his eyes shifted back to his desk, I quietly left the room.

~~~~***~~~~

As soon as I had mentioned Paul Oesur to Al Hackl he replied he'd be delighted to meet me. I glanced down at the directions Al Hackl had given me and drove up 16th Street, past stately mansions built during Washington's gilded age. I slowed as I passed Kolorama Street, not far from Meridian Hill, and turned left on Euclid Avenue. Abruptly the castle-like homes gave way to a spate of shabby row houses. I wondered if I'd made a wrong turn as I adjusted to the change in surroundings.

Finally I spotted it, a tiny white sign marked Colortone with an arrow pointing up a long alleyway. A series of circles, mostly faded, in red, blue, yellow and black had been stenciled along the asphalt.

At the top of the alleyway I took my place among a dozen cars. Ahead another row of dilapidated houses backed toward the small parking lot. It seemed on odd place to locate a business. I looked at the Colortone building. I didn't expect it to be pretty but neither did I expect it to be so plain. Low and flat, the windowless structure of solid concrete stretched for a distance up an adjacent alley. Along its wall someone had scrawled, "No addicts permitted in this area or we call the police!" Further up a young couple in love had sketched a heart and their initials.

Next to the front door, which I now approached warily, were two signs, one bright and colorfully marked, "Colortone Press," and to my delight, one slightly smaller with the words etched in brass, "Acropolis Books." Inside, a smiling receptionist greeted me. We strode briskly up a hallway until suddenly she made a sharp turn into a large office. "Mr. Hackl, Mr. MacVicar is here to see you."

From behind a desk, surrounded by a ceiling-high stack of books and papers, a small man leapt to his feet. As he approached, his eyes almost sparkled. Short and round, I noticed he was stylishly dressed in a three-piece, vested suit.

"Mr. MacVicar, sit down," he said, pointing to an old sofa. I sat down and he took a seat opposite me, perching eagerly on the edge of an upholstered chair. Still smiling, he leaned forward, his eyes squinting in concentration. "So tell me, how do you know Paul Oesur?"

I hated to disappoint him, but I didn't have a whole lot of choice. "Actually, I don't. I mean I don't really know him. My father had met him a few times and suggested to me that he might have a lead into publishing."

"I see," he said, holding onto most of his smile. "Well, tell me what I can do for you?"

I quickly relayed my background, intimating perhaps my promotional experience could be useful in helping him sell books. He peered at me over his glasses, giving me the impression he was studying me as much as listening, yet if I said anything remotely amusing he'd burst into a short, nervous laugh. "I'd like you to meet a few people," he suddenly said.

I waited in anticipation. This was definitely a good sign. A few minutes later I followed him up a corridor, past cubicles, and into a large conference room. Seated at a table were three men whom he quickly introduced, the chief estimator; a salesperson, not much older than me, and Don Hoffman, a soft-spoken man with a dark mustache, who I was told was the sales manager. They all worked for Colortone.

"What would you think about selling printing?" Al asked, all atwinkle again.

Startled, since this wasn't what I'd come to speak to him about, yet excited they were taking an interest, I stammered, "Yes . . . I know a little about printing. I think I'd be good at it." What I kept to myself was my view that printing was what happened when all the fun stuff had already been done. They each asked a few questions. Then Al Hackl gave me a tour. The smell of wet ink on paper filled the air as we passed the presses and returned past the bindery department, where sets of double pages were noisily being folded, collated and stitched. "That's the operation!" he shouted, and we retreated down a second set of steps.

"Thank you," I said, shaking his hand. "Thank you for your consideration."

I walked out into the bright sunlight. And as I tried to focus my eyes I noticed a little boy standing in the parking lot. He was staring at me so I looked over and smiled, and from a distance he seemed to smile back. He was wearing a football helmet and he stood there swaying back and forth. As I approached my car he came closer so I sauntered over, but when he looked up I noticed his face was covered with mucus and most of his teeth were broken. I smiled again, this time awkwardly, and hoped his poor retarded mind could transfer to his heart a moment of human kindness.

Sitting alone in my apartment the next afternoon, the phone rang. "Jamie, this is Don Hoffman. Al Hackl and I talked and we'd like to have you join us."

An offer. I'd finally gotten an offer. "Can I ask what is the salary?"

"Of course. We'll start you out at $10,000 per year. That's a draw against a six percent commission."

"When can I start?"

"Monday, if you like."

Four months had passed and this wasn't where I thought I would be. It wasn't even a job I was sure I wanted to do . . . but I'd finally had an offer. Finally I had a job. "I'll take it."

Chapter 68
YOU'VE GOT TO BE KIDDING

Don Hoffman pulled up a chair beside me in my tiny cubicle and in a tone reminiscent of a kindly professor proceeded to enlighten me. "Washington doesn't make anything. There is nothing manufactured here. What Washington does is *communicate*. There are four thousand trade associations and countless government agencies, not to mention hundreds of unions and nonprofit organizations, and they all have one thing in common—they have to communicate to a constituency . . . and that means printing."

He handed me two books. One was a four-inch-thick listing of every association in town and the other was what he referred to as, "the industry Bible," *Pocket Pal*. "It's a technical guide to the entire printing process from separations and film to press time and bindery. When you're not calling on print buyers from the first book," he said, glancing suggestively at the phone on my desk, "you should be studying *Pocket Pal*. Some of the buyers are art directors. They'll test your knowledge, and if you don't know what you're talking about you'll look pretty foolish."

"One final thing," he added, and he handed me a sheet of paper with several blank lines. I noticed his voice never wavered, as though choosing a monotone allowed him the freedom to say anything, no matter how distasteful it might sound. "Be sure to turn this in to me every evening. There is a box outside my door." I looked down at the sheet. "You earn one-half point for every phone call you make," he said. "One point for each letter you mail, three points for every appointment you get and five points for each estimate you turn in. Each day you're expected to achieve fifty-one points."

I stared at the lined piece of paper and fought the urge to reply, "You've got to be kidding?"

He stood up and left the room. I looked back down at the sheet. This was clearly going to take some adjustment. For two years no one had questioned what I did all day, let alone when and how I did it. Was I really supposed to record every phone call I made? I picked up the phone, wondering how I was going to do a job I already hated. An eternity later, I turned in my call report, fifty-three points.

"You got two appointments?" Don Hoffman said, smiling as he reviewed my sheet. "By the way, I'll give you a tip. Fill up your Mondays and Tuesdays and the rest of the week will take care of itself."

My first appointment was with the National Firefighters Union, lodged comfortably in a small building on Capitol Hill. After a short presentation their print buyer announced she didn't have anything right now but would certainly consider me in the future. I left her my card and a small brochure and walked out onto East Capitol Street. It was sunny and windy and at noon the sidewalks had begun to fill up with people.

I looked to my left. A Roy Rogers restaurant was nestled against the Commodore Hotel. Across the street from the restaurant, a swarm of cars circled around flags in front of Union Station. The restaurant was already packed with office workers and what appeared to be young legislative aides when I took my place in line. Tray in hand, I selected a table warmed by the sunlight near the center of the room.

I surveyed the fresh faces of the young men and women dressed in conservative suits, walking in. Probably graduates of universities like Princeton and Yale, I reflected, by-products no doubt of old-money wealth with lawyerly ambitions. They all seemed bright-eyed and focused.

I took a bite of my cheeseburger and looked up again, surprised this time to suddenly see a disheveled figure from the corner of the room begin shuffling in my direction. It appeared as though he was probably homeless. I avoided his gaze but suddenly realized he was hovering above.

"Excuse me, sir," he muttered politely. "Do you have a twenty for two tens?" No sooner had he asked than he plunked two neatly folded ten-dollar bills on the center of my tray.

I looked at the tens and I looked at him. What could he be trying to pull? But there they were—bigger than life—two ten-dollar bills. Had I become so hardened I couldn't take a simple request at face value? Especially from a man lingering nearby in rags, a man who has nothing.

I studied his face. His expression of sincerity hadn't changed. "I think so," I said, and I fished out my wallet. Inside I spotted a twenty along with a few other bills. I pulled out the twenty and handed it to him while slipping the two tens in my wallet.

Just then I heard him say, "Sir?"

I looked up. While staring down at me incredulously, he slowly unfolded a one-dollar bill. His expression was now one of confusion, disbelief, bordering upon alarm. My God, had I accidentally handed him a one-dollar bill instead of a twenty? Did he think I intentionally tried to cheat him?

"I'm sorry," I sputtered, and immediately handed him back his two tens. "I thought I'd given you a twenty!" He dropped the one-dollar bill on my table and indignantly turned and marched out the front door. Just as the door closed I realized what had happened. Dammit! I started to go after him and then sat down and laughed. What the hell? It was worth every cent just watching him pull it off.

As I drove back to the office, I couldn't help smiling, for unlike most scams where mutual avarice is the key to success, this one depended on the mark being honest, not just a little honest . . . lily white honest.

***

Al Hackl kept his private life private. What little I learned over the first few months was that after his father had died when Al was only one, he'd spent the rest of his childhood in Austria, reared by his mother. What brought him to the United States, I wasn't quite sure, but I suspected his journey was the result of Nazi aggression.

In 1946, he'd opened a tiny, one press operation above an auto repair shop. Giddily, he announced to me one morning in a rare reflective moment, "My pressman was also my secretary!" Four moves and thirty expansionary years later, he ended up running a four-million-dollar per year printing company. But what became obvious was that other than some late-night scribblings of encouragement he left in our boxes, he had little interest in the day-to-day runnings of Colortone Press. Al had confided in me one day that Acropolis Books had begun ten years earlier as a means to keeping his presses running. But what he didn't say was that it now absorbed most of his time and attention. Perhaps because he felt book publishing was simply more glamorous than offset printing or maybe for him it was the thrill of a big-time score a successful book could sometimes bring. Or maybe he just needed a diversion. But whatever the reason, from what I could see, running a publishing company didn't seem to suit his temperament.

Watching Al was like watching a pinball machine in play. Even when sitting he seemed to be in perpetual motion. Workers would exclaim, "He's a heart attack waiting to happen," a bundle of emotions in what clearly was a turbulent business. I couldn't quite fathom what fueled his energy.

Maybe, like the Ringling brothers, running his own show was simply what immigrants did, and once he started, no matter how hard it got, he couldn't imagine doing anything else.

I had to do something, I realized, about Dr. Gray's group sessions. Over the past month I'd attended the meetings sporadically, and now I hadn't been to a session in nearly two weeks. I just couldn't see where they were getting me, what with Dr. Gray's silent, endless gazing and the group's tendency to cover the same ground over and over again. Besides that, the building itself reminded me of the whole horrible nightmare. But it appeared as though I wasn't going to be able to just drift away. Whether I showed up or not, I was billed forty dollars, and on this month's invoice, Dr. Gray had written, "Please pay!"

This wasn't going to be easy. After all, this was the man who'd brought me back. I drew a deep breath and picked up the phone. "Dr. Gray. This is Jamie," I said, trying to sound cheerful, hoping it would depict how healthy I felt. "I've given this a great deal of thought, and I've decided I won't be coming to the sessions anymore. I feel I'm ready to let go."

"Don't you think you should come in and say goodbye to the group?"

I wasn't expecting this. For a moment I couldn't think of anything to say. He wasn't implying that I wasn't ready, he was simply requesting I come in one more time . . . bring the whole process to closure . . . and if I didn't, I'd be leaving without his full blessing.

"I suppose I could."

"Good. Then we'll see you on Thursday."

I didn't want to be like the departing young woman who'd stated her case yet sounded so rote and rehearsed. But as I walked down the street I found myself rehearsing my exact words, wondering how to say what I felt in a way that would result in their nods of agreement.

I sat through the session, thinking more about what I had to do than what anyone was saying, carefully avoiding any interest in the discussion for fear I could be drawn back in. Finally, a few minutes before the end of the hour, Dr. Gray looked over. My signal, as our eyes met, that if I had anything to say, it was my time to say it.

"I've made a decision. After careful consideration, I won't be coming to any more sessions. I feel I'm ready to move forward."

The two men on the sofa, the young business woman and Dr. Gray and his assistant all just looked at me, quietly acknowledging my statement. There was no affirmation, no disagreement, just a few half smiles in response to my decision.

"Time's up," Dr. Gray said.

I slowly rose and lingered for a moment, until only Dr. Gray and

I were alone. "If I should ever need to," I asked, feeling suddenly uneasy, "can I give you a call?"

"Of course," he said, glancing up from his desk, and I left the room without the slightest idea of whether he felt I was ready or not.

***

Colortone Press and Acropolis had been abuzz all morning. Chuck Crimaldi, the protagonist himself of the *Contract Killer*, would be arriving any moment.

A variety of authors, agents and worldly publishing types intermittently visited Al, but in terms of sheer curiosity, none were more provocative than Chuck Crimaldi.

Despite the title of his book, *Crimaldi, Contract Killer*, which Al had placed in blood-red type near the subhead *Mafia Enforcer*, the author, for obvious reasons, only alluded to a past of fatal misdeeds. Instead, Chuck Crimaldi's claim to fame was the enforcement of loan payments from "deadbeats" with the thick end of a baseball bat. On occasion, he wrote, he'd even confront his debtors in the presence of their wives and children. I envisioned a short, violent whack breaking the shinbone, neat and clean . . . as well as a forearm, should the victim attempt to defend himself. But to the author's self-acclaimed credit, Crimaldi would apologize to the family, often leaving a few bucks behind just to show he wasn't really that bad of a guy.

For this ghoulish career and his soon-to-be notoriety, several employees—in hopes of an autograph—had purchased his book and were giddily, if not unseemly, awaiting his arrival. I was damn curious myself. But when he walked in the front door he was far different than what I'd expected. Short and wiry, somewhere in his late forties, he seemed almost gentle as he graciously embraced his newfound fame. But it was his hands in which I found myself fixated. The truth would be in his hands. Just as I suspected they weren't normal hands. They were broad and powerful with thick, stubby fingers, and despite the blue crinkle in his eyes, I instantly believed he was just who he said he was.

———

It was late in the afternoon when I exited my cubicle on the way out the door. Al suddenly appeared, rounding the corner with a thin, pretty woman by his side. He introduced her as his publicist for Acropolis Books. Almost gleefully he added, "Jamie used to work for Ringling Brothers Circus."

"Is that so?" she said, glancing up at me with a look of surprise. "I have a friend who works for Ringling, Joe Kastner. He works in accounting. Do you know him?"

My stomach unexpectedly stiffened. "I think I may have met him," I muttered, quickly trying to change the subject. "How long have you worked for Acropolis?"

"Almost two years," Al interrupted, and to my relief, he hurriedly ushered her out the front door.

I climbed into my car and sat motionless. What if she calls Kastner? What if she tells him she met me? He'd tell her everything. How long would it be before the whole office knew? I felt myself start to panic. And suddenly one fear tumbled into another. I backed down the alleyway. Three men were standing on the corner. One peered at me and I shuddered, remembering how crazy it was to think I was the center of everyone's universe. I thought again of Al's publicist. What if bumping into me was no accident? What if they already knew? What if they were just testing me? "Jesus! What kind of thinking is that?" Two weeks out of Dr. Gray's sessions and I was already coming unglued.

Locating a phone booth, I pulled over to the side of the road. Suddenly I felt weary. Charlene picked up the phone. I could hear laughter in the background. I asked her all about her day, wanting to hear even the most mundane of details. "I don't know what's with me today," I finally eased out. "I'm feeling really tired. Is it okay to be tired?"

"What do you mean?"

"I don't know. I guess it just scares me when I feel really tired. What if I don't get enough rest?"

"You worry too much," she exclaimed. "Just listen to your body. It will naturally respond to whatever it needs."

I felt myself gradually grow calm. And then I hung up the phone and decided I'd leave the office a few hours earlier than usual.

The next day, Don Hoffman cornered me in the hallway. "You haven't been turning in your call reports."

"Pardon?"

"Your call reports. The fifty one points," he said in his flat, yet demanding tone. "You're supposed to be turning them in every day."

"You're right," I said, trying not to sound belligerent, while thinking, "What a ludicrous, Mickey Mouse system! Do you have any idea how demeaning it feels?"

***

Winter turned into spring and gradually some distance set in between what had happened and now. I'd try not to think about it, repeating to myself the rules I'd learned. Get plenty of rest. Set achievable goals. Deal only in reality. Don't put all your eggs in one basket . . . and slowly, the chilling affects would temporarily subside.

Don Hoffman quit asking for my call reports. I'd gradually worn him down, along with achieving the coup d'état, securing just enough accounts to make me ignorable. But whatever spark was required to perform the job enjoyably, I still hadn't found. In fact my restlessness was growing by the day, and this morning for some reason I was particularly irked. For the second time in an hour I'd been banished to the bowels of the shop in search of alternative paper stocks.

The client had brought in her artwork, neatly covered in amber-lith and overlays, and was now waiting in the reception area while I strolled to the room near the loading dock, where the cold, dusty samples were shelved.

I leafed through the boxes, my total extent of creative involvement, and again felt frustrated. This just isn't me!

How long can I kid myself? No matter how hard I tried, my impression of printing still hadn't changed. I could imagine Johannes

Gutenberg himself, watching his work endlessly repeat itself—far removed from the kernel of the idea, the design and layout of the page, the very message itself. I selected three coated cover stocks, along with their matching text weights, and presented her with the samples. She chose one. And with as much enthusiasm as I could muster, I marched the job into production.

The afternoon had become cloudy and cool, verging on rain, when I walked out the office front door. Oblivious to the weather, I spotted the little boy sitting on a curb near his yard. His head was dipped, as though the helmet had finally become too heavy a burden. I feared he was crying but he looked up and smiled, though it wasn't his usual, effusive grin. It was more of a lonely smile. I waved at him as his head drooped again, feeling guilty that that was all I was willing to do, wishing I carried a magic wand.

At the end of the alleyway, I wandered up 17th Street and walked past a row of neglected homes. Further up the hill, the street intersected with Columbia Road, which spilled into an ethnic community. I could hear Latino music emanating from the restaurants as I strolled by. A few of the patrons still wore their native garb, western shirts and white flowery dresses. And amidst the music and the bright dancing colors the streets seemed almost festive.

It had rained during lunch, leaving behind a murky steam that hung as though it wasn't sure what to do. I meandered down 17th Street, stopping to admire an old, brick elementary school, its name nobly engraved in stone. Children had decorated its tall windows with paper tulips in red and yellow.

I turned up the alley to Colortone, wondering if the little boy with the helmet was still there, hoping for some reason he was, but all that remained where he'd sat was an empty patch of grass.

It wasn't easy concentrating the rest of the day. My normal lack of enthusiasm had turned into a lingering sadness. Occupationally, I'd gone from all my eggs in one basket to all my eggs in no basket.

I walked out to my car, wondering if a beer on the way home

would cheer me up. Just the thought of it answered my question. What purpose would a lonely place for lonely people serve? Brooding perhaps? Feigning deep thoughts, as though at the moment I had them to think?

I drifted along more than I drove, not caring if the light turned red, or the traffic backed up, or even if I was going the shortest route. I wasn't in any hurry to get anywhere. In fact, as it started to rain again, the steady sweep of the wipers gave the city a moody look, making it unnecessary to think . . . just feel.

I switched on the radio and turned right on L Street, feeling strangely removed from the sounds and the steady red stream of lights ahead. An occasional umbrella darting through the dark was all that reminded me I wasn't alone. I stared out at the glassy streets, surprised at how numb I felt, how purposeless everything seemed. But just then, a song came on the radio breaking through the din. And from the very first note, I was glued to the seat. Judy Collins sang out the words as though every syllable symbolized all the pain she'd ever felt.

My throat knotted up as she continued to sing *Send In The Clowns*, flowing easily through the words—concluding each verse with a sad refrain.

Tears filled my eyes. I didn't know why. All I knew was that the lyrics were about loss—mind-numbing, heart-pounding loss—and like a lover who'd left and suddenly realized he had to go back, I thought about Michu, King Charles and his crazy band of unicyclists, the show girls, the dancing colors and all the excitement . . . even Charlie Bauman running around, roaring like one of his lions. And I realized that was where I belonged. If there was any way possible . . . any chance at all . . . I had to go back!

I quickly switched lanes, looking for a way out of the traffic. I had to tell Charlene! Now I knew what I had to do and this time it would be different.

By the time I got home I'd worked out all the details. I called Charlene and told her I was coming over.

"I'm going back," I said, "that is if they'll have me!"

She listened attentively, smiling in response to my announcement, yet I could tell she was understandably leery. How, she must have been thinking, would she fit into the picture?

"Here's the arrangement," I added. "I'll only go back if I can come home on the weekends. I'll either fly back here or you can join me." Charlene nodded. "Who knows?" I went on, "maybe later you can join me permanently."

I could tell she was getting excited. "Mondays through Thursdays? What's the big deal in that?" I said. "I can easily handle it if I know that I have a base, a normal life I can return to."

I paused to take a breath. Charlene looked concerned. "Are you sure they'll take you back?"

I hesitated for a moment. Up to now I'd been riding on the intensity of my revelation. "I don't know . . . I guess it would depend on their current staffing. That, and I guess I'd have to convince them I'm all right."

I searched for a further rationalization. "At least they wouldn't have to train me, and as for the hospital it's now been well over a year."

"Why don't you call Mike Franks?" Charlene said, suddenly sounding more optimistic than me.

"Now?"

"Why not? He might be in town and we might as well know what he thinks."

I gathered up my courage and dialed his number. To my surprise he answered the phone. I glanced at Charlene, nervously, but Mike seemed genuinely delighted to hear from me.

"There is something I'd like to discuss with you. It's kind of important. Is there a chance we can get together?"

"I'm leaving for Houston tomorrow. Why don't you come by tonight?"

Charlene and I drove to Mike's house. It was far less extravagant than I expected, a small town house nested amongst an ivy garden. As I eased to a stop I knew that any self doubts I harbored had to be erased. What was needed right now was conviction.

"Come in," Mike's girlfriend smiled, opening the door and offering us a drink. We both declined as she walked lightly across the room joining Mike on a leather sofa, curious no doubt, as much as Mike, about what I had come to say.

I sat on the edge of the chair and spoke in as deliberate a tone as I could render. "Mike, I've put a lot of thought into this. It may sound crazy but I'd like to come back." I paused for affect and then proceeded again. "I've learned a lot over the past eighteen months and what I've discovered is that being an advance man is what I love to do."

To my relief Mike wasn't surprised. His girlfriend even volunteered that he'd been short handed lately.

"There is one thing," I said, and I wanted to be sure we reached an understanding. "I need to have a home base. I want to be able to come home on the weekends."

Mike nodded. "Something could probably be arranged."

I took his statement to mean he'd turn a blind eye versus declaring it a formal endorsement. But if that's what it took and the company paid for my commute, I didn't much care how it was authorized.

"I'll have to talk with Allen . . . you'll have to convince him. But if it's okay with Allen, it's okay with me." He stood up and I knew he'd at least approach Allen with a favorable point of view.

"I'll call you tomorrow," he said. "We'll take it from there."

The next morning and into the afternoon, I anxiously awaited his call. I already felt distanced from Colortone Press. It was just after three when the phone rang.

"Allen will see you."

"Fantastic! What did he say?"

"He said he'd see you. Beyond that, he couldn't say."

"Well, at least he didn't say no."

Mike agreed while being careful not to encourage false hopes. "The day after tomorrow, at ten a.m.," Mike said, and then added, "Good luck."

All the next day I thought about what had transpired in so short a time. If Allen said yes, my life would again be turned inside out, but there was another reason I wanted the job. Somehow I knew that if I didn't go back, if I didn't try it again, I'd wonder the rest of my life if it was the job or me. Could I handle a demanding job and still hold on to my health?

By the next morning I'd twirled my decision around in my mind long enough. I needed an objective opinion from someone who knew me, somebody who had my best interest at heart, someone whose opinion I respected. Gingerly, I picked up the phone and called my father.

"I'm going back," I said.

"Going back where?"

"To the circus, to Ringling Brothers. I've decided I need to go back. I'm going to be an advance man again."

There was a long pause on the other end, followed by a short, perfunctory question.

"Are you out of your mind?"

PART SEVEN

GOING BACK

Chapter 69
SPANISH MOSS AND THE SUPERDOME

"Well, Gargantua, I guess it's just me and you again." I studied him, looking out at me from his glass cage. Funny how two-and-a-half years can change your perspective. He didn't look quite as ferocious. Upright and chest thrust forward, he was forever fixed, but it seemed kind of cruel. Even gorillas deserved a rest.

Power is a strange thing, I thought, as I waited for Allen. Some people crave it, need it, and if not enjoy it, at least covet it once they get it. For those people, I envied their material rewards, sometimes resentfully, and feared their ability to affect my life, but I seldom stood in awe of they themselves. Others just seemed to go through the motions, rising through the ranks having little effect on those around them. And then there were people like Allen. Not many. Just a few. People like Allen never asked for it. In fact, I couldn't imagine Allen reading a textbook on management skills. For Allen, power just came with the territory, the result of following Irvin's coattails to the number-two slot in the organization. I never got the impression he liked it. He just did it because the job had to be done, and for Allen, the task was never easy. When it came to difficult decisions affecting other people, he would anguish over their pain as much as he would rejoice over their pleasure. It was management by the gut not just by the head, and if Allen wielded power, he also wielded compassion. It was something he was resolved to do. And for that I was in awe.

Maureen walked out and announced that Allen was ready to see me. I was surprised at how calm I felt. Allen stood up and smiled, not a warm welcoming smile, more of a wary smile. It was obvious he'd reached no preliminary decision. Just like Mike had said, whatever he decided, it would be the result of our face-to-face meeting.

Allen rarely tackled difficult decisions directly, preferring instead to converse indirectly, allowing the decision to unfold itself naturally. He took out a cigar from the box behind his desk, offering me one once again. I politely declined.

"Did you see the Redskins game yesterday?" he asked, lighting his cigar.

Fortunately I had, since like most Washingtonians I was an avid Redskins fan.

"I don't know about George Allen," he said, pretending he didn't have an opinion. "How can you build a football team trading all your draft picks for these older guys?"

For the next ten minutes, we bantered back and forth about the coach, the quarterback, the merits of experience over stamina, and the upcoming game against Dallas, and gradually we relaxed in each other's company.

Sensing my timing wasn't going to get any better, I summoned up my courage. "I'd like to come back," I said. "This is what I'm good at. It's what I love to do. I've learned some valuable lessons." Then repeating what I'd come to believe, I murmured, "Maybe I'm even better off than those that never have."

Deciding I'd said enough, I watched as Allen leaned back in his chair, solemnly studying his cigar, and for the life of me, I couldn't tell whether I was in or out.

Nervously I waited, allowing the silence in the room to pressure a decision. Allen stared at the ceiling, slowly exhaling a stream of white smoke. "Okay," he said, "we'll give it a try," and then he swiveled around and fixed his gaze. "But I don't want a repeat of what happened last time. If I even think it could happen again, I'm pulling you off the road."

"That's only fair," I said, and then realizing the impact of what had just happened, I exclaimed, "Don't worry, I won't disappoint you!"

He slowly stood and shook my hand, relieved, it appeared, at having made his decision. "Welcome back," he said. "Mike Franks will be pleased."

I could barely work when I returned to the office knowing I was an advance man once again. I resisted the urge to call Charlene, deciding instead to tell her in person. On the way home, I picked up a bottle of champagne, then carefully arranged two wine glasses on a small table in front of the sofa. I dimmed the lights and lit two candles and eagerly awaited her arrival.

She walked in and I looked up and grinned.

"You got it! You're going back!"

I raised up a wine glass, bursting out laughing.

"Where are you going? What's your first city? What did Mike say? Have you told Colortone yet?"

"I've no idea. I'll call Mike tomorrow. For now, I just want to savor the moment."

Mike reached me before I could locate him. "Congratulations!"

"Thank you," I said, happily accepting his praise.

"I'm calling from Houston," he said. "I was hoping I'd catch you bright and early. When can you start?"

"I'll give notice today, two full weeks, which I assume they will take. What will be my first city?"

"I don't know. We'll talk about that later. You can assist me for the time being in New Orleans. The show will be starting there the week after next."

I paused for a moment, unsure whether to be disappointed or not.

"You've got to walk," Mike interjected, "before you can run."

"You're right," I agreed, embarrassed he already had to temper my enthusiasm.

"Have you been to the Superdome?"

"No, in fact, I've never been to New Orleans."

"You'll love it. The arena is huge. We actually ride golf carts to monitor the doors. Just let my secretary know what day you'll be arriving. I'll be working out of the promoter's office."

I hung up the phone and strolled out the door. For the first time, it seemed real. In two short weeks, I'd be back in the midst of it all, the performers, the crowds, the colors and all the excitement. Now all I had to do was tell Al Hackl.

I pulled into Colortone's parking lot, and suddenly the excitement that had been propelling me forward stalled. This was going to be harder than I thought. As I peered at Al's building, it occurred to me this wasn't some multi-layered corporation I was leaving. It was a man who, despite all his quirks and flailings about, was doing the best he could.

I sat down at my desk and looked at the list of leads I'd set aside to call for the day and was quickly reminded of how much I disliked the job. I stood up, fortifying myself with the adage, "there's no time like the present," and ambled back to Al's office.

"May I have a word?"

Al looked up, preoccupied, but he seemed to sense this was something requiring his attention. He nodded and moved to a chair in front of his desk, motioning me to join him.

I thought I'd ease into my announcement with small talk. I noticed he was holding some papers having to do with Acropolis. "Is it a tough business?"

"All business is tough," he sighed.

Well, that didn't help matters, I thought. "Al, I don't know how to tell you this, but I'm afraid I'm resigning. I've decided to go back with the circus."

A look of bafflement crept over his face. "But you've been doing so well."

"I know, but it just isn't me. It has nothing to do with Colortone . . . and I couldn't be more grateful for all that you've done, but my heart just isn't in it."

Al leaned forward, with a look of consternation I wasn't prepared for. "What am I doing wrong? What can I do?"

I knew his question wasn't about me. He was just frustrated at making another investment in someone only to come up short. I thought of the fifty-one point system, how perhaps he could trust his account executives a little more fully, but decided it would only blemish my leaving.

"Nothing," I replied. "It just wasn't for me." I told him I would stay a full two weeks, introducing anyone he'd like to my accounts, and then muttered an apology and quietly left his office. As I wandered down the hall, I wondered which was harder, firing someone you didn't admire or quitting a job from someone you did.

I was disheartened to hear it was the "Red" show that was performing in New Orleans. My reunion with Michu, Charlie King and the other performers I was more familiar with would just have to wait until the "Blue" show and I were reunited. Then again, it occurred to me there might be some merit in easing back in, as I remembered, with embarrassment, Axel Gautier and his herd of elephants whom I'd led astray for eight miles and Bill Pruyn, the outraged music director, not to mention Billy Williams or Harold Ronk whom I'd screamed at along with his lover in an Evansville restaurant.

From my hotel, I walked across a catwalk to the New Orleans Superdome. Mike Franks was right. The Superdome was huge. It was more of a canyon than a building, which I suppose it needed to be as the first fully enclosed building to house its own football team. From the top tier, I looked down at the tiny circus rigging below. It seemed strange to see the three rings concealing only half of the arena floor, and I tried to imagine a football being kicked from one end to the other. From the standpoint of size alone, it was obviously large enough, but playing football indoors was like eating ice cream in the middle of winter. It just didn't seem as inviting.

I turned and made my way through the incoming crowds. "Third floor to the right," the usher told me, and I picked up my pace. Just as I was approaching the promoter's office, Mike rolled up in a golf cart, screeching to a stop.

"Does anyone know your driving record?"

"I've only run over three people so far."

"New shoes?" I asked, surprised to see he was wearing a pair of brown, thick soled shoes instead of his trademark patent-leather loafers.

"It was either these or surgery," he said, and suddenly I remembered how it felt, like treading barefoot on bamboo. "These concrete floors were killing my arches! Did you check in okay across the street?"

I confirmed I had and he handed me a program.

"Why don't you relax for the afternoon? We've only got four days to go. Get acquainted with the show. You can help me watch doors later tonight."

"Thanks," I said, and I strolled into the arena and eased into a seat. I'd already studied the program so I had a pretty good idea of what to expect. It was the year of the American Bicentennial, and Irvin had crafted the main production number around patriotism, 1776, and the signing of the Declaration of Independence. I watched as performers on stilts paraded around the hippodrome track dressed in Uncle Sam top hats and tails, while show girls swung from their ropes in costumes depicting the Statue of Liberty, pointed hats and all. The rest of the performers marched around the track attired in an array of colonial garb, all of which climaxed in the center ring with a rousing rendition of "America the Beautiful," bringing the audience stampeding to its feet. The whole thing seemed to work. Yet, if there was anything odd about the entire spectacle, it was the vacant expressions on the performers' faces, peering out from the sparkle and glitter and the red, white and blue, most of whom couldn't speak a word of English.

In addition to the perennial tiger trainer, Gunther Gebel Williams, the two major attractions that were now receiving top billing were a Frenchman named Phillip Petit and an eleven-year-old boy that Irvin had discovered in England. Phillip Petit, the previous year, had made world headlines by walking a tightrope between the tops of the two World Trade Center towers, while the young boy, after riding a number of two-wheeled contraptions, capped off his act by balancing on a three-inch tricycle.

After the show, I hastened back to the promoter's office and was surprised to see Mike's girlfriend lazily sitting in one of the chairs, reading a fashion magazine. She looked up and beamed. Her nails appeared recently manicured, and I couldn't help noticing a sizable diamond ring on her finger.

"Are congratulations in order?"

"Didn't you know? We're engaged. Mike gave it to me last week!"

"Fantastic!" I said, trying to transfer my amazement that Mike was truly getting married to my congratulatory response. "When is the date?"

"June," she said. "By the way, where is Charlene?"

"Back in Washington," I said, pleased that she asked.

"Call her and have her come down! I'm bored to tears. Tell her the shopping here is wonderful."

Charlene and Mike's fiancé couldn't be less alike. We'd barely be able to afford the plane ticket, let alone shopping, but the more I thought about it, the more it seemed like a fun idea. So with two hours remaining until the evening performance, I marched back to the hotel and called Charlene.

"Would you like to fly down?"

"I'd love to!" she said. "But you just got started."

"I know but now is as good a time as any if we're going to spend weekends on the road together."

"I'll call the airlines," she exclaimed. "Let me see what I can arrange."

I finished dinner and then scurried back to the arena in time to help Mike with the doors. We rode around the concourse, stopping to watch the ticket takers at various intervals, then waited in the office for the deadwood to arrive.

"There's a meeting in Atlanta next week for all the promoters to discuss the new show," he said. "I'll have a better idea then where I'm sending you."

"That's fine," I said, feeling suddenly more patient.

The deadwood arrived, and for the next two hours we counted the tickets. It was after eleven when I crossed the catwalk back to the hotel. I was surprised to feel how familiar it all was. It seemed as though I'd never left. But as I walked slowly down the hotel corridor, there was another reminder that was also familiar. It was my first full day and I was bone tired.

A light was blinking on my bedside phone.

"Yes," the desk clerk said, "a Charlene called. She'll be arriving Saturday morning at ten a.m. She said to leave her a key."

"Thank you," I said, and feeling gladdened, I hung up the phone.

My energy returned after a full night's sleep and a morning spent lounging by the pool. I'll just have to adjust to the new hours, I reminded myself, taking refuge in the fact that it wasn't even my town or responsibility. The real test would come later.

Saturday morning Charlene bounced into the promoter's office and I'd have thought she and Mike's fiancé were the best of old friends. Within minutes, they announced, "We're off." And as they disappeared around the corner, I hollered, "Be back by dinner and we'll explore Bourbon Street."

Charlene's shopping bags were considerably lighter than her companion's when she returned, as was Mike's wallet, I presumed. "I'll meet you at the hotel," I started to say, "right after the deadwood," and I watched as she jauntily returned to the room.

New Orleans in August was hot. Shirt-clinging hot. Even the Spanish moss hanging from the trees looked exhausted. Fortunately, by nightfall the temperature had dropped to a breathable level. Bourbon Street was only a few blocks away. As we walked the short distance to the old French Quarter, I found myself glancing at the side streets apprehensively. Mike had commented that the crime was so bad that each day on page two the newspaper listed all the muggings, thefts and murders from the night before, and it read like the phone book.

I could see signs of life up ahead, tourists walking between rows of ornate wooden buildings, two-story structures with ivy and wrought iron, and I wondered how much of the original flavor still existed. Not the flavor of two-hundred years ago, but the flavor of twenty years earlier when Pete Fountain and the Mardi Gras and the great jazz scene were still in their prime.

I lowered my expectations for, excepting New England, the more

I traveled the country the more I came to expect the real thing to be merely a copy of its former self—and usually a dim one at that. It was the thematic nature of our culture, always trying to recapture the past while somehow cheapening it in the process.

But then again, hadn't Irvin Feld's Ringling Brothers and Barnum and Bailey Circus been accused of the same crime? A touch of the old authenticity, with lion tamers and clowns and European acrobats, but much of it a tinselly version of itself, a window to the past but with a view from the lifeless confines of the modern day arena.

We rounded the corner, and I wondered what relics of our time someone in the future will nostalgically try to replicate. As an onslaught of neon lights appeared, some advertising "Live Sex Acts" and others "Shooters" and "Two Beers for One," I had a hard time thinking of much.

Charlene departed Sunday afternoon. That night Mike and I stepped reluctantly toward a row of elevators leading to the arena's skydome suites. It was the last day of an eight-day run and the box office, for some reason, wanted to close out the matinee and the evening performance simultaneously. It was already nine o'clock and that meant we'd have both shows of deadwood to count.

We opened the door and what was normally an immaculate room, with enclosed seating and a plate glass view of the arena, was now obstructed by boxes and strewn with used paper cups and leftover snacks. Three men—the general manager, the box office manager and what appeared to be their auditor—were already seated amidst the boxes of deadwood that were stacked high on top of one another.

"The boxes on that side of the room are from the matinee," the general manager volunteered. "And the boxes on this side of the room are from the evening performance. We've already counted the matinee tickets, so ya'll can go ahead and count while we add up the deadwood from the evening performance."

This was all said with a conciliatory gesture in an air of cordiality he, in all likelihood, hoped to sustain. But three hours later, with all the tickets counted, there was one small problem. Somehow, despite the machines, our relentless double checking and our peering over one another's shoulders, we ended up eighteen-thousand dollars apart. And it was eighteen-thousand dollars in Ringling's favor.

"Let's take a break," one of the men sighed, and he got up and stretched, retrieving another Coca-Cola from the refrigerator. A black woman who had been sweeping the rows of seats outside the suite was also having a rest and had stopped to look out at the arena floor below. The manager watched her for a minute, then exaggerated his stance so that everyone knew he was observing her, and leaned forward and shouted, "Boo!"

This cracked him up, along with his two colleagues. I looked over at Mike to see his reaction. Despite all the laughter, Mike's quiet expression never changed. And I knew that if grace could be measured by restraint, he did a remarkable job of hiding his distaste.

The manager plopped back down in his chair and looked over at Mike. "We'll have to recount all the tickets. We're all pretty tired. Why don't we lock up the room and we'll meet back here in the morning?"

Mike smiled, perhaps to soften his refusal. "No, if you're going to recount the tickets, you're going to have to do it now."

The manager looked askance. Everyone knew Mike was testing their endurance, but according to the contract, it was within his rights. The manager stood up and exhaled. "All right, let's start."

Mike glanced over at me, as I braced myself for three more hours. "Why don't you turn in," Mike whispered, "I can do the rest."

"That's all right," I said. "I'll be okay."

Then warmly, more emphatically, he said, "Go ahead. Get some sleep. I'll take care of it from here."

The next morning I waited for Mike in the lobby. He strode in a few minutes later looking tired, but surprisingly alert.

"What happened?" I asked.

"They found the discrepancy. I had to agree with their numbers."

"What was the mistake?"

"There was a whole slew of complimentary passes they had neglected to count."

"How did they find them?"

"I don't know. But they did."

As soon as I arrived at the Atlanta Marriott I phoned Chris Bursky. We agreed to meet in the downstairs bar. He gave me a big bear hug and welcomed me back, cautioning me not to take things so seriously. Having discussed with an equal measure of incredulity the impending nuptials of Mike Franks, I couldn't resist asking, "So what's this I hear about Michu getting married?"

I had perused a copy of the Blue show's program, and low and behold, Michu had fallen in love with and married a fellow lilliputian only five inches taller than he. They looked so puckishly alike she could have passed easily for his sister.

Stealing a page from P.T. Barnum's shameless promotion of Tom Thumb's earlier wedding to Lavinia Warren, Bursky said that Irvin had concocted a scheme where during each and every show, a glorious reenactment of Michu's wedding would be featured. In all their marital bliss, the diminutive couple repeated their vows in what the program described as a ceremony befitting royalty itself.

The only difference, Bursky now relished in telling me, was unlike P.T. Barnum's promotion of the real thing, Michu's wedding was totally contrived. Not only had there never been a wedding or courtship, word had it they couldn't stand each other, or at least according to Chris she couldn't abide him. Perhaps when she agreed to the sham, I thought, she didn't know Michu, as lovable as he could be, enjoyed his vodka with a liberal dose of crankiness.

"Come on," Chris said. "It's time to go upstairs."

All of the promoters had already gathered in the room. From the sounds of the raucous laughter and mingling about, it seemed more like a knights of the round table gone awry than an executive meeting. Mike Franks, Art Ricker and Allen Bloom were seated at the head table. After a few half-hearted attempts, Allen clinked his glass more forcibly and called the meeting to order.

"Irvin will be stopping by in a few minutes to tell you about the new show," Allen said. "In the meantime, are there any items or issues you'd like to discuss?"

Art Ricker inadvertently set the tone of the meeting. "Before we talk about the Blue show, what's with the kid in the Red show on the three-inch tricycle? Who in the world can see a three-inch tricycle?"

Chris Bursky shouted out in parliamentary fashion. "Here! Here!"

Sounding emboldened, Art started again. "And while we're at it, what's with Phillip Petit? It was certainly impressive walking between the two World Trade Center towers, but height isn't a factor inside an arena. All he does now is sidestep across a tightrope thirty feet up in the air. The audience falls asleep!"

I had to admit he had a point, at least when it came to the impossibility of duplicating an outrageous feat inside an arena. It called to mind a similar tour de force by another Frenchman a hundred years before. This daredevil, in a moment of either sheer lunacy or supreme self confidence, announced he would cross Niagara Falls on a tightrope, a maneuver that had never before been attempted.

Despite meticulous preparations, there was more than the psychological impact of height about which to be concerned. There was the very real danger of the turbulent air that swirls constantly over the falls. And though even the main rope was reinforced with leads attached to rocks and trees along the banks to lessen the swaying back and forth, the primary rope still dipped nearly sixty feet in the center. Given all this, I wondered now if the eighteen minutes it took him to cross the thirteen hundred feet—in front of thousands of morbidly curious onlookers—was excruciatingly slow or, relatively speaking, frighteningly fast.

Other promoters joined Art in agreement, and just as it appeared Allen was losing control of the meeting, the doors swung open and Irvin Feld walked in. A noticeable hush engulfed the room as we sat up and Irvin took his seat at the head table. Irvin made a point of acknowledging a few of the promoters he knew, and I sensed he was far more comfortable in front of an audience than he was one to one.

Most of what he went on to say seemed unexceptional, a new polar bear act and a few new balancing acts from Eastern Europe, but then he paused and said there was one more act he was especially proud to present. "For the first time in years," Irvin said, "Ringling Brothers, in the form of Elvin Bale, is bringing back the human cannonball. Not since the days of the famous Zacchinis has the human cannonball been the grand finale of the show!"

I leaned over and whispered to Chris, "Isn't being shot out of a cannon rather dangerous?"

Chris smiled. "It's not actually a shot. The smoke and the bang are simply for show. Think of it as being propelled forward by a giant slingshot."

"I see," I said. "For a moment I thought it was foolish."

The meeting adjourned and several of us reconvened in the bar. Mike Franks dropped in and pulled me aside. "Detroit and Toledo, back-to-back dates, that's where I'm sending you."

Tommy Crangle chimed in. "Détwah. Ah, Yes!"

"How many shows?" I asked.

"I don't know. About six in Toledo and eighteen in Detroit. We'll promote it together."

The bartender wiped away a pool of water. I ordered another beer and watched as Mike slipped away. Twenty-four shows? That was even more than in Indiana. Whatever they thought triggered my breakdown they clearly didn't think it was back-to-back dates and too many shows.

I finished my drink, recalling with a queasy feeling something about wanting to be tested, and quietly placed the bottle back on the counter.

Chapter 70
THE LIGHT OF A LAMP

Sifting through the previous year's Detroit and Toledo binders, I suddenly stumbled upon an interesting item. Buried among the listings of media trade-outs and complimentary passes, I noticed a sizable block of tickets had been given to the Hyatt Regency in Deerborn, Michigan. The explanation simply read "Room Trade-Out/Promoter," next to the name and phone number of a Marjorie Harris, Marketing Director.

I didn't know much about Deerborn, other than the fact that it was an upscale suburb of Detroit, but the Hyatt Regency, with its see-through glass elevators, was as swanky as it gets. What did I have to lose? Having called ahead, I drove up to the front entrance and calmly strode into the main lobby.

"May I help you?" a white-gloved man in a black and gold uniform asked graciously.

"Yes, I'm here to see Marjorie Harris."

"Of course, right this way," he said. I gazed up at a vaulted ceiling that drifted effortlessly above. "Will you be staying with us?" he asked. Then he voiced something about a concierge and bellhop at my disposal as we strolled past a fancy fountain.

He escorted me through a door marked "Private Offices" and I found myself standing in front of a petite and friendly dark-haired woman. Returning her greeting, I took a seat, then muttered a bit awkwardly, "I'm not sure of the details. . . ."

"Well, last year," she interjected, "the promoter gave us one thousand coupons, redeemable mid-week for two dollars each."

"I see," I said, astonished to hear the passes weren't offered for free. The agreement was the equivalent of a huge group sale. "Out of curiosity, what did you do with them?"

"We gave them to our employees!"

I nodded in assent, hoping to convey an appreciation for their generosity, then quickly indicated I didn't see any problem with that arrangement again this year.

"Good!" she said. "I've already reserved you one of our penthouse suites."

"Penthouse suite?"

"That will be Suite 114G. When will you be joining us?"

I searched for the right words, wondering if there was some elegant way to put it. "Today?"

She handed me a bronze key and instructed me to insert the key next to the letter P, inside the elevator. Then she told me each morning I'd find a copy of the *Detroit Free Press* outside my door along with a complimentary continental breakfast of juices and muffins just down the hall. "There's one other thing," she added. "Don't forget to try our monorail on the fourth floor. It connects directly to Detroit's newly minted shopping mall."

"Thank you," I said politely, while conjuring up memories of the Alamo Motel. I meandered out of her office, trying to conceal my amazement, and quickly returned to the main lobby.

"Will you be needing a bellhop, sir?"

"Why not?" I replied, feeling slightly disoriented. Moments later, with luggage and bellhop behind, we boarded a crowded glass elevator.

People pushed in their floor numbers, and I conveniently remembered her instructions. I searched for the letter P and found it perched atop a row of numbers. I inserted the key in the slot and gave it a quick turn. Like a Christmas tree, the entire word Penthouse suddenly lit up in lights. I slipped the key back in my pocket and as the lobby grew smaller and smaller, with all the prudence I could summon, I tried to suppress a grin.

One-hundred and fifty-thousand dollars. The sound of it rolled off my tongue like a candied apple. It was a hell of a lot of money to spend in one city, but then again, Detroit was the sixth largest market in the country. Toledo, an hour's drive south, carried a budget of another thirty-thousand dollars. And as a further enticement, I'd been granted my wish. The Blue show was coming to town, first to Toledo before traveling north to Detroit. My projection, Mike said, was $900,000 for Detroit and $190,000 for Toledo. But as I drove into downtown Detroit, already dreaming of the possibilities ahead, I nervously reminded myself not to set impossible goals.

I rolled down the window, breathing in the smells of the city as I drove into the heart of town. It was obvious from the start, Detroit today was a far cry from its glory years—the 1920s—when the city shined as the entrepreneurial center of America. After all, this was where Henry Ford had built a manufacturing empire constructed on the ownership of the American dream—the automobile—based on a philosophy that what was good for the American worker was good for his Ford Motor Company.

I wondered what he'd think now, fifty years later, if he could see block after block of boarded up houses and buildings, not to mention vacant alleys that were once thriving streets but were now home to drug pushers and prostitutes. Racial tensions and devastating riots only a few years earlier had left downtown Detroit virtually abandoned. And now the white middle classes, from everything I'd heard, were deathly afraid to venture into the inner city. But unfortunately, unlike Cleveland, one of the institutions that hadn't fled the city was the Detroit Coliseum, home to the legendary Detroit Red Wings hockey team. And, of course, home to the annual pilgrimage of Ringling Brothers and Barnum and Bailey Circus.

I parked across the street from the Coliseum and stared at the morose, gray building. A marquee announced an upcoming boxing match. The building to my surprise didn't even stand on its own. Instead, it abutted two office buildings, equally as gloomy.

As I sat in my car, weighing my options, I decided the only chance I had was to somehow wrap Ringling Brothers and Barnum and

Bailey Circus around the same flag embracing Detroit's civic pride. Why ignore the city's decline? Play it up! Nothing like the wholesome, family-oriented, "Greatest Show on Earth" performing in downtown Detroit to prove that the city was on the comeback trail. This, I decided, would be my mantra each and every time the press questioned me about this year's event. Hell, maybe if I said it enough I'd even begin to believe it myself.

I turned off the car engine and hiked up several stone steps leading to the front entrance. Inside the doors, the coliseum's white walls were badly in need of paint and looked as decrepit as the city itself. I peeked inside the arena and then veered to the right up a broad set of stairs where a sign indicated general offices. I was anxious to meet Lee Hamilton, the general manager. Allen had laughed when he'd mentioned him. "Be sure to ask Lee," he said, "how we first met!"

I was ushered by a friendly woman into a large, plush office, an office that could easily have belonged to the Executive Suites of General Motors. A man rose comfortably from his seat. In contrast to the formality of the room, he was casually attired in a white shirt and cardigan sweater. He motioned me to a chair and I couldn't help noticing a freshness about him, as if he'd just returned from a reunion at an ivy league school.

"How is Allen?" he asked, settling back down behind a large polished desk.

"Fine," I said.

"He may have told you we're good friends. We try to play golf together at least once a year."

For some reason, I had a hard time picturing Allen and this nice but carefully coiffed man as close friends. "He insisted I ask how you two first met," I said, now even more curious than ever.

Lee Hamilton leaned forward in his chair and laughed. "Allen was just a kid, and so was I for that matter. He was here with Irvin Feld promoting a rock concert. I was in charge of concessions and got a small commission on everything I sold. Intermission started and I was determined to keep the concessions open as long as people were buying. Allen was equally determined to get the band back on stage. After fifteen minutes he demanded I turn off the lights. I refused. The argument escalated. Allen got angrier and angrier, louder and louder, so finally, with no other option, I ended the discussion. I punched him in the nose."

"You punched him in the nose? What happened then?"

"He let me keep the concessions open."

Lee Hamilton and I talked about Detroit. He agreed with my assessment that peoples' fear had to be mitigated about coming downtown, "It's an issue that can't be disregarded." Then he told me what I already knew. "Since the arena is contributing a portion of the advertising dollars, you need to coordinate your thoughts with our in-house advertising department. You'll be working with a young woman named Julie Hanson. She's a little high strung but I'm sure you'll get along fine. I'll take you downstairs and introduce you."

Mike Franks had already warned me about Julie. He said she was seeing a man from Ringling she'd met the previous year. But from Mike's subtle hints I'd begun to suspect she could be a thorn in my side. My only hope was that her dating relationship would lessen any tensions. But like Claire Rothman in Cleveland, we'd already decided we'd confide in her little—a formula bound to infuriate her if I didn't throw her a few bones.

"This is Julie," Lee Hamilton said, introducing us, and I was taken aback by how pretty she was. Brown eyed and delicate, I couldn't help thinking how easy it would have been to fall for her myself. But what quickly became evident behind her soft features was a competitive edge, fueled I suspected, by a resentment that she wasn't the one to have final say. An irritation that would become especially grating when she learned it was her role to set up any appointments I needed for the major promotions and media. Kindness, at least at this stage, I decided, was my opening gambit. "I've heard wonderful things about you. I'm looking forward to your advice and what I'm sure will be a mutually beneficial working relationship."

Toledo evoked an unexpected feeling. As I crossed over one of its bridges, I could see miles of docks and warehouses along with refineries and power plants dotting the shoreline where the Maumee River flowed through the city, spilling into the western foot of Lake Erie. The city was another rust belt remnant of the massive industrial age when the Great Lakes were the "Anvil of America," producing the majority of the world's iron and steel and petroleum products. Unfortunately, as I looked out my open window and breathed in the pungent smells of chemicals billowing from one of its numerous smokestacks, I was reminded that, like an old, discarded war horse, Toledo was now known more for its contaminants infiltrating the air and its waterways than for anything else.

But as I drove through the city, adhering to my habit of becoming hopelessly lost, I could see old, wooden houses with ragged porches alongside Mom and Pop grocery stores. Nearby were hardware stores and pizza parlors and, to my amazement, a barbershop that still advertised its location with a revolving pole of red and white stripes. Haircuts were only three dollars.

Multi-ethnic and family oriented, this didn't require a grand marketing strategy. Just get the word out and the people will come. In fact, with a little luck, I could probably do most of the leg work via phone from Detroit instead of dashing back and forth.

The sun was casting long shadows by the time I arrived in front of Toledo's arena. Red brick and drab, it looked more like a windowless schoolhouse than a modern city arena. Yet with a recurring sense of wonderment, I strolled inside. The general manager's office was easy to spot but what intrigued me the most was the arena itself. I stepped into the corridor and into the first set of entrance doors, and as though I was seeing the inside of an arena for the first time I gazed out at the thousands of empty seats. But as my eyes drifted upward I was startled to discover that I'd been assigned to the only other arena in the country in which the top tier of seats were worn, wooden bleachers.

I called Charlene. "You won't believe the penthouse suite with its A-framed view of the city." She happily agreed to fly up to Detroit for the weekend. I was quickly discovering, when it came to assuaging loneliness, that a hundred casual relationships didn't add up to one special one, someone I cared about and someone who cared about me.

I hung up the phone and strolled over to the center of the room for my daily routine of exercises, fifteen minutes of calisthenics followed by twenty pushups. No cheating. The chest had to touch the floor. If I was going to make it through the next three months in one piece, I had to start now and think of it more like a marathon than a sprint. I stood still and looked in the mirror, pinching my flesh between my ribs. Worried I'd already lost a pound or two, I vowed I'd force-feed myself if I had to.

I lifted my suitcase and did twenty reps each of one-arm curls, followed by three-dozen sit ups, then finished by leaning backwards against the dresser, placing both hands on the edge and slowly lowering and raising my weight ten times.

Mike Franks had that bewildered look on his face when he burst into my office, plopping his briefcase on my desk. Although I'd kept him appraised on a weekly basis, I hadn't seen him in over a month.

"I've arranged all the major promotions and I'm already negotiating with the radio stations," I said, diplomatically supporting the illusion we were promoting the city together. "I hope you don't mind my proceeding ahead."

"No, that's fine," he said. "I'd have been here more often but frankly I've been amazed at how fast it's all come back to you."

Julie was sitting on a small sofa on the opposite side of the room, trying her best to look happy.

"Julie is going to chaperon the advance clown and handle our press releases," I said, knowing this probably wouldn't appease her. "I've also asked her to help with the animal walk."

Mike smiled at her, approvingly, and for a moment she seemed to lower her guard, but Mike's inability to further the conversation led to an awkward silence. It was obvious that wherever he'd been working, he was feeling overwhelmed. And once again I couldn't help feeling sorry for him, even knowing his dilemma was largely due to his own hopeless disorganization.

I was struggling for something else to say when a red-faced man appeared in the doorway. Suddenly in a resonating, scolding tone he grumbled at Mike, "Do you know how hard it was to set up that appointment for you with Bill Hodges?"

Mike looked up, clearly confused, while the man puffed out his chest. "The next time you are too busy to meet with the marketing director of a major department store, you can kindly tell me in advance!" And with a cold, steady stare he turned on his heels.

I couldn't tell whether Mike was embarrassed or just baffled. He looked over at Julie and quietly asked, "What does that man do again?"

"He sells ads for the Red Wings program," she said, and then instantly sensing, despite the fact Mike's demeanor hadn't changed, that her co-worker's ranking might diminish his indignation, she quickly sputtered, "and he's a very nice guy!"

⇒━━

Julie was miffed again. She hadn't spoken to me for the last forty-eight hours, which didn't surprise me since for the past several days I'd been withholding what she considered invaluable information— the allocation of my television dollars. It wasn't that the scheduling of the television was any big mystery. It was just that the simplest discussion with Julie invariably ended in chilly disagreement, and I'd run out of patience for such nonsense. I had more important things to worry about, such as holding onto my sanity for one. So I was taken aback when she popped her head into my office and happily declared that one of the radio reps had gotten permission from her station to ride in the animal walk.

"That's nice," I said, aiming to hide the obvious, that I'd been flirting with the radio rep and had offered her one of the elephants as if it were a box of chocolates. Julie knew about Charlene, and although I was trying to be faithful, I couldn't deny my memories of unabashed freedom tarried barely beneath the surface.

"By the way, she's an ex-Playboy bunny," Julie said, leaning against the door. "Did you know that?"

"No, I didn't," I said, trying to sound indifferent while immediately envisioning her lusty figure in Playmate attire and wondering what about all this amused Julie so.

"I just thought I'd let you know," she said, and then acting as though we were the best of compatriots, she turned and disappeared out the door.

———

Mike's one-day visit, a month ago, was the last that I'd seen of him but I couldn't help agreeing with his impression. The work had all come readily back to me. And given Mike's tendency to leave me with the unfinished details, it was probably best that he had left me alone from the beginning. Anyway, he'd said he'd be back for Toledo's opening night and that in itself gave me well needed comfort.

Steve Smith and Robin would be arriving tomorrow, generating, I hoped, plenty of advance clown publicity. All the media buys had long been placed and the multitude of promotions confirmed. Now it was finally a matter of seeing how the numbers held up. Tickets had been on sale for two weeks in Toledo and one week in Detroit. In both cities the numbers were running neck-and-neck with last year's figures. But I was particularly focused on the past two days of sales, wondering if a small upward tick could represent a sudden surge forward. Fortunately I was rescued from the heady "what ifs" by the ring of the phone. I instantly recognized Chris Bursky's voice. "So how are you holding up?" he asked.

"I'm doing okay, better than I expected."

"If you need any help I'll be there," he said, and I gratefully noted his sincerity. "By the way," he continued, and by the lilt in his voice I could tell I was in for an interesting story. "Did you hear about Irvin's Saturday night massacre?"

"Pardon?" I said.

"Irvin just fired the entire accounting department."

"The entire department?"

"All eight people . . . though I think he kept one."

"What the hell for?"

"Someone screwed up. For six weeks accounting accidentally issued inflated payroll checks to several of the performers. The problem is that one of the performers was Gunther Gebel Williams and he refused to give it back. Not only wouldn't he give the money back, he demanded he keep the raise!"

"You're kidding," I said. "What did Irvin do?"

"There was nothing he could do. Gunther's the star moneymaker of the show. They had to let him keep it. Irvin was furious. He marched downstairs and promptly fired the whole department."

"Unbelievable!" I said. Chris Bursky echoed my sentiments. Then I hung up the phone and wondered if Irvin's temper tantrums knew any earthly boundaries.

No sooner had Steve and Robin pulled up in their camper than Robin jumped out of the passenger side. "We called the office every day when we heard what had happened!"

"I know, they told me," I said. "It meant a lot to me."

"We didn't know . . . you looked fine. A little thin but you always look thin," Steve sputtered, as if he was holding himself partially responsible.

"No one could have known," I said, uneasy a little at the remembrance of Steve and Robin racing through Sears at my behest. "I'm okay now. I've learned a lot, including the need to pace myself."

I told them all about Charlene and how I was doing my best to structure a better life on the road. "I'm staying in shape and keeping a balance in life," I said, fully realizing I was trying to reassure myself as much as them. Then I caught them up on what little I knew about the office, especially Irvin's recent tirade.

We shared a few more stories while Robin cooked hamburgers on a grill outside the camper and Steve and I relaxed on lawn chairs a few feet away. I told him Julie would be by to pick him up in the morning. Then the three of us talked until late in the evening, until all that remained of the outside world was a veil of darkness illuminated by the light of a lamp that Robin had thoughtfully placed on the center of the table.

Chapter 71

THE RIGGING STILL
GLIMMERED INTACT

The autumn trees were still flowering in shades of red and yellow as I drove toward Toledo for the animal walk and tonight's opening night performance. Once again I found myself wondering what kind of reception I'd receive from the performers, taking refuge in a comment I'd once heard, "If you really knew how little people thought about you, you'd be a lot less concerned about what they think." Perhaps, it occurred to me, my reunion will go easier if I think more about them than me.

Axel Gautier was leaning on his hooked stick when I arrived, watching the roustabouts wrestle the elephants from the train cars. I briefly caught his eye as the roustabouts unlatched the chains from the elephants' feet. If he held any animosity for the eight-mile detour, or for that matter, even recognized who I was, I couldn't detect it. I had thought it was Axel's gait when he walked, fast-paced and straight, or his posture when he stood, his head held high, that made him seem so imperious, but at the moment he looked almost humble. Then I realized his haughty demeanor had little to do with either. It was his smile, or to be more exact, his lack thereof. It occurred to me I'd never seen him smile. It was what made Axel Gautier conspicuous, especially during the show. All the other performers had been mentally cattle prodded to never stop smiling. Even Charlie Bauman, while inside his lion cage, routinely broke into a wide grin. Michu never stopped smiling the entire time he danced his Hungarian jig and Elvin Bale burst into a grin the second his heels locked onto the bar. But not Axel Gautier. Whatever he did was serious business. And knowing Irvin's meticulous attention to detail, I couldn't help wondering how he got away with it.

I smiled in his direction but he just stared past me, undisturbed. The dust settled momentarily. He barked a command in German and the elephants breezed by the crowd making their way the short distance to the Toledo Coliseum.

Darkness had fallen, returning with a cool chill in the air. I walked down the back ramp, pulled along by performers arriving for the opening night performance. I was anxious to see Charlie King and a few of the familiar faces before joining Mike Franks upstairs to monitor the doors.

As I picked my way down the ramp I gradually overtook two men in overcoats shuffling along in front. Curiously we glanced at one another. And if Axel Gautier had forgotten or feigned ignorance, Harold Ronk, the ringmaster, and his sour-faced boyfriend, Bob Harrison, had obviously not. Harold, in a replay of his restaurant demeanor, recoiled in fright, as though he'd just seen a ghost, while his companion just glowered disdainfully. I was too far below contempt to warrant a further acknowledgment. More amused than surprised I nodded hello and skirted unapologetically past.

As I wandered through clown alley and into the maze of blue curtain dressing rooms, I heard a commotion emanating from a passageway to my right. I rounded the corner. Up ahead a cluster of performers were applauding while congregating in front of one of the dressing rooms. As I neared I noticed a sign had been hoisted, "Happy Birthday—Charlie Bauman." Charlie was standing outside the curtain, reacting good naturedly. What I couldn't see until I peered over the shoulder of one of the performers was what everyone was laughing about. Knee-high Michu was goose stepping back and forth, wearing a tiny German helmet and shouldering a rifle while presenting Charlie Bauman with a ludicrous Nazi salute.

I joined in the fun for a few minutes, then continued my way down the corridor in search of Charlie King. He was relaxing on a stool inside his dressing room. I suspected he was used to people suddenly reappearing in his life for he looked up and grinned as though he'd only seen me yesterday.

"How do I thank you?" I said, knowing what I felt couldn't possibly be put into words.

"There's nothing to thank me for," he said, accepting my heartfelt thanks.

Neither of us knew quite what to say. "I'd better go," I said, resisting the urge to stay. "Mike Franks is waiting for me upstairs."

I strolled past my office to find Mike standing by the front entrance. "Let's split up," he said. "We'll meet back here in an hour." The doors opened and people wove in through the turnstiles. The box office windows, I noticed, were steady, and as the show began to start, I hurried back to the front entrance.

"Come on! Let's see the size of the crowd," Mike said. We marched through the nearest portal. To my surprise, even as the band played the opening number, people were still milling about, filling up the lower tier of seats.

"It looks like a sellout!" I exclaimed.

Mike scanned the audience. "Those are just people from the bleachers filling up the higher priced seats."

We watched for a few minutes and agreed it was a sizeable crowd, but as we strolled back toward the promoter's office Mike's observation still lingered in my thoughts. I wondered how things might have changed if in Evansville I'd heard those same simple words.

Billy Williams was waiting outside the door with his ticket-counting machine when we arrived.

"I'm sorry about Indiana," I volunteered, feeling especially embarrassed about my actions in front of Billy.

Luckily the awkwardness I felt was quickly countered by something to do. The box office manager walked in with a single box of deadwood. It didn't take us long to determine that we ended up only five hundred seats short of a sellout. I called Allen while Mike exited and announced he was retiring to his hotel room. I said good-night to Billy and found myself delighted to be left alone.

I sat back for a few minutes, savoring my opening night success, then wandered into the arena, selecting a seat high enough up to enjoy the view. The second half slowly wound to a finish. But just as the Flying Gaonas were climbing down from their flying trapeze, a huge contraption that looked more like a cylinder on two wheels than a war-time cannon, rolled onto the arena floor.

It appeared Elvin Bale had gotten his wish. As he strolled out from behind the curtain I reflected back to the radio interview when he'd indicated he'd be trying to please Irvin with a brand new act. Elvin carefully circled the giant cylinder. He was dressed in a white leather jumpsuit and cape. He carried his helmet under one arm. I couldn't help wondering, as he bowed to the crowd and sprang gracefully up the ladder, how much his father's rebuke, admonishing him to risk life and limb without even the security of a safety harness, still penetrated his thoughts.

"May we have a drum roll please!" Harold Ronk roared, and as the drums' cadence filled the air, the barrel rose slowly to a steep incline. Then a jarring bang sounded and sparks shot out from beneath the cannon. Through a cloud of gray smoke Elvin was propelled a hundred miles per hour, over the three rings and onto a net two-hundred feet on the opposite side. Before anyone could question if he was still in one piece, Elvin bounced off the ropes, beamed to the spellbound audience and disappeared still waving through the back door curtain.

⌁

To Mike Franks, Toledo might as well have been Albuquerque. For someone who lived his life on the road, Mike was surprisingly indifferent to his surroundings. Perhaps in a certain way, I reflected, it was to his advantage. If he didn't particularly notice where he was, it was unlikely he'd spend much time sentimentalizing where he'd just been.

I could tell this morning he was restless, bored, as he leafed through his newspaper.

"I think I'll be all right if you'd like to head back to Washington."

He glanced over and put down the paper. "Are you sure?"

"I'm sure," I said. "But how about if we make a deal? If later I discover I'm running into trouble I'll give you a call."

"No problem," he said. "I won't hesitate to fly back in."

Thirty minutes before the evening performance I stumbled downstairs in search of Charlie Bauman. With only one day remaining in Toledo, it was time to submit my list of performer interviews for Detroit.

With only the curtain to knock upon I stood in front of Charlie's dressing room and listened for sounds he was there. Charlie muttered "come in" and I gingerly parted the curtains. Never knowing what to expect I was surprised to see a warm, tired smile sweep across his face.

"Sit down," he said, pointing to a chair in front of his table. He had stripped to a T-shirt and slacks. Behind him, I noticed a rack of sequined costumes and tuxedos depicting his double life.

I handed over my list of performer interviews, bracing myself for his reaction. But almost indifferently he brushed the paper aside, saying he'd take care of it. He slipped out a white handkerchief and wiped moisture from his upper lip. Unexpectedly I found myself asking, "How have you been?"

He leaned forward and as though he'd been waiting all day to unburden himself he blurted, "This job is giving me ulcers. Irvin has no idea what I go through."

I sat motionless and listened.

"I can never get rest. I'm bothered all times of the night and day. The performers are always fighting with one another. They're all just a bunch of egotists!"

He sat back, momentarily catching his breath, then stammered, "And if that's not enough, three days ago I had to bail out two of the roustabouts from jail just minutes before the train left! I should have let them stay there and rot!"

He wiped his mouth again and sat back and looked at me. It suddenly occurred to me he was reaching out to me for an answer, the solution to somehow coping while chaotic events swirl all around him. "Perhaps," I said, "you need to care . . . but not so much." It was an answer, I realized, that wasn't going to satisfy him in a million years. "You've got to get away from it," I continued. "Is there anything outside the circus you enjoy?"

"Fishing," he replied, and for a moment I saw a glimmer of hope. "I've always loved fishing. It's the only thing that's ever let me relax."

"How long has it been since you've gone fishing?"

Charlie reached for his shirt. "It's been years," he lamented. "But how can I take the time? I wouldn't even know where to go."

"You have to make the time. If you're performing in one of my towns, just let me know. I'll gladly make all the arrangements."

He nodded, breathing a little easier, and though I suspected he'd rarely go fishing, the thought of it seemed to calm his nerves.

That night Billy and I closed out the show. $191,000.00. The total was barely over Allen's projection but it was good enough for me. I walked back to the hotel, and for the first time in days I didn't feel frightened. Toledo I'd always known I could handle, but Detroit, with its eighteen shows, was another matter. But somehow my conversation with Charlie Bauman had given me a sense of wholeness that I needed.

There are days when the wind blows through the trees and the sun sparkles so brightly you'd swear Mother Nature was exclaiming, "Today all is well with the world." I drove up I-75 on my way to Detroit for the two o'clock animal walk.

The train had pulled to a stop near the center of town. Tall office buildings loomed overhead in the background. I parked alongside a busy street.

Axel Gautier was already hoisting the riders, one of whom I noticed was the pretty ex-Playboy bunny. She was fidgeting on the back of the elephant's neck, trying to get a hand grip, when I caught her attention and waved.

I scanned the crowd searching for Julie and found her among the spectators conversing with one of the television reporters. I nodded a greeting, then watched from a distance since for once she seemed happily in charge.

Axel shouted a command and the elephants lurched forward lumbering across the street. I turned and darted back to my car but not before catching a glimpse of my favorite rider whose hips were thrusting forward in sync to the elephant's rhythm.

I sped into traffic, anxious to see the lines at the box office on opening day. There were brisk lines, seven and eight people deep. But what interested me most was not just the number of people, but more importantly, the diversity. Just as I'd hoped it wasn't only the inner-city blacks buying tickets, there were businessmen, women in suits and blue-collar workers standing comfortably in line. I grabbed my briefcase and hurried inside thinking maybe my mantra, "downtown was safe" may have worked!

Lloyd Morgan was busily rigging the show as I strolled into the general manager's office. "Could someone show me to my office?"

"Of course," one of the administrative assistants said. He escorted me to a tiny, cramped cubicle not far from the arena box office.

"A little small?" I murmured, and I wondered for a moment if Julie had a hand in this.

"Oh, it's only for today, sir. We're clearing out a larger space for you to move into tomorrow!"

I spread out my binders and notes, thankful tonight's opening was scheduled on a Friday. Opening on a weekend almost guaranteed a sellout performance. All I had to do now was wait for a few more hours.

"May I come in?" I looked up from reviewing my notes. Lloyd Morgan stuck his head in my cubicle.

"Of course," I said, as he slipped into a chair in front of my desk.

"I think I've seen it all," he sighed, propping his elbow on the edge of my desk. "I don't like ethnic jokes but I swear I just watched six Polacks pick up a roll of canvas and carry it twenty yards to a forklift."

I started to laugh but it was obvious he was more frustrated than amused. He slumped in his chair, quieter than usual. I tried to make small talk but he seemed too preoccupied to converse. Finally, he pronounced with a worried expression, "I'd better be getting back to the train," and he ambled back out of the office.

The head usher, a solid, gravelly voiced man, was cracking an inside joke when I arrived with my gold and silver foil hats. I'd forgotten how incestuous the ushering business was. You could usually take your cue from the head usher. If he was a sweet, elderly gentleman then chances are you'd have a slew of sweet, elderly ushers. Or instead, as in this case, if he sounded like an aging hoodlum you could expect to find slouched in their seats several of his boyhood chums.

The supervisor finally acknowledged me. I proceeded to explain to the group how they would have to select fifty-two children from the audience and escort them down to the arena floor just before intermission. But other than a few half-attentive nods most of them just stared at me apathetically.

I waited for a moment to see if there were any questions. "The doors are now open," the head usher snapped. "Let's take our positions."

I hurried through the portal and observed Billy Williams had already taken his position by the front entrance. I quickly began circling the arena, but calm as I tried to be, the shouts and the jostling of people unexpectedly quickened my pace. Midway around the concourse, I glanced at my watch and hurriedly swung by my office. The TV anchor, our honorary ringmaster, was waiting along with a cameraman.

"Come on! Follow me," I shouted, and as they started to move in my direction, he blurted out, "We'd like to do an interview with you!" I noticed another woman, more demure, had joined us.

"I'm with the *Detroit Free Press*," she said, shaking my hand. "Would you mind if I also asked a few questions?"

"I'd be delighted!" I said. The cameraman looked around and suggested we do the interview inside the arena.

"This will be fine," he said, as we stopped near an inside railing. "We can get a full sweep of the audience from here."

Suddenly he switched on a blinding light and I realized I was still out of breath.

"How do you explain this stunning crowd?" the TV reporter asked, extending the microphone toward me.

"It's easy," I replied. "This is living proof downtown Detroit is on the rebound. Just look at the crowd. They're from the suburbs and the outskirts as well as the inner city!" Then I carefully repeated the message I'd been trumpeting from the beginning.

As the interview wound to an end I noticed the reporter from the daily newspaper still had not asked any questions. She just folded her notebook and quietly walked away.

During intermission Billy Williams came in carrying a box of deadwood from the box office. "You can start adding the complimentary passes while I count the kids' stubs," he said.

One hour later Billy penciled in the figure. We'd exceeded last year's opening night total by $5,300.00. I quickly picked up the phone and dialed Allen.

"How did we do?" Allen asked.

"Fantastic!" I said, and I gave him the numbers. Then thinking of the $900,000 projection I interjected, "How would you feel if we did a million?"

"If we did a million, I'd be happy."

"Yes, but would you be ecstatic?"

Suddenly there was a pause on the other end. "Why don't we just worry about hitting this year's projection?"

I opened the hotel door and retrieved a copy of the *Detroit Free Press*. The opening night review had been placed in the style section. "Ringling Circus Performs to Sold Out Crowd!" The review was positive with plaudits for all the main acts. But when I reached the second column I was surprised to see a quote directly from me. "Jamie MacVicar, promoter of this year's show, attributes part of the success to a rebound of downtown Detroit." The next two paragraphs embellished the point. It was obvious that, although it may or may not be true, the press loved the possibility that our achievement was a symbol of the city's resurgence. I picked up an extra copy to mail to Irvin and hurried downtown to the coliseum.

I plopped myself down at my desk and reminded myself it was time to settle into a routine. Just as I was trying to figure out what exactly that could be the telephone rang. To my delight it was Chris Bursky.

"How are you holding up?"

"Fine," I said. Then I asked him all about the town he was promoting, and I mentioned the review in this morning's *Detroit Free Press*.

"Uh oh," Chris said, "Irvin doesn't like it when promoters are quoted. When it comes to the business end he doesn't like sharing the spotlight."

The matinee had just ended when the young man who had shown me to my cubicle stepped into my office. "I'll show you to your new quarters?" I followed him past the box office and watched as he unlocked the door to a spacious room, subdued by a dark red carpet.

"We sometimes use this as a spare lounge," he said, and I noticed a long bar running along the left-hand side. A small desk with a lamp and a phone had been placed in the center of the room.

"Much improved," I said. "Thank you."

I glanced at the time, debating whether to move my things now or later, and elected instead to get something to eat while I still had two hours before the evening performance.

I wandered out to the front of the building and turned left down a wide sidewalk. The sky had turned dark and cloudy. What few people were out didn't look very friendly. Wouldn't it be ironic if I got mugged two blocks from the Coliseum? What would the paper write then?

Sam's Hamburgers looked like as good a place as any, and I took a seat at the counter. Yellow grease stains splattered the wall but it didn't much matter as long as the hamburger was edible and the place didn't look anything like the arena. I finished my french fries and lingered as long as I could, then paid the old man in the apron and slowly walked back to the arena.

I swung by the box office and noticed there were only a few tickets left in the rack for the evening performance. "Looks like a sell-out!" I shouted from outside the window.

"I'd be surprised if it wasn't," the box office manager replied. I still had a few minutes to kill so I leaned back in my chair in the cubicle, propped my feet on the desk and reveled in my impending success.

Just then I heard the outer door open and the faint shuffling of feet. I got up and strode out of my cubicle. Suddenly, standing in front of me, was the implacable figure of Irvin Feld. His son, Kenneth, stood at his side and to his right, towering over both of them, stood a man I'd never seen before wearing a sports coat and a cowboy hat.

Without a handshake or even a simple hello, Irvin said, "Where is an office we can use?"

"Right this way," I answered, and I quickly led them down the hallway to my new office. "Things are going great," I exclaimed. "It looks like tonight's a sellout performance!"

I opened the door. Irvin glanced inside.

"All right," he said. "We'll be back later." And I watched them stride, three abreast, back down the corridor. It looked like a scene from the Shootout at the O.K. Corral, except Wyatt Earp was half the size of his deputy.

I moved my binders from the cubicle to my new office and hurriedly took my position by the front entrance. The doors opened and I circled round the concourse, checking into my quarters intermittently to see if they had returned. But the room remained as deserted as when I had left it. Finally, the last of the crowd trickled in and I strode back to my office. Just as I was opening the door Irvin and his companions emerged from one of the exits. "I thought you said it was a sellout!" Irvin snapped, glaring at me angrily.

"It's not?" I asked, as he brushed past. I turned and rushed into the arena. Irvin was right. There were several hundred seats still noticeably empty. I ran down to the box office.

"I thought you told me tonight was a sellout?"

The box office manager looked up. "No, I said it *could* be a sellout."

"But there were hardly any tickets in the racks."

"That's because we were still putting them in."

"Well, I look like an idiot! I told Irvin Feld it was a sellout." I closed the door feeling frustrated before realizing it was simply an innocent mistake.

I arrived back at the office and Irvin and Kenny were sitting by themselves at a table. Neither was speaking. They were just sitting there still dressed in their wool overcoats.

I sat down at my desk, nervously aware of their silence. Then thinking it might improve Irvin's mood, I pulled out the morning's review.

"Here's the review," I said, "It's very complimentary." Then I walked back to my desk and sat down. I watched to see if there was any reaction, but Irvin read the write-up and without commenting handed the review to his son. A moment later, Irvin rose and announced they were going inside to watch the show.

I busied myself with paperwork while wondering what brought them here. And more importantly how long did they intend to stay?

Soon I heard the sounds of intermission and voices begin filling the corridor. I stood up, stretched my frame and began moving toward the door. Suddenly the door flew open and Irvin burst into the room.

"The carts were half-empty! One of them didn't have any kids in it at all. I counted them! There were only thirty-four kids in the carts!"

I started to speak. Irvin pivoted, red faced, and positioned himself under my chin, "Do you have any idea how much those carts cost me?"

I stared at him, paralyzed. So that's what this is all about. All this time I had thought he was starting an alumni, an experience that these kids would never forget. But all he could think about was how much the carts cost.

He spun away from me and stormed over to my desk. He picked up the phone and dialed. Incredulously, I realized he was now yelling at Allen Bloom. Finally, he returned his attention to me and held up the receiver. "Here, Allen wants to talk to you!"

I started to explain. "The ushers just didn't do it."

"Jamie, it's your job!"

I listened in silence and then hung up the receiver. Irvin and Kenny had retreated to their table on the far side of the room. Irvin just sat there, simmering.

Expecting any second I'd be fired, I focused on the hundreds of things over the past three months I'd done right, including the fact that tonight was almost a sold out performance. And as I gradually tried to make sense of it, it occurred to me it made no sense. If this was my first tour perhaps I'd be cowering in fear, but as I sat there, measuring my reaction, all I could think was how crazy it seemed.

I returned to my hotel room and found a message to call Mike Franks.

"I just wanted to let you know Irvin Feld might be coming to town."

"You're too late. He's already here," I said, and I proceeded to tell him what happened.

"I forgot to tell you to keep a low profile when Irvin's around."

"Why is he here anyway?"

"He came in to fire Lloyd Morgan."

"What did Lloyd do?"

"I don't know. They just lost faith in him."

"So who is the guy in the cowboy hat?"

"That's Lloyd's replacement."

The next morning I ran into Lee Hamilton. He told me he'd loaned Irvin and Kenny his office to do what they'd come to do. "Irvin and Kenny flew out last night," he said, "leaving Lloyd's successor behind." I stepped downstairs to see if Lloyd was still around. "I'm afraid not," Charlie Bauman said, "Lloyd and his wife already cleaned out their train car. As far as I know, they're halfway to their home in Florida."

A petal had fallen off the rose, not with a sudden descent, more with a gentle fluttering to the ground. Thanks to Irvin, I cared, but not as much. It was time to settle down. Keep my priorities straight. Make it to the end with mind and body intact. I was tired. I could feel it. Not mind-numbing body-aching tired, but tired nevertheless.

I called in the numbers to Allen, telling him I'd gotten the ushers better organized. He shrugged it off, perhaps not caring as much or at least not holding a grudge.

Monday I took the day off, and while the performers rested, I slept late and then strolled down to the hotel pool. No one was there and I swam long, delicious strokes, feeling the water enliven me as I glided back and forth.

Tuesday came and went, as did Wednesday and Thursday, and the numbers continued to hold. Finally it was Friday afternoon, with only the weekend to go, and I was sitting in my office when the phone rang. It was the general manager, Lee Hamilton, asking if I could come up for a few minutes since he and Julie wouldn't be there when I left on Sunday.

For the past several days, I'd avoided Julie and walked upstairs with a certain trepidation. But Julie was sitting on the sofa, at-ease, with her hands folded neatly on her lap. "Will you be coming back next year?" Lee asked.

"I don't know," I said. "You know Ringling. They don't often send us to the same town twice."

A secretary walked in, distracting him for a moment. I turned to Julie and said in my most gracious tone, "It's been a pleasure working with you." And to my surprise, she handed me a neatly wrapped gift.

"Just so there are no hard feelings," she said. "It's a box of stationery."

"How nice of you," I said.

"By the way," she added, "I neglected to tell you. That day when the radio rep called to confirm she'd be riding in the animal walk." She paused and my interest piqued as I was again reminded of the curvy ex-Playboy bunny. "She had told me to tell you if you ever got lonely to give her a call. I forgot to mention it."

I held Julie's gaze just long enough to give her the satisfaction she'd succeeded. She'd had the final word. And then I leaned back in good humor. What the hell? At least I hadn't woken a sleepy conscience.

Saturday, with its three shows, was always a long day, yet I found myself going through the motions wistfully detached. Occasionally I'd peek inside the arena to catch Charlie Bauman standing guard in his black tuxedo or Michu being carted to the center ring on the shoulders of one of the clowns or Charlie King and his unicyclists racing around the hippodrome track, but oddly enough, I was comfortable viewing it from afar. Perhaps, it occurred to me, I won't even say goodbye. I'll just wish it from here.

I wandered back to the hotel room. It was almost midnight, and I slept through the night soundly. The next day, the performers all seemed relaxed. It was that end-of-another-journey feeling that put everyone in a more jovial mood. And like the preceding day, everything seemed a little richer. The colors, the costumes, the music. The faces on the people. Everything I'd come to feel a part of now fit like a warm glove.

The last performance was nearing its end when Billy walked in with the box of deadwood. We counted the last of the unsold tickets and then Billy tallied the numbers, adding the figure to the cumulative total. "$904,000.00," he said. I'd broken the projection. Not by much, but enough.

I took the final numbers and called Allen Bloom. "Congratulations," he said, and then I folded the sheet of paper and carefully placed it in my briefcase, snapping the latches shut.

"I'll see you in the next town," Billy said, shaking my hand.

I stood alone in the middle of the room for just a minute, and then I walked out into the empty corridor. The turnstiles and popcorn machines seemed strangely still while outside the entrance door I watched a few leaves being swept along by the wind.

I turned and headed down the hall and then snuck into one of the portals, passing through the short, dark tunnel, and pausing at the railing for one last glance at the three rings below. All the rigging still glimmered intact, a magical moment of beauty between the time the performers depart and the roustabouts return to tear it all apart. I looked down at my hand holding my briefcase firm and steady and took a deep breath. I did it. By damn . . . I did it. And then I realized it was over, I'd climbed back on the horse that threw me, and here I was alive and well and still standing. Suddenly, looking out across the vast empty space, a smile as sweet as I'd ever felt swept across my face, and a voice rose exalted from within, "Yes . . . Yes, you son of a bitch, Yes!

Author's Note

The Advance Man is a true story and with the exception of minor details I have tried to be as faithful as possible to my memory of conversations and events. In some cases names and descriptions of individuals have been changed in order to protect their privacy and in one case, for the same reason, a composite character was created. For scholars and circus historians, though history can often be contradictory, I have been particularly careful to stick to the records as chronicled, including giving Ringling Bros. & Barnum and Bailey Circus the opportunity to offer any comments or corrections.

Acknowledgements

Few books achieve any merit without the invaluable contributions of many. My editors, Lori Crockett and Carolyn Blakemore, tightened and streamlined the text, and in the process greatly enhanced the narrative flow. Wayne Kabak read the manuscript twice, providing insights and constructive criticism that significantly improved the book. Early on, my researcher, Allen Buergenthal, uncovered a treasure trove of interesting nuggets, from facts about Gargantua to little-known details about Savannah. Others, who appear in the book, searched their memories and their knowledge and provided important information. It is here that I thank Peter Halbin, Carl Bruce and John Husskisson. I also thank Juanita Green, whose experience growing up in LaGrange, Georgia provided the background for the passages about the travails of a young, black counterpart.

The crafting of the book would not have been nearly as enjoyable without the sunny disposition of my assistant, Bonnie Hart, who side-by-side typed and re-typed the manuscript. I am also indebted to Laura McGinty, Ben Ohmart, Elaine Farinacci, Dr. Harland Randolf, Mildred MacVicar, Fred MacVicar, Marcia Strausel, Scott McBride, Florence Auld, my daughters Courtney and Kristin, Florence Homasson and Brian Benson. And I especially thank Connie Beatson whose unwavering advice and support was immeasurable. All of these people, at various intervals over a long, long period, gave me their wisdom, counsel and encouragement. Without them this book would never have been published. And for that I am profoundly grateful. All errors and shortcomings are solely mine.

I also must credit an industry that I have thoroughly enjoyed; for me, the perfect blend of art and business. And though much, some would argue, has changed, in fundamental ways, little has changed at all.

And finally I am indebted to the readers who have accompanied me along the way, for as Emerson replied when asked to whom he writes, "I write to an unknown friend."

THE ADVANCE MAN

THE ADVANCE MAN
A Journey Into the World of the Circus
Jamie MacVicar

To order additional copies:
Call 1-800-345-6665   orders@pathwaybook.com
To contact the author please write:
jmacvicar@cox.net

A companion DVD "A Look Back,"
narrated by the author, is also available.
History excerpted from *The Advance
Man* and over 160 images bring the
fascinating people and events of the circus to life!
$23.95 plus shipping: Call 1-800-345-6665.
or email: macvicarenterprises@cox.net

BEAR MANOR MEDIA
ALBANY, GEORGIA

• *Publishers of Quality Entertainment Biographies* •

Narrative Non-Fiction
ISBN: 1-59393-203-0
U.S.A. $32.50   Canada $35.00

"*A Gift of Laughter*"

ISBN: 0-87491-974-6
$17.95 + $3.00 shipping
– Hardcover

CROSSED PENS
Jamie MacVicar • Frederick MacVicar
Peter A. B. Taylor

"*Unique, hilarious, great imagination!*"
– USA TODAY

"*Funny, Bawdy and Delightfully Insightful!*"
– THE AMERICAN SPECTATOR

Join father, son and a sculptor friend for a rollicking romp through manhood. It's about art, love, spirituality, the craft of writing, and a host of other topics as wits are matched and insights shared. And in the end, it's tenderly poignant, as father and son unite through humor and the lost art of letters.

To order, e-mail Business Agent:
macvicarenterprises@cox.net

Acropolis Books

Bibliography

※

Barnum, P.T., *The Life of Barnum*, Autobiography, 1855, Globe Bible Publishing Co., Philadelphia, PA

Bauman, Charly, *Tiger, Tiger, My 25 Years With the Big Cats*, 1975, Playboy Press

Billington, Monroe Lee, *The American South*, 1971, Charles Scribner and Sons, New York

Cooper, Courtney Riley, *Lions 'n' Tigers 'n' Everything*, 1924, Little, Brown and Company, Boston

Drake, Sir Garland Tyrwhitt, *Beasts and Circuses*, 1936, J.W. Arrowsmith Ltd., Great Britain

Eliot, Mack, *Down Thunder Road, The Making of Bruce Springsteen*, 1992, Simon and Schuster, New York, New York

Fenner, Mildred Sandison and Wolcott, *The Circus Lure and Legend*, 1970, Prentice Hall, Inc., Englewood Cliffs, New Jersey

Hammerstrom, David Lewis, *Behind the Big Top*, 1980, A.S. Bonner & Co., Inc., New York, New York

Kunhardt, Philip B., Jr., Philip B. III, Peter W., *P.T. Barnum, America's Greatest Showman*, an illustrated biography, 1995, Alfred A. Knopf, New York, New York

Murray, Marion, *Circus*, 1956, Greenwood Press Publishers, Westport, Connecticut

Murray, Marion, *From Rome to Ringling Circus*, 1956, Greenwood Press Publishers, Westport, Connecticut

North, Henry Ringling and Alden Hatch, *The Circus Kings*, 1960, Doubleday & Company, Garden City, New York

Penning, Stefario and Dominic, *Then and Now*, MacMillan Publishing Co., New York, New York

Plowden, Gene, *Gargantua, Circus Star of the Century*, 1972, E.A. Seeman Publishing, Inc., Miami, Florida

Plowden, Gene, *Those Amazing Ringlings and Their Circus*, Bonanza Books, New York

Shout, William Lawrence, *Theatre in a Tent, The Development of a Professional Entertainment*, 1972, Bowling Green University Popular Press, Bowling Green, Ohio

Soloman, Abby, *Lord of the Rings*, February, 1983, Inc. Publishing Company

An Introduction to Savannah, distributed by Dixie Souveniers

Sojourn in Savannah, 1990, Historic Savannah Foundation

104th Edition Program, Ringling Brothers and Barnum and Bailey Circus, 1975

106th Edition Program, Ringling Brothers and Barnum and Bailey Circus, 1977

Cullinane, John, "Lord of the Rings," March 1981, *Regardies* magazine

Pottker, John, "The Family Circus," August 1990, *Regardies* magazine

"You Carry the Cure in Your Own Heart," *Parade* magazine, August 28, 1994

Thomas, Bill, "King Big Top," *The Washingtonian* magazine, December, 1986

Williams, Juan, "Holding Back the Shadows," *The Washington Post* (Circus Wars, Irvin Feld), Abe Pollin Dispute-February 17, 1991

Riersh, Edward, "The Two Faces of Abe (Pollin)," *Regardies* magazine, March 1990, (Pollin vs. Irvin Feld)

Klemensaud, Judy, "Animal Trainers are Unsung Stars of the Big Top at the Garden," April 16, 1982, *New York Times*

"Circus Lives," March 29, 1983, *The Washington Post*, Style Section, D1

Harrington, Richard, "Rock's Rough and Ready Promoter," *The Washington Post*, Sunday, October 27, 1991

Schore, Mark, "In Nashville, the Eagles' Pedestal Perch," *The Washington Post*, Sunday, October 24, 1993

Trescott, Jacqueline, "A Splendid Setting for Black History," *The Washington Post*, April 13, 1997

Jones, Tamara, "Cannon Fodder," *The Washington Post*, September 15, 1996

Phillips, Dan, "Two Killed, 15 Injured in Circus Train Wreck," *The Washington Post*, January 14, 1994

Robinson, Eugene, "Clowning Around is Taken Seriously in England," *The Washington Post*, January 4, 1993

"Col. Tom Parker Dies at 87; Was Elvis Presley Manager," *The Washington Post*, January 22, 1997

Harrington, Richard, "One for the Money, Elvis Presley," *The Washington Post*, January 1997

Salerno, Heather, "Ready to Take the Show on to New Roads," *The Washington Post*

"A Smooth Transition, How Archie Leach Became Cary Grant," *The Washington Post*, Book World, February 12, 1997

"Dennis Kucinich, Keeping a Civilized Tongue," *The Washington Post*, The Reliable Source, 1996

Duggan, Paul, "Much Ado About Pachyderm Poo," *The Washington Post*, April 21, 1995

Powers, William F., "Business Under the Big Top," *The Washington Post*, July 11, 1994

Thomas, Bill, "King Big Top," *The Washington Post*, December 1986

"American Impressario Irvin Feld Dies; Was Owner of Ringling Brothers Circus," obituary, *The Washington Post*

"Irvin Feld's Eye for Talent," Appreciation, *The Washington Post*

"Irvin Feld, Circus Operator," *New York Times*, September 1984

"Feld Buys Circus," PR Newswire, March 18, 1982

Newspaper Opening Night Reviews, Evansville, Indiana; Terre Haute, Indiana, 1975

Williams, Peggy, "The Lady is a Clown," *Cleveland Plain Dealer*, November 1, 1974

Scott, Jane, "Stevie Wonder Rocks Coliseum,"*Cleveland Plain Dealer*, October 29, 1974

Mastroiani, Tony, "Shiny New Circus Offers Thrills, Chills," *Cleveland Plain Dealer*, November 1, 1974

Mileti, Nick, *The Toronto Star*, 1991; *Los Angeles Times*, March 8, 1987; *Los Angeles Times*, October 18, 1986; UP International, June 13, 1985; UP International, December 17, 1980; *The Washington Post*, 1980; *McGraw Hill, Inc. Business Week*, March 17, 1975

"Colisseum Hockey Opener Delayed," *Cleveland Plain Dealer*, October 28, 1974

"Celts First Coliseum Foe," *Cleveland Plain Dealer*, October 29, 1974

Straussmeyer, Mary, "Coliseum is for Sports Fans Who Want the Best," *Cleveland Plain Dealer*, August 25, 1974

Barnam, George, "Mileti, Sinatra Share Spotlight," *Cleveland Plain Dealer*, October 27, 1974

"Easy In, Easy Out is Coliseum Parking Plan," *Cleveland Plain Dealer*, October 24, 1974

Guuenther, Wally, "Nick Mileti's Dream Comes True Tonight," *Cleveland Plain Dealer*, October 26, 1974

"Coliseum and Mileti Win Raves," *Cleveland Plain Dealer*, November 6, 1974

Straussmeyer, Mary, "Frankly, Nick has Knack for Giving Colossal Party," *Cleveland Plain Dealer*, October 28, 1974

Feagler, Dick, "Coliseum Sounds Sour Note for Steamed Up Motorists," *Cleveland Plain Dealer*, October 28, 1974

Preston, Howard, "Opening of Big C Means End of Era at Arena," *Cleveland Plain Dealer*, October 26, 1974

Miller, William, "Mileti Coliseum Officials Say Building Will be Ready for Sinatra," *Cleveland Plain Dealer*, August 30, 1974

Adams, Ray, "Saturday is 'C Day' for Mileti and Coliseum," *Cleveland Plain Dealer*, October 24, 1974

Hickey, William, "Second Roman Coliseum Opens," *Cleveland Plain Dealer*, October 25, 1974

Straussmeyer, Mary, "A Spirit Befitting the Coliseum," *Cleveland Plain Dealer*, October 20, 1974

"Plain Dealer Asks U.S. Court for an Order to Head off Strike," *Cleveland Plain Dealer*, October 30, 1974

"Guild Strikes Plain Dealer," *The Cleveland Press*, November 1, 1974

"Strike Shuts Plain Dealer," *The Cleveland Press*, November 2, 1974

Allen, Henry, "What it Felt Like—Living in the American Century," *Washington Post*, September 20, 1999

Videotapes:"Circus"

"Barnum, 1986"

"The Life of P.T. Barnum"

Cleveland, Ohio; Savannah, Georgia; Terre Haute and Evansville, Indiana Chambers of Commerce

Photo Credits

Every effort has been made to trace sources and copyright holders, but where this has been unsuccessful, if notified, the author will be pleased to rectify any omissions at the earliest opportunity.

DIVIDER PAGES - The Beginning: *Circus Poster.* California: *Train*, Tom Boylan, Train Order Publishing. Cleveland: *Cuyahoga River*, Wikimedia Commons. Savannah: *Wrought Iron Balcony*, author's collection. Indiana: *Midwest Farm*, Posted by Zanne, Farmer's Wife Blog "weather." Going Home: *Wash. D.C. Park*, author's collection. Going Back: *Circus Arriving*, Circus World Museum, Baraboo, Wisconsin. CENTER INSERT – *P.T. Barnum and wife*, Bridgeport Public Library. *American Museum*, William England. *Fiji Cannibals*, Sideshow World. *Albino children*, Bridgeport Public Library. *Chang and Eng in chair* and *with wives*, Bridgeport Public Library. *Chang and Eng house*, Steve Noga, Stone Mountain Broker. *James Bailey,* Circus World Museum, Baraboo Wisconsin. *Cooper and Bailey Circus,* Howard Tribbals. *James Bailey home*, Marty Shore, Manhattan Walks. *Circus Parade*, Neenah Public Library, Wisconsin. *Boy Peeking Under Tent*, unknown. *Boy in Straw Hat*, The Marion County Historical Society, Marion, Ohio. *Tody Hamilton*, Circus World Museum, Baraboo, Wisconsin. *Barnum and Bailey Band*, unknown. *Ringling family,* Wisconsin Historical Society. *Ringling Sideshow*, Sideshow World. *Circus clowns*, unknown. *Postered building*, Circus World Museum, Baraboo, Wisconsin. *Circus tent*, Red Sky Shelters. *Jumbo By Train*, Bridgeport Public Library. *John Ringling and John Ringling's mansion*, John and Mable Ringling Museum, Sarasota, Florida. *John Ringling North on yacht*, John and Mable Ringling Museum, Sarasota, Florida. *Hartford fire*, Emergency Management. LAST PAGE – *Circus Leaving*, Circus World Museum, Baraboo, Wisconsin.

Index

About the Author

JAMIE MACVICAR is the President of an award-winning communications firm. He has published several articles and short stories. He is the co-author of *Crossed Pens*, a humorous book of letters among three men. The author divides his time between Washington, D.C. and the Canadian Rockies.

Butler Area Public Library
218 North McKean Street
Butler PA 16001